AUDITING
CONCEPTS
AND
STANDARDS

REVISED SECOND EDITION

AUDITING
CONCEPTS AND STANDARDS

DAVID N. RICCHIUTE
University of Notre Dame

A99
PUBLISHED BY
SOUTH-WESTERN PUBLISHING CO.
CINCINNATI   WEST CHICAGO, IL   CARROLLTON, TX   LIVERMORE, CA

Material from Uniform CPA Examination Questions and Unofficial Answers,
copyright © 1983–1985 by the American Institute of Certified Public Accountants,
Inc., is reprinted or adapted with permission.

Material from CIA Examination Questions and Answers, copyright © 1977–1982 by
the Institute of Internal Auditors, is reprinted or adapted with permission.

Material from the Certificate in Management Accounting Examination, copyright
© 1974–1984 by the National Association of Accountants, is reprinted or
adapted with permission.

PREFACE

In comparison with the topical content of most accounting courses, Auditing is somewhat less quantitative, less structured, and more subjective in nature. As a result, there is considerable diversity in the focus and approach of most auditing texts: some are conceptual, some pragmatic, and some integrate concepts with practice. The focus and approach of this text are best characterized by its subtitle, "Concepts and Standards." *Auditing: Concepts and Standards,* revised second edition, is completely updated to include all of the Auditing Standards Board's nine "expectation gap" pronouncements (SAS Nos. 53–61) and the AICPA's Code of Professional Conduct. Like the second edition, this revised edition emphasizes both the concepts and standards of independent auditing, integrating each with contemporary audit method and with the complex decisions and judgment processes inherent in audit practice. In addition, the text, particularly Parts II (Audit Technology) and III (Audit Method), explicitly incorporates the risk model from SAS No. 47, "Audit Risk and Materiality in Conducting an Audit," and the financial statement assertions from SAS No. 31, "Evidential Matter." The text is intended for use in introductory undergraduate or graduate auditing courses, and can also be used in continuing professional education seminars for CPAs.

FEATURES

Following are several major features incorporated in the text, some of which are unique:

▲ The text provides extensive discussion of and references to the professional literature, including the Auditing Standards Board's *Statements on Auditing Standards* (through SAS No. 61), contemporary articles from professional and academic journals like the *Journal of Accountancy* and *Auditing: A Journal of Practice & Theory,* and important monographs such as Mautz and Sharaf's *The Philosophy of Auditing.*

▲ Separate chapters provide extensive coverage of professional judgment and auditor responsibilities (Chapter 3), materiality and audit risk (Chapter 5), the audit process and working papers (Chapter 6), internal and governmental auditing (Chapter 21), and researching nonroutine audit practice problems (Chapter 22).

▲ Chapters 9 and 10 on audit sampling are consistent with SAS No. 39, "Audit Sampling," and the AICPA's *Audit Sampling Guide.* Chapters 11 through 14 include appendices which present case studies that illustrate audit sampling applications in tests of controls over billing, accounts receivable, cash disbursements, and accounts payable.

▲ Seven chapters are devoted to tests of controls and substantive tests within four major transaction cycles: the revenue/receipt cycle (Chapters 11 and 12), the expenditure/disbursement cycle (Chapters 13, 14, and 15), the conversion cycle (Chapter 16), and the financing cycle (Chapter 17). Most of the working papers illustrated in these chapters are automated rather than manual, as is common in practice. Chapters 11, 12, 13, 14, and 16 include appendices that illustrate computer-assisted audit procedures.

▲ Extensive references, review questions, multiple choice questions, and problems are provided at the end of each chapter. Most of the multiple choice questions are adapted from professional examinations. Both author-prepared and professional examination problems are included.

▲ An introductory overview is presented for each chapter to answer the questions: What is this chapter about? How does the material flow and fit together?

ORGANIZATION

The revised second edition of *Auditing: Concepts & Standards* is organized in five parts, each with a specific intent and purpose.

Part One — *Professional Responsibilities*

Chapters 1 through 4 introduce the public accounting profession and an auditor's professional responsibilities for ethical behavior, sound judgment, and legal liability. Chapter 1, an overview of auditing and the public accounting profession, addresses the need for and evolution of auditing in the U.S., audit standards setting, the role of quality control and peer review within public accounting firms, and the form and content of audit reports. Chapter 2, "Professional Conduct," focuses on the principles and rules of conduct underlying the AICPA's Code of Professional Conduct, and the formal mechanisms used to enforce the AICPA and state society codes of conduct. Chapter 3, "Professional Judgment and Auditor Responsibilities," introduces the role of professional judgment in auditing and the audit decision making process; decision aids, "heuristics" and biases prevalent in audit practice; and an auditor's responsibilities under generally accepted auditing standards. Chapter 4, "Auditor's Legal Liability," identifies the major issues central to the legal liability cases involving independent auditors and describes an auditor's potential liability under common law, the Securities Act of 1933, and the Securities Exchange Act of 1934.

Part Two — *Audit Technology*

Chapters 5 through 8 introduce generally accepted auditing standards, the audit process, and the auditor's consideration of internal control structure in a financial statement audit. Chapter 5, "Standards, Materiality, and Audit Risk," discusses the relationship among auditing concepts, standards, and audit procedures; the evolution, nature, and scope of the AICPA's generally accepted auditing standards (including the attestation standards); and the importance of materiality and audit risk in contemporary audit practice. Chapter 6, "Evidence, the Audit Process, and Working Papers," addresses audit evidence and its relationship to financial statement assertions, audit objectives, and audit procedures; the nature of tests of controls, substantive tests, and analytical procedures; the major activities in the audit process — including the decision to accept an engagement, planning, and interim and year-end audit work — and the purpose and content of manual and automated working papers. Chapter 7, "Internal Control Structure in a Financial Statement Audit," discusses the elements of internal control structure — the control environment, the accounting system, and control procedures — and how an auditor considers an entity's internal control structure when planning and performing a financial statement audit. Chapter 8, "Internal Control Structure in EDP Systems," continues the discussion of internal control structure, focusing on differences between EDP and manual accounting systems, the nature and function of EDP controls, an auditor's approach to considering internal control structure in EDP systems, and microcomputer applications in auditing.

Part Three — *Audit Method*

Chapters 9 through 18 focus attention on the audit procedures used in tests of controls and in substantive tests of financial statement account balances. Chapter 9, "Audit Sampling in Tests of Controls," introduces and illustrates three statistical sampling for attributes plans — attribute estimation, sequential (stop-or-go) sampling, and discovery sampling — and a nonstatistical sampling plan. Chapter 10, "Audit Sampling in Substantive Tests of Account Balances," addresses four statistical sampling plans for variables — difference estimation, ratio estimation, mean-per-unit estimation, and probability proportional to size (PPS) sampling — and a nonstatistical sampling plan. Chapters 11 through 17 introduce, discuss, and illustrate the detailed tests of controls and substantive tests used in contemporary audit practice. Chapters 11 and 12 address the revenue/receipt cycle, including sales and cash receipts transactions, accounts receivable, and cash balances. Chapters 11 and 12 address the revenue/receipt cycle, including sales and cash receipts transactions, accounts receivable, and cash balances. Chapters 13 and 14 turn attention to the expenditure/disbursement cycle, including purchases and cash disbursement transactions, accounts payable, prepaid expenses, and accrued liabilities. Chapters 15, 16, and 17 introduce tests of controls and substantive tests applicable to personnel and payroll, to inventory and plant assets, and to investments, debt, and equity, respectively. Chapter 18 completes the discussion of audit procedures, addressing an auditor's considerable responsibilities when completing an audit — for example, auditing accounting estimates, the review for subsequent events, communicating with the audit committee, inquiries of a client's legal counsel, management representation letters, and forming an opinion on financial statements.

Part Four — *Reporting*

Chapters 19 and 20 introduce audit reports and reports issued for other types of engagements. Chapter 19, "Reports on Audited Financial Statements," discusses the evolution and major components of standard audit reports, modifications of standard reports, reporting requirements for comparative financial statements, and an auditor's responsibility for reporting on information accompanying audited financial statements and on statements prepared for use in foreign countries. Chapter 20, "Other Reports," discusses reporting in a variety of nonaudit engagements, including: compilations and reviews of financial statements, interim financial information, internal control structure, letters for underwriters, and reports on personal financial statements, financial forecasts and projections, and the application of accounting principles.

Part Five — *Research, Internal and Governmental Auditing*

The final two chapters discuss the role of research in audit practice, and two additional and highly prominent types of auditing in the U.S. Chapter 21, "Internal and Governmental Auditing," introduces the internal auditor's operational audit and the governmental auditor's financial-and-compliance, economy-and-efficiency, and program results audits. The chapter also discusses the Single Audit Act of 1984. Chapter 22, "Researching Audit Practice Problems," describes an auditor's approach to researching nonroutine accounting and auditing problems, and introduces several manual and computer-assisted research sources commonly used in practice.

ACKNOWLEDGMENTS

I gratefully acknowledge the AICPA, the Association of Government Accountants, the Institute of Internal Auditors, the Institute of Management

Accounting, Deloitte Haskins & Sells, Ernst & Whinney, and Peat Marwick Main for permission to quote from their pronouncements and publications.

In addition, I am indebted to the following people for insightful comments, suggestions, and assistance: Joyce Allen, Xavier University; James Brown, Crowe Chizek & Company; John Delaney, University of Texas at San Antonio; Philip Driscoll, Syracuse University; John Edwards, Louisiana Tech University; Keith Ehrenreich, California State Polytechnic University, Pomona; Robert Eskew, Purdue University; Linda Marquis, Northern Kentucky University; Alan Reinstein, Wayne State University; Robert Rouse, Auburn University; Glenn Sumners, Louisiana State University; Carl Warren, University of Georgia; and H. James Williams, Georgetown University.

David N. Ricchiute
University of Notre Dame

CONTENTS IN BRIEF

CONTENTS

PART I PROFESSIONAL RESPONSIBILITIES

AUDITING AND THE PUBLIC ACCOUNTING PROFESSION

1

Major topics discussed in this chapter are the:

▲ *Nature of auditing and the attest function.*
▲ *Need for independent audits.*
▲ *Evolution of auditing in the United States.*
▲ *Audit standard-setting process.*
▲ *Nature and services of public accounting firms.*
▲ *Role of quality control and peer review for public accounting firms.*
▲ *Relationship between accounting and auditing and the organizations that influence both disciplines.*
▲ *Form and basic content of audit reports.*

Within the past several decades, accounting and auditing have matured into complex and controversial professional activities: complex, because accounting and auditing have become increasingly sophisticated; and controversial, because several public- and private-sector organizations have strongly criticized the performance and regulation of accountants and auditors. One could have picked no better time to study accounting and auditing, no better time to become a professional accountant or auditor. The profession has matured, yet it continues to grow.

This chapter is an introduction to auditing and the public accounting profession. The chapter begins with a discussion of the nature of auditing, the types of audits performed in the United States, and the need for auditing. The historical evolution of auditing is addressed next, followed by a description of the standard-setting process and the role of the Auditing Standards Board and generally accepted auditing standards. In turn, the public accounting profession is introduced, and quality control and peer review, the profession's means for monitoring the effectiveness of public accounting firms, are discussed. The chapter concludes by describing the professional organizations influencing auditing and by briefly introducing the auditor's report, the end product of a financial statement audit.

NATURE OF AUDITING

There are several different types of audits, each distinguished by its purpose and scope. Financial statement audits performed by independent auditors are the main focus of this book. However, the fundamental concepts of auditing are applicable to all types of audits, whether performed by independent auditors or by internal or public-sector (governmental) auditors.

Auditing Defined

Over the years, the term "auditing" has been defined by a variety of organizations and individuals. In 1972, the American Accounting Association's Committee on Basic Auditing Concepts developed a definition that is not only clear, concise, and logical, but sufficiently broad to encompass many different types of audits. The Committee's report, entitled *A Statement of Basic Auditing Concepts* (ASOBAC), defines auditing as follows:

> Auditing is a systematic process of objectively obtaining and evaluating evidence regarding assertions about economic actions and events to ascertain the degree of correspondence between those assertions and established criteria and communicating the results to interested users.[1]

As this definition implies, auditing encompasses both an *investigative process* and a *reporting process*. Investigation involves the systematic gathering and evaluation of evidence as a basis for determining whether assertions made, for example, in a company's financial statements, correspond with established criteria, such as generally accepted accounting principles (GAAP). In turn, reporting involves communicating an evaluation or opinion in an audit report to interested users.

In the context of a financial statement audit, the opinion conveyed in an audit report is referred to as an *attestation* and defined in ASOBAC as follows:

> Attestation is a communicated statement of opinion (judgment), based upon convincing evidence, by an independent, competent, authoritative person, concerning the degree of correspondence in all material respects of accounting information communicated by an entity (individual, firm, or governmental unit) with established criteria.[2]

The opinion conveyed in an audit report depends upon the results of the audit, and may indicate either that the financial statements are presented fairly

---

[1] Committee on Basic Auditing Concepts, "A Statement of Basic Auditing Concepts," *The Accounting Review,* supplement to vol. 47, 1972, p. 18.

[2] *Ibid.*, p. 22.

in conformity with GAAP or that the statements are not presented fairly. Alternatively, an auditor may conclude that the statements cannot be attested to, for example if sufficient evidence cannot be obtained.

Auditing and the Scientific Method of Inquiry

A financial statement audit is a systematic process which begins with a client's request for audit services and culminates in an attestation. In the sciences, a similar systematic process occurs when a scientist is confronted with a research problem that must be solved; the process referred to is the *scientific method of inquiry*. Of course, there are differences between the activities of auditors and scientists. However, there are remarkable similarities, suggesting that auditors can learn much about audit method from a scientist's method of investigation.

The judgments of both auditors and scientists rely heavily upon the quality and quantity of evidence obtained. Thus, despite differences between scientists' and auditors' activities, the common dependence upon evidence suggests that ". . . we should keep in mind the well-deserved prestige of scientific methods and consider the extent to which they suggest the possibility of improvement in the auditing method."[3]

The scientific method of inquiry is a logical, evaluative framework for reaching reasoned, supportable conclusions. Cohen and Nagel, in *An Introduction to Logic and Scientific Method*, capture the essence of the scientific method:

> Scientific method . . . is the persistent application of logic as the common feature of all reasoned knowledge.
>
> . . . but in essence scientific method is simply the pursuit of truth as determined by logical considerations.[4]

If the phrase "scientific method" were replaced by "auditing," Cohen and Nagel's comments would capture the essence of auditing as well.

To illustrate the similarities between the scientific method of inquiry and auditing, the following equates each step in the scientific method to a typical auditing scenario. As the illustration implies, auditing is nothing more than a special application of the scientific method of inquiry.

---

[3]R. K. Mautz and H. A. Sharaf, *The Philosophy of Auditing* (Sarasota: American Accounting Association, 1961), p. 23.

[4]M. R. Cohen and E. Nagel, *An Introduction to Logic and Scientific Method* (New York: Harcourt, Brace, and Company, 1934), p. 192.

Scientific Method	Independent Audit
• Observe and recognize a problem	Client requests an opinion about whether financial statements present fairly the financial position as of December 31, 19xx, the results of operations, and cash flows in conformity with GAAP.
• Formulate overall and composite hypotheses	Overall hypothesis: Financial statements present fairly . . . . Composite hypotheses: Individual financial statement accounts and other disclosures are fairly stated.
• Gather relevant, verifiable evidence to test hypotheses	Select appropriate audit procedures and gather sufficient competent evidential matter to test each composite hypothesis.
• Evaluate evidence • Develop conclusions	Evaluate evidential matter to determine if the composite hypotheses and, therefore, the overall hypothesis are supported, refuted, or inconclusive.

Other Types of Audits

In addition to independent financial statement audits, there are other types of audits, including operational audits, financial and compliance audits, economy and efficiency audits, and program results audits. Each of these audits is described briefly here and discussed in detail in Chapter 21.

Operational Audits. An operational audit is designed to assess the efficiency and effectiveness of management's operating procedures, but is usually conducted by a company's internal auditors, rather than by independent auditors. Thus, internal operational audits focus on operating procedures, not on recorded dollar amounts or reported financial information. In general, an operational audit can address a company's entire scope of operating procedures, or selected procedures. For example, management might request that the internal audit department appraise controls over sensitive and highly valued inventory, such as microprocessing chips or precious metals. Regardless of the internal auditor's charge, though, an operational audit should always result in clearly defined recommendations to aid management in correcting inefficient or ineffective operating procedures.

Financial and Compliance Audits. A financial and compliance audit is quite similar to a financial statement audit, but is performed for public-sector entities, such as state and local government agencies, and by either independent auditors or public-sector (governmental) auditors. In general, a financial and compliance audit is designed to determine whether a public-sector entity's financial statements are presented fairly in accordance with generally accepted accounting principles, which is similar to independent audits. An additional objective is to determine whether the governmental entity has complied with applicable laws and regulations that may have a material effect on financial statements. For example, many state governments receive direct grants from the federal government which impose specific requirements on how grant funds are to be disbursed. Thus, a financial and compliance audit for the recipient state would focus not only on whether the state's financial statements conform with generally accepted accounting principles, but also on whether the state complied with the federal government's restrictions on disbursing grant funds.

Economy and Efficiency Audits. An economy and efficiency audit is similar to an operational audit, but is typically performed for public-sector entities, such as state and local governmental agencies, and by either public-sector (governmental) auditors or by independent auditors. In general, a public-sector economy and efficiency audit is designed to determine whether a governmental entity, such as a state highway department, is managing and utilizing resources economically and efficiently, what the causes of diseconomies or inefficiencies are, and whether the entity has complied with laws and regulations concerning matters of economy and efficiency. For example, for a particular state agency, a state government may authorize an economy and efficiency audit if the legislature decides there is sufficient cause to believe the agency is potentially purchasing goods and services at uneconomical prices or is mismanaging resources purchased.

Program Results Audits. Program results audits are performed for governmental entities, such as state and local governmental agencies, and by either independent or public-sector auditors, but are unlike any of the types of audits introduced thus far. In general, a program results audit is open-ended, is relatively subjective, and is designed to determine whether an entity is achieving the results and benefits desired by the legislature, and whether the entity has considered alternatives that might yield desired results at lower cost. For example, if a city were to receive a federal grant for the purpose of "improving the quality of life in the west side of town," the program results auditor would have to judge first how to measure "quality of life" and then whether the city had indeed met the granting federal agency's criteria. Thus, program results audits are typically more subjective than financial statement audits and require a considerable amount of creativity on the auditor's part.

NEED FOR INDEPENDENT AUDITS

Independent auditors conduct financial statement audits because the users of reported financial information have a need for these services. In short, there is a demand, and therefore an established market, for independent audits.

The Market for Independent Audit Services

In the United States, both general-purpose financial statements and an independent auditor's report are included within the annual report of a publicly traded corporation. The need for an auditor's report derives from the fact that stockholders turn over resources to a corporation's management who presumably invests resources in the best interests of stockholders. However, stockholders do not have direct access to internal accounting records and therefore are unaware of whether reported financial information has been biased by management. As a result, there is a need for a "monitor," the independent auditor, to report on whether the financial statements prepared by management present fairly in all material respects the financial position, results of operations, and cash flows of the corporation. In fact, so prevalent is the need for independent auditing, that the Securities and Exchange Commission requires an independent audit in order to protect the interests of security holders of publicly traded corporations.

Even though financial statements are audited by independent auditors, the statements are the representations and responsibility of management, not the auditor. An independent auditor is responsible for reporting on financial statements. Management, in contrast, is responsible for adopting sound policies, safeguarding assets, devising an adequate internal control structure, and, equally important, determining the form and content of financial statements.

Users of Financial Information

Users of financial information can be classified as either internal or external to an entity: *internal users* include corporate controllers, management accountants, and internal auditors, among others. Because they are directly involved in achieving the company's goals, these users are willing to rely initially upon internally generated financial information. Ultimately, however, internal users require an unbiased opinion as a check upon management, employees, and the financial accounting and reporting system.

In contrast, *external users* typically are far removed from the operation of the company and are, at best, only indirectly involved in achieving the company's goals. Thus, external users are reluctant to rely upon internally generated financial information; rather, they prefer the "comfort" of an audit. Although many and varied in their needs, external users can be categorized generally as investors (e.g., present and potential debt and equity security holders), creditors (e.g., banks and suppliers), analysts (e.g., underwriters and credit rating bureaus), and financial information monitors (e.g., regulatory agencies and stock exchanges).

An independent auditor's opinion provides both internal and external users with input to making reasoned, logical, and informed decisions about a variety of financial matters, including a company's earnings performance, financial position, liquidity position, managerial performance, and economic vulnerability. Without auditors, decisions such as these are more likely to be made from biased financial information. Auditing helps to minimize biases by acting as a monitor of financial information reported by management.

THE EVOLUTION OF AUDITING IN THE U.S.

Throughout this book, the discussion centers on contemporary audit practice in the United States. From what beginnings, though, did auditing in the U.S. evolve? The following sections discuss the influence of British audit practice on U.S. practice and the early authoritative pronouncements.

The British Influence

Although the genesis of financial auditing is not known with certainty, evidence of early audit activity has been documented. For example, ancient Egyptians are known to have required that tax receipts be recorded by two independent officials, and Romans are known to have cross-checked expenditure authorizations with actual payments. Despite this early evidence of isolated audit activity, there is only sketchy evidence of systematic auditing prior to the nineteenth century.

The first contemporary audit-related legislation appeared in the British Joint Stock Companies Act of 1844. The 1844 Act, revised and reissued as the Companies Clauses Consolidation Act of 1845, required that one or more stockholders examine balance sheets prepared by company directors. Stockholders were given authority to examine company books and records and to question officers, management, and employees as necessary. The balance sheet and accompanying stockholder-auditor report were filed with the Registrar of Joint Stock Companies, with copies forwarded to all stockholders.

The Companies Acts of 1855–56 provided that auditors no longer need be stockholders. Rather, an auditor could be appointed at the company's option. Only a petition signed by 20 percent of the stockholders could compel a company to appoint an outside auditor. Through this provision in the 1855–

56 Acts, the seed was planted for a movement toward compulsory audits. Surprisingly, the Companies Acts of 1862, 1900, and 1928–29 made no effort to require audits. It was not until the Companies Act of 1947, some nine decades after the 1855–56 Acts, that British law required compulsory opinions that financial statements give a "full and fair" view of financial position and results of operations.

Nineteenth and twentieth century auditing in Great Britain had a marked impact upon the professional practice of auditing in the United States. Many British public accounting firms opened U.S. offices when British investments expanded overseas. In fact, the evolution of auditing in the United States had a decided British influence; several of today's major U.S. public accounting firms were once branches of British firms (e.g., Price Waterhouse & Co.).

The Early Pronouncements

The first authoritative auditing pronouncement in the U.S. was published in the April 1917 Federal Reserve Bulletin under the title "Uniform Accounting: A Tentative Proposal Submitted by the Federal Reserve Board." The 1917 bulletin, prepared at the request of the Federal Trade Commission, was described as a "memorandum on balance-sheet audits" and was intended to promote "a uniform system of accounting."

Subsequent revisions of the 1917 bulletin were not particularly substantive. However, the titles of the 1918, 1929, and 1936 bulletins reflected changes in the profession's view toward auditing during that period. The title change in 1918, "Approved Methods for the Preparation of Balance-Sheet Statements" from "Uniform Accounting . . ." in 1917, suggests a realization that uniform accounting methods for all business entities is unattainable; accounting should serve a business entity, not vice versa.

The 1929 bulletin, "Verification of Financial Statements," referred to financial statements rather than balance sheets, as had been the case in the 1917 and 1918 bulletins, suggesting that the 1929 bulletin was intended to apply to income statements as well as balance sheets. This reflects a particularly important shift in thinking within the first three decades of the twentieth century. At the turn of the century and thereafter, a business entity's liquidity position was a major financial barometer used by financial information users. Thus, the balance sheet was the preeminent financial statement of the day. In the late twenties, however, due in part to the stock market crash of 1929, operating performance and net income became equally important financial barometers, along with liquidity. Thus, during the period 1917 through 1929, the income statement gained equal prominence with the balance sheet.

The title of the 1936 bulletin, "Examination of Financial Statements by Independent Public Accountants," is perhaps the most revealing indication of the profession's changing view toward auditing. Whereas the 1929 bulletin was entitled *"Verification* of Financial Statements," the 1936 bulletin related to *examinations*. A verification is entirely different from an examination; verification implies auditing every transaction and event underlying financial statements, and examination implies auditing selected transactions and events. Contemporary auditors do not verify financial statements; they examine them. Clearly, "examination" more closely approximates the independent auditor's function.

AUDIT STANDARD SETTING

The preceding discussion outlines some of the early history of audit practice in the U.S. The following sections introduce the organizations and authoritative bodies that exercise the most influence on audit practice today: the American Institute of Certified Public Accountants (AICPA), the national organization of certified public accountants (CPAs); the Securities and Exchange Commission (SEC), a federal agency empowered to protect investors by promoting reliable financial information; and the Auditing Standards Board, a senior technical body of the AICPA designated to issue authoritative auditing pronouncements.

American Institute of Certified Public Accountants

The AICPA is a national voluntary-membership, professional organization with approximately 200,000 members. Although all members are CPAs, not all practice as independent accountants or auditors; some hold financial positions in industry or government — for example, as controllers, financial officers, and internal auditors — others teach in colleges and universities, and some hold other positions.

Since its formation in the late nineteenth century, the AICPA has exerted a strong influence on accounting and auditing thought, particularly through its research, publications, and pronouncements on accounting, auditing, professional ethics, management advisory services, and taxes and its programs for continuing professional education. For example, research conducted by or for the AICPA has resulted in publications such as Auditing Research Monographs, Auditing Procedures Studies, and Audit and Accounting Guides, none of which are authoritative, but all of which are available to guide practicing auditors. In addition, the AICPA publishes a monthly periodical, *The Journal of Accountancy,* regarded by many as the leading professional publication devoted to current developments in accounting and auditing practice.

Securities and Exchange Commission

The Securities and Exchange Commission was created by Congress in 1934 to regulate the registration and exchange of securities under the Securities Act of 1933 and Securities Exchange Act of 1934. The SEC is not empowered with the authority to issue authoritative auditing pronouncements per se, but the Commission does issue publications which must be followed by publicly traded corporations in periodic filings to the SEC, including *Form 10-K,* the annual financial report; *Form 10-Q,* the quarterly financial report; and *Form 8-K,* a form filed at the end of any month in which significant events have occurred, such as the sale of a subsidiary or addition of a new product line.

Until 1982, the major SEC publication of interest to independent auditors was *Accounting Series Releases (ASRs),* which represented both informational and enforcement-related pronouncements that had to be followed in the published financial reports of publicly traded corporations. Although some ASRs are still relevant today, the Commission now issues two separate series of publications which replaced the ASRs: *Financial Reporting Releases,* which announce accounting and auditing matters of general interest, and *Accounting and Auditing Enforcement Releases,* which announce accounting and auditing matters related to the SEC's enforcement activities. The SEC also issues *Staff Accounting Bulletins,* which are unofficial interpretations that provide guidance in the application of SEC regulations. Today, the AICPA, through its Auditing Standards Board, is the most influential organization in the audit standard-setting process. However, the SEC's position is always considered by the AICPA in developing audit standards.

Authoritative Bodies

Since 1939, four succeeding authoritative bodies have been empowered by the AICPA to create guidelines for audit and accounting services:

▲ Committee on Auditing Procedure, 1939–1972.
▲ Auditing Standards Executive Committee, 1972–1978.
▲ Auditing Standards Board, 1978 to present.
▲ Accounting and Review Services Committee, 1977 to present.

In 1939, the AICPA authorized appointment of the Committee on Auditing Procedure (CAP) to ''. . . examine into auditing procedure and other related questions in the light of recent public discussions.'' The ''public discussions'' related in part to the McKesson & Robbins, Inc. $19 million overstatement of inventory and accounts receivable. Although common practice today, McKesson & Robbins' auditors neither observed physical inventory on hand nor confirmed accounts receivable balances with debtors. In 1939, the CAP issued a report, "Extensions of Auditing Procedure," which recommended physical inventory observations and accounts receivable confirmations as accepted audit practice. The report became the CAP's first *Statement on Auditing Procedure (SAP);* and fifty-four statements were issued by the CAP from 1939 to 1972.

In 1972, the name of the committee was changed to the Auditing Standards Executive Committee (AudSEC), and the fifty-four SAPs were codified into *Statement on Auditing Standards (SAS) No. 1.* The name change recognized AudSEC as the senior technical AICPA committee authorized to issue auditing pronouncements. The title change from Statements on Auditing *Procedure* to Statements on Auditing *Standards* suggests that the statements interpret standards, rather than promulgate procedures. This shift in title was more substantive than cosmetic, since standards deal with guidelines or measures of quality, and procedures deal with methods and techniques. That is, the title change underscored the role of AudSEC as a standard-setting body. From 1972 to 1978, AudSEC issued SAS Nos. 2 through 23, covering such issues as reports on audited financial statements, related party transactions, the auditor's responsibility for detecting errors or irregularities, and illegal acts by clients.

Creation of Auditing Standards Board. In 1978, the AICPA's independent Commission on Auditors' Responsibilities issued a 195-page report on the appropriate responsibilities of independent auditors. Section 10 of the report, "The Process of Establishing Auditing Standards," offered several criticisms of AudSEC, including:

▲ *Quality of guidance* — to be more useful to practicing auditors, the guidance in SASs should be more specific.
▲ *Timeliness of guidance* — SASs are typically issued long after a project first appears on AudSEC's technical agenda.
▲ *Orientation to public company audit* — most SASs are oriented toward public company audits, thereby ignoring nonpublic company audits, the major focus of many CPA firms.

As a partial response to these criticisms, the AICPA disbanded AudSEC and appointed two senior technical committees: the Auditing Standards Board, designated to issue *SASs* and *Interpretations* of SASs, and the Accounting and Review Services Committee (discussed more fully in Chapter 20), designated to issue *Statements on Standards for Accounting and Review Services (SSARS),* relating to unaudited financial information for nonpublic entities. The individual pronouncements of both bodies are numbered sequentially when issued, and the provisions of each new pronouncement are codified, i.e. incorporated within appropriate code sections of the *AICPA Professional Standards.* An updated *Codification of Statements on Auditing Standards* is published annually, containing the currently effective SASs and Interpretations of SASs. Major divisions within the codification are divided into sections, each with its own section number, and paragraphs within a section are numbered decimally. For example, AU Section 110.01 refers to the first paragraph of Section 110.[5]

Charge and Structure of Auditing Standards Board. At the time of its formation in October 1978, the Auditing Standards Board was given the following charge:

> The AICPA Auditing Standards Board shall be responsible for the promulgation of auditing standards and procedures to be observed by members of the AICPA in accordance with the Institute's rules of conduct.
>
> The board shall be alert to new opportunities for auditors to serve the public, both by the assumption of new responsibilities and by improved ways of meeting old ones, and shall as expeditiously as possible develop standards and procedures that will enable the auditor to assume those responsibilities.
>
> Auditing standards and procedures promulgated by the board shall:
> a. Define the nature and extent of the auditor's responsibilities.
> b. Provide guidance to the auditor in carrying out his duties, enabling him to express an opinion on the reliability of the representations on which he is reporting.
> c. Make special provision, where appropriate, to meet the needs of small enterprises.
> d. Have regard to the costs which they impose on society in relation to the benefits reasonably expected to be derived from the audit function.
>
> The auditing standards board shall provide auditors with all possible guidance in the implementation of its pronouncements, by means of interpretations of its statements, by the issuance of guidelines, and by other means available to it.

The Board consists of twenty-one AICPA members, who are compensated and reimbursed for expenses. Board members are appointed for rotating terms with the consent of the AICPA's Directors.

An AICPA Vice President-Auditing and a Director of Auditing Research work closely with the Board. The VP-Auditing has administrative responsibility for the Board's support staff and works directly with the Board's chairman on such matters as setting the agenda and overseeing project task forces. The Director of Auditing Research oversees research projects central to the Board's technical agenda. Although they do not vote in ASB matters, both

---

[5] Throughout this book, references to sections and paragraphs of the AICPA's *Codification of Statements on Auditing Standards* are made parenthetically after the sentence or passages referenced, with "Section" abbreviated *Sec.*

the VP-Auditing and Director of Auditing Research are important to the Board's operations and, therefore, to the audit standard-setting process in the United States.

Generally Accepted Auditing Standards (GAAS)

In 1941, the Securities and Exchange Commission (SEC) issued Accounting Series Release No. 21, which in part required that an auditor state within an audit report whether the audit was conducted in accordance with generally accepted auditing standards applicable in the circumstances. However, no such written standards existed. As a result, the Committee on Auditing Procedure began deliberating on a series of standards for auditing. The work was interrupted by World War II, and it was not until 1947 that the Committee finalized nine generally accepted standards in its report, "Tentative Statement of Auditing Standards — Their Generally Accepted Significance and Scope." The nine standards were approved by vote of the AICPA's membership in 1948, and a tenth standard was adopted in 1949. In 1988, two of the standards were revised.

The ten generally accepted auditing standards (GAAS), presented in Figure 1-1, remain applicable today. The Statements on Auditing Standards issued by the Auditing Standards Board are considered interpretations of the ten GAAS. As illustrated in Figure 1-1, the standards are classified as general standards, standards of field work, and standards of reporting. The three *general standards* relate to the auditor's professional qualifications and the quality of his or her audit work. In turn, the three *standards of field work* relate to the conduct of an audit in the "field" — that is, at the client's place of business. The four *standards of reporting* relate to an auditor's report on the results of an independent audit. The ten standards are interrelated and interdependent and represent the measures of quality for conducting an independent audit. These ten generally accepted standards will be referred to frequently throughout this book, as they are throughout the auditing literature, and in Chapter 5 they will be interpreted in detail and related to the underlying concepts of auditing.

Public or Private Sector?

As noted above, there have been four private-sector standard-setting bodies since 1939: the Committee on Auditing Procedure, AudSec, and now the Auditing Standards Board and the Accounting and Review Services Committee. Despite this preponderance of private-sector bodies, there has been a long-standing debate within the financial community regarding who should set auditing standards — the public sector (e.g., the federal government) or the private sector, as is the case today. For example, as far back as the early

---

FIGURE 1-1
Generally Accepted Auditing Standards

General Standards

1. The examination is to be performed by a person or persons having adequate technical training and proficiency as an auditor.
2. In all matters relating to the assignment, an independence in mental attitude is to be maintained by the auditor or auditors.
3. Due professional care is to be exercised in the performance of the examination and the preparation of the report.

Standards of Field Work

1. The work is to be adequately planned and assistants, if any, are to be properly supervised.
2. A sufficient understanding of internal control structure is to be obtained to plan the audit and to determine the nature, timing, and extent of tests to be performed.
3. Sufficient competent evidential matter is to be obtained through inspection, observation, inquiries, and confirmations to afford a reasonable basis for an opinion regarding the financial statements under examination.

Standards of Reporting

1. The report shall state whether the financial statements are presented in accordance with generally accepted accounting principles.
2. The report shall identify those circumstances in which such principles have not been consistently observed in the current period in relation to the preceding period.
3. Informative disclosures in the financial statements are to be regarded as reasonably adequate unless otherwise stated in the report.
4. The report shall contain either an expression of opinion regarding the financial statements, taken as a whole, or an assertion to the effect that an opinion cannot be expressed. When an overall opinion cannot be expressed, the reasons therefor should be stated. In all cases where an auditor's name is associated with financial statements, the report should contain a clear-cut indication of the character of the auditor's examination, if any, and the degree of responsibility he is taking.

1930s, there was a movement within Congress to charter auditors and to mandate annual audits by government-affiliated auditors. In the 1970s, the Senate Subcommittee on Reports, Accounting, and Management issued a report, *The Accounting Establishment,* recommending that both auditing and accounting standards be developed in the public sector. More recently, and as a result of several well-publicized audit failures in the 1980s, the House Subcommittee on Oversight and Investigations, chaired by Congressman John D. Dingell (D-Mich.), conducted hearings on the quality and effectiveness of corporate financial disclosures, including the role of private-sector standard setting and the responsibilities of independent auditors.

Despite this controversy, there has been no widespread effort to remove audit standard setting from the private sector, primarily because it is not clear that self-regulation has failed. However, if the standard-setting process should fail, self-regulation would appear unsuccessful and therefore suspect. In addition, to the extent that audit failures result from auditor deficiencies alone, rather than from deficiencies in the standard-setting process, the profession would suffer nevertheless since, again, self-regulation would appear suspect. In short, it is in the best interest of every practicing auditor to uphold the profession's standards and thereby enhance the profession's credibility. If the profession is not successful in demonstrating effective self-regulation to the public-sector protectors (e.g., the SEC) of third-party rights (e.g., security holders), public-sector regulation could well supplant private-sector self-regulation.

THE PUBLIC ACCOUNTING PROFESSION

The phrase "public accounting" describes the separate body of knowledge and related services provided to clients by independent certified public accountants. In general, certified public accounting (CPA) firms are categorized as national, regional, or local, depending upon a firm's size and geographical scope. The "Big 8" national firms are: Arthur Andersen & Co.; Arthur Young & Co.; Coopers & Lybrand; Deloitte Haskins & Sells; Ernst & Whinney; Peat, Marwick, Main; Price Waterhouse & Co.; and Touche Ross & Co. Other national firms include Grant Thornton, Laventhol & Horwath, and Seidman and Seidman.

Most CPA firms are organized as partnerships (or professional service corporations) and are structured such that there are fewer partners (or shareholders) than managers in a firm, fewer managers than senior accountants, and fewer senior accountants than staff accountants. In a CPA firm, promotions are usually made from within; direct entry into a firm at a rank above staff accountant is less common than promotion within a firm.

Certified Public Accountants

To become a CPA, an individual must satisfy selected *educational requirements*, pass the *Uniform CPA Examination*, and satisfy selected *experience requirements*. The educational and experience requirements are determined individually by state boards of accountancy and vary among states. The Uniform CPA Examination is prepared by the AICPA, administered by the individual state boards of accountancy, and graded by the AICPA. A license to practice as a CPA is granted by the state board of accountancy, a state regulatory agency empowered to regulate the practice of public accounting within a state. Because licenses to practice are granted by state rather than national regulatory agencies, a license must be obtained from each state in which a CPA practices. However, because there is reciprocity among most state boards of accountancy, a CPA can obtain a license to practice in another state assuming he or she is in "good standing" in all other states from which a license was issued and meets the requirements of the state granting reciprocity.

Educational requirements are not uniform among the states. However, most states require that a CPA candidate hold at least the equivalent of a four-year baccalaureate degree with a minimum number of credit hours in accounting. The *Uniform CPA Examination* is administered twice annually, in May and November. The exam consists of four sections — Accounting Practice, Accounting Theory, Law, and Auditing — and is administered over a three-day period. A grade of seventy-five is required to pass a section of the exam, and conditional credit (i.e., credit for passing individual sections) is allowed in all states.

The *experience requirements* to become a CPA also vary among the states. The requirements range from a high of three years with a CPA firm to, as is the case in some states, no requirements at all. In most states the experience requirements can be fulfilled either before or after passing the CPA examination.

The services of certified public accountants are provided to the general public and include auditing, tax services, management advisory services, and accounting services. Other services are also provided by public accountants, but are less prominent.[6]

Auditing

Financial statement audits result in a public accounting firm attesting that financial statements are presented fairly in conformity with GAAP, that they

---

[6]For discussions of contemporary and emerging services see: J. L. Arnold, A. A. Cherry, M. A. Diamond, and J. A. Walker, "Small Business: An Area Ripe for Practice Development," *Journal of Accountancy* (August, 1984), pp. 74–82; R. D. Dillon, W. R. Feldhaus, and R. P. Farrell, "A Special Area of Service: Risk Management," *Journal of Accountancy* (February, 1984), pp. 50–58.; S.Goldberg, "Pension Planning and the CPA," *Journal of Accountancy* (May, 1984), pp. 68–72; D. Palluis and R. K. Elliot, "Prospective Financial Statements: Guidelines for a Growing Practice Area," *Journal of Accountancy* (January, 1984), pp.56–69; and C. C. Verschoor, "Personal Financial Planning and the CPA," *Journal of Accountancy* (January, 1985), pp. 52–58.

are not so presented, or that an opinion cannot be given. Auditing has long been the predominant service offered by the larger public accounting firms, though there is less emphasis on auditing in smaller firms.

The personnel assigned to an audit engagement varies depending on the size of the entity audited, the nature of its business, and the complexity of the engagement. For example, an audit team assigned to a medium-size client might include one partner, one manager, one senior accountant, and three staff accountants. The *partner* is directly responsible for planning and reviewing all phases of the engagement, even though he or she may not be involved directly in the engagement's day-to-day operations. When the engagement is completed, the partner signs the audit report in the firm's name and performs other roles, such as reviewing the audit work performed and approving the firm's billing to the client.

The *manager* reports directly to the partner and typically has much closer contact with the client's operational personnel, such as the corporate controller, and with the senior and staff accountants. Much like the partner, the manager performs little detailed audit work. Most of the manager's work relates to planning, supervision, detailed reviews of all work performed by the senior and staff accountants, and billings to the client.

The *senior accountant* reports directly to the manager and is closely involved in the day-to-day operations of the engagement. He or she supervises the detailed audit work of the staff accountants and performs audit procedures requiring a higher degree of experience and expertise. *Staff accountants* report to the senior accountant and are directly responsible for, and provide conclusions about, each phase of the audit engagement to which they are assigned. For example, a staff accountant may be assigned to examine evidence supporting the balances of receivable or payable accounts as of the balance sheet date.

Tax Services

Because a client's tax liability is dependent upon accounting records, public accounting firms are particularly qualified to provide a variety of tax preparation and planning services. Tax services are usually provided for audit clients, although public accounting firms also serve a large number of individuals and companies that are not audit clients.

Although a client's financial reporting and tax compliance responsibilities are closely related, it is important to understand that each serves different objectives. An objective of financial reporting is determining net income; an objective of tax compliance is determining taxable income. These two concepts of income are quite different: financial net income is determined by applying generally accepted accounting principles, and taxable income by applying tax laws and regulations. Understanding this difference is important to an auditor, because it can often explain the motivation for choosing particular alternative accounting policies over others.

Management Advisory Services

Public accounting firms also provide clients with non-audit-related advice, such as how to design and implement a cost accounting or data processing system. These management advisory services have been criticized by the government and others. Essentially, the critics have argued that it is inconsistent for a public accounting firm to audit an accounting system designed and/or implemented by that firm.[7] Although a rather complex issue, the essential question is: "At what point does advice become managerial decision making?" An answer to that question could go a long way toward resolving the management advisory services controversy, since advice is compatible with audit services, but making decisions for management is not.

Accounting Services

Public accounting firms, particularly smaller firms, frequently provide accounting services to clients. These services are not related to auditing and may involve the compilation or review of a company's financial statements or may encompass the entire accounting function, including preparation of all or most journal entries from source documents, posting to ledger accounts, and year-end adjusting and closing procedures. A CPA firm's association with unaudited statements is discussed in Chapter 20.

MONITORING PUBLIC ACCOUNTING FIRMS: QUALITY CONTROL AND PEER REVIEW

Quality control is the process of assuring consistent performance and achievement within an individual CPA firm, and *peer review* is the process

---

[7]More complete discussions of the debate appear in several early articles: D. R. Carmichael and R. J. Sweiringa, "Compatability of Auditing Independence and Management Services — An Identification of the Issues," *The Accounting Review* (October, 1968), pp. 697–706; R. V. Hartley and T. L. Ross, "MAS and Audit Independence: An Image Problem," *Journal of Accountancy* (November, 1972), pp. 42–52; S. P. Klion, "MAS Practice: Are the Critics Justified?" *Journal of Accountancy* (June, 1978), pp. 72–78; and P. Titard, "Independence and Management Advisory Services — Opinions of Financial Statement Users," *Journal of Accountancy* (July, 1971), pp. 47–52.

of encouraging quality control across all firms. Over the past decade, quality control and peer review have become increasingly important to the management of a public accounting practice as a result of growing criticism by congressional subcommittees, among others, during the 1970s and 1980s. The success and continued acceptance of private-sector regulation of the public accounting profession may depend heavily upon the effectiveness of established quality control and peer review programs.

Relating Quality Control and GAAS

The quality of a CPA firm's audit practice is dependent upon the quality of each audit engagement — a whole is equal to the sum of its parts. Since generally accepted auditing standards are recognized as the measures of an audit's quality, it can also be argued that the quality of a CPA firm's audit practice is therefore dependent upon the application of generally accepted auditing standards to each audit engagement. Quality control is the vehicle used by CPA firms to assure that GAAS are followed on each engagement, and as a result, that the firm maintains a quality practice. Thus, as stated in *Statement on Auditing Standards No. 25,* "The Relationship of Generally Accepted Auditing Standards to Quality Control Standards" (AU Sec. 161):

▲ A firm should establish quality control policies and procedures to provide reasonable assurance of conformity with GAAS in its audit engagements.

▲ GAAS and quality control standards are related, and the quality control policies and procedures adopted by a firm may affect both the conduct of individual audit engagements and the conduct of a firm's audit practice as a whole.

In 1978, the AICPA established the now disbanded Quality Control Standards Committee, a senior technical committee of the AICPA designated to issue pronouncements on quality control standards. The Committee's only *Statement on Quality Control Standards,* "System of Quality Control for a CPA Firm," was issued in 1979 and stated that a firm should have a comprehensive and suitably designed quality control system, encompassing the firm's organization structure, policies, and procedures. In general, the nature and extent of a firm's system of quality control will depend upon its size, degree of operating autonomy allowed operating personnel and practice offices, nature of practice, organizational structure, and appropriate cost-benefit considerations. Nevertheless, despite the nature and extent of a firm's quality control system, the firm should consider each of the nine elements of quality control identified in *Statement on Quality Control Standards No. 1* and presented in Figure 1-2, pages 22 and 23.

FIGURE 1-2
Elements of Quality Control

   A firm shall consider each of the elements of quality control discussed below, to the extent applicable to its practice, in establishing its
quality control policies and procedures. The elements of quality control
are interrelated. Thus, a firm's hiring practices affect its policies as to
training. Training practices affect policies as to promotion. Practices in
both categories affect policies as to supervision. Practices as to supervision, in turn, affect policies as to training and promotion.

a. *Independence.* Policies and procedures should be established to provide the firm with reasonable assurance that persons at all organizational levels maintain independence to the extent required by the rules
   of conduct of the AICPA. Rule 101 [ET section 101.01] of the rules
   of conduct contains examples of instances wherein a firm's independence will be considered to be impaired.

b. *Assigning Personnel to Engagements.* Policies and procedures for assigning personnel to engagements should be established to provide the
   firm with reasonable assurance that work will be performed by persons
   having the degree of technical training and proficiency required in the
   circumstances. In making assignments, the nature and extent of supervision to be provided should be taken into account. Generally, the
   more able and experienced the personnel assigned to a particular engagement, the less is the need for direct supervision.

c. *Consultation.* Policies and procedures for consultation should be established to provide the firm with reasonable assurance that personnel
   will seek assistance, to the extent required, from persons having appropriate levels of knowledge, competence, judgment, and authority.
   The nature of the arrangements for consultation will depend on a number of factors, including the size of the firm and the levels of knowledge, competence, and judgment possessed by the persons performing
   the work.

d. *Supervision.* Policies and procedures for the conduct and supervision
   of work at all organizational levels should be established to provide
   the firm with reasonable assurance that the work performed meets the
   firm's standards of quality. The extent of supervision and review appropriate in a given instance depends on many factors, including the
   complexity of the subject matter, the qualifications of the persons performing the work, and the extent of consultation available and used.
   The responsibility of a firm for establishing procedures for supervision
   is distinct from the responsibility of individuals to adequately plan and
   supervise the work on a particular engagement.

(continued)

e. *Hiring.* Policies and procedures for hiring should be established to provide the firm with reasonable assurance that those employed possess the appropriate characteristics to enable them to perform competently. The quality of a firm's work ultimately depends on the integrity, competence, and motivation of personnel who perform and supervise the work. Thus, a firm's recruiting programs are factors in maintaining such quality.

f. *Professional Development.* Policies and procedures for professional development should be established to provide the firm with reasonable assurance that personnel will have the knowledge required to enable them to fulfill responsibilities assigned. Continuing professional education and training activities enable a firm to provide personnel with the knowledge required to fulfill responsibilities assigned to them and to progress within the firm.

g. *Advancement.* Policies and procedures for advancing personnel should be established to provide the firm with reasonable assurance that those selected for advancement will have the qualifications necessary for fulfillment of the responsibilities they will be called on to assume. Practices in advancing personnel have important implications for the quality of a firm's work. Qualifications that personnel selected for advancement should possess include, but are not limited to, character, intelligence, judgment, and motivation.

h. *Acceptance and Continuance of Clients.* Policies and procedures should be established for deciding whether to accept or continue a client in order to minimize the likelihood of association with a client whose management lacks integrity. Suggesting that there should be procedures for this purpose does not imply that a firm vouches for the integrity or reliability of a client, nor does it imply that a firm has a duty to anyone but itself with respect to the acceptance, rejection, or retention of clients. However, prudence suggests that a firm be selective in determining its professional relationships.

i. *Inspection.* Policies and procedures for inspection should be established to provide the firm with reasonable assurance that the procedures relating to the other elements of quality control are being effectively applied. Procedures for inspection may be developed and performed by individuals acting on behalf of the firm's management. The type of inspection procedures used will depend on the controls established by the firm and the assignment of responsibilities within the firm to implement its quality control policies and procedures.

In 1980, the Quality Control Standards Committee issued a guide, "Establishing Quality Control Policies and Procedures," which, although not possessing the authority of a *Statement on Quality Control Standards,* provides examples of procedures a firm might establish for each element of quality control. Figure 1-3, pages 24 and 25, summarizes the examples.

FIGURE 1-3
Summary Examples of Quality Control Procedures For CPA Firms

Independence

A. Require that personnel at all organizational levels adhere to the independence rules, regulations, interpretations, and rulings of the AICPA, state
   CPA society, state board of accountancy, state statute, and, if applicable,
   the Securities and Exchange Commission and other regulatory agencies.
B. Communicate policies and procedures relating to independence to personnel
   at all organizational levels.
C. Confirm, when acting as principal auditor, the independence of another firm
   engaged to perform segments of an engagement.
D. Monitor compliance with policies and procedures relating to independence.

Assigning Personnel to Engagements

A. Delineate the firm's approach to assigning personnel, including the planning of overall firm and office needs and the measures employed to achieve
   a balance of engagement manpower requirements, personnel skills, individual development, and utilization.
B. Designate an appropriate person or persons to be responsible for assigning
   personnel to engagements.
C. Provide for approval of the scheduling and staffing of the engagement by
   the person with final responsibility for the engagement.

Consultation

A. Identify areas and specialized situations where consultation is required, and
   encourage personnel to consult with or use authoritative sources on other
   complex or unusual matters.
B. Designate individuals as specialists to serve as authoritative sources, and
   define their authority in consultative situations. Provide procedures for resolving differences of opinion between engagement personnel and specialists.
C. Specify the extent of documentation to be provided for the results of consultation in those areas and specialized situations where consultation is required. Specify documentation, as appropriate, for other consultations.

Supervision

A. Provide procedures for planning engagements.
B. Provide procedures for maintaining the firm's standards of quality for the
   work performed.
C. Provide procedures for reviewing engagement working papers and reports.

Hiring

A. Maintain a program designed to obtain qualified personnel by planning for personnel needs, establishing hiring objectives, and setting qualifications for those involved in the hiring function.
B. Establish qualifications and guidelines for evaluating potential hirees at each professional level.
C. Inform applicants and new personnel of the firm's policies and procedures relevant to them.

Professional Development

A. Establish guidelines and requirements for the firm's professional development program and communicate them to personnel.
B. Make available to personnel information about current developments in professional technical standards and materials containing the firm's technical policies and procedures and encourage personnel to engage in self-development activities.
C. Provide, to the extent necessary, programs to fill the firm's needs for personnel with expertise in specialized areas and industries.
D. Provide for on-the-job training during the performance of engagements.

Advancement

A. Establish qualifications deemed necessary for the various levels of responsibility within the firm.
B. Evaluate performance of personnel, and periodically advise personnel of their progress. Maintain personnel files containing documentation relating to the evaluation process.
C. Assign responsibility for making advancement decisions.

Acceptance and Continuance of Clients

A. Establish procedures for evaluation of prospective clients and for their approval as clients.
B. Evaluate clients at the end of specific periods or upon the occurrence of specified events to determine whether the relationships should be continued.

Inspection

A. Define the scope and content of the firm's inspection program.
B. Provide for reporting inspection findings to the appropriate management levels and for monitoring actions taken or planned.

Source: Quality Control Standards Committee, ''Establishing Quality Control Policies and Procedures,'' *AICPA Professional Standards, Vol. 2* (New York: American Institute of Certified Public Accountants), Sec. 90.10–90.26.

Peer Review

There is perhaps no better way to monitor a CPA firm's system of quality control than for members of other CPA firms to review the system's scope, appropriateness, and effectiveness — that is, *peer review*. Partly for this reason, the AICPA in 1977 established a membership division for CPA firms, categorizing member firms as SEC practice firms or private company practice firms. *SEC practice firms* are those which provide services to any publicly traded clients, i.e., companies whose securities are traded on national or regional stock exchanges or over the counter and therefore must file periodic financial reports with the SEC. *Private company practice firms* provide services to nonpublicly traded, privately owned companies. Membership in the divisions has been voluntary since 1977. However, effective in 1988, a CPA firm cannot audit a publicly held company unless the firm is a member of the SEC practice firms section. The philosophy underlying the AICPA's division for CPA firms is to encourage self-regulation and self-discipline within the profession by imposing practice requirements for all member firms.

In addition to establishing and maintaining a program of peer review for member firms, the AICPA firm membership sections are intended to improve the quality of each member firm's services to clients by sanctioning practice requirements and potential disciplinary action. The collective performance of all SEC practice section firms is monitored through a Public Oversight Board, composed of individuals outside the accounting profession, which meets and issues reports on section activities and oversights.

The peer review programs of the SEC practice section and private company practice section are somewhat similar. In general, peer reviews for either section are conducted by peer review teams consisting of appointed individuals from several different member firms or from the professional staff of one member firm. Regardless of how peer review teams are formed, they are charged with the following responsibilities:

- ▲ Study and evaluate the reviewed firm's system of quality control.
- ▲ Examine the reviewed firm's compliance with its quality control procedures.
- ▲ Examine appropriate documentation for the reviewed firm's compliance with section membership requirements.

Review teams report their findings to the reviewed firm; the findings are also made public through the sponsoring section. Deficiencies in quality control policies or procedures or in compliance with section membership requirements can result in fines, suspensions, expulsion from membership, or other actions against the reviewed member firm.

RELATING ACCOUNTING AND AUDITING

Largely because auditing is studied in "accounting" curricula and practiced by public "accountants," it is often viewed as a subdivision of accounting. However, accounting and auditing are related because auditors are accountants first, not because auditing is accounting first. R. K. Mautz and H. A. Sharaf comment:

> Auditing is analytic, not constructive; it is critical, investigative, concerned with the basis for accounting measurements and assertions. Auditing emphasizes proof, the support for financial statements and data. Thus auditing has its principal roots, not in accounting which it reviews, but in logic on which it leans heavily for ideas and methods.[8]

Thus, accounting and auditing are two separate disciplines with unrelated foundations and dissimilar bodies of knowledge.

Although accounting and auditing are separate disciplines, a familiarity with audit method is not wholly sufficient to render an auditor competent. Because an auditor examines financial statements, he or she must also be familiar with accounting principles and practices. Thus, the organizations that influence accounting also influence auditing. While the AICPA, followed by the SEC, has the most direct influence on auditing practice, the Financial Accounting Standards Board and several professional organizations also affect auditing, though to a lesser extent. These organizations are introduced briefly in the following sections.

The Financial Accounting Standards Board

The Financial Accounting Standards Board (FASB), an independent accounting standard-setting body, issues authoritative *Statements of Financial Accounting Standards* on controversial accounting and reporting issues. For example, the FASB has issued statements on leases, oil and gas accounting, pensions, and accounting for income taxes — all extremely controversial issues. Except in unusual circumstances, an independent auditor is precluded from expressing an opinion that financial statements are presented in conformity with GAAP if the statements contain any material departure from accounting principles promulgated by the FASB. Thus, auditors must be familiar with the provisions of FASB Statements or risk violating GAAP.

---

[8]Mautz and Sharaf, *op. cit.,* p. 14.

Professional Organizations

The professional organizations that influence auditing standards and practice are the Institute of Internal Auditors, the National Association of Accountants, the Financial Executives Institute, and the American Accounting Association.

The Institute of Internal Auditors (IIA) is a voluntary membership organization. The Institute conducts and sponsors research and continuing education programs, sponsors the Certified Internal Auditor examination, and publishes a bimonthly journal, *The Internal Auditor*. Internal auditors and the Institute are discussed more fully in Chapter 21.

The National Association of Accountants (NAA) is an organization composed primarily of management accountants, which also conducts and sponsors research and continuing education programs. The NAA publishes a monthly journal, *Management Accounting*, and, through the Institute for Management Accounting, sponsors the Certificate in Management Accounting examination. Among its many and varied nonperiodic publications, the NAA issues position papers on a variety of accounting and reporting topics. Although these papers are not binding on accountants, they do influence accounting thought.

The Financial Executives Institute (FEI) is an organization of corporate financial and accounting officers. Although the FEI does not sponsor a professional certification examination, it does publish a variety of influential publications, including the *Financial Executive*, a bimonthly journal.

The American Accounting Association (AAA) is an organization of accounting educators. In addition to its quarterly journal, *The Accounting Review*, the AAA also publishes research monographs and committee reports, including the Report of the Committee on Basic Auditing Concepts discussed earlier in this chapter.

AUDIT REPORTS: THE END PRODUCT

In education, it is often useful to explain the end product of a body of knowledge early on, rather than at the end of a discussion; the body of knowledge can then become much more relevant and understandable. As suggested earlier, the end product of an audit is the opinion communicated in an audit report, i.e., the attestation. This section introduces the auditor's report. Chapter 19 discusses the report in much more detail; the purpose here is to promote understanding of the concepts, standards, and procedures which constitute Chapters 2 through 18, and which form the basis for the auditor's report.

In practice today, there are four different types of audit reports: three give an opinion on financial statements, and one, the disclaimer of opinion, gives no opinion at all. Figure 1-4 interprets the intended meaning of each type of report.

FIGURE 1-4
Types of Audit Reports

Type of Report	Interpretation
Unqualified Opinion	Financial statements taken as a whole *present fairly* the financial position, results of operations, and cash flows in conformity with generally accepted accounting principles.
Qualified Opinion	*"Except for"* the effects of a particular matter, the financial statements *present fairly* the financial position, results of operations, and cash flows in conformity with generally accepted accounting principles.
Adverse Opinion	Financial statements *do not present fairly* the financial position, results of operations, or cash flows in conformity with generally accepted accounting principles.
Disclaimer of Opinion	Auditor *does not express an opinion* on the financial position, results of operations, or cash flows.

Unqualified Opinion

An unqualified opinion communicates a favorable signal about financial position, results of operations, and cash flows. Auditors generally use fairly uniform language when issuing a standard, three-paragraph, unqualified report. The first, or introductory, paragraph identifies the financial statements audited and distinguishes the auditor's responsibility from that of management. The second paragraph of the report describes the scope of the audit engagement, and the third paragraph expresses the auditor's opinion.

An example of the standard wording of a report expressing an unqualified opinion follows:

Report of Independent Auditors

To Share Owners and Board of Directors
of Wilson Equipment Company

We have audited the accompanying balance sheets of Wilson Equipment Company and consolidated affiliates as of December 31, 1990 and 1989, and the related statements of income, retained earnings, and cash flows for each of the years in the three-year period ended December 31, 1990. These financial statements are the responsibility of the company's management. Our responsibility is to express an opinion on these financial statements based on our audits.

We conducted our audits in accordance with generally accepted auditing standards. Those standards require that we plan and perform the audit to obtain reasonable assurance about whether the financial statements are free of material misstatement. An audit includes examining, on a test basis, evidence supporting the amounts and disclosures in the financial statements. An audit also includes assessing the accounting principles used and significant estimates made by management, as well as evaluating the overall financial statement presentation. We believe that our audits provide a reasonable basis for our opinion.

In our opinion, the financial statements referred to above present fairly, in all material respects, the financial position of Wilson Equipment Company as of December 31, 1990 and 1989, and the results of its operations and its cash flows for each of the years in the three-year period ended December 31, 1990 in conformity with generally accepted accounting principles.

Cheever, Taylor & Co., CPAs
345 Park Avenue, New York, N.Y. 10154

February 14, 1991

Note that the report covers financial statements for more than one period, which is typical in practice, since most companies present comparative rather than single-year statements. In the example, the report covers balance sheets prepared as of the end of the two most recent fiscal years and statements of earnings and cash flows for three years, as required by the SEC.

Qualified Opinion

A qualified opinion communicates a favorable signal about financial statements, but with modifications. For example, an auditor may wish to alert users that financial position, results of operations, and cash flows are fairly presented "except for" the effects of misapplying an accounting principle.

A qualified opinion requires rewording of the opinion paragraph, and the report includes an additional paragraph explaining the nature of the issue leading to the qualification. Of course, the signal communicated in a qualified report is less favorable than that of an unqualified opinion, but more favorable than an adverse opinion.

Adverse Opinion

An adverse opinion communicates an unfavorable signal. Usually an adverse opinion is issued when the conditions are appropriate for a qualified opinion, yet the issue leading to qualification is so material that a less favorable signal is warranted. For example, an auditor may wish to alert users that the effects of misapplying an accounting principle are so material that financial position, results of operations, and cash flows are not fairly presented. As in the case of a qualified opinion, an adverse opinion requires rewording of the opinion paragraph and an explanatory paragraph.

Disclaimer of Opinion

A disclaimer of opinion signals that an auditor does not express an opinion. For example, a disclaimer is appropriate when an auditor has not performed an audit sufficient in scope to enable him or her to form an opinion on the financial statements. A disclaimer of opinion typically results in an explanatory paragraph followed by a paragraph stating that no opinion is expressed.

SUMMARY

Financial statement audits are the primary function of independent auditors. Because users demand an independent, unbiased opinion on financial statements, there is a well-established market for the services of independent auditors.

As with any unfamiliar area of study, it is useful to draw analogies with familiar areas. The scientific method of inquiry, a logical problem-solving framework associated with the sciences, is highly analogous to audit practice; an audit represents nothing more than a special application of the scientific method.

The origin of auditing in the U.S. is predominantly British, having evolved from the Companies Acts of the mid-to-late nineteenth century. Early twentieth century U.S. auditing pronouncements are particularly revealing about the profession's maturation during that period. For example, the profession recognized that the use of uniform accounting methods for all business entities was not fruitful, and that "examination" — rather than "verification" — was a more appropriate description of an independent auditor's function.

Certified public accountants in CPA firms provide a variety of services including audit, tax, MAS, and accounting services. CPA firms can be classified as national, regional, or local, and the organizational levels within CPA firms generally include partner, manager, senior accountant, and staff accountant.

Today, several rule-making bodies or professional organizations impact accounting and auditing thought. Prominent among them are the Auditing Standards Board, Accounting and Review Services Committee, Financial Accounting Standards Board, Securities and Exchange Commission, Institute of Internal Auditors, National Association of Accountants, Financial Executives Institute, and American Accounting Association.

Quality control, the process of assuring consistent performance and achievement within an individual CPA firm, and peer review, the process of encouraging quality control across all firms, are designed to strengthen the quality of audit activities. Together they represent the profession's major efforts toward self-regulation.

The end product of an audit is the audit report, i.e., the attestation. The audit report is designed to communicate one of four signals: favorable (unqualified opinion); favorable, with qualification (qualified opinion); unfavorable (adverse opinion); or neither favorable nor unfavorable (disclaimer of opinion). Familiarity with the end result of an audit facilitates understanding of the concepts, standards, and procedures underlying auditing.

REFERENCES

American Institute of Certified Public Accountants. *Codification of Statements on Auditing Standards*. New York: American Institute of Certified Public Accountants, 1987.

Bremser, W. G. "Peer Review: Enhancing Quality Control." *Journal of Accountancy* (October, 1983), pp. 78–85.

Carey, J. L. *The Rise of the Accounting Profession from Technician to Professional*. New York: American Institute of Certified Public Accountants, 1969.

Chatfield, M. *A History of Accounting Thought*. Hinsdale, Illinois: The Dryden Press, 1974.

Cohen, M. R., and E. Nagel. *An Introduction to Logic and Scientific Method*. New York: Harcourt, Brace, and Company, 1934.

Commission on Auditors' Responsibilities. *Report, Conclusions, and Recommendations*. New York: Commission on Auditors' Responsibilities, 1978.

Committee on Basic Auditing Concepts. "A Statement of Basic Auditing Concepts." *The Accounting Review*, supplement to vol. 47, 1972.

Cook, J. M., and H. G. Robinson, "Peer Review: The Accounting Profession's Program." *The CPA Journal* (March, 1979), pp. 11–16.

Guy, D. M. and J. D. Sullivan, "The Expectation Gap Auditing Standards," *Journal of Accountancy* (April 1988), pp. 36–46.

Hall, W. D. "What Does It Take To Be An Auditor?" *Journal of Accountancy* (January, 1988), pp. 72–80.

Hickok, R. S. "Looking to the Future: A Key to Success." *Journal of Accountancy* (March, 1984), pp. 63–76.

Larson, R. E. "Self Regulation: A Professional Step Forward." *Journal of Accountancy* (September, 1983), pp. 58–64.

Lee, B. Z., R. E. Larson, and P. B. Chenok. "Issues Confronting the Accounting Profession." *Journal of Accountancy* (November, 1983), pp. 78–85.

Loscalzo, M. A. "What Is Peer Review All About?" *Journal of Accountancy* (October, 1979), pp. 78–82.

Mautz, R. K. "Self Regulation: Perils and Problems." *Journal of Accountancy* (May, 1983), pp. 76–84.

Mautz, R. K. "Self Regulation: Criticisms and a Response." *Journal of Accountancy* (April, 1984), pp. 56–66.

Mautz, R. K., and H. A. Sharaf. *The Philosophy of Auditing*. Sarasota: American Accounting Association, 1961.

Roy, R. H., and J. H. MacNeil. *Horizons for a Profession*. New York: American Institute of Certified Public Accountants, 1967.

QUESTIONS

1. In your own words define (a) auditing and (b) attestation.
2. What is the scientific method of inquiry, and how does it relate to auditing?
3. Identify the major types of audits performed in the U.S. today.
4. Why is there a need for the services of independent auditors?
5. What services are generally provided to clients by public accounting firms?
6. What are the professional levels generally found in medium and large CPA firms?

7. What requirements must a candidate satisfy in order to become a certified public accountant?

8. What is significant about the titles of the bulletins of 1917, 1918, 1929, and 1936?

9. What roles are served by the AICPA's two authoritative standard-setting bodies?

10. How are auditing and accounting related?

11. Briefly explain the AICPA's program for peer review.

12. Explain how quality control and generally accepted auditing standards are related.

13. Identify the four different types of audit reports and the signal intended by each.

14. How should each type of report be interpreted?

MULTIPLE CHOICE QUESTIONS (AICPA Adapted)

1. Independent auditing can best be described as

   a. A branch of accounting.
   b. A discipline which attests to the results of accounting and other functional operations and data.
   c. A professional activity that measures and communicates financial and business data.
   d. A regulatory function that prevents the issuance of improper financial information.

2. The independent audit is important to readers of financial statements because it

   a. Determines the future stewardship of the management of the company whose financial statements are audited.
   b. Measures and communicates financial business data included in financial statements.
   c. Involves the objective examination of and reporting on management-prepared statements.
   d. Reports on the accuracy of all information in the financial statements.

3. An independent audit aids in the communication of economic data because the audit

   a. Confirms the accuracy of management's financial representations.
   b. Lends credibility to the financial statements.
   c. Guarantees that financial data are fairly presented.
   d. Assures the readers of financial statements that any fraudulent activity has been corrected.

4. Which of the following best describes the reason why an independent auditor reports on financial statements?

   a. A management fraud may exist, and it is more likely to be detected by independent auditors.
   b. Different interests may exist between the company preparing the statements and the persons using the statements.

c. A misstatement of account balances may exist and is generally corrected as the result of the independent auditor's work.

d. A poorly designed internal control structure may be in existence.

5. The major reason an independent auditor gathers audit evidence is to

  a. Form an opinion on the financial statements.

  b. Detect fraud.

  c. Evaluate management.

  d. Evaluate internal control structure.

6. The primary responsibility for the adequacy of disclosure in the financial statements and accompanying notes rests with the

  a. Audit partner assigned to the engagement.

  b. Senior auditor in charge of field work.

  c. Staff auditor who drafts the statements and notes.

  d. Client management.

7. A basic objective of a CPA firm is to provide professional services to conform with professional standards. Reasonable assurance of achieving this basic objective is provided through

  a. Continuing professional education.

  b. A system of quality control.

  c. Compliance with generally accepted reporting standards.

  d. A system of peer review.

8. A CPA firm's primary purpose for performing management advisory services is to

  a. Prepare the CPA firm for the changing needs and requirements of the business community.

  b. Establish the CPA firm as a consultant, which will enable the CPA firm to ensure future viability and growth.

  c. Provide advice and technical assistance which will enable a client to conduct its business more effectively.

  d. Enable staff members of the CPA firm to acquire the necessary continuing education in all areas of business.

9. The objective of quality control mandates that a public accounting firm should establish policies and procedures for professional development which provide reasonable assurance that all entry-level personnel

  a. Prepare working papers which are standardized in form and content.

  b. Have the knowledge required to enable them to fulfill responsibilities assigned.

  c. Will advance within the organization.

  d. Develop specialties in specific areas of public accounting.

10. A CPA establishes quality control policies and procedures for deciding whether to accept a new client or continue to perform services for a current client. The primary purpose for establishing such policies and procedures is

a. To enable the auditor to attest to the integrity or reliability of a client.
b. To comply with the quality control standards established by regulatory bodies.
c. To minimize the likelihood of association with clients whose managements lack integrity.
d. To lessen the exposure to litigation resulting from failure to detect irregularities in client financial statements.

11. In pursuing its quality control objectives with respect to assigning personnel to engagements, a CPA firm may use policies and procedures such as

a. Rotating employees from assignment to assignment on a random basis to aid in the staff training effort.
b. Requiring timely identification of the staffing requirements of specific engagements so that enough qualified personnel can be made available.
c. Allowing staff to select the assignments of their choice to promote better client relationships.
d. Assigning a number of employees to each engagement in excess of the number required so as not to overburden the staff and interfere with the quality of the audit work performed.

PROBLEMS

1-1 Within the chapter, five different types of audits were identified:
- Financial statement audit
- Operational audit
- Financial and compliance audit
- Economy and efficiency audit
- Program results audit

Each type of audit is designed for a particular purpose and is selected depending on the specific objectives of report users.

Required:
For each of the following circumstances, indicate the type of audit required.
a. Management is interested in whether the purchasing department is functioning economically.
b. The state legislature is concerned that the requirements of a federal grant may have been violated.
c. A commercial bank will not approve a working capital loan without a report on whether the company's financial statements are presented fairly.
d. A state agency is not eligible for federal grants lacking a report on whether the agency's financial statements are presented fairly.
e. Management is interested in whether controls over highly sensitive inventory are reasonable and adequate.
f. Management is required to obtain a report indicating whether the objectives of a direct grant have been achieved.

1-2 During the past several decades, auditing has gained a considerable amount of attention both within the financial community and within academic curricula. For example, independent audits are now commonly conducted for all publicly traded and many privately owned corporations. Further, not only do undergraduate accounting curricula typically include an introductory auditing course, but many colleges and universities also offer advanced undergraduate and graduate auditing courses. Thus, there appears to be an established and unquestioned need for auditing.

Required:
Explain why there is an established need for auditing services for each of the following organizations:
a. Publicly owned corporations.
b. Privately owned corporations.
c. State and local governmental agencies.
d. Partnerships.

1-3   One of your classmates, Kristin Lea, a chemistry major, is puzzled about what an auditor does. She says to you, "My only impression about auditors comes from Bob Cratchit, Tiny Tim's father, in Charles Dickens' *A Christmas Carol*. It sure seems to me as though there's little science in an auditor's work!"

Required:
Explain the role of an auditor through an illustration that would be understandable to a chemistry major.

1-4   The following two statements are representative of attitudes and opinions sometimes encountered by CPAs in their professional practices:
a. Today's audit consists of test checking. This is dangerous because test checking depends upon the auditor's judgment, which may be defective. An audit can be relied upon only if every transaction is verified.
b. An audit by a CPA is essentially unproductive and contributes to neither the gross national product nor the general well-being of society. The auditor does not create, but merely checks what someone else has done.

Required:
Evaluate both of the above statements and indicate:
1. Areas of agreement with the statement, if any.
2. Areas of misconception, incompleteness, or fallacious reasoning included in the statement, if any.

(AICPA Adapted)

1-5   Feiler, the sole owner of a small hardware business, has been told that the business should have financial statements reported on by an independent CPA. Feiler, having some bookkeeping experience, has personally prepared the company's financial statements and does not understand why such statements should be examined by a CPA. Feiler discussed the matter with Farber, a CPA, and asked Farber to explain why an audit is considered important.

Required:
1. Describe the objectives of an independent audit.
2. Identify ten ways in which an independent audit may be beneficial to Feiler.

(AICPA Adapted)

1-6   Marc David is an employee-stockholder of the Lexington Corporation. Because he has extensive acounting experience, David proposes to the other stockholders that he, rather than a public accounting firm, be appointed independent auditor for Lexington Corporation. David argues that because of his ownership in the company, the other owners' interests would be served best by his appointment. At a meeting of stockholders, David states, "I'd be much better for the job. For one thing, I can do the work, and for another, it won't cost us a small fortune."

Required:
Indicate the deficiencies in David's arguments. Be specific.

1-7   In response to the AICPA's quality control program for individual CPA firms, many public accounting firms have drafted audit and accounting quality control documents which describe policies and procedures designed to provide reasonable assurance that the firm is complying with generally accepted auditing standards on all audit engagements. Following is a selected list of policies and procedures taken from a public accounting firm's quality control document.

a. As a member of both practice divisions of the AICPA, the firm is subject to and cooperates in the Quality Control Peer Review Program. The firm's Audit Monitoring Committee is responsible for scheduling periodic working paper reviews for completed engagements and for ensuring that all professional personnel are made aware of the knowledge gained by the reviews.

b. The firm is not to express an opinion on an organization's financial statements if professional staff serve as executor, trustee, officer, or director of the organization. Other appointments to these positions in either client or nonclient organizations must be in agreement with the AICPA's Code of Professional Ethics.

c. Situations occur or questions arise which require certain technical accounting and/or auditing knowledge, or specialized industry knowledge that may not exist within the audit team. In these cases, the engagement partner or others associated with the engagement shall consult with the Partner for Technical Services or other designated personnel to obtain the assistance needed or to otherwise resolve the issue.

d. The following factors are considered by the Scheduling Partner in achieving a balance of the personnel elements of the engagement: staffing requirements, personnel skills, individual development, and staff utilization during the job.

e. At the annual partners meeting, the Administrative Partner assures that no audit partner has any loan from a client other than those specifically permitted by professional ethics.

f. On each audit engagement, adequate review is to be performed at all organizational levels, as appropriate, considering the training, ability, and experience of the personnel assigned and the complexity of the engagement.

g. Each year, all professional staff are responsible to develop a personal plan which includes goals for participating in on-the-job training through challenging and diversified assignments, formal programs prepared and conducted by the firm and by professional organizations, individual development through self-study and other activities, and participation in and service to professional, community, and public and/or private organizations and activities.

h. The personal attributes sought in entry-level professional staff include but are not limited to the following: motivation, professional potential, language skills, demonstrated involvement, and leadership.

i. Personnel are periodically evaluated and are advised formally of their progress. Staff personnel files are maintained for each professional staff member and contain written evaluations of performance.

j. The reputation of a company's directors, officers, and principal shareholders or owners is of great importance. The firm seeks to minimize the likelihood of associating with a client whose management lacks integrity and a fair degree of stability over time. In addition, the nature of the business, its sources of financing and financial need, its internal control structure and the purpose for and nature of the audit or other engagement are all considerations in evaluating the relative risk of our professional liability in serving the company.

Required:

1. Explain the relationship between quality control and peer review for a public accounting firm.

2. For each of the policies and procedures listed above, indicate the element of quality control addressed by the firm.

1-8   In discussing the historical evolution of auditing within the United States, the following statement was made within the chapter.

"A verification is entirely different from an examination. . . . Contemporary auditors do not verify financial statements; they examine them."

Something appears wrong with this statement. Certainly, when an auditor examines evidence — for example, when an auditor examines a vendor's invoice — he or she verifies it.

Required:

Explain the difference between a "verification" and an "examination." Is the statement within the text incorrect?

1-9   Appointment in 1939 of the AICPA's Committee on Auditing Procedure, the first authoritative audit standard-setting body in the U.S., was a response to public-sector demands that the private sector ". . . examine into auditing procedure and other related questions in the light of recent public discussions." As discussed in the text, the "public discussions" related in part to the McKesson & Robbins, Inc. $19 million overstatement of inventory and accounts receivable. McKesson & Robbins auditors neither observed physical inventory on hand nor confirmed accounts receivable balances with debtors. In 1939, the Committee on Auditing Procedure responded with Statement on Auditing Procedure No. 1, which recommended physical inventory observation and accounts receivable confirmation, both of which have since become common practice.

Required:

Do these beginnings — that is, a response to a highly publicized fraud — have any implications for audit standard setting today, which is essentially the same today with the Auditing Standards Board as it was in 1939 with the Committee on Auditing Procedure?

1-10   In general, there are four different types of audit reports that an independent auditor could issue for any given audit client: unqualified, qualified, adverse, and disclaimer of opinion. In the context of audit reports, following are a series of circumstances, as well as an indication of likely materiality, for separate audit engagements:

Circumstance	Likely Materiality	
	Moderate	High
1. Financial statements depart from generally accepted accounting principles.	X	
2. Financial statements depart from generally accepted accounting principles.		X
3. Future commitments relating to long-term operating leases are not disclosed in the financial statments.	X	
4. Part of the audit engagement has been completed by another CPA firm.	X	
5. Outside counsel has indicated that pending litigation against the client is likely to result in a judgment against the client.		X

Required:
For each of the circumstances listed above, indicate the type of audit report required, i.e., unqualified, qualified, adverse, or disclaimer of opinion.

PROFESSIONAL CONDUCT

2

Major topics discussed in this chapter are the:

▲   *Relationship between general and professional ethics.*
▲   *Structure and content of the AICPA Code of Professional Conduct.*
▲   *Principles underlying the AICPA Rules of Conduct.*
▲   *Nature and purpose of each of the Rules of Conduct.*
▲   *Process of enforcing the AICPA and state society codes of profes-sional conduct.*

M ost issues in accounting and auditing are predominantly technical, rather than ethical, in nature. Examples include choices among alternative accounting policies, such as inventory or depreciation methods, and alternative audit procedures, such as confirmation and direct observation. However, some decisions made in audit practice relate primarily to professional conduct and are based either wholly or in part on ethical choice. In fact, public accountants are often confronted with ethical decisions regarding independence, integrity, and objectivity; applications of general and technical professional standards; and responsibilities to clients and colleagues. This chapter considers these issues in light of the AICPA Code of Professional Conduct, enacted by member vote in 1988.

The chapter begins with a brief introduction to general and professional ethics and a discussion of events in the 1980s that led to a complete restructuring of professional standards regarding an accountant's conduct. In turn, the Principles, Rules, Interpretations, and Rulings of the AICPA Code of Professional Conduct are discussed, and each of the Code's Rules of Conduct is presented and interpreted. Finally, ethics enforcement and the national joint enforcement efforts of the AICPA, the state societies of CPAs, and the National Joint Trial Board are described.

GENERAL ETHICS, PROFESSIONAL ETHICS, AND REFORM

General ethics is the study of ideal conduct, the reflection of right versus wrong, good versus bad. More specifically, general ethics involve choices of conduct determined by balancing "outer conditions," such as peer reaction

41

or extrinsic rewards, with "inner self," i.e., one's value system. General ethics, then, include both choice and the consequences of choice. Likewise, ethical conduct among professionals also involves making choices in light of the consequences of alternatives. Thus, professional conduct is very closely related to general ethics, as indicated in the following quote:

> Ethical behavior in auditing or in any other activity is no more than a special application of the general notion of ethical conduct devised by philosophers for men generally. Ethical conduct in auditing draws its justification and basic nature from the general theory of ethics.[1]

General ethics, then, provide a model or rationale for deriving, explaining, and justifying professional conduct. However, unlike general ethics, professional codes of conduct typically do not describe ideal standards of behavior; rather, they describe minimum standards. Ignoring ideal conduct in favor of threshold standards can be detrimental to a profession by sanctioning the bare minimum and thereby encouraging mediocrity. In fact, several critics of the profession had charged that the now superseded AICPA Code of Professional Ethics, in force prior to 1988, no longer served the public interest. For example, observers within the financial community had strongly criticized some of the Rules of Conduct, arguing that the rules did not adequately encompass either the profession's expanding scope of services or the rather aggressive new client development practices of some CPAs. Compounding these criticisms, the financial press and popular press raised the public consciousness by publicizing a series of audit failures and business failures, most notably in the banking and government securities industries.

Responding to this criticism, the AICPA in 1983 appointed a special committee on standards of professional conduct for CPAs. The committee, chaired by George D. Anderson, a former chairman of the AICPA, was charged with the responsibility of evaluating the relevance of the Rules of Conduct to the profession's commitment to professionalism, quality service, and the public interest. The committee observed that the previous Rules of Conduct were negatively worded minimum standards (all but two of the Rules used the words "shall not") which neither encouraged ideal professional conduct nor addressed the expanding array of non-audit services provided by CPAs. Although a goal of the Rules was to maintain high-quality performance and weed out substandard practices, the committee concluded that the existing thirteen rules were not meeting this objective.

As a result, the committee recommended reform. To restructure the code, the committee recommended that the AICPA develop a positively worded,

---

[1]R. K. Mautz and H. A. Sharaf, *The Philosophy of Auditing* (Sarasota: American Accounting Association, 1961), p. 232.

goal-oriented code and that the code be monitored by a mandatory quality assurance review program that would replace the then existing voluntary peer review program. The new Code would apply to all AICPA members, not just those in public practice as the prior Code did.

The committee's recommendation represented a challenge to the profession, a mandate to develop a code that encouraged ideal ethical and performance standards rather than negatively worded minimum standards that tolerate minimum behavior. The profession responded. In January 1988, 92 percent of 183,400 voting AICPA members (about seventy percent of the membership) voted in favor of establishing a new Code of Professional Conduct. In the next sections of the chapter the new AICPA Code of Professional Conduct is discussed in detail. The discussion begins with an overview of the Code, introduces the Principles underlying the Code, and continues with detailed interpretations of the new Rules of Conduct.

AICPA CODE OF PROFESSIONAL CONDUCT: AN OVERVIEW

The AICPA Code of Professional Conduct consists of two sections:

▲ Principles
▲ Rules of Conduct

And two related items:

▲ Interpretations of Rules of Conduct
▲ Rulings

The *Principles* underlie the Rules of Conduct and obligate independent accountants to a level of self-discipline above and beyond the minimum requirements imposed by laws and regulations. The Principles consist of six articles relating to professional responsibilities, the public interest, integrity, objectivity and independence, due care, and the scope and nature of professional services rendered by AICPA members.

The *Rules of Conduct* govern the performance of all AICPA members — including those in public practice, industry, government, and education — in five general areas: independence, integrity, and objectivity; professional auditing and accounting standards; responsibilities to clients; responsibilities to colleagues; and other responsibilities and practices. The Rules are to professional conduct what generally accepted auditing standards are to audit performance: both are sets of guidelines or measures of quality for professional practitioners. Because the Rules of Conduct are enforceable upon AICPA members, new or revised Rules require member approval by formal mail ballots before becoming effective.

Interpretations of the Rules of Conduct are issued by the Executive

Committee of the Institute's Professional Ethics Division and are intended to interpret the scope and applicability of specific Rules of Conduct. Prior to adoption, all proposed Interpretations are first exposed to state societies (or associations) of CPAs and state boards of accountancy for comment. Ethics *Rulings* are also issued by the Professional Ethics Division's Executive Committee after exposure to state societies and boards of accountancy. The Rulings summarize the applicability of Rules of Conduct and Interpretations to particular factual situations. AICPA members must justify departures from Rules of Conduct, Interpretations, and Ethics Rulings.

The content of the AICPA Code of Professional Conduct can and likely will change from time to time. Proposals to amend the Code may be made by the Institute's Professional Ethics Division or Board of Directors, five percent or more of the Institute's members, or any thirty members of the AICPA Council.

The Principles and Rules are discussed more fully in the following sections.

PRINCIPLES OF PROFESSIONAL CONDUCT

The following quote was made by Marcus Aurelis in the context of ethical behavior:

A man should *be* upright; not be *kept* upright.

This quote suggests that ideal conduct should be expected, not mandated by formal rules and regulations. Unfortunately, however, the "ideal" does not always equate with "reality;" people are motivated by a variety of conflicting pressures. For this reason, most of the professions, including law and medicine, have developed formal codes of ethical conduct, and public accounting is no exception.

Not only is a code of conduct a cornerstone of ethical behavior for professional practitioners, it also underlies the trust placed in accountants by the public, the financial community, and other internal and external users of financial information. Users cannot audit financial information themselves; they lack the necessary skills and access to financial information. Thus, users rely upon auditors to perform the audit and attest functions. In short, users trust the independent auditor, and the Code of Conduct symbolizes the profession's faith in that trust. If users could not assume some standard of ethical conduct by professional accountants, the audit and attest functions would be meaningless.

The two fundamental thoughts expressed above — ideal conduct and trust — underlie the broad principles within the AICPA Code of Professional Conduct. The six principles are:

▲ *Responsibilities* — In carrying out their responsibilities as professionals, members should exercise sensitive professional and moral judgments in all their activities.

▲ *The Public Interest* — Members should accept the obligation to act in a way that will serve the public interest, honor the public trust, and demonstrate commitment to professionalism.

▲ *Integrity* — To maintain and broaden public confidence, members should perform all professional responsibilities with the highest sense of integrity.

▲ *Objectivity and Independence* — A member should maintain objectivity and be free of conflicts of interest in discharging professional responsibilities. A member in public practice should be independent in fact and appearance when providing auditing and other attestation services.

▲ *Due Care* — A member should observe the profession's technical and ethical standards, strive continually to improve competence and the quality of services, and discharge professional responsibility to the best of the member's ability.

▲ *Scope and Nature of Services* — A member in public practice should observe the Code of Professional Conduct in determining the scope and nature of services to be provided.

The principles are explicit, but somewhat abstract as principles should be. They express the profession's recognition of its responsibilities to the public, to clients, and to colleagues — the basic tenets of ethical and professional conduct. These six broad principles are the basis, the underlying rationale, for the Rules of Conduct.

RULES OF CONDUCT

Section 7.4 of the AICPA Bylaws provides the authority for the Code of Professional Conduct in general and for the Rules of Conduct in particular. The Bylaws state that following a hearing, an ethics trial board may admonish, suspend for a period of not more than two years, or expel a member found guilty of violating any provision of the Rules of Conduct. Of course, an AICPA member cannot engage a nonmember to carry out acts in his or her behalf that would violate a Rule of Conduct; acts carried out in a member's behalf are deemed to be performed by the member.

The Rules of Conduct apply to all professional services rendered by AICPA members — including tax and management advisory services — except where the wording of the rule obviously indicates otherwise or a member is practicing in a foreign country and following additional rules imposed by a foreign accounting body's code of conduct. The Rules of Conduct were adopted by the entire membership of the AICPA, and therefore provide guidance to all members in the performance of their professional responsibilities, including members in public practice, industry, government, and education.

Independence, Integrity, and Objectivity

Independence, integrity, and objectivity relate to an accountant's professional and personal character and, as such, are unobservable qualities; behaviors can be observed but motives cannot. Because these qualities are unobservable, Rules 101 and 102 are often difficult to measure in practice — you can not observe someone being independent of an audit client and you can not observe integrity. As a result, more Interpretations and Rulings were issued about independence, integrity, and objectivity, specifically about Rule 101, than any other rule of the Code of Professional Ethics in force before 1988.

Rule 101 — Independence

A member in public practice shall be independent in the performance of professional services as required by standards promulgated by bodies designated by Council.

Independent auditing is predicated upon a public accountant's independence from audited financial information and from financial information preparers and users. However, independence is required not only in financial statement audits, but in other servcies as well, such as review engagements and reports on prospective financial statements, both of which are discussed in Chapter 20.

Interpretation 101-1 provides examples of situations that would impair an accountant's independence:

> Independence will be considered to be impaired if, for example, a member had any of the following transactions, interests, or relationships:
> A. During the period of a professional engagement, or at the time of expressing an opinion, a member or a member's firm
>   1. Had or was committed to acquire any direct or material indirect financial interest in the enterprise.

2. Was a trustee of any trust or executor or administrator of any estate if such trust or estate had or was committed to acquire any direct or material indirect financial interest in the enterprise.

3. Had any joint, closely held business investment with the enterprise or with any officer, director, or principal stockholders thereof that was material in relation to the member's net worth or to the net worth of the member's firm.

4. Had any loan to or from the enterprise or any officer, director, or principal stockholder of the enterprise. This proscription does not apply to the following loans from a financial institution when made under normal lending procedures, terms, and requirements:

   a. Loans obtained by a member or a member's firm that are not material in relation to the net worth of such borrower.

   b. Home mortgages.

   c. Other secured loans, except loans guaranteed by a member's firm which are otherwise unsecured.

B. During the period covered by the financial statements, during the period of the professional engagement, or at the time of expressing an opinion, a member or a member's firm:

1. Was connected with the enterprise as a promoter, underwriter, or voting trustee, a director or officer in any capacity equivalent to that of a member of management or of an employee.

2. Was a trustee for any pension or profit-sharing trust of the enterprise.

The interpretation notes that the above examples are not intended to be all-inclusive. In fact, an accountant's independence could be questioned in a variety of other situations including non-audit related accounting services, actual or threatened litigation by a client, and when an accountant serves as an honorary director or trustee, all of which are discussed next.

Accounting Services. In addition to auditing, public accountants also provide accounting-related services, such as automated bookkeeping or data processing services to clients who lack adequate internal accounting staff. Accountants who perform these services remain subject to the Rules of Conduct, just as if an audit were being conducted. A sensitive issue that is often raised by critics of the profession is whether these nonaudit services impair audit independence. That is, does the performance of bookkeeping or data processing services for any one client cause an auditor either to overlook the mechanical accuracy of recorded data or to compromise judgments about recorded transactions?

In practice, the Securities and Exchange Commission specifically precludes an accountant from performing both accounting and audit services for publicly traded clients. However, SEC regulations do not apply to privately owned companies. For privately owned clients, meeting the following re-

quirements would be sufficient to give the appearance to reasonable observers
that independence is not impaired:

▲ The CPA must not have any relationship or combination of relationships with the client or any conflict of interest which would impair his
or her integrity and objectivity.

▲ The client must accept responsibility for the financial statements. A
small client may not have a competent employee to maintain accounting records and may rely on the CPA for this purpose. Nevertheless,
the client must be sufficiently knowledgeable of the enterprise's activities and financial condition and the applicable accounting principles
to reasonably accept such responsibility, including, specifically, fairness of valuation and presentation and adequacy of disclosure. When
necessary, the CPA must discuss accounting matters with the client to
be sure that the client has the required degree of understanding.

▲ The CPA must not assume the role of employee or of management
conducting the operations of an enterprise. For example, the CPA shall
not consummate transactions, have custody of assets, or exercise authority on behalf of the client. The client must prepare the source
documents on all transactions in sufficient detail to identify clearly the
nature and amount of such transactions and maintain an accounting
control over data processed by the CPA such as control totals and
document counts. The CPA should not make changes in such data
without the concurrence of the client.

▲ The CPA, in making an examination of financial statements prepared
from books and records which he or she has maintained completely or
in part, must conform to generally accepted auditing standards. The
fact that he or she has processed or maintained certain records does
not eliminate the need to make sufficient tests.

Assuming a public accountant meets all the above requirements for a nonpublicly held client, he or she would retain the appearance of independence
under the AICPA Rules of Conduct.

Actual or Threatened Litigation. If the auditor is to fulfill his or her fundamental obligation to render an informed, objective opinion on financial
statements, the relationship between client management and the auditor must
be characterized by complete candor, full disclosure, and an undisputed absence of bias. However, because of the expressed or implied contractual relationship between an auditor and client and the auditor's status as an independent contractor, both of which are addressed more fully in Chapter 4,
clients sometimes sue auditors for allegedly failing to carry out the duties of
an audit services contract — that is, for breach of contract, among other things.
When client management commences, or expresses an intention to commence, legal action against an auditor, the auditor and client are suddenly

placed in adversary positions, thereby raising questions about the client's candor and willingness to disclose, about the auditor's objectivity and self-interest, and therefore about auditor independence.

Following are guidelines for interpreting auditor independence when client management sues or threatens to sue an auditor:

▲ The commencement of litigation by the present management alleging deficiencies in audit work would be considered to impair independence.

▲ The commencement of litigation by the auditor against the present management alleging management fraud or deceit would be considered to impair independence.

▲ An expressed intention by the present management to commence litigation against the auditor alleging deficiencies in audit work for the client is considered to impair independence if the auditor concludes that there is a strong possibility that a claim will be filed.

▲ Litigation not related to audit work for the client for an amount not material to the CPA's firm or to the financial statements of the client company would not usually be considered to affect the relationship in such a way as to impair independence. Such claims may arise, for example, out of disputes about billing for services, results of tax or management advisory services, or similar matters.

Thus, in most instances, actual or threatened litigation would generally impair independence in appearance, if not independence in fact.

Honorary Directorships and Trusteeships. Accountants are often asked to serve as honorary directors or trustees for, and therefore to lend the prestige of their names to, not-for-profit charitable, religious, or civic organizations. The question raised is whether the accountant can serve both as an honorary trustee or director and as auditor and still maintain the appearance of independence.

The profession assumes that not-for-profit organizations which request only the prestige of an accountant's name also have sufficiently large boards of directors/trustees to limit the accountant's participation in board activities. Therefore, under the Code of Professional Conduct, independence is not impaired as long as:

▲ The accountant's position is purely honorary.

▲ It is identified as honorary in all letterheads and externally circulated materials.

▲ The accountant restricts involvement to the use of his or her name.

▲ The accountant does not vote or otherwise participate in management functions.

> **Rule 102 — Integrity and Objectivity**
>
> In the performance of any professional service, a member shall maintain objectivity and integrity, shall be free of conflicts of interest, and shall not knowingly misrepresent facts or subordinate his or her judgment to others.

Integrity relates to uprightness, honesty, and sincerity; objectivity, in contrast, relates to impartiality. Much like independence (Rule 101), however, both integrity and objectivity are difficult to measure. For example, errors or omissions made by an auditor could result from random unintentional mistakes just as they could from a lack of integrity and objectivity. Distinguishing unintentional mistakes from those due to a lack on integrity or objectivity can be difficult; nevertheless, the Code of Professional Conduct appropriately views integrity and objectivity as imperative, as absolute prerequisites to ethical conduct.

General and Technical Standards

The general and technical standards of the Rules of Conduct relate to an AIPCA member's professional obligation to be competent and to follow the profession's general and technical standards. A CPA certificate obtained today is not a guaranty of competence a decade from now; it implies only that a candidate satisfied the then-current minimum standards of competence. A CPA must continually strive to remain competent.

Further, a CPA certificate does not suggest that a CPA is qualified to undertake all types of professional engagements. The ability to render competent professional service is also dependent upon a CPA's being aware of, and complying with, the profession's published, authoritative standards (e.g., GAAS and GAAP). However, the published standards do not cover all aspects of accounting and auditing. Thus, to remain competent, a CPA must be broadly informed.

> **Rule 201 — General Standards**
>
> A member shall comply with the following standards and with any interpretations thereof by bodies designated by Council.
> A. *Professional Competence*. Undertake only those professional services that the member or the member's firm can reasonably expect to be completed with professional competence.

B. *Due Professional Care.* Exercise due professional care in the performance of professional services.
C. *Planning and Supervision.* Adequately plan and supervise the performance of professional services.
D. *Sufficient Relevant Data.* Obtain sufficient relevant data to afford a reasonable basis for conclusions or recommendations in relation to any professional services performed.

Rule 201 is intended to preclude a member from accepting engagements beyond the realm of his or her competence and expertise. The thrust of this intent is embodied explicitly in Rule 201 A, B, and D. However, Rule 201 does not preclude members from improving their competence (for example, through continuing education courses) in order to accept engagements beyond the realm of their present skills.

Rules 201 B, C, and D relate to issues addressed also in the generally accepted auditing standards, specifically, the third general standard (201 B), the first field work standard (201 C), and the third field work standard (201 D). Thus, the Code of Professional Conduct recognizes and emphasizes the importance of these standards to professional practice.

Rule 201 encompasses one of the more significant issues that confronted the profession in the 1970s and 1980s: "shopping" for accounting and auditing "opinions." In practice, auditors and clients sometimes disagree; they may disagree over the interpretation of accounting principles, over the need for disclosure, or over other accounting and auditing matters. When there are disagreements, some clients will request that competing public accounting firms provide professional advice to them on the disputed matters, thereby raising questions of integrity and objectivity on the part of the responding firm. The Code of Professional Conduct does not preclude an accountant from providing advice to nonclients, but SAS No. 50, "Reports on the Application of Accounting Principles," recognizes that questions from nonclients are often prompted by disagreements, and therefore that the accountant should first consult with the engaged accountant before providing advice. In short, advice should not be given without first considering all of the facts and both sides of the issue.

Rule 202 — Compliance with Standards

A member who performs auditing, review, compilation, management advisory, tax, or other professional services shall comply with standards promulgated by bodies designated by Council.

Rule 202 requires that AICPA members comply with all professional standards relevant to a service rendered. For example, in a financial statement audit, the ten generally accepted auditing standards (GAAS) introduced in Chapter 1 — and all Statements on Auditing Standards, the profession's interpretation of GAAS — must be followed by AICPA members not only because the standards are guidelines and measures of quality for financial statement audits, but also because Rule 202 specifically states that they must. Violating a generally accepted auditing standard, or the standards for any of the other services cited in the Rule, in turn violates the Code of Professional Conduct.

Rule 203 — Accounting Principles

A member shall not (1) express an opinion or state affirmatively that the financial statements or other financial data of any entity are presented in conformity with generally accepted accounting principles or (2) state that he or she is not aware of any such material modifications that should be made to such statements or data in order for them to be in conformity with generally accepted accounting principles, if such statements or data contain any departure from an accounting principle promulgated by bodies designated by Council to establish such principles that has a material effect on the statements or data taken as a whole. If, however, the statements or data contain such a departure and the member can demonstrate that due to unusual circumstances the financial statements or data would otherwise have been misleading, the member can comply with the rule by describing the departure, its approximate effects, if practicable, and the reasons why compliance with the principle would result in a misleading statement.

Rule 203 relates to all engagements for which financial statements or other financial data are reported on by an AICPA member. Thus, the rule applies to financial statement audits and to special engagements for which generally accepted accounting principles are reported on, such as reports on a comprehensive basis of accounting other than GAAP (e.g., cash basis statements) or reports on specified elements of a financial statement (e.g., gross sales), both of which are introduced in Chapter 20. Departures from FASB Statements of Financial Accounting Standards, Opinions of the Accounting Principles Board, and Accounting Research Bulletins are specifically prohibited under Rule 203.

There is a strong presumption that adherence to officially promulgated accounting principles, like Statements of Financial Accounting Standards, would in nearly all instances result in financial statements that are not misleading. However, in rare and unusual circumstances not considered within an official pronouncement, an accountant may believe that the literal interpretation and application of an accounting pronouncement might result in misleading financial statements. It is difficult for authoritative bodies to anticipate all of the circumstances to which promulgated accounting principles might be applied. Rule 203 therefore recognizes that on occasion there may be circumstances so unusual that the literal application of an accounting pronouncement would have the effect of rendering the financial statements or financial data misleading. In such cases, the proper accounting treatment is that which will render the financial statements not misleading.

Responsibilities to Clients

An AICPA member is obligated to be fair, candid, and professionally concerned with his or her client's best interests. However, this obligation should be interpreted in light of the member's obligation of independence, integrity, and objectivity to the public. In short, an AICPA member has a dual responsibility to clients and to users, and compromising the interests of one group in favor of the other is implicitly prohibited by the Code.

Rule 301 — Confidential Client Information

A member in public practice shall not disclose any confidential client information without the specific consent of the client.

This rule shall not be construed (1) to relieve a member of his or her professional obligations under rules 202 and 203, (2) to affect in any way the member's obligation to comply with a validly issued and enforceable subpoena or summons, (3) to prohibit review of a member's professional practice under AICPA or state CPA society authorization, or (4) to preclude a member from initiating a complaint with or responding to any inquiry made by a recognized investigative or disciplinary body.

Members of a recognized investigative or disciplinary body and professional practice reviewers shall not use their own advantage or disclose any member's confidential client information that comes to their attention in carrying out their official responsibilities. However, this prohibition shall not restrict the exchange of information with a recognized investigative or disciplinary body or affect, in any way, compliance with a validly issued and enforceable subpoena or summons.

In the course of a financial statement audit or other professional engagement, an accountant typically encounters confidential client information. For example, when reviewing for potential legal claims against a client, an auditor may learn from attorneys that a patent has been obtained by the company to manufacture a revolutionary new product. Other examples of confidential information include officers' salaries, unreleased advertising campaigns, and product cost information. Disclosing this information could be detrimental to the entity's competitive edge within the industry and therefore is specifically prohibited. As the Rule states, confidential client information can not be disclosed without the specific consent of the client. However, as stated within the text of Rule 301, confidential client information would have to be disclosed in some circumstances, such as a response to a court-issued subpoena or summons. The purpose of Rule 301 is to encourage a client to provide financial information freely to an independent accountant without threat of confidential information being disclosed unnecessarily.

Closely related to confidentiality is the issue of privileged information. Information communicated between physicians and patients and between attorneys and clients is privileged and therefore cannot be requested even by a court of law. Information communicated between a CPA and client, however, is not privileged under common law, but is under the statutes of some states. That is, there is no right of privileged communication in federal jurisdictions, but there is in some states.

Rule 302 — Contingent Fees

Professional services shall not be offered or rendered under an arrangement whereby no fee will be charged unless a specified finding or result is attained, or where the fee is contingent upon the findings or results of such services. However, a member's fees may vary depending, for example, on the complexity of the service rendered.

Fees are not regarded as being contingent if fixed by courts or other public authorities or, in tax matters, if determined based on the results of judicial proceedings or the findings of governmental agencies.

Rule 302 specifically prohibits fee arrangements whereby no fee is paid unless a particular outcome is attained (e.g., no fee unless the audit opinion is unqualified) or the fee is contingent upon a particular outcome (e.g., 10 percent of reported net income). Obviously, the logic of Rule 302 is to remove AICPA members from potentially compromising positions.

A member's fees, however, may be based upon the outcome of a tax proceeding or a contract renegotiation claim; in these cases the member cannot directly influence the results of the proceedings. Also, a fee may be dependent upon the complexity of an engagement. For example, because of the accounting and auditing issues involved, a member may charge more per hour of work for a major oil and gas refinery than for a local retail gas station that sells refined oil and gas products.

Responsibilities to Colleagues

The general acceptance of public accountants as important contributors to the financial community results primarily from the collective efforts of all AICPA members over time. Individual members are each obligated to portray an image of mutual cooperation in order to maintain and further enhance the profession's public image. Members should support their colleagues through responsible contributions to professional organizations, such as the AICPA and state societies of CPAs, and through cooperation in resolving professional and technical accounting and auditing issues.

Contributions to the profession and cooperation among colleagues, however, do not excuse a member from testifying as an expert witness against another CPA, for example in a judicial proceeding or inquiry. In the long run, ignoring a colleague's incompetence or unethical acts can be more damaging to both the profession and the public than revealing alleged weaknesses through honest and objective testimony. A member is obligated to follow and, in the case of acting as an expert witness, uphold the Code of Professional Conduct.

Unquestionably, a member must be competitive in developing a client base. The public can only benefit from competition among CPAs. A natural byproduct of competition, however, is that some members will gain new clients and others will lose clients. This temporary shift in client base, however, is healthy for the profession; competition within an industry almost always results in an optimum blend of costs and benefits to the industry's benefactors (e.g., financial statement users and some clients). Nevertheless, competition should not be so intense that the interests of the profession as a whole are undermined. As a result, members should be competitive in the sense of providing quality professional services, yet responsible in the sense of avoiding unscrupulous means for attracting potential clients.

Aside from competitive situations, CPAs should also act responsibly when communicating with colleagues about professional matters. For example, *Statement on Auditing Standards No. 7*, "Communication Between Predecessor and Successor Auditors" (AU Sec. 315), deals with communication between predecessor and successor auditors either when a change of auditors is in process or after the change actually occurs. The Statement defines a successor auditor as one who has accepted an engagement or been invited to submit a proposal, and places the initiative for communication between the auditors upon the successor. However, the predecessor must first obtain the client's permission before responding. Further, as suggested by Rule 301, a predecessor may not disclose confidential client information without a client's specific permission.

Two rules were issued under Section 400 prior to the 1980s. Both, however, were deleted by member vote, leaving no currently effective rules relating to responsibilities to colleagues.

Other Responsibilities and Practices

Rules 501–505 deal with the profession's image from the viewpoint of a member's individual professional and personal activities. An AICPA member is a representative of the profession, a focal point from which the public draws general and specific conclusions about the profession as a whole. Thus, a member should avoid professional and personal activities which may erode public confidence.

Although financial compensation can affect one's standard of living and lifestyle, a member should emphasize the quality of professional services over amount of compensation. A CPA should strive to optimize the relationship between quality and compensation, not maximize compensation to the detriment of quality. These thoughts underscore the "spirit" of Rules 501–505. The rules related to other responsibilities and practices follow.

Rule 501 — Acts Discreditable

A member shall not commit an act discreditable to the profession.

In general, Rule 501 relates to discreditable acts not specifically covered by other rules of conduct. Although not specifically mentioned within either the Rule or related Interpretations, Rule 501 presumably prohibits financial statements intentionally misstated in a client's behalf, fraudulently prepared tax returns, and criminal offenses.

Client's Records and Accountant's Workpapers. Working papers are the accountant's property and, as a result, need not be surrendered to the client. However, in some instances, accountants prepare working papers that contain information not included or recorded within the client's books and records, such as listings of cash receipts/disbursements and depreciation schedules. Interpretation 501-1, "Clients Records and Accountant's Workpapers," recognizes that some working papers actually constitute part of the client's records, and copies should therefore be made available to the client upon request. Examples of working papers that are considered to be part of the client's records include:

▲ Worksheets used in place of original entries (e.g., listings and distributions of cash receipts or cash disbursements on columnar working papers).
▲ Worksheets used in place of the general ledger or subsidiary ledgers, such as accounts receivable, job cost and equipment ledgers, or similar depreciation records.
▲ All adjusting entries and closing journal entries (i.e., correcting entries made by the auditor) and supporting details.
▲ Consolidating or combining journal entries and worksheets and supporting detail used in arriving at final figures incorporated in an end product such as financial statements or tax returns.

Any working papers developed by the accountant which do not result in changes to the client's records or are not in themselves part of the records ordinarily maintained by the client are not the client's property.

Discrimination. Equal opportunity is a fundamental, inalienable right of all members of a free society, and if denied, constitutes an inequity on not only the injured person but also society as a whole. Interpretation 501-2, "Discrimination in Employment Practices," states that discrimination based on race, color, sex, age, or national origin in hiring, promotion, or salary practices is presumed to constitute an act discreditable to the profession in violation of Rule 501.

Negligence in the Preparation of Financial Statements or Records. As noted earlier, Rule 501 presumably prohibits preparing fraudulent financial statements in a client's behalf. Interpretation 501-4, however, goes further, by addressing negligence — rather than intentional fraud — in the preparation of a client's financial statements or records. The Interpretation states that an accountant who negligently makes, or permits or directs another to make, false and misleading entries in the financial statements or records of a client is considered to have committed an act discreditable to the profession in violation of Rule 501.

Rule 502 — Advertising and Other Forms of Solicitation

A member in public practice shall not seek to obtain clients by advertising or other forms of solicitation in a manner that is false, misleading, or deceptive. Solicitation by the use of coercion, overreaching, or harassing conduct is prohibited.

For over fifty years, the Code of Professional Ethics specifically prohibited solicitation and advertising. Prior to amendment in 1979, the text of Rule 502 stated: ''A member shall not seek to obtain clients by solicitation. Advertising is a form of solicitation and is prohibited.'' However, in 1976 the Institute's Professional Ethics Division became aware that state attorneys general, the Justice Department, and the Federal Trade Commission were beginning to advise several professional groups to repeal or at least not enforce their prohibitions against advertising.[2]

Advertising by Professionals: The U.S. Supreme Court Responds. Bates vs State Bar of Arizona[3] was a pivotal U.S. Supreme Court opinion which, in conjunction with other cases, helped pave the way toward advertising by professionals, including AICPA members. The Bates case involved two Arizona attorneys who, in defiance of the Arizona State Bar Association, advertised routine professional services in a Phoenix newspaper. Although common today, the paid advertisement for legal services was quite uncommon at the time. In 1977, the U.S. Supreme Court ruled 5-to-4 in favor of Bates, stating that the Arizona Bar, a state agency, could not deprive the two attorneys of their First Amendment (free speech) rights.

The Bates case was not unique; other professional organizations had faced similar challenges to their prohibitions against advertising. Interestingly, the conclusions reached in these challenges were similar to the Bates case. A partner in a major public accounting firm comments:

> To the best of my knowledge, all professional associations that have faced legal challenges to their ethical rules on advertising during the past few years have lost their cases in trial courts. Though there are a number of appeals pending, it is an open question as to whether their prohibitions on advertising can be sustained.[4]

---

[2]A. C. Ostlund, ''Advertising — In the Public Interest?'' *Journal of Accountancy* (January, 1978), p. 59.

[3]*Bates vs. State Bar of Arizona* (97 S. Ct. 2691).

[4]A. C. Ostlund, *op. cit.,* p. 61.

In 1978, the AICPA membership voted overwhelming to modify Rule 502. The current version of the Rule was adopted by member vote in January 1988.

Interpretations of Rule 502. Three Interpretations under Rule 502 are currently in effect and relate to (1) what represents informational advertising, (2) what constitutes false, misleading, or deceptive acts, and (3) engagements obtained through the efforts of third parties. Two other Interpretations were issued but have since been rescinded. The three currently effective Interpretations are presented below.

Interpretation 502-1: Informational Advertising. Advertising that is informative and objective is permitted. Such advertising should be in good taste and be professionally dignified. There are no other restrictions, such as on the type of advertising media, frequency of placement, size, art work, or type style. Some examples of informative and objective content are:

1. Information about the member and the member's firm such as
   a. Names, addresses, telephone numbers, number of partners, shareholders, or employees, office hours, foreign language competence, and date the firm was established.
   b. Services offered and fees for such services, including hourly rates and fixed fees.
   c. Educational and professional attainments, including date and place of certifications, schools attended, dates of graduation, degrees received, and memberships in professional associations.
2. Statements of policy or position made by a member or a member's firm related to the practice of public accounting or addressed to a subject of public interest.

Interpretation 502-2: False, Misleading, or Deceptive Acts. Advertising or other forms of solicitation that are false, misleading, or deceptive are not in the public interest and are prohibited. Such activities include those that

1. Create false or unjustified expectations of favorable results.
2. Imply the ability to influence any court, tribunal, regulatory agency, or similar body or official.
3. Consist of self-laudatory statements that are not based on verifiable facts.
4. Make comparisons with other CPAs.
5. Contain testimonials or endorsements.
6. Contain any other representations that would be likely to cause a reasonable person to misunderstand or be deceived.

Interpretation 502-5: Engagements Obtained through Efforts of Third Parties. Members are often asked to render professional services to clients or customers of third parties. Such third parties may have obtained such clients or customers as the result of their advertising and solicitation efforts.

Members are permitted to enter into such engagements. The member has the responsibility to ascertain that all promotional efforts are within the bounds of the Rules of Conduct. Such action is required because the members will receive the benefits of such efforts by third parties, and members must not do through others what they are prohibited from doing themselves by the Rules of Conduct.

Rule 503 — Commissions

The acceptance by a member in public practice of a payment for the referral of products or services of others to a client is prohibited. Such action is considered to create a conflict of interest that results in a loss of objectivity and independence.

A member shall not make a payment to obtain a client. This rule shall not prohibit payments for the purchase of an accounting practice or retirement payments to individuals formerly engaged in the practice of public accounting or payments to their heirs or estates.

Rule 503 prohibits a member from receiving or paying a commission for client referrals. For example, financial institutions and attorneys frequently refer clients to AICPA members for accounting and auditing services. This practice is perfectly acceptable and can represent an important source for new clients. However, under Rule 503, a member is precluded from paying referral fees or commissions to the referring institution or attorney. Likewise, a member is also precluded from accepting a commission for client referrals to others, e.g., to another CPA more experienced in the services required by the client.

Although Rule 503 prohibits commissions for client referrals, it does allow the payment of fees to a referring public accountant for professional services rendered either to the successor public accountant or to the client in connection with the engagement. That is, Rule 503 is intended to preclude fees when an accountant does not provide commensurate services, as is the case in referral fees. But if a referring public accountant provides services, either to the successor accountant or to the client, reasonable fees are justified.

In addition, Rule 503 does not prohibit the practice of public accounting firms compensating staff for securing new client engagements. New client development is not inconsistent with a staff member's professional activities — thus, payments to staff for securing new clients is part of the staff member's normal compensation.

Prior to 1988, the now superseded Rule 504, entitled "Incompatible Occupations," provided that "A member who is engaged in the practice of public accounting shall not concurrently engage in any business or occupation which would create a conflict of interest in rendering professional services." Rule 504 recognized that an incompatible occupation could result in a conflict of interest, thereby potentially impairing an accountant's independence, integrity, and objectivity. For example, if an accountant were also an audit client's attorney, Rule 504 would be violated, since attorneys act as advocates for their clients, and auditors act as independent attestors. That is, the accountant's role in objectively evaluating audit evidence about a contingent liability related to a patent infringement could be compromised if he or she were also engaged to defend the client in the related court suit. Rule 504 was deleted by member vote in 1988 because the Code of Professional Conduct's Principles, specifically Objectivity and Independence, provide guidance on conflicts of interest, and Rule 102, Integrity and Objectivity, requires that members avoid conflicts of interest.

Rule 505 — Form of Practice and Name

A member may practice public accounting only in the form of a proprietorship, a partnership, or a professional corporation whose characteristics conform to resolutions of Council.

A member shall not practice public accounting under a firm name that is misleading. Names of one or more past partners or shareholders may be included in the firm name of a successor partnership or corporation. Also, a partner or shareholder surviving the death or withdrawal of all other partners or shareholders may continue to practice under such name which includes the name of past partners or shareholders for up to two years after becoming a sole practitioner.

A firm may not designate itself as "Members of the American Institute of Certified Public Accountants" unless all of its partners or shareholders are members of the Institute.

Form of Practice. A firm of certified public accountants may take the form of a proprietorship, partnership, or corporation. Before 1969, public accounting firms were prohibited from organizing as corporations. But at a May 1969 AICPA Council meeting, a seven-point resolution was passed, and then revised in 1979, which allowed a firm to organize as a professional corporation.

Like traditional corporations, professional corporations enjoy the tax benefits of pensions and profit sharing, among other things. But unlike traditional corporations, professional corporations do not enjoy the benefit of limited liability.

The AICPA's 1979 professional corporation resolution was revised by member vote in 1988 and appears in Figure 2-1. Note particularly from the four points listed in Figure 2-1 that professional corporations actually represent corporations in form, but partnerships in substance.

Name of Practice. The name of a public accounting firm can be fictitious or indicate a specialization, provided that the firm name or specialization is not misleading. In this context, Rule 505 is consistent with Rule 502 on advertising: only firm names or specializations that are false, misleading, or deceptive are prohibited. Also, all firm partners or shareholders must be AICPA members in order for the firm to carry the designation "Members of the AICPA."

ENFORCEMENT

Until the late 1970s three bodies operated somewhat independently to enforce ethical conduct among CPAs: the AICPA, the state societies of CPAs (both voluntary membership organizations), and the state boards of accountancy (state regulatory agencies). The AICPA enforces the AICPA Code of Professional Conduct, and the state societies enforce their own codes; each organization can, after a hearing, admonish, suspend, or expel a violator and publicize a member's ethics violations. In contrast, the state boards of accountancy are empowered to regulate the practice of public accounting within their own states and therefore can revoke a CPA's license to practice. Thus, from the standpoint of enforcement, the state boards of accountancy are the most powerful of the three organizations, because a CPA can practice regardless of membership in the AICPA or a state society, but cannot practice without a license.

Over the years, and particularly prior to the 1980s, enforcement of the AICPA Code of Professional Ethics and the state codes had been largely ineffective. In part, the ineffectiveness stemmed from CPAs' reluctance to report a fellow CPA's alleged ethics violations, varying disciplinary punishment from state to state, and ineffective communication among the AICPA, state societies, and state boards concerning violations and disciplinary action.

In an effort to dispel the effects of the last two criticisms, most state societies joined forces with the National Joint Trial Board to develop a national ethics enforcement system. The joint ethics enforcement system allows

FIGURE 2-1
Council Resolution Permitting Professional Corporations or
Associations

RESOLVED, that the characteristics of a professional corporation as referred
to in Rule 505 of the Code of Professional Conduct are as follows:
1. *Ownership.* All shareholders of the corporation or association shall be persons engaged in the practice of public accounting as defined by the Code of
   Professional Conduct. Shareholders shall at all times own their shares in
   their own right and shall be the beneficial owners of the equity capital as-
   cribed to them.
2. *Transfer of Shares.* Provision shall be made requiring any shareholder who
   ceases to be eligible to be a shareholder to dispose of all of his or her shares
   within a reasonable period to a person qualified to be a shareholder or to
   the corporation or association.
3. *Directors and Officers.* The principal executive officer shall be a shareholder and a director, and to the extent possible, all other directors and
   officers shall be certified public accountants. Lay directors and officers shall
   not exercise any authority whatsoever over professional matters.
4. *Conduct.* The right to practice as a corporation or association shall not change
   the obligation of its shareholders, directors, officers, and other employees
   to comply with the standards of professional conduct established by the
   American Institute of Certified Public Accountants.

the AICPA Ethics Division Subcommittee and the state society ethics committees to act independently or refer a case to the National Joint Trial Board.

As depicted in Figure 2-2, alleged violations that involve more than one
state, that involve potential litigation, or that are of national concern are handled by the AICPA Ethics Division Subcommittee; others are handled by the
state society ethics committee. Cases involving litigation are placed in a sus-
pense file until settled; if convicted in court, a CPA's AICPA and state society memberships are automatically suspended on conviction and terminated
upon final judgment.

Cases reach the Joint Trial Board if (1) both the AICPA and state society
concur on their findings, yet do not issue a joint administrative reprimand, or
(2) either the AICPA or state society takes action individually and refers a
case on its own. Following a disciplinary hearing, the Joint Trial Board may
take any one of the following courses of action: acquittal, censure, suspension (up to two years) or expulsion of a member, or a judgment requiring
continuing professional education. Of course, a member may appeal an adverse decision.

FIGURE 2-2
Joint Ethics Enforcement: AICPA, State Societies, and Joint National
Trial Board

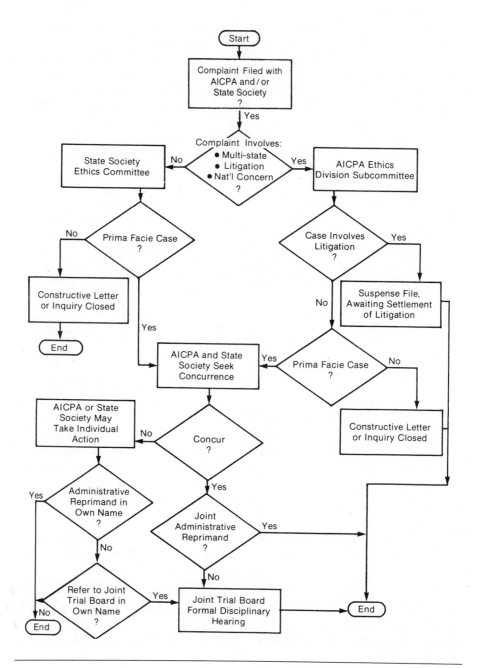

SUMMARY

General ethics relate to ideal conduct, choice, and the consequences of choice, and are closely related to professional ethics and, correspondingly, to professional conduct.

The AICPA Code of Professional Conduct consists of two sections, Principles and Rules of Conduct, and also includes Interpretations and Ethics Rulings. Six principles underlie the Code: (1) responsibilities, (2) the public interest, (3) integrity, (4) objectivity and independence, (5) due care, and (6) the scope and nature of services. The Rules of Conduct relate to independence, integrity and objectivity; general and technical standards; responsibilities to clients and colleagues; and other responsibilities. Like Interpretations and Ethics Rulings, the Rules of Conduct are enforceable by the AICPA upon members. Interpretations are intended to interpret the scope and applicability of specific Rules of Conduct, and Ethics Rulings are intended to summarize the applicability of Rules and Interpretations to specific factual situations; both Interpretations and Ethics Rulings are issued by the AICPA's Professional Ethics Division.

Enforcement of the AICPA and individual state society codes had been relatively ineffective. As a result, the AICPA and a number of states developed a joint ethics enforcement system in conjunction with the National Joint Trial Board. This system allows the AICPA and the state societies to act either independently or jointly to review complaints and reprimand ethics violators.

REFERENCES

AICPA. *Restructuring Professional Standards to Achieve Professional Excellence in a Changing Environment.* Report of the Special Committee on Standards of Professional Conduct for Certified Public Accountants (New York: AICPA, 1986).

AICPA Professional Standards, Vol. 2 (New York: AICPA).

Anderson, G. D. "A Fresh Look at Standards of Professional Conduct." *Journal of Accountancy* (September, 1985), pp. 91–106.

Carey, J. L., and W. O. Doherty. *Ethical Standards of The Accounting Profession.* New York: American Institute of Certified Public Accountants, 1966.

Graber, D. E. "Ethics Enforcement — How Effective?" *The CPA Journal* (September, 1979), pp. 11–17.

Larson, R. E. "For The Members, By The Members." *Journal of Accountancy* (October 1987), pp. 116–122.

Mautz, R. K., and H. A. Sharaf. *The Philosophy of Auditing.* Sarasota: American Accounting Association, 1961.

Olson, W. E. "How should a Profession Be Disciplined?" *Journal of Accountancy* (May, 1978), pp. 59–66.

Ostlund, A. C. "Advertising — In the Public Interest?" *Journal of Accountancy*
    (January, 1978), pp. 59–63.
Windal, F. W., and R. N. Corley. *The Accounting Professional: Ethics, Responsi-
    bility, and Liability.* Englewood Cliffs, N.J.: Prentice-Hall, Inc., 1980.
Wood, T. D., and D. A. Ball. "New Rule 502 and Effective Advertising by CPAs."
    Journal of Accountancy (June, 1978), pp. 65–71.

QUESTIONS

1. What are general ethics, and how do they relate to professional ethics?
2. Identify and briefly describe the four components of the AICPA Code of Professional Conduct.
3. Relate (1) Principles of Professional Conduct, (2) ideal conduct, and (3) trust. Be specific.
4. Discuss the applicability of the AICPA Rules of Conduct.
5. Identify at least four examples of situations in which an AICPA member would not be deemed independent.
6. Is it ethical for an AICPA member to act also as an attorney for a client?
7. What is the purpose of the general and technical standards section of the AICPA Code of Professional Conduct?
8. Does Rule 301, "Confidential Client Information," preclude AICPA members who serve on AICPA Ethics Division subcommittees and members of state society ethics committees from exchanging confidential client information that is central to an ethics investigation? Explain.
9. Who should initiate communication between predecessor and successor auditors when a change in auditors either is in process or actually occurs? Explain. What impact does Rule 301, "Confidential Client Information," have on communication between predecessor and successor auditors?
10. Rule 502, "Advertising and Other Forms of Solicitation," precludes a member from advertising in a manner that is false, misleading, or deceptive. What is meant by "false, misleading, or deceptive" advertising?
11. When referring a client to another CPA, can an AICPA member accept a commission from the CPA if (a) the amount is clearly immaterial, and (b) it merely covers the AICPA member's costs (i.e., time and expenses) of referral?
12. Why had enforcement of the AICPA Code of Professional Ethics and state society codes been relatively ineffective in the past?
13. Explain the current national joint ethics enforcement system.

MULTIPLE CHOICE QUESTIONS

1. Which of the following most completely describes how independence has been defined by the profession?

    a. Performing an audit from the viewpoint of the public.
    b. Avoiding the appearance of significant interests in the affairs of an audit client.

    c. Possessing the ability to act with integrity and objectivity.
    d. Accepting responsibility to act professionally and in accordance with a
       professional Code of Conduct.   (AICPA Adapted)

2. The AICPA Code of Professional Conduct states, in part, that a CPA should
   maintain integrity and objectivity. Objectivity in the code refers to a CPA's
   ability

    a. To maintain an impartial attitude on all matters which come under the CPA's
       review.
    b. To independently distinguish between accounting practices that are acceptable
       and those that are not.
    c. To be unyielding in all matters dealing with auditing procedures.
    d. To independently choose between alternative accounting principles and audit-
       ing standards.   (AICPA Adapted)

3. Which of the following publications does not qualify as a statement of generally
   accepted accounting principles under the AICPA Code of Professional Conduct?

    a. Accounting interpretations issued by the FASB.
    b. Accounting interpretations issued by the AICPA.
    c. AICPA Accounting Research Bulletins.
    d. Statements of Financial Accounting Standards issued by the FASB.
                                            (AICPA Adapted)

4. In which of the following circumstances would a CPA be bound by ethics to
   refrain from disclosing any confidential information obtained during the course
   of a professional engagement?

    a. The CPA is issued a summons enforceable by a court order which orders the
       CPA to present confidential information.
    b. A major stockholder of a client company seeks accounting information from
       the CPA after management declined to disclose the requested information.
    c. Confidential client information is made available as part of a quality review
       of the CPA's practice by a review team authorized by the AICPA.
    d. An inquiry by a disciplinary body of a state CPA society requests confidential
       client information.   (AICPA Adapted)

5. The AICPA Code of Professional Conduct states that a CPA shall not disclose
   any confidential information obtained in the course of a professional engagement
   except with the consent of the client. This rule should be understood to preclude
   a CPA from responding to an inquiry made by

    a. The trial board of the AICPA.
    b. An investigative body of a state CPA society.
    c. A CPA-shareholder of the client corporation.
    d. An AICPA voluntary quality review body.   (AICPA Adapted)

6. Richard, CPA, performs accounting services for Norton Corporation. Norton
   wishes to offer its shares to the public and asks Richard to audit the financial
   statements prepared for registration purposes. Richard refers Norton to Cruz,
   CPA, who is more competent in the area of registration statements. Cruz performs the audit of Norton's financial statements and subsequently thanks Richard

for the referral by giving Richard a portion of the audit fee collected. Richard accepts the fee. Who, if anyone, has violated professional ethics?

   a. Only Richard.
   b. Both Richard and Cruz.
   c. Only Cruz.
   d. Neither Richard nor Cruz.   (AICPA Adapted)

7. In which of the following situations would a CPA be in violation of the AICPA Code of Professional Conduct in determining his or her fee?

   a. A fee based on whether the CPA's report on the client's financial statements results in the approval of a bank loan.
   b. A fee based on the outcome of a bankruptcy proceeding.
   c. A fee based on the nature of the service rendered and the CPA's particular expertise instead of the actual time spent on the engagement.
   d. A fee based on the fee charged by the predecessor auditor.
                                                         (AICPA Adapted)

8. The AICPA Code of Professional Conduct would be violated if a CPA accepted a fee for services and the fee was

   a. Fixed by a public authority.
   b. Based on a price quotation submitted in competitive bidding.
   c. Determined, based on the result of judicial proceedings.
   d. Payable after a specified finding was attained.   (AICPA Adapted)

9. Inclusion of which of the following in a promotional brochure published by a CPA firm would be most likely to result in a violation of the AICPA rules of conduct?

   a. Names and addresses, telephone numbers, numbers of partners, office hours, foreign language competence, and date the firm was established.
   b. Services offered and fees for such services, including hourly rates and fixed fees.
   c. Educational and professional attainments, including date and place of certification, schools attended, dates of graduation, degrees received, and memberships in professional associations.
   d. Names, addresses, and telephone numbers of the firm's clients, including the number of years served.   (AICPA Adapted)

10. Inclusion of which of the following statements in a CPA's advertisement is *not* acceptable pursuant to the AICPA Code of Professional Conduct?

   a. Paul Fall
      Certified Public Accountant
      Fluency in Spanish and French.
   b. Paul Fall
      Certified Public Accountant
      J. D., Evans Law School 1964
   c. Paul Fall
      Certified Public Accountant
      Free Consultation

<u>d.</u> Paul Fall
     Certified Public Accountant
     Endorsed by the AICPA   (AICPA Adapted)

11. Which of the following is prohibited by the AICPA Code of Professional Conduct?

<u>a.</u> A firm that designates itself "Members of the AICPA" when one partner has been expelled from the AICPA.
b. Practice of public accounting in the form of a professional corporation.
c. Use of the partnership name for a limited period by one of the partners in a public accounting firm after the death or withdrawal of all other partners.
d. Holding as an investment ten of 1,000 outstanding shares in a commercial corporation which performs bookkeeping services.   (AICPA Adapted)

12. Which of the following is required for a firm to designate itself "Member of the American Institute of Certified Public Accountants" on its letterhead?

a. At least one of the partners must be a member.
b. The partners whose names appear in the firm name must be members.
<u>c.</u> All partners must be members.
d. The firm must be a dues paying member.   (AICPA Adapted)

PROBLEMS

2-1   Certified public accountants have imposed upon themselves a rigorous code of professional conduct.

Required:
Discuss the underlying reasons for the accounting profession's adopting a code of professional conduct.   (AICPA Adapted)

2-2   An auditor must not only appear to be independent, but also be independent in fact.

Required:
1. Explain the concept of an "auditor's independence" as it applies to third-party reliance upon financial statements.
2. a. What determines whether or not an auditor is independent in fact?
   b. What determines whether or not an auditor appears to be independent?
3. Explain how an auditor may be independent in fact but not appear to be independent.
4. Would a CPA be considered independent for an examination of the financial statements of a:
   a. Church for which he or she is serving as treasurer without compensation? Explain.
   b. Civic club for which the CPA's spouse is serving as treasurer-bookkeeper if the CPA is not to receive a fee for the examination? Explain.
                                                          (AICPA Adapted)

2-3   The attribute of independence has been traditionally associated with the CPA's function of auditing and expressing opinions on financial statements.

Required:
1. What is meant by "independence" as applied to the CPA's function of auditing and expressing opinions on financial statements? Explain.
2. CPAs have imposed upon themselves certain rules of professional conduct that induce their members to remain independent and to strengthen public confidence in their independence. Which of the rules of professional conduct are concerned with the CPA's independence? Explain.
3. The Wallydrag Company is indebted to a CPA for unpaid fees and has offered to issue to the CPA unsecured interest-bearing notes. Would acceptance of these notes have any bearing upon the CPA's independence in relations with the Wallydrag Company? Discuss.
4. The Rocky Hill Corporation was formed on October 1, 1989, and its fiscal year will end on September 30, 1990. A CPA has audited the corporation's opening balance sheet and had rendered an unqualified opinion on it.

   A month after submitting the report, the CPA is offered the position of secretary of the Company because of the need for a complete set of officers and for convenience in signing various documents. The CPA will have no financial interest in the company through stock ownership or otherwise, will receive no salary, will not keep the books, and will have no influence on its financial matters other than occasional advice on income tax matters and similar advice normally given a client by the CPA.
   a. Assume that the CPA accepts the offer but plans to resign the position prior to conducting the annual audit with the intention of again assuming the office after rendering an opinion on the statements. Can the CPA render an independent opinion on the financial statements? Discuss.
   b. Assume that the CPA accepts the offer on a temporary basis until the corporation has gotten under way and can employ a secretary, but in any event would permanently resign the position before conducting the annual audit. Can the CPA render an independent opinion on the financial statements? Discuss.

                                                                    (AICPA Adapted)

2-4   Ruth Shafer, CPA, is auditing the Nelson Company. Her son, aged 16, owns 100 shares of the 50,000 shares of the Nelson Company common stock outstanding at the balance sheet date.

Required:
Discuss the effect, if any, the son's stock ownership would have on the auditor's opinion.   (AICPA Adapted)

2-5   Your client, Nuesel Corporation, requests that you conduct a feasibility study to advise management of the best way for the corporation to utilize electronic data processing equipment and which computer, if any, best meets the corporation's requirements. You are technically competent in this area and accept the engagement. Upon completion of your study, the corporation accepts your suggestions and installs the computer and related equipment that you recommended.

Required:
1. Discuss the effect that the acceptance of this management services engagement would have upon your independence in expressing an opinion on the financial statements of the Nuesel Corporation.
2. Data Print, Inc., a local printer of data processing forms, customarily offers a commission for recommending Data Print as a supplier. The client is aware of the commission offer and suggests that you accept it. Would it be proper for you to accept the commission with the client's approval? Discuss. (AICPA Adapted)

2-6   Benjamin Leon, a retired partner of your CPA firm, has just been appointed to the board of directors of Palmer Corporation, your firm's client. Leon is also a member of your firm's income tax committee which meets monthly to discuss income tax problems of the partnership's clients. The partnership pays Leon $100 for each committee meeting he attends and a monthly retirement benefit of $1,000.

Required:
Discuss the effect of Leon's appointment to the board of directors of Palmer Corporation on your partnership's independence in expressing an opinion on the Palmer Corporation's financial statements.   (AICPA Adapted)

2-7   Audrey Campbell, CPA, has examined the financial statements of the Grimm Company for several years. Grimm's president now has asked Campbell to install an inventory control system for the company.

Required:
Discuss the factors that Campbell should consider in determining whether to accept this engagement.   (AICPA Adapted)

2-8   Charles Adams, CPA, has been practicing public accounting for several years, but feels uncomfortable with electronic data processing. As a result, he contemplates hiring an additional professional staff member who specializes in systems analysis and computers.

Required:
Must Adams be personally able to perform all of the services that the specialist can perform in order to be able to supervise the new hire? Explain.

2-9   Paulette Martin, CPA, had been approached by a staff assistant regarding the applicability of the AICPA Rules of Conduct to unaudited financial statements. The assistant notes that Rule 202, "Compliance with Standards," does not permit an AICPA member's name to be associated with financial statements in such a manner as to imply that the member is acting as an independent public accountant unless he or she has complied with the applicable standards. The assistant then asks:
> "Since generally accepted auditing standards appear to relate to audited and not to unaudited financial statements, does Rule 202 effectively prohibit an AICPA member from being associated with unaudited financial statements?"

Required:
Is the assistant's interpretation of Rule 202 correct? Explain.

2-10   Donald Bowie, CPA, is the assistant controller for Aberdeen Industries, a highly diversified conglomerate operating in the U.S. and abroad. Bowie has been asked by Aberdeen's corporate controller to perform examinations and express an opinion on several of Aberdeen's more significant holdings. The opinions are for distribution to, and use by, Aberdeen's officials only.

Required:
Is Bowie in violation of the AICPA Code of Professional Conduct if he conducts the examinations and issues an internal-use opinion? Explain.

2-11   Doris Sweeny, CPA, is engaged by the local municipal government to conduct periodic personal property tax audits of companies operating within the municipality. The property tax relates to business inventories, equipment, and machinery; thus, Sweeny will examine accounts and records related to sales, purchases, and gross profit percentages, among other things.

Ashton Manufacturing Company, a local producer of tool and die equipment, resents the fact that Sweeny is conducting the property tax audits because she also provides audit services to several competing tool and die manufacturing companies. Ashton fears that, while conducting the property tax audit, Sweeny may encounter trade secrets beneficial to some of her audit clients. As a result, Ashton approaches the Ethics Division of the AICPA arguing that it is unethical for Sweeny to conduct its property tax audit.

Required:
Does Sweeny violate the AICPA Code of Professional Conduct by conducting a property tax audit of Ashton, a tool and die equipment manufacturer, and providing audit services to competing companies within the same industry? Explain.

2-12   Judy Hanlon, CPA, is engaged to prepare the federal income tax return for the Guild Corporation for the year ended December 31, 1990. This is Hanlon's first engagement of any kind for the Guild Corporation.

In preparing the 1990 return, Hanlon finds an error on the 1989 return. The 1989 depreciation was overstated significantly — accumulated depreciation brought forward from 1988 to 1989 was understated, and thus the 1989 base for declining balance depreciation was overstated.

Hanlon reports the error to Guild's controller, the officer responsible for tax returns. The controller states: "Let the revenue agent find the error," and further instructs Hanlon to carry forward the material overstatement of the depreciable base to the 1990 depreciation computation. The controller notes that this error also had been made in the financial records for 1989 and 1990 and offers to furnish Hanlon with a letter assuming full responsibility for this treatment.

Required:
1. Evaluate Hanlon's action in this situation.
2. Discuss the additional action that Hanlon should now undertake.

(AICPA Adapted)

2-13   Certified public accountants often serve as expert witnesses in damage suits involving accounting and auditing matters. For example, accountants acting as expert witnesses could be asked to testify about appropriate auditing procedures or applicable accounting principles in given nonroutine circumstances.

Required:
When acting as an expert witness in a damage suit, may a CPA receive compensation based on the amount awarded a plaintiff?

2-14   Each of the following situations relate to Rule 502, "Advertising and Other Forms of Solicitation":
a. A trade association engages a CPA to analyze specific problems affecting members of the association. The results of the CPA's analysis will bear the CPA's name, be reproduced by the association, and be distributed to association members.

Required:
Does Rule 502 prohibit distribution of results of the CPA's analysis? Explain.

b. A CPA is engaged by the local chapter of a national accounting association to conduct a continuing education course for its members. The CPA is identified in promotional material distributed by the association.

Required:
What responsibility does the CPA have for information included within the promotional material? Explain.

c. A CPA is retained by a stock brokerage client to prepare a booklet on the tax aspects of security transactions. The client bears all printing costs and compensates the CPA for time expended on the project. A legend on the cover of the booklet states that it was prepared by the CPA. Booklets are mailed to the brokerage client's customers with end-of-month statements.

Required:
Is there any objection to this practice? Explain.

2-15   Several CPAs within the firm of Harding & Co. specialize in professional services related to client acquisitions and mergers. Because of these special talents, the policy committee of Harding & Co. decides to form a separate partnership to perform acquisition and merger services. Harding & Co. believes that the separate partnership can indicate a specialization on its business stationery because the acquisition and merger partnership will not practice public accounting, per se.

Required:
May the separate partnership indicate a specialization on its business stationery? Explain.

2-16   A CPA in public practice wishes to be a representative of a computer company which services tax practitioners. The CPA will utilize contacts with professional tax practitioners to introduce and promote use of the service. The CPA will receive a fee from the computer tax service for each tax return processed for a practitioner referred by the CPA.

Required:
Does this arrangement violate Rule 503, "Commissions"? Explain.

2-17   Tom Jencks, CPA, conducts a public accounting practice. In 1990 Jencks and Raymond Carver, a non-CPA, organized Electro-Data Corporation to specialize in computerized bookkeeping services. Jencks and Carver each supplied 50% of Electro-Data's capital, and each holds 50% of the capital stock. Carver is the salaried general manager of Electro-Data. Jencks is affiliated with the corporation only as a stockholder; he receives no salary and does not participate in day-to-day management. However, he has transferred all of his bookkeeping accounts to the corporation and recommends its services whenever possible.

Required:
Organizing your presentation around Jencks' involvement with Electro-Data Corporation, discuss the propriety of:
1. A CPA's participation in an enterprise offering computerized bookkeeping services.
2. A CPA's transfer of bookkeeping accounts to a service company.
3. A CPA's recommendation of a particular bookkeeping service company.

(AICPA Adapted)

2-18   A CPA in public practice is considering running for the elected office of state controller. Principal functions of the state controller include maintaining control over all state fund accounts, administering disbursements, and allocating revenue among county and local governments. The CPA intends to continue practicing public accounting if elected.

Required:
Can the CPA practice public accounting and serve as state controller? Explain.

2-19   Your CPA firm decides to form a partnership with Faye Reitz, a non-CPA management consultant, which would result in a "mixed partnership" of a CPA and a non-CPA.

Required:
Under what circumstances, if any, would it be ethically proper for a CPA to form a "mixed partnership?" Discuss.   (AICPA Adapted)

2-20   Although not partners, two CPAs share an office, maintain joint bank accounts, and work together on each other's engagements. As a result, they decide to have a joint letterhead showing both names, their address, and the designation "Certified Public Accountants."

Required:
Is the joint letterhead (including the address and the designation "Certified Public Accountants") proper? Explain.

2-21   Frank Gilbert and Gloria Aponte formed a corporation called Financial Services, Inc., each taking 50% of the authorized common stock. Gilbert is a CPA and a member of the American Institute of CPAs. Aponte is a CPCU (Chartered Property

Casualty Underwriter). The corporation performs auditing and tax services under Gilbert's direction and insurance services under Aponte's supervision. The opening of the corporation's office was announced by a three-inch, two-column "card" in the local newspaper.

One of the corporation's first audit clients was the Grandtime Company. Grandtime had total assets of $600,000 and total liabilities of $270,000. In the course of his examination, Gilbert found that Grandtime's building with a book value of $240,000 was pledged as security for a 10-year note in the amount of $200,000. The client's statements did not mention that the building was pledged as security for the note. However, since the failure to disclose the lien did not affect either the value of the assets or the amount of the liabilities, and since his examination was satisfactory in all other respects, Gilbert rendered an unqualified opinion on Grandtime's financial statements. About two months after the date of his opinion, Gilbert learned that an insurance company was planning to loan Grandtime $150,000 in the form of a first-mortgage note on the building. Realizing that the insurance company was unaware of the existing lien on the building, Gilbert had Aponte notify the insurance company of the fact that Grandtime's building was pledged as security for the note.

Shortly after the events described above, Gilbert was charged with a violation of professional ethics.

Required:
Identify and discuss the ethical implications of those acts by Gilbert that were in violation of the AICPA Code of Professional Conduct.   (AICPA Adapted)

2-22   Lakeview Development Corporation was formed on January 2, 1989 to develop a vacation-recreation area on land purchased the same day by the corporation for $100,000. The corporation also purchased for $40,000 an adjacent tract of land which the corporation plans to subdivide into fifty building lots. When the area is developed, the lots are expected to sell for $10,000 each.

The corporation borrowed a substantial portion of its funds from a bank and gave a mortgage on the land. A mortgage covenant requires that the corporation furnish quarterly financial statements.

The quarterly financial statements prepared at March 31 and June 30 by the corporation's bookkeeper were unacceptable to the bank officials. The corporation's president now offers you the engagement of preparing unaudited quarterly financial statements. Because of limited funds your fee would be paid in Lakeview Development Corporation common stock rather than in cash. The stock would be repurchased by the corporation when funds become available. You would not receive enough stock to a major stockholder.

Required:
1. Discuss the ethical implications of your accepting the engagement and the reporting requirements which are applicable if you should accept the engagement.
2. Assume that you accept the engagement to prepare the September 30 statements. What disclosures, if any, would you make of your prospective ownership of corporation stock in the quarterly financial statements?
3. The president insists that you present the fifty building lots at their expected sales price of $500,000 in the September 30 unaudited statements as was done in prior statements. The write-up was credited to Contributed Capital. How would you respond to the president's request?

4. The corporation elected to close its fiscal year September 30, 1989 and you are requested to prepare the corporation's federal income tax return. Discuss the implication of signing the return and the disclosure of your stock ownership in Lakeview Corporation (disregard the write-up of the land).

5. Assume that you accept the engagement to prepare the tax return. In the course of collecting information for the preparation of the return you find that the corporation's president paid the entire cost of a family vacation from corporate funds and listed the expense as travel and entertainment. You ascertain that the corporation's board of directors would not consider the cost of the vacation as either additional compensation or a gift to the president if the facts were known. What disclosure would you make in (a) the tax return and (b) the financial statements?

6. After accepting your unaudited September 30 financial statements, the bank notified the corporation that the December 31 financial statements must be accompanied by a CPA's opinion. You were asked to conduct the audit and told that your fee would be paid in cash. Discuss the ethical implications of accepting the engagement.

PROFESSIONAL JUDGMENT AND
AUDITOR RESPONSIBILITIES

3

Major topics discussed in this chapter are the:

▲ *Role of professional judgment in auditing and the audit decision making process.*

▲ *Decision models, decision aids, "heuristics," and biases prevalent in audit practice.*

▲ *Meaning and source of the "expectation gap."*

▲ *Auditor's responsibility for detecting client errors, irregularities, and illegal acts.*

▲ *Scope and provisions of the Foreign Corrupt Practices Act.*

▲ *Reports of the National Commission on Fraudulent Financial Reporting and the Commission on Auditors' Responsibilities.*

Despite the technology and methodology available to an auditor, contemporary professional auditing is best characterized as a complex decision making process involving a series of interrelated judgments. In short, the most effective auditors are not necessarily master technicians; rather, they are competent decision makers.

This chapter begins by addressing the importance of professional judgment in auditing, the audit decision making process, and the role of statistical decision models and structured decision aids in audit practice. In turn, the chapter discusses three cognitive heuristics ("rules of thumb"): representativeness, availability, and anchoring, which have been found by psychologists and auditing researchers to cause biases in decision making.

The independent auditor's somewhat controversial responsibilities for detecting and disclosing client errors, irregularities, and illegal acts are also discussed in this chapter. In general, the controversy results from the public's perception of the role of independent auditors within the financial community. Many individuals believe an auditor should search diligently for material client errors, irregularities, and illegal acts, even if the search conflicts with the auditor's primary objective of issuing an opinion. Not surprisingly, many auditors take a different view. The thrust of the controversy is reviewed in this chapter, as are the auditor's responsibilities under *Statements on Auditing Standards* (SAS) Nos. 53 and 54 and the Foreign Corrupt Practices Act (FCPA). Finally, the chapter introduces recommendations made by the National Commission on Fraudulent Financial Reporting and by the Commission on Auditors' Responsibilities about the independent auditor's responsibility for detecting and disclosing management fraud. Thus, the discussion focuses on auditor responsibilities as they are today (i.e., SAS Nos. 53 and 54 and the FCPA) and as some believe they should be (i.e., the National Commission on Fraudulent Financial Reporting and the Commission on Auditors' Responsibilities).

PROFESSIONAL JUDGMENT IN AUDITING

Unquestionably, keen professional judgment is a fundamental prerequisite of all competent professional auditors. In fact, the Auditing Standards Boards' *Statements on Auditing Standards,* the profession's interpretive guidelines for the ten generally accepted auditing standards, include almost 100 specific references to the need for professional judgment in audit practice. For example, the AICPA's *Codification of Statements on Auditing Standards* states that:

▲ "The auditor should obtain a level of knowledge of the entity's business that will enable him . . . to obtain an understanding of the events, transactions, and practices that, in his *judgment,* may have a significant effect on the financial statements."

▲ "The auditor should plan the audit so that audit risk will be limited to a low level that is, in his *professional judgment,* appropriate for issuing an opinion on the financial statements."

▲ "The assessment of possible error as of the balance sheet date should be based on the auditor's *judgment* of the state of the particular account(s) as of that date. . . ."

Thus, the hallmark of auditing is neither the audit technology addressed in Chapters 5 through 8 nor the detailed audit tests introduced in Chapters 9 through 18. Rather, the hallmark of auditing is the sequence of complex judgments which constitute audit decision making. Much as physicians are compensated for their professional judgments about the relationship among identifiable symptoms, probable cause, and likely diagnosis, auditors are recognized and compensated for complex professional judgments about the collection, interpretation, and integration of audit evidence.

THE AUDIT DECISION MAKING PROCESS

The audit decision making process consists of six basic components. These components are stated in general terms in Figure 3-1 and are discussed in the following sections.

FIGURE 3-1
The Audit Decision Making Process

- Identification of pertinent prior information.
- Identification of pertinent current information.
- Evaluation of prior and current information.
- Prediction of alternative future outcomes.
- Assessment of the likelihood that particular future outcomes will occur.
- Weighting and combining information to choose among alternative courses of action.

Prior and Current Information: Identification and Evaluation

When an auditor has conducted an audit for a particular client in past years, the auditor has knowledge of prior information pertinent to the current year's audit. Thus, when planning the current engagement, the auditor should identify and consider prior information that serves to improve current judgments. For example, when planning the nature, timing, and extent of audit procedures, an auditor should consider the types of client errors and control deficiencies detected during the previous year's audit — otherwise, important prior evidence about audit risk may go unnoticed and, therefore, unconsidered. That is, a large number of errors detected in the previous year may prompt the auditor to believe audit risk is higher in the current year than would have been anticipated otherwise.

In turn, current information is used to update and revise prior information. For example, the prior year's audit may have indicated high error rates in the manual posting of cash receipts to accounts receivable subsidiary records, thereby leading the auditor to expect high error rates in the current year's engagement. However, if management has implemented a reliable computer posting system during the current year, then the auditor would likely revise his or her expected error rates for the current year, and plan the audit accordingly.

Future Outcomes: Prediction and Assessment

From prior and current information, an auditor predicts particular future outcomes and assesses the likelihood that the future outcomes will occur. For example, if prior information for a client indicated recurring operating losses and negative cash flows from operations, and current information revealed both a defaulted loan and the denial of trade credit from a supplier, the auditor would predict that the client had solvency problems. From this information, the auditor would have to assess the likelihood that the client was not a going concern.

Alternative Courses of Action

Finally, an auditor must weight and combine prior and current information and then choose among alternative courses of action. For example, prior and current information is used by auditors to make a myriad of audit judgments, including: the selection of appropriate audit procedures (e.g., observation, inquiry, confirmation), the type of audit report necessary in the circumstances (e.g., unqualified opinion, qualified opinion, etc.), and types of alternative financial statement disclosures (e.g., footnotes, separate line items within the financial statements). However, because most audit judgments are made under conditions of uncertainty, auditors sustain a risk that material errors, irregularities, or illegal acts may go undetected, and the related risk that inappropriate judgments may result in legal liability to injured clients and third parties. The auditor's responsibility for client errors, irregularities, and illegal acts is discussed later in this chapter, and legal liability is addressed in Chapter 4.

DECISION MODELS, DECISION AIDS, HEURISTICS, AND BIASES

To augment and guide the decision-making process in auditing, some auditors use *statistical decision models* such as multiple regression, time series analysis, and other statistical sampling plans. These decision models do not supplant professional judgment; rather, they are intended to result in more consistent judgments over time for similar, repetitive types of decisions. They are particularly advantageous for large firms with offices throughout the country and around the world. The use of similar statistical decision models in all offices helps assure that the judgment process is consistent throughout the firm.

Of course, not all judgments made in auditing are susceptible to statistical analysis. However, the advantages of decision models, such as consistent judgment processes, can be achieved through *structured decision aids*, which are preprinted, standardized forms, such as checklists and questionnaires, that guide the auditor through the evidence gathering and information evaluation processes. Structured decision aids are used frequently in practice to help in making decisions about the effectiveness of a client's internal control structure and the results of nonstatistical audit sampling plans. For example, one major public accounting firm uses a structured decision aid to assimilate large volumes of current information about internal control structure and to consider misstatements that could occur in the financial statements. Another large public accounting firm uses a decision aid to determine sample sizes when nonstatistical sampling is used.

As indicated earlier, auditors should use both prior and current information to assess the likelihood that particular future outcomes, such as insolvency, will occur. However, research in experimental psychology suggests that decision makers often rely on *heuristics*, or "rules of thumb," to simplify and thus potentially bias, otherwise complex cognitive processes, such as audit decision making. Two psychologists, Amos Tversky and Daniel Kahneman, have identified three such heuristics—representativeness, availability, and anchoring—all of which are revealing and therefore instructive about how audit decision making can be biased despite the good intentions of auditors.[1]

Representativeness

Decision makers who unknowingly rely on the representativeness heuristic tend to evaluate the likelihood of, say, item B belonging to class A by determining how much item B resembles class A, rather than consider the laws of probability — that is, "how representative is item B of class A," rather than "what is the probability that item B came from class A." For example, a baseball player may be experiencing a hitting streak, causing people to overestimate the likelihood that he will get a hit the next time at bat.

One of the biases that can result from the representativeness heuristic is that auditors may fail to consider prior information appropriately when predicting future outcomes. For example, research in auditing[2] has found that, in hypothetical cases, practicing auditors overstated the likelihood that a client manager was involved in fraud by overweighting (i.e., overstating the importance of) the similarity between the manager's psychological profile and the profile of admitted perpetrators, and by underweighting the fact that not one of the one hundred managers had been involved in material fraud previously. That is, the practicing auditors' judgments were based more on representativeness than on prior probabilities.

---

[1]Tversky and Kahneman's research on heuristics and biases is summarized in: A. Tversky and D. Kahneman, "Judgment under Uncertainty: Heuristics and Biases," *Science* (1984), pp. 1124–1131. Accounting and auditing research on heuristics and biases is reviewed in: R. Libby, *Accounting and Human Information Processing: Theory and Applications*. Englewood Cliffs, N.J.: Prentice-Hall, 1981, Chapter 3; and R. H. Ashton, *Research in Audit Decision Making: Rationale, Evidence, and Implications*. Vancouver, British Columbia: Canadian Certified General Accountants' Research Foundation, 1983, Chapter 5.

[2]E. J. Joyce and G. C. Biddle, "Are Auditors' Judgments Sufficiently Regressive?" *Journal of Accounting Research* (Autumn, 1981), pp. 323–349.

Availability

Decision makers who unknowingly rely on the availability heuristic tend to evaluate the likelihood of a particular outcome by the ease with which similar instances or occurrences are brought to mind—that is, by how easy it is to recall familiar circumstances. For example, an individual who has just read about a plane crash is likely to overstate the probability of similar events occurring in the future.

In auditing, rare and sensational events such as highly publicized frauds involving cash embezzlements are likely to be judged as occurring disproportionately more often than they really do occur. Thus, decision makers, such as auditors, are more apt to overestimate the likelihood of sensational events and to underestimate less sensational events.

Anchoring

The anchoring heuristic suggests that decision makers often assess the likelihood of an outcome by making initial, and sometimes biased, estimates about the likelihood of the outcome (the anchor) and then revising the likelihood, though insufficiently, when presented with new information. For example, in practice, auditors often consult prior year working papers when designing current year audit procedures, thereby raising questions of whether the procedures are adequately adjusted for changing circumstances, such as newly hired accounting personnel or significantly revised control procedures. Although somewhat mixed, the results of prior research in auditing tend to suggest that auditor behavior is generally consistent with the anchoring heuristic.[3]

Implications

Most decisions in auditing are complex, are made under conditions of uncertainty, and therefore require that auditors explicitly or implicitly consider the likelihood that particular future outcomes will occur. However, as discussed above, practicing auditors may unknowingly rely on heuristics which tend to simplify otherwise complex judgments, but which may also result in biased and unreliable probability assessments.

Because the heuristics are cognitive in nature, they may occur unknowingly to the unsuspecting auditor. Thus, educating current and future auditors

---

[3]E. J. Joyce and G. C. Biddle, ''Anchoring and Adjustment in Probabilistic Inference in Auditing.'' *Journal of Accounting Research* (Spring, 1981), pp. 120–145; W. R. Kinney and W. C. Uecker, ''Mitigating the Consequences of Anchoring in Auditor Judgments.'' *The Accounting Review* (January, 1982), pp. 55–69.

may be the most effective means of avoiding the potential biases associated with simplifying heuristics such as representativeness, availability, and anchoring. To that end, audit managers in one large public accounting firm are now indoctrinated both to the cognitive heuristics and to the potential biases which the heuristics tend to create. In short, as this one instance suggests, the profession recognizes the significance of behavioral heuristics and is responding accordingly.

✶ THE EXPECTATION GAP

In the 1970s, the AICPA issued pronouncements on the independent auditor's responsibility for detecting client errors, irregularities, and illegal acts (SAS Nos. 16 and 17: issued in 1977, superseded in 1988), and Congress enacted legislation related to questionable and illegal practices by management (Foreign Corrupt Practices Act of 1977). However, despite these authoritative pronouncements and Congressional Act, a central overriding question lingered: Are the expectations of independent auditors and financial information users consistent regarding the auditor's responsibilities for detecting and reporting client errors, irregularities, and illegal acts? In short, is there an "expectation gap"?

Why Do Expectations Differ?

The expectation gap is a natural outgrowth of the fact that few people enjoy accepting responsibility for another's shortcomings. On one hand, financial information users would like to place responsibility for detecting and disclosing client errors, irregularities, and illegal acts upon independent auditors, perceiving them as the "watchdogs" or "guarantors" of financial information released by publicly traded companies. In contrast, auditors are reluctant to accept responsibility for detecting the questionable acts of management, the true "steward" of reported financial information, because the objective of an audit under generally accepted auditing standards is to report on the presentation of financial statements, not to form conclusions about irregularities and illegal acts.

From the viewpoint of financial information users, such as investors and creditors, several factors lead to the expectation gap. First, it is not clear that the public understands the role and limitations of auditors and independent audits. In large measure, auditing is viewed as a clerical exercise, one in which reported financial information is either correct or incorrect. In the 1930s auditors contributed to this viewpoint by describing the audit report as a "certificate," thereby implying a degree of accuracy not really attainable in external financial reports.[4] Second, the trend in litigation involving independent auditors has been to increase rather than decrease the public's expectations of auditors. For example, within the past three decades, auditors have been held liable for failing to disclose significant transactions and events occurring between the date of an audit report and the effective date of an SEC registration statement[5] and have been fined and jailed for allegedly conspiring to violate federal securities statutes.[6] Clearly, recent court decisions have tended to expand the public's expectations, and this well established trend is not likely to reverse.[7]

Research within the past two decades also underscores the ever-widening expectation gap. For example, in the 1970s researchers surveyed large-firm audit partners and small-firm CPAs, bank loan officers, financial analysts, and corporate financial managers about the auditor's responsibility for detecting and disclosing corporate irregularities and illegal acts.[8] The survey results suggested significantly different perceptions of auditors' responsibilities between auditors and the three non-audit groups. After this study was conducted, however, the Auditing Standards Board issued SAS Nos. 16 and 17, and Congress passed the Foreign Corrupt Practices Act (FCPA). Although the two SASs and the FCPA further defined the auditor's responsibilities for detecting errors, irregularities, and illegal acts, they did not eliminate or reduce the expectation gap. Rather, the gap was further expanded in the 1980s by a series of highly publicized business and audit failures in the government securities and banking industries, resulting in hearings conducted by the House Subcommittee on Oversight and Investigations and in far-reaching pronouncements issued by the Auditing Standards Board in 1988.

The Auditing Standards Board Responds

SAS Nos. 16 and 17, both issued in 1977 and superseded in 1988, related to client errors, irregularities, and illegal acts and were intended as a direct response to the gap between the performance of independent auditors and the expectations of financial statement users. However, in the 1980s the expectation gap grew not only wider but in a different direction as some observers in the financial community began to equate business failure with

---

[4]C. D. Liggio, "The Expectation Gap: The Accountant's Legal Waterloo?" *The CPA Journal* (July, 1975), p. 24.

[5]*Escott et al. v. BarChris Construction Corporation,* 283 F. Supp. 643 (S.D.N.Y. 1968).

[6]*United States v. Simon,* 425 F. 2nd 796 (1969).

[7]The independent auditor's legal liability and some significant court cases are discussed more fully in Chapter 4.

[8]C. D. Baron *et al.,* "Uncovering Corporate Irregularities: Are We Closing the Expectation Gap?" *Journal of Accountancy* (October, 1977), pp. 56–66.

audit failure. That is, some observers believed that if a corporation is approaching business failure, a financial statement audit should serve as an early warning system for impending financial collapse. A former chairman of the Auditing Standards Board commented:

> . . . that expectation gap still exists, aided and abetted by some difficult economic times in certain industries and several notable bankruptcies traceable to questionable practices or to management's lack of awareness of the risks it was incurring. In the minds of many, a business failure equates to an audit failure, and it is this perception or expectation that the profession must address — regardless of whether or not that expectation is well founded.[9]

In 1988 the Auditing Standards Board issued nine new Statements on Auditing Standards as part of "expectation gap agenda," one of which, SAS No. 53, addresses an auditor's responsibility for discovering and reporting client errors and irregularities, and another, SAS No. 54, addresses responsibilities related to illegal acts by clients. These controversial responsibilities, each central to the public's expectations of independent auditors, are discussed next.

DETECTING ERRORS AND IRREGULARITIES

SAS No. 53, "The Auditor's Responsibility To Detect and Report Errors and Irregularities," provides guidance about an auditor's responsibility for detecting client errors, such as unintentional mathematical mistakes, and irregularities, including management fraud. In SAS No. 53 *errors* are defined as unintentional misstatements or omissions in financial statements. Examples include mistakes in gathering or processing accounting data, mistakes in the application of accounting principles, and incorrect accounting estimates, such as the allowance for uncollectible receivables, arising from oversight or misinterpretation of facts. *Irregularities,* in contrast, are intentional misstatements or omissions of amounts or disclosures in financial statements. Examples of irregularities include the manipulation, falsification, or alteration of accounting records; the misrepresentation or intentional omission of events; and the intentional misapplication of accounting principles.

As indicated by the definitions and examples, *intent* is the primary difference between an error and an irregularity. In practice, however, intent is often difficult to determine. For example, an unreasonable estimate of the

---

[9]J. D. Sullivan, "A Program for Progress in Standards Setting," *In Our Opinion* (October, 1985), pp. 1–2.

allowance for uncollectible accounts receivable could result from an unintentional bias, which would constitute an error, or from an intentional attempt to misstate the financial statements, an irregularity. Distinguishing whether an act is an error or an irregularity is difficult, but particularly important, because irregularities are intentional and, as a result, raise concerns about management's integrity, attitude, and operating style.

Responsibility

Under the former standard, SAS No. 16, an auditor was responsible, within the inherent limitations of the auditing process, to *plan to search* for material errors or irregularities and to *exercise due skill and care* in the conduct of the audit; an auditor extended auditing procedures only if the audit indicated that material errors or irregularities may exist. In contrast, SAS No. 53, the current standard, requires that an audit be *designed to provide reasonable assurance of detecting* material errors and irregularities, and addresses the detection of errors and irregularities in terms of *audit risk:*

> The auditor should assess the risk that errors and irregularities may cause the financial statements to contain a material misstatement. Based on that assessment, the auditor should design the audit to provide reasonable assurance of detecting errors and irregularities that are material to the financial statements (SAS No. 53, par. 05).

Despite the requirement of designing an audit to detect material errors or irregularities, a properly designed and executed audit may still fail to detect a cleverly concealed irregularity, particularly those involving forgery or collusion among employees or management. For example, auditors are neither trained nor expected under generally accepted auditing standards to judge the authenticity of forged documents. An auditor is not an insurer and an audit report does not constitute a guarantee, because an audit opinion and audit procedures are based on the concept of reasonable, not absolute, assurance. Nevertheless, an auditor should exercise both due care and professional skepticism to provide reasonable assurance that material errors and irregularities will be detected.

Considering the Risk of Errors and Irregularities in Audit Planning

Audit risk, discussed more fully in Chapter 5, is the likelihood that an auditor may unknowingly fail to modify an opinion on materially misstated financial statements — for example, the risk that material error in accounts receivable may go undetected, leading the unknowing auditor to issue an unqualified opinion on the financial statements even though the statements are materially misstated because of the undetected error. To assess the risk that errors or irregularities may cause material misstatements in financial statements, SAS No. 53 states that, while planning an engagement, an auditor should consider factors that influence risk both at the overall financial statement level and at the account balance level.

At the financial statement level, the auditor should consider factors such as those listed at Figure 3-2 and judge whether the level of risk may affect the overall strategy of the audit. Although the presence of one of the factors from Figure 3-2 would not necessarily indicate increased risk, the presence

---

FIGURE 3-2

Factors Affecting the Risk of Material Misstatements Arising From Errors and Irregularities

Characteristics of Management:
- Management operating and financing decisions are dominated by a single person.
- Management's attitude toward financial reporting is unduly aggressive.
- Management, particularly senior accounting personnel, turnover is high.
- Management places undue emphasis on meeting earnings projections.
- Management's reputation in the business community is poor.

Characteristics of the Entity's Operations and Industry:
- Profitability relative to industry profitability is inadequate or inconsistent.
- Sensitivity of operating results to economic factors (inflation, interest rates, unemployment, etc.) is high.
- Rate of change in entity's industry is rapid.
- Direction of change in entity's industry is declining with many business failures.
- Internal or external matters that raise substantial doubt about the entity's ability to continue in existence as a going concern are present.

Characteristics of the Audit Engagement:
- Many contentious or difficult accounting issues are present.
- Significant difficult-to-audit transactions or balances are present.
- Significant and unusual related party transactions not in the ordinary course of business are present.
- Nature, cause (if known), or the amount of known and likely misstatements detected in the audit of prior period's financial statements is significant.
- It is a new client with no prior audit history or sufficient information is not available from the predecessor auditor.

Source: *Statement on Auditing Standards No. 53*, ''The Auditor's Responsibility to Detect and Report Errors and Irregularities.''

of several could affect the auditor's strategy. For example, if management places undue emphasis on meeting earnings projections, the rate of change in the industry is rapid, and management's reputation in the business community is poor, the auditor would likely alter his or her overall strategy by expanding the extent of audit procedures applied, engaging experienced staff, and encouraging assigned staff to exercise more than the usual level of professional skepticism.

At the account balance level, an auditor should consider the effects of the financial statement level risk factors (Figure 3-2) on the specific financial statement accounts or classes of transactions affected. For example, if the rate of change in an industry is rapid, an auditor should consider whether any inventory is obsolete and therefore reported at inflated carrying values. In addition, the auditor should consider other factors that may influence the risk of material misstatements, such as complex calculations related to pension and warranty liabilities, imputed interest rates on receivables and payables, and loan loss reserves in the banking industry.

Professional Skepticism

An auditor should not presume without reason that management is dishonest; a presumption of dishonesty in all cases would be contrary to the accumulated experience of practicing auditors. In fact, in considering the risk of material misstatements from errors and irregularities, honesty is not the issue. Rather, the issue is that an audit should be planned and performed with an attitude of professional skepticism — that is, an attitude which recognizes that, honesty aside, management may have incentives to intentionally misstate amounts or disclosures in the financial statements, incentives which derive for example from the factors appearing in Figure 3-2.

Professional skepticism should be exercised both at the planning stage of an engagement and while performing audit procedures and gathering evidence. For example, if an auditor concludes during the planning stage that there is significant risk of material misstatement, audit strategy should be altered by designing appropriate audit procedures and assigning sufficiently experienced audit staff. In addition, if ratio analysis performed during the audit discloses unexpected findings, the auditor should obtain additional corroborating evidence rather than rely exclusively on management's explanations to determine whether the ratio suggests material misstatements.

Evaluating Audit Test Results and Reporting

Material errors detected by applying audit procedures should be corrected through journal entries. Material irregularities, in contrast, have additional implications because they are intentional. If an auditor detects an irregularity, but has also determined that the effect on the financial statements could not be material, as for example in the case of misappropriations of small amounts of cash from an imprest fund, the auditor should:

▲ Refer the matter to an appropriate level of management that is at least one level above those involved, and

▲ Be satisfied that, in view of the organizational position of the likely perpetrator, the irregularity has no implications for other aspects of the audit or that those implications have been adequately considered.

However, if the auditor detects a material irregularity or has been unable to evaluate materiality, he or she should:

▲ Consider the implications for other aspects of the audit,

▲ Discuss the matter and the approach to further investigation with an appropriate level of management that is at least one level above those involved,

▲ Attempt to obtain evidence to determine whether in fact material irregularities exist and, if so, their effect, and

▲ If appropriate, suggest that the client consult with legal counsel on matters concerning questions of law.

If an auditor concludes that an entity's financial statements are affected materially by an irregularity, he or she should insist that financial statements be revised. If management refuses, the auditor should express a qualified or an adverse opinion, disclosing all substantive reasons for the opinion. In turn, if the auditor is precluded from applying necessary audit procedures or is unable to reach a conclusion about materiality, he or she should qualify or disclaim an opinion and indicate the findings to the board of directors or its audit committee. Disclosing irregularities to parties other than senior management and the audit committee of the board of directors is not ordinarily part of an auditor's responsibility, but may be necessary in some circumstances such as disclosure in response to a subpoena and disclosure in response to an inquiry from a successor auditor.

ILLEGAL ACTS BY CLIENTS

The auditor's responsibility for detecting client errors and irregularities has long been a major preoccupation of regulatory agencies such as the SEC; the financial markets; professional accounting organizations such as the AICPA; and the financial press. In contrast, the auditor's responsibility for illegal acts by clients gained widespread prominence only within the last two decades. Prior to the 1970s, conventional wisdom held that material illegal corporate payments, such as bribes to influence political officials, were virtually nonexistent. But in a dramatic turn of events, a 1976 SEC-sponsored voluntary compliance program disclosed that over 250 U.S. corporations had made questionable or illegal payments both in the U.S. and abroad. In 1977 Congress responded by enacting the Foreign Corrupt Practices Act, discussed later in the chapter, and the AICPA issued SAS No. 17, which was superseded in 1988 by SAS No. 54, "Illegal Acts By Clients," a part of the Auditing Standards Boards' expectation gap agenda. SAS No. 54 defines *illegal acts* as violations of laws or governmental regulations and provides guidance in three general areas: an auditor's responsibility for detecting and disclosing illegal acts, the audit procedures an auditor should consider both in the apparent absence of illegal acts and when illegalities are possible, and how an auditor should respond to detected illegal acts.

Responsibility

Two important issues underscore an auditor's responsibility for illegal acts: dependence on legal judgment and the proximity of a questionable act to the financial statements. *Dependence on legal judgment* simply means that determining the legality or illegality of specific client acts is normally beyond the scope of an independent auditor's professional competence. Auditors are proficient in accounting and auditing, not the law. True, an auditor's experience and understanding of a client's industry may provide a basis for recognizing some illegal acts — for example, violations of tax or federal securities laws — but determining legality should generally be left to attorneys or await final determination by a court.

The likelihood of potential detection depends on the *proximity of the act* to recorded transactions and events. The further removed an illegal act is from the transactions and events normally reflected in financial statements, the less likely an auditor is to become aware of the act. For example, although violations of federal tax laws are likely to be detected during an audit, violations of other laws and regulations — such as the Occupational Safety and Health Act, or regulations of the Food and Drug Administration or the Environmental Protection Agency — are beyond the scope of an audit and therefore are far less likely to be detected. Even if they are detected, an auditor considers such laws from the perspective of their relation to audit objectives, not from the perspective of legality. Not surprisingly, many of the questionable or illegal payments disclosed through the SEC's voluntary compliance program were made through off-the-books accounts and therefore were not susceptible to reasonable audit investigation.

Under SAS No. 54, an auditor's responsibility to detect and report misstatements resulting from illegal acts that have a *direct and material* effect on financial statement amounts is identical to that for errors and irregularities:

to assess the risk that they may cause the financial statements to contain a material misstatement, and design the audit to provide reasonable assurance of detecting them. Examples of illegal acts having a direct and material effect include violations of tax laws or of government grant contracts. Regarding illegal acts that have a *material but indirect* effect on the financial statements — those that are removed from the transactions and events reflected in financial statements — the auditor should be aware that they may have occurred, although an audit provides no assurance that they will be detected. Examples of illegal acts having a material but indirect effect include violations of equal employment and antitrust laws.

Audit Procedures

A financial statement audit normally does not include procedures designed specifically to detect illegal acts. However, some audit procedures that are motivated by audit objectives unrelated to illegal acts could provide evidence of possible violations of laws and regulations. For example, reading the minutes of the board of directors' meetings, a procedure not motivated by its potential to reveal illegal acts, may provide the auditor's first evidence of an impending investigation by a governmental agency for violations of federal laws that impose fines and therefore that may require disclosure as a contingent liability. When there is no reason to believe illegal acts exist, the auditor should make inquiries of management about the entity's compliance with laws and regulations and, where applicable, also inquire about management's policies for preventing illegal acts and for issuing policy directives internally. No other audit procedures are necessary, in the absence of evidence suggesting that possible illegal acts exist.

When an auditor becomes aware of information concerning a possible illegal act, he or she should obtain an understanding of the circumstances of the act and enough evidence — including inquires of management at levels above those involved — to judge the effect of the act on the financial statements. If evidence provided by management is not convincing — that is, does not convince the auditor that no illegal act occurred — the auditor should consult with the entity's legal counsel and consider other procedures. For example, the auditor might consider confirming significant information with intermediaries, such as bankers and lawyers, or with other parties to the transaction.

Responding to Detected Illegal Acts

When an illegal act has or is likely to occur, an auditor should consider the effect of the act on the financial statements and on the audit report. This requires an evaluation of the materiality of the act. As discussed more fully in Chapter 5, materiality is a somewhat elusive concept in accounting and auditing, and this is no less the case when applied to illegal acts. For example, during the 1970s, several relatively high-ranking corporate officials dismissed their company's questionable payments as immaterial and therefore of little consequence to financial information users. Although specific acts alone may be immaterial in amount, SAS no. 54 identifies two related factors — contingent monetary effects and loss contingencies — which may render an act material.

Contingent monetary effects include fines, penalties, and damages which, in some circumstances, such as violations of the Foreign Corrupt Practices Act (discussed later in this chapter), may be quite substantial. *Loss contingencies,* such as the threat of expropriation of assets, enforced discontinuance of foreign operations, or possible litigation, are frequently more substantial than either contingent monetary effects or, for example, an illegal payment itself. Thus, when considering the materiality of an illegal act, an auditor should consider the contingent monetary effects and loss contingencies, not just the dollar amount of the payment itself.

Acts that are not clearly inconsequential should be reported to the audit committee of the board of directors or to others with equivalent authority, such as federal cognizant agencies that monitor direct federal grants to state and local governments. Disclosure to other parties is not ordinarily the auditor's responsibility, although there is a duty to notify successor auditors and there may be a duty to respond to a subpoena. If an illegal act has not been accounted for or disclosed properly, the auditor should express a qualified opinion or adverse opinion. If precluded by management from obtaining evidence, the auditor should disclaim an opinion on the financial statements.

THE FOREIGN CORRUPT PRACTICES ACT

In December 1977, President Carter signed into law the Foreign Corrupt Practices Act (FCPA) of 1977. The Act covers two major areas, both relevant to accountants and auditors: foreign corrupt practices and accounting standards. The foreign corrupt practices sections of the Act made it unlawful for SEC registrants (entities subject to registration and reporting requirements of the Securities Exchange Act of 1934), both domestic and foreign, and domestic nonregistrants to influence foreign governments or officials through payments or gifts. The accounting standards section requires that SEC registrants comply with certain record-keeping and internal control requirements, and applies to all SEC registrants, even those with no international operations.

Background

The FCPA evolved from several circumstances, including investigations by the Office of the Watergate Special Prosecutor and the SEC's voluntary disclosure program discussed earlier. The intent of Congress in legislating the Act was to respond directly as critics of corporate governance and corporate responsibility through legislation that would require corporations to develop and apply internal control procedures sufficient to detect illegal payments and to enable preparation of accurate and fairly stated financial reports. As a result of the FCPA, internal control structure was no longer a matter of technical proficiency, it was a matter of law.

Several events within the public sector played a particularly significant role in the deliberations leading to final enactment of the FCPA. In March, 1976, Senator William Proxmire (D.-Wisconsin) introduced legislation which, if enacted, would have charged the SEC with the responsibility to establish rules and regulations regarding a corporation's obligation to maintain accurate books, records, or accounts for business transactions. However, on May 12, 1976, the SEC responded through its *Report on Questionable and Illegal Corporate Payments and Practices* to the Senate Banking, Housing, and Urban Affairs Committee. The SEC's "May 12 Report" in part recommended that Congress enact legislation that would accomplish objectives similar to those outlined by Senator Proxmire. The SEC apparently believed that Congressional legislation would have far more impact within the private sector than would SEC rules and regulations. Approximately one year later, following extensive hearings on questionable and illegal payments, the Senate Banking, Housing, and Urban Affairs Committee proposed legislation in its Senate Report No. 95-114. Part of the Committee's proposed legislation appears in the FCPA.

Interestingly, the text of the FCPA does not introduce new thinking on the relationship among illegal payments, corporate governance, and corporate responsibility. Rather, the Act codifies and legislates previously existing concepts and procedures. For example, language within the *internal control* provisions of the Act is taken almost verbatim from then-current *Statements on Auditing Standards*. Thus, Congress apparently intended to underscore the importance of concepts and practices already well established within the financial community, rather than to revolutionize corporate accounting, reporting, and auditing.

As noted earlier, the FCPA includes provisions relating to foreign corrupt practices and accounting standards. The foreign corrupt practices sections contain *unlawful influence* provisions, and the accounting standards section contains *record-keeping and internal accounting control* provisions, both of which are discussed next.

Unlawful Influence

The unlawful influence provisions of the Act make it illegal for an entity or its officers, directors, employees, agents, or stockholders to arrange payments or gifts to foreign governments, officials, political parties, or political candidates for purposes of obtaining or retaining business by influencing any official act or decision or inducing the recipient to use his or her influence over any official act or decision. The unlawful influence provisions apply to all domestic entities and foreign SEC-registrant entities and prohibit bribes intended to influence foreign acts or decisions.

It is important to note that the Act prohibits payments to influence official acts or decisions. The Act does not prohibit so-called "grease" or "facilitating" payments made to ministerial or clerical government employees for the purpose, for example, of expediting government processing of shipments through customs or securing police protection.

An entity convicted of a bribe — whether willful or not — can be fined up to $1,000,000. An officer, director, or stockholder of a convicted entity can be fined up to $10,000 and/or imprisoned up to five years, although bribes by these parties must be willful. Fines imposed upon individuals may not be paid by a company.

Record Keeping and Internal Control

The record-keeping and internal control provisions of the Act are as follows:

▲ **Record-Keeping Requirements** — Entities must make and keep books, records, and accounts which, in reasonable detail, accurately reflect the transactions and dispositions of the assets of the company.

▲ **Internal Accounting Control Requirements** — Entities must devise and maintain a system of internal accounting controls sufficient to provide reasonable assurances that:

— Transactions are executed in accordance with management's general and specific authorization.
— Transactions are recorded as necessary (1) to permit preparation of financial statements in conformity with generally accepted accounting principles or any other criteria applicable to such statements, and (2) to maintain accountability for assets.
— Access to assets is permitted only in accordance with management's general and specific authorization.
— The recorded accountability for assets is compared with the existing assets at reasonable intervals, and appropriate action is taken with respect to any differences.

These provisions apply to SEC-registrant entities and, because they amend Section 13(b) of the Securities Exchange Act of 1934, are administered and enforced by the SEC. In general, the intent of the record-keeping provisions is to enable preparation of accurate and fairly stated financial reports; the intent of the internal control provisions is to provide a basis for detecting questionable or illegal payments.

An entity violating the internal accounting control or record-keeping provisions of the Act can be fined up to $10,000. An officer, director, or stockholder of a violating entity can be fined up to $10,000 and/or imprisoned up to five years. Again, fines imposed upon individuals may not be paid by the corporation.

FALSIFICATION OF RECORDS AND REPRESENTATIONS TO AUDITORS

Since enactment of the FCPA, Congress has deliberated on modifying and simplifying the Act, and the Securities and Exchange Commission has finalized or proposed authoritative releases which impose additional restrictions upon SEC registrants. Prominent among the SEC's actions was Release No. 34-15570, "Falsification of Records and Representations to Auditors." As its title implies, this release specifically prohibits falsifying accounting records or making false or misleading representations to auditors.

With regard to falsification of accounting records, the release provides that:

> No person shall, directly or indirectly, falsify or cause to be falsified, any book, record or account subject to Section 13(b)(2)(a) of the Securities Exchange Act.

(The FCPA is included, in part, in Section 13(b) of the Securities Exchange Act of 1934.)

The provision relating to representations to auditors states that:

> No director or officer of an issuer shall, directly or indirectly,
> (a) make or cause to be made a materially false or misleading statement, or
> (b) omit to state, or cause another person to omit to state, any material fact necessary in order to make statements made, in the light of the circumstances under which such statements were made, not misleading, to an accountant in connection with (1) any audit or examination of the financial statements of the issuer required to be made pursuant to this subpart or (2) the preparation or filing of any document or report required to be filed with the Commission pursuant to this subpart or otherwise.

Thus, Release No. 34-15570 prohibits the falsification of books and records and the omission of statements or misleading statements to accountants.

Because the FCPA is not limited to intentional acts (i.e., with "scienter," or the intent to deceive), neither of the provisions in Release No. 34-15570 includes a scienter requirement. Some critics believe the lack of a scienter requirement could impede communication between a company's management and its auditors since management may fear unintentional violations of the Release. However, the SEC believes that a scienter provision is unwarranted since an individual could negligently, though unintentionally, falsify a transaction. In short, the SEC believes that negligence should be "actionable," i.e., subject to adjudication, regardless of intent.

Both written and oral statements are covered under the representations-to-auditors provision, and representations to internal auditors are also covered. The falsification-of-records provision covers not only journals and ledgers but also correspondence, memorandums, tapes, papers, and other documents, whether expressed in ordinary or machine language.

Although the representations-to-auditors provision includes a materiality standard, i.e., applies to material items only, the falsification-of-records provision does not. The SEC believed that a materiality standard for the falsification-of-records rule would result in an unintended loophole by providing room for a class of "harmless falsifications" which, in the SEC's view, would be counterproductive to the objectives of the FCPA. The FCPA does not include a materiality standard either.

TOWARD EXPANDED STANDARDS ON MANAGEMENT FRAUD

In response to the expectation gap, two independent commissions were formed — one in the 1970s and another in the 1980s — in part to develop conclusions and recommendations for the independent auditor's responsibility to detect and report client errors and irregularities. The first, the Commission on Auditors' Responsibilities, popularly called the "Cohen Commission," after its chairman, Manual F. Cohen, issued a final report in 1978. The second, the National Commission on Fraudulent Financial Reporting, the "Treadway Commission," after James C. Treadway, Jr., chairman, issued its final report in 1987. Each of these reports made thoughtful recommendations regarding auditor responsibilities and are outlined here as a basis for appreciating how independent bodies outside the profession of public accountancy view the responsibilities of public accountants. The report of the National Commission on Fraudulent Financial Reporting is reviewed first, since it impacted on the Auditing Standards Boards' deliberations in SAS No. 53, the current standard regarding an auditor's responsibility for client errors and irregularities.

NATIONAL COMMISSION ON FRAUDULENT FINANCIAL REPORTING

Coincident with hearings conducted by the House Subcommittee on Oversight and Investigations — the Dingell Committee — the AICPA, the American Accounting Association, the Institute of Internal Auditors, the Financial Executives Institute, and the National Association of Accountants reached agreement in 1985 to form an independent National Commission on Fraudulent Financial Reporting, chaired by James C. Treadway, Jr., a former commissioner of the Securities and Exchange Commission. Over its two year existence, the Commission considered the extent to which management fraud undermines the integrity of financial reporting, the extent to which fraud can be prevented, the role of independent auditors in detecting management fraud, and whether changes in auditing standards are necessary. Although influential to the Auditing Standards Board in their deliberations related to SAS No. 53 on client errors and irregularities, the scope of the Commission's charge was far broader than the Board's expectation gap agenda. The Commission made recommendations for public companies, for the SEC, for education, and for independent auditors. The following reviews two of the Commission's recommendations, one relating to the independent auditor's responsibility for detecting fraudulent financial reporting and a second relating to improving the auditor's detection capabilities.

Responsibility for Detecting Fraudulent Financial Reporting

Independent auditors have long accepted their responsibility to detect material monetary error within financial statements, but their acknowledged responsibility for detecting intentional client irregularities has been debated continuously and remained for years a major source of contention in the expectation gap. Based in part on Congressional pressure and the report of the Commission on Auditors' Responsibilities, discussed later, the Auditing Standards Executive Committee, forebear to today's Auditing Standards Board, issued SAS No. 16 in 1977 which, as noted earlier in the chapter, required that an auditor plan an audit to search for irregularities, but did not specify how a search should be conducted. As some critics noted, SAS No. 16 merely expressed what previously existing professional literature implied and, as such, did not reach far enough.

Although the Commission appreciated that an auditor cannot be held responsible for detecting all material irregularities, particularly those involving a carefully concealed forgery or collusion, they recommended that auditors should be held responsible for actively considering the likelihood of intentional irregularities and for designing specific audit tests to recognize the risk of irregularities. As a result (and before the Auditing Standards Board issued SAS No. 53 in 1988), the National Commission on Fraudulent Financial Reporting made the following recommendation:

> *Recommendation:* The Auditing Standards Board should revise standards to restate the independent public accountant's responsibility for detection of fraudulent financial reporting, requiring the independent public accountant to (1) take affirmative steps in each audit to assess the potential for such reporting and (2) design tests to provide reasonable assurance of detection. Revised standards should include guidance for assessing risk and pursuing detection when risks are identified.

SAS No. 53, the auditor's current responsibility for client errors and irregularities, is generally responsive to the Commission's recommendation, in that the pronouncement requires both that the auditor assess the risk that irregularities may cause materially misstated financial statements and that the audit be designed to provide reasonable assurance of detecting material irregularities. Having noted that the majority of intentional irregularities involve top management, the Commission suggested that the auditor not assume management integrity but, rather, apply professional skepticism, also a requirement of SAS No. 53.

Improving Detection Capabilities

Typical financial statement audits can and often do detect instances of fraudulent financial reporting but, in the Commission's view, auditors can do more. The Commission made two recommendations about improving an auditor's detection capabilities: one related to analytical procedures and a second related to timely reviews of an entity's quarterly financial data.

Analytical Procedures. Analytical procedures, discussed more fully in chapter 6, are audit procedures that study plausible relationships among both financial and nonfinancial data and, as such, are intended to identify accounts that are likely to contain monetary error rather than to identify accounts that actually do contain monetary error. Examples of analytical procedures include ratio analysis and simple comparisons of related accounts such as sales and accounts receivable. In the Commission's view, monetary misstatements are often difficult to detect when an auditor examines the accounts that contain concealed irregularities. But because of double entry bookkeeping, deliberate manipulations of accounting estimates and misstatements of revenues and assets often introduce aberrations in otherwise predictable ratios or trends that will remain concealed in detailed tests of account balances but that will stand out to the skeptical auditor when reviewing ratios and trends. As a result, the Commission recommended a far more prominent role for analytical procedures in auditing:

> *Recommendation:* The Auditing Standards Board should establish standards to require independent public accountants to perform analytical review procedures in all audit engagements and should provide improved guidance on the appropriate use of these procedures.

In response, the Auditing Standards Board issued SAS No. 56, "Analytical Procedures," which requires that an auditor use analytical procedures in both the planning and overall review stages of all audits and, therefore, is generally responsive to the Commission's recommendation.

Quarterly Financial Data. Investors often rely heavily on and react quickly to quarterly financial results released by public companies. However, unlike annual financial statements, quarterly financial information is not audited or even reviewed in most instances by independent public accountants before published. As a result of the financial community's heavy reliance on quarterly financial information, the Commission recommended that independent accountants review, though not audit, quarterly information before it is released to the public:

> *Recommendation:* The Securities and Exchange Commission should require independent public accountants to review quarterly financial data of all public companies before release to the public.

The Auditing Standards Board's nine expectation gap pronouncements issued in 1988 did not address the Commission's recommendation explicitly. SAS No. 36, "Review of Interim Financial Information" (AU Sec. 722) does provide guidance on the nature and extent of procedures the independent accountant should apply when engaged to review interim financial information. However, in contrast with the Commission's recommendation, SAS No. 36 does not require that public accountants review interim financial information, and neither do currently effective directives of the Securities and Exchange Commission.

THE COMMISSION ON AUDITORS' RESPONSIBILITIES

Interestingly, during the 1970s, the Commission on Auditors' Responsibilities also deliberated about and reported on fraud detection and corporate accountability. Rather than emphasize an auditor's inherent limitations when conducting a financial statement audit, the Commission on Auditors' Responsibilities proposed a much higher level of responsibility. Their aggressive proposal is reviewed next.

A Standard of Care for Fraud Detection

The Commission's recommendations regarding the auditor's responsibility for fraud detection relate not to a specific degree of responsibility, but rather to a desired standard of care when conducting an audit. Thus, a central theme of the Commission's recommendations is that the higher an auditor's degree of care, the more likely he or she is to detect client errors or irregularities. The recommendations revolve around eight separate guidelines for auditors, which are listed in Figure 3-3 and discussed in the following sections.

Client Investigations and Doubts about Management's Integrity. The relationship between auditor and client is based upon mutual cooperation and trust. If a potential client is neither cooperative nor trustworthy, the audit engagement should not be accepted. An auditor, therefore, should develop a systematic approach to investigating the integrity and reputation of all prospective clients, take all reasonable actions to resolve doubt, and reject audit engagements when an investigation reveals strong negative signs. An uncooperative or untrustworthy client probably cannot be audited effectively and should be avoided since the probability of client errors or irregularities may be too high.

FIGURE 3-3
A Standard of Care for Fraud Detection

- Establish a program for investigating clients.
- Respond to doubts about management's integrity.
- Be alert to conditions suggesting management fraud.
- Understand a client's business and industry.
- Extend the scope of typical studies and evaluations of internal control.
- Develop and disseminate information on frauds and methods of detecting fraud.
- Be alert to possible deficiencies in audit techniques.
- Understand the limitations of incomplete audits.

Conditions Suggesting Management Fraud. Under now-superseded SAS No. 16, an auditor was to plan an audit to search for material errors or irregularities. The Commission reiterated the desirability of such planning, suggesting that an auditor be cognizant of unusual circumstances or relationships which, although not irregularities themselves, may predispose management toward committing irregularities. Several examples follow of unusual circumstances or relationships that could motivate management to misrepresent earnings or solvency:

▲ Industry is declining or experiencing a large number of business failures.

▲ Industry is overbuilt or its market is otherwise saturated.

▲ Entity lacks sufficient working capital or credit to continue operations.

▲ Entity requires a favorable earnings record to support its stock price.

▲ Entity is close to violating restrictive debt covenants (e.g., loan becomes due immediately if current ratio falls below a specified minimum).

An auditor should be alert to these and other questionable circumstances and consider related potential irregularities and the need for extending audit procedures.

Client's Business and Industry. A competent and effective audit requires that an auditor understand a client's business and industry. A company's economic condition and inherent industry peculiarities can be informative indicators of potential financial or business-related risks. For example, in many capital goods industries, proper quality control is an important determinant of a finished product's carrying value; poorly manufactured products should be carried at net realizable value, which may be below cost. Seemingly non-audit-related conditions, such as quality control, can affect the planning and conduct of an audit. In short, an audit should not be conducted in a vacuum.

Consideration of Internal Control Structure. The second standard of fieldwork, discussed in Chapter 5, requires consideration of an entity's internal control structure as a basis for determining the nature, timing, and extent of necessary audit procedures. The Commission, however, believed that audit work conducted under the second standard of field work should be focused toward client errors and irregularities, as well as toward determining necessary audit procedures. Accordingly, the Commission recommended extending an auditor's responsibility by requiring consideration of all internal controls that bear upon the prevention and detection of errors and irregularities. Thus, under the Commission's recommendation, the objective of an auditor's assessment of internal control structure would be twofold: to determine the extent of audit procedures and to detect and prevent errors and irregularities.

Information on Frauds and Methods of Detection. As business has become increasingly sophisticated, so too have the schemes for perpetrating fraud. For example, although widespread adoption of computer systems has revolutionized information processing, it has also resulted in a new wave of white collar crime. In fact, some accountants might argue that computer crime has reached epidemic proportions. The computer may have created a new hurdle for perpetrators, but certainly not an insurmountable one.

In light of the ever-changing business environment and myriad of internal control override schemes, the Commission recommended that members of the profession cooperate by cataloging methods of perpetrating, concealing, and detecting fraud. For example, an AICPA clearinghouse could collect and coordinate fraud information, periodically distributing update information to members.

Possible Deficiencies in Audit Techniques. Audit procedures change in response to changes in the environment. However, audit procedures will not change if auditors do not realize that the environment is changing. In light of the ever-changing environment and potential ineffectiveness of some contemporary audit procedures, the Commission recommended that auditors constantly reconsider the effectiveness of audit techniques and respond to potential deficiencies.

Limitations of Incomplete Audits. Auditors frequently perform limited reviews of interim financial information. These reviews are essentially incomplete audits which provide limited assurance about an entity's interim financial reports and normally generate much less evidence than financial statement audits. A complete audit cannot be relied upon to detect all material errors or irregularities, and detection is even less likely in a limited review. As a result, the Commission recommended that auditors and clients be aware of the limitations of incomplete audits.

A Framework for Auditor Participation in Achieving Corporate Accountability

The Commission believed that an auditor must approach the detection and disclosure of questionable or illegal client acts within a specified framework, beginning with a clear specification of what is considered questionable and what is considered illegal. In general, the Commission's framework revolves around necessary *actions* by corporations and recommendations as to the *auditor's responsibilities.*

FIGURE 3-4
Corporate Codes of Conduct: Sample Topics

· Political contributions, domestic and foreign
· Gifts and entertainment
· Bribes and questionable payments
· Conflicts of interest
· Confidentiality of financial and accounting information
· Compliance with domestic laws, rules, and regulations

Corporate Actions. Primary responsibility for preventing questionable or illegal corporate acts should fall upon the corporations themselves, not upon the auditors. However, this responsibility should be accepted aggressively and communicated throughout the organization through, as the Commission recommended, a corporate code of conduct.

As a result of widespread publicity surrounding illegal corporate payments and enactment of the Foreign Corrupt Practices Act, many corporations either developed corporate codes of conduct or amended existing codes. Since the scope and content of corporate codes vary, a model code is not feasible. Figure 3-4, however, includes selected topics that should be considered. For example, in light of the FCPA, it would be advisable for a code to include company policy related to the intent and dollar amount of political contributions, gifts, and entertainment and the definition of bribes and questionable payments.

Auditor's Responsibilities. The report of the Commission stated that unless management adopts a code of conduct, an auditor cannot reasonably be expected to assume additional responsibility. Lacking a code, the auditor would not have an appropriate model from which to judge corporate conduct.

Questionable or illegal payments are often more difficult to detect than errors or irregularities because bribes are typically small in relation to financial statement amounts, and collusion is common. Thus, the Commission concluded that an auditor should not be placed in the same legal jeopardy for failing to detect a questionable or illegal act as the individuals perpetrating the act. The Commission did believe, however, that auditors should be responsible for detecting those acts that the exercise of professional care would normally uncover.

The Commission made a clear distinction between detecting and disclosing questionable or illegal acts. Although the Commission recommended limited detection responsibility in the absence of a corporate code, upon detecting a questionable or illegal act, the auditor should:

▲ Discuss the act at an appropriate level of corporate authority.
▲ Determine the impact of the act upon financial statements.
▲ Compare the act with the corporation's code of conduct, if any.
▲ Consider the extent of public disclosures.

If a corporate code of conduct exists, the Commission recommended a report by management in the corporation's annual report stating that a code exists, that it was reviewed, and that compliance is monitored. Further, the auditor's report would also indicate whether the corporation's monitoring system was reviewed, what conclusions were reached regarding aspects of the code that are auditable, and what violations were found during the audit.

SUMMARY

Rather than audit technology and audit method, professional judgment is the hallmark of auditing. Several statistical decision models, such as multiple regression, and structured decision aids, such as questionnaires and checklists, are available to guide practitioners, but professional judgment — not technology or method — is what distinguishes the most effective auditors.

Research in experimental psychology and auditing has revealed three cognitive heuristics — representativeness, availability, and anchoring — which tend to simplify the decision making process, but which may also create biases in audit judgment. At least one public accounting firm has underscored the importance of understanding these heuristics by introducing them in training courses offered to audit managers.

Financial information users and independent auditors often disagree regarding the auditor's responsibilities for client errors, irregularities, and illegal acts. In large measure, this "expectation gap" has contributed much to the misunderstanding within the financial community of the independent auditor's role.

SAS No. 53, "The Auditor's Responsibility to Detect Errors and Irregularities," issued in 1988, requires that an auditor assess the risk that errors and irregularities may cause materially misstated financial statements and, based on that assessment, requires that an audit be designed to provide reasonable assurance of detecting material errors and irregularities. SAS No. 54, "Illegal Acts by Clients," describes an auditor's responsibility for illegal acts by clients, but distinguishes between acts that may have a direct and material effect on the financial statements and acts that have a material but indirect effect. Even though determining illegality is beyond the scope of an auditor's expertise, he or she should have a reasonable basis for identifying potentially improper acts. Of course, the likelihood of detection is dependent upon the proximity of the act to the transactions and events underlying an entity's financial statements.

The Foreign Corrupt Practices Act is perhaps the single most significant corporate governance and accountability legislation enacted within the past several decades. The Act makes it unlawful for SEC registrants or domestic nonregistrants to influence foreign governments or officials through gifts or payments, and requires that SEC registrants comply with certain internal control and record-keeping requirements. The latter provision affects independent auditors because, as a result of the Act, internal control structure is now a matter of law.

SAS Nos. 53 and 54 and the FCPA address auditors' responsibilities as they exist today. However, both the National Commission on Fraudulent Financial Reporting in 1987 and the Commission on Auditors' Responsibilities in 1978 developed nonauthoritative but thoughtful models of auditor responsibilities. SAS No. 53, which describes the profession's current responsibility for detecting and reporting material errors and irregularities is generally responsive to the recommendations of the National Commission on Fraudulent Financial Reporting.

REFERENCES

Professional Judgment

Ashton, R. H. "Human Information Processing Research in Auditing: A Review and Synthesis." In D. R. Nichols and H. F. Stettler, eds., *Auditing Symposium VI*, Lawrence, Ks.: University of Kansas, 1982, pp. 71–83.

Ashton, R. H. *Research in Audit Decision Making: Rationale, Evidence, and Implications*. Vancouver, British Columbia: Canadian Certified General Accountants' Research Foundation, 1983.

Ashton, R. H. "Integrating Research and Teaching in Auditing: Fifteen Cases on Judgment and Decision Making." *The Accounting Review* (January, 1984), pp. 78–97.

Joyce, E. J., and R. Libby. "Behavioral Studies of Audit Decision Making." *Journal of Accounting Literature* (Spring, 1982), pp. 103–123.

Libby, R. *Accounting and Human Information Processing*. Englewood Cliffs, N.J.: Prentice-Hall, 1981.

Libby, R., and B. L. Lewis. "Human Information Processing Research in Accounting: The State of the Art in 1982." *Accounting, Organizations and Society* (Vol. 7, No. 3, 1982), pp. 231–285.

Auditor Responsibilities

Allen, B. "The Biggest Computer Frauds: Lessons for CPAs." *Journal of Accountancy* (May, 1977), pp. 52–63.

American Institute of Certified Public Accountants. *Codification of Statements on Auditing Standards.* New York: American Institute of Certified Public Accountants.

Baron, C. D., *et al.* "Uncovering Corporate Irregularities: Are We Closing the Expectation Gap?" *Journal of Accountancy* (October, 1977), pp. 56–66.

Baruch, H. "The Foreign Corrupt Practices Act." *Harvard Business Review* (January–February, 1979), pp. 32–50.

Chira, R. "Deception of Auditors and False Records." *Journal of Accountancy* (July, 1979), pp. 61–72.

Commission on Auditors' Responsibilities. *Report, Conclusions, and Recommendations,* Sections 4 and 5 (New York: Commission on Auditors' Responsibilities, 1978).

Cook, J. M., and T. P. Kelly. "Internal Control: A Matter of Law." *Journal of Accountancy* (January, 1979), pp. 56–64.

Levy, M. M. "Financial Fraud: Schemes and Indicia." *Journal of Accountancy* (August, 1985), pp. 78–87.

Liggio, C. D. "The Expectation Gap: The Accountant's Legal Waterloo?" *The CPA Journal* (July, 1975), pp. 23–29.

Mautz, R. K., and H. A. Sharaf. *The Philosophy of Auditing.* Sarasota: American Accounting Association, 1961.

Mednick, R. "The Auditor's Role in Society: A New Approach to Solving the Perception Gap." *Journal of Accountancy* (February, 1986), pp. 70–75.

Moser, S. T. "Sensitive Corporate Actions: Toward a Resolution." *The CPA Journal* (April, 1977), pp. 17–21.

National Commission on Fraudulent Financial Reporting. *Report,* Chapter 3 (National Commission on Fraudulent Financial Reporting, 1987).

Pomeranz, F. "A Corporate Response to the Foreign Corrupt Practices Act." *Journal of Accounting, Auditing and Finance* (Fall, 1978), pp. 70–75.

Reed, J. L. "Are Auditors Sentinels for Society?" *The CPA Journal* (June, 1976), pp. 15–18.

Solomon, K. I., and H. Muller. "Illegal Payments: Where the Auditor Stands." *Journal of Accountancy* (January, 1977), pp. 51–57.

QUESTIONS

1. What are the components of the audit decision making process?
2. Why should an auditor consider information obtained in prior audits when planning the current audit?
3. What are statistical decision models? Give examples.
4. What are structured decision aids? Give an example.
5. What are "heuristics," and why are they of concern to practicing auditors?
6. Explain the "expectation gap." Why does it exist?
7. Do past events and research suggest the expectation gap has narrowed?
8. Distinguish between client errors and irregularities.
9. What is the independent auditor's responsibility for client errors or irregularities?
10. In light of material undetected errors or irregularities, what inherent risk does an auditor sustain by not examining all of an entity's transactions and events during a financial statement audit? How do current auditing standards deal with that risk?

11. Identify the 1976 event which first disclosed the magnitude of questionable or illegal payments made by U.S. corporations.

12. Discuss the independent auditor's responsibility for detecting illegal acts by clients.

13. How should an independent auditor proceed if the effect of an illegal act on financial statements is not susceptible to reasonable investigation?

14. U.S. corporations are either publicly traded registrants of the Securities and Exchange Commission or privately owned nonregistrants. Which of these classifications of U.S. corporations are subject to the unlawful influence and internal accounting control and record-keeping provisions of the Foreign Corrupt Practices Act of 1977?

15. Identify the significant public-sector events which led to enactment of the Foreign Corrupt Practices Act.

16. What is the unlawful influence provision of the Foreign Corrupt Practices Act?

17. What are the intended purposes of the record-keeping and internal control provisions of the Foreign Corrupt Practices Act?

18. What are "grease" or "facilitating" payments, and how are they treated within the Foreign Corrupt Practices Act?

19. What penalties may be imposed upon an entity, officers, directors, or stockholders for violating the Foreign Corrupt Practices Act?

20. Describe the Commission on Auditors' Responsibilities' proposed standard of care for fraud detection.

21. What is the purpose of developing or amending corporate codes of conduct in response to the Foreign Corrupt Practices Act?

MULTIPLE CHOICE QUESTIONS

1. An auditor decides to extend testing in the cash disbursements area because the client's accounts receivable clerk appears suspicious. This is an example of which heuristic?

   a. Availability.
   b. Anchoring and adjustment.
   c. Representativeness.
   d. Calibration.

2. In 1988 and 1989, an auditor found that approximately 4 percent of processed sales invoices for a given client were not mathematically accurate. In late 1989, the client implemented a control requiring that all sales invoices be extended mathematically by two independent employees. When planning the 1990 engagement, the auditor estimated a 4 percent error rate for processed sales invoices. This is an example of which heuristic?

   a. Availability.
   b. Anchoring and adjustment.
   c. Representativeness.
   d. Calibration.

3. If an independent auditor's examination leading to an opinion on financial statements causes the auditor to believe that material errors or irregularities exist, the auditor should

<u>a.</u> Consider the implications and discuss the matter with appropriate levels of management.

b. Make the investigation necessary to determine whether the errors or irregularities have in fact occurred.

c. Request that management investigate to determine whether the errors or irregularities have in fact occurred.

d. Consider whether the errors or irregularities were the result of a failure by employees to comply with existing internal control procedures.

(AICPA Adapted)

4. Which of the following, if material, would be an irregularity as defined in Statements on Auditing Standards?

a. Errors in the application of accounting principles.

b. Clerical errors in the accounting data underlying the financial statements.

c. Misinterpretation of facts that existed when the financial statements were prepared.

<u>d.</u> Misappropriation of an asset or groups of assets.   (AICPA Adapted)

5. With respect to errors and irregularities, which of the following should be part of an auditor's planning of the audit engagement?

a. Plan to search for errors or irregularities that would have a material or immaterial effect on the financial statements.

b. Plan to discover errors or irregularities that are either material or immaterial.

c. Plan to discover errors or irregularities that are material.

<u>d.</u> Plan to consider factors affecting the risk of material misstatement both at the financial statement and the account balance level.   (AICPA Adapted)

6. Which of the following statements best describes the auditor's responsibility for detecting irregularities?

a. The auditor is responsible for failure to detect irregularities when such failure clearly results from nonperformance of audit procedures specifically described in the engagement letter.

b. The auditor must extend auditing procedures to actively search for evidence of irregularities in all situations.

<u>c.</u> The auditor must extend auditing procedures to actively search for evidence of irregularities where the examination indicated that irregularities may exist.

d. The auditor is responsible for failure to detect irregularities only when an unqualified opinion is issued.   (AICPA Adapted)

7. An audit conducted in accordance with generally accepted auditing standards generally should

a. Be expected to provide assurance that illegal acts will be detected where internal control structure is effective.

b. Be relied upon to disclose violations of truth in lending laws.

c. Encompass a plan to actively search for illegalities which relate to operating aspects.

<u>d.</u> Not be relied upon to provide assurance that illegal acts will be detected.

(AICPA Adapted)

8. If as a result of auditing procedures an auditor believes that the client may have committed illegal acts, which of the following actions should be taken immediately by the auditor?

   a. Consult with the client's counsel and the auditor's counsel to determine how the suspected illegal acts will be communicated to the stockholders.
   b. Extend normal auditing procedures to ascertain whether the suspected illegal acts may have a material effect on the financial statements.
   c. Inquire of the client's management and obtain an understanding of the circumstances of the acts and sufficient other evidence to determine the effects of the acts on the financial statements.
   d. Notify each member of the audit committee of the board of directors of the nature of the acts and request that they give guidance with respect to the approach to be taken by the auditor.   (AICPA Adapted)

9. If an illegal act is discovered during the audit of a publicly held company, the auditor should

   a. Notify the regulatory authorities.
   b. Determine who was responsible for the illegal act.
   c. Intensify the examination.
   d. Report the act to high level personnel within the client's organization.
                                                                      (AICPA Adapted)

10. The audit client's board of directors and audit committee refused to take any action with respect to an immaterial illegal act which was brought to their attention by the auditor. Because of their failure to act, the auditor withdrew from the engagement. The auditor's decision to withdraw was primarily due to doubts concerning

   a. Inadequate financial statement disclosures.
   b. Compliance with the Foreign Corrupt Practices Act.
   c. Scope limitations resulting from their inaction.
   d. Reliance on management's representations.   (AICPA Adapted)

11. The Foreign Corrupt Practices Act of 1977 prohibits briberey of foreign officials. Which of the following statements correctly describes the Act's application to corporations engaging in such practices?

   a. It only applies to multinational corporations.
   b. It applies to all domestic corporations engaged in interstate commerce.
   c. It only applies to corporations whose securities are registered under the Securities Exchange Act of 1934.
   d. It only applies to corporations engaged in foreign commerce.
                                                                      (AICPA Adapted)

12. The Foreign Corrupt Practices Act requires that

   a. Auditors engaged to examine the financial statements of publicly held companies report all illegal payments to the SEC.
   b. Publicly held companies establish independent audit committees to monitor the effectiveness of their system of internal control.
   c. U.S. firms doing business abroad report sizable payments to non-U.S. citizens to the Justice Department.

d. Publicly held companies devise and maintain an adequate system of internal control.   (AICPA Adapted)

PROBLEMS

3-1   Andrew Mills, an entry-level staff auditor with less than six months' professional experience, is assigned to audit the Cash accounts of Drexel Industries, a long-standing audit client of Rollins, Huntersfield, and Dodge, CPAs. Dodge, the audit partner on the Drexel engagement, tells Mills, "Drexel is a rather low risk client. In fact, in all the years I've been associated with the Drexel audit, I don't recall any serious problems, particularly in Cash — controls are tight and management is trustworthy. Tell you what: I've got to be away for a few days. I haven't been out to Drexel or even talked with management in the past few months, but why don't you just follow last year's work, and run with it." Following Dodge's advice, Mills copies last year's audit program and follows the audit procedures explicitly.

Upon returning, Dodge calls Mills, and asks, "How did it go?" Mills responds, "Fine — things seemed so clean, I only had to talk with management once, and that was just to locate the cash receipts and cash disbursements records."

Required:
1. Evaluate Dodge's audit approach in the context of the decision making process normally expected of professional auditors.
2. Which, if any, of the cognitive heuristics was relied on by both Dodge and Mills. Explain.

3-2   Alpine Roofing Company, an audit client of Marques, CPA, manufactures two products: tar shingles and aluminum gutters. In examining Alpine's *Reserve for Warranty Guarantees* as of December 31, 1990 — that is, the estimated liability for warranty repairs and allowances resulting from 1990 sales — Marques reviews internal quality control and engineering reports and learns the following:
• Alpine processes approximately 75 sales orders per business day for tar shingles and 25 orders for aluminum gutters.
• Warranty repairs and allowances are claimed on about 20% of the recorded sales orders for shingles and on 10% for gutters, both of which are of concern to management.
Because sales were unusually high in October and more than 25% warranty claims for either product could prove damaging to Alpine's reputation, Alpine management asks Marques which product, shingles or gutters, is more likely to have more than 25% warranty claims resulting from October sales. Marques concludes that tar shingles are more likely to have more than 25% claims because shingle sales outperformed gutter sales 3 to 1 in October, just as in the above daily estimates.

Required:
1. Which one or more of the cognitive heuristics — representativeness, availability, or anchoring — may have caused biases in Marques' response.
2. Is Marques correct? Why, or why not?

3-3   From data available in the public press, a public accounting firm estimates that undetected management fraud may occur in 20 out of every 1,000 large, publicly traded companies (2%) and in 80 out of every 1,000 small, privately owned companies (8%). But because the data may not be wholly reliable, the firm's Executive Committee decides to poll its regular and small business audit partners at the annual partners meeting; regular partners will be surveyed about publicly traded companies and small business partners will be surveyed about privately owned companies. The survey results will be used to redesign the firm's audit planning checklist, which, in the Executive Committee's view, does not adequately address the auditor's responsibility for detecting and reporting irregularities under SAS No. 53.

At the annual partners meeting, all regular audit partners are given a questionnaire which asks the following two questions:

1. From your experience, do you believe that the incidence of management irregularities in large, publicly traded companies is:
   a. *More* than 20 out of every 1,000 companies — i.e., more than 2%?
   b. *Less* than 20 out of every 1,000 companies — i.e., less than 2%?
2. What is your estimate of the percentage of large, publicly traded companies involved in management irregularities?
   _____%.

Small business partners were given the following questionnaire, which was identical except that it related to privately owned companies:

1. From your experience, do you believe that the incidence of management irregularities in small, privately owned companies is:
   a. *More* than 80 out of every 1,000 companies — i.e., more than 8%?
   b. *Less* than 80 out of every 1,000 companies — i.e., less than 8%?
2. What is your estimate of the percentage of small, privately owned companies involved in management irregularities?

Compiled responses from each partner group indicated the incidence of management irregularities to be .025 (2.5%) for large, publicly traded companies and .18 (18%) for small, privately owned companies.

Required:

1. For the survey described above, which one(s) of the cognitive heuristics — representativeness, availability, or anchoring — could potentially bias the responding partners? Explain.
2. From the results indicated, has either or both of the partner groups apparently been biased by the heuristic(s) identified in (1) above? Explain.
3. How could the firm have avoided any suspicion that a particular heuristic might bias the survey results?

3-4   Several years ago Dale Holden organized Holden Family Restaurants. Holden started with one restaurant that catered to the family trade. Holden Family Restaurant became very popular because the quality of the food and service was excellent, the restaurant was attractive yet modest, and the prices were reasonable.

The success with his first restaurant encouraged Dale Holden to expand by opening additional Holden Family Restaurants in other metropolitan locations throughout the state. Holden has opened at least one new restaurant each year for the last five years, and there are now a total of eight restaurants. All of the restaurants are successful because Holden has been able to maintain the same high standards that were achieved with the original restaurant.

With the rapid expansion of the business, Holden has hired a controller and supporting staff. The financial operations of the restaurants are managed by the controller and staff. This allows Holden to focus his attention on the restaurant operations and to plan for future locations.

Holden has applied to the bank for additional financing to open another restaurant this year. For the first time ever the bank asked him to provide financial statements audited by a CPA. The bank assured Holden that the audited statements were not being required because they doubted his integrity or thought him to be a poor credit risk. The loan officer explained that bank policy required all businesses over a certain size to supply audited statements with loan applications, and Holden's business had reached that size.

Holden was not surprised by the bank's requirement. He had ruled out an audit previously because he has great respect for his controller's ability, and he wanted to avoid the fee associated with the first audit as long as possible. However, the growth of his business and the increased number of restaurant locations make an audit a sound business requirement. He also believes that an additional benefit of the independent audit will be the probable detection of any irregularities which may be occurring at his restaurants.

To fulfill the bank request for audited statements, Dale Holden has hired Hill & Associates, Certified Public Accountants.

Required:
1. Discuss Hill & Associates' responsibilities for the detection of irregularities in a financial statement audit.
2. What effect, if any, would the detection of irregularities by Hill & Associates have on their expression of an opinion on the financial statements? Give the reasons for your answer.   (CMA Adapted)

3-5   Several months prior to beginning an audit engagement of the Taunton Manufacturing Company, you point out to Taunton's corporate controller, Marsha Wade, that, as part of your normal responsibilities, you will design the audit to provide reasonable assurance of detecting any material errors or irregularities that may exist. The controller, somewhat alarmed by your statement, responds that all of her employees are trustworthy and very much above reproach; thus, she refuses to pay any portion of the audit fee relating to a search for material errors or irregularities. Further, she states her understanding that auditors are not responsible for detecting irregularities, assuming generally accepted auditing standards are followed.

Required:
Respond to each of the corporate controller's statements.

3-6   The partner in charge of your firm is concerned that staff members may not be aware of current professional standards regarding the communication of material errors, irregularities, and illegal acts to individuals or organizations outside of the client's organization.

Required:
Draft a memorandum for distribution to all staff members regarding proper procedures for reporting both to insiders in the client's organization and to outsiders when errors, irregularities, or illegal acts may exist.

3-7   The CPA firm of Winston & Mall was engaged by the Fast Cargo Company, a retailer, to audit its financial statements for the year ended August 31, 1990. The auditors followed generally accepted auditing standards and examined transactions on a test basis. A sample of 100 disbursements was used to test vouchers payable, cash disbursements, and receiving and purchasing procedures. An investigation of the sample disclosed several instances where purchases had been recorded and paid for without the required receiving report being included in the file of supporting documents. This was properly noted in the working papers by Martin, the junior auditor who did the sampling. Mall, the partner in charge, called these facts to the attention of Harris, Fast Cargo's chief accountant, who told Mall not to worry about it and promised to make certain that these receiving reports were properly included in the voucher file. Mall accepted this and did nothing further to investigate or follow up on this situation.

The chief accountant was engaged in a fraudulent scheme whereby merchandise was diverted to a private warehouse where Harris leased space, and the invoices were sent to Fast Cargo for payment. The scheme was discovered later by a special investigation, and a preliminary estimate indicates that the loss to Fast Cargo will be in excess of $50,000.

Required:
1. What is the liability, if any, of Winston & Mall in this situation? Discuss.
2. What additional steps, if any, should have been taken by Mall? Explain.

(AICPA Adapted)

3-8   The CPA firm of Martinson, Brinks & Sutherland, a partnership, was the auditor for Masco Corporation, a medium-size wholesaler. Masco leased warehouse facilities and sought financing for leasehold improvements to these facilities. Masco assured its bank that the leasehold improvements would result in a more efficient and profitable operation. On the basis of these assurances, the bank granted Masco a line of credit.

The loan agreement required annual audited financial statements. Masco submitted to the bank its 1989 audited financial statements which showed an operating profit of $75,000, leasehold improvements of $250,000, and net worth of $350,000. In reliance thereon, the bank loaned Masco $200,000. The audit report which accompanied the financial statements disclaimed an opinion because the cost of the leasehold improvements could not be determined from the company's records. The part of the audit report dealing with leasehold improvements reads as follows:

> Additions to fixed assets in 1989 were found to include principally warehouse improvements. Practically all of this work was done by company employees and the cost of materials and overhead were paid by Masco. Unfortunately, fully completed, detailed cost records were not kept of these leasehold improvements, and no exact determination could be made as to the actual cost of said improvements. The total amount capitalized is set forth in Note 4.

In late 1990 Masco went out of business, at which time it was learned that the claimed leasehold improvements were totally fictitious. The labor expenses charged as leasehold improvements proved to be operating expenses. No item of building material cost had been recorded. No independent investigation of the existence of the leasehold improvements was made by the auditors.

If the $250,000 had not been capitalized, the income statement would have reflected a substantial loss from operations and the net worth would have been correspondingly decreased.

The bank has sustained a loss on its loan to Masco of $200,000 and now seeks to recover damages from the CPA firm, alleging that the accountants negligently audited the financial statements.

Required:
Answer the following, setting forth reasons for any conclusions stated.
1. Will the disclaimer of opinion absolve the CPA firm from responsibility for not detecting the irregularity?
2. Are the individual partners of Martinson, Brinks & Sutherland, who did not take part in the audit, liable?

(AICPA Adapted)

3-9   The Foreign Corrupt Practices Act of 1977 can have a serious impact upon the business operations of many corporations, especially Securities and Exchange Commission registrants who are subject to both the unlawful influence and the internal accounting control and record-keeping provisions of the Act. Assume that you are manager of internal auditing for a major publicly traded U.S. corporation which manufactures and distributes aluminum alloy products throughout the world. The corporation's chief executive officer requests that you draft a plan for complying with the Foreign Corrupt Practices Act.

Required:
Draft a plan for complying with the FCPA. The plan should emphasize a corporate strategy for encouraging and monitoring compliance with the Act, rather than detailed procedures for complying with specific provisions of the Act.

3-10   Retail Corporation, a ten-store men's haberdashery chain, has a written company policy which states that company buyers may not have an investment in nor borrow money from an existing or potential supplier. Louise Chan, the independent auditor, learns from a Retail employee that Williams, a buyer, is indebted to Park, a supplier, for a substantial amount of money. Retail's volume of business with Park increased significantly during the year. Chan believes the debtor-creditor relationship of Williams and Park constitutes a conflict of interest that might lead Williams to perpetrate a material fraud.

Required:
Discuss what immediate actions Chan should take upon discovery of these facts.

(AICPA Adapted)

AUDITOR'S LEGAL LIABILITY

4

Major topics discussed in this chapter are the:

▲ *Issues underlying an auditor's legal liability to clients and third parties.*

▲ *Auditor's common law liability to clients, primary beneficiaries, foreseen beneficiaries, and other third parties.*

▲ *Scope of an auditor's involvement with the Securities Acts.*

▲ *Auditor's statutory liability to securities purchasers and sellers under the Securities Acts.*

▲ *Auditor's liability for criminal offenses.*

▲ *Precautions an auditor should consider to minimize the risk of legal liability.*

E fficient allocation of resources within a competitive, free-market economy is dependent upon objective, verifiable, and relevant financial information. Independent auditors attest to much of this financial information and, if deficient in carrying out the attest function, may be legally liable to users who suffer damages from relying upon misstated or misleading financial information.

This chapter addresses the independent auditor's civil and criminal liability, beginning with an introduction to the current legal environment and a review of the basic issues underscoring most auditor liability cases. In turn, an auditor's common law civil liability to clients and third parties is described. Following is an introduction to the Securities Act of 1933 and the Securities Exchange Act of 1934 and a discussion of an auditor's statutory liability to securities purchasers and sellers under the 1933 and 1934 Acts. The chapter concludes with a discussion of the auditor's role in minimizing the risk of legal liability. An appendix briefly outlines several major liability cases not specifically discussed within the chapter.

At the outset, one should note that the generalizations drawn within this chapter are based upon constantly changing and evolving standards of auditor liability, and in some instances represent majority rather than unanimous views. Generalizations are useful in understanding complex legal issues. However, they can be dangerous if used to draw defendable conclusions in actual legal liability cases. Individual cases must be based upon the specific facts and legal issues and principles applied, not upon generalizations.

THE LEGAL ENVIRONMENT

The mid-1960s marked the beginning of a period of rising consumerism and increasing litigation. Since then, auditors and other professionals have experienced an onslaught of scrutiny, criticism, and legal liability suits. Although legal liability cases involving independent auditors were less common prior to the sixties, several earlier cases were significant in shaping the legal environment surrounding the auditing profession.

One early case was a civil action involving McKesson & Robbins, Inc., and Price Waterhouse & Co. Although the case was settled out of court, it had a profound impact on the profession. McKesson & Robbins' 1937 financial statements disclosed $87 million in assets, although approximately $10 million of inventory and $9 million of accounts receivable were fictitious. In keeping with acceptable audit procedure of the era, Price Waterhouse neither observed inventories nor confirmed receivables with debtors, and thereby failed to detect that McKesson & Robbins' officials had fictitiously overstated the company's financial condition. McKesson & Robbins' treasurer discovered and reported the overstatement to the company's president, who disclosed the fraud. The company went into receivership in 1938.

Price Waterhouse repaid over $520,000 in professional fees for services rendered after January 1, 1933. However, as noted in Chapter 1, the most significant developments resulting from the case were appointment of the Committee on Auditing Procedure, forebear of today's Auditing Standards Board, and issuance of the first Statement on Auditing Procedure, forebear of today's Statements on Auditing Standards. *Statement on Auditing Procedure No. 1,* ''Extensions of Auditing Procedure'' (October, 1939), recommended observation of inventories and confirmation of receivables, both firmly established auditing procedures today. Since the McKesson & Robbins case, thousands of civil actions have been filed against independent auditors, and the number of actions is increasing.

Criminal actions against independent auditors have been less prevalent than civil actions, although, as a result of provisions within several federal statutes, the threat of criminal liability does exist. The most prominent criminal liability case, *United States v. Simon,* decided in 1969, firmly established an auditor's criminal liability and is discussed more fully later in the chapter.

A particularly significant point underscoring this chapter is that independent auditors are now, and will continue to be, potentially liable to clients and third parties in both civil and criminal actions. The nature and extent of liability are examined in the remainder of the chapter.

LIABILITY UNDER COMMON AND STATUTORY LAW: AN OVERVIEW

Clients and certain third parties may bring common law civil action against auditors. Clients may sue for breach of contract or for tort, which is the breach of a noncontractual duty. In contrast, only tort actions may be brought against auditors by third parties including primary beneficiaries, foreseen beneficiaries, and other foreseeable third parties.

Purchasers of securities may bring action against auditors under statutory law for violating the Securities Act of 1933, usually Section 11. Purchasers or sellers of securities may bring action for violating the Securities Exchange Act of 1934, usually Section 10(b), SEC Rule 10b-5, or Section 18.

Under either common or statutory law, an auditor may be liable for ordinary negligence, gross negligence, or fraud, and either the plaintiff or defendant (auditor) may have the burden of proving or disproving that (1) damage or loss resulted from relying upon financial statements or advice, (2) financial statements were misstated or advice was erroneous, (3) financial statements or advice were in fact relied on, and/or (4) auditor conduct was deficient. In summary, the following issues are relevant in most civil liability cases involving auditors:

▲ Source of law:
  —Common law
  —Statutory law (Securities Act of 1933 and Securities Exchange Act of 1934)
▲ Identity of plaintiff:
  —Common law: client, third party primary beneficiary, third party foreseen beneficiary, or other foreseeable third party
  —Securities Act of 1933: purchaser of securities
  —Securities Exchange Act of 1934: purchaser or seller of securities
▲ Potential liability, common and statutory law:
  —Ordinary negligence
  —Gross negligence
  —Fraud
▲ Burden of proof upon either plaintiff or defendant:
  —Damage or loss
  —Misstated financial statements or erroneous advice
  —Reliance upon financial statements or advice
  —Deficient auditor conduct

These issues are discussed in the following sections and are summarized in Figures 4-1 and 4-2, under common and statutory law, respectively.

FIGURE 4-1
Liability under Common Law

Plaintiff	Minimum Basis For Potential Auditor Liability	Burden of Proof upon Plaintiff
Client	Ordinary negligence	Damage or loss
Third party:		Misstated financial statements or erroneous advice
Primary beneficiary	Ordinary negligence	Reliance upon financial statements or advice
Foreseen beneficiary	Ordinary (majority view) or gross negligence	
Foreseeable third parties	Gross negligence	Deficient auditor conduct

---

Source of Law

A plaintiff may bring action against an auditor under either common or statutory law. *Common law* refers to "unwritten" law evolving from legal precedent, i.e., judgments in prior court cases, rather than state or federal statutes. In contrast, *statutory law* refers to "written" law established by legislative bodies and published in state and federal statutes. The Securities Act of 1933 and Securities Exchange Act of 1934, both administered by the SEC, are the two most prominent federal statutes affecting an auditor's potential legal liability.

Identity of Plaintiff

Under common law an action may be initiated against auditors by a client or by third parties. A client may bring action against an auditor for breach of contract or tort. Clients may sue for *breach of contract* because clients and auditors are parties to an express or implied contract for services, i.e., "privity of contract" exists. Such actions usually result from an auditor's violation of either generally accepted auditing standards or the auditor-client confidential relationship. A *tort* is a wrongful act, other than breach of contract, resulting in injury to another person.

Primary beneficiaries are specifically identified to auditors as beneficiaries of audit services, i.e., the auditor would not have been engaged were it not for the primary beneficiary. For example, many closely held, nonpublicly

FIGURE 4-2
Liability under Statutory Law

Plaintiff	Minimum Basis for Potential Auditor Liability	Burden of Proof	
		Upon Plaintiff	Upon Defendant
Under 1933 Act, Section 11: Security purchaser	Ordinary negligence	Damage or loss Financial statements misstated or advice erroneous	Lack of reliance or Auditor conduct not deficient (due diligence)
Under 1934 Act, Section 10(b) Rule 10b-5: Security purchaser or seller	Gross negligence or fraud	Damage or loss Financial statements misstated or advice erroneous Reliance Deficient auditor conduct	
Under 1934 Act, Section 18: Security purchaser or seller	Gross negligence	Damage or loss Financial statements misstated or advice erroneous Reliance	Auditor conduct not deficient (due diligence)

traded entities engage auditors primarily because a third party, such as a specifically named bank, requires audited financial statements. In these cases, clients hire auditors to conduct an audit for the third party's primary benefit. Closely related to primary beneficiaries are *foreseen beneficiaries,* who are not specifically identified as benefactors of audit services although their general identity and specific purpose for relying upon an audit report are known to the auditor. For example, if a client intended to use audited financial statements to secure a loan from an unnamed creditor, any party extending credit would be a foreseen beneficiary. Of course, if a creditor were specifically named prior to or during the audit engagement, the creditor would be a primary beneficiary.

The final classification of plaintiffs under common law is *foreseeable third parties,* and includes parties such as investors and potential investors. Whereas common law actions by clients may be brought for breach of contract or for torts, actions by third parties are usually brought under tort law.

Under statutory law, plaintiffs may bring action against auditors for violating either of the Securities Acts. A plaintiff in an action under the Securities Act of 1933 may be any person purchasing securities identified within a registration statement. A registration statement includes both (1) a prospectus describing the entity and securities offered and (2) other detailed information such as balance sheets and earnings summaries. In contrast, a plaintiff in an action under the Securities Exchange Act of 1934 may be any person purchasing or selling publicly traded securities.

Potential Liability

Under either common or statutory law, an auditor may be liable for ordinary negligence, gross negligence, or fraud. These terms are abstract and, as a result, have been interpreted inconsistently by different courts in different jurisdictions. The following definitions are adapted for discussion purposes:

▲ *Ordinary negligence* — lack of reasonable care when performing services; when used alone, the term "negligence" is generally understood to mean ordinary negligence.

▲ *Gross negligence* — lack of even minimum care when performing services.

▲ *Fraud* — intentional misrepresentation of a material fact resulting in another party being deceived and then injured.

Ordinary negligence implies a higher degree of responsibility than gross negligence, and gross negligence higher than fraud. This is the case because "reasonable care" (ordinary negligence) is a higher degree of care than "minimum care" (gross negligence), and so on.

In 1931 the Court of Appeals of New York noted in *Ultramares Corp. v. Touche* that gross negligence could be so great as to constitute constructive (as opposed to actual) fraud. Constructive fraud lacks intent, an essential condition in actual fraud; however, the result of constructive and actual fraud is identical — another party is deceived and then injured.

Burden of Proof

In general, the extent of an independent auditor's liability under common and statutory law rests on four essential elements. The burden of proving any or all of the elements differs under common law and various sections of the Securities Acts.

The first element relates to *damage or loss* resulting from relying upon financial statements or advice. Damages or losses vary from case to case and may be represented by a decline in a security's value or in the amount of an audit fee. As noted in Figures 4-1 and 4-2, the burden of proving damage or loss always falls upon the plaintiff.

The second element, *misstated financial statements or erroneous advice,* is the basis for claiming damage or loss. Like proof of damage or loss, the plaintiff always has the burden of proving that financial statements are misstated or advice erroneous.

Reliance upon financial statements or advice, the third element to be proven, entails two separate but related issues:

▲ Did the plaintiff actually rely on the statements or advice to reach a decision?

▲ Did reliance on the statements or advice actually lead to damage or loss?

The burden of proving reliance falls upon the plaintiff under both common law (Figure 4-1) and the Securities Exchange Act of 1934 (Figure 4-2). However, under the Securities Act of 1933, the plaintiff does not have to prove reliance; rather, the defendant (auditor) has the burden of proving that a plaintiff's damage or loss did not result from relying upon financial statements or advice.

The fourth element of proof relates to an *auditor's conduct* when performing audit and other accounting-related services. The level of conduct owed to a plaintiff depends upon an auditor's knowledge of a plaintiff's existence and identity and the plaintiff's reason for relying on financial statements or advice. For example, in comparison with some third parties, a client's existence, identity, and reason for relying upon financial statements are more clearly known to an auditor. Thus, an auditor's expected level of conduct is higher for clients than for some third parties.

Under the Securities Act of 1933 and Section 18 of the Securities Ex-

change Act of 1934, an auditor has the burden of proving that a reasonable
investigation was made and, therefore, that his or her level of conduct was
adequate. This is referred to as the "due diligence" defense and is closely
aligned with due professional care. In contrast, the plaintiff must prove deficient auditor conduct under common law and Section 10(b) of the Securities
Exchange Act of 1934.

COMMON LAW LIABILITY

Common law is based in the doctrine of *stare decisis* — that is, handing
down precedent to succeeding cases and abiding by the principles in precedent-setting cases. Thus, common law derives from legal precedent, which
in turn reflects contemporary social values, and because social values change
over time, so too does common law.

Under common law, an auditor may be liable to a party contracting for
audit services, i.e., the client, and to third parties who, although not party to
a contractual relationship, nevertheless are users of audited external financial
information. As shown in Figure 4-1, third parties may be classified as primary beneficiaries, who are treated as clients under common law; foreseen
beneficiaries, also treated similarly to clients; and other foreseeable parties.
A discussion of the auditor's potential liability to clients and third parties
follows.

Clients

An auditor's common law liability to clients is based on the express or
implied contractual relationship between an auditor and client and on the
auditor's status as an independent contractor. The contractual relationship results from an agreement between an auditor and client regarding prescribed
audit services; the status as independent contractor, rather than agent or employee, results because an auditor's activities are not controlled by the client.
A client may initiate a common law civil action when an auditor is alleged
to have failed in carrying out the duties of an audit services contract. The
action may be for breach of contract or tort.

The auditor's common law liability to clients is rooted in English statutes. D. Y. Causey reports that the earliest English case involving an auditor
occurred in 1887 — *Leeds Estate, Building and Investment Co. v. Shepherd.*[1]
The company, a lending institution, sued an auditor for breach of duty, win-
ning primarily on grounds that the auditor was wrongful in not inquiring into

---

[1] D. Y. Causey, Jr., *Duties and Liabilities of Public Accountants* (rev. ed.; Homewood,
Ill.: Dow Jones-Irwin, 1982).

a balance sheet's "substantial accuracy." The tenets of this early case are quite reflective of today's legal climate.

Figure 4-1 summarizes an auditor's liability to clients under common law. An auditor is liable under common law for ordinary negligence and, therefore, gross negligence and fraud. Thus, an auditor is liable not only for intentional misrepresentations and lack of minimum care, but also for lack of reasonable care — the highest degree of care. To win damages, a client has the burden of proving damage or loss, that financial statements are misstated or advice erroneous, reliance on financial statements or advice, and deficient auditor conduct. Damages are usually awarded in monetary terms.

An auditor's liability to clients also extends to parties who acquire a client's rights by subrogation (substitution). For instance, if a bonding company reimburses a client for an employee's embezzlement, the bonding company succeeds to the client's right to sue the auditor for failing to detect the embezzlement. A 1940 case, *Maryland Casualty Co. v. Jonathon Cook,* illustrates this situation.

Over a period of seven years, the Flint, Michigan, city treasurer embezzled monies from municipal funds. Jonathon Cook & Company accepted the 1932 audit engagement which was to be based on specifications included within an audit services contract. The specifications would have been sufficient to uncover the embezzlement; however, Cook essentially ignored them. As a result, Maryland Casualty, which carried a surety bond on the treasurer, reimbursed the city of Flint and initiated action against Cook. The court ruled in favor of Maryland Casualty, arguing that the engagement should have been conducted in accordance with the audit specifications, i.e., in accordance with the terms of the contract.

Maryland Casualty Co. v. Jonathon Cook also illustrates the importance of written contracts for audit services. These contracts, typically called *engagement letters,* are central to an auditor's liability and should be prepared and fully understood prior to every engagement. A more prominent and precedent-setting case regarding engagement letters was *1136 Tenants' Corp. v. Max Rothenberg & Co.* 1136 Tenants Corporation was an apartment cooperative which engaged Max Rothenberg & Co., without an engagement letter, to conduct nonaudit accounting services. Services were provided from 1963 to 1965, when it was discovered that a former manager had absconded with funds from the corporation. 1136 Tenants sued Max Rothenberg, arguing that an audit should have been performed. In defense, Rothenberg unsuccessfully argued that an audit was not agreed upon. Although the professional fees for this engagement amounted to only $600 per year, Rothenberg was ordered to pay over $230,000 in damages. Clearly, failure to secure an engagement letter can be devastating. The role of engagement letters in the audit process is discussed more fully in Chapter 6.

Primary Beneficiaries

Even though audit engagement letters identify the auditor and client as parties to the contract, audit reports prepared for the express benefit of primary beneficiaries are sometimes addressed to the primary beneficiary. In short, primary beneficiaries often enjoy a status similar to that of clients.

English common law, the forebear of U.S. legal precedent, has traditionally held that only parties to a contract — i.e., those specifically named — may enforce the contract. However, in the mid-nineteenth century, U.S. courts began to equate primary beneficiaries with clients. For example, an 1859 case, *Lawrence v. Fox,* effectively ruled that privity was not essential for primary beneficiaries to sue, assuming that contractual duties were limited to third parties rather than clients. Some six decades later, however, in *Glanzer v. Shepard,* the court firmly established a primary beneficiary's right to sue for damages even though contractual duties extended only between the parties to the contract. Although *Glanzer v. Shepard* did not involve an auditor, it is generally recognized as an important influence on an auditor's legal liability to primary beneficiaries.

Ultramares Corp. v. Touche (1931), a landmark New York Court of Appeals case, established that auditors are liable to third parties for fraud — intentional misrepresentations and deceit — but they are not liable to unidentified third parties for negligence. Relying on financial statements audited by Touche, Ultramares Corporation made loans to Fred Stern & Co., a rubber importer that in reality was insolvent. Stern was unable to repay the loans and subsequently declared bankruptcy. The court ruled that accountants are liable for negligence only to those parties in privity — that is, to clients and to those third parties whom the accountant knows will rely on the financial statements (primary beneficiaries).

In a New Jersey Supreme Court case, *H. Rosenblum Inc. v. Adler,* the court strayed from the privity concept established in *Ultramares,* ruling that accountants can be held liable not only to clients and primary beneficiaries, but to foreseeable third parties as well. But a 1981 New York Court of Appeals case, *Credit Alliance v. Arthur Andersen & Co.,* has been viewed by the profession as a strong reaffirmation of the privity concept in *Ultramares,* also a New York Court of Appeals case. Credit Alliance, a finance company, loaned large sums of money to L. B. Smith, Inc., a heavy equipment lessor and audit client of Arthur Andersen. L. B. Smith subsequently went bankrupt and was unable to repay approximately $9 million. Credit Alliance prevailed, arguing it was in privity since L. B. Smith had used the audited financial statements to solicit financing throughout the financial community. The court acknowledged that other courts throughout the nation had moved away from Ultramares, but reaffirmed preexisting New York law by ruling that negligence suits against auditors required privity or a relationship "so close as to approach that of privity." Thus, *Credit Alliance* reaffirms the privity concept established in *Ultramares,* but its significance nationwide must await further court cases.

Figure 4-1 summarizes an auditor's common law liability to primary beneficiaries. As is the case with clients, an auditor is liable to primary beneficiaries for lack of reasonable care (ordinary negligence), and primary beneficiaries have the burden of proving: damage or loss, that financial statements are misstated or advice erroneous, reliance on financial statements or advice, and deficient auditor conduct. Again, the critical point is that the courts have imposed the same liability upon auditors for primary beneficiaries as for clients.

Foreseen Beneficiaries

Some third parties are not specifically identified to auditors, and yet their general identity and specific purpose for relying upon financial statements can be reasonably foreseen. Conceptually, there is a difference between a primary and a foreseen beneficiary. However, the difference is sometimes unclear because the foreseen beneficiary concept is not as well established judicially as the primary beneficiary concept.[2]

Two cases, decided within one year of each other, provide precedent for the majority view in cases involving foreseen beneficiaries. In *Rusch Factors, Inc. v. Levin* (1968), the defendant had audited financial statements which were used to support a corporation's loan application with Rusch Factors. The statements erroneously showed the borrower to be solvent. The loan was granted, and the borrower subsequently went into receivership. As a result, Rusch Factors took action against the auditor, claiming negligent misrepresentation. The Rhode Island court held the auditor liable for ordinary negligence, ruling that Rusch was a foreseen beneficiary. The language of the decision was quite clear:

> . . . the Court holds that an accountant should be liable in negligence for careless financial misrepresentations relied upon by actually foreseen and limited classes of persons. According to the plaintiff's complaint in the instant case, the defendant knew that his certification was to be used for, and had as its very aim and purpose, the reliance of potential financiers of the Rhode Island corporation.

The auditor's defense of "lack of privity" — i.e., that Rusch Factors was not a party to the contract — did not hold.

---

[2]J. J. Schultz, Jr., and K. Pany, "The Independent Auditor's Civil Liability — An Overview," *The Accounting Review* (April, 1980), p. 323.

One year later, in *Ryan v. Kanne,* James A. Kanne, a lumber companies operator, hired Ryan to prepare an unaudited balance sheet for Kanne's businesses. If the statements warranted, Kanne intended to incorporate his business for purposes of raising additional capital. Because of its importance to Kanne, Ryan orally guaranteed the accuracy of "Accounts Payable — Trade" within $5,000. On the basis of the resulting balance sheet, Kanne incorporated his businesses.

Ryan subsequently sued the corporation for unpaid professional fees and won. However, the corporation countersued Ryan, because upon reaudit the originally reported balance in "Accounts Payable — Trade" was found misstated by more than $5,000. Ryan's defense was based on lack of privity; i.e., the corporation was not a party to the contract for professional services with Kanne, a sole proprietor. The Iowa court, however, found Ryan liable to the corporation for ordinary negligence, throwing out Ryan's lack of privity defense.

Although these two cases are important for their consistent and precedent-setting majority views, the Florida Second District Court of Appeals in *Investment Corp. of Florida v. Buchman* (1968) took a dim view of holding auditors liable for ordinary negligence to foreseen beneficiaries. The Florida court's minority view upheld gross, but not ordinary, negligence. Three important points derive from the court's positions in *Rusch Factors, Inc. v. Levin, Ryan v. Kanne,* and *Investment Corp. of Florida v. Buchman.* First, the courts do not agree. Although ordinary negligence seems to represent a majority view and gross negligence a minority view, it is not clear how other courts will rule. Second, each decision was reached in a different jurisdiction. Thus, once again, it is not clear how other jurisdictions will react. Finally, unlike the precedent-setting decisions underlying liability to primary beneficiaries (each of which is at least five decades old), the decisions underlying liability to foreseen beneficiaries are relatively recent. Thus, the legal precedent underlying the majority view regarding liability to foreseen beneficiaries (i.e., ordinary negligence) has not yet "withstood the tests of time."

Figure 4-1 summarizes an auditor's common law liability to foreseen beneficiaries. Because of the competing views expressed in these cases, an auditor's liability may be for either ordinary or gross negligence, although ordinary negligence reflects the current majority view. It is clearer, however, that foreseen beneficiaries maintain the burden of proving: damage or loss, that financial statements are misstated or advice erroneous, reliance on financial statements or advice, and deficient auditor conduct.

Foreseeable Third Parties

Foreseeable third parties are the furthest removed from a contractual agreement for audit services. Thus, it is not surprising that they enjoy the least favorable position in auditor legal liability cases. However, even though unforeseen in the sense that they are not specifically identified to auditors, other third parties are nevertheless "foreseeable." The notion of "foreseeability" explains an auditor's liability to other third parties.

Figure 4-1 summarizes an auditor's common law liability to foreseeable third parties. An auditor is responsible for lack of minimum care (gross negligence); this responsibility derives from *Ultramares Corp. v. Touche*. Third parties have the burden of proving: damage or loss, that financial statements are misstated or advice erroneous, reliance on financial statements or advice, and deficient auditor conduct.

THE SECURITIES ACTS

As of 1933, most states had adopted so-called "blue-sky" laws to regulate the exchange of debt and equity securities. Although adequate for intrastate exchanges, the "blue-sky" laws were less effective in regulating interstate exchanges. As a result of this, the 1929 stock market crash, and President Franklin Roosevelt's "New Deal" administration, the Securities Acts were enacted and the SEC was created. An auditor's potential legal liability under the Securities Acts ". . . is a Congressional attempt to hold accountants and others involved in Securities Acts registrations more strictly liable to third parties than they would be under the common law."[3]

The SEC was created under the Securities Exchange Act of 1934 and charged to administer both the 1934 Act and the Securities Act of 1933, which had been administered by the Federal Trade Commission. The SEC, headquartered in Washington, D.C., consists of five appointed Commissioners, one of which is designated chairman, a number of administrative divisions or offices, one of which is the Office of the Chief Accountant, and nine regional branches throughout the U.S. Today, in addition to the Securities Acts, the Commission also administers the Public Utility Holding Company Act of 1935, the Trust Indenture Act of 1939, the Investment Company Act of 1940, the Investment Advisors Act of 1940, the National Bankruptcy Act (Chapter XI), the Securities Investor Protection Act of 1970, and portions of the Foreign Corrupt Practices Act of 1977, among others.

The Securities Act of 1933

The Securities Act of 1933, often referred to as the "truth in securities" law, regulates the initial offering and sale of securities through the mails and

---

[3]K. F. Skousen, *An Introduction to the SEC* (3d. ed.; Cincinnati: South-Western Publishing Co., 1983), p. 113.

other forms of interstate commerce. Once a security is offered and sold, the 1933 Act no longer applies. In general, the Act's purpose is to promote full and fair disclosure and to prohibit fraudulent misrepresentations regarding initial offers and sales of securities. To achieve this purpose, the SEC requires that an entity first file a registration statement, including prospectus, with the Commission before offering securities publicly. Figure 4-3 (pages 130–131) illustrates the filing process.

The Registration Process. A registration statement is filed on a prescribed form and reports required information, including:

▲ An entity's nature, history, and capital structure.
▲ Descriptions of the securities offered and underwriting arrangements.
▲ Officers' and directors' salaries and security holdings.
▲ Estimated net proceeds from the offering and their intended use.
▲ Detailed financial information.

Registration forms are not of the "fill-in-the-blank" variety; rather, narrative responses are required, and the completion process is demanding and time consuming. Once filed, a registration statement is examined by a review team of the SEC's Division of Corporation Finance. The team typically consists of an accountant, an attorney, and a financial analyst.

Following review, the SEC forwards a letter of comment to the offering entity, requesting changes in the registration statement or other action if necessary. If the statement is corrected, the registration process continues. However, if it is not corrected, the SEC can accept the original filing (rarely done); issue a refusal order, which does not halt the registration process (sometimes done); issue a stop order, which halts the registration process. Most entities, however, respond properly to letters of comment; thus, these alternatives are not often used. The filing process, like the registration process, is time consuming and complex.

The Independent Auditor. An auditor's liability under the Securities Act of 1933 derives from his or her involvement in the registration process. In connection with a registration statement, an auditor will ordinarily (1) examine financial statements in accordance with generally accepted auditing standards, (2) read the registration statement for material inconsistencies with financial statements, (3) review events from the date of the audited financial statements to the registration statement's effective date, and (4) issue a letter for underwriters, a so-called "comfort letter." The comfort letter discusses selected representations appearing in the registration statement and should be prepared in accordance with *Statement on Auditing Standards No. 49,* "Letters for Underwriters."

FIGURE 4-3
Illustrative Example of Registration Process: Securities Act of 1933

Event	Participants	Agenda	Timetable
Preliminary meeting to discuss issue	President, VP-Finance, independent accountants, underwriters, counsel	Discuss financial needs; introduce and select type of issue to meet needs.	1 July (Begin)
Form selection	Management, counsel	Select appropriate form for use in registration statement.	3 July (3 days)
Initial meeting of working group	President, VP-Finance, independent accountants, underwriter, counsel for underwriter, company counsel	Assign specific duties to each person in working group; discuss underwriting problems with this issue; discuss accounting problems with the issue.	8 July (8 days)
Second meeting of working group	Same as for initial meeting	Review work assignments; Prepare presentation to board of directors.	22 July (22 days)
Meeting of board of directors	Board of directors, members of working group	Approve proposed issue and increase of debt or equity; Authorize preparation of materials.	26 July (26 days)
Meeting of company counsel with underwriters	Company counsel, counsel for underwriters, underwriters	Discuss underwriting terms and blue sky problems.	30 July (30 days)
Meeting of working group	Members of working group	Review collected material and examine discrepancies.	6 Aug. (37 days)
Prefiling conference with SEC staff	Working group members, SEC staff, other experts as needed	Review proposed registration and associated problems: legal, financial, operative.	9 Aug. (40 days)
Additional meeting of working group	Members of working group	Prepare final registration statement and prospectuses.	12–30 Aug. (61 days)

Event	Participants	Action	Date
Meeting with board of directors	Board of directors, members of working group	Approve registration statement/prospectuses; discuss related topics/problems.	6 Sept. (68 days)
Meeting of working group	Members of working group	Draft final corrected registration statement	10 Sept. (72 days)
Filing registration statement with SEC	Company counsel or representative and SEC staff	File registration statement and pay fee.	12 Sept. (74 days)
Distribution of "red herring" prospectus*	Underwriters	Publicize offering.	16 Sept. (78 days)
Receipt of letter of comments	Members of working group	Relate deficiencies in registration statement.	15 Oct. (107 days)
Meeting of working group	Members of working group	Correct deficiencies and submit amendments.	21 Oct. (113 days)
"Due diligence" meeting	Management representatives, independent accountants, company & underwriter's counsel, underwriters, other professionals as needed	Exchange final information and discuss pertinent problems relating to underwriting and issue.	24 Oct. (116 days)
Pricing amendment	Management, underwriters	Add the amounts for the actual price, underwriter's discount or commission, and net proceeds to company to the amended registration statement	25 Oct. (117 days)
Notice of acceptance	SEC staff	Report from SEC staff on acceptance status of price-amended registration statement	28 Oct. (120 days)
Statement becomes effective			30 Oct. (122 days)

*A "red herring" is a preliminary prospectus (title stamped in red, thus accounting for the name).

Source: K. F. Skousen, An Introduction to the SEC (4th ed.; Cincinnati: South-Western Publishing Co., 1987), pp. 58–59.

Relevant Section. Most suits against auditors under the Securities Act of 1933 relate to Section 11. The statutory basis for an auditor's liability is contained in Section 11(a), which states in part:

Section 11(a)

In case any part of the registration statement, when such part became effective, contained an untrue statement of a material fact or omitted to state a material fact required to be stated therein or necessary to make the statements therein not misleading, any person acquiring such security . . . may sue . . . every accountant . . . who has with his consent been named as having prepared or certified any part of the registration statement. . . .

In general, Section 11 is designed to protect potential investors by imposing liability on anyone who makes untrue statements or omits material facts in connection with a registration statement.

The Securities Exchange Act of 1934

Whereas the 1933 Act regulates the initial offering and sale of securities, the Securities Exchange Act of 1934 regulates the trading of previously issued securities. Under the 1934 Act, an entity must register securities with and report to the SEC if there are 500 or more shareholders or if assets exceed $3 million or more. In general, the Act's purpose is to promote adequate and accurate disclosure of material facts on a continuing basis.

The Registration and Periodic Reporting Process. Entities subject to the 1934 Act must register classes of traded securities and report selected information periodically. Of the registration forms available for different situations, Form 10-K is the most commonly used.

Form 10-K is filed by every entity for which another form is not specified, and entities that file Form 10-K also file Form 10-Q, a quarterly financial report. Entities which file registration forms other than Form 10-K are required to use specially designated forms for periodic reporting. However, all entities, regardless of the registration form filed, are required to file Form 8-K, a current report to be filed within fifteen days after the occurrence of a material event. Through these various reports, the 1934 Act effectively provides continuous disclosure to interested parties.

The Independent Auditor. An auditor's liability under the Securities Exchange Act of 1934 derives from his or her involvement in the disclosure process. Typically, an auditor is most involved with Forms 10-K and 10-Q; thus, most suits involving an auditor result from involvement with these forms.

Relevant Sections. Most suits against auditors under the 1934 Act relate to either Section 10(b) or Section 18.

Section 10(b)

It shall be unlawful for any person, directly or indirectly, by the use of any means or instrumentality of interstate commerce or of the mails, or of any facility of any national securities exchange —

(b) To use or employ, in connection with the purchase or sale of any security registered on a national securities exchange or any security not so registered, any manipulative or deceptive device or contrivance in contravention of such rules and regulations as the Commission may prescribe as necessary or appropriate in the public interest or for the protection of investors.

Under Section 10(b) the SEC issued Rule 10b-5, "Employment of Manipulative and Deceptive Devices," which states:

Rule 10b-5

It shall be unlawful for any person, directly or indirectly, by the use of any means or instrumentality of interstate commerce, or of the mails, or of any facility of any national securities exchange,

(a) to employ any device, scheme, or artifice to defraud,

(b) to make any untrue statement of a material fact or to omit to state a material fact necessary in order to make the statements made, in the light of the circumstances under which they were made, not misleading, or

(c) to engage in any act, practice, or course of business which operates or would operate as a fraud or deceit upon any person, in connection with the purchase or sale of any security.

In general, Section 10(b) and Rule 10b-5 are antifraud provisions designed to protect purchasers and sellers of securities against manipulation and deception by an auditor or any other person.

Section 18 of the 1934 Act is a disclosure provision which states in part:

Section 18

Any person who shall make or cause to be made any statement in any application, report, or document filed . . . which . . . was . . . false or misleading with respect to any material fact, shall be liable to any person (not knowing that such statement was false or misleading) who, in reliance upon such statement, shall have purchased or sold a security at a price which was affected by such statement, for damages caused by such reliance, unless the person sued shall prove that he acted in good faith and had no knowledge that such statement was false or misleading.

Section 18 is designed to protect purchasers and sellers from false and misleading statements.

STATUTORY LIABILITY

An auditor may be liable to securities purchasers under the Securities Act of 1933 for his or her involvement in the registration process and to securities purchasers and sellers under the Securities Exchange Act of 1934 for involvement in the disclosure process.

Liability: 1933 Act, Section 11

Under Section 11 of the 1933 Act, an auditor may be liable to any purchaser of securities identified in a registration statement, e.g., Form S-1. The purchaser's suit must be based upon a material false or misleading statement within the registration statement.

Figure 4-2 summarizes an auditor's statutory liability to securities purchasers under Section 11 of the 1933 Act. An auditor is liable for lack of reasonable care (ordinary negligence) and, in contrast with common law, also sustains the burden for proving either (1) the purchaser's damages or losses resulted from relying upon information other than the registration statement, or (2) the auditor acted in good faith. The latter is referred to as the "due diligence" defense and is typically the defense chosen, since proving reliance upon other information can be quite difficult. The plaintiff (purchaser) on the other hand sustains the burden of proving damage or loss and that financial statements are misstated or advice erroneous.

A particularly important case involving an auditor's liability under Section 11 was *Escott v. BarChris Construction Corp.* BarChris, which constructed recreational bowling centers, filed an S-1 registration statement on

March 30, 1961. Peat, Marwick, Mitchell & Co. had previously audited BarChris' 1960 financial statements. In connection with the S-1 filing, a subsequent events review (called an ''S-1 review'' by the SEC) covering the period from the balance sheet date to the registration statement's effective date was required.

Most of the S-1 review was performed by a senior accountant who was not yet a CPA, was inexperienced in the construction industry, and was supervising his first engagement as a senior accountant. The senior and his assistants failed to discover material transactions and events occurring in the subsequent period. On October 29, 1962, after registered securities (debentures) were offered and sold, BarChris filed for bankruptcy. Purchasers of the debentures subsequently filed suit against Peat, Marwick, Mitchell & Co. (among others) alleging the registration statement contained false and misleading statements. The auditors elected the due diligence defense.

The court ruled in favor of the purchasers, rejecting the auditors' due diligence defense. Pertinent sections of the opinion follow:

> There had been a material change for the worse in BarChris's financial position. That change was sufficiently serious so that the failure to disclose it made the 1960 figures misleading. (The senior) did not discover it. As far as results were concerned, his S-1 review was useless.
>
> Accountants should not be held to a standard higher than that recognized in their profession. I do not do so here. (The senior's) review did not come up to that standard. He did not take some of the steps which Peat, Marwick's written program prescribed. He did not spend an adequate amount of time on a task of this magnitude. Most important of all, he was too easily satisfied with glib answers to his inquiries.
>
> . . . the burden of proof is on Peat, Marwick. I find that the burden has not been satisfied. I conclude that Peat, Marwick has not established its due diligence defense.

The court's opinion not only established an auditor's potential liability for ordinary negligence under the 1933 Act, but also prompted *Statement on Auditing Procedure No. 47,* ''Subsequent Events'' (AU Sec. 560), discussed in Chapter 18.

Liability: 1934 Act, Section 10(b), Rule 10b-5

An auditor's liability under Section 10(b) is quite broad, since a plaintiff (purchaser or seller) may sue based upon any alleged false statement, whether the statement is filed with the SEC or not. Thus, even though, as explained in the following paragraphs, an auditor is not liable for ordinary negligence, there is significant exposure to liability under Section 10(b), since any form of statement may result in liability.

Figure 4-2 summarizes an auditor's statutory liability to security purchasers and sellers under Section 10(b) and Rule 10b-5. In contrast with Section 11 of the 1933 Act, an auditor is liable under the 1934 Act for lack of minimum care (gross negligence), not lack of reasonable care (ordinary negligence). The plaintiff purchaser or seller has the burden of proving damage or loss, that financial statements are misstated or advice erroneous, reliance on the statements or advice, and deficient auditor conduct.

The courts have been inconsistent on the issue of negligent conduct under Section 10(b) and Rule 10b-5. Although *Ernst & Ernst v. Hochfelder* (1976), a landmark U.S. Supreme Court case, helped to resolve the issue, the court chose not to address every aspect of the issue.

Ernst & Ernst (now Ernst and Whinney) were auditors for the First Securities Company of Chicago from 1946 through 1967. In 1968, Leston B. Nay, president and ninety-two percent stockholder of First Securities, left a suicide note stating that First Securities was bankrupt and describing his embezzlement from several escrow accounts. Nay perpetrated the embezzlement by inducing customers to invest in nonexistent high-yield accounts.

Customers were instructed to make checks payable to Nay, who through his "mail rule" restricted employees from opening mail addressed to him, even during his absence. Nay diverted the proceeds to his own use; thus the accounts were neither known nor available to Ernst & Ernst. Following Nay's suicide disclosure, investors sued Ernst & Ernst, claiming the firm was negligent in not discovering the mail rule. The investors reasoned that once discovered, the rule would have prevented a proper audit, prompting disclosure of the rule to the SEC and subsequent exposure of the embezzlement. Ernst & Ernst noted that the mail rule had no bearing on First Securities' internal control structure, which was claimed to be adequate otherwise. On the other hand, the plaintiff produced three expert witnesses, all of whom agreed the mail rule reflected a significant inadequacy in internal control.

The U.S. Supreme Court ruled in favor of Ernst & Ernst, concluding that the plaintiff had to prove intent to deceive, manipulate, or defraud, i.e., "scienter," in order for Ernst & Ernst to be held liable under Section 10(b) and Rule 10b-5. As a result of the *Hochfelder* decision, accountants are not liable under Section 10(b) and Rule 10b-5 in the absence of scienter, thus eliminating ordinary negligence as a basis for liability. However, the court left open the question of whether gross negligence can satisfy the scienter requirement, stating that:

> In certain areas of the law recklessness is considered to be a form of intentional conduct for purposes of imposing liability for some act. We need not address here the question whether, in some circumstances, reckless behavior is sufficient for civil liability under 10(b) and 10b-5.

Since the *Hochfelder* decision, liability has been imposed on accountants in some cases under Section 10(b) and Rule 10b-5 for reckless or willful misconduct. In one such case, *McLean v. Alexander,* the U.S. District court of Delaware held the accountant liable for recklessness, characterizing his conduct as "far more than mere negligence" but less than "a preconceived actual intent to defraud."

The issue of accountants' liability under Section 10(b) and Rule 10b-5 in the absence of intent remains unsettled. However, the *McLean* and other decisions subsequent to *Hochfelder* suggest that accountants are potentially liable for reckless misconduct, i.e., gross negligence.

Liability: 1934 Act, Section 18

An auditor's legal liability is narrower under Section 18 than under Section 10(b). A Section 18 action may be taken only with respect to alleged false statements filed with the SEC while a Section 10(b) action may be based on any alleged false statements, even those not filed.

Figure 4-2 summarizes an auditor's statutory liability to securities purchasers and sellers under Section 18. As under Section 10(b), an auditor is liable under Section 18 for lack of minimum care (gross negligence). The plaintiff purchaser or seller has the burden of proving damage or loss, that financial statements are misstated or advice erroneous, and reliance on the statements or advice. In contrast with Section 10(b), an auditor must prove due diligence, that is, that he or she acted in good faith and without knowledge that the statements were false or misleading.

CRIMINAL LIABILITY

An auditor can be held criminally liable under several federal statutes, including the Securities Act of 1933 (Section 24), the Securities Exchange Act of 1934 (Section 32(a)), the Federal False Statements Statute, and the Federal Mail Fraud Statute. Section 24 of the 1933 Act holds an auditor criminally liable for willfully making a false statement or omitting a material fact in connection with a registration statement. Section 32(a) of the 1934 Act also holds an auditor criminally liable for willfully making a false or misleading statement in reports filed under the Act. Criminal penalties against individuals under either section can be not more than $10,000, or five years' imprisonment, or both. Under the Federal False Statements Statute, criminal liability can result from any issue within a federal department's or agency's jurisdiction, and under the Federal Mail Fraud Statute, from any mailing or conspiracy to mail false financial statements.

Continental Vending

Over the years there have been only a few criminal liability cases involving auditors; the overwhelming majority of cases have been for civil liability. A particularly prominent criminal liability case involving auditors was decided in 1969, *United States v. Simon,* popularly known as the "Continental Vending" case, and involved both Section 32(a) of the 1934 Act and the Federal Mail Fraud Statute.

Harold Roth was president of Continental Vending and owner of about twenty-five percent of both Continental and its affiliate, Valley Commercial Corporation. From 1958 to 1962, Continental loaned over $3 million to Roth through Valley Commercial, whose operations were supervised by Roth. Because Roth could not repay Valley, Valley could not repay Continental. Thus, Roth pledged collateral, about eighty percent of which was Continental stock. Although the receivable from Valley was recorded by Continental, it was not collectible because Roth was unable to pay Valley, and the market value of Roth's collateral was less than the amount owed.

Bankruptcy followed, and the government sued the auditors, alleging that a footnote in Continental's September 30, 1962 financial statements did not adequately disclose that (1) Roth ultimately received money loaned by Continental to Valley and (2) Roth's collateral consisted largely of Continental securities.

The auditors argued that they had followed generally accepted accounting principles and thus were free of criminal liability. However, the court ruled in the government's favor, stating that improper activities should be disclosed. In part the court stated:

> But it simply cannot be true that an accountant is under no duty to disclose what he knows when he has reason to believe that, to a material extent, a corporation is being operated not to carry out its business in the interests of all the stockholders but for the private benefit of its president.

Further, regarding an auditor's obligations, the court stated:

> Generally accepted accounting principles instruct an accountant what to do in the usual case when he has no reason to doubt that the affairs of the corporation are being honestly conducted. Once he has reason to believe that this basic assumption is false, an entirely different situation confronts him.

Thus, the court effectively ruled that the standard of an auditor's obligation should extend beyond generally accepted accounting principles and should be based on disclosure, i.e., "fair" presentation. The auditors were convicted of willfully making a false or misleading statement and for using the mails to distribute false, misleading financial statements, although they subsequently received a presidential pardon.

As noted earlier, Continental Vending is one of only a few criminal liability cases involving auditors. Thus, no generalizations or conclusions can be drawn about an auditor's potential criminal liability. Unfortunately, generalizations and conclusions will require more criminal cases.

Racketeer Influenced and Corrupt Organizations Act

In addition to the federal statutes listed earlier, an independent auditor can also be held liable under the Racketeer Influenced and Corrupt Organizations Act (RICO), passed originally as part of the Organized Crime Control Act of 1970. The intent of the rather broadly worded RICO Act was to curtail the movement of organized crime into legitimate business. Although RICO is a federal criminal statute, a last-minute change by Congress added a civil provision that has been used widely against legitimate businesses and professionals, including independent accountants.

Rather than define the nebulous term "organized crime," Congress chose to list the acts typically associated with organized crimes, such as murder, arson, and extortion, and other acts such as mail fraud, wire fraud, and fraud in the sale of securities, all of which were growing in prominence in the late 1960s. Although targeted toward organized crime, RICO has greatly impacted the professions because the Act is broadly worded, defines a "pattern of racketeering activity" as two or more accusations (not convictions) within a 10-year period, and contains a provision that permits private parties, such as stockholders, to bring civil suits that include treble damages and attorneys' fees. As Congressman Frederick C. Boucher (D.-Va.) has stated, ". . . the result of combining this broadly worded statute with the unfettered use made of it by private parties has been an explosion of RICO treble-damage claims in cases against people Congress never intended to be victimized by this powerful weapon."[4] Among those who may be victimized are professionals, such as certified public accountants, who are not even remotely connected with organized crime. In fact, through late 1985, RICO had affected most of the national public accounting firms, and no less than twenty-two suits had been filed against small accounting firms throughout the United States.[5]

In 1985, the U.S. Supreme Court, in a 5–4 decision *(Sedima v. Imrex Company),* ruled that RICO's civil provisions could be applied to virtually any commercial dispute, which effectively increased the potential exposure of professional accountants, since suits against auditors typically involve a commercial dispute. However, the Court also noted that RICO has been legally applied to defendants not intended by Congress, and that any correction of the Act's defects must lie with Congress.

---

[4]F. C. Boucher, "Why Civil RICO Must Be Reformed," *Journal of Accountancy* (December, 1985), p. 103.

[5]L. Berton. "Small CPA Firms' Liability Rates Soar," *The Wall Street Journal* (November 19, 1985), p. 6.

COPING WITH POTENTIAL LIABILITY

An auditor sustains the risk of litigation on virtually every engagement. Thus, haphazard professional conduct is foolhardy; litigation by clients or third parties is always a potential danger.

The following briefly describes several precautions an auditor should consider in an attempt to minimize the risk of potential litigation.

Engagement Letters

Both *Maryland Casualty Co. v. Jonathon Cook* and *1136 Tenants' Corp. v. Max Rothenberg & Co.*, discussed earlier, illustrate the importance of engagement letters. Among other things, engagement letters (1) provide an explicit agreement of professional services expected and intended and (2) serve to eliminate, or at least minimize, any misunderstandings between auditor and client regarding the scope of the engagement. As a result, an engagement letter should be prepared for every professional engagement, audit or otherwise. Engagement letters are illustrated in Chapter 6.

GAAS

Generally accepted auditing standards are the measures of quality, the professional guidelines for audit engagements. Nevertheless, some courts have ruled that auditors should reach for a higher standard of care, a standard assuring fairness to all users. It is not clear whether courts will in the future require a higher standard. However, it is clear the courts will not accept a lower standard of care. Today, generally accepted auditing standards are the model. The standards are discussed more fully in Chapter 5.

Quality Control

Quality control is the vehicle through which an auditor attempts to apply the same standard of care to all professional engagements, i.e., a "measuring stick" designed to minimize substandard performance on individual engagements. Obviously, the stronger a system of quality control, the less likely a substandard engagement.

As a result of the AICPA Quality Control Standards Committee's *Statement on Quality Control Standards No. 1,* "System of Quality Control for a CPA Firm" (1979), a system of quality control is required of all firms, regardless of size. This statement describes nine elements of quality control which, in addition to *Statement on Auditing Standards No. 25,* "The Relationship of GAAS to Quality Control Standards" (1979), was discussed in Chapter 1.

Balancing Practice Development and Quality Control

Unlimited growth does not necessarily yield a successful audit practice. In fact, it can lead to haphazard performance and potential legal action. Practice development should not flourish at the expense of quality control. New clients should be carefully scrutinized for integrity, and competent professional staff must be available to properly discharge the responsibilities of both new and continuing engagements.

Defensive Auditing

The purpose of an external audit is to issue an opinion on financial information. That opinion, however, is dependent upon the quality and quantity of audit evidence obtained. Defensive auditing implies that an auditor be mindful of potential litigation when conducting an engagement, thereby clearly documenting the basis for all audit decisions and conclusions. It is one thing to obtain oral responses from management regarding questionable transactions, and quite another to document corroborative support for management's responses.

Closely related to defensive auditing is the awareness that some questions relate to the law and not to accounting or auditing. An auditor should retain legal counsel for consultation when necessary. Auditors are generally neither trained nor experienced in the law, and therefore should reserve judgment until legal counsel is consulted.

Professional Liability Insurance

In many instances over the years, independent accountants have been unsuccessful in coping with legal liability, resulting in highly publicized court cases and substantial settlements against public accounting firms. In fact, a recent study by the House Subcommittee on Oversight and Investigations indicates that since 1980, the "Big 8" public accounting firms have paid nearly $180 million in out-of-court settlements related to independent audits.[6] As a result of the large settlements involving the large national firms, malpractice insurance rates are skyrocketing for all firms, and insurance companies are becoming increasingly reluctant to underwrite professional liability insurance for independent accountants. For example, insurance premium increases of 200 to 400 percent in one year are not uncommon, and the number of insurance companies offering liability insurance to small and medium-size firms has dropped from almost a dozen in 1980 to three in 1986. Even Lloyd's

---

[6]S. H. Collins, "Professional Liability: The Situation Worsens," *Journal of Accountancy* (November, 1985), p. 57.

of London, the major insurer of the national public accounting firms, has threatened to drop coverage unless awards against accountants are restrained.[7] In short, the soaring malpractice suits once associated primarily with the medical profession have now spread to public accounting.

In response to the high costs and diminishing sources of accountants' liability insurance, the AICPA established a special committee to consider the nature and extent of accountants' liability in general, and potential remedies to the explosion in liability suits in particular. Among the profession's more far-reaching proposals has been a movement to seek Congressional legislation that would limit the liability of independent accountants in individual cases. This proposal is not without precedent. For example, the Atomic Energy Act of 1954 limits liability for nuclear accidents to $650 million, and more compelling, the liability of accountants in some foreign countries is limited by statute.

SUMMARY

Over the past two decades, independent auditors and other professionals have become increasingly vulnerable to legal liability. In all likelihood, this trend will continue.

In any civil liability case involving auditors, several issues are relevant, including: (1) the source of law (common or statutory), (2) the identity of the plaintiff, (3) potential liability, and (4) who sustains the burden of proving (a) damage or loss, (b) that financial statements are misstated or advice erroneous, (c) reliance on financial statements or advice, and (d) deficient auditor conduct. Concluding upon these issues depends on the facts involved in individual cases.

Under common law, an independent auditor may be liable to clients, primary beneficiaries, foreseen beneficiaries, and other foreseeable third parties. Under Section 11 of the Securities Act of 1933, an auditor may be liable to purchasers of securities, and under Sections 10b and 18 of the Securities Exchange Act of 1934, an auditor may be liable to purchasers of securities, sellers, or both.

An independent auditor's criminal liability extends from several federal (and state) statutes, the most prominent being: Section 24 of the 1933 Act, Section 32(a) of the 1934 Act, and the Federal False Statements and Mail Fraud Statutes. In addition, auditors may be held liable under the Racketeer Influenced and Corrupt Organizations Act. Few cases have been decided regarding an auditor's criminal liability; however, it is clear that criminal penalties have been and may continue to be levied.

---

[7]L. Berton. "Small CPA Firms' Liability Rates Soar," *The Wall Street Journal* (November 19, 1985), p. 6.

Given today's legal environment, auditors should take precautions to minimize potential legal exposure, such as: (1) preparing engagement letters for all audit and accounting-related engagements, (2) adhering to GAAS, (3) promoting quality control through a firm's practice, (4) balancing practice development and quality control, and (5) documenting all audit decisions and conclusions. In short, an auditor should practice defensive auditing. Despite the above precautions, however, the risk of legal liability cannot be totally eliminated. Professional liability insurance may protect a practitioner from devastating financial losses, but such coverage is becoming increasingly expensive and difficult to obtain.

APPENDIX
OTHER SIGNIFICANT LEGAL LIABILITY CASES

Following are brief descriptions of several significant legal liability cases not discussed specifically within the chapter.

Smith v. London Assurance Corp. (1905) — Auditors were found liable to their client for breach of contract for failure to discover an embezzlement of a large sum of money by one of the client's employees. The court noted that:

— Public accountants constitute a skilled professional class and are therefore subject to the same risks of liability for negligence in the practice of their profession as are members of other skilled professions. The degree of skill implied by one who holds himself or herself out as a professional is that commonly possessed by others in the same employment.
— The contract expressly called for certain auditing procedures that were not actually carried out with reasonable care and diligence.

State Street Trust Co. v. Ernst (1938) — Auditors examined accounts receivable but failed to discover the fact that the receivables were overstated because many of the accounts were uncollectible. The court noted that:

— An auditor may be liable to third parties for fraud even where there is no deliberate or active fraud on the auditor's part. The court indicated that fraud on the part of the auditor may be inferred from any or all of the following:

▲ Certifying as true to the knowledge of the auditor when he or she possessed insufficient knowledge as a basis for the certification
▲ Reckless misstatement
▲ Flimsy grounds for an opinion
▲ A failure to investigate doubtful facts or circumstances
▲ Heedlessness and reckless disregard of consequences.

National Surety Corp. v. Lybrand (1939) — The auditors failed to discover embezzlements of cash that were concealed through lapping and kiting practices. The court indicated that:

> — The contract for services explicitly required a determination of the client's cash position and therefore implied that certain auditing procedures should be undertaken.
> — Expert testimony established that ordinary professional care and the use of proper auditing methods would have identified well-known danger signals and that follow-up inquiries would have led to discovery of the embezzlement.

United States v. White (1941) — The auditor was convicted of criminal fraud under Section 17 of the Securities Act of 1933 for his failure to disclose several instances of questionable accounting practices in connection with a registration statement. The court expressed the following thought with respect to the sufficiency of evidence in a criminal case:

> — Items of questionable accounting, which taken individually do not demonstrate knowledge of falsity, may acquire greater significance as proof when considered together.

Speed v. Transamerica Corp. (1951) — This case did not involve auditors. Nevertheless, it is of significance because of the standard that the court used to evaluate the usefulness of financial information. The case involved an offer by majority shareholders to buy out the minority interest. Although the adequacy of generally accepted accounting principles was not a major issue in this case, the court's treatment of a specific generally accepted accounting principle related to inventory valuation is significant. The court found that:

> — Majority shareholders had violated Section 10, Rule 10b-5, of the 1934 Act by failing to disclose that the current value of inventory was significantly higher than historical cost, which was reported in the financial statements in accordance with generally accepted accounting principles.

United States v. Benjamin (1964) — The auditor was convicted in a criminal action under Section 24 of the 1933 Act for his failure to exercise due diligence that would have revealed misrepresentations in pro forma financial statements used in conjunction with sales of unregistered securities. The court stated:

> In our complex society the accountant's certificate and the lawyer's opinion can be instruments for inflicting pecuniary loss more potent than the chisel or the crowbar. Of course, Congress did not mean that any mistake of law or misstatement of fact should subject an attorney or an accountant

to criminal liability simply because more skilled practitioners would not have made them. But Congress equally could not have intended that men holding themselves out as members of these ancient professions should be able to escape criminal liability on a plea of ignorance when they have shut their eyes to what was plainly to be seen or have represented a knowledge they knew they did not possess.

Fischer v. Kletz (1967) — In this case, which involved actions under common law and Section 10b, Rule 10b-5, and Section 18 of the 1934 Act, the court noted that:

— An auditor has a duty to anyone still relying on his or her report to disclose subsequently discovered errors in the report. This duty exists regardless of the auditor's lack of financial interest in any transactions to which the information relates. The obligation arises because of the auditor's special relationship that provides access to the information.

Gerstle v. Gamble-Skogmo (1969) — This case, which was an action under Section 14 of the 1934 Act, involved the merger of General Outdoor Advertising Co., Inc., into Gamble-Skogmo. The case did not involve auditors. Although the following finding was not central to the case, it is further evidence of the courts' willingness to challenge the adequacy of generally accepted accounting principles. The court found that:

— Proxy statements were misleading because they failed to disclose the appreciation in value of certain fixed assets that management intended to sell after the merger.

SEC v. Bangor Punta Corp. (1974) — This case did not involve auditors. The action was brought under Section 11 of the 1933 Act and involved a registration statement pertaining to an offer to exchange Bangor Punta stock for stock of Piper Aircraft Co. The court indicated that:

— The registration statement was false and misleading because it reflected an investment in a railroad at a book value that was approximately four times the current market value.
— Any differences between generally accepted accounting principles and fair disclosure in a prospectus must be resolved in favor of the disclosure requirements of the securities laws.

Herzfeld v. Laventhol, Kreckstein, Horwath & Horwath (1974) — This case involved a private placement of securities by a corporation engaged in real estate syndication. The auditors were found liable under Section 10b, Rule 10b-5, of the 1934 Act for failure to fully disclose the facts and circumstances underlying their qualified opinion. The court noted that:

— The accountant's professional duty to investors cannot be fulfilled by merely following generally accepted accounting principles.

— The financial reports must fairly present the true financial position to the "untutored eye of an ordinary investor."

— An auditor's qualified opinion should disclose the reasoning and facts which prompted it.

United States v. C.W. Randell, et al. (1974) — In this case, auditors were found criminally liable by a jury under Section 32 of the 1934 Act for willfully and knowingly making false and misleading statements with respect to material facts in a proxy statement. In instructing the jury, the judge stated that:

> Knowing and willful action can be inferred from an auditor's deliberately closing his eyes to the obvious or from recklessly stating as fact matters of which he was ignorant.

United States v. Natelli (1975) — As a result of failing to disclose uncollectible receivable write-offs, auditors were held criminally liable under Section 32 of the 1934 Act. In this case, commonly referred to as National Student Marketing, the court held that criminal liability can be imposed under Section 32 when an auditor willfully and knowingly conceals material prior errors.

Fund of Funds Ltd. v. Arthur Andersen (1982) — In the late 1970s, the Fund of Funds mutual investment company, a client of Arthur Andersen, diversified its investment portfolio to include large investments in oil- and gas-producing properties purchased under an agreement with King Resources Company, also an Arthur Andersen client. Importantly, some of Andersen's audit personnel were assigned to both the Fund of Funds and the King Resources Company audits.

While auditing King Resources, Andersen auditors discovered that King's profits on sales to Fund of Funds were actually higher than on sales of similar oil and gas properties to other King customers; however King management was not notified. When Fund of Funds management discovered the disparity sometime later, Fund of Funds sued Andersen, contending that Andersen had a duty either to notify management or to resign from one of the engagements. Andersen contended that the Code of Professional Ethics precluded divulging confidential client information. In the largest settlement ever made against a public accounting firm in the U.S., the court awarded $80 million plus accrued interest to Fund of Funds' shareholders.

Cenco, Inc. v. Seidman & Seidman (1982) — New management at Cenco sued Seidman & Seidman for failing to uncover a $25 million inventory fraud perpetrated by Cenco's former management. In a three-judge decision, the U.S. Court of Appeals for the Seventh Circuit in Chicago upheld a lower federal court, ruling that Seidman & Seidman was not negligent for failing to uncover inventory fraud, since "auditors aren't detectives hired to ferret out fraud," and the fraud was quite difficult to detect because former management turned the company "into an engine of theft against outsiders."

Cedars of Lebanon Hospital Corp. v. Touche Ross (1982) — The hospital and its board of directors brought suit against Touche Ross for failing to detect an embezzlement scheme — in this case, a collusive fraud — perpetrated by the hospital's administrator. A Circuit Court of Dade County, Florida, found that Touche Ross was not guilty, and also awarded Touche Ross legal and accounting fees and $500,000 in punitive damages from Cedars of Lebanon Hospital. In a *Journal of Accountancy* News Report (May, 1982, page 12) commenting on both *Cedars of Lebanon Hospital Corp. v. Touche Ross* and on *Cenco, Inc. v. Seidman & Seidman,* the editors observed that the two cases ". . . may indicate a change in the public perception of [auditors' liability] for detecting management fraud, according to major accounting firms."

REFERENCES

Causey, D. Y., Jr. *Duties and Liabilities of Public Accountants,* rev. ed. Homewood, Ill.: Dow Jones-Irwin, 1982.

Chazen, C., and K. I. Solomon, "The Art of Defensive Auditing." *Journal of Accountancy* (October, 1975), pp. 66–71.

Collins, S. H. "Professional Liability: The Situation Worsens," *Journal of Accountancy* (November, 1985), pp. 57–66.

Fiflis, T. J. "Current Problems of Accountants' Responsibilities to Third Parties." *Vanderbilt Law Review* (January, 1975), pp. 31–145.

Gormley, R. J. *The Law of Accountants and Auditors: Rights, Duties, and Liabilities.* New York: Warren, Gorham & Lamont, 1981.

Hampson, J. J. "Accountants' Liability — The Significance of *Hochfelder.*" *Journal of Accountancy* (December, 1976), 69–74.

Isbell, D. B. "The Continental Vending Case: Lessons for the Profession." *Journal of Accountancy* (August, 1970), pp. 33–40.

———, and D. R. Carmichael. "Disclaimers and Liability — The Rhode Island Trust Case." *Journal of Accountancy* (April, 1973), pp. 37–42.

Jaenicke, H. R. *The Effect of Litigation on Independent Auditors, Research Study No. 1.* New York: Commission on Auditors' Responsibilities, 1978.

Levy, S. *Accountants' Legal Responsibility*. New York: American Institute of Accountants, 1954.

Minow, N. N. "Accountants' Liability and the Litigation Explosion." *Journal of Accountancy* (September, 1984), pp. 70–86.

Peat, Marwick, Mitchell & Co. *Research Opportunities in Auditing*. New York: Peat, Marwick, Mitchell & Co., 1976.

Reiling, H. B., and R. A. Taussig. "Recent Liability Cases — Implications for Accountants." *Journal of Accountancy* (September, 1970), pp. 39–53.

Schlesinger, M. "The Hochfelder Decision: How It Will Effect Future Malpractice Suits against Accountants." *Practical Accountant* (September–October, 1976), pp. 77–81.

Schnepper, J. A. "The Accountant's Liability under Rule 10b-5 and Section 10(b) of the Securities Exchange Act of 1934: The Hole in Hochfelder." *The Accounting Review* (July, 1977), pp. 653–657.

Schultz, J. J., Jr., and K. Pany. "The Independent Auditor's Civil Liability — An Overview." *The Accounting Review* (April, 1980), pp. 319–326.

Skousen, K. F. *An Introduction to the SEC*, 3d ed. Cincinnati: South-Western Publishing Co., 1983.

Slavin, N. S. "The Elimination of 'Scienter' in Determining the Auditor's Statutory Liability." *The Accounting Review* (April, 1977), pp. 360–368.

Stein, A. M., and J. M. Wolosky. "Accountant's Liability: An Overview of Your Current Exposure." *The Practical Accountant* (June, 1985), pp. 33–40.

Stoppelman, J. S. "Accountants and Rule 10b-5: After Hochfelder." *Journal of Accountancy* (August, 1977), pp. 49–54.

QUESTIONS

1. What impact did the McKesson & Robbins, Inc., case have upon the profession?
2. Identify the major issues involved in a civil action against an auditor.
3. Distinguish ordinary negligence, gross negligence, and fraud.
4. In general, what elements must be proved by various parties to a legal liability case involving auditors?
5. What is the auditor's common law liability to clients? What is the basis for liability?
6. What lesson to auditors emerges from both *Maryland Casualty Co. v. Jonathon Cook* and *1136 Tenants' Corp. v. Max Rothenberg & Co.?*
7. Briefly describe the facts in *Ultramares Corp. v. Touche* and cite the significance of the case.
8. Summarize an auditor's common law liability to primary beneficiaries.
9. Explain how primary beneficiaries differ from foreseen beneficiaries. Give examples.
10. What are the majority and minority views on an auditor's liability to foreseen beneficiaries?
11. Summarize the auditor's common law liability to other foreseeable third parties.
12. Describe the origin, function, and general structure of the Securities and Exchange Commission.

13. In what ways is an auditor involved with a registration statement under the Securities Act of 1933?
14. What is the purpose of Section 11 of the Securities Act of 1933?
15. What are the purposes of Section 10(b) and Rule 10b-5 and Section 18 of the Securities Exchange Act of 1934?
16. Describe an auditor's alternative defenses under Section 11 of the Securities Act of 1933.
17. What lessons does *Escott v. BarChris Construction Corp.* offer with regard to an inexperienced audit staff?
18. Summarize an auditor's statutory liability to securities purchasers and sellers under Section 10(b) and Rule 10b-5 of the Securities Exchange Act of 1934.
19. How does the burden of proof under Section 18 of the Securities Exchange Act of 1934 differ from that under Section 10(b) and Rule 10b-5?
20. What is the significance to auditors of Section 24 of the Securities Act of 1933 and Section 32(a) of the Securities Exchange Act of 1934?
21. What is the significance of *United States v. Simon* to an independent auditor?
22. Identify several precautions an auditor might take to avoid litigation.

MULTIPLE CHOICE QUESTIONS (AICPA Adapted)

1. Martin Corporation orally engaged Humm & Dawson to audit its year-end financial statements. The engagement was to be completed within two months after the close of Martin's fiscal year for a fixed fee of $2,500. Under these circumstances what obligation is assumed by Humm & Dawson?

   a. None, because the contract is unenforceable since it is not in writing.
   b. An implied promise to exercise reasonable standards of competence and care.
   c. An implied obligation to take extraordinary steps to discover all defalcations.
   d. The obligation of an insurer of its work which is liable without fault.

2. Winslow Manufacturing, Inc., sought at $200,000 loan from National Lending Corporation. National Lending insisted that audited financial statements be submitted before it would extend credit. Winslow agreed to this and also agreed to pay the audit fee. An audit was performed by an independent CPA who submitted an audit report to Winslow to be used solely for the purpose of negotiating a loan from National. National, upon reviewing the audited financial statements, decided in good faith not to extend the credit desired. Certain ratios, which as a matter of policy were used by National in reaching its decision, were deemed too low. Winslow used copies of the audited financial statements to obtain credit elsewhere. It was subsequently learned that the CPA, despite the exercise of reasonable care, had failed to discover a sophisticated embezzlement scheme by Winslow's chief accountant. Under these circumstances, what liability does the CPA have?

   a. The CPA is liable to third parties who extended credit to Winslow on the basis of the audited financial statements.
   b. The CPA is liable to Winslow to repay the audit fee because credit was not extended by National.

c. The CPA is liable to Winslow for any losses Winslow suffered as a result of failure to discover the embezzlement.

d. The CPA is not liable to any of the parties.

3. Major, Major & Sharpe, CPAs, are the auditors of MacLain Industries. In connection with the public offering of $10 million of MacLain securities, Major expressed an unqualified opinion as to the financial statements. Subsequent to the offering, certain misstatements and omissions were revealed. Major has been sued by the purchasers of the stock offered pursuant to the registration statement which included the financial statements audited by Major. In the ensuing lawsuit by the MacLain investors, Major will be able to avoid liability if

a. The errors and omissions were caused primarily by MacLain.

b. It can be shown that at least some of the investors did not actually read the audited financial statements.

c. It can prove due diligence in the audit of the financial statements of MacLain.

d. MacLain had expressly assumed any liability in connection with the public offering.

4. Donalds & Company, CPAs, audited the financial statements included in the annual report submitted by Markum Securities, Inc., to the Securities and Exchange Commission. The audit was improper in several respects. Markum is now insolvent and unable to satisfy the claims of its customers. The customers have instituted legal action against Donalds based upon Section 10b and Rule 10b-5 of the Securities Exchange Act of 1934. Which of the following is likely to be Donalds' best defense?

a. They did **not** intentionally certify false financial statements.

b. Section 10b does **not** apply to them.

c. They were **not** in privity of contract with the creditors.

d. Their engagement letter specifically disclaimed any liability to any party which resulted from Markum's fraudulent conduct.

5. If a CPA firm is being sued for common law fraud by a third party on the basis of materially false financial statements, which of the following is the best defense which the accountants could assert?

a. Lack of privity.

b. Lack of reliance.

c. A disclaimer contained in the engagement letter.

d. Contributory negligence on the part of the client.

6. Under the Securities Act of 1933, an accountant may be held liable for any materially false or misleading financial statements, including an omission of a material fact therefrom, provided the purchaser

a. Proves reliance on the registration statement or prospectus.

b. Proves negligence or fraud on the part of the accountant.

c. Brings suit within four years after the security is offered to the public.

d. Proves a false statement or omission existed.

7. Which of the following statements concerning the scope of Section 10(b) of the Securities Exchange Act of 1934 is correct?

a. In order to come within its scope, a transaction must have taken place on a national stock exchange.

b. It applies exclusively to securities of corporations registered under the Securities Exchange Act of 1934.

c. There is an exemption from its application for securities registered under the Securities Act of 1933.

d. It applies to purchases as well as sales of securities in interstate commerce.

8. Sylvia Martinson is a duly licensed CPA. One of her clients is suing her for negligence, alleging that she failed to meet generally accepted auditing standards in the current year's audit, thereby failing to discover large thefts of inventory. Under the circumstances:

a. Martinson is not bound by generally accepted auditing standards unless she is a member of the AICPA.

b. Martinson's failure to meet generally accepted auditing standards would result in liability.

c. Generally accepted auditing standards do **not** currently cover the procedures which must be used in verifying inventory for balance sheet purposes.

d. If Martinson failed to meet generally accepted auditing standards, she would undoubtedly be found to have committed the tort of fraud.

9. The traditional common law rules regarding accountants' liability to third parties for negligence:

a. Remain substantially unchanged since their inception.

b. Were more stringent than the rules currently applicable.

c. Are of relatively minor importance to the accountant.

d. Have been substantially changed at both the federal and state levels.

10. A third-party purchaser of securities has brought suit based upon the Securities Act of 1933 against a CPA firm. The CPA firm will prevail in the suit brought by the third party even though the CPA firm issued an unqualified opinion on materially incorrect financial statements if:

a. The CPA firm was unaware of the defects.

b. The third-party plaintiff had **no** direct dealings with the CPA firm.

c. The CPA firm can show that the third-party plaintiff did **not** rely upon the audited financial statements.

d. The CPA firm can establish that it was not guilty of actual fraud.

11. An investor, seeking to recover stock market losses from a CPA firm on the basis of an unqualified opinion on financial statements which accompanied a registration statement, must establish that:

a. There was a false statement or omission of material fact contained in the audited financial statements.

b. He or she relied upon the financial statements.

c. The CPA firm did not act in good faith.

d. The CPA firm would have discovered the false statement or omission if it had exercised due care in its examination.

12. A CPA is subject to criminal liability if the CPA:

   a. Refuses to turn over the working papers to the client.
   b. Performs an audit in a negligent manner.
   c. Willfully omits a material fact required to be stated in a registration statement.
   d. Willfully breaches the contract with the client.

PROBLEMS

4-1   Millard & Hans, CPAs, have been engaged for several years by Happy Toys, Inc., to perform the "usual" examination of its financial statements and provide other accounting services. The understanding was oral, and the fee was based on an annual retainer.

Millard & Hans regularly prepared unaudited quarterly financial statements and examined and reported on Happy Toys' annual financial statements. During the current year's examination, Happy Toys decided to go public and requested that Millard & Hans assist in preparing all the necessary financial statements and other financial information and supply the independent auditor's reports as necessary for inclusion in a registration statement to be filed with the Securities and Exchange Commission (SEC). Millard & Hans are independent in accordance with SEC rules and regulations. Millard & Hans complied with Happy Toys' request and subsequently submitted a bill to Happy Toys for $15,000 for the additional work performed in connection with the SEC filing. Happy Toys refused to pay, claiming the additional work was a part of the "usual" engagement and was covered by the annual retainer.

Required:
Discuss how Millard & Hans can avoid similar problems in the future with Happy Toys and other clients.

(AICPA Adapted)

4-2   Barney & Co., CPAs, has been engaged to perform an examination of the financial statements of Waldo, Inc., for several years. The terms of the engagement have been set out in an annual engagement letter signed by both parties. The terms of each engagement included the following:

> This being an ordinary examination, it is not primarily or specifically designed, and cannot be relied upon, to disclose defalcations and other similar irregularities, although their discovery may result.

Three years ago Harold Zamp, head cashier of Waldo and an expert in computer operations, devised a previously unheard of method of embezzling funds from his employer. At first Zamp's thefts were small, but increased as time went on. During the current year, before Barney began working on the engagement, the thefts became so large that serious variances in certain accounts came to the attention of the controller. When questioned about the variances, Zamp confessed and explained his unique embezzlement scheme. Investigation revealed that Zamp had stolen $257,550. Zamp has no assets with which to repay the thefts.

Waldo submitted its claim for $257,550 to Multi-State Surety Company in accordance with the terms of the fidelity bond covering Zamp. Fulfilling its surety obligation, Multi-State paid the claim and now seeks to recover its losses from Barney.

In defense, Barney asserts the following:

a. Multi-State has no standing in court to sue because it was not a party to the contract (i.e., lacking in privity) between Barney and its client, Waldo.

b. Even if Multi-State had the standing to sue, its claim should be dismissed because Barney's engagements with Waldo did not specifically include the discovery of defalcations other than those discoveries which might arise in the process of an ordinary examination.

Required:
Discuss the validity of each of Barney's defenses.

(AICPA Adapted)

4.3   Charlotte Worthington, the founding and senior partner of a successful and respected CPA firm, is a highly competent practitioner who always emphasizes high professional standards. One of the policies of the firm is that all reports by members or staff be submitted to Worthington for review.

Recently, Arthur Craft, a junior partner in the firm, received a phone call from Herbert Flack, a close personal friend. Flack informed Craft that he, his family, and some friends were planning to create a corporation to engage in various land development ventures, that various members of the family are presently in a partnership (Flack Ventures) which holds some land and other assets, and that the partnership would contribute all of its assets to the new corporation, and the corporation would assume the liabilities of the partnership.

Flack asked Craft to prepare a balance sheet of the partnership that he could show to his family who were in the partnership and friends to determine whether they might have an interest in joining in the formation and financing of the new corporation. Flack said he had the partnership general ledger in front of him and proceeded to read to Craft the names of the accounts and their balances at the end of the latest month. Craft took the notes he made during the telephone conversation with Flack, classified and organized the data into a conventional balance sheet, and had his secretary type the balance sheet and an accompanying letter on firm stationery. He did not consult Worthington on this matter nor submit his work to her for review.

The transmittal letter stated: "We have reviewed the books and records of Flack Ventures, a partnership, and have prepared the attached balance sheet at March 31, 1989. We did not perform an examination in conformity with generally accepted auditing standards, and therefore do not express an opinion on the accompanying balance sheet." The balance sheet was prominently marked "unaudited." Craft signed the letter and instructed his secretary to send it to Flack.

Required:
What legal problems are suggested by these facts? Explain.

(AICPA Adapted)

4-4   Jackson, a junior staff member of an accounting firm, began the audit of the Bosco Corporation which manufactured and sold expensive watches. In the middle of the audit Jackson quit. The accounting firm hired another person to continue the audit of Bosco. Due to the changeover and the time pressure to finish the audit, the firm violated certain generally accepted auditing standards when it did not follow adequate procedures with respect to the physical inventory. Had the proper procedures been used during the examination the auditors would have discovered that watches worth more than $20,000 were missing. The employee who was stealing the watches was able to steal an additional $30,000 worth before the thefts were discovered six months after the completion of the audit.

Required:
Discuss the legal problems of the accounting firm as a result of these events.

(AICPA Adapted)

4-5   Factory Discount Prices, Inc., is a chain store discount outlet which sells women's clothes. It has an excessively large inventory on hand and is in urgent need of additional cash. It is bordering on bankruptcy, especially if the inventory has to be liquidated by sale to other stores instead of to the public. Furthermore, about 15 percent of the inventory is not resalable except at a drastic discount below cost. Faced with this financial crisis, Factory approached several of the manufacturers from whom it purchases. Dexter Apparel, Inc., one of the parties approached, indicated a willingness to loan Factory $300,000 under certain conditions. First, Factory was to submit audited financial statements for the express purpose of providing the correct financial condition of the company. The loan was to be predicated upon these financial statements and Factory's engagement letter with Dunn & Clark, its CPAs, expressly indicated this.

The second condition insisted upon by Dexter was that it obtain a secured position in all unsecured inventory, accounts, and other related personal property. In due course a security agreement was executed and a financing statement properly filed and recorded.

In preparing the financial statements, Factory valued the inventory at cost, which was approximately $100,000 over the current fair market value. Also, Factory failed to disclose two secured creditors to whom substantial amounts were owed and who took priority over Dexter's security interests.

Dunn & Clark issued an unqualified opinion on the financial statements of Factory which they believed were fairly presented.

Six months later Factory filed a voluntary bankruptcy petition. Dexter received $125,000 as its share of the bankrupt's estate. It is suing Dunn & Clark for the loss of $175,000. Dunn & Clark deny liability on the basis of lack of privity and lack of negligence.

Required:
Answer the following, setting forth reasons for any conclusions stated: Is Dexter entitled to recover its loss from Dunn & Clark?

(AICPA Adapted)

4-6   Meglow Corporation manufactured women's dresses and blouses. Because its cash position was deteriorating, Meglow sought a loan from Busch Factors. Busch had previously extended $25,000 credit to Meglow but refused to lend any additional money without obtaining copies of Meglow's audited financial statements.

Meglow contacted the CPA firm of Watkins, Winslow & Watkins to perform the audit. In arranging for the examination, Meglow clearly indicated that its purpose was to satisfy Busch Factors as to the corporation's sound financial condition and thus to obtain an additional loan of $50,000. Watkins, Winslow & Watkins accepted the engagement, performed the examination in a negligent manner, and rendered an unqualified auditor's opinion. If reasonable care had been exercised in performing the examination, the financial statements would have been found to be misleading.

Meglow submitted the audited financial statements to Busch Factors and obtained an additional loan of $35,000. Busch refused to lend more than that amount. After several other factors also refused, Meglow finally was able to persuade Maxwell Department Stores, one of its customers, to lend the additional $15,000. Maxwell relied upon the financial statements examined by Watkins, Winslow & Watkins.

Meglow is now in bankruptcy, and Busch seeks to collect from Watkins, Winslow & Watkins the $60,000 it loaned Meglow. Maxwell seeks to recover from Watkins, Winslow & Watkins the $15,000 it loaned Meglow.

Required:
1. Will Busch recover? Explain.
2. Will Maxwell recover? Explain.

(AICPA Adapted)

4-7   Jones, CPA, was engaged by Dee Co. to examine and report on its financial statements which were required by the National Bank to accompany Dee's application for a $50,000 loan. Jones was informed that the primary purpose of the financial statements was to obtain the bank loan. National Bank previously had loaned Dee Co. $100,000 for five years at 12 percent with the typical call provisions requiring immediate repayment upon default or for failing to meet certain current ratio tests. This loan was still outstanding when Jones was engaged.

Jones discovered that Dee's accounting records were seriously deficient. He informed Dee's president of the deficiencies and that he would have to disclaim an opinion on any financial statements which might be prepared from the records. The president then prevailed upon Jones to assist the company accountant to "get the books in shape and, if possible, to prepare unaudited financial statements for internal use only."

With the assistance of Dee's accountant, Jones was able to compile a set of unaudited statements. During this time Jones learned that a physical inventory count had not been taken and that the inventory per books was an estimate made by management. This disclosure was not made in the financial statements. The inventory reported in the balance sheet was material in relation to the financial statements taken as a whole.

Jones had the statements typed on his stationery without marking each statement "unaudited — for internal use only." He delivered a copy of the statements, accompanied by his report disclaiming an opinion on the statements, to each member of the board of directors (all were members of management).

Dee's president removed Jones' report and used the financial statements to obtain the additional loan from National Bank. Jones had no knowledge of these acts.

It was subsequently learned that Dee's book inventory was significantly overstated. Dee became insolvent, and suit was brought against Jones by National.

Required:
Discuss the possibilities, including counter arguments, of Jones being liable to National.

(AICPA Adapted)

4-8   Cragsmore & Company, a medium-size partnership of CPAs, was engaged by Marlowe Manufacturing, Inc., a closely held corporation, to examine its financial statements for the year ended December 31, 1989.

Prior to preparing the auditor's report, Susan Cragsmore, a partner, and Fred Willmore, a staff senior, reviewed the disclosures necessary in the footnotes to the financial statements. One footnote involved the terms, costs, and obligations of a lease between Marlowe and Acme Leasing Company.

Willmore suggested that the footnote disclose the following: "The Acme Leasing Company is owned by persons who have a 35% interest in the capital stock and who are officers of Marlowe Manufacturing, Inc."

On Cragsmore's recommendation, this was revised by substituting "minority shareholders" for "persons who have a 35% interest in the capital stock and who are officers."

The auditor's report and financial statements were forwarded to Marlowe Manufacturing for review. The officer-shareholders of Marlowe who also owned Acme Leasing objected to the revised wording and insisted that the footnote be changed to describe the relationship between Acme and Marlowe as merely one of affiliation. Cragsmore acceded to this request.

The auditor's report was issued on this basis with an unqualified opinion. But the working papers included the drafts that showed the changes in the wording of the footnote.

Subsequent to delivery of the auditor's report, Marlowe suffered a substantial uninsured fire loss and was forced into bankruptcy. The failure of Marlowe to carry any fire insurance coverage was not noted in the financial statements.

Required:
What legal problems are suggested by these facts for Cragsmore & Company? Discuss.

(AICPA Adapted)

4-9   A CPA firm has been named as a defendant in a class action by purchasers of the shares of stock of the Newly Corporation. The offering was a public offering of securities within the meaning of the Securities Act of 1933. The plaintiffs allege that the firm was either negligent or fraudulent in connection with the preparation of the audited financial statements which accompanied the registration statement filed with the SEC. Specifically, they allege that the CPA firm either intentionally disregarded or failed to exercise reasonable care to discover material facts which occurred subsequent to January 31, 1989, the date of the auditor's report. The securities were sold to the public on March 16, 1989.

Required:
Discuss the liability of the CPA firm in respect to the events which occurred in the period between the date of the auditor's report and the effective date of the public offering of the securities. Set forth reasons for any conclusions stated.

(AICPA Adapted)

4-10   Whitlow and Wyatt, CPAs, have been the independent auditors of Interstate Land Development Corporation for several years. During these years, Interstate prepared and filed its own annual income tax returns.

During 1989, Interstate requested Whitlow and Wyatt to examine all the necessary financial statements of the corporation to be submitted to the Securities and Exchange Commission (SEC) in connection with a multistate public offering of one million shares of Interstate common stock. This public offering came under the provisions of the Securities Act of 1933. The examination was performed carefully, and the financial statements were fairly presented for the respective periods. These financial statements were included in the registration statement filed with the SEC.

While the registration statement was being processed by the SEC but prior to the effective date, the Internal Revenue Service subpoenaed Whitlow and Wyatt to turn over all its working papers relating to Interstate for the years 1986–1988. Whitlow and Wyatt initially refused to comply for two reasons. First, Whitlow and Wyatt did not prepare Interstate's tax returns. Second, Whitlow and Wyatt claimed that the working papers were confidential matters subject to the privileged communications rule. Subsequently, however, Whitlow and Wyatt did relinquish the subpoenaed working papers.

Upon receiving the subpoena, Wyatt called Dunkirk, the chairman of Interstate's board of directors, and asked him about the IRS investigation. Dunkirk responded, ''I'm sure the IRS people are on a fishing expedition and that they will not find any material deficiencies.''

A few days later Dunkirk received written confirmation from the IRS that it was contending that Interstate had underpaid its taxes during the period under review. The confirmation revealed that Interstate was being assessed $800,000, including penalties and interest for the three years.

This $800,000 assessment was material relative to the financial statements as of December 31, 1989. The amount for each year individually exclusive of penalty and interest was not material relative to each respective year.

Required:
Discuss the additional liability assumed by Whitlow and Wyatt in connection with this SEC registration engagement.

(AICPA Adapted)

4-11   Gordon & Groton, CPAs, were the auditors of Jordan & Company, a brokerage firm and member of a national stock exchange. Gordon & Groton examined and reported on the financial statements of Jordan which were filed with the Securities and Exchange Commission.

Several of Jordan's customers were swindled by a fraudulent scheme perpetrated by Jordan's president, who owned 90 percent of the voting stock of the company. The facts established that Gordon & Groton were negligent but not reckless or grossly negligent in the conduct of the audit and neither participated in the fraudulent scheme nor knew of its existence.

The customers are suing Gordon & Groton under the antifraud provisions of Section 10(b) and Rule 10b-5 of the Securities Exchange Act of 1934 for aiding and abetting the fraudulent scheme of the president. The customers' suit for fraud is predicated exclusively on the auditors failing to conduct a proper audit, thereby failing to discover the fraudulent scheme.

Required:
What is the probable outcome of the lawsuit? Set forth reasons for any conclusions stated.

(AICPA Adapted)

4-12   The CPA firm of Bigelow, Barton and Brown was expanding very rapidly. Consequently it hired several junior accountants, including Robert Small. Subsequently, the partners of the firm became dissatisfied with Small's production and warned him that they would be forced to discharge him unless his output increased significantly.

At that time Small was engaged in audits of several clients. He decided that, to avoid being fired, he would reduce or omit entirely some of the standard audit programs prepared by the partners. One of the CPA firms' clients, Newell Corporation, was in serious financial difficulty and had adjusted several of its accounts being examined by Small to appear financially sound. Small prepared fictitious working papers in his home at night to support purported completion of auditing procedures assigned to him although he in fact did not examine the adjusted entries. The CPA firm rendered an unqualified opinion on Newell's financial statements, which were grossly misstated. Several creditors subsequently loaned large sums of money to Newell Corporation, relying upon the audited financial statements.

Required:

Would the CPA firm be liable to the creditors who extended the loans in reliance on the erroneous financial statements if Newell Corporation should fail to pay them? Explain.

(AICPA Adapted)

4-13   Crane and Co. has been engaged to audit the financial statements for Mirror Manufacturing Corporation for the year ended September 30, 1990. Mirror Manufacturing needed additional cash to continue its operations. To raise funds it agreed to sell its common stock investment in a subsidiary. The buyers insisted upon having the proceeds placed in escrow because of the possibility of a major contingent tax liability. Don Carter, president of Mirror, explained this to Joan Crane, the partner in charge of the Mirror audit. Carter indicated that he wished to show the proceeds from the sale of the subsidiary as an unrestricted current account receivable. He stated that in his opinion the government's claim was groundless and that he needed an "uncluttered" balance sheet and a "clean" auditor's opinion to obtain additional working capital. Crane acquiesced in this request. The government's claim proved to be valid, and, pursuant to the agreement with the buyers, the purchase price of the subsidiary was reduced by $450,000. This coupled with other adverse developments, caused Mirror to become insolvent with assets to cover only some of its liabilities. Crane and Co. is being sued by several of Mirror's creditors who loaned money in reliance upon the financial statements upon which it rendered an unqualified opinion.

Required:

What is the liability, if any, of Crane and Co. to the creditors of Mirror Manufacturing? Explain.

(AICPA Adapted)

PART II AUDIT TECHNOLOGY

STANDARDS, MATERIALITY, AND AUDIT RISK

5

Major topics discussed in this chapter are the:

▲ *Role of theory in auditing.*
▲ *Relationship among auditing concepts, standards, and procedures.*
▲ *Major concepts underlying auditing standards.*
▲ *Evolution, nature, and scope of the AICPA's generally accepted auditing standards.*
▲ *Importance of materiality and risk to applications of generally accepted auditing standards.*

J ust as constitutional law is based upon interpretations of a single document, the U.S. Constitution, so too is auditing. Although considerably less profound than the Constitution in both breadth and impact, generally accepted auditing standards are to the practice of auditing what the Constitution is to the practice of constitutional law. Practitioners in either discipline are guided by a single basic document.

This chapter introduces the role of theory in auditing and discusses the concepts and generally accepted standards of audit practice. Subsequently, the impact of materiality and audit risk on the auditor's interpretation of auditing standards is discussed. The concepts and standards developed within this chapter represent the basic foundation, the underlying model, for the chapters to follow.

THEORY IN AUDITING

Despite its rather lofty implications, the term "theory" represents nothing more than a way to do something — that is, a framework or guide to action. Thus, a theory of auditing is a guide to performing an audit.

In general, theories can be classified as either *normative,* suggesting that the theory explains how something should be done, or *descriptive,* implying that the theory explains how something is actually done in practice. For example, a normative theory of accounting could prescribe a discounted present-value model of income determination for business enterprises; in contrast, a descriptive theory of accounting could recount the income determination models actually used by business enterprises.

Significant Studies

In accounting, numerous efforts have been made by various individuals and organizations to develop normative and descriptive theories of accounting.[1] However, few individuals or organizations have even considered the need for a theory of auditing. Unfortunately, many people ". . . think of auditing as a completely practical, as opposed to theoretical, subject. To them, auditing is a series of practices and procedures, methods and techniques, a way of doing with little need for the explanations, descriptions, reconciliations, and arguments so frequently lumped together as 'theory' ".[2]

Despite this attitude, three significant efforts have been made to develop normative theories of auditing. The earliest, Professors R. K. Mautz and H. A. Sharaf's *The Philosophy of Auditing,* was an introductory, though exhaustive, study of the nature and possibility of a theory of auditing. Mautz and Sharaf's pioneering monograph, published in 1961, investigated what they believed to be the primary concepts of auditing: evidence, due audit care, fair presentation, independence, and ethical conduct, and each of these concepts is discussed and developed further in this chapter. Perhaps no auditing publication prior to or since Mautz and Sharaf's monograph has been quite so influential and widely quoted.

In 1972, the American Accounting Association's Auditing Concepts Committee published *A Statement of Basic Auditing Concepts* (ASOBAC), a report influenced significantly by Mautz and Sharaf's monograph. Among other things, ASOBAC developed objectives and criteria to guide the planning, conduct, and discharge of the audit function and explored the theoretical foundations and methodology of collecting and evaluating audit evidence. ASOBAC is also widely quoted, although it is narrower in scope than the 1961 monograph.

In 1978, Professor C. W. Schandl published *Theory of Auditing: Evaluation, Investigation, and Judgment,* also an extension of Mautz and Sharaf.

---

[1] For example, normative accounting theories include: R. J. Chambers, *Accounting, Evaluation, and Economic Behavior* (Englewood Cliffs, N.J.: Prentice-Hall, Inc., 1966); E. O. Edwards and P. W. Bell, *The Theory and Measurement of Business Income* (Berkeley: University of California Press, 1961); M. Moonitz, *The Basic Postulates of Accounting* (New York: AICPA, 1961); R. T. Sprouse and M. Moonitz, *A Tentative Set of Broad Accounting Principles for Business Enterprises* (New York: AICPA, 1962). Descriptive theories include: P. Grady, *Inventory of Generally Accepted Accounting Principles for Business Enterprises* (New York: AICPA, 1965); Y. Ijiri, *The Foundations of Accounting Measurement. A Mathematical, Economic, and Behavioral Inquiry* (Englewood Cliffs, N.J. Prentice-Hall, Inc., 1967); *Statement of the Accounting Principles* Board No. 4, Basic Concepts and Accounting Principles Underlying Financial Statements of Business Enterprise (New York: AICPA, 1970).

[2] R. K. Mautz and H. A. Sharaf, *The Philosophy of Auditing* (Sarasota: American Accounting Association, 1961), p. 1.

Schandl developed a theory of auditing based upon what he identified as the fundamental elements of theory:

▲ Postulates — fundamental concepts required to be accepted without proof.
▲ Theorems — propositions that are explained by postulates.
▲ Structure — the component parts of a discipline and their interrelationship.
▲ Principles — conventions commonly associated with a discipline, serving as explanations for practices.
▲ Standards — required quality of practice.

In Schandl's framework, theorems are derived from postulates, structure from theorems, and so forth. Together, *The Philosophy of Auditing*, *ASOBAC*, and *Theory of Auditing* represent important contributions to normative auditing theory; they underscore a movement toward appreciating auditing on a conceptual, as well as practical, level.

Standards: A Framework

Auditing practice involves applying scores of detailed procedures to test an auditor's specific audit objectives. However, because of the overwhelming proportion of audit time spent applying procedures, auditors rarely consider the "theory" underlying an audit. The emphasis in practice is on generating sound, cost-efficient audit conclusions. Thus, if an auditor can be successful without considering "theory," why is it necessary to study theory as Mautz and Sharaf, the Auditing Concepts Committee, and Schandl have done or as this chapter does? The reason is that theory can be useful. Theory generalizes, rationalizes, and explains a discipline's activities; therefore, auditing theory can generalize, rationalize, and explain auditing practice. As stated earlier, theory is a framework or guide to action.

To further highlight the role of a theory or framework, consider this simple analogy between a home builder and an auditor. A builder does not haphazardly arrange lumber, electrical wiring, and plumbing components in constructing a house; rather, the builder uses a blueprint (framework) to guide the selection and installation of materials. Likewise, an auditor should not haphazardly apply hastily selected audit procedures in the hope of conducting a competent audit; he or she should proceed within a prescribed framework in the expectation of selecting and applying the most appropriate and efficient audit procedures. The following quote underscores the usefulness of theory:

> A number of isolated facts does not produce a science any more than a lump of bricks produces a house. The isolated facts must be put in order and brought into mutual structural relations in the form of some theory.

Then, only, do we have a science, something to start from, and analyze, ponder on, criticize and improve.[3]

There is no generally accepted theory of auditing. Although influential, *The Philosophy of Auditing, ASOBAC,* and *Theory of Auditing* have not gained widespread acceptance among audit practitioners. Independent, internal, and public-sector auditors, however, have each adopted a set of standards as guides for conducting audits. The standards for internal and public-sector audits are reproduced in Appendices A and B, respectively, of Chapter 21.

The balance of this chapter focuses upon the AICPA's generally accepted auditing standards. The following section discusses the major concepts underlying the standards: Mautz and Sharaf's evidence, due audit care, fair presentation, independence, and ethical conduct. Subsequent sections of the chapter trace the historical development of and interpret the GAAS, describe the audit standard-setting process in the U.S., and discuss two elements which underlie application of the standards, materiality and risk.

AUDITING CONCEPTS

Concepts are abstractions derived from experience and observation and are designed to aid understanding of the similarities within a subject matter and the differences from other subject matters. Much like engineering, physics, economics, sociology, and other physical and social sciences, auditing is based upon a series of fundamental concepts.

The importance of auditing *concepts* is that they are the basis for *standards,* the guidelines or measures of quality from which audit *procedures* are derived. Audit standards differ from audit procedures. Audit standards are measures of quality and objectives and, as such, rarely change over time. In contrast, procedures are detailed methods or techniques for discharging standards and, as such, change as the audit environment changes. For example, a computer accounting system and a manual system require somewhat different audit procedures; however, the quality and objectives of each audit, i.e., the standards, would not differ. Audit procedures provide the means to fulfill audit standards. Auditing concepts, standards, and procedures are related in hierarchical form as follows:

---

[3]A. Korzybski, *Science and Sanity* (4th ed.; The International Non-Aristotelian Library Publishing Co., 1958), p. 55.

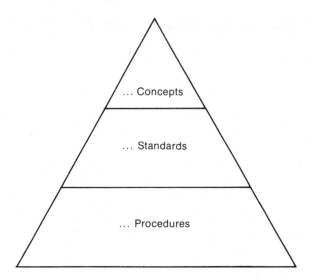

As the illustration suggests, standards are more numerous than the fundamental concepts from which they were derived, and procedures are considerably more numerous than standards. The most important point from the illustration, however, is that all audit procedures applied in practice are based upon a general model, i.e., concepts and standards. Thus, there is a theoretical basis for selecting and applying audit procedures in practice.

Mautz and Sharaf identify five fundamental concepts central to the structure of auditing theory:

▲ Evidence
▲ Due Audit Care
▲ Fair presentation
▲ Independence
▲ Ethical Conduct

A discussion of each concept follows.

Evidence

Gathering and evaluating evidence, the third and fourth steps to the scientific method of inquiry, consume the overwhelming majority of audit time and are, therefore, critical to an auditor's examination. The purpose of gathering and evaluating evidence is to acquire knowledge as a basis for reaching a conclusion about an audit hypothesis — for example, to conclude whether receivables exist. The purpose is not to "prove" that the audit hypothesis is true, but rather to determine with a reasonable degree of assurance whether the hypothesis is true, is false, or cannot be concluded upon. Understanding the basic difference between these two competing points of view can be quite instructive concerning the frame of mind an auditor should possess. Conducting an audit with a preconceived notion as to the conclusions to be reached — e.g., financial statements *are* presented in accordance with GAAP — can detract significantly from an auditor's impartiality, and therefore from an auditor's ability to interpret potential danger signals.

Mautz and Sharaf interpreted several logical ways of acquiring knowledge or truth about a subject from W. P. Montague's *The Ways of Knowing*.[4] On the surface these ways of acquiring knowledge appear unrelated to auditing; yet they can be quite useful for rationalizing how audit evidence is gathered and evaluated in practice. These logical methods of acquiring knowledge are authoritarianism, mysticism, rationalism, empiricism, and pragmatism; the relationship of each to auditing is discussed in the following sections and is recapped in Figure 5-1.

Authoritarianism represents evidence based on the written or oral testimony of others. Auditing examples include statements by third parties or by officers and employees of the entity, and authoritative documents prepared either outside or inside the entity. Closely related to authoritarianism is *mysticism*, or intuitively obtained evidence. Examples include the common audit practice of "scanning" books or records for unusual or revealing relationships among accounting data. The basic difference between these two ways of acquiring knowledge is that authoritarianism is based upon evidence provided by others, and mysticism upon a sense of intuition, instinct, and imagination.

Rationalism involves reasoning from generally accepted assumptions. For example, in mathematics, the numbering system and certain mathematical expressions are well established and accepted. Likewise, in auditing, it is more likely, and therefore assumed, that fairly stated financial statements are more apt to result from a satisfactory internal control structure than from an unsatisfactory system.

Empiricism, a fourth way of acquiring knowledge, involves perceptual experience, i.e., generalizations drawn from observations. For example, auditors often observe the physical inventory recorded within the accounts. The inventory account is expressed in the general ledger in terms of dollars; however, items of inventory are in the form of physical objects at various stages of completion and must be observed.

---

[4]W. P. Montague, *The Ways of Knowing* (4th ed.; New York: The Macmillan Company, 1953).

FIGURE 5-1
Ways of Acquiring Evidence

Authoritarianism — evidence based on testimony
  • Testimony of people
    • Statements of independent third parties
    • Statements of officers and employees
  • Testimony of documents
    • Documents prepared outside the entity
    • Documents prepared inside the entity
    • Subsidiary or detail records

Mysticism — intuitively obtained evidence
  • Scanning
    • Books and records
    • Documents
  • Critical review of testimony of others

Rationalism — reasoning from accepted assumptions
  • Recalculation by auditor
  • Existence of internal control structure
  • Retracing bookkeeping procedures

Empiricism — perceptual experience
  • Physical examination and count

Pragmatism — practical results
  • Subsequent actions by the entity, its officers, employees, customers, etc.

Finally, *pragmatism* relates to practical results, and is based in the realization that what works well must be true. For example, auditors are concerned that all accounts receivable recorded as of the balance sheet date are actually collectible; otherwise they are not assets and therefore should be removed from the balance sheet. Pragmatism suggests that the best means of testing collectibility is to examine subsequent collections. If the receivable was collected, the auditor need then only determine if the receivable actually existed as of the balance sheet date.

These five ways of acquiring knowledge are useful to a conceptual discussion of evidence because they suggest a logical theme to the various practical approaches to evidence gathering and evaluation. They provide an interesting and refreshing basis for introducing the concept of evidence, which is indeed the conceptual foundation of auditing. The nature of audit evidence is discussed more completely in Chapter 6.

Due Audit Care

Clearly, auditors are not infallible. Like physicians, attorneys, and other responsible professionals, independent auditors are subject to human error. However, also like other professionals, independent auditors are expected to perform their duties with a high degree of care. The concept of due audit care is rooted in the fundamental issue of *the degree of care expected of the prudent auditor.*

In the legal profession, the notion of a "reasonable person" is often applied by the courts to determine the extent and limits of an individual's responsibility. The "prudent auditor" serves a similar purpose in auditing. Unfortunately, precise operational definitions of a prudent auditor do not exist; the notion is subject to judgment and interpretation as is the "reasonable person" concept. Thus, it is quite difficult to establish the extent and limits of an independent auditor's responsibility to clients and other financial information users. As guidelines, however, Mautz and Sharaf offer several thoughts about the care to be exercised by a prudent audit practitioner: [5]

▲ The prudent audit practitioner will take steps to obtain any knowledge readily available which will enable him or her to foresee unreasonable risk or harm to others.

▲ To the extent that audit experience (the auditor's own or that of others) or the history of the organization under examination suggests the existence of extra risk in connection with the work of any employee, department, type of transaction, or asset, the auditor should give that risk special attention.

▲ Any unusual circumstances or relationships should be considered by the auditor in planning and performing the audit.

▲ The prudent auditor must recognize unfamiliar situations and take any precautionary measures warranted by the circumstances.

▲ The prudent auditor will take all appropriate steps to resolve any doubtful impressions or unanswered questions concerning matters material to his or her opinion.

▲ The prudent auditor will keep abreast of developments in his or her area of competence.

▲ The prudent auditor will recognize the necessity for reviewing the work of assistants and will perform such review with full understanding of its importance.

Though not necessarily complete, these guidelines do provide a framework for understanding the nature of due audit care. However, applying the concept of due care in practice can be difficult. For example, a particularly dif-

---

[5]Mautz and Sharaf, *op. cit.,* pp. 135–138.

ficult question rooted in due care relates to an independent auditor's responsibility for detecting client errors, irregularities, and illegal acts. This rather thorny issue has been addressed by the profession and was discussed extensively in Chapter 3.

Fair Presentation

Fair presentation is an accounting-related concept requiring that reported financial information be impartial and unbiased and reflect an organization's results of operations, financial position, and cash flows. However, fair presentation is central to auditing as well since (1) impartial (independent) auditors are engaged primarily to reduce the probability of bias in reported financial information and (2) the opinion paragraph of a standard audit report states in part that "financial statements . . . present fairly."

Mautz and Sharaf divide the concept of fair presentation into three related subconcepts: accounting propriety, adequate disclosure, and audit obligation. Each subconcept is fundamental to an understanding of the nature of fair presentation from an independent auditor's, as opposed to an accountant's, point of view.

Accounting propriety refers to the applicability (propriety) of specific accounting principles to specific situations. An auditor must determine (1) whether a particular financial statement presentation reflects GAAP and (2) whether GAAP, as presented, reflects the transaction or event as it actually occurred. *Adequate disclosure,* a closely related subconcept, refers to the amount and scope of information disclosed. An auditor must determine whether financial information is sufficiently summarized, thereby minimizing unnecessary detail, yet sufficiently detailed, thereby optimizing information content. Thus, accounting propriety relates primarily to reflections of "truth," and adequate disclosure, to the extent of information disclosed.

A third subconcept of fair presentation, *audit obligation,* refers to the independent auditor's obligation to issue an opinion, i.e., the attest function. The auditor is responsible both for fair presentation in an audit report and for passing judgment on the accounting propriety and disclosure of financial statement information. Thus, the concept of fair presentation extends not only to financial statements but also to the auditor's report.

Independence

The status of auditing as a useful service to the public is based on the fact that the financial community perceives auditors to be independent of both (1) the financial information audited and (2) the financial information's preparers and users. Were it not for independence, an auditor's attest function would be meaningless.

The concept of independence relates both to the real independence of individual audit practitioners (practitioner-independence) and to the apparent independence of all audit professionals collectively (profession-independence).[6] *Practioner-independence* is a state of mind, an attitude of impartiality and self-reliance that pervades an auditor's approach to audit examinations. To successfully maintain an impartial attitude toward financial information, preparers, and users, an auditor must be aware of conditions or factors that might impair independence. Mautz and Sharaf identify three fundamental dimensions of practitioner-independence which can minimize or eliminate potential threats to the auditor's impartiality:[7]

▲ *Programming independence* — freedom from control or undue influence in the selection of audit techniques and procedures and in the extent of their application. This requires that the auditor have freedom to develop his or her own program, both as to steps to be included and the amount of work to be performed, within the over-all bounds of the engagement.

▲ *Investigative independence* — freedom from control or undue influence in the selection of areas, activities, personal relationships, and managerial policies to be examined. This requires that no legitimate source of information be closed to the auditor.

▲ *Reporting independence* — freedom from control or undue influence in the statement of facts revealed by the examination or in the expression of recommendations or opinions as a result of the examination.

Thus, practitioner-independence requires freedom from restrictions regarding audit techniques, the areas audited, and the auditor's reporting obligation. To be independent, an auditor's professional judgment should be neither subordinated to nor influenced by any other interested parties.

Profession-independence, in contrast, is a perception held by members of the financial community and the general public about practitioners as a group. Perceptions, however, are sometimes inaccurate and occasionally damaging. To the extent that the profession is perceived as lacking independence, the impartiality of individual practitioners is suspect. Thus, profession-independence has a direct impact on the effectiveness and indeed the livelihood of an auditor. As a result, maintaining an image of independence has been a major preoccupation of the profession.

---

[6]*Ibid.,* p. 205.
[7]*Ibid.,* pp. 205–206.

Ethical Conduct

As discussed in Chapter 2, ethical conduct within a profession is a special application of general ethics, the study of ideal conduct. In turn, general ethics is but one of five fields of study in philosophy — the others being esthetics, the study of ideal form or beauty; logic, the study of ideal method in thought and research; metaphysics, the study of ultimate reality; and politics, the study of ideal social organization. Thus, ethics in auditing refers to the *ideal conduct* of a professional independent auditor and is a philosophical issue rooted in the study of general ethics.

Although an abstract issue, ethical conduct in auditing requires reasoned and logical solutions to practical audit questions. These questions and solutions were discussed extensively in Chapter 2.

Although discussed separately, the above concepts — evidence, due audit care, fair presentation, independence, and ethics — are very much related. They provide a way of thinking about auditing, a conceptual overview for understanding audit practice.

GENERALLY ACCEPTED AUDITING STANDARDS

In February, 1941, the SEC issued Accounting Series Release No. 21, which in part required that an auditor state within an audit report whether the examination was conducted in accordance with generally accepted auditing standards applicable in the circumstances. However, no such written standards existed. As a result, the AICPA's Committee on Auditing Procedure began deliberating on a series of standards for auditing. Interrupted by World War II, it was not until October, 1947, that the Committee finalized nine generally accepted standards in its report, "Tentative Statement of Auditing Standards — Their Generally Accepted Significance and Scope." The nine standards were approved by vote of the AICPA's membership in 1948, and a tenth was adopted from *Statement on Auditing Procedure No. 23* and approved by membership vote in 1949. In 1988, the second field work standard and the second reporting standard were revised by SAS No. 55 and SAS No. 58, respectively.

The AICPA's ten generally accepted auditing standards are classified as general, field work, and reporting standards. Following is a discussion of the standards, which are presented along with related auditing concepts in Figure 5-2.

General Standards

The three general standards are based primarily on the concepts of due audit care, independence, and ethical conduct. Essentially, they relate to an auditor's professional qualifications and the quality of his or her work, and pervade applications of the field work and reporting standards. The general standards (Figure 5-2) require:

▲ Adequate technical training and proficiency.
▲ Independence in mental attitude.
▲ Due professional care.

Adequate Technical Training and Proficiency. An independent auditor is expected to be proficient in both accounting and auditing. Accounting and auditing are separate fields; however, an auditor must be proficient in accounting in order to audit accounting information competently.

An auditor becomes proficient through formal preprofessional education (e.g., baccalaureate or graduate degrees) and continuing professional education (e.g., AICPA or CPA firm-sponsored seminars) and through properly supervised on-the-job experience. Education and experience complement each other and are the basis for developing sound professional judgment, a prerequisite of a competent professional auditor.

Independence in Mental Attitude. The second general standard requires that an auditor be independent. That is, an auditor should be impartial and have no biases about either the financial information audited or the financial information's preparers and users.

Because it is an attitude or state of mind, independence is difficult to demonstrate objectively; only an auditor's actions can be used by observers to evaluate independence. Even though independence requires that an auditor be intellectually honest, an auditor can demonstrate independence only by remaining free of any obligation or interest in a client's financial information and information preparers and users. Thus an auditor must be independent both "in fact" and "in appearance." For example, an auditor who owns an interest in a business might be intellectually honest when conducting the annual audit; however, it is doubtful that a commercial bank would be willing to rely upon the auditor's report. Such ownership would cloud the bank's interpretation of the audit report since the auditor has a financial interest in the bank's lending decision.

Over the years the SEC has issued several pronouncements related to auditor independence. Most prominent among them are Accounting Series Releases (ASR) 126 (July, 1972) and 234 (December, 1977), which set forth the SEC's guidelines for resolving independence questions. The guidelines relate to such issues as an auditor's financial interests, family and business relationships with clients, occupations with conflicting interests, interests in nonclient affiliates, and unpaid prior professional fees.

FIGURE 5-2
Generally Accepted Auditing Standards (GAAS)

General Standards	Related Auditing Concepts

General Standards

1. The examination is to be performed by a person or persons having adequate technical training and proficiency as an auditor.
2. In all matters relating to the assignment, an independence in mental attitude is to be maintained by the auditor or auditors.
3. Due professional care is to be exercised in the performance of the examination and the preparation of the report.

Due audit care
Independence
Ethical conduct

LOOKS AT AUDITOR AS PERSON

Standards of Field Work

1. The work is to be adequately planned, and assistants, if any, are to be properly supervised.
2. A sufficient understanding of internal control structure should be obtained to plan the audit and to determine the nature, timing, and extent of tests to be performed.
3. Sufficient competent evidential matter is to be obtained through inspection, observation, inquiries, and confirmations to afford a reasonable basis for an opinion regarding the financial statements under examination.

Evidence

PLAN OF AUDIT

Standards of Reporting

1. The report shall state whether the financial statements are presented in accordance with generally accepted accounting principles.
2. The report shall identify those circumstances in which such principles have not been consistently observed in the current period in relation to the preceding period.
3. Informative disclosures in the financial statements are to be regarded as reasonably adequate unless otherwise stated in the report.
4. The report shall contain either an expression of opinion regarding the financial statements, taken as a whole, or an assertion to the effect that an opinion cannot be expressed. When an overall opinion cannot be expressed, the reasons therefor should be stated. In all cases where an auditor's name is associated with financial statements, the report should contain a clear-cut indication of the character of the auditor's examination, if any, and the degree of responsibility he or she is taking.

AUDIT REPORT

Fair presentation

In the 1970s and early 1980s, a rather pointed debate surfaced over a particularly sensitive issue to public accounting firms: nonaudit services. Critics argued that independence is impaired when a firm realizes significant nonaudit fees from an audit client. For example, some public accounting firms provided executive-search services to help clients find and hire financial executives, such as controllers and treasurers, thereby raising the question: "Is an auditor really independent of financial executives placed with audit clients?" As a result of this question and the ensuing debate, one national public accounting firm spun off its executive search practice, quieting some critics of executive search, but refocusing attention on other nonaudit services, primarily management consulting.

In 1978, the Securities and Exchange Commission responded to the nonaudit services issue with Accounting Series Release No. 250, which required disclosure in Form 10-K (the annual report to the SEC) of the nature of all nonaudit services and the percentage of nonaudit to audit fees. Three years later, in 1981, the SEC rescinded ASR No. 250, and as a result, public disclosure of nonaudit services is no longer mandatory.

Clearly, nonaudit services such as executive search and management consulting have raised serious questions about auditor independence. However, as discussed earlier in the chapter, profession-independence focuses not on independence "in fact," but on the financial community's "perception" of auditor independence, thereby raising the question: "What is the financial community's perception of auditor independence?" Recent research suggests that, despite repeated criticisms, both sophisticated financial information users, such as financial analysts, and educated but inexperienced readers, such as MBA students, have relatively high confidence in auditor independence, even in cases involving nonaudit services.[8]

Rule 203 of the AICPA's Code of Professional Conduct also addresses the issue of independence and was discussed extensively in Chapter 2.

Due Professional Care. The third general standard is concerned with how an auditor's work is performed. The standard requires that auditors observe each of the field work and reporting standards and supervise all work performed by assistants.

To demonstrate the scope and intent of the third general standard, the AICPA cites the following lengthy though perceptive quote from *Cooley on Torts.*

---

[8]P. M. J. Reckers and A. J. Stagliano, "Non-Audit Services and Perceived Independence: Some New Evidence," *Auditing: A Journal of Practice & Theory* (Summer, 1981), pp. 23–47.

Every man who offers his service to another and is employed assumes the duty to exercise in the employment such skill as he possesses with reasonable care and diligence. In all these employments where peculiar skill is prerequisite, if one offers his service, he is understood as holding himself out to the public as possessing the degree of skill commonly possessed by others in the same employment, and, if his pretentions are unfounded, he commits a species of fraud upon every man who employs him in reliance on his public profession. But no man, whether skilled or unskilled, undertakes that the task he assumes shall be performed successfully, and without fault or error. He undertakes for good faith and integrity, but not for infallibility, and he is liable to his employer for negligence, bad faith, or dishonesty, but not for losses consequent upon pure errors of judgment.

Perhaps no other quote so clearly mirrors the essence of due professional care. In short, although not infallible, an auditor is responsible nevertheless to exercise reasonable care and to possess requisite skills, or risk committing an inexcusable "fraud" upon all who rely on his or her work.

Standards of Field Work

The three standards of field work are based primarily on the auditing concept of evidence. They encompass the guidelines and measures of quality for conducting audit work in the "field" and are applied in conjunction with the general standards. The standards of field work (Figure 5-2) require:

▲ Adequate planning and supervision.
▲ Consideration of the internal control structure.
▲ Sufficient competent evidential matter.

Planning and Supervision. The first standard of field work encompasses the timing, planning, and supervision of audit work.

Preferably, an auditor should be appointed before or soon after the year under audit begins. Early appointment allows an auditor ample time to plan an expeditious audit and to consider completing some audit field work before the balance sheet date. Even though early appointment is advantageous, an auditor can accept an audit engagement near or after the balance sheet date. However, the auditor should alert the client that an unqualified opinion cannot be issued unless an adequate examination can still be performed.

Auditors often conduct certain auditing procedures, such as tests of control procedures, at interim dates prior to the balance sheet date. One purpose of interim audit work is to determine the extent to which a business entity's internal control structure can be relied upon. In fact, when controls are found to be effective, year-end work may consist mainly of analytical procedures, such as comparison of current with prior year account balances, and less extensive detailed tests, assuming controls are still effective. Emphasis on tests of controls is more appropriate for accounts with large numbers of transactions, and emphasis on detailed testing is more appropriate for accounts with few transactions. Extensive, time-consuming tests of controls for accounts with only a small number of transactions would be inefficient, since less audit time would be consumed by simply examining all or most of the transactions directly.

In March, 1978, the Auditing Standards Executive Committee issued *Statement on Auditing Standards No. 22,* "Planning and Supervision" (AU Sec. 311), providing interpretation of the first field work standard. SAS No. 22 describes *audit planning* as the process of developing an overall strategy, a strategy dependent upon the size and complexity of the client entity, experience with the entity, and knowledge of the entity's business. Audit planning considerations include:

▲ Matters relating to the entity's business and the industry in which it operates.
▲ The entity's accounting policies and procedures.
▲ Preliminary estimates of materiality levels for audit purposes.
▲ Financial statement items likely to require adjustment.

Above all, an auditor should become thoroughly familiar with the client's organization and operating characteristics. Familiarity breeds both understanding and a sense of perspective. An auditor is best prepared to discharge the audit and attest functions when thoroughly familiar with the client; an audit should not be conducted in a vacuum.

Supervision is described in SAS No. 22 as the process of directing the efforts of assistants, in conjunction with the objectives of the audit, and determining whether the objectives are achieved. All work performed by assistants should be thoroughly reviewed, and their conclusions should be consistent with the opinion communicated in the audit report. Procedures should also be established to determine how differences of opinion among staff members regarding accounting and auditing issues are to be resolved.

Internal Control Structure. The second standard of field work requires that an auditor consider an entity's internal control structure as a basis for planning the audit. The standard points to an important inverse relationship between (1) the effectiveness of internal control structure and (2) the extent of detailed audit procedures. That is, as the effectiveness of an entity's internal control structure increases, the need for detailed audit procedures should decrease. This relationship is based on the premise that effective internal control structures can be relied upon, and ineffective structures cannot.

Considering internal control structure in accordance with the second standard of field work can, and often does, result in recommendations about significant deficiencies in an entity's internal control structure. In fact, *Statement on Auditing Standards* No. 60, ''Communication of Internal Control Structure Related Matters Noted in an Audit,'' requires, as its title suggests, that significant deficiencies in internal control structure be communicated to the board of directors; the form of communication is optional, but it should be made at the earliest practicable date. The deficiencies communicated, however, should not be construed as all possible deficiencies; they represent only those deficiencies found while considering internal control structure under the second standard of field work. There is a difference between complying with the second field work standard and conducting a full-scale examination for deficiencies as part of a special engagement. The scope of a full-scale examination would be directed exclusively toward detecting deficiencies and therefore would be much more apt to detect them.

The design and implementation of internal control structure is very closely related to the nature, extent, and timing of audit procedures. Internal control structure and its relationship to audit work are discussed in detail in Chapter 7.

Evidential Matter. According to *Statement on Auditing Standards No. 31,* ''Evidential Matter'' (AU Sec. 330), audit evidence consists of underlying accounting data and all related corroborating information available to an auditor. Underlying accounting data include such items as journals, ledgers, reconciliations, and related accounting manuals; corroborating information includes checks, invoices, contracts, and minutes of meetings.

Sufficient competent evidential matter is the only basis for reaching reasoned, informed audit conclusions. Determining the sufficiency and competence of audit evidence, however, is left solely to the independent auditor's professional judgment. In this sense, audit evidence is somewhat more difficult to interpret than legal evidence. Legal evidence is guided by formal rules of admissibility, while audit evidence is guided solely by the auditor's judgment. Thus, independent auditors must reinterpret the terms ''sufficient'' and ''competent'' for every audit engagement.

''Sufficiency'' refers to the quantity of audit evidence obtained, although it does not suggest ''the more, the better.'' An audit opinion must be reached within a reasonable length of time and at a reasonable cost. Therefore, an auditor should balance the cost of obtaining additional evidence with the usefulness of information generated. In contrast, ''competence'' refers to the validity and relevance of evidence. The validity of audit evidence depends on the circumstances in which it is obtained. Recognizing the possibility of ex-

ceptions due to existing circumstances, the following general presumptions
can be made regarding the validity of evidence:

▲ Evidential matter obtained from independent sources outside an entity
   is more reliable than evidence secured from within the entity.
▲ A satisfactory internal control structure is more likely to result in reliable accounting data and financial statements than is an unsatisfactory control structure.
▲ Direct personal knowledge of the independent auditor obtained through
   physical examination, observation, computation, and inspection is more
   persuasive than information obtained indirectly.

Of course, independent auditors would much prefer to obtain convincing
audit evidence. However, because the cost of obtaining evidence should not
exceed the usefulness of evidence obtained, audit evidence is often persuasive
rather than wholly convincing. This situation is quite acceptable though, since
an audit is designed to provide reasonable, as opposed to absolute, assurance
about a company's financial statements.

The nature, types, and documentation of audit evidence are discussed
more fully in Chapter 6.

Standards of Reporting

The AICPA's four standards of reporting are based on the auditing concept of fair presentation. They encompass the guidelines and measures of
quality for reporting on the results of an audit and, therefore, are the standards for the auditor's attest function. Like the field work standards, the standards of reporting are applied in conjunction with the general standards discussed earlier.

The standards of reporting (Figure 5-2) relate to:

▲ Conformity of financial statements with GAAP.
▲ Consistent application of accounting principles.
▲ Informative disclosures.
▲ Expression of opinion.

Conformity of Financial Statements with GAAP. The first standard of
reporting requires that an auditor issue an opinion, not a statement of fact,
about whether financial statements are presented in accordance with generally
accepted accounting principles. If an opinion cannot be formulated, the auditor's report should reflect this disclaimer of opinion.

Generally accepted accounting principles include financial accounting
principles within extant authoritative accounting pronouncements (e.g., Accounting Research Bulletins, Opinions of the Accounting Principles Board,

and Statements of Financial Accounting Standards) as well as other principles which appear to be generally accepted. Thus, as noted in APB Statement No. 4, GAAP results from general consensus:

> Generally accepted accounting principles incorporate the consensus at a particular time as to which economic resources and obligations should be recorded as assets and liabilities . . . , which changes in assets and liabilities should be recorded, when these changes should be recorded, how the assets and liabilities and changes in them should be measured, what information should be disclosed and how it should be disclosed, and which financial statements should be prepared.[9]

In short, no one really knows what the entire "pool" of generally accepted accounting principles is at any given point in time. GAAP is dynamic, rather than static, and is constantly evolving in response to changes in the environment:

> Present generally accepted accounting principles are the result of an evolutionary process that can be expected to continue in the future. . . . Generally accepted accounting principles change in response to changes in economic and social conditions, to new knowledge and technology, and to demands of users for more serviceable financial information.[10]

Because GAAP may change and new, more creative transactions emerge continually, no single reference source exists for all accounting principles in all industries. In response, *Statement on Auditing Standards No. 43*, "Omnibus SAS-1982," clarifies the order of sources that an auditor should consult when attempting to determine GAAP for nonroutine accounting and reporting questions (AU Sec. 411.05-.08). The sources and related examples are listed at the top of page 182.

Consistent Application of Accounting Principles. The second standard of reporting requires that the auditor identify circumstances in which accounting principles have not been applied consistently for all periods presented in the financial statements. However, the basis for the standard is not simply consistency in and of itself; rather, the basis is the relationship between consistency and comparability.

"Comparability" is a general term encompassing both intracomparability, the comparability of an entity's financial statements from period to period, and intercomparability, the comparability of an entity's financial statements with those of other entities. Consistency is closely related to

---

[9] *Statement of the Accounting Principles Board No. 4*. "Basic Concepts and Accounting Principles Underlying Financial Statements of Business Enterprises" (New York: American Institute of Certified Public Accountants, 1970), par. 137.

[10] *Ibid.*, par. 208–209.

Sources of GAAP	Examples
1. Pronouncements of an authoritative body designated by AICPA Council to establish accounting principles.	FASB Statements and Interpretations; APB Opinions; AICPA Accounting Research Bulletins.
2. Pronouncements of bodies composed of expert accountants that follow a due process, including exposure of proposed principles for public comment, for the intended purpose of establishing accounting principles or describing current practices that are generally accepted.	AICPA Industry Audit and Accounting Guides; AICPA Statements of Position; FASB Technical Bulletins.
3. Practices or pronouncements that are widely recognized as being generally accepted because, for example, they represent prevalent practice in a particular industry.	AICPA Accounting Interpretations.
4. Other accounting literature.	APB Statements; AICPA Issues Papers; FASB Statements of Financial Accounting Concepts; pronouncements of various professional associations or regulatory agencies; accounting textbooks; journal articles.

intracomparability. For example, if a company changes from the sum-of-the-years-digits method of depreciation to straight-line in 1989, the company's application of accounting principles is not consistent, and therefore, the 1989 financial statements may not be comparable with statements for prior years. Thus, the objective of the second standard of reporting is to provide assurance that the comparability of an entity's financial statements is not materially affected by inconsistent application of accounting principles from period to period.

Informative Disclosures. Financial statements and related notes should include adequate disclosure of all material matters. In accordance with *Statement on Auditing Standards No. 32,* "Adequacy of Disclosure in Financial Statements" (AU Sec. 431), disclosures should be adequate in form, arrangement, and content.

Deciding whether disclosure is informative or adequate should be based on whether additional information would have a material impact upon a reasonably informed decision maker. Thus, an auditor's decision rule should be: What impact, if any, is the information likely to have upon decision makers? Are decisions apt to be different? If information is apt to affect decision making, it should be included in the financial statements; if management chooses not to disclose the information, the independent auditor's report should express a qualified or adverse opinion.

Auditors frequently receive information in confidence regarding sensitive company matters, such as executive compensation and new product development. Informative disclosure does not require disclosure of such confidential information, since the information is not relevant to whether a company's financial statements are presented fairly in accordance with GAAP. Financial statement disclosures should be informative about a company's results of operations, financial position, and cash flows; disclosures beyond the realm of financial reporting are superfluous.

Expression of Opinion. The fourth standard of reporting requires that an independent auditor either express an opinion on an entity's financial statements taken as a whole or assert that an opinion is not expressed. Note that an opinion is expressed on financial statements "taken as a whole." Piecemeal opinions on portions of individual financial statements are not appropriate since they tend to detract from the overall signal intended by the auditor's report. However, an auditor could express an unqualified opinion on one of an entity's financial statements and a qualified or adverse opinion or disclaimer of opinion on the others.

The fourth standard of reporting also requires that a report indicate the character of an examination and the degree of an auditor's responsibility in all cases where an auditor's name is "associated" with financial statements. *Statement on Auditing Standards No. 26,* "Association with Financial Statements" (AU Sec. 504), indicates an accountant is associated with financial statements when he or she: (1) has consented to the use of the accountant's name in a report, document, or written communication containing the statements, or (2) submits to a client, or others, financial statements the accountant prepared or assisted in preparing, even though the accountant's name is not appended to the statements.

In general, the objective of the fourth standard of reporting is to prevent misinterpretations of the degree of responsibility assumed by an independent auditor. The auditor is responsible only for the report issued; management is responsible for the accompanying financial statements and notes. Audit report writing is discussed extensively in Chapter 19.

THE BOUNDARIES OF GAAS

The AICPA's ten generally accepted auditing standards are not without critics. As discussed below, some of the critics have argued that the standards are not sufficiently specific, and others have argued the standards are not sufficiently broad to encompass the ever expanding scope of a CPA's services.

Critics of GAAS

When first issued in 1948, the standards were specifically entitled "tentative" and were considered an initial step toward developing standards for the profession. However, for almost forty years, the standards were neither reconsidered nor revised. Mautz and Sharaf comment:

> If Generally Accepted Auditing Standards had been viewed as a first step in the development of realistic and useful standards for the profession it would have been a milestone indeed. Apparently, however, it is currently accepted as a final and sufficient statement of such standards. In our judgment, a critical reading of these standards finds them unsatisfactory for this purpose. They are not sufficiently specific to provide guidance to any of the several interests in audit work.[11]

Although Mautz and Sharaf's criticism of the standards was published in 1961, no serious effort was made to reconsider the standards until the mid-1980s.

In 1984, Jacobson and Elliott,[12] among others, urged the profession to reconsider GAAS, in part because the Auditing Standards Board's Statements on Auditing Standards are intended to interpret the standards, yet SASs have been and continue to be issued on services that are not explicitly within the bounds of the attest function as envisioned by GAAS. That is, the boundaries of GAAS are not sufficiently broad to encompass either the range of services currently offered by CPAs or several of the interpretive SASs issued by the Auditing Standards Board. For example, the Board has issued SASs on changing prices (SAS No. 28), interim financial information (SAS No. 36), and mineral reserves (SAS No. 40), none of which relates specifically to the independent auditor's financial statement attest function, the primary focus of GAAS.

---

[11] Ibid., p. 112.

[12] Jacobson, P. D. and R. K. Elliott, "GAAS: Reconsidering the 'Ten Commandments'," *Journal of Accountancy* (May, 1984), pp. 77–88.

Attestation Standards

In response to a need for standards that could encompass future expansion of the auditor's attest function beyond external financial statements, the Auditing Standards Board and the Accounting and Review Services Committee in 1986 issued jointly a Statement on Standards for Attestation Engagements, "Attestation Standards." The statement defines an attestation engagement as ". . . one in which a practitioner is engaged to issue or does issue a written communication that expresses a conclusion about the reliability of a written assertion that is the responsibility of another party" and identifies eleven attestation standards that provide guidance both to independent accountants when performing new or evolving attest services and to AICPA standard-setting bodies when establishing interpretative standards for attestation engagements.

The eleven attestation standards, which are listed and compared with GAAS in Figure 5-3, are a natural extension of existing GAAS, since they apply to the growing array of attest services which extend beyond the auditor's financial statement attest function. For example, the attestation standards would apply to such attest services as reports on descriptions of internal control structure; reports on descriptions of computer software; reports on investment performance statistics; and reports on compliance with statutory, regulatory, and contractual requirements, among other things. Importantly, the attestation standards do not supersede any of the ten GAAS discussed in this chapter. Rather, the attestation standards serve as an umbrella over the entire range of attest services performed by auditors, and GAAS apply exclusively to one type of attest service: opinion audits of external financial statements.

FIGURE 5-3
Comparison Between Attestation Standards and GAAS

Attestation Standards	Generally Accepted Auditing Standards
General Standards	
1. The engagement shall be performed by a practitioner or practitioners having adequate technical training and proficiency in the attest function.	1. The examination is to be performed by a person or persons having adequate technical training and proficiency as an auditor.

continued on page 184

FIGURE 5-3 (*cont.*)
Comparison Between Attestation Standards and GAAS

Attestation Standards	Generally Accepted Auditing Standards

General Standards

2. The engagement shall be performed by a practitioner or practitioners having adequate knowledge in the subject matter of the assertion.
3. The practitioner shall perform an engagement only if he or she has reason to believe that the following two conditions exist:
   - The assertion is capable of evaluation against reasonable criteria that either have been established by a recognized body or are stated in the presentation of the assertion in a sufficiently clear and comprehensive manner for a knowledgeable reader to be able to understand them.
   - The assertion is capable of reasonably consistent estimation or measurement using such criteria.

4. In all matters relating to the engagement, an independence in mental attitude shall be maintained by the practitioner or practitioners.

   2. In all matters relating to the assignment, an independence in mental attitude is to be maintained by the auditor or auditors.

5. Due professional care shall be exercised in the performance of the engagement.

   3. Due professional care is to be exercised in the performance of the examination and the preparation of the report.

Standards of Field Work

1. The work shall be adequately planned and assistants, if any, shall be properly supervised.

   1. The work is to be adequately planned and assistants, if any, are to be properly supervised.

   2. A sufficient understanding of internal control structure should be obtained to plan the audit and to de-

continued on page 185

2. Sufficient evidence shall be obtained to provide a reasonable basis for the conclusion that is expressed in the report.

termine the nature, timing, and extent of tests to be performed.

3. Sufficient competent evidential matter is to be obtained through inspection, observation, inquiries, and confirmations to afford a reasonable basis for an opinion regarding the financial statements under examination.

Standards of Reporting

1. The report shall identify the assertion being reported on and state the character of the engagement.
2. The report shall state the practitioner's conclusion about whether the assertion is presented in conformity with the established or stated criteria against which it was measured.

1. The report shall state whether the financial statements are presented in accordance with generally accepted accounting principles.

2. The report shall identify those circumstances in which such principles have not been consistently observed in the current period in relation to the preceding period.
3. Informative disclosures in the financial statements are to be regarded as reasonably adequate unless otherwise stated in the report.

3. The report shall state all of the practitioner's significant reservations about the engagement and the presentation of the assertion.
4. The report on an engagement to evaluate an assertion that has been prepared in conformity with agreed-upon criteria or on an engagement to apply agreed-upon procedures should contain a statement limiting its use to the parties who have agreed upon such criteria or procedures.

4. The report shall either contain an expression of opinion regarding the financial statements, taken as a whole, or an assertion to the effect that an opinion cannot be expressed. When an overall opinion cannot be expressed, the reasons therefore should be stated. In all cases where an auditor's name is associated with financial statements, the report should contain a clear-cut indication of the character of the auditor's examination, if any, and the degree of responsibility he is taking.

Source: Statement on Standards for Attestation Engagements, "Attestation Standards" (New York: AICPA, March 1986), pp. 26–28.

AUDIT RISK AND MATERIALITY

As noted in Statement on Auditing Standards No. 47, "Audit Risk and Materiality in Conducting an Audit" (AU Sec. 312), the opinion paragraph of an audit report makes explicit reference to materiality and implicit reference to audit risk, as illustrated by the underscored phrases below:

> Opinion Paragraph
> In our opinion, the aforementioned financial statements present fairly, in all material respects, the financial position of ABC Corporation and consolidated affiliates at December 31, 1990 and 1989, and the results of its operations and its cash flows for each of the years then ended, in conformity with generally accepted accounting principles.

The phrase "in our opinion" implies to readers of the report that the auditor may unknowingly fail to appropriately modify his or her opinion for material undetected misstatements. That is, because of misapplications of generally accepted accounting principles, recorded transactions which depart from fact, and/or omissions of necessary information, the auditor sustains a risk that the financial statements may contain undetected errors or irregularities which result in financial statements that are not presented fairly in conformity with generally accepted accounting principles.

In turn, the phrase "present fairly" indicates to readers of the report that the auditor's opinion relates only to transactions, events, or disclosures which are important — i.e., material — for fair presentation of the financial statements in conformity with generally accepted accounting principles. That is, some matters, by either their nature or amount, are not deemed important by the auditor and, therefore, the phrase "present fairly, in all material respects, . . ." implicitly indicates the auditor's belief that the financial statements taken as a whole are not materially misstated.

Thus, both audit risk and materiality are closely related to the field work and reporting standards in general, and to the fourth reporting standard in particular: to the field work and reporting standards because they should be interpreted in light of the auditor's assessment of risk and materiality, and to the fourth reporting standard because, as discussed above, it communicates the notions of risk and materiality to financial statement users through the audit report's opinion paragraph.

Inherent Risk, Control Risk, and Detection Risk

For an entire set of financial statements taken as a whole, *audit risk* is the probability that ". . . the auditor may unknowingly fail to appropriately modify his opinion on financial statements that are materially misstated'' (AU Sec. 312.02). Audit risk is assessed either in quantitative terms — for example, five percent or ten percent — or in nonquantitative terms — for example, high, moderate, or low. In general, an auditor should plan an audit so that audit risk will be limited to a level that is low enough to issue an opinion confidently, without undue risk that the financial statements may be materially misstated.

However, for any one individual account balance, such as Accounts Receivable or Inventory, audit risk consists of the (AU Sec. 312.20):

▲ *inherent* and *control risks* that the account contains error that could be material when combined with error in other accounts, and
▲ *detection risk* that the auditor will not detect material error.

Inherent, control, and detection risk are discussed individually below, followed thereafter by a model for measuring audit risk for individual financial statement accounts.

Inherent Risk. Inherent risk represents the susceptibility of an account balance to error that could be material, assuming there are no related control procedures. For example, technological developments in an industry could render some inventory obsolete, thereby increasing the inherent risk that Inventory is overstated.

Some accounts are more inherently risky than others as a result of their very nature alone, rather than from observable external influences, such as technology. For example, liquid assets such as cash and marketable securities are more susceptible to theft, and therefore are more inherently risky, than nonliquid assets such as coal or timber.

Control Risk. Control risk represents the risk that error could occur and will not be prevented or detected by the internal control structure. The more effective an internal control structure, the less control risk sustained by the auditor.

In practice, auditors sometimes combine inherent and control risk in a single inherent/control risk assessment, and sometimes they assess the two risks separately. However, regardless of whether the risks are assessed separately or in combination, the auditor should have some basis for judging risk. For example, as a basis for assessing control risk, an auditor could use evidence gathered when documenting a client's internal control structure under the second standard of field work. In addition, an auditor could use a specially designed technological-obsolescence questionnaire to assess inherent risk for high-tech inventory.

Detection Risk. Detection risk represents the risk that error could occur and not be detected by the auditor's procedures. In practice, detection risk results from ineffective or misapplied auditing procedures, and arises partly because auditors do not often test one hundred percent of the transactions comprising an account balance and partly because of other uncertainties, such as inadequate supervision or poor judgment, that arise even when testing all transactions.

Because auditors select and are free to change audit procedures, detection risk exists independently of inherent and control risk, neither of which are directly controllable by the auditor. As a result, detection risk should bear an inverse relationship to inherent and control risk, since the greater the inherent and control risks, the less detection risk an auditor could accept. For example, if a client's control procedures over precious metals are inadequate, an auditor would be willing to accept only a very low detection risk, primarily because (1) precious metals are highly susceptible to theft and therefore have a higher level of inherent risk, and (2) controls are inadequate, indicating a high control risk. In this case, the auditor's procedures would have to be particularly effective to minimize detection risk.

Measuring Audit Risk

In practice, audit risk is often judged subjectively (e.g., high, medium, or low) by auditors primarily because inherent, control, and detection risk are often judged subjectively. However, assuming inherent, control, and detection risk can be quantified for a given audit client, an auditor could measure audit risk for particular accounts according to the following expression, implied in SAS No. 47.

$$AR = IR \times CR \times DR$$

where: AR = Audit risk for an account

IR = Inherent risk *material error in account*

CR = Control risk

DR = Detection risk

For example, assume that from evidence obtained in prior years' audits, an auditor estimates that inherent risk is .50, control risk .40, and detection risk .10 for inventory, which is stated at $1 million. In this case, audit risk for inventory is .02 [.50 × .40 × .10], indicating there is a two percent risk that Inventory will be materially misstated despite the auditor's procedures. Of course, the reliability of quantitatively determined measures of audit risk, such as the two percent risk in the illustration, is directly dependent on the accuracy of the component risks, each of which is usually estimated subjectively.

Defining Materiality

The question of "what is material in what situations" has never really been resolved with certainty and, given the profession's emphasis on professional judgment, probably won't be in the near future. However, on a conceptual level, there is consensus as to what materiality means. For example, the Securities and Exchange Commission defines materiality in Rule 1-02 of Regulation S-X:

> The term "material," when used to qualify a requirement for the furnishing of information as to any subject, limits the information required to those matters about which an average prudent investor ought reasonably to be informed.

In addition, several court cases have defined materiality. For example, in *Escott v. BarChris Construction Corp.*, the court defined a material fact as:

> . . . a fact that if it had been correctly stated or disclosed would have deterred or tended to deter the average prudent investor from purchasing the securities in question.[13]

Similarly, the court in *SEC v. Texas Gulf Sulphur Co.* stated:

> The basic test of materiality . . . is whether a reasonable man would have attached importance . . . in determining his choice of action in the transaction in question.[14]

And more recently, the Financial Accounting Standards Board defined materiality as:

> the magnitude of an omission or misstatement of accounting information that, in the judgment of a reasonable person relying on the information would have been changed or influenced by the omission or misstatement.[15]

Thus, as these quotes suggest, there is general agreement among the SEC, the courts, and the FASB that a transaction, event, or disclosure is material if it would affect a decision made by an average prudent investor, a reasonable person, or the like. However, although appealing on a conceptual level,

---

[13]*Escott et al. v. BarChris Construction Corp.*, 283 F. Supp. 681 (S.D.N.Y., 1966).

[14]*SEC v. Texas Gulf Sulphur Co.*, 401 F. 2d 849 (C.A. 2nd, 1968).

[15]*Statement of Financial Accounting Standards No. 2*, "Qualitative Characteristics of Accounting Information" (Samford: FASB, 1980), par. 132.

these definitions provide little practical guidance about how to make materiality decisions in real-world audit practice situations. The following sections address these practical considerations by discussing when an auditor makes materiality decisions in financial statement audits, how an auditor arrives at an overall preliminary estimate of materiality for an entire set of financial statements taken as a whole, and how an auditor allocates the overall estimate to individual financial statement components.

Making Materiality Decisions in Practice

As explained in Statement on Auditing Standards No. 47, ''Audit Risk and Materiality in Conducting an Audit'' (AU Sec. 312), there is an inverse relationship between audit risk and materiality. For example, the risk that a particular financial statement account, such as Receivables, could be misstated by an extremely large amount might be very low, but the risk that the account could be misstated by an extremely small amount might be very high. Holding other considerations constant, either a decrease in the allowable level of audit risk or a decrease in the amount of error deemed material would cause the auditor to do one or more of the following: select more effective audit procedures, perform auditing procedures closer to the balance sheet date, or increase the extent of the particular procedures applied (AU Sec. 312.17).

During a financial statement audit, an auditor considers materiality at least twice: once while planning the engagement, and again after all audit procedures have been completed. While planning an engagement, the auditor determines a *preliminary estimate of materiality* for the entire set of financial statements taken as a whole; if altered during the engagement, the new estimate is called a revised estimate of materiality. The preliminary estimate represents the maximum amount by which a set of financial statements could be misstated and still not cause the auditor to believe that the decisions of reasonable users would be affected. For example, if a preliminary estimate was $100,000, then combined misstatements of less than $100,000 would be immaterial. The purpose of determining a preliminary estimate is to help the auditor plan the extent of audit evidence to accumulate during the engagement. For example, if the preliminary estimate were revised downward to $75,000, then the extent of audit procedures would increase, since the auditor would need to examine more evidence in order to find smaller misstatements.

Toward the end of an engagement, after all audit evidence has been gathered and evaluated, an auditor again considers materiality by comparing the combined misstatement for all accounts with the preliminary (or revised) estimate for the entire set of financial statements taken as a whole. If the combined misstatement exceeds the preliminary estimate, then the financial statements would be materially misstated, and the auditor could either perform additional audit procedures or request that the client adjust the misstated accounts. Of course, if additional procedures are not performed and the client refuses to adjust the misstated accounts, then the auditor could issue a qualified or adverse opinion.

Determining a preliminary estimate of materiality is a crucial decision in audit practice because it affects both the extent of audit procedures performed and, ultimately, whether combined misstatement is likely to affect users' decisions. But, how do auditors determine a preliminary estimate? The following discussion addresses this question.

Preliminary Estimates of Materiality

Statement on Auditing Standards No. 22, "Planning and Supervision" (AU Sec. 311), states that an auditor should consider a preliminary judgment (estimate) of materiality when planning an audit engagement. The preliminary judgment need not be quantified necessarily, but many practitioners find quantification useful for assuring that all professional staff assigned to the engagement view materiality similarly. For example, if the preliminary judgment were determined by the audit partner to be "high" rather than stated numerically, not all members of the audit staff may interpret "high materiality" identically.

In practice, auditors sometimes determine a preliminary estimate of materiality using quantitative decisions aids and selected quantitative and qualitative materiality criteria, as discussed in the following sections.

A Decision Aid From Practice. Over the years, practicing auditors have designed and implemented various *decision aids,* not to supplant professional judgment, but to guide decision making. For example, based on data from a sample of actual audit engagements, one such decision aid was developed by Peat, Marwick, Main to guide the firm's auditors in developing preliminary estimates of materiality.[16]

The Peat, Marwick, Main decision aid requires that the auditor first determine the larger of estimated revenues or assets and then calculate a preliminary estimate of materiality from the following table:

---

[16]R. K. Elliott, "Author's Response to 'Materiality in Audit Planning'," *Journal of Accountancy* (July, 1983), p. 104.

If the Larger of Estimated Revenues or Assets Is		The Preliminary Estimate Is the Larger of Estimated Revenues or Assets	
Over	But Not Over	Times	Plus
$ 0	$ 30,000	.054	0
30,000	100,000	.029	750
100,000	300,000	.018	1,850
300,000	1,000,000	.0125	3,500
1,000,000	3,000,000	.0083	7,700
3,000,000	10,000,000	.006	14,600
10,000,000	30,000,000	.004	34,600
30,000,000	100,000,000	.00272	73,000
100,000,000	300,000,000	.0019	155,000
300,000,000	1,000,000,000	.00125	350,000
1,000,000,000	3,000,000,000	.00087	730,000
3,000,000,000	10,000,000,000	.00058	1,600,000
10,000,000,000	30,000,000,000	.0004	3,400,000
30,000,000,000	—	.00027	7,300,000

For example, if a client had estimated revenues of $22,500,000 and estimated assets of $15,750,000, then the preliminary estimate of materiality would be:

$$(\$22,500,000 \times .004) + \$34,600 = \$124,600$$

Of course, this estimate is merely input to the auditor's final judgment about materiality and would be revised based on other information.

Quantitative Materiality Criteria. Research conducted within the past several years has isolated quantitative materiality criteria often used by selected practicing auditors, all of whom responded to hypothetical case studies in controlled experiments or in mail survey questionnaires.[17] The criteria are:

▲ Percentage effect on net income
▲ Percentage effect on total revenues
▲ Percentage effect on total assets

---

[17]Major studies include: J. R. Boatsman and J. C. Robertson, "Policy-Capturing on Selected Materiality Judgments," *The Accounting Review* (April, 1974), pp. 342–352; M. Firth, "Consensus Views and Judgment Models in Materiality Decisions," *Accounting, Organizations and Society* (Vol. 4, No. 4, 1979), pp. 283–295; and S. Moriarity and F. Barron, "Modeling the Materiality Judgments of Audit Partners," *Journal of Accounting Research* (Autumn, 1976), pp. 320–341. For a review of empirical research on materiality, see: G. L. Holstrum and W. F. Messier, Jr., "A Review and Integration of Empirical Research on Materiality," *Auditing: A Journal of Practice and Theory* (Fall, 1982), pp. 45–63.

By far, the most common quantitative materiality criterion used by practicing auditors has been the percentage effect on net income. Although many auditors differ as to what percentage is material, most agree that combined error of less than five percent of net income is normally immaterial, and combined error of more than ten percent is normally material.

Both the effect on total revenues and the effect on total assets are also important quantitative criteria, particularly when used in conjunction with net income. For example, if a large, publicly traded company were to report net income of $2,000,000 in one year and $1,000 in the following year, with total assets approximating $20,000,000 in both years, an auditor would be foolish to conclude in the latter year that ten percent of net income, or $100, is material. Rather, the auditor would focus on total revenues and total assets, neither of which are normally subject to such wide fluctuations.

Qualitative Factors. In making materiality decisions, an auditor considers not only quantitative criteria, but also qualitative factors, particularly those which may cause a quantitatively immaterial transaction to be material in a qualitative sense. One common example is a quantitatively immaterial adjustment to working capital that would result in violation of a debt covenant if recorded on the books. To illustrate, assume that a client held a long-term bank loan which carried a debt covenant requiring the client to maintain a current ratio of 3 to 2 or better, and violation of the covenant would result in the loan becoming due and payable immediately. In this case, the disclosure issue is not so much the debt covenant violation as the fact that the long-term debt would have to be reclassified as a current liability assuming the bank called the note due and payable immediately.

A second qualitative factor, reversal of an earnings trend, is sometimes used by auditors as a materiality criterion, even when the percentage effect on net income, total revenues, and total assets is immaterial. To illustrate, assume that in four consecutive years, a company's earnings per share had been $2.50, $2.75, $3.03, and $3.33, respectively — an approximate increase of ten percent per year. An otherwise quantitatively immaterial audit adjustment that altered this trend negatively might be considered material because of the potential effect on financial statement users. A commercial loan officer, for example, might consider the reversal to be the "tip of the iceberg", or the beginning of a long-term downward trend. That is, the loan officer might be concerned that financial position may deteriorate over the loan repayment period, thereby reducing the likelihood of repayment. In this case, the loan officer might not deny the loan necessarily but might require a higher interest rate to compensate the bank for increased risk.

Another qualitative criterion is a quantitatively immaterial illegal payment which violates the Foreign Corrupt Practices Act (FCPA) among other federal and state laws. Disclosing a quantitatively immaterial illegal payment may be necessary for at least two reasons. First, financial statement users may be influenced by the fact that management is involved in questionable or illegal payments. Second, as noted in Chapter 3, the FCPA carries rather severe fines which may result in material contingent liabilities if the Justice Department or Securities and Exchange Commission prosecutes.

Allocating Preliminary Estimates of Materiality to Individual Accounts

Although an auditor's opinion relates to an entire set of financial statements taken as a whole, an audit is conducted piece-by-piece on individual financial statement components. As a result, some auditors allocate the preliminary estimate of materiality among financial statement components, such as income statement and balance sheet accounts. In practice, though, most auditors allocate materiality to balance sheet rather than income statement accounts, because (1) usually there are fewer balance sheet than income statement accounts, and (2) most income statement errors also affect the balance sheet.

In general, there are several approaches to allocating the preliminary estimate of materiality to individual financial statement accounts. Examples include:

▲ Relative magnitude of financial statement accounts.
▲ Relative variability of financial statement accounts.
▲ Professional judgment.

Each is illustrated below.

Relative Magnitude. One method is to allocate the preliminary estimate based on the relative dollar balance in each balance sheet account. However, the allocation should ignore accounts that will not be audited, such as retained earnings, and accounts that will be audited 100 percent. A simplified model which incorporates all of these considerations follows [18]:

$$\begin{matrix} \text{Preliminary} \\ \text{estimate of} \\ \text{materiality} \\ \text{for an} \\ \text{individual} \\ \text{balance sheet} \\ \text{account} \end{matrix} = \begin{matrix} \text{Preliminary} \\ \text{estimate of} \\ \text{materiality} \\ \text{for all} \\ \text{accounts} \end{matrix} \times \sqrt{\frac{\text{Amount of balance sheet account}}{\begin{matrix}\text{Sum of all balance sheet accounts} \\ \text{less (1) accounts not audited and} \\ \text{(2) accounts audited 100 percent}\end{matrix}}}$$

---

[18] G. R. Zuber, R. K. Elliott, W. R. Kinnery, Jr., and James J. Leisenring, "Using Materiality in Audit Planning," *Journal of Accountancy* (March, 1983), p. 50.

Other, more comprehensive, relative-magnitude models can be developed to allocate materiality more efficiently, although the cost to develop a more comprehensive model may exceed the benefits, given particularly that the model should be used to generate "initial," not final, allocations. That is, rather than blindly accept each allocation, an auditor should consider other factors affecting each account audited. For example, some balance sheet accounts, such as Cash, process relatively large volumes of transactions, but do not normally carry dollar balances representative of the volume of transactions processed. Thus, regardless of which relative-magnitude model is applied, the allocation of materiality to Cash is apt to be adjusted.

Relative Variability. The relative-magnitude approach discussed above considers the dollar balance of each account, but not the relative variability of each account's transactions. As a result, some auditors allocate materiality on the basis of a measure of variability — for example, the standard deviation of transactions processed — under the theory that as variability rises, so does an auditor's uncertainty, and, therefore, so does audit risk. For example, if two balance sheet accounts, such as Accounts Receivable and Accounts Payable, each had recorded book values of $1 million, then a relative-magnitude model would yield identical materiality allocations. However, if the standard deviation was $150 for Accounts Receivable and $950 for Accounts Payable, an auditor would likely conclude that payables transactions were less homogeneous than receivables transactions, and therefore might desire different materiality allocations for each account.

Professional Judgment. Most auditors use subjective professional judgment, only, to assess materiality for each financial statement account and then compare the sum of all materiality assessments with the overall preliminary estimate of materiality, revising as necessary. The essential difference between the relative magnitude and relative variability approaches on one hand and the professional judgment approach on the other is that the former approaches determine quantitative estimates of materiality first and then revise on the basis of other information, and the latter bypass the decision aid stage. Of course, regardless of the method used, an auditor should consider the cost of auditing specific accounts before actually allocating materiality.

Materiality in Auditing and in Accounting

Although both accountants and auditors employ similar criteria, their ultimate decisions regarding materiality often differ. In general, auditors have a higher threshold of materiality than do accountants. For example, a $1,000 understatement of advertising expense for a medium-size client is more apt to be material to the controller than to an independent auditor. The controller may be more concerned, for example, because a division manager's annual bonus is based on net income, or the advertising department's expenditures for the period are about to exceed amounts budgeted. In contrast, an auditor may be less concerned because the decisions of external financial information users are not likely to be affected. Regardless of how an auditor makes materiality decisions, the significant point is that materiality is inherent in most audit practice decisions and, therefore, is a particularly important consideration requiring keen professional judgment.

SUMMARY

Theory, a way of doing something, is not typically associated with auditing practice. At least three efforts, however, have been made to develop theories of auditing; although significant contributions, none have gained widespread acceptance among practitioners.

The most prominent concepts in auditing are evidence, due audit care, fair presentation, independence, and ethical conduct. In turn, these concepts are the basis for auditing standards. First developed in the 1940s, the AICPA's ten generally accepted auditing standards still stand today as the basic framework, the measures of quality and objectives, for contemporary audit practice in the U.S.

Materiality and risk are two primary considerations affecting applications of generally accepted auditing standards and are important because an auditor has neither the time nor resources to examine all of an entity's transactions and events. Thus, decisions must be made about which transactions and events will be examined. Of course, the most material areas and those involving the greatest risk receive the most audit attention.

REFERENCES

American Institute of Certified Public Accountants. *Report of the Special Committee of the AICPA to Study the Structure of the Auditing Standards Executive Committee.* New York: American Institute of Certified Public Accountants, 1978.

Commission on Auditors' Responsibilities, *Report, Conclusions, and Recommendations* (Section 10). New York: Commission on Auditors' Responsibilities, 1978.

Committee on Basic Auditing Concepts. "A Statement of Basic Auditing Concepts," *The Accounting Review,* supplement to vol. 47, 1972.

Cushing, B. E., and J. K. Loebbecke. "Analytical Approaches to Audit Risk," *Auditing: A Journal of Practice & Theory* (Fall, 1983), pp. 23–41.

Financial Accounting Standards Board Discussion Memorandum. "An Analysis of

Issues Related to Criteria for Determining Materiality.'' Stamford: Financial Accounting Standards Board, 1975.

Grobstein, M., and P. W. Craig. ''A Risk Analysis Approach to Auditing,'' *Auditing: A Journal of Practice & Theory* (Spring, 1984), pp. 1–16.

Holstrum, G. L., and W. F. Messier, Jr. ''A Review and Integration of Empirical Research on Materiality,'' *Auditing: A Journal of Practice & Theory* (Fall, 1982), pp. 45–63.

Jacobson, P. D., and R. K. Elliott. ''GAAS: Reconsidering the 'Ten Commandments.' '' *Journal of Accountancy* (May, 1984), pp. 77–88.

Jiambalvo, J., and W. Waller. ''Decomposition and Assessments of Audit Risk,'' *Auditing: A Journal of Practice & Theory* (Spring, 1984), pp. 80–88.

Mautz, R. K., and H. A. Sharaf. *The Philosophy of Auditing.* Sarasota: American Accounting Association, 1961.

Muller, H. ''The Auditing Standards Division: Responsibilities, Authority, and Structure.'' *Journal of Accountancy* (September, 1975), pp. 50–54.

Reckers, P. M. J., and A. J. Stagliano. ''Non-Audit Services and Perceived Independence: Some New Evidence.'' *Auditing: A Journal of Practice & Theory* (Summer, 1981), pp. 23–37.

Schandl, C. W. *Theory of Auditing: Evaluation, Investigation, and Judgment.* Houston: Scholars Book Co., 1978.

Strother, J. F. ''The Establishment of Generally Accepted Accounting Principles and Generally Accepted Auditing Standards.'' *Vanderbilt Law Review* (January, 1975), pp. 201–233.

Toba, Y. ''A General Theory of Evidence as the Conceptual Foundation in Auditing Theory. *The Accounting Review* (January, 1975), pp. 7–24.

U.S. Senate, Subcommittee on Reports, Accounting, and Management of the Committee on Government Operations. *The Accounting Establishment: A Staff Study.* Washington: U.S. Government Printing Office, 1976.

Zuber, G. R., R. K. Elliott, W. R. Kinney, Jr., and James J. Leisenring. ''Using Materiality in Audit Planning.'' *Journal of Accountancy* (March, 1983), pp. 42–54.

QUESTIONS

1. Identify and briefly discuss three significant studies of auditing theory reviewed in the chapter.
2. Why is it necessary to study auditing theory?
3. Identify the five fundamental concepts of auditing described by Mautz and Sharaf. What is the significance of these concepts to audit standards and procedures?
4. What is the purpose of an auditor's gathering and evaluating audit evidence?
5. Identify the fundamental issue underlying the concept of due audit care.
6. What fundamental precautions can be expected of a ''prudent auditor'' when exercising due audit care?
7. Identify and briefly describe the three subconcepts of ''fair presentation.''
8. Distinguish between practitioner-independence and profession-independence.
9. Briefly trace the historical development of generally accepted auditing standards.

10. What concepts underlie the three general standards, and what, in general, do these standards relate to?

11. What concept underlies the standards of field work, and what, in general, do the standards encompass?

12. Ignoring specific procedures, what matters should an auditor consider when planning an audit?

13. What concept underlies the reporting standards, and what, in general, do the standards encompass?

14. Identify and describe the quantitative criteria often used by practicing auditors when making materiality decisions.

15. What approaches are available for allocating the preliminary estimate of materiality to individual financial statement accounts?

16. Identify and describe the three component risks underlying audit risk for an individual financial statement account.

MULTIPLE CHOICE QUESTIONS (AICPA Adapted)

1. Which of the following best describes what is meant by generally accepted auditing standards?

   a. Acts to be performed by the auditor.
   b. Measures of the quality of the auditor's performance.
   c. Procedures to be used to gather evidence to support financial statements.
   d. Audit objectives generally determined on audit engagements.

2. A CPA should comply with applicable generally accepted auditing standards on every engagement:

   a. Without exception.
   b. Except in examinations that result in a qualified report.
   c. Except in engagements where the CPA is associated with unaudited financial statements.
   d. Except in examinations of interim financial statements.

3. Which of the following statements best describes the primary purpose of Statements on Auditing Standards?

   a. They are guides intended to set forth auditing procedures which are applicable to a variety of situations.
   b. They are procedural outlines which are intended to narrow the areas of inconsistency and divergence of auditor opinion.
   c. They are authoritative statements, enforced through the code of professional conduct, and are intended to limit the degree of auditor judgment.
   d. They are interpretations which are intended to clarify the meaning of "generally accepted auditing standards."

4. A CPA is most likely to refer to one or more of the three general auditing standards in determining:

  a. The nature of the CPA's report qualification.
  b. The scope of the CPA's auditing procedures.
  c. Requirements for the consideration of internal control structure.
  d. Whether the CPA should undertake an audit engagement.

5. Which of the following is mandatory if the auditor is to comply with generally accepted auditing standards?

  a. Possession by the auditor of adequate technical training.
  b. Use of analytical procedures in audit engagements.
  c. Use of statistical sampling whenever feasible on an audit engagement.
  d. Confirmation by the auditor of material accounts receivable balances.

6. The first general standard requires that a person or persons have adequate technical training and proficiency as an auditor. This standard is met by:

  a. An understanding of the field of business and finance.
  b. Education and experience in the field of auditing.
  c. Continuing professional education.
  d. A thorough knowledge of the Statements of Auditing Standards.

7. What is the meaning of the generally accepted auditing standard which requires that the auditor be independent?

  a. The auditor must be without bias with respect to the client under audit.
  b. The auditor must adopt a critical attitude during the audit.
  c. The auditor's sole obligation is to third parties.
  d. The auditor may have a direct ownership interest in the client's business if it is not material.

8. A CPA, while performing an audit, strives to achieve independence in appearance in order to

  a. Reduce risk and liability,
  b. Maintain public confidence in the profession.
  c. Become independent in fact.
  d. Comply with the generally accepted standards of field work.

9. The third general standard states that due care is to be exercised in the performance of the examination. This standard should be interpreted to mean that a CPA who undertakes an engagement assumes a duty to perform

  a. With reasonable diligence and without fault or error.
  b. As a professional who will assume responsibility for losses consequent upon error of judgment.
  c. To the satisfaction of the client and third parties who may rely upon it.
  d. As a professional possessing the degree of skill commonly possessed by others in the field.

10. What is the general character of the three generally accepted auditing standards classified as standards of field work?

  a. The competence, independence, and professional care of persons performing the audit.

b. Criteria for the content of the auditor's report on financial statements and related footnote disclosures.

c. The criteria of audit planning and evidence gathering.

d. The need to maintain an independence in mental attitude in all matters relating to the audit.

11. The first standard of field work, which states that the work is to be adequately planned, and assistants, if any, are to be properly supervised, recognizes that:

   a. Early appointment of the auditor is advantageous to the auditor and the client.
   b. Acceptance of an audit engagement after the close of the client's fiscal year is generally not permissible.
   c. Appointment of the auditor subsequent to the physical count of inventories requires a disclaimer of opinion.
   d. Performance of substantial parts of the examination is necessary at interim dates.

12. In connection with the third generally accepted auditing standard of field work, an auditor examines corroborating evidential matter which includes all of the following except:

   a. Client accounting manuals.
   b. Written client representations.
   c. Vendor invoices.
   d. Minutes of board meetings.

13. The sufficiency and competency of evidential matter ultimately are based on the:

   a. Availability of corroborating data.
   b. Generally accepted auditing standards.
   c. Pertinence of the evidence.
   d. Judgment of the auditor.

14. Which of the following underlies the application of generally accepted auditing standards, particularly the standards of field work and reporting?

   a. The elements of materiality and risk.
   b. The element of internal control structure.
   c. The element of corroborating evidence.
   d. The element of reasonable assurance.

15. The fourth generally accepted auditing standard of reporting requires an auditor to render a report whenever an auditor's name is associated with financial statements. The overall purpose of the fourth standard of reporting is to require that reports

   a. Assure that the auditor is independent with respect to the financial statements under examination.
   b. State that the auditor's examination of the financial statements has been conducted in accordance with generally accepted auditing standards.
   c. Indicate the character of the auditor's examination and the degree of responsibility assumed.
   d. Express whether the accounting principles used in preparing the financial statements have been applied consistently in the period under examination.

16. The auditor's judgment concerning the overall fairness of the presentation of financial positions, results of operations, and cash flows is applied within the framework of

    a. Quality control.
    b. Generally accepted auditing standards which include the concept of materiality.
    c. The auditor's evaluation of the audited company's internal control structure.
    d. Generally accepted accounting principles.

17. Which one of the following statements is correct concerning the concept of materiality?

    a. Materiality is determined by reference to guidelines established by the AICPA.
    b. Materiality depends only on the dollar amount of an item relative to other items in the financial statements.
    c. Materiality depends on the nature of an item rather than the dollar amount.
    d. Materiality is a matter of professional judgment.

18. The concept of materiality would be least important to an auditor in determining the

    a. Transactions that should be reviewed.
    b. Need for disclosure of a particular fact or transaction.
    c. Scope of the CPA's audit program relating to various accounts.
    d. Effects of direct financial interest in the client upon the CPA's independence.

PROBLEMS

5-1   Generally accepted auditing standards are an auditor's guidelines for selecting and designing detailed audit procedures, and an auditor typically applies selected procedures to determine whether an entity's financial statements are presented in accordance with generally accepted accounting principles. Thus, generally accepted auditing standards, audit procedures, and generally accepted accounting principles are fundamentally related to one another in an opinion audit.

Required:
1. What is the difference between (a) generally accepted auditing standards and (b) auditing procedures?
2. Why is it important that the auditor's report state whether an entity's financial statements are presented "in conformity with generally accepted accounting principles"?

5-2   Andrea Farell, a local CPA, has been approached by Whitely Corporation concerning audited financial statements for the year ended September 30, 1990. Whitely, a relatively new company, maintains a computerized data processing system. Not having been exposed to electronic data processing (EDP) systems previously, Farell enrolls in professional development courses designed to provide participants with an understanding of:

a. A computer programming language identical to the one used by Whitely.
b. The capability of computers and how automated data are processed.
c. How to examine the controls typically associated with EDP systems and to use the computer to achieve compliance with generally accepted auditing standards.
d. Auditing problems peculiar to EDP systems.
e. The types of system documentation typically employed in an EDP environment.

  Farell completes the rather extensive course and is pleased with both the quality of instruction and depth and extent of topical coverage.

Required:
1. The first general standard requires that an auditor have "adequate technical training and proficiency." Has Farell complied with the standard? Discuss.
2. Why is training in computer-based systems necessary before Farell can accept the Whitely engagement? Discuss.

5-3   The second general standard states that "In all matters relating to the assignment, an independence in mental attitude is to be maintained by the auditor or auditors." In addition to the AICPA's Code of Professional Conduct Rule 101 (discussed in Chapter 2) and selected Securities and Exchange Commission Accounting Series Releases, the second general standard is the profession's primary guideline relating to independence.

Required:
Discuss the importance of, and difficulties in achieving, independence in mental attitude.

5-4   The CPA firm Rodgers and Burge conducted an audit of the Lexington Manufacturing Company's December 31, 1990 financial statements. The scope paragraph of the unqualified report read as follows:

"We conducted our audits in accordance with generally accepted auditing standards. Those standards require that we plan and perform the audit to obtain reasonable assurance about whether the financial statements are free of material misstatement. An audit includes examining, on a test basis, evidence supporting the amounts and disclosures in the financial statements. An audit also includes assessing the accounting principles used and significant estimates made by management, as well as evaluating the overall financial statement presentation. We believe that our audits provide a reasonable basis for our opinion."

Required:
What does the scope paragraph imply about (1) the professional qualifications of Rodgers and Burge and the quality of their work and (2) the conduct of their audit work?

5-5   You are the managing partner of Berke & Co., CPAs. On February 2, 1990, you receive a letter from the president of Barbizon, Inc., requesting the following:

  We have made arrangements with Farmers Loan and Trust to borrow $125,000 to finance the purchase of new equipment. The bank has asked us to submit audited financial statements for the fiscal year ended December 31, 1989.

  Barbizon has not previously been audited and requests that you conduct the audit.

Required:
1. Can you accept the engagement? Explain.
2. Assuming you accept the engagement, what can be done about confirming December 31, 1989 accounts receivable balances with debtors and observing December 31, 1989 physical inventory quantities, two auditing procedures that you would have conducted if the engagement were accepted prior to December 31.

5-6   The third generally accepted auditing standard of field work requires that the auditor obtain sufficient competent evidential matter to afford a reasonable basis for an opinion regarding the financial statements under examination. In considering what constitutes sufficient competent evidential matter, a distinction should be made between underlying accounting data and all corroborating information available to the auditor.

Required:
1. Discuss the nature of evidential matter to be considered by the auditor in terms of the underlying accounting data, all corroborating information available to the auditor, and the methods by which the auditor tests or gathers competent evidential matter.
2. Discuss briefly the meaning of competence in relation to audit evidence, and state the three general presumptions that can be made about the validity of evidential matter.

(AICPA Adapted)

5-7   You have been assigned by your firm to complete the examination of the financial statements of Carter Manufacturing Corporation, because the senior accountant and an inexperienced assistant who began the engagement were hospitalized because of an accident. The engagement is about one-half completed. Your auditor's report must be delivered in three weeks as agreed when your firm accepted the engagement. You estimate that by utilizing the client's staff to the greatest possible extent you can complete the engagement in five weeks. Your firm cannot assign an assistant to you.

The working papers show the status of work on the examination as follows:
a. Completed — cash, fixed assets, depreciation, mortgage payable, and stockholders' equity.
b. Completed except as noted later — inventories, accounts payable, tests of purchase transactions, and payrolls.
c. Nothing done — trade accounts receivable, inventory receiving cutoff and price testing, accrued expenses payable, unrecorded liability test, tests of sales transactions, payroll deductions test and observation of payroll check distribution, other expenses, analytical procedures, vouching of December purchase transactions, auditor's report, consideration of internal control structure, letter on control structure deficiencies, minutes, preparation of tax returns, procedural recommendations for management, subsequent events, supervision and review.

Your review discloses that the assistant's working papers are incomplete and were not reviewed by the senior accountant. For example, the inventory working papers present incomplete notions, incomplete explanations, and no cross-referencing.

Required:
1. What field work standards have been violated by the senior accountant who preceded you on this assignment? Explain why you feel the standards you list have been violated.
2. In planning your work to complete this engagement, you should scan work papers and schedule certain work as soon as possible and also identify work which may be postponed until after the report is issued to the client.
   a. List the areas on which you should plan to work first, say in your first week of work, and for each item explain why it deserves early attention.
   b. State which work you believe could be postponed until after the report is issued to the client, and give reasons why the work may be postponed.

(AICPA Adapted)

5-8   You are engaged in the examination of the financial statements of Rapid, Inc., and its recently acquired subsidiary, Slow Corporation. In acquiring Slow Corporation during 1990, Rapid, Inc., exchanged a large number of its shares of common stock for 90% of the outstanding common stock of Slow Corporation in a transaction that was accounted for as a pooling of interests. Rapid, Inc., is now preparing the annual report to shareholders and proposes to include in the report combined financial statements for the year ended December 31, 1990 with a footnote describing its exchange of stock for that of Slow Corporation. Rapid, Inc., also proposes to include in its report the financial statements of the previous year as they appeared in Rapid, Inc.'s, 1989 annual report along with a five-year financial summary from Rapid's prior annual reports, all of which had been accompanied by your unqualified auditor's opinion.

Required:
1. Discuss the objectives or purposes of the standard of reporting which requires the auditor's report to identify circumstances in which generally accepted accounting principles have not been consistently observed over the past two periods.
2. Briefly discuss whether Rapid's proposed presentation of financial statements in the 1990 annual report would affect comparability.

(AICPA Adapted)

5-9   Leer, CPA, has discussed various reporting considerations with two audit clients. The two clients presented the following situations and asked how they would affect the audit report.
A. A client has a loan agreement that restricts the amount of cash dividends that can be paid and requires the maintenance of a particular current ratio. The client is in compliance with the terms of the agreement, and it is not likely that there will be a violation in the foreseeable future. The client believes there is no need to mention the restriction in the financial statements because such mention might mislead the readers.
B. During the year, a client correctly accounted for the acquisition of a majority-owned domestic subsidiary but did not properly present the minority interest in retained earnings or net income of the subsidiary in the consolidated financial statements. The client agrees with Leer that the minority interest presented in the consolidated financial statements is materially misstated but takes the position that the minority shareholders of the subsidiary should look to that subsidiary's financial statements for information concerning their interest therein.

Required:

Each of these situations relates to one of the four generally accepted auditing standards of reporting.

Identify and describe the applicable reporting standard in each situation, and discuss how the particular client situation relates to the standard and to Leer's report.

Organize your answer as follows:

Situation	Applicable Standard of Reporting	Discussion of Relationship of Client Situation to Standard of Reporting and to Leer's Report
A		
B		

(AICPA Adapted)

5-10   Smith, the owner of a small company, asked Holmes, a CPA, to conduct an audit of the company's records. Smith told Holmes that an audit is to be completed in time to submit audited financial statements to a bank as part of a loan application. Holmes immediately accepted the engagement and agreed to provide an auditor's report within three weeks. Smith agreed to pay Holmes a fixed fee plus a bonus if the loan was granted.

Holmes hired two accounting students to conduct the audit and spent several hours telling them exactly what to do. Holmes told the students not to spend time reviewing the controls but instead to concentrate on proving the mathematical accuracy of the ledger accounts, and summarizing the data in the accounting records that support Smith's financial statements. The students followed Holmes' instructions and after two weeks gave Holmes the financial statements, which did not include footnotes. Holmes reviewed the statements and prepared an unqualified auditor's report. The report, however, did not refer to generally accepted accounting principles nor to the year-to-year application of such principles.

Required:

Briefly describe each of the generally accepted auditing standards and indicate how the actions of Holmes resulted in a failure to comply with each standard.

Organize your answer as follows:

Brief Description of Generally Accepted Auditing Standards	Holmes' Actions Resulting in Failure to Comply with Generally Accepted Auditing Standards

(AICPA Adapted)

5-11   Audit risk, the probability that an auditor may unknowingly fail to modify
her or his opinion on materially misstated financial statements, occurs on all external
audit engagements, partly because auditors do not usually test all transactions underlying an account balance and partly because of other uncertainties, such as inadequate
planning and supervision.

Required:
1. Briefly describe inherent risk, control risk, and detection risk, the three component risks underlying audit risk for individual financial statement accounts.
2. Why are some financial statement accounts more inherently risky than others?
3. Explain why detection risk bears an inverse relationship to inherent and control
   risk.
4. Assuming inherent, control, and detection risks are judged by an auditor to be
   .75, .50, and .25 respectively, for trade accounts receivable, what is audit risk
   for the account?
5. In regard to (4) above, assume inherent risk is revised downward to .50.
   a. What is audit risk?
   b. In comparison with (4). above, how will the new audit risk level affect the
      auditor's revised estimate of materiality for trade accounts receivable?

5-12   The concept of materiality is important to the CPA in the examination of
financial statements and expression of opinion on the statements.

Required:
Discuss the following:
1. How is materiality (and immateriality) related to the proper presentation of financial statements?
2. In what ways will considerations of materiality affect the CPA in
   a. Developing an audit program?
   b. Performance of auditing procedures?
3. What factors and measures should the CPA consider in assessing the materiality
   of an exception to financial statement presentation?
4. How will the materiality of a CPA's exceptions to financial statements influence
   the type of opinion expressed?

(AICPA Adapted)

5-13   Richard Yates, CPA, is auditing the Levitan Corporation's financial statements for the year ended December 31, 1990. In prior years, Levitan's financial
statements were audited by other auditors. Levitan's unaudited Accounts Receivable,
Inventory, and Plant Assets are $2,500,000, $7,750,000, and $15,000,000, respec-
tively, and all other assets total $12,750,000. Total current liabilities are $9,900,000,
and net income is expected to be $4,500,000 on $35,000,000 of total revenues.
Levitan Corporation is publicly traded on a national stock exchange.

Because Yates had not previously audited Levitan, he decides to audit all of the
balance sheet accounts, and to audit Accounts Payable, with a recorded balance of
$3,000,000, 100 percent, since controls are weak and the balance represents a small
number of individual accounts.

Required:

1. Determine a preliminary estimate of materiality for Levitan Corporation's financial statements taken as a whole.
2. What portion of the preliminary estimate of materiality should be allocated to Accounts Receivable, Inventory, and Plant Assets, assuming Yates uses the *relative-magnitude* approach to determine the allocation.

5-14   During the course of an audit engagement an independent auditor gives serious consideration to the concept of materiality. This concept is inherent in the work of the independent auditor and is important for planning, preparing, and modifying audit programs. The concept of materiality underlies the application of all the generally accepted auditing standards, particularly the standards of field work and reporting.

Required:

1. Briefly describe what is meant by the independent auditor's concept of materiality.
2. What are some common financial statement relationships and other considerations used by the auditor in judging materiality?
3. Describe how the planning and execution of an audit program might be affected by the independent auditor's concept of materiality.

EVIDENCE, THE AUDIT PROCESS, AND WORKING PAPERS

6

Major topics discussed in this chapter are the:

▲   *Nature of audit evidence and its relationship to financial statement assertions, audit objectives, and audit procedures.*

▲   *Nature of tests of controls, substantive tests, and analytical procedures.*

▲   *Major activities in the audit process, including the decision to accept an engagement, first- and second-level planning, and interim and year-end audit work.*

▲   *Purpose, content, and form of manual and automated working papers.*

This chapter introduces the nature of audit evidence, the audit process, and audit working papers. In general, the chapter describes the nature of independent financial statement audits, thereby providing a basis for appreciating and understanding the details of audit method developed in subsequent chapters.

AUDIT EVIDENCE

The purpose of gathering and evaluating audit evidence is to acquire data and information to be used as a basis for concluding whether an entity's financial statements are presented fairly in accordance with generally accepted accounting principles. Note that the purpose is not to "prove" that an entity's financial statements are presented fairly, but to make an informed decision based on an impartial evaluation of the evidence gathered. This subtle distinction between "proving" financial statements are fairly stated versus impartial evaluation is important in understanding the role of evidence in the independent audit of financial statements. With this distinction as background, the following sections discuss the nature of audit evidence and its relationship to audit assertions, objectives, and procedures. Evidence based on the work of specialists and problems associated with related party transactions — two important issues in the evaluation of audit evidence — are considered as well.

208

The Nature of Audit Evidence

The third standard of field work states:

Sufficient competent evidential matter is to be obtained through inspection, observation, inquiries, and confirmations to afford a reasonable basis for an opinion regarding the financial statements under examination.

As defined in SAS No. 31 (AU Sec. 326), *evidential matter* consists of the underlying accounting data and corroborating information available to an auditor. *Underlying accounting data* include: books of original entry, general and subsidiary ledgers, related accounting manuals, and informal records such as work sheets. *Corroborating information* includes: documentary materials such as checks, invoices, contracts, and minutes of meetings; confirmations and other written representations by knowledgeable parties; and information obtained from inquiry, observation, inspection, and physical examination.

Sufficiency, as used in the third standard of field work, refers to the amount and kinds of evidence obtained, and *competence* refers to validity and relevance. The sufficiency and competence of evidence must be judged by an independent auditor, and in this context an auditor's judgment is based primarily on the persuasiveness of evidence. Although the persuasiveness of evidence must be judged in light of the particular circumstances at hand, the following generalizations are appropriate:

▲ Evidence obtained from independent external sources is more reliable than evidence obtained from within the entity.
▲ Evidence obtained directly by the auditor through examination, observation, computation, or inspection is more reliable than evidence obtained indirectly.
▲ Evidence obtained when control risk is low is more reliable than evidence obtained when control risk is high.

Because an audit must be conducted within a reasonable time frame and at reasonable cost to the client, an auditor cannot examine evidence supporting every transaction or event underlying an entity's financial statements. As a result, an auditor's conclusions are reached by examining a sample of transactions and events. Conclusions drawn from samples are then generalized to the related populations. For example, an auditor might examine evidence supporting 100 randomly selected accounts payable and conclude from these results that the entire population of 5,000 accounts is fairly presented. However, because conclusions are drawn from examining some rather than all available evidence, audit evidence is seldom wholly convincing. Rather, audit evidence is persuasive, and an auditor attempts to gather the most persuasive evidence available.

Relating Audit Evidence, Assertions, Objectives, and Procedures

Much of an auditor's work during an independent audit consists of obtaining and evaluating evidence about the explicit and implicit assertions embodied in financial statements. Since financial statements are management's responsibility, financial statement assertions are management's representations and can be broadly categorized as in Figure 6-1.

From the assertions contained within an entity's financial statements, an auditor develops specific *audit objectives*. Audit objectives vary from one engagement to another depending upon an entity's specific circumstances, including the nature of its economic activity and the accounting practices unique to its industry. For example, selected audit objectives related to a manufacturing company's inventory might include:

Financial Statement Assertion	Illustrative Audit Objective
Existence... *observation*	Inventories included in the balance sheet physically exist.
Completeness . *observation &* .. *documentation*	Inventory quantities include all products, materials, and supplies on hand.
Rights	The entity has legal title or similar rights of ownership to inventories.
Valuation	Inventories are properly stated at the lower of cost or market.
Presentation	Inventories are properly classified in the balance sheet as current assets.

FIGURE 6-1

Financial Statement Assertions

- *Existence or occurrence:* all recorded assets, liabilities, and equities exist at a given date, and all recorded transactions occurred during a given period.
- *Completeness:* all transactions and accounts that should be presented in the financial statements are so included.
- *Rights and obligations:* assets are the rights of the entity, and liabilities are the obligations of the entity at a given date.
- *Valuation or allocation:* assets, liabilities, equities, revenues, and expenses have been included in the financial statements at appropriate amounts.
- *Presentation and disclosure:* financial statement components are properly classified, described, and disclosed.

To achieve audit objectives, an auditor selects *audit procedures,* considering the nature of the objectives, the types and reliability of evidence available, materiality, and the assessed level of control risk. A single audit procedure may be used to satisfy one or more objectives, or more than one procedure may be needed to satisfy a single objective. The following basic procedures are used by auditors to gather evidence needed to satisfy audit objectives.

▲ *Observation:* physically examine a tangible asset, or develop impressions from circumstances.
▲ *Documentation:* examine documents and records.
▲ *Confirmation:* obtain written statements from independent third parties.
▲ *Mechanical tests of accounting data:* recompute amounts previously calculated by client personnel, or trace transactions through the accounting system.
▲ *Comparisons:* develop and analyze trends and relationships among data.
▲ *Inquiries:* obtain written or oral statements from client personnel.

Observation. An auditor can acquire direct personal knowledge about the existence of assets such as cash, inventory, and fixed assets through physical examination. In addition, physical examination may provide an auditor with useful information about the quality or condition of assets, for example, when an auditor identifies obsolete or damaged inventory during a physical inventory observation.

Observation extends not only to tangible assets, but also to client activities and events, often a valuable source of impressions and insights. For example, observing client personnel may be useful in an auditor's assessment of control risk, particularly in determining whether client employees perform assigned duties.

Documentation. By inspecting documents and records, an auditor can determine whether recorded data are adequately supported and transactions properly authorized. In applying this procedure, often referred to as *vouching,* an auditor selects certain items of recorded financial information and then locates and examines the documents supporting the items selected.

Confirmation. Some account balances and other information can be substantiated or confirmed by securing written statements from independent parties. For example, an auditor might confirm receivable and payable balances with debtors and creditors, respectively, or might confirm the terms of a lease agreement with the lessor.

Mechanical Tests of Accounting Data. An auditor can verify the mathematical accuracy of underlying accounting data by *recomputing* calculations performed by client personnel. For example, an auditor might total or "foot" the columns in the cash receipts journal, or recalculate depreciation expense. *Tracing,* another type of mechanical test applied by auditors, involves following a transaction through the accounting system — e.g., from source document to journal to subsidiary and general ledgers — and is used primarily to determine whether transactions are properly recorded and classified.

Comparisons. Selected items can be compared with similar items from prior periods to reveal trends, or with other items in the same period to establish informative relationships. Analyses of trends and relationships can be particularly useful in identifying areas requiring further examination, and are discussed later in the context of analytical procedures.

Inquiries. An auditor typically obtains a significant amount of written and oral information from client personnel. In general, such information can be quite informative; however, it is often less reliable than information obtained from external sources and should be corroborated through other procedures.

TESTS OF CONTROLS, SUBSTANTIVE TESTS, AND AUDIT RISK

Depending on an auditor's objectives, the basic auditing procedures — observation, documentation, confirmation, mechanical tests, comparisons, and inquiries — can be used in performing either tests of controls or substantive tests. *Tests of controls* are auditing procedures intended to assess the effectiveness of an internal control structure policy (or procedure) in preventing or detecting material misstatements. In turn, *substantive tests* consist of tests of details and analytical procedures and are auditing procedures intended to detect material misstatements, or to identify accounts likely to contain material misstatements.

Tests of Controls and Control Risk. When evaluating an entity's internal control structure, an auditor performs procedures designed to provide knowledge necessary for audit planning and procedures, called tests of controls, designed to provide evidence used in assessing control risk. Procedures used for planning usually include inquiries of management, inspection of documents such as invoices, and observing employees at work.

Tests of controls, in contrast, are concerned with how internal control structure policies or procedures are applied, the consistency of application during the period, and by whom they are applied. Through tests of controls, an auditor reaches a conclusion about the *assessed level of control risk,* which is the auditor's assessment of the effectiveness of an entity's internal control structure in preventing or detecting material misstatements in the financial statements. The assessed level of control risk is then used in determining an acceptable level of detection risk. As the assessed level of control risk increases, the acceptable level of detection risk decreases. Examples of tests of controls are illustrated and discussed in detail in Chapters 11, 13, 15, 16, and 17.

Most control procedures can be classified into one of two categories, controls that "leave an audit trail," i.e., create documentation, and those that do not. The distinction between the two is essential to understanding the nature of tests of controls. For example, consider two control procedures implemented by a company: (1) sales orders are approved and initialed by the credit manager before goods are shipped, and (2) monthly bank reconciliations are prepared by an employee not otherwise involved in the approval or recording of cash transactions. The first control procedure — credit approval — is an example of a control that creates documentation: sales orders with the credit manager's initials. In contrast, the second control procedure — bank reconciliations prepared by independent employees — provides documentation (the reconciliation), but the documentation does not provide evidence about whether the preparer is independent of the cash function (Who actually prepared the reconciliation?). As a result, for this control procedure, as well as other procedures which rely on segregation of duties, an auditor would likely rely on the auditing procedures of observation and/or inquiries as tests of controls. That is, the auditor could physically observe who prepares the reconciliation and/or make inquiries of other appropriate personnel.

Substantive Tests and Detection Risk. After considering inherent risk and control risk, an auditor performs substantive tests to restrict detection risk to an acceptable level. Substantive tests provide evidence about monetary misstatements and are founded in the third standard of field work, which requires that an auditor obtain sufficient, competent, evidential matter as a basis for reaching an opinion on whether financial statements are presented fairly. However, the extent of substantive testing is dependent on the results of tests of controls, because the extent of substantive tests depends on the acceptable level of detection risk which, in turn, depends on the assessed level of control risk. For example, if tests of controls indicated that the two control procedures identified above — credit approval and bank reconciliations — are operating as planned, then related substantive tests can be reduced, although not eliminated, because control risk is low.

Substantive tests can be classified either as *tests of details* of transactions and balances or as *analytical procedures*. Each type of substantive test is discussed below.

Substantive Tests of Details. An auditor's substantive tests of details are intended to detect material misstatements in financial statements. For example, to test whether recorded receivables exist at the balance sheet date, an auditor could confirm balances directly with customers and perform other tests (procedures) to determine whether sales and receivables transactions are recorded in the proper accounting period.

Tests of details and tests of controls differ in one critical respect: tests of controls provide evidence about whether misstatement is *likely* (as a means to assess control risk), and substantive tests of details provide evidence about whether misstatement actually *exists* (as a means to control detection risk). For example, if a test of controls indicates that a control procedure is not reliable, and therefore that control risk is high, then the auditor would conclude only that material misstatement at the balance sheet date is likely, and therefore that substantive tests of details must be extended to control detection risk. But, if tests of details reveal material monetary error, then the auditor would conclude that misstatement actually exists and that further tests should be conducted or the financial statements adjusted. Examples of substantive tests of details are discussed and illustrated in Chapters 12, 14, 15, 16, and 17.

Analytical Procedures. The auditing procedures identified as "comparisons" and discussed briefly on page 212 are commonly referred to in practice as *analytical procedures* and are defined in *Statement on Auditing Standards No. 56*, "Analytical Procedures," as "evaluations of financial information made by a study of plausible relationships among both financial and nonfinancial data." Analytical procedures range from simple comparisons to complex statistical models that incorporate vast amounts of data, such as regression analysis. Unlike tests of controls and substantive tests of details, analytical procedures are based on the presumption that plausible relationships among data may reasonably be expected to exist since, in double entry accounting, two or more financial statement accounts are affected for each recorded transaction. For example, debits to accounts receivable require a corresponding credit to another account, often sales, thereby suggesting that accounts receivable and sales should bear a plausible relationship to one another. That is, if gross sales for a company decrease from one period to the next by fifty percent, an auditor might reasonably expect a substantial decrease in accounts receivable as well. However, if accounts receivable did not decrease by a substantial amount, the auditor would probably make inquiries of management and/or perform additional tests of details designed to determine whether monetary misstatement exists in recorded gross sales, recorded receivables, or both. Thus, analytical procedures are not necessarily intended to isolate monetary misstatements, as for example a substantive test of details might, but rather to identify accounts that are likely to contain monetary misstatements.

Under SAS No. 56, analytical procedures should be applied to some extent for purposes of assisting the auditor during the planning stage of an engagement and as an overall review of the financial statements during the final review stage. In addition, in some cases, analytical procedures used as substantive tests can actually be more effective or efficient for achieving some audit objectives than a substantive test of details, since analytical procedures allow the auditor to reach conclusions about the details in an account by testing aggregated data within the account. Tests of details, in contrast, allow an auditor to draw conclusions about aggregated data from testing details. Regardless of the auditor's intent in using a particular analytical procedure — i.e., planning, overall review, or as a substantive test — all analytical procedures involve comparisons of recorded amounts or ratios to expectations. The auditor's expectations are derived from plausible relationships and are based on the auditor's understanding of the client and the client's industry. Examples of information an auditor uses in developing expectations include:

▲ Financial information for comparable prior periods giving consideration to known changes.
▲ Anticipated results — for example, projections or forecasts including extrapolations from interim or annual data.
▲ Relationships among elements of financial information within the period — for example, the relationship between sales and accounts receivable.
▲ Information regarding the industry in which the client operates — for example, gross margin information.
▲ Relationships between financial information and relevant nonfinancial information — for example, the relationship between sales and a client's share of the market.

Analytical procedures used in the planning stage of an engagement are discussed later in this chapter. Examples of analytical procedures used as substantive tests are discussed and illustrated in Chapters 12, 14, 15, 16, and 17. Analytical procedures used in the final review stage of an engagement are discussed in Chapter 18.

Dual Purpose Tests. In practice, auditors often perform *dual-purpose tests* which are intended to provide evidence about both control risk and likely monetary error. For example, when recomputing the mathematical extensions on sales invoices (e.g., quantity $\times$ unit price), an auditor is actually performing both a test of controls and a substantive test of details: a test of controls in the sense that the auditor is determining whether client personnel are properly extending sales invoices, and a substantive test in the sense that the auditor is determining whether monetary error exists.

Applying Substantive Tests Prior to the Balance Sheet Date

Tests of control are typically performed during an interim period prior to the balance sheet date, while most substantive tests are performed at year-end shortly after the balance sheet date. Some substantive tests, however, may be performed prior to the balance sheet date in order to permit early consideration of significant matters (e.g., recent pronouncements that require extensive disclosures), or to avoid excessive year-end workloads and time constraints. In either case, performing substantive tests at interim to determine monetary error increases detection risk in that undetected errors or irregularities may exist at the balance sheet date, and the risk becomes greater as the period between interim tests and year-end increases. *Statement on Auditing Standards No. 45,* "Omnibus Statement on Auditing Standards: 1983 (AU Sec. 313)," addresses factors to consider before applying substantive tests at interim and extending interim audit conclusions to the balance sheet date.

Factors to Consider. Essentially an auditor should consider no less than four factors before concluding that interim substantive tests are desirable. First, since the period between interim tests and the balance sheet date — the "remaining period" — cannot be ignored, the auditor should consider: (1) whether the benefits of applying substantive tests at interim would exceed the costs of year-end follow-up procedures to reassess control risk for the remaining period and (2) whether evidence obtained at interim and for the remaining period will be sufficiently persuasive. If the answer to either or both questions is "No," the auditor should conclude that applying substantive tests at interim is undesirable, since the audit is likely to be either uneconomical or ineffective, or both.

Second, if an auditor does not intend to rely on an entity's internal control structure during the remaining period — for example, when control risk is high — he or she should consider whether the effectiveness of substantive procedures applied to the remaining period will be impaired. For example, if an entity lacks sufficient control over the custody and movement of inventory, interim substantive tests related to existence may be ineffective.

Third, rapidly changing business conditions during the remaining period may predispose management to misstate year-end financial statements. For example, competitors may have introduced new products that seriously eroded the market share of a company's existing product line, prompting management to overstate sales for the year. If business conditions are changing or changes are anticipated, the auditor may judge control risk intolerable, electing to apply substantive tests of details at year-end (rather than at interim), thereby reducing detection risk.

Finally, when applying substantive tests at interim, an auditor should consider whether the related year-end account balances are reasonably predictable (through, for example, analytical procedures) and whether questionable balances, if any, can be identified and investigated. For example, statistical techniques such as regression analysis can be used to estimate an upper and lower bound for a year-end account balance. If the recorded account balance falls within the upper and lower bounds, and interim substantive tests did not detect material misstatements — suggesting low control risk — regression analysis would have confirmed the results of interim tests, and there would be no reason to believe that audit risk is intolerable.

Extending Interim Conclusions to the Balance Sheet Date. If an auditor decides to apply substantive tests at interim, he or she must determine whether the accumulated audit evidence gathered from (1) interim tests of controls and (2) substantive tests applied for the remaining period adequately addresses the financial statement assertions introduced earlier: existence or occurrence, completeness, rights and obligations, valuation or allocation, and presentation and disclosure. If interim audit conclusions are to be extended to the balance sheet date, year-end substantive tests should at a minimum include: (1) comparing information concerning year-end balances with comparable interim information in order to identify and investigate unusual amounts and (2) other analytical procedures and/or substantive tests of details. Otherwise, an auditor would not have a reasonable basis for extending interim audit conclusions to the balance sheet date.

Using the Work of Specialists

Occasionally, an auditor may call upon a specialist — a person possessing a special skill or knowledge in a particular nonaccounting field — to examine evidence related to an audit engagement. For example, an auditor might engage actuaries to determine actuarial gains and losses, appraisers to determine the net realizable value of art objects, or chemists to determine the composition and value of chemical solutions. *Statement on Auditing Standards No. 11,* "Using the Work of a Specialist" (AU Sec. 336), provides guidance when specialists are used, focusing specifically on the decision to use a specialist, selecting a specialist, and using a specialist's findings.

Decision to Use a Specialist. The third standard of field work requires that audit evidence be competent. Auditors, however, are not always in a position to judge competence. For example, an auditor may not be able to determine whether a portion of an oil refinery's inventory represents crude oil or colored salad oil. Obviously, the difference in values between crude oil and salad oil can have a significant impact upon the carrying value of inventory. Thus, when an audit judgment requires special knowledge, an auditor should use the work of a specialist.

Selecting a Specialist. A specialist should be qualified, reputable, and, except in unusual instances, unrelated to a client. When selecting a specialist, an auditor should consider:

▲ The professional certification, license, or other appropriate recognition of the specialist's competence.
▲ The reputation and standing of the specialist in the views of peers and others familiar with his or her capability or performance.
▲ The relationship, if any, of the specialist to the client.

In all cases, the auditor, client, and specialist should reach an understanding about the nature of the work to be performed by the specialist. Ideally, the understanding should be in writing and include:

▲ The objectives and scope of the specialist's work.
▲ The specialist's representations as to his or her relationship, if any, to the client.
▲ The methods or assumptions to be used.
▲ A comparison of methods or assumptions to be used with those used in the preceding period.
▲ The specialist's understanding of the auditor's use of the specialist's findings.
▲ The form and content of the specialist's report.

Using a Specialist's Findings. A specialist's methods and techniques are his or her responsibility. However, even though not possessing a specialist's skills, an auditor should obtain an understanding of the specialist's methods or assumptions in order to judge whether the findings are suitable for corroborating financial statement assertions. In short, an auditor should not blindly accept a specialist's findings but should consider whether the findings support financial statement assertions and make appropriate tests of accounting data provided to the specialist by the client. If an auditor's consideration and tests suggest a specialist's findings are unreasonable, the findings should not be relied upon. In contrast, if an auditor's consideration and tests suggest findings are reasonable, the auditor may assume that the findings constitute sufficient competent evidential matter.

Related Party Transactions

A transaction is an exchange of promises, commitments, or economic resources between or among parties. In most cases, parties to a transaction are independent, thereby increasing the likelihood that the transaction is at "arm's length" — that is, a bargained exchange. Occasionally, however, parties to a transaction are not independent. Rather, they are related and may include the reporting entity, its affiliates, principal owners, managers, and their immediate family members, and other parties in a position to influence or be influenced by another party. The significance of related party transactions is that the legal form and therefore the disclosure of such a transaction may not accurately reflect its economic substance. Thus, an auditor is concerned that financial statements reflect the economic substance, not just the legal form, of material related party transactions. *Statement on Auditing Standards No. 45,* "Omnibus Statement on Auditing Standards: 1983" (AU Sec. 334) addresses related party transactions.

Motivation for Related Party Transactions. A relationship between or among related parties does not necessarily mean a transaction is not at arm's length; an auditor must obtain and carefully evaluate evidence before drawing such a conclusion. Nevertheless, an auditor should be aware that the likelihood of a related party transaction not being at arm's length increases in situations similar to the following (AU Sec. 334.04):

▲ Lack of sufficient working capital or credit to continue business.
▲ An urgent desire for a continued favorable earnings record in the hope of supporting the price of the company's stock.
▲ An overly optimistic earnings forecast.
▲ Dependence on a single or relatively few products, customers, or transactions for the ongoing success of the venture.
▲ A declining industry characterized by a large number of business failures.
▲ Excess capacity.
▲ Significant litigation, especially litigation between stockholders and management.
▲ Significant obsolescence dangers because the company is in a high-technology industry.

Any of these situations could be sufficient motivation for a client to engage in a related party transaction that is not at arm's length.

Determining the Existence of Related Parties. Certain relationships such as parent-subsidiary or investor-investee are obvious to an auditor, and any material transactions between these parties should be investigated. However, to determine the existence of less obvious related parties, the auditor needs to follow specific audit procedures, such as (AU Sec. 334.07):

▲ Evaluate the company's procedures for identifying and properly accounting for related party transactions.

▲ Request from appropriate management personnel the names of all related parties and inquire whether there were any transactions with these parties during the period.

▲ Review filings by the reporting entity with the Securities and Exchange Commission and other regulatory agencies for the names of related parties and for other businesses in which officers and directors occupy directorship or management positions.

▲ Determine the names of all pension and other trusts established for the benefit of employees and the names of their officers and trustees.

▲ Review stockholder listings of closely held companies to identify principal stockholders.

▲ Review prior years' working papers for the names of known related parties.

▲ Inquire of predecessor, principal, or other auditors of related entities concerning their knowledge of existing relationships and the extent of management involvement in material transactions.

▲ Review material investment transactions during the period under examination to determine whether the nature and extent of investments during the period create related parties.

Identifying Transactions with Related Parties. Once the existence of related parties has been determined, the auditor then identifies material transactions with these parties and identifies transactions that may suggest previously undetermined relationships. The following procedures provide guidance for identifying these transactions (AU Sec. 334.08):

▲ Provide audit personnel performing segments of the examination or examining and reporting separately on the accounts of related components of the reporting entity with the names of known related parties so that they may become aware of transactions with such parties during their examinations.

▲ Review the minutes of meetings of the board of directors and executive or operating committees for information about material transactions authorized or discussed at their meetings.

▲ Review proxy and other material filed with the Securities and Exchange Commission and comparable data filed with other regulatory agencies for information about material transactions with related parties.

▲ Review conflict-of-interests statements obtained by the company from its management.

▲ Review the extent and nature of business transacted with major customers, suppliers, borrowers, and lenders for indications of previously undisclosed relationships.

▲ Consider whether transactions are occurring, but are not being given accounting recognition, such as receiving or providing accounting, management or other services at no charge or a major stockholder absorbing corporate expenses.

▲ Review accounting records for large, unusual, or nonrecurring transactions or balances, paying particular attention to transactions recognized at or near the end of the reporting period.

▲ Review confirmations of compensating balance arrangements for indications that balances are or were maintained for or by related parties.

▲ Review invoices from law firms that have performed regular or special services for the company for indications of the existence of related parties or related party transactions.

▲ Review confirmations of loans receivable and payable for indications of guarantees. When guarantees are indicated, determine their nature and the relationships, if any, of the guarantors to the reporting entity.

After identifying related party transactions, an auditor should apply the audit procedures necessary to assess the purpose, nature, and extent of the transactions and their effect on the financial statements. In general, the procedures should extend beyond simply making inquiries of management and might include obtaining an understanding of the business purpose of the transactions, examining documentation such as invoices or contracts, and determining whether the transactions were approved by the board of directors. The accounting considerations and required disclosures for related party transactions are discussed in FASB *Statement of Financial Accounting Standards No. 57,* ''Related Party Disclosures.''

THE AUDIT PROCESS: AN OVERVIEW

All financial statement audits are similar in logic and in scope — similar in logic because they are based on the scientific method of inquiry, and similar in scope because they are designed to enable the auditor to formulate an opinion on financial statements. As a result of these similarities, generalizations can be drawn about the audit process. Of course, the audit process varies with individual audit engagements since no two clients are identical. Nevertheless, generalizations about the audit process are useful in understanding how an independent auditor conducts a financial statement audit.

Figure 6-2 lists the major steps in the audit process and includes representative dates (assuming a December 31 fiscal year-end and either a continuing engagement or a new engagement accepted early in the year) and refer-

---

FIGURE 6-2
An Overview of the Audit Process

Approximate Dates	Activity
March	Communication with audit committee
	Decision to accept or continue engagement
	Engagement letter
	General understanding of client's business and industry
April–May	First-level planning (Figure 6-4, page 228)
July–August	Second-level planning (Figure 6-4, page 228)
September–November	Interim audit work (Figure 6-5, page 231)
December–February	Year-end audit work (Figure 6-6, page 232)
	Subsequent events review
Last day of field work	Management representation letters and legal letters
	Reports

---

ences to more detailed illustrations within the chapter. Importantly, Figure 6-2 and the related illustrations and discussion pertain to a financial statement audit, not to internal or public-sector audits, both of which are discussed in Chapter 21. Discussion of each step in the audit process follows.

Communication with Corporate Audit Committee

An auditor's initial contact with a publicly traded client is often through a corporate audit committee. The audit committee is composed of selected members of an entity's board of directors and serves as intermediary between external auditors and the full board of directors in matters relating to the external audit, the internal audit function, and other financial and accounting matters.

An audit committee can be a valuable tool for promoting direct and effective communication between audit professionals and corporate directors. Typically, audit committee members are outside directors, i.e., individuals having no relationship with the entity other than their directorship. Thus, officers who serve as board members would not ordinarily serve on the audit committee, since they are involved in management.

Although not common until the 1970s, corporate audit committees were encouraged as early as 1940 in SEC *Accounting Series Release No. 19.* The Release recommended that registrants establish audit committees composed of nonofficer members of the board of directors to nominate audit firms and to arrange and monitor details of the engagement. In 1967, an AICPA Executive Committee *Statement on Audit Committees of Boards of Directors* also encouraged audit committees composed of outside directors, emphasizing the advantages of promoting communications between auditors and the board of directors. In 1972 the SEC reiterated its support for audit committees in *Accounting Series Release No. 123,* "Standing Audit Committees Composed of Outside Directors." Thus, for a number of years audit committees were strongly encouraged, though not mandatory. However, as of June 30, 1978, the New York Stock Exchange required all listed companies to appoint audit committees consisting of outside directors only.

To date, no definitive description of an audit committee's duties and responsibilities has appeared. However, Harold Williams, a former SEC Commissioner, has discussed a committee's basic responsibilities, recommending that an audit committee should:[1]

▲ Review the scope of an audit.
▲ Review audit results and discuss financial statements in depth with external auditors.
▲ Recommend to the board of directors and/or approve changes in accounting policies that have a significant effect on the entity's financial reports.
▲ Have the authority to nominate or terminate external auditors.
▲ Examine the entity's internal control structure.
▲ Assure the existence of a framework for internal auditors to express their concerns, either directly to the audit committee or through the external auditors.
▲ Assume a responsibility for the quality of earnings reported.

Although this list of responsibilities is not necessarily all-inclusive, it clearly indicates the far-reaching role an audit committee can play. Audit committees are neither ceremonial nor perfunctory; they can serve a useful purpose and can affect an auditor's decision to accept or continue an engagement.

---

[1]H. M. Williams, "Audit Committees — The Public Sector's View," *Journal of Accountancy* (September, 1977), pp. 73–74.

Decision to Accept or Continue an Engagement

An auditor cannot conduct an objective and competent audit if a client lacks integrity. *Statement on Quality Control Standards No. 1,* "System of Quality Control for a CPA Firm" (AICPA, 1979), recommends that a firm establish policies and procedures for deciding whether to accept or continue an engagement, thereby minimizing the likelihood of associating with an untrustworthy client. However, as a result of investigating a client's integrity, a firm is in a position only to decide whether to accept or continue an engagement, not to vouch for a client's or potential client's integrity.

A firm may use a variety of policies and procedures for deciding whether to accept or continue an engagement. For example, in considering acceptance of a new engagement, an auditor could:[2]

▲ Review proposed client's financial statements.
▲ Inquire of third parties, such as banks and legal counsel, about a proposed client's reputation.
▲ Evaluate the firm's ability to service the proposed client properly.

Given the potential for civil and criminal liability discussed in Chapter 4, a firm should continually monitor, and reevaluate when appropriate, a client's integrity. A firm should never accept or continue an engagement when there is a strong likelihood of material errors, irregularities, or illegal acts. No such engagement is worth the attendant risk.

When a potential new engagement involves replacing a predecessor auditor, the successor auditor should communicate with the predecessor before accepting the engagement. *Statement on Auditing Standards No. 7,* "Communications between Predecessor and Successor Auditors" (AU Sec. 315), places the initiative for communicating on the successor auditor; a predecessor auditor is not otherwise required to communicate important information to successor auditors.

The successor auditor should explain to the prospective client the need to communicate with the predecessor and request permission to do so. Since an auditor may not disclose confidential information without the client's permission, the successor should ask the prospective client to authorize the predecessor auditor to respond fully to the successor's inquiries. If the prospective client refuses to authorize communication with the predecessor auditor or limits the information which the predecessor may disclose, the successor should determine the reasons for refusal and the impact upon the decision to accept the engagement.

---

[2]Quality Control Standards Committee, *Statement on Quality Control Standards No. 1,* "System of Quality Control for a CPA Firm" (New York: American Institute of Certified Public Accountants, 1979).

Following authorization, the successor auditor should ask the predecessor specific and reasonable questions about the proposed client. Inquiries may be oral or written and should include, among other things, questions regarding (AU Sec. 315.06):

▲ Management's integrity.
▲ Disagreements with management about accounting principles, audit procedures, and other relevant matters.
▲ The reasons for a change in auditors.

The predecessor should respond promptly and fully to all reasonable and specific questions. However, if the predecessor decides not to respond fully due to unusual circumstances, such as pending litigation, he or she should inform the successor auditor that responses are limited. The successor then should consider the impact of the limitations on the decision to accept the engagement.

Engagement Letter

After a decision is made to accept or continue an engagement, an agreement should be reached with the client, preferably through the audit committee, about the professional services desired, and an engagement letter prepared. As illustrated in Figure 6-3, an engagement letter is a written contract between an auditor and client and generally serves to minimize misunderstandings, alert the client to the purpose of the engagement and role of the external auditor, and help minimize legal liability for services neither contracted for nor performed. Engagement letters are not required by professional standards; however, they should be prepared for every professional engagement. As illustrated by *Maryland Casualty Co. v. Jonathon Cook* and *1136 Tenant's Corp. v. Max Rothenberg & Co.* (see Chapter 4), the costs of not preparing an engagement letter can be substantial.

General Understanding of Client's Business and Industry

Effective audits cannot be conducted in a vacuum. An auditor must have a general understanding of a client's business, industry, and other relevant environmental considerations, allowing the engagement to be tailored to the specific situation and conditions at hand. While all audits are similar in logic and scope, each individual client's business, industry, and environmental factors differ, suggesting that the details of any two audits are rarely if ever identical.

Initially, an auditor should tour a client's office and manufacturing facilities, becoming familiar with the general layout and specific location of

FIGURE 6-3
Engagement Letter

FARREL & CO., CPAs
5101 Madison Road
Cincinnati, Ohio 45227

May 23, 1990

Mr. Robert Wolpert
Chairman of the Audit Committee
Shannon Industries
Buxton Street
Cincinnati, OH 45212

Dear Mr. Wolpert:

This will confirm our understanding of the arrangements for our audit of the financial statements of Shannon Industries for the year ended December 31, 1990.

We will audit the company's balance sheet at December 31, 1990, and the related statements of income, retained earnings, and cash flows for the year then ended, for the purpose of expressing an opinion on them. Our audit will be made in accordance with generally accepted auditing standards.

Our procedures will include tests of documentary evidence supporting the transactions recorded in the accounts, tests of the physical existence of inventories, and direct confirmation of receivables and certain other assets and liabilities by correspondence with selected customers, creditors, legal counsel, and banks. At the conclusion of our audit, we will request certain written representations from management about the financial statements and related matters.

Our engagement is subject to the risk that material errors, irregularities, or illegal acts, if they exist, will not be detected. However, we will inform you of any such matters that come to our attention.

We will review the company's federal and state income tax returns for the fiscal year ended December 31, 1990. These returns, we understand, will be prepared by the controller.

Further, we will be available during the year to consult with you on the tax effects of any proposed transactions or contemplated change in business policies.

Our fee for these services will be at our regular per diem rates, plus travel and other out-of-pocket costs. Invoices will be rendered every two weeks and are payable on presentation.

We are pleased to have this opportunity to serve you.

If this letter correctly expresses your understanding, please sign the enclosed copy where indicated and return it to us.

Very truly yours,

_____

FARREL & CO., CPAs

Arrangements accepted:

_____   _____

Chairman of the Audit Committee   Date
Shannon Industries

---

facilities and with key managerial and operating personnel. In turn, an auditor should make inquiries and examine documents related to the client's business, industry, and environment. *Statement on Auditing Standards No. 22,* "Planning and Supervision" (AU Sec. 311), lists several business- and industry-related factors which should be considered:

▲ *Business factors* — type of business, type of products and services, capital structure, and production, distribution, and compensation methods.
▲ *Industry factors* — economic conditions, government regulations, changes in technology, common accounting practices, competitive conditions, and financial trends and ratios.

In addition, other environmental considerations related to both a client's business and industry should be considered, such as:

▲ Dependability of supply sources and predictability of lead times for purchased goods and services.
▲ Characteristics of supply sources, such as number and size of vendors regarding price, quality, availability, and services.
▲ Ownership concentration and degree of ownership control by officers, directors, and affiliated companies.

Lacking a clear understanding of a client's business, industry, and environment, an auditor can neither plan nor conduct a thoughtful, efficient, and effective audit.

First-Level Planning

An auditor's typical first-level planning activities are summarized in Figure 6-4. First-level planning begins with reviews of prior-year documentation (assuming a continuing engagement) and first-quarter financial information for the current year.

The *review of prior-year audit work* is designed to assess potentially risky audit areas, identify audit areas to be emphasized during the engagement, and consider improvements that could be made in the current year. The *review of first-quarter financial results* is similarly motivated in that the auditor attempts to isolate unusual fluctuations or inconsistencies from prior-year statements that may signal potentially risky audit areas. Thus, the objectives of reviewing prior-year audit work and first-quarter financial results are to identify problem areas, minimize audit risk, and optimize audit effort.

During the first-level planning stage an auditor also prepares a *preliminary audit time budget*, an estimate of total planned audit time by staff level

---

FIGURE 6-4
Audit Planning Acitivities

Approximate Dates	Activity

April–May	First-Level Planning:
	    Review prior-year audit work
	    Review first-quarter financial results
	    Prepare a preliminary audit time budget

July–August	Second-Level Planning:
	    Review second-quarter financial results
	    Prepare final audit time budget
	    Perform analytical procedures
	    Prepare preliminary audit planning memorandum
	    Coordinate with professional staff assigned to engagement
	    Coordinate with client
	    Prepare interim audit programs

---

and audit activity. For example, a preliminary time budget for Cash, Marketable Securities, and Receivables might appear in part as follows:

	Partial Preliminary Time Budget:					
	Total Estimated Hours		Estimated Hours by Staff Level			
Audit Area	Interim	Year-End	Junior	Senior	Manager	Partner
Cash	40	(35)	36 (31)	2 (2)	1 (1)	1 (1)
Marketable Securities	20	(15)	17 (12)	1 (1)	1 (1)	1 (1)
Accounts Receivable	40	(30)	34 (25)	4 (3)	1 (1)	1 (1)
.	.	.	.	.	.	.
.	.	.	.	.	.	.

First-level planning focuses on generating preliminary evaluations and follows from the auditor's general understanding of a client's business, industry, and other relevant factors.

Second-Level Planning

Figure 6-4 also summarizes an auditor's second-level planning activities. Second-level planning begins by updating results of first-level planning, i.e., *reviewing second-quarter financial results* and *finalizing the audit time budget.*

During second-level planning, the auditor also *performs analytical procedures* that are used to assist in planning the nature, timing, and extent of anticipated auditing procedures and in drafting the preliminary audit planning memorandum. Under SAS No. 56, "Analytical Procedures," analytical procedures used in planning should focus on enhancing the auditor's understanding of the entity's transactions and on identifying risky audit areas. The sophistication of analytical procedures applied during planning will vary depending on the client, and may range from simple comparisons of account balances between the current and prior year to extensive statistical analyses designed to estimate ranges of expected account balances.

The auditor then prepares a *preliminary audit planning memorandum,* which represents an overview of planned audit activity by staff level and includes the final audit time budget. Typically, the planning memorandum describes in general terms the audit approach intended for each audit area.

For example, the memorandum might state the following for a hypothetical client's income tax related transactions and accounts:

> A tax department representative will participate with the audit staff at interim, completing a tax planning checklist designed to isolate specific tax planning and disclosure problems. The tax department representative will prepare a memorandum of the findings for distribution to and discussion with the audit partner, manager, and if necessary, the client.
>
> At year-end, the audit staff will review the client's calculation of accumulated income tax prepayments, deferred income taxes, and income tax expense, consulting the tax department when necessary. A tax department representative will review year-end audit working papers and prepare a memorandum on the adequacy of related tax accounts. The audit supervisor will reach a conclusion as to whether all tax accounts are fairly stated at the balance sheet date.

The planning memorandum includes similar paragraphs for each audit area and is distributed to each professional staff member assigned to the engagement.

Following completion and approval of the planning memorandum, an auditor schedules available staff members for the audit, and a meeting is held to *coordinate with professional staff assigned to the engagement*. The purpose of the meeting is to introduce each staff member to the engagement and discuss the planned audit approach. Since the meeting is ideally held in advance of interim and year-end audit work, the assigned staff should have sufficient time to prepare for the engagement by, for example, reviewing the planning memorandum, the correspondence and permanent files, and prior-year working papers, all of which are introduced later in the chapter. It is also necessary to *coordinate with the client* with respect to the scheduled dates of audit activity.

The final second-level planning activity involves drafting *interim audit programs* for tests of controls. An *audit program* is a detailed list of procedures to be performed for a particular aspect of an engagement. Individually, an audit program assists an auditor in estimating the time required for a particular audit area, in determining staff requirements, and in scheduling audit work. Collectively, all of the programs prepared for an engagement assist in maintaining control as the audit progresses.

In general, interim audit programs cannot be designed until the auditor has reviewed and documented the client's internal control structure. However, in continuing engagements, interim audit programs can be drafted in advance of field work, since the auditor has prior knowledge of the client's control structure and prior information about the results of previous assessments of control risk. Of course, if necessary, the programs may be revised when actually used, although the reasons for revision should be justified (e.g., unreliable information during second-level planning or accounting system changes). For initial engagements, interim audit programs are not usually prepared until the client's control structure has been reviewed and documented, since the auditor has no prior information about the system.

Importantly, audit planning does not end with second-level planning activities; in fact, it should continue throughout the engagement. A plan is an overall strategy, subject to revision as more reliable information becomes available.

Interim Audit Work

Figure 6-5 summarizes an auditor's typical interim audit activities. The objective of interim audit work, which derives from the second standard of field work, is to assess the level of control risk the auditor will assume in determining the level of year-end detection risk to accept.

A thorough assessment of control risk usually requires that an auditor (1) obtain an understanding of the control environment, the accounting system, and the control procedures, and (2) document the control structure. The auditor's consideration of internal control structure is discussed in detail in Chapter 7.

The final interim audit activity involves drafting *preliminary year-end audit programs*. The year-end programs are heavily dependent upon the engagement's objectives, risky audit areas, audit areas to be emphasized, and most importantly, results of the auditor's assessment of control risk. Thus, year-end audit programs cannot be drafted during the first- and second-level planning stages, because a critical determinant of year-end detection risk — control risk — is not yet known.

FIGURE 6-5
Interim Audit Activities

Approximate Dates	Activity
September– October	▲ Obtain an understanding of the internal control structure ▲ Document internal control structure ▲ Assess control risk
November	Prepare preliminary year-end audit programs

Year-End Audit Work

Figure 6-6 summarizes an auditor's typical year-end audit activities. The objective of year-end audit work, which derives from the third standard of fieldwork, is to obtain sufficient competent evidential matter to afford a reasonable basis for an opinion on financial statements.

Because of time pressures typically associated with year-end activities, it is particularly critical to *coordinate with the client*. The auditor should meet with client personnel to confirm year-end audit dates, finalize working paper schedules to be prepared by the client, and arrange for "cutoff" (as of a particular day, e.g., January 10) bank statements to be mailed directly to the auditor. Coordination is much more critical at year-end than at interim, since year-end work must be completed early enough to result in a timely audit report. Interim audit work, in contrast, can be conducted at almost any time during the year under audit (although interim work is usually done during the second half of the fiscal year).

Prior to performing year-end audit procedures, the auditor should *finalize year-end audit programs* initially prepared at the end of the interim review. The auditor should review and evaluate any significant system changes or other circumstances occurring since interim and update the audit programs as appropriate.

Finally, an auditor undertakes the most time-consuming year-end audit activity: performing year-end substantive tests which, as explained earlier in the chapter, include (1) tests of details of transactions and balances and (2) analytical procedures. The purpose of all substantive tests is to obtain evidence concerning the validity and propriety of the accounting treatment of transactions and balances. Specific substantive tests are discussed more thoroughly in later chapters.

FIGURE 6-6
Year-End Audit Activities

Approximate Dates	Activity
December	Coordinate with client Finalize year-end audit programs
January–February	Perform substantive tests of details and analytical procedures

---

Subsequent Events

An audit report is usually dated as of the last day of field work, e.g., February 7, 1990 for a December 31, 1989 fiscal year-end. Although the audit report and audit work relate to the period January 1 through December 31, 1989 the auditor is also responsible for transactions and events occurring between January 1 and February 7, 1990 — the so-called *subsequent period* — that have an effect on the December 31, 1989 financial statements. For example, if an auditor learns on January 21, 1990 that a customer of an audit client is unable to pay a debt which arose in 1989, adjustment and/or disclosure of the December 31, 1989 account receivable may be necessary depending on the circumstances. An auditor is responsible for, and must plan to search for, subsequent events, as discussed more fully in Chapter 18.

Representation Letters

During the course of an audit, management and other parties make many representations to an auditor, both oral and written. SAS No. 19, "Client Representations" (AU Sec. 333), requires that an auditor obtain certain written representations from management, in the form of a *management representation letter*. The specific representations to be obtained by an auditor depend on the circumstances of the engagement. Auditors also request written representations from other parties, such as *legal letters* from a client's lawyer, as required by SAS No. 12, "Inquiry of a Client's Lawyer Concerning Litigation, Claims, and Assessments" (AU Sec. 337). Management representation letters and legal letters are discussed more fully in Chapter 18.

Reports

The concluding activity within the audit process is to prepare and issue (1) a report on the financial statements (i.e., the audit report) and (2) a report on internal control structure related matters noted during the audit. The audit report, which expresses the auditor's opinion on the financial statements results from evidence examined; the report on internal control structure results from control deficiencies discovered during the audit engagement.

The auditor's opinion on financial statements and reported deficiencies in control structure should be clearly documented in the audit working papers and communicated on a timely basis. The audit report, required by the fourth standard of reporting, is dated as of the last day of field work and can be addressed to the company, the board of directors, or the stockholders. The report on internal control structure — or internal control structure memorandum — can be issued on any practicable date, and is required by *Statement on Auditing Standards No. 55,* "The Communication of Internal Control Structure Related Matters Noted in an Audit." Audit reports are discussed more fully in Chapter 19, and internal control structure memoranda in Chapter 7.

AUDIT WORKING PAPERS

Audit working papers are an auditor's principal record of work performed and conclusions reached, and as noted in *Statement on Auditing Standards No. 41,* "Working Papers" (AU Sec. 339), an auditor ". . . should prepare and maintain working papers." An audit working paper may take virtually any form, including, for example, a manual ("pencil and paper") or computer-prepared schedule documenting ownership of an asset; a technical memorandum prepared by the tax staff about the accounting treatment of a complicated interperiod income tax allocation problem; or a schedule extracting significant matters from a client's board of directors meeting. In short, any documentary evidence supporting a financial statement assertion could potentially be presented as an audit working paper.

The specific quantity, form, and content of working papers varies from one engagement to another. For example, the working papers for a large, publicly traded client are certain to be far more extensive than for a small, privately owned company. The auditor's judgment about the quantity, form, and content of working papers for a particular engagement should be guided by factors such as the:

▲ Nature of the engagement (e.g., publicly traded versus privately owned company)
▲ Nature of the auditor's report (e.g., audit report versus limited review report)
▲ Nature of the financial statements, schedules, or other information on which the auditor is reporting (e.g., accrual basis versus another comprehensive basis of accounting, such as cash)
▲ Nature and condition of the client's financial records
▲ Degree of reliance on internal control structure
▲ Needs in the particular circumstances for supervision and review of work performed

Working Papers and Related Files

Working papers remain in the custody, and are the property, of the auditor. In fact, in some states the auditor is designated by statute as owner of the working papers. However, the auditor's property rights are subject to the limitations of AICPA Ethics Rule 301 (Chapter 2), which prohibits disclosure of confidential client information without the specific consent of the client. Completed working papers related to a particular engagement are usually retained in the auditor's office files until no longer considered of use to a current engagement. Most firms retain working papers in their office files for at least two years following an engagement, after which the papers are moved to a remote location for storage (e.g., special storage area or warehouse), sometimes in microfilm form and sometimes on computer disks. For example, working papers compiled for a December 31, 1989 year-end engagement might be retained in the audit firm's office files until completion of the December 31, 1991 audit. The retention period thereafter should be sufficient for the firm's needs and consistent with applicable federal and state statutes of limitation.

Certain information relating to an audit engagement is maintained separately from the working papers because the information is of continuing interest year after year or relates directly to the preparation of income tax returns. Although groupings and classification of information may vary somewhat among firms, the following are representative of the types of files maintained for each client apart from the current audit working paper file:

▲ Correspondence file.
▲ Permanent file.
▲ Tax file.

Each type of file is described below.

Correspondence File. The correspondence file contains all correspondence to, from, or on behalf of a client, and is especially useful for planning an audit engagement. For example, prior to the year-end phase of an engagement, a client may have communicated with the auditor about specific accounting and reporting problems. Correspondence related to the problems should be included in the correspondence file, creating a "signal" to the audit staff that the current engagement should be planned with consideration for the problems.

Permanent File. The permanent file contains information of continuing interest and relevance to an audit engagement. For example, the file might include a client's background and history, organization charts, articles of incorporation, bylaws, charter, outstanding bond indenture agreements, contracts, and flowcharts of transaction cycles. Permanent files should be reviewed by all staff members unfamiliar with the client and should be updated during each engagement.

Tax File. The tax file contains information relevant to a client's past, current, and future income tax obligations, and serves as a basis for preparing current-year returns or performing other tax-related services, such as amending prior-year returns or representing the client in an IRS audit. For example, the file might include prior-year state and federal income tax returns, tax-related correspondence, research and rulings, and schedules of significant temporary differences between pretax financial or "book" income and taxable income. All relevant tax information arising during an audit engagement should be included in the tax file.

Functions, Content, and Arrangement of Working Papers

As noted in SAS No. 41, working papers serve mainly to:

▲ Provide the principal support for an auditor's opinion and for his or her representation regarding compliance with the standards of field work, which is implicit in the reference to generally accepted auditing standards in an audit report.
▲ Aid in the conduct and review of an auditor's work.

In short, working papers represent a means — in most cases the only means — for organizing, cataloging, and cross-referencing documented evidence; for supervising and reviewing a staff member's performance on individual engagements and professional development on a series of engagements; for documenting compliance with generally accepted auditing standards; and for planning subsequent audits.

Content of Working Papers. Although specific content varies from engagement to engagement, working papers ordinarily should include documentation indicating that the standards of field work were accomplished, i.e., that

▲ The work was adequately planned, supervised, and reviewed, in observance of the first standard of field work.
▲ The internal control structure was considered as a basis for determining the extent of substantive tests in observance of the second standard of field work.
▲ The audit evidence obtained, the auditing procedures applied, and the testing performed provided sufficient competent evidential matter to afford a reasonable basis for an opinion, in observance of the third standard of field work.

Working papers should support an auditor's conclusions and, in an effort to promote understanding and minimize preparation time, should be clear, concise, and above all unambiguous. The sheer volume of working papers generated during an audit engagement is inconsequential; quantity is no substitute for quality. The information contained in working papers, however, is of great consequence because it (1) is the primary support for an auditor's opinion and (2) can represent an auditor's primary means for proving due diligence under Section 11 of the Securities Act of 1933 and Section 18 of the Securities Exchange Act of 1934 (see Chapter 4).

An auditor's general criteria for determining whether to document something in the working papers derive from the purpose of audit working papers. An item should be documented and included in working papers if it (1) aids the auditor in the conduct of his or her work and/or (2) provides important support for his or her opinion.

Arrangement of Working Papers. There is no standard order of presentation for working papers; thus the arrangement of papers varies among firms. Indeed, even the physical form of completed sets of working papers varies. For example, some firms bind working papers, and others arrange loose, unbound papers within file folders.

Of course, the physical form of completed working papers is of no real significance. However, the arrangement should be logical and the working papers should be indexed and referenced to allow easy access to detailed information.

Figure 6-7 depicts a logical and typical arrangement of a set of working papers. In Figure 6-7, a *draft of financial statements* is the first group of working papers presented, followed by an *engagement letter* and a *preliminary audit planning memorandum*. The *working financial statements* are the source for the draft of financial statements, and all dollar amounts within the working financial statements are referenced to detailed schedules within the working papers.

Adjustments and reclassifications, an auditor's "correcting" journal entries, are presented next. *Adjusting entries* represent corrections to the client's books and are given to the client to record. In contrast, *reclassification entries* are made within the auditor's working papers for financial statement reporting purposes and are not given to the client for recording in the client's books.

Detailed audit working papers are subdivided and grouped by financial statement accounts (Figure 6-7), which, in turn, are filed in order of appearance in the financial statements. Hence, the Cash account working papers are typically first, followed by Marketable Securities, Accounts Receivable, and so on.

Working papers for each asset, liability, and equity account begin with a *lead schedule* summarizing the account's balance per the general ledger, adjusting and reclassification entries, and the final balance per audit. The lead

FIGURE 6-7
Arrangement of Audit Working Papers

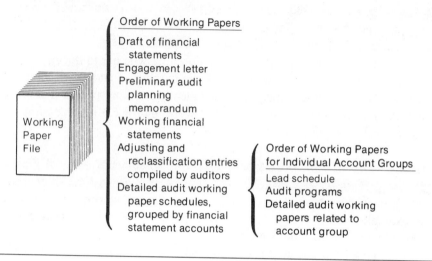

schedule also includes the auditor's conclusion about whether the account is fairly stated. These conclusions become the basis for an auditor's opinion on financial statements taken as a whole.

Audit programs represent listings of detailed procedures applied to specific financial statement accounts or activities. Usually, a separate program is prepared for each significant account or activity examined. For example, there might be a separate program for Cash, a separate program for Accounts Receivable, and so on. As depicted in Figure 6-7, programs typically follow the related lead schedules, although programs for specific activities, such as a review for subsequent events, might be filed elsewhere (e.g., following adjusting and reclassification entries).

A portion of a sample audit program appears in Figure 6-8. Several observations about the sample program are noteworthy:

▲ Listed program steps (audit procedures) are explicit and detailed.
▲ A reference is provided to other working paper schedules containing related detailed audit work.
▲ The staff member completing a program step initials the step when completed, thereby taking responsibility.

Detailed audit working papers, documenting completion of audit program steps, are presented after the audit programs and represent the bulk of working paper files.

Figure 6-9 illustrates a typical detailed audit working paper in the form

FIGURE 6-8
Sample Audit Program

Program Steps (Uncollectible Receivables)	Working Paper Reference	Performed By
.		
.		
.		
.		
7. Obtain prior-year ending balance from general ledger.	B6	KLR
8. Review accounts written off during the year.	B7	KLR
9. Calculate provision for uncollectible accounts.	B10	KLR
.		
.		
.		
.		

of a schedule. The significance of Figure 6-9 is not in the schedule itself, but in the following items, which are common to most working papers: indexes, references, preparer and reviewer intials, dates, and tick marks and explanations.

The *index* serves the same purpose as the page number of a book. However, working papers are numbered sequentially within account groups with page numbers preceded by an account code. For example, the alphanumeric index *B6* in Figure 6-9 indicates the sixth page of the Accounts Receivable working papers. Account groups within the working papers could be identified as follows:

▲ Single letters (A, B, C, etc.) = asset accounts.
▲ Double letters (AA, BB, CC, etc.) = liability and equity accounts.
▲ Numerals (10, 20, 30, etc.) = revenue and expense accounts (e.g., 10-1 might represent the schedule for sales revenue accounts).

References are a means for transferring information within the working papers. For example, in Figure 6-9, the $2,750 for Adams Company is referenced *from* working paper B7, and the $29,025, total uncollectible receivables, is referenced *to* B1, the Accounts Receivable lead schedule. The direction of transfer (to or from) can be determined by the location of index

FIGURE 6-9
Sample Audit Working Paper

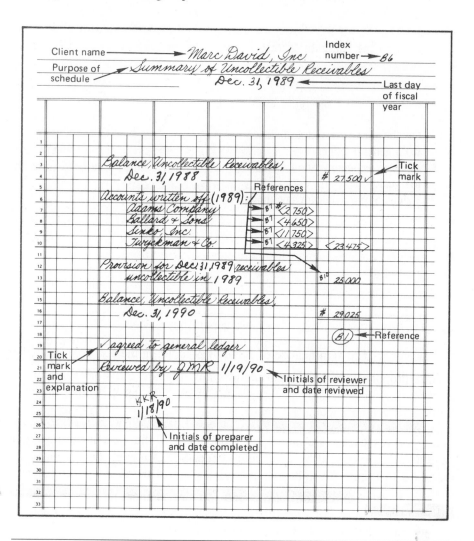

references. A reference to the left of or above an item indicates "transferred from"; a circled reference to the right of or below an item indicates "transferred to." Other approaches are also common. For example, some auditors specifically state "From B7" and "To B1."

Indexing and referencing provide a basic road map through audit working papers. A reviewer should be able to follow his or her way through an entire set of properly indexed and referenced working papers without diffi-culty.

Initials of preparers and reviewers of working papers are included to affix primary responsibility for work performed. As a result, the manager or partner in charge of the engagement can direct specific inquiries about work performed to the individuals responsible. The preparer and reviewer should also indicate the *dates of completion and review,* respectively. The comple-tion date is particularly important because it indicates the last day on which related audit work was performed. Thus, transactions and events from this date to the audit report date should be reviewed before leaving the client's office on the last day of fieldwork.

Another date appearing on each working paper is the entity's fiscal year-end. The *year-end date* identifies the year under audit, distinguishing the working paper from similar ones prepared in other years.

Unless self-explanatory, all information or data contained in working papers should be referenced from another schedule or "tick marked" and explained. *Tick marks* are symbols used in working papers. An example of a tick mark and related explanation appears in Figure 6-9.

Automated Working Papers

For generations, audit working papers have been prepared manually, stored, and used as a single-copy record of audit evidence. However, with the advent of full-screen microcomputers (discussed more fully in Chapter 8), a large proportion of practicing auditors now prepare and store some or vir-tually all of their working papers on floppy or hard disks. Unlike manually prepared working papers, automated working papers provide the distinct ad-vantages of (1) considerably easier data manipulation, since data entry, cal-culations, and postings can be accomplished instantaneously, and (2) signifi-cantly reduced storage costs, since even floppy disks can hold over 100 pages of working papers on a single disk.

Many public accounting firms and software vendors have developed au-tomated working paper programs which provide standard tabular formats for selected working paper schedules, thereby requiring that the auditor merely input dollar amounts for the current engagement and manipulate data as nec-essary. For example, a common but tedious year-end audit activity often as-signed to entry-level staff is the preparation of a *working trial balance* for all general ledger accounts and *lead schedules* for each individual balance sheet account. Preparing the trial balance and lead schedules manually not only is time consuming, but can result in mathematical errors, particularly when the auditor posts adjusting journal entries through the lead schedules to the work-ing trial balance. However, when an auditor uses preformatted schedules, each task is accomplished in significantly less time, and posting is accomplished simply by depressing predetermined function keys on the microcomputer.

When working papers are prepared on microcomputers, the auditor has the option of either "keying in" audit information, such as tick marks, index numbers, references, and explanations, or handwriting the required information on printed-out "hard copy." For example, Figure 6-10 illustrates an automated version of the manually prepared working paper illustrated in Figure 6-9. Note that the automated version (Figure 6-10) includes exactly the same information as Figure 6-9; only the format is different.

Automated working papers can be advantageous on either small or large engagements. However, for large multinational clients, there are additional advantages since the auditor must generate evidence from locations around the globe rather than from a single, centrally located accounting department. For example, the physical inventory observations for several international retail stores are now accomplished on preformatted microcomputer schedules — often called "electronic spreadsheets" — which are prepared in various stores and warehouses around the world and then transferred through telephone communications channels to a centrally located office of the firm conducting the audit, usually the office in charge of the U.S. audit. Since the schedules are preformatted, all inventory data are in a common form, thereby allowing easy manipulation and efficient reconciliation with the client's final priced inventory.

Despite whether an auditor prepares working papers manually or with the aid of a microcomputer or other computer, the purposes and objectives are identical: to aid in the conduct and review of audit work and to provide the principal support for the auditor's report. The form of working papers — manual or electronic — is irrelevant.

IRS Access to Audit Working Papers

In March, 1984, following nine years of judicial proceedings, the U.S. Supreme Court ruled in *United States v. Arthur Young & Co. et al.*,[3] that an auditor's tax accrual working papers — that is, working papers used to determine a client's current and deferred tax liability — *are* relevant to an Internal Revenue Service (IRS) tax audit, and therefore *are not* protected from disclosure under the theory of accountant-client privileged communications. Other cases have addressed the issue, but the Arthur Young case is particularly noteworthy because it has caused considerable concern within the profession and is the first case to reach the U.S. Supreme Court.

---

[3] *United States v. Arthur Young & Co. et al.* U.S. Sup. Ct., no. 82-687 (March 21, 1984).

FIGURE 6-10
Sample Automated Audit Working Paper

Marc David, Inc.   B6
Summary of Uncollectible Receivables
December 31, 1989

Balance, Uncollectible
Receivables,
  Dec. 31. 1988 $27,500*

accounts written off
(1989):

	Ref:		
Adams Company	B7	$(2,750)	
Ballard & Sons	B7	(4,650)	
Sinko Inc.	B7	(11,750)	
Twyckman & Co.	B7	(4,325)	(23,475)

Provision for Dec. 31,
1989 receivables
  uncollectible in 1990   B10   25,000

Balance, Uncollectible
Receivables,
  Dec. 31, 1989 $29,025
                                                     To B1

*agreed to general ledger

KLR
1/18/90

Reviewed by JMR: 1/19/90

The case first received attention in 1975 when the IRS, in an audit of Amerada Hess Corporation's 1972–1974 tax returns, detected questionable payments of $7,830. As a result of the questionable payments, what had been a routine tax audit became a criminal investigation, and the IRS issued an administrative summons seeking the tax accrual working papers prepared by Arthur Young. Amerada Hess, however, instructed Young not to comply with the summons, prompting the IRS to seek enforcement in the U.S. District Court. The District Court ruled in favor of the IRS, arguing that the tax accrual working papers were relevant to the IRS audit and that the accountant-client privilege did not protect the papers. On appeal, the U.S. Court of Appeals agreed the tax accrual working papers were relevant to the IRS audit, but held that the public interest and the integrity of the securities markets were best served by protecting a client's confidential communications from public scrutiny.

The dispute ended on further appeal when the U.S. Supreme Court ruled that tax accrual working papers (1) are relevant to an IRS audit within the meaning of Internal Revenue Code (IRC) section 7602, and (2) are not protected from disclosure under IRC section 7602. In general, the Court reasoned that an IRS summons should be judged by the *potential relevance* of tax accrual working papers to an IRS tax audit, and not by the relevance standards typically used in judging the admissibility of evidence in court.

The financial community reacted to the Court's opinion with considerable concern and some alarm, since the ruling may discourage audit clients from communicating openly with auditors about tax matters. However, in a related journal article, two informed observers noted that: "In view of the client's clear responsibility for preparing and issuing financial statements, as well as the fact that the IRS has access to and seeks first a taxpayer's documentation, it seems unlikely that managements would choose not to communicate openly in a major area with the accountants who audit these financial statements and issue opinions on them."[4] Thus, the impact of the case on the accountant-client relationship may not be substantial. However, the more far-reaching question is the likely impact of the case on how auditors prepare and maintain working papers, particularly working papers that may be subjected to public scrutiny through the courts.

SUMMARY

Auditors examine evidence to acquire knowledge about whether an entity's financial statements are presented fairly. Thus, evidence — the underlying accounting data and corroborating information supporting financial statement assertions — is the basis for an auditor's opinion. Evidence should be sufficient and competent and thus persuasive, and should support an auditor's basic audit objectives for all financial information tested.

The audit process is logical and systematic and is designed to generate audit evidence. The process begins with communication between auditors and the audit committee, a decision to accept or continue an engagement, and

---

[4]D. L. Buchholz and J. F. Moraglio, "IRS Access to Auditors' Work Papers: The Supreme Court Decision," *Journal of Accountancy* (September, 1984), p. 94.

preparation of an engagement letter. An auditor then proceeds to obtain an understanding of a client's business and industry, and conducts first- and second-level planning activities over the next few months. Interim audit work, designed to assess control risk, begins after the planning stages, though usually well before year-end. Year-end audit work, designed to control detection risk through substantive tests of account balances and disclosures, begins near the end of the fiscal year and includes a review for subsequent events. Representation letters and reports are the final activities of the audit process.

Audit working papers are an auditor's record of work performed and are required for every engagement. Working papers are the auditor's means for organizing and cataloging evidence obtained and thus provide the principal support for an auditor's opinion.

REFERENCES

American Accounting Association. "Report of the Committee on Basic Auditing Concepts." *The Accounting Review,* Supplement to Vol. XLVII, 1972.

Buchholz, D. L., and J. F. Moraglio, "IRS Access to Auditors' Work Papers: The Supreme Court Decision." *Journal of Accountancy* (September, 1984), pp. 91–100.

Dungan, C. W., G. T. Friedlob, and R. W. Rouse. "The Supreme Court on Tax Accrual Workpapers." *The CPA Journal* (February, 1985), pp. 20–26.

Hadnott, B. L. "Audit Evidence — What Kind and How Much?" *The CPA Journal* (October, 1979), pp. 23–29.

Hull, J. C. "A Guide to Better Workpapers." *Journal of Accountancy* (February, 1969), pp. 44–52.

Jaenicke, H. R. "A New Approach to Engagement Management." Journal of Accountancy (April, 1980), pp. 68–78.

Kissinger, J. N. "A General Theory of Evidence as the Conceptual Foundation in Auditing Theory: Some Comments and Extensions." *The Accounting Review* (April, 1977), pp. 322–339.

Label, W. A., and A. A. Arens. "Guidelines for More Effective Workpaper Review," *The Practical Accountant* (April, 1984), pp. 49–54.

Mautz, R. K. "The Nature and Reliability of Audit Evidence." *Journal of Accountancy* (May, 1958), pp. 40–47.

Mautz, R. K., and D. L. Mini. "Internal Control Evaluation and Audit Program Modification." *The Accounting Review* (April, 1966), pp. 283–291.

Mautz, R. K., and R. D. Neary. "Corporate Audit Committee — Quo Vadis." *Journal of Accountancy* (October, 1979), pp. 83–88.

Mautz, R. K., and F. L. Neuman, *Corporate Audit Committees.* Champaign: University of Illinois, 1970.

Mautz, R. K., and H. A. Sharaf, *The Philosophy of Auditing.* New York: American Accounting Association, 1961.

Palmer, R. E. "Audit Committees — Are They Effective? An Auditor's View." *Journal of Accountancy* (September, 1977), pp. 76–79.

Ricchiute, D. N. "A Case for Automated Workpapers." *Journal of Accountancy* (January, 1981), pp. 71–75.

Tipgos, M. A. "Prior Year's Working Papers: Uses and Dangers." *The CPA Journal* (September, 1978), pp. 19–25.

Toba, Y. "A General Theory of Evidence as the Conceptual Foundation in Auditing Theory." *The Accounting Review* (January, 1975), pp. 7–24.

Williams, H. M. "Audit Committees — The Public Sector's View." *Journal of Accountancy* (September, 1977), pp. 71–74.

QUESTIONS

1. Identify the purpose of gathering and evaluating evidence.
2. Explain the terms *sufficient, competent,* and *evidential matter* as used in the third standard of field work.
3. An auditor attempts to obtain the most persuasive evidence available. What general criteria can an auditor apply in evaluating the persuasiveness of evidence?
4. Identify and briefly explain the major types of assertions or management representations made in financial statements.
5. Briefly explain the relationship between financial statement assertions and audit objectives and procedures.
6. Identify and briefly describe the basic procedures used by auditors for gathering evidence.
7. What should an auditor consider when selecting a specialist to examine evidence requiring special knowledge and expertise?
8. What is the audit significance of related party transactions?
9. Explain the nature and purpose of an audit committee.
10. Briefly describe an auditor's decision process when deciding to accept or continue an engagement.
11. What are the purposes of an engagement letter?
12. Why does an auditor obtain an understanding of a client's business and industry before beginning an audit engagement?
13. What are an auditor's objectives in reviewing prior-year audit work and first-quarter financial information during the first-level planning stage?
14. What are the purpose and typical contents of a preliminary audit planning memorandum?
15. What is the objective of the interim phase of an audit engagement?
16. Why is coordination with the client prior to beginning year-end audit work especially important?
17. What is the objective of year-end audit work?
18. "Subsequent events" occur after the last day of a client's fiscal year and on or before the report date. Why would an auditor be concerned about transactions and events subsequent to the period reported on?
19. Identify and briefly describe the major client information files maintained separately from audit working papers.
20. Explain the functions and general content of audit working papers.
21. Describe a typical arrangement of working papers.

MULTIPLE CHOICE QUESTIONS

1. Audit evidence can come in different forms with different degrees of persuasiveness. Which of the following is the least persuasive type of evidence?

   a. Vendor's invoice.
   b. Bank statement obtained from the client.
   c. Computations made by the auditor.
   d. Prenumbered client invoices.   (AICPA Adapted)

2. Which of the following statements relating to the competence of evidential matter is always true?

   a. Evidential matter gathered by an auditor from outside an enterprise is reliable.
   b. Accounting data developed when control risk is low are more relevant than data developed when control risk is high.
   c. Oral representations made by management are not valid evidence.
   d. Evidence gathered by auditors must be both valid and relevant to be considered competent.

3. The following statements were made in a discussion of audit evidence between two CPAs. Which statement is not valid concerning evidential matter?

   a. "I am seldom convinced beyond all doubt with respect to all aspects of the statements being examined."
   b. "I would not undertake that procedure because at best the results would only be persuasive and I'm looking for convincing evidence."
   c. "I evaluate the degree of risk involved in deciding the kind of evidence I will gather."
   d. "I evaluate the usefulness of the evidence I can obtain against the cost to obtain it."   (AICPA Adapted)

4. Which of the following is not a specialist upon whose work an auditor may rely?

   a. Actuary.
   b. Appraiser.
   c. Internal auditor.
   d. Engineer.   (AICPA Adapted)

5. In which of the following instances would an auditor be least likely to require the assistance of a specialist?

   a. Assessing the valuation of inventories of art works.
   b. Determining the quantities of materials stored in piles on the ground.
   c. Determining the value of unlisted securities.
   d. Ascertaining the assessed valuation of fixed assets.   (AICPA Adapted)

6. Which of the following would not necessarily be a related party transaction?

   a. Sales to another corporation with a similar name.
   b. Purchases from another corporation that is controlled by the corporation's chief stockholder.

c. Loan from the corporation to a major stockholder.

d. Sale of land to the corporation by the spouse of a director. (AICPA Adapted)

7. As generally conceived, the audit committee of a publicly held company should be made up of

   a. Representatives from the client's management, investors, suppliers, and customers.

   b. The audit partner, the chief financial officer, the legal counsel, and at least one outsider.

   c. Representatives of the major equity interests (bonds, preferred stock, common stock).

   d. Members of the board of directors who are not officers or employees.

   (AICPA Adapted)

8. When a CPA is approached to perform an audit for the first time, the CPA should make inquiries of the predecessor auditor. This is a necessary procedure because the predecessor may be able to provide the successor with information that will assist the successor in determining

   a. Whether the predecessor's work should be utilized.

   b. Whether the company follows the policy of rotating its auditors.

   c. Whether, in the predecessor's opinion, the company's internal control structure has been satisfactory.

   d. Whether the engagement should be accepted.   (AICPA Adapted)

9. Preliminary arrangements agreed to by the auditor and the client should be reduced to writing by the auditor. The best place to set forth these arrangements is in:

   a. A memorandum to be placed in the permanent section of the audit working papers.

   b. An engagement letter.

   c. A client representation letter.

   d. A confirmation letter attached to the constructive services letter.

   (AICPA Adapted)

10. Which of the following elements ultimately determines the specific auditing procedures that are necessary in the circumstances to afford a reasonable basis for an opinion?

    a. Auditor judgment.

    b. Materiality.

    c. Audit risk.

    d. Reasonable assurance.   (AICPA Adapted)

11. Analytical procedures are

    a. Substantive tests designed to assess control risk.

    b. Tests of controls designed to evaluate the validity of management's representation letter.

    c. Substantive tests designed to evaluate the reasonableness of financial information.

    d. Tests of control designed to evaluate the reasonableness of financial information. (AICPA Adapted)

12. Which of the following is not a factor affecting the independent auditor's judgment as to the quantity, type, and content of audit working papers?

    a. The needs in the particular circumstances for supervision and review of the work performed by any assistants.
    b. The nature and condition of the client's records and internal control structure.
    c. The expertise of client personnel and their expected audit participation.
    d. The type of the financial statements, schedules, or other information upon which the auditor is reporting. (AICPA Adapted)

13. During an audit engagement, pertinent data are compiled and included in the audit working papers. The working papers primarily are considered to be:

    a. A client-owned record of conclusions reached by the auditors who performed the engagement.
    b. Evidence supporting financial statements.
    c. Support for the auditor's representations as to compliance with generally accepted auditing standards.
    d. A record to be used as a basis for the following year's engagement. (AICPA Adapted)

PROBLEMS

6-1 In an examination of financial statements, an auditor must judge the validity of audit evidence obtained.

Required:
Assume that you have assessed a low level of control risk.
1. In the course of an examination, the auditor asks many questions of client officers and employees.
    a. Describe the factors that the auditor should consider in evaluating oral evidence provided by client officers and employees.
    b. Discuss the validity and limitations of oral evidence.
2. An auditor's examination may include computation of various balance sheet and operating ratios for comparison with prior years and industry averages. Discuss the validity and limitations of ratio analysis.
3. In connection with an examination of the financial statements of a manufacturing company, an auditor is observing the physical inventory of finished goods, which consists of expensive, highly complex electronic equipment. Discuss the validity and limitations of the audit evidence provided by this procedure.

(AICPA Adapted)

6-2 Auditors frequently refer to the terms "standards" and "procedures." Auditing standards deal with measures of the quality of the auditor's performance. Auditing procedures refer to the methods or techniques used by the auditor to gather evidence in the conduct of the examination.

Required:

Identify the basic types of auditing procedures that an auditor would use during an audit of financial statements.

6-3   The third generally accepted auditing standard of field work requires that the auditor obtain sufficient competent evidential matter to afford a reasonable basis for an opinion regarding the financial statements under examination. In considering what constitutes sufficient competent evidential matter, a distinction should be made between underlying accounting data and all corroborating information available to the auditor.

Required:

Discuss the nature of evidential matter to be considered by the auditor in terms of the underlying accounting data, all corroborating information available to the auditor, and the methods by which the auditor tests or gathers competent evidential matter.

(AICPA Adapted)

6-4   Tom Majors, an entry-level staff auditor, has been assigned to observe the physical inventory of the Lewiston Chemical Company, a December 31 year-end audit client. Lewiston processes and distributes industrial chemicals.

Upon arriving at Lewiston's manufacturing plant, Tom learns that there are fifteen above-ground cylindrical-shaped storage tanks, each fifty feet tall. In addition, there are three rectangular storage tanks located underground. The above-ground tanks are connected in lots of five, and there are three different chemicals at the site; the underground pipes stretch over two miles in length. The underground pipes can be accessed at each of the tanks, and also at various access ports throughout the plant.

In addition to the tanks and pipes, there is a shipping/receiving depot. Three separate pipelines run to the depot so that each of the chemicals can be accessed for shipping and receiving. Tank trucks are used to both deliver and ship chemicals to and from the depot.

Required:

1. Indicate the special audit problems Tom faces when observing Lewiston's chemical inventory.
2. Discuss what specialist(s) Tom should consider using to assist in the physical inventory observation. Specifically state what problems the specialist(s) will be assigned to solve.

6-5   In any audit engagement, an auditor is concerned that financial statements properly reflect the economic substance of material related party transactions. To achieve this objective, auditors attempt to determine the existence of related parties and the nature of transactions entered into between the audit client and the related parties.

During the course of an audit engagement, you have identified two potential related party transactions. The first involves a significant stockholder of the client who has borrowed cash to purchase a new home. The second is an affiliated company which has agreed to supply your audit client with raw materials.

Required:

Describe how each of the two potential related party transactions should be structured so that its legal form accurately reflects the economic substance. Include the items an auditor would review to assure that the transaction is made at "arm's length."

6-6   The first generally accepted auditing standard of field work requires, in part, that "the work is to be adequately planned." An effective tool that aids the auditor in adequately planning the work is an audit program.

Required:
What is an audit program, and what purposes does it serve?

(AICPA Adapted)

6-7   In late spring of 1989, you are advised of a new assignment as in-charge accountant of your CPA firm's recurring annual audit of a major client, the Lancer Company. You are given the engagement letter for the audit covering the calendar year December 31, 1989, and a list of personnel assigned to this engagement. It is your responsibility to plan and supervise the field work for the engagement.

Required:
Discuss the necessary preparation and planning for the Lancer Company annual audit *prior to* beginning field work at the client's office. In your discussion include the sources you should consult, the type of information you should seek, the preliminary plans and preparation you should make for the field work, and any actions you should take relative to the staff assigned to the engagement.

(AICPA Adapted)

6-8   The audit committee of the Board of Directors of Unicorn Corp. asked Tish & Field, CPAs, to audit Unicorn's financial statements for the year ended December 31, 1989. Tish & Field explained the need to make an inquiry of the predecessor auditor and requested permission to do so. Unicorn's management agreed and authorized the predecessor auditor to respond fully to Tish & Field's inquiries.

After a satisfactory communication with the predecessor auditor, Tish & Field drafted an engagement letter that was mailed to the audit committee of the Board of Directors of Unicorn Corp. The engagement letter clearly set forth arrangements concerning the involvement of the predecessor auditor and other matters.

Required:
1. What information should Tish & Field have obtained during their inquiry of the predecessor auditor prior to acceptance of the engagement?
2. Describe what other matters Tish & Field would generally have included in the engagement letter.

(AICPA Adapted)

6-9   For many years the financial and accounting community has recognized the importance of the use of audit committees and has endorsed their formation. At this time the use of audit committees has become widespread. Independent auditors have become increasingly involved with audit committees and consequently have become familiar with their nature and function.

Required:
1. Describe what an audit committee is.
2. Identify the reasons why audit committees have been formed and are currently in operation.
3. What are the functions of an audit committee?

(AICPA Adapted)

6-10   Jones, CPA, is approached by a prospective client who desires to engage Jones to perform an audit which in prior years was performed by another CPA.

Required:
Identify the procedures which Jones should follow in accepting or declining the engagement.

(AICPA Adapted)

6-11   In conducting an audit leading to the expression of an opinion on the financial statements, the independent auditor must obtain evidence to establish that the items listed on the financial statements actually exist and are valued properly. Among the items an independent auditor could encounter during an audit that would have to be verified are (1) inventory on consignment, (2) insurance expense, (3) interest payable, and (4) common stock outstanding.

Required:
For any three of the four items listed, indicate the types of audit evidence the independent auditor primarily would depend upon in verifying these items.

(CMA Adapted)

6-12   The preparation of working papers is an integral part of the CPA's examination of financial statements.

Required:
1. a. What are the purposes or functions of audit working papers?
   b. What records may be included in audit working papers?
2. What factors affect the CPA's judgment of the type and content of the working papers for a particular engagement?
3. Discuss the relationship of audit working papers to each of the standards of field work.
4. You are instructing an inexperienced staff member whose first auditing assignment is to examine an account. An analysis of the account has been prepared by the client for inclusion in the audit working papers. Prepare a list of the information and notations that the staff member should include in the account analysis to provide an adequate working paper as evidence of the examination. (Do not include a description of auditing procedures applicable to the account.)

(AICPA Adapted)

INTERNAL CONTROL STRUCTURE IN A FINANCIAL STATEMENT AUDIT

7

Major topics discussed in this chapter are the:

▲ *Nature of an entity's internal control structure.*

▲ *Elements of internal control structure — the control environment, the accounting system, and control procedures.*

▲ *Potential deficiencies in internal control structure.*

▲ *Auditor's consideration of internal control structure in assessing control risk under the second standard of field work.*

▲ *Requirements for communicating internal control structure related matters noted during the audit, such as deficiencies in an entity's control procedures.*

Lacking an effective internal control structure, an entity's accounting system could be unreliable and its reported financial information suspect. This chapter addresses the auditor's approach to considering internal control structure in a financial statement audit, focusing on the question: Can an entity's controls be relied on to restrict the extent of substantive tests of details? The chapter begins by introducing internal control structure and its three elements: the control environment, the accounting system, and control procedures. In turn, the chapter describes and illustrates an auditor's responsibilities for considering internal control structure in a financial statement audit, including how an auditor performs tests of controls, assesses control risk, and communicates reportable conditions such as deficiencies in internal control. The chapter is consistent with SAS No. 55, "Consideration of the Internal Control Structure in a Financial Statement Audit," and SAS No. 60, "Communication of Internal Control Structure Related Matters Noted in an Audit."

INTERNAL CONTROL STRUCTURE

An entity's *internal control structure* consists of the policies and procedures established by management to provide reasonable assurance that specific objectives of the entity will be achieved. An auditor considers internal control structure in every financial statement audit. However, the responsibility for establishing and maintaining internal control structure is management's, not the auditor's.

Reasonable Assurance. Even the most carefully designed internal control structure cannot insure that the entity's objectives will be accomplished. Thus, an auditor can expect the internal control structure to provide only reasonable, not absolute, assurance that objectives will be accomplished. The concept of reasonable assurance recognizes that the benefits (for example, reduced risk of employee theft) expected from a policy or procedure may not be worth the cost of implementation. This cost-benefit relationship should be considered by management when designing, implementing, and monitoring the system and should be recognized by the auditor when considering the system's effectiveness.

Inherent Limitations. The effectiveness of an internal control structure can be diminished by inherent limitations. For example, even the most logically designed and carefully implemented system may be undermined by employee errors or intentional acts which circumvent the system. A second limitation, unrelated to employee behavior, relates to the fact that changes in an entity's business may necessitate changes in controls. For example, controls over a manual data processing system may not be appropriate for a newly designed and implemented computer system. Thus, the results of an auditor's current evaluation of the effectiveness of internal control structure cannot necessarily be projected to future periods.

ELEMENTS OF INTERNAL CONTROL STRUCTURE

From an auditor's perspective, internal control structure includes three elements: the control environment, the accounting system, and control procedures, each of which consists of the policies and procedures established by management to provide reasonable assurance that specific objectives will be achieved. The auditor's interest, however, lies only in those policies and procedures that affect the assertions embodied within the entity's financial statements — that is, policies and procedures related to the assertions of existence or occurrence, completeness, rights and obligations, valuation or allocation, and presentation and disclosure.

Control Environment

An entity's *control environment* represents management's and the board of director's attitude toward, awareness of, and actions concerning internal control structure. It reflects the importance of control in management's operating style. For example, an active audit committee, a competent internal audit department, and direct management control over the authority delegated to employees would suggest that management is committed to an effective internal control structure.

The auditor's objective in considering an entity's control environment is to obtain an understanding of management's and the board of director's attitude, awareness, and actions concerning:

▲ Management philosophy and operating style.
▲ Organizational structure.
▲ The audit committee.
▲ Methods used to communicate authority and responsibility.
▲ Management control methods.
▲ The internal audit function.
▲ Personnel policies and procedures.
▲ External influences on the entity, such as government regulations.

Accounting System

The *accounting system* consists of the methods and records established by management to record and report transactions and events and to maintain accountability for assets and liabilities. To be effective, an accounting system should include methods and records that will identify all valid transactions and record them in the proper accounting period, describe transactions on a timely basis and in sufficient detail to permit proper classification, measure the transaction properly, and present the transactions and related disclosures in the financial statements. The auditor's objective regarding an entity's accounting system is to obtain an understanding of:

▲ Major classes of transactions processed by the system,
▲ How transactions are initiated,
▲ Records, documents, and accounts used in the processing and reporting of transactions,
▲ The processing of transactions, and
▲ Financial reporting procedures.

The central activity of most businesses typically involves a series of related business functions, all of which must be captured within the accounting system. Although sometimes complex, these functions can be described in general as follows: Capital funds are received from debt and equity security holders (creditors and owners) and either held for use in operations or invested; funds for operations are used to acquire resources (goods and services) from vendors and employees in exchange for obligations to pay; resources are used in operations or held or transformed and distributed to outsiders in exchange for promises of future payments; outsiders pay for resources distributed to them; and obligations to vendors and employees are paid.

Figure 7-1 categorizes these functions into four *transaction cycles,* the vehicles through which repetitive transactions are processed by an entity's accounting system: (1) financing, (2) expenditure/disbursement, (3) conversion, and (4) revenue/receipt. Because cycles consist of related, homogeneous, and repetitive transactions that can be grouped together conveniently, the number and nature of cycles will vary from industry to industry and from company to company. Thus, these four cycles are representative, not definitive. They include most, but not necessarily all, of any manufacturing, merchandising, or service entity's business functions; the functions may differ for particular entities, and so too may the cycles. In fact, if sufficiently significant to an entity's business activity, any one of the functions could represent a separate transaction cycle. In addition, the four cycles are not appropriate for specialized industries such as banking and real estate. The fact that cycles vary suggests that in considering internal control structure, an auditor must determine which cycles are operating.

An external financial reporting cycle is also common to many entities and relates to: preparing journal entries and posting transactions to the general ledger (to the extent such functions are not performed within other cycles); deciding the generally accepted accounting principles an entity should follow; gathering and summarizing information for preparing financial statements and other historical financial reports; and preparing and reviewing financial statements and other external reports. This cycle is not considered in this book, however, since it does not relate directly to the processing of transactions.

FIGURE 7-1

Relating Business Functions and Transaction Cycles

Functions	Cycles
Capital funds are received from investors and creditors.	Financing
Capital funds are held for use in operations or invested.	
Resources (goods and services) are acquired from vendors and employees in exchange for obligations to pay.	Expenditure/ Disbursement
Obligations to vendors and employees are paid.	
Resources are used, held, or transformed.	Conversion
Resources are distributed to outsiders in exchange for promises of future payments.	Revenue/ Receipt
Outsiders pay for resources distributed to them.	

Focusing on transaction cycles does not mean that individual financial statement accounts are ignored; it means an auditor focuses on processes (cycles) in order to understand end results (accounts). Accounts are location devices in which processed transactions are recorded, classified, and summarized. In short, transactions processed through cycles determine the dollar balances within financial statement accounts.

The dollar balances in some accounts actually result from transactions processed through more than one cycle. For example, debits to Cash result from cash received from customers, a function of the revenue/receipt cycle, and from creditors and investors, a function of the financing cycle. Credits to Cash result from cash disbursements, a function of the expenditure/disbursement cycle. Thus, the dollar balance in Cash reflects the net result of transactions processed through three cycles. Accounts are much more meaningful to an auditor if he or she understands the processes (cycles) relating to accounts and their dollar balances. Figure 7-2 illustrates the account groups or components that are generally contained within each cycle, and also indicates the chapters in this book devoted to each cycle.

Control Procedures

Control procedures are those policies and procedures in addition to the control environment and the accounting system that management establishes to provide reasonable assurance that specific objectives are achieved. The auditor's objective is to obtain a knowledge of control procedures necessary to plan the audit after considering the knowledge obtained about the control environment and the accounting system.

In practice, control procedures have various objectives and take various forms depending on the entity's business and industry. Generally, though, control policies and procedures should be established over the authorization and execution of transactions, segregation of duties, the design and use of documents and records, access to assets and records, and independent checks on performance.

Transaction Authorization. All transactions should be authorized by responsible personnel acting within the scope of their prescribed authority and responsibility. Without a formal system of transaction authorization, any employee could commit resources without regard to the entity's operating objectives.

The required authorization for a transaction (or series of related transactions) depends on the nature, scope, and frequency of occurence. *Specific authorization* means authorization is required each time the transaction is pro-

FIGURE 7-2
Relating Transaction Cycles and Financial
Statement Accounts

Cycles	Major Related Account Groups/Components
Revenue/ Receipt (Chapters 11, 12)	Sales Receivables Cash Receipts Cash Balances
Expenditure/ Disbursement (Chapters 13, 14, 15)	Purchases Payables Personnel and Payroll Cash Disbursements
Conversion (Chapter 16)	Inventory Cost of Sales Fixed Assets
Financing (Chapter 17)	Investments Long-Term Debt Capital Stock

posed and is typically associated with unusual, material, or infrequent projects. For example, specific authorization might be required for plant expansion, purchases or sales of subsidiaries, or capital asset purchases in excess of a designated amount. In contrast, *general authorization* means the entity has established policies and procedures which personnel should follow to determine if a proposed transaction or project is authorized in general. For example, an entity may have authorized pricing and credit sale policies, and personnel may complete transactions meeting these prescribed policies without first obtaining specific authorization. General authorization avoids the inefficiencies of specifically reauthorizing routine transactions. Without general or specific authorization, a proposed transaction should not be executed.

Authorization is not the same as approval; authorization and approval are sequential though related activities. Authorization means authority has been given to acquire or expend resources. Approval, in contrast, means the predetermined conditions of authorization have been met and resources may therefore be acquired or expended. For example, an employee might approve payment of a vendor's invoice for materials acquired in conjunction with a capital asset purchase specifically authorized by the board of directors. Transaction authorization usually precedes approval, although they may occur simultaneously.

Segregation of Duties. No system of policies and procedures can prevent *collusion,* an irregularity or illegal act committed by two or more employees, each of whom is necessary to complete the fraudulent scheme. For example, even if different employees authorize, execute, and record cash payments, no accounting system could prevent them from conspiring to transact a fraudulent payment and sharing the misappropriated funds. As a result, preventing collusion is not an objective of an internal control structure. The best alternative is the segregation of functional responsibilities to prevent any one employee, acting alone, from committing and concealing irregularities or illegal acts. Optimum segregation of duties exists when collusion is necessary to circumvent the control structure.

To achieve optimum segregation of functional responsibilities, an entity's management, custodial, accounting, and internal accountability functions should be performed by different employees. That is, the following responsibilities would be separated:

▲ Transaction authorization (a management function).
▲ Transaction execution (a custodial function).
▲ Transaction recording (an accounting function).
▲ Independent checks on performance (an internal accountability function).

If any one employee were responsible for all four of these functions, his or her opportunities to misappropriate assets would be almost endless. If any one employee were responsible for three or for two functions, his or her opportunities would diminish progressively, but would not be eliminated completely. Optimum segregation of duties would suggest that no employee be responsible for any more than one function because:

▲ Restricting employee responsibility to one function means at least four different, independent employees are required to authorize, execute, record, and periodically account for transactions. Thus, a system of checks and balances exists to reevaluate the validity of a transaction four separate times. If two, three, or four functions are performed by a single employee, the system of checks and balances becomes progressively weaker.
▲ The more employees required to complete a transaction, the more employees necessary to commit and conceal irregularities. Importantly, it is reasonable to assume that employees are less apt to attempt collu-

sion as the number of employees required to commit fraud increases.
In cases of fraud, there is no safety in numbers.

Documents and Records. To obtain accurate and reliable accounting data,
transactions must be recorded promptly in the accounting periods and dollar
amounts actually executed, and classified properly in control and subsidiary
accounts. Satisfying these requirements, however, in turn depends on documents and accounting records that accurately reflect all executed transactions.
Records and documents are physical evidence of executed transactions and
collectively represent the *audit trail* that is so critical to an auditor when
tracing transactions through an accounting system.

The design of documents and accounting records can have considerable
impact on how efficiently an accounting system operates, and therefore how
efficiently an audit can be conducted. As a result, documents and records —
the components of the audit trail — should be:

▲ Designed for multiple use if possible, thereby minimizing the number
of different forms.
▲ Prenumbered consecutively when printed, thereby providing a control
over unused and missing forms.
▲ Relatively easy to complete, thereby encouraging employees to complete them accurately.

The transaction recording process and the accounting records should be
clearly and unambiguously described in a *procedures manual.* The purpose
of a procedures manual is to encourage consistent use and completion of
prescribed accounting records and documents and to provide a ready reference for newly hired personnel. A procedures manual can also represent an
important reference source for auditors attempting to determine how an entity's accounting procedures are intended to operate.

Access to Assets and Records. Only authorized personnel should have access to assets and accounting records. One means of limiting access to both
assets and related acounting records is the use of physical controls, such as
protection devices and automatic transaction recording equipment.

Protection devices restrict unauthorized personnel from gaining either
direct access to assets or indirect access through accounting records which
could be used to misappropriate assets. For example, locked storerooms could
restrict access to parts inventories, and fireproof vaults to petty cash vouchers.

Mechanical and electronic *transaction recording equipment* limits access
to assets by limiting the number of employees involved in recording and
posting transactions, thereby minimizing the likelihood of irregularities. For

example, electronic cash registers record cash sales both on cash register tapes and in off-site electronic storage equipment, creating two records of a single transaction.

Independent Checks. The reliability of the accounting system should be assessed periodically by independent employees who compare recorded assets with actual assets. For example, perpetual inventory records can be tested by comparing recorded quantities with actual quantities on hand. Independent checks on performance are intended to reveal unrecorded or improperly recorded transactions and, equally important, to make corrections.

To maximize potential effectiveness, independent checks should take advantage of the element of surprise, be conducted by personnel independent of the functions tested, and result in appropriate action. The element of surprise encourages employees to execute and record transactions accurately, since their work may be "audited" at any time. Of course, periodic accountability would be much less effective if conducted by employees responsible for the functions tested; the results could lack objectivity. Thus, periodic comparisons should be conducted by personnel independent of the functions tested.

Discrepancies noted between recorded and actual assets should be followed up by responsible levels of management, resolved, and corrected if necessary. Lacking follow-up procedures, independent checks on performance would be meaningless.

IDENTIFYING DEFICIENCIES IN INTERNAL CONTROL STRUCTURE

In view of the concept of reasonable assurance and the limitations inherent in any control structure, an auditor must have a general understanding of how employees could make errors or intentionally commit and conceal irregularities. Potential control deficiencies could be indicated by a number of situations that need exist only occasionally to result in an error or irregularity. Some of these possible situations follow:

▲ Transactions are not appropriately authorized.

▲ Transactions are approved but do not conform with authorization as to essential conditions and terms, or documentation of transactions is not checked or adequately tested as to pertinent details.

▲ Transactions are not recorded in the amounts and in the accounting periods in which they are executed.

▲ Assets recorded in the accounts do not agree with actual assets due to errors in recording transactions.

▲ Conditions affecting accounting values are not recognized on a timely basis.

▲ Tangible assets, unissued securites, blank forms, or accounting records are exposed to unauthorized access.

▲ Tangible assets written off are exposed to unauthorized use or disposal.

▲ Accounting policies are not formally authorized and documented, or financial presentations do not conform to authorized policies.

Any of these situations could present opportunities for errors or irregularities and therefore should be considered by an auditor when evaluating control effectiveness.

In order to commit and conceal an irregularity, an employee would need access both to assets and to records. Access to assets is needed to commit an irregularity, and access to records is needed to conceal the irregularity. Figure 7-3 illustrates how commission and concealment are possible. Each column of *x*s identifies a situation which provides opportunity for errors or irregularities. Each situation is interpreted as follows: "Persons who *(x)* may cause a shortage of cash or other tangible assets by *(x)* and attempt concealment of the shortage by *(x)*." Boxed *x*s mean the related situations are to be read as if connected by the word *or*. Together, the situations listed above and Figure 7-3 (pages 264–265) provide a model for an auditor when considering the possibility of errors or irregularities.

THE AUDITOR'S CONSIDERATION OF INTERNAL CONTROL STRUCTURE

Before designing substantive tests of account balances, an auditor first considers the question: Can the entity's internal control structure be relied on to restrict the extent of substantive tests? If the control structure can be relied on to prevent or detect aggregate client errors in excess of the auditor's tolerable error, then the auditor may restrict the extent of substantive tests of account balances, but not below a level sufficient to reduce audit risk to an amount judged appropriate for issuing an opinion on financial statements. The auditor's consideration of internal control structure is not a substitute for substantive tests of details; rather, tests of controls and substantive tests complement each other.

The second standard of field work, introduced in Chapter 5, provides the basis for an auditor's consideration of an entity's internal control structure in a financial statement audit:

A sufficient understanding of the internal control structure is to be obtained to plan the audit and to determine the nature, timing, and extent of tests to be performed.

An auditor's consideration of an entity's internal control structure includes three phases: (1) *obtain an understanding* of how management has designed policies and procedures for the control environment, accounting system, and control procedures, (2) *assess control risk* for the policies and procedures that have been placed in operation, and (3) *determine the nature, timing, and extent of substantive tests*. Figure 7-4 flowcharts the three phases of the auditor's consideration of internal control structure and indicates the objective of each phase. The following discussion addresses each phase separately, although some portions of each may actually be performed concurrently in practice.

Obtain an Understanding of Internal Control Structure

In every financial statement audit, an auditor should obtain an understanding of internal control structure sufficient to plan the audit. An understanding of control structure is necessary for the auditor (1) to determine whether there are control procedures that can be relied on when planning the nature, timing, and extent of substantive tests, and (2) if controls cannot be relied on, to gather information that will aid in designing substantive tests. Obtaining an understanding consists of: performing a preliminary review, documenting the internal control structure and identifying transaction cycles, performing a transaction "walk-through," and identifying control procedures that are potentially reliable.

Performing a Preliminary Review. Before expending time and effort to document an entity's internal control structure, an auditor first reviews prior-year audit working papers and client procedures manuals, makes appropriate inquiries of management, and observes client personnel to obtain a general understanding of the control environment, the flow of transactions through the accounting system, and control procedures. An understanding of the control environment, the accounting system, and the control procedures provides the auditor with a general knowledge of the entity's organizational structure, of methods used to communicate responsibility and authority, and of methods used by management to supervise the system. In turn, an understanding of the flow of transactions provides the auditor with a general knowledge of the various classes of transactions and the methods by which each significant class of transactions is authorized, executed, initially recorded, and subsequently processed.

Based on his or her understanding of an entity's control environment, control procedures, and the flow of transactions, the auditor decides for each major class of transactions whether it is reasonable to plan to rely on internal control structure, and therefore whether to continue considering internal con-

FIGURE 7-3 Summary of Basic Possibilities for Errors and Irregularities

Persons Who

Handle cash receipts before initial recording ....
Handle cash receipts after initial recording...........
Prepare vouchers supporting cash disbursements.......
Issue checks singly ....
Handle signed checks ....
Participate in payroll preparation or disbursement
Have custody of imprest or other funds ....
Have sole custody of other tangible assets ....

May Cause a Shortage of Cash or
Other Tangible Assets by

Losing or intercepting unrecorded cash receipts.........
Losing or abstracting recorded cash receipts.........
Preparing improper vouchers to support cash
  disbursements...
Issuing unsupported checks ....
Misdirecting or diverting proper checks ....
Making improper payroll disbursements ....
Losing or abstracting imprest or other funds.........
Losing or misappropriating other tangible assets.........

By reducing accountability for cash or other tangible assets through...

Cash receipts records ....

Cash disbursements records ....

Vouchers supporting cash disbursements .....

Payroll disbursements records ....

Journal entries or general ledger postings ....

Other records ....

And transferring the shortage to

Operating accounts ....

Trade receivables ....

Trade payables ....

Other balance sheet accounts ....

Payroll distribution or related accounts ......

Without reducing accountability for cash or other tangible assets and permitting the shortage to remain in

Cash on hand or on deposit ....

Other tangible assets ....

Adapted from: Deloitte Haskins & Sells, *Internal Accounting Control: An Overview of the DH&S Study and Evaluation Techniques*, (New York: Deloitte Haskins & Sells, 1979), pp. 18–19.

FIGURE 7-4
Considering Internal Control Structure in a Financial Statement Audit

Objective: To obtain an understand-   To determine an assessed   To determine the na-
                ing of internal control   level of control risk   ture, timing, and ex-
                structure sufficient to   tent of substantive
                plan the audit   tests

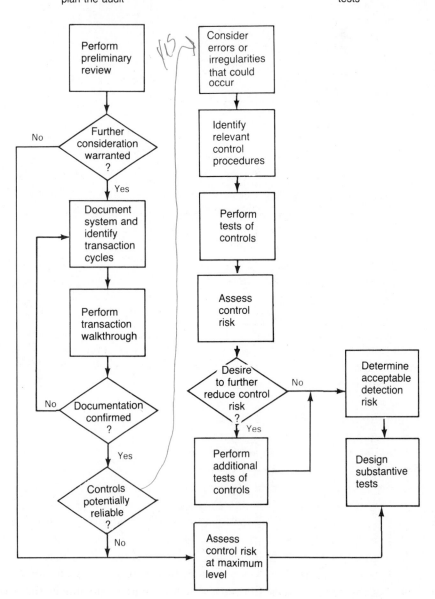

trol structure as shown in Figure 7-4. The decision is based on the auditor's answer to the following two questions:

▲ Is further consideration of internal control structure likely to justify restricting substantive tests of details?

▲ Is the audit effort needed to continue considering internal control structure likely to be less than the reduction in audit effort achieved by reliance on the system?

Answering "No" to either question would cause an auditor to discontinue further consideration of internal control structure and to design substantive tests of account balances assuming a maximum level of control risk. If the auditor does not rely on the control structure and therefore assumes a maximum level of control risk, he or she should document that conclusion in the audit working papers. In contrast, answering "Yes" to both questions would cause the auditor to continue considering internal control structure as follows.

Documenting the System. To document an entity's internal control structure, an auditor relies on discussions with appropriate client personnel and reviews accounting records, documents, and employee procedures manuals. For example, an auditor might talk to the corporate controller, to internal auditors, and to employees responsible for particular accounting functions (e.g., the manager of accounts receivable and his or her employees), review organization charts and transaction documentation (e.g., purchase orders, receiving reports, and vendor invoices), and consult procedures manuals to confirm the procedures discussed or observed.

In practice today, auditors use one or more of three means to document internal control structure: narrative memoranda, flowcharts, and questionnaires. A *narrative memorandum* is a written description of a particular phase or phases of an accounting system. Figure 7-5 illustrates a narrative description for a company's cash collections on credit sales. Although useful for describing uncomplicated systems, narratives may be inappropriate when a system is complex or frequently revised.

Flowcharts consist of interrelated symbols which diagram the flow of transactions and events through a system, or portions thereof. Although different flowchart symbols can be used to depict the same operation, a firm of certified public accountants should adopt standardized symbols in order to promote understanding and communication among auditors within the firm. Figure 7-6 illustrates several common flowcharting symbols, and in Figure 7-7 the symbols are used to flowchart the system described previously in narrative form in Figure 7-5. Note, though, that in practice an auditor would not use both a narrative description and a flowchart to document the same system or class of transactions; rather, one or the other would be used.

FIGURE 7-5

Narrative Description of Accounting System

Karolus Lighting Fixtures, Inc.

Memorandum: Cash Collections on Credit Sales

December 31, 1990

Two departments are involved in the cash collection function: the mail room and Cash Receipts. In the mail room, envelopes containing remittance advices and the customer's checks are opened. Each check is restrictively endorsed, and a mail-room employee prepares two copies of a list of the day's receipts. Copy 1 of the list of receipts and all remittance advices are forwarded to Accounts Receivable for posting; Copy 2 and all checks are forwarded to Cash Receipts.

In Cash Receipts, Copy 2 of the list of receipts and the checks are used to prepare a bank deposit slip and two copies of a cash summary sheet, and to update cash records. Checks and the deposit slip are hand-carried to the First National Bank for deposit, and Copy 1 of the cash summary is forwarded to Accounts Receivable and General Accounting for recording. Copy 2 of the cash summary and Copy 2 of the list of receipts are filed in Cash Receipts.

BLK 9/30/90

Unlike flowchart symbols, flowchart logic cannot be standardized. When preparing system flowcharts, an auditor should strive to be efficient, by displaying operations as concisely as practicable, and informative, by clearly indicating employee responsibilities and document flow. Flowcharting is a creative process, requiring keen imagination and thoughtful preparation.

Internal control structure *questionnaires* consist of a series of questions designed to detect control deficiencies. Questionnaires require *Yes, No,* or *Not Applicable* (N/A) responses: *Yes* responses suggest satisfactory control conditions, and *No* responses signal potential material deficiencies that could lead to errors, irregularities, or illegal acts. Figure 7-8 illustrates an internal control questionnaire related to the cash collection procedures described in narrative form in Figure 7-5 and flowcharted in Figure 7-7. Note that the internal control questionnaire in Figure 7-8 indicates one *No* response and therefore suggests one potential deficiency: that cash collection employees are not bonded, which means that the company is not insured against losses from employees misappropriating cash receipts.

Questionnaires can be adapted to almost any system, since they usually contain questions about many conceivable potential deficiencies, thereby in-

FIGURE 7-6
Some Common Flowchart Symbols

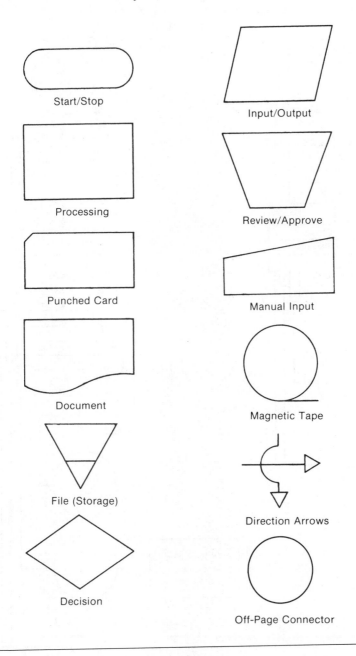

Start/Stop

Input/Output

Processing

Review/Approve

Punched Card

Manual Input

Document

Magnetic Tape

File (Storage)

Direction Arrows

Decision

Off-Page Connector

FIGURE 7-7
Flowchart of Accounting System

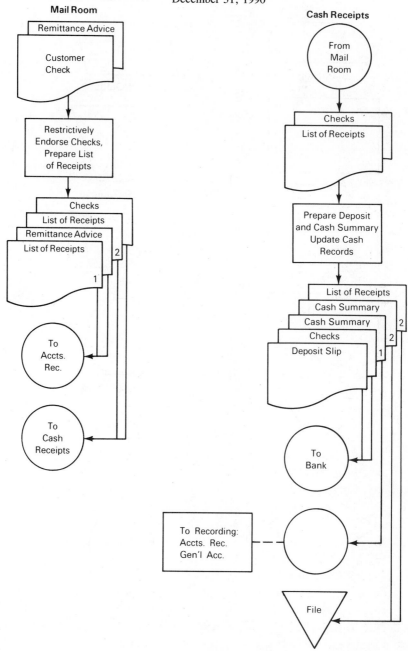

Karolus Lighting Fixtures Inc.
Cash Collection on Credit Sales Procedures
December 31, 1990

FIGURE 7-8
Questionnaire

Karolus Lighting Fixtures, Inc.
Cash Collections on Credit Sales
December 31, 1990

Question	Answer: Yes, No, or N/A	Remarks	Performed By
			BLK
1. Are mail receipts opened by personnel independent of shipping, billing, sales invoice processing, and recording?	*yes*		
2. Are checks restrictively endorsed immediately upon opening the mail?	*yes*		
3. Are lists of receipts prepared when all mail receipts are opened?	*yes*		
4. Are checks forwarded promptly to personnel responsible for preparing bank deposits?	*yes*		
5. Are checks deposited daily?	*yes*		
6. Are cash summaries prepared and forwarded to recording?	*yes*		
7. Are all employees who handle cash adequately bonded?	*no*	*Cash collection employees are not bonded*	

creasing the likelihood of detection. On the other hand, questionnaires can result in unreliable documentation, since employees may respond inaccurately to questions asked by the auditor. This may occur particularly when an employee attempts to provide the "expected" answer or responds to questions that should be directed to other employees. To avoid inaccurate responses, an auditor should attempt to verify responses with supervisory personnel and with the entity's procedures manual.

Of course, an auditor could use any combination of narratives, flowcharts, and/or questionnaires to document an entity's internal control structure, thereby maximizing the advantages of each. For example, an auditor might decide to flowchart the major aspects of an entity's accounting system and use narratives to describe less important operations.

Identifying Transaction Cycles. Because the number and nature of transaction cycles vary from industry to industry and from company to company, an auditor must identify each client's major transaction cycles. Identifying cycles involves five steps:

- ▲ Review account components for homogeneity.
- ▲ Identify representative cycles.
- ▲ Flowchart each cycle, supplementing with narratives and questionnaires as necessary.
- ▲ Trace one or a few representative transactions through each cycle (transaction walk-through).
- ▲ Revise flowcharts if necessary.

Every financial statement account has two components: a debit side and a credit side. *Reviewing account components for homogeneity* involves examining the normal business function associated with each major account component. *Transaction cycles are then identified* by components with similar business functions. For example, normally Accounts Receivable is debited and Sales credited when resources are distributed to outsiders in exchange for promises of future payments. Likewise, normally Cash is debited and Accounts Receivable credited when outsider's pay for resources distributed to them. Because resource distribution and outsiders' payments are both functions of the revenue/receipt cycle, debits to Cash, credits to Sales, and debits and credits to Accounts Receivable are homogeneous account components related to the revenue/receipt cycle, as the following illustrates:

Revenue/Receipt Cycle

| | Related Account Component | |
Account	Dr.	Cr.
Cash	X	
Sales		X
Accounts Receivable	X	X

The process of reviewing account components is continued until all major cycles are identified. As noted earlier, a particular business function may be significant enough to represent a cycle by itself; others may justify grouping into one cycle, as in the preceding hypothetical illustration.

After all major cycles are identified, each should be *flowcharted*, supplementing with narratives and questionnaires as necessary. The flowcharts are pictures of the cycles, and can be invaluable to an auditor in attempting to understand the logic and complexities of an entity's accounting system and control procedures. Flowcharts are often far superior to narratives and questionnaires exclusively, since the information for an entire control structure is compressed into so few cycles. In short, a picture is "worth a thousand words."

Performing a Transaction "Walk-Through." Following documentation, a single transaction (or a small number of transactions) for each major segment of the internal control structure is selected and followed, or "walked through," the accounting system. The purpose of the walk-through is to verify narrative, questionnaire, and/or flowchart documentation and to familiarize the auditor with the audit trail. Documentation is followed from beginning to end, tracing transactions through the complete authorization, execution, and recording process. If the transaction walk-through isolates differences from narratives, questionnaires or flowcharts, the reason for the differences should be resolved and the auditor's documentation revised if necessary.

Identifying Controls That Are Potentially Reliable. From information gathered by documenting the system, an auditor evaluates whether the entity's prescribed control procedures can be relied on when designing substantive tests of account balances, assuming client employees satisfactorily comply with the procedures. If control procedures are not suitably designed to justify reliance, the auditor would not perform tests of controls, and therefore would discontinue considering the internal control structure. Hence control risk would be assessed at the maximum level, and the auditor would design substantive tests that do not rely on the internal control structure. In addition, the auditor would communicate any apparent "reportable conditions" to the board of director's audit committee as required by *Statement on Auditing Standards No. 60*, "Communication of Internal Control Structure Related Matters Noted in an Audit," discussed later in this chapter.

If control procedures are suitably designed and potentially reliable, the auditor would continue to consider internal control structure by assessing control risk.

Assess Control Risk

Control risk (along with inherent risk) is the basis for determining the nature, timing, and extent of substantive procedures. To assess control risk, the auditor:

▲ Considers the errors or irregularities that could occur and that could result in misstatements in the financial statements,

▲ Identifies relevant control procedures designed to prevent the errors or irregularities, and

▲ Performs tests of controls on the control procedures to be relied on in designing substantive tests.

Errors, Irregularities, and Control Procedures. For each major transaction cycle, an auditor considers the errors or irregularities that could occur in an entity's control structure and then identifies control procedures that could serve either to prevent or to detect the errors or irregularities. For example, an auditor might identify the following errors or irregularities and control procedures for cash receipts transactions:

Types of Errors or Irregularities That Could Occur	Controls Designed to Prevent or Detect the Error or Irregularity
Cash receipts on credit sales could be lost or diverted, potentially resulting in overstated receivables and unrecorded cash.	Establish the cash receipts function in a centralized location.
	Require daily reconciliation of cash receipts records with bank deposit slips.
Cash shortages could go unreported, potentially resulting in lost cash and overstated cash balances.	Prepare lists of cash receipts in the mail room.
	Establish periodic procedures for reconciling cash records with bank statements.

The auditor would apply tests of controls to each of the control procedures that he or she intends to rely on when designing substantive tests.

Tests of Controls. In a financial statement audit, tests of controls consist of audit procedures directed toward the effectiveness of both the design and operation of an entity's internal control structure. They are applied only to those controls on which the auditor intends to rely when designing substantive tests of account balances. An auditor would not rely on, and therefore not test, a particular control if the audit effort required to test the control exceeded the reduction in year-end audit effort that could be achieved by reliance.

Tests of controls are intended to answer three questions:

▲ Were the necessary control procedures performed?
▲ How were they performed?
▲ By whom were they performed?

In general, an auditor answers these questions by making inquiries of responsible personnel, observing personnel perform assigned duties, and inspecting documentation. For example, there is frequently no documentary evidence (no "audit trail") related to who receives and deposits cash or who records and posts customer accounts. Thus, an auditor would rely on observation and inquiry to answer the questions above. However, to determine whether cash receipts are recorded and deposited promptly, an auditor might rely on the tests of controls illustrated in Figure 7-9, all of which require inspecting documentation.

Ideally, tests of controls should be applied to transactions and detailed records that were executed and prepared throughout the entire fiscal year under audit. However, auditors often perform tests of controls at interim, e.g., September or October for a December 31 year-end engagement, thereby raising the question of whether additional tests are necessary for the remaining period. In deciding whether to perform tests of controls for the remaining period, an auditor should consider the following:

▲ The results of tests of controls at interim.
▲ Management's responses to inquiries concerning the remaining period.
▲ The length of the remaining period.
▲ The nature and amount of the transactions or balances involved.
▲ Evidence of the control within the remaining period that may be obtained from substantive tests performed by the auditor, by the internal auditors, or both.

When examining documentation, an auditor does not examine all of the transactions and detailed records related to the controls tested, but selects a sample from the population of all available transactions or records for the period. Audit sampling in tests of controls is discussed in detail in Chapter 9.

When performing tests of controls, an auditor may find differences between what was expected, based on the documentation obtained, and what actually occurred. For example, a vendor's invoice may have been paid without the accounts payable manager's initials of approval. Such differences are appropriately called *exceptions, deviations,* or *occurrences,* rather than errors, because an "exception" does not necessarily mean that an "error" had been made in the accounting records. Thus, the fact that a vendor's invoice lacks approving initials does not necessarily mean that the invoice should not have been paid.

FIGURE 7-9
Tests of Controls

Karolus Lighting Fixtures, Inc.
Cash Collections and Deposits
December 31, 1990

Program Step	Performed By
Collections	
1. On a surprise basis, take control of the bank deposit (deposit slip and checks) just before delivery by client personnel to the bank.	*BLK*
2. Compare the total dollar amount of the checks to the total recorded on the deposit slip.	*BLK*
3. Compare the checks (in the deposit package) to details in the cash receipts records and the accounts receivable subsidiary ledger (e.g., customer names, and amounts), and determine whether the lapse of time between cash receipt and deposit is reasonable.	*BLK*
Deposits	
4. For sampled deposits:	
a. Compare the entries in the cash receipts journal with the deposits listed on the monthly bank statement to determine whether all cash receipts are deposited promptly.	*BLK*
b. Determine whether cash receipts not listed on the bank statement are listed as deposits in transit in the bank reconciliation and are included with the deposits in the subsequent month's bank statement.	*BLK*
5. Trace the totals in the cash receipts journal to the postings in the general ledger.	*BLK*
6. Document any weaknesses or discrepancies observed.	*BLK*

Control Risk. An auditor assesses control risk from his or her understanding of internal control structure in general, and from evidential matter obtained by tests of controls in particular. Generally, the lower the level of control risk an auditor desires, the more assurance he or she will require from evidential matter obtained in tests of controls.

On occasion, an auditor may desire a further reduction in the assessed level of control risk — that is, below the level indicated by completed tests of controls — in order to reduce the extent of substantive tests to be applied to year end account balances. In such cases, additional tests of controls would be necessary. However, the additional tests would be performed only if the auditor believes evidential matter is available to support a further reduction and if the expected effort to perform additional tests would result in less audit effort for substantive tests.

Determine the Nature, Timing, and Extent of Substantive Tests

After considering the assessed level of control risk (and inherent risk) for financial statement accounts or assertions, the auditor next determines the nature, timing, and extent of substantive tests necessary to restrict detection risk to an acceptable level. As explained in Chapter 5, control risk and detection risk are inversely related. As the assessed level of control risk increases, the acceptable level of detection risk decreases. Correspondingly, in planning substantive tests an auditor would perform more extensive tests, perform tests at the balance sheet date rather than at interim dates, and would test more extensively. Figure 7-10 depicts the relationship between detection risk and the nature, timing, and extent of substantive tests.

Regardless of how low the assessed level of control risk, the acceptable level of detection risk could not be so high as to preclude the need for any substantive tests at all. The auditor would always perform some substantive tests for all significant account balances and transactions.

COMMUNICATING INTERNAL CONTROL STRUCTURE RELATED MATTERS NOTED IN AN AUDIT

Management is responsible for establishing, maintaining, and monitoring an entity's internal control structure. Nevertheless, an auditor is required to communicate to the audit committee any "reportable conditions" identified while performing the financial statement audit. *Reportable conditions* are defined in SAS No. 60 as:

> . . . significant deficiencies in the design or operation of the internal control structure, that could adversely affect the organization's ability to record, process, summarize, and report financial data consistent with the assertions of management in the financial statements.

FIGURE 7-10

Relationship of Detection Risk to the Nature, Timing, and Extent of Substantive Tests

Effect of Detection Risk on	Acceptable Level of Detection Risk:	
	Lower	Higher
Nature of Substantive Tests	Should use more persuasive tests (e.g., confirmations from independent parties)	Could use less persuasive tests (e.g., examine documentation within the entity)
Timing of Substantive Tests	Perform tests at balance sheet date	Perform tests at an interim date
Extent of Substantive Tests	Test more extensively (e.g., increase sample size)	Test less extensively (e.g., decrease sample size)

Reportable conditions may involve deficiencies in the control environment such as management's override of control procedures, in the accounting system such as inadequate recordkeeping, and in the control procedures such as failure to prepare reconciliations on a timely basis. A deficiency may be of such a magnitude as to be considered a *material weakness in internal control*, defined in SAS No. 60 as:

> . . . a condition in which the design or operation of the specific internal control structure elements do not reduce to a relatively low level the risk that errors or irregularities in amounts that would be material in relation to the financial statements being audited may occur and not be detected within a timely period by employees in the normal course of performing their assigned functions.

Essentially, material weaknesses in internal control are a subset of reportable conditions.

Only an engagement designed specifically to report on internal control structure, discussed more fully in Chapter 20, could be expected to give reasonable assurance that all potentially reportable conditions — and, therefore, all significant deficiencies — are detected. Nevertheless, reportable conditions may come to an auditor's attention during an audit and, under SAS No. 60, should be communicated to the board of director's audit committee or, lacking an audit committee, to individuals with equivalent authority and responsibility. The communication preferably should be written, but if done orally should be documented by memoranda or notations in the working papers. An illustrative written report appears in Figure 7-11 and identifies the one reportable condition — which, in this case, is also a material weakness in internal control — indicated by the questionnaire in Figure 7-8: employees who handle cash are not bonded.

Regardless of the form of communication, the reportable conditions communicated are those detected as a result of considering internal control structure in accordance with the second standard of field work only. Additional conditions may exist and not be detected. An auditor's primary audit objective is to issue an opinion on financial statements. An audit engagement is designed and conducted with that objective in mind and cannot be relied upon to detect all significant deficiencies in internal control.

SUMMARY

The design, implementation, and monitoring of internal control structure — including the control environment, the accounting system, and control procedures — are the responsibilities of management, not the independent auditor. The auditor's responsibility is to obtain an understanding of the internal control structure sufficient to plan the audit and to determine the nature, timing, and extent of tests to be performed. Reportable conditions, including material weaknesses in internal control, should be communicated to the audit committee.

REFERENCES

American Institute of Certified Public Accountants. *Report of the Special Advisory Committee on Internal Control*. New York: American Institute of Certified Public Accountants, 1979.

American National Standards Institute. *Flowchart Symbols and Their Usage in Information Processing*. New York: American National Standards Institute, Inc., 1971.

Arthur Andersen & Co. *A Guide for Studying land Evaluating Internal Accounting Controls*. New York: Arthur Andersen & Co., 1978.

Deloitte, Haskins & Sells. *Internal Accounting Control: An Overview of the DH&S Study and Evaluation Techniques*. New York: Deloitte, Haskins & Sells, 1979.

Grollman, W. K., and R. W. Colby. "Internal Control for Small Businesses." *Journal of Accountancy*. (December, 1978), pp. 64–67.

Loebbecke, J. K., and G. R. Zuber. "Evaluating Internal Control." *Journal of Accountancy* (February, 1980), pp. 49–56.

FIGURE 7-11
Communication of Internal Control Structure Related Matters Noted in
an Audit

February 7, 1991

Board of Directors
Karolus Lighting Fixtures, Inc.

In planning and performing our audit of the financial statements of the Karolus
Lighting Fixtures, Inc., for the year ended December 31, 1990, we considered
its internal control structure. Our consideration was to determine our auditing
procedures for the purposes of expressing our opinion on the financial statements and not to provide assurances on the internal control structure. However,
in that connection, we noted certain matters involving the internal control structure and its operation that we consider to be reportable conditions under standards established by the American Institute of Certified Public Accountants.
Reportable conditions involve matters coming to our attention relating to significant deficiencies in the design or operation of the internal control structure
that, in our judgment, could adversely affect the organization's ability to record, process, summarize, and report financial data consistent with the assertions of management in the financial statements. These may involve aspects of
the control environment, the accounting system, or specific control procedures.

Our consideration of internal control structure disclosed the following condition
that we believe results in more than a relatively low risk that errors or irregularities in amounts that would be material in relation to the financial statements
of Karolus Lighting Fixtures, Inc. may occur and not be detected within a
timely period: Employees who handle cash are not bonded. This internal control weakness could result in material loss to the company if cash is diverted.

This report is intended solely for the information and use of the audit committee, management, and others in the organization.

Lynne Nicholas, CPA

Miotto, N. J. "Evaluating Internal Accounting Controls." *Management Accounting* (July, 1980), pp. 15–18.

Mock, T. J., and J. L. Turner. *Internal Acounting Control Evaluation and Auditor Judgment.* Auditing Research Monograph No. 3. New York: AICPA, 1981.

Mock, T. J., and J. J. Willingham. "An Improved Method of Documenting and Evaluating a System of Internal Accounting Controls." *Auditing: A Journal of Practice & Theory* (Spring, 1983), pp. 91–99.

Morris, W. J., Jr., and H. M. Anderson. "Audit Scope Adjustments for Internal Accounting Control." *The CPA Journal* (July, 1976), pp. 15–20.

Srinidhi, B. N., and M. A. Vasarhelyi. "Auditor Judgment Concerning Establishment of Substantive Tests Based on Internal Control Reliability." *Auditing: A Journal of Practice & Theory* (Spring 1986), pp. 64–76.

Touche Ross & Co. *Touche Ross Accounting Control Evaluation: Controlling Assets and Transactions.* New York: Touche Ross & Co., 1979.

QUESTIONS

1. Why is it necessary that an entity design and implement an internal control structure?
2. Briefly explain the elements of internal control structure.
3. Briefly explain the concept of management responsibility as it relates to internal control structure.
4. Why is a formal system of transaction authorization necessary?
5. Distinguish between specific and general authorization.
6. How does the design of an entity's documents and accounting records affect the conduct of an audit? Identify some basic design characteristics which promote efficiency.
7. What is a "procedures manual"? what purpose does it serve?
8. Identify the two types of physical controls over assets and accounting records, giving examples for each.
9. What is the purpose of periodically comparing recorded assets with actual assets?
10. Which functions must be separated in order to achieve optimum segregation of functional responsibilities? Why?
11. Briefly explain the concept of reasonable assurance.
12. Briefly describe the limitations inherent in any internal control structure.
13. Describe three different schemes that an employee could use to override internal control structure. Indicate who might override the system, and how he or she might cause a shortage of cash or other tangible assets and attempt concealment. Use Figure 7-3 as a guideline.
14. What is a transaction cycle? Identify four cycles and the business functions related to each.
15. Identify and indicate the major components of each phase of an auditor's consideration of internal control structure.
16. What methods can an auditor use to document internal control structure?
17. What is the purpose of a transaction "walk-through"?
18. Briefly describe the process of identifying transaction cycles.
19. Under what circumstances might an auditor not perform tests of controls that he or she otherwise intended to rely upon?

20. In your own words briefly define what is meant by a "material weakness in internal control."

MULTIPLE CHOICE QUESTIONS

1. Transaction authorization within an organization may be either specific or general. An example of specific transaction authorization is the:

   a. Setting of automatic reorder points for material or merchandise.
   b. Approval of a detailed construction budget for a warehouse.
   c. Establishment of requirements to be met in determining a customer's credit limits.
   d. Establishment of sales prices for products to be sold to any customer.
                                                                       (AICPA Adapted)

2. It is important for the CPA to consider the competence of the audit client's employees because their competence bears directly and importantly upon the

   a. Cost-benefit relationship of internal control structure.
   b. Achievement of the objectives of the internal control structure.
   c. Comparison of recorded accountability with assets on hand.
   d. Timing of the tests to be performed.   (AICPA Adapted)

3. When considering internal control structure, an auditor must be aware of the concept of reasonable assurance, which recognizes that:

   a. The employment of competent personnel provides assurance that the objectives of internal control structure will be achieved.
   b. The establishment and maintenance of internal control structure is an important responsibility of the management and not of the auditor.
   c. The cost of control procedures should not exceed the benefits expected to be derived from the procedures.
   d. The segregation of incompatible functions is necessary to obtain assurance that the internal control structure is effective.   (AICPA Adapted)

4. When considering the effectiveness of internal control structure, the auditor should recognize that inherent limitations do exist. Which of the following is an example of an inherent limitation in internal control structure?

   a. The effectiveness of procedures depends on the segregation of employee duties.
   b. Procedures are designed to assure the execution and recording of transactions in accordance with management's authorization.
   c. In the performance of most control procedures, there are possibilities of errors arising from mistakes in judgment.
   d. Procedures for handling large numbers of transactions are processed by electronic data processing equipment.   (AICPA Adapted)

5. The primary purpose of the auditor's consideration of internal control structure is to provide a basis for

a. Determining whether procedures and records that are concerned with the safe-guarding of assets are reliable.
b. Constructive suggestions to clients concerning improvements in internal control structure.
c. Determining the nature, extent, and timing of audit tests to be performed.
d. The expression of an opinion.   (AICPA Adapted)

6. Which of the following audit tests would be regarded as a test of controls?

   a. Tests of the specific items making up the balance in a given general ledger account.
   b. Comparisons of the inventory pricing to vendors' invoices.
   c. Comparisons of the signatures on canceled checks to board of directors' authorizations.
   d. Tests of the additions to property, plant, and equipment by physical inspections.   (AICPA Adapted)

7. The sequence of steps in gathering evidence as the basis of the auditor's opinion is:

   a. Substantive tests, documentation of control structure, and tests of controls.
   b. Documentation of control structure, substantive tests, and tests of controls.
   c. Documentation of control structure, tests of controls, and substantive tests.
   d. Tests of controls, documentation of control structure, and substantive tests.
                                                                        (AICPA Adapted)

8. The primary purpose of performing tests of controls is to provide reasonable assurance that

   a. The design and operation of internal control structure is effective.
   b. The flow of transactions through the accounting system is understood.
   c. Transactions are recorded at the amounts executed.
   d. All control procedures leave visible evidence.   (AICPA Adapted)

9. Which of the following is essential to determining whether the necessary control procedures were prescribed and are being followed?

   a. Developing questionnaires and checklists.
   b. Studying and evaluating administrative control policies.
   c. Documenting the control structure and testing controls.
   d. Observing employee functions and making inquiries.   (AICPA Adapted)

10. An auditor's flowchart of a client's internal control structure is a diagramatic representation that depicts the auditor's

    a. Understanding of the structure.
    b. Program for tests of controls.
    c. Documentation of having considered the structure.
    d. Understanding of the types of irregularities that are probable, given the present structure.   (AICPA Adapted)

11. An auditor who becomes aware of a material weakness in internal control is required to communicate this to the

a. Audit committee of the board of directors.
b. Senior management and board of directors.
c. Board of directors and internal auditors.
d. Internal auditors and senior management.   (AICPA Adapted)

12. After considering a client's internal control structure, an auditor has concluded that the structure is well designed and is functioning as anticipated. Under these circumstances the auditor would most likely

a. Cease to perform further substantive tests.
b. Not increase the extent of predetermined substantive tests.
c. Increase the extent of anticipated analytical procedures.
d. Perform all tests of controls to the extent outlined in the preplanned audit program.   (AICPA Adapted)

13. After considering internal control structure, an auditor might decide to

a. Increase the extent of tests of controls and substantive tests in areas where internal control structure is strong.
b. Reduce the extent of tests of controls in areas where the internal control structure is strong.
c. Reduce the extent of both substantive tests and tests of controls in areas where internal control structure is strong.
d. Increase the extent of substantive tests in areas where the internal control structure is weak.   (AICPA Adapted)

PROBLEMS

7-1   An entity's internal control structure should be designed to achieve a variety of objectives. Assume that an entity wishes to accomplish the following four specific control objectives:
1. Transactions should be executed in accordance with management's general or specific authorization.
2. Transactions should be recorded as necessary (1) to permit preparation of financial statements in conformity with generally accepted accounting principles and (2) to maintain accountability for assets.
3. Access to assets should be permitted only in accordance with management's authorization.
4. The recorded accountability for assets should be compared with the existing assets at reasonable intervals, and appropriate action taken with respect to any differences.

To achieve these objectives, management could institute a number of specific control procedures, including the following:
a. Unused, blank checks are stored in locked safes.
b. A bank reconciliation is prepared monthly by personnel independent of the cash function.
c. Credit approval is required for all new customers and for all credit purchases over $10,000.

d. Accounts receivable postings are made from a listing of remittances prepared daily.

e. Perpetual inventory records are updated daily from manufacturing reports.

f. A physical inventory observation is performed monthly.

g. All capital asset acquisitions are reviewed by the board of directors.

h. Only authorized personnel are allowed to enter manufacturing sites.

Required:

For each of the above control procedures, a through h, indicate which objective, 1 through 4, is achieved.

7-2   An auditor must have a general understanding of how employees could make errors or intentionally commit and conceal irregularities; otherwise, he or she would be unable to recognize potential deficiencies in internal control structure. To that end, Figure 7-3 in the text and the related discussion provide a summary of basic possibilities for client-related errors and irregularities.

Required:

Evaluate each of the following cases independently. For each case discuss:

1. How an employee could attempt concealment.

2. What control(s) should be present to prevent concealment.

Case A

Checks from customers are received by the company's receptionist, whose job it is to stamp each check received with a restrictive endorsement, and to prepare a list of all funds received and the name of each corresponding customer.

Case B

A company has three accounts payable clerks. It is the job of each clerk to prepare vouchers for payment. Supporting documents, such as receiving reports and bills of lading, are attached to each voucher as backup for the payment request. The vouchers and support are then forwarded to the company's controller for approval and check signing.

Case C

A company maintains an imprest petty cash fund in order to pay for small, miscellaneous items such as office supplies or postage. The amount of the fund is maintained at $500. Whenever funds are disbursed, a signed request form is filed with the remaining cash. One office clerk is designated as the fund's custodian, and all withdrawals and reimbursements are made by this employee.

7-3   You have been assigned to the audit of the F&S Savings and Loan Association. In preparing for the audit, you learn the following about F&S:

Total assets for the institution are approximately $400 million. F&S has a main office downtown, and thirteen branch offices throughout the city. Four hundred people are employed by F&S, with a total payroll of $6 million.

F&S derives revenue from two principal sources. The major source is interest and fee income from loans. As a savings and loan company, F&S is restricted to making loans only to consumers for purposes such as home mortgages, auto loans, and other personal loans; that is, it cannot make loans to commercial enterprises.

The second revenue source is income from investments. F&S invests funds in short-term instruments such as government securities and certificates of deposit in order to have a ready source of available funds. Interest earned on such investments may or may not be a material component of earnings, depending on the amount of funds invested during a period.

F&S has two major expense components. Administrative costs, such as the previously mentioned payroll costs, constitute one group of expenses; other administrative costs include building maintenance, utilities, and taxes. The second component of expenses involves interest paid to depositors. The dollar magnitude of these interest payments varies considerably, depending on current market rates of interest.

Required:
Using Figure 7-1, as a guide, identify the major business functions and related transaction cycles for the F&S Savings and Loan Association.

7-4   Jones, CPA, who has been engaged to examine the financial statements of Ajax Inc., is ready to begin consideration of Ajax's internal control structure and is aware of the inherent limitations that should be recognized.

Required:
1. What are the objectives of an internal control structure?
2. What are the reasonable assurances that are intended to be provided by internal control structure?
3. When considering the potential effectiveness of internal control structure, what are the inherent limitations that should be recognized?   (AICPA Adapted)

7-5   Susan Barnes, CPA, is considering Tillson Company's internal control structure in conjunction with the annual audit of the company's financial statements.

Required:
1. Describe the inherent limitations that should be recognized in considering the potential effectiveness of any internal control structure.
2. Under generally accepted auditing standards, what is Barnes' obligation with respect to communicating any significant deficiencies detected in the course of considering internal control structure?

7-6   Internal control structure consists of the policies and procedures established by management to provide reasonable assurance that specific objectives will be achieved.

Required:
1. What is the purpose of the auditor's consideration of internal control structure?
2. What are the objectives of a preliminary evaluation of internal control structure?
3. How is the auditor's understanding of internal control structure documented? Discuss the advantages of each type of documentation.
4. What is the purpose of tests of controls?
5. If an auditor is satisfied after considering internal control structure that no significant deficiencies exist, is it necessary to perform substantive tests of details?
                                                                    (AICPA Adapted)

7-7   Ronald Ondeyko, CPA, is preparing a seminar on internal control structure for his entry-level audit staff. His predominant concern is to present the staff with an overview of critical issues confronted during an auditor's consideration of internal control structure under the second standard of field work.

Required:
To aid in developing the seminar's materials, Ondeyko asks you to respond to the following questions.
1. Why and how does an auditor consider internal control structure?
2. For each major class of transactions, how does an auditor decide whether to continue obtaining an understanding of internal control structure?
3. How does an auditor document internal control structure?
4. How does an auditor identify an entity's relevant transaction cycles?
5. What is the purpose of a transaction walk-through?
6. After obtaining an understanding, how would an auditor proceed if control procedures are not suitably designed to justify reliance?
7. What is the purpose of tests of controls, and what general questions do tests of controls attempt to answer?
8. In tests of controls, what is the difference between an "exception" and an "error"?
9. How does an auditor evaluate internal control structure from having obtained an understanding of the system and performed tests of controls?

7-8   You are reviewing audit working papers containing a narrative description of the Tenney Corporation factory payroll system. A portion of that narrative is as follows:

Factory employees punch time clock cards each day when entering or leaving the shop. At the end of each week the timekeeping department collects the time cards and prepares duplicate batch-control slips by department showing total hours and number of employees. The time cards and original batch-control slips are sent to the payroll accounting section. The second copies of the batch-control slips are filed by date.

In the payroll accounting section, payroll transaction cards are keypunched from the information on the time cards, and a batch-total card for each batch is keypunched from the batch control slip. The time cards and batch-control slips are then filed by batch for possible reference. The payroll transaction cards and batch total card are sent to data processing where they are sorted by employee number within batch. Each batch is edited by a computer program which checks the validity of employee number against a master employee tape file and the total hours and number of employees against the batch-total card. A detailed printout by batch and employee number is produced which indicates batches that do not balance and invalid employee numbers. This printout is returned to payroll accounting to resolve all differences.

In searching for documentation you found a flowchart of the payroll system which included all appropriate symbols (American National Standards Institute, Inc.) but was only partially labeled. The portion of this flowchart described in the narrative appears on page 289.

Required:
1. Label your answers (a) through (q). Next to the corresponding letter, supply the appropriate labeling (document name, process description, or file order) applicable to each of the letters on the flowchart.

2. Flowcharts are one of the aids an auditor may use to document and evaluate a client's internal control structure. List advantages of using flowcharts in this context.   (AICPA Adapted)

7-9   A partially completed charge sales systems flowchart appears on pages 290–291. The flowchart depicts the charge sales activities of the Bottom Manufacturing Corporation.

A customer's purchase order is received, and a six-part sales order is prepared therefrom. The six copies are initially distributed as follows:

Copy No. 1 — Billing copy — to billing department.
Copy No. 2 — Shipping copy — to shipping department.
Copy No. 3 — Credit copy — to credit department.
Copy No. 4 — Stock request copy — to credit department.
Copy No. 5 — Customer copy — to customer.
Copy No. 6 — Sales order copy — File in sales order department.

When each copy of the sales order reaches the applicable department or destination, it calls for specific internal control procedures and related documents. Some of the procedures and related documents are indicated on the flowchart. Other procedures and documents are labeled letters a to r.

Required:
List the procedures or the internal documents that are labeled letters c or r in the flowchart of Bottom Manufacturing Corporation's charge sales system. Organize your answers as follows (note that an explanation of the letters a and b which appear in the flowchart are entered as examples):

Flowchart Symbol Letter	Procedures or Internal Document
a.	Prepare a six-part sales order.
b.	File by order number.

                                                                  (AICPA Adapted)

7-10   The town of Commuter Park operates a private parking lot near the railroad station for the benefit of town residents. The guard on duty issues annual prenumbered parking stickers to residents who submit an application form and show evidence of residency. The sticker is affixed to the auto and allows the resident to park anywhere in the lot for twelve hours if four quarters are placed in the parking meter. Applications are maintained in the guard office at the lot. The guard checks to see that only residents are using the lot and that no resident has parked without paying the required meter fee.

Once a week the guard on duty, who has a master key for all meters, takes the coins from the meters and places them in a locked steel box. The guard delivers the box to the town storage building, where the box is opened and the coins are manually counted by a storage department clerk who records the total cash counted on a "Weekly Cash Report." This report is sent to the town accounting department. The storage department clerk puts the cash in a safe, and on the following day the cash is picked up by the town's treasurer, who manually recounts the cash, prepares the bank deposit slip, and delivers the deposit to the bank. The deposit slip, authenticated by the

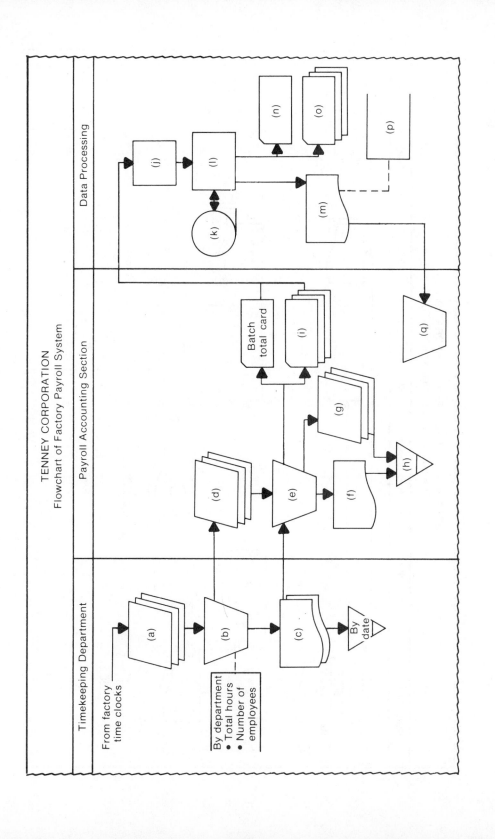

TENNEY CORPORATION
Flowchart of Factory Payroll System

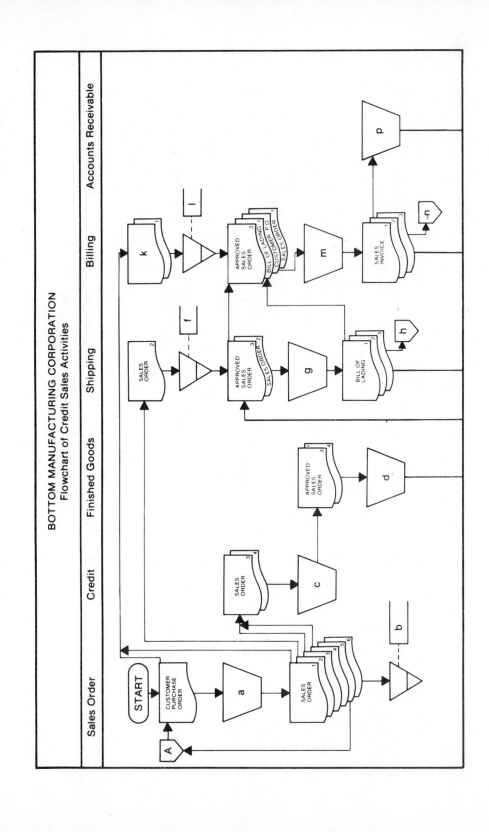

BOTTOM MANUFACTURING CORPORATION
Flowchart of Credit Sales Activities

Sales Order | Credit | Finished Goods | Shipping | Billing | Accounts Receivable

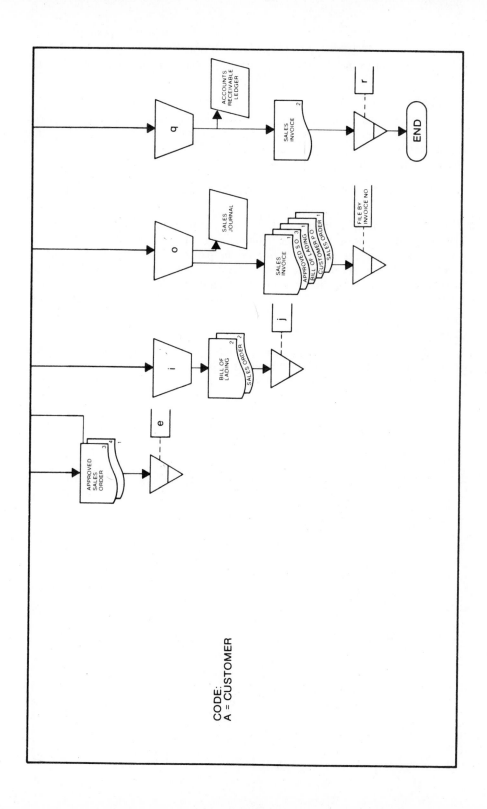

CODE:
A = CUSTOMER

bank teller, is sent to the accounting department where it is filed with the "Weekly Cash Report."

Required:
Describe deficiencies in the existing system and recommend one or more improvements for each of the deficiencies to strengthen control procedures over the parking lot cash receipts.

Organize your answer sheet as follows:

Weakness	Recommended Improvement(s)

7-11   As part of your annual audit of Call Camper Company, you have the responsibility for preparing a report communicating internal control structure related matters noted in the engagement. Your working papers include a completed internal control questionnaire and documentation of tests of controls. Your tests of controls and substantive tests identified a number of significant deficiencies in the internal control structure; for some of these, corrective action by management is not practicable.

Required:
Discuss the form and content of the report on internal control structure related matters and the reasons or purposes for such a report. *Do not write a report.*

CONSIDERING INTERNAL CONTROL STRUCTURE IN EDP SYSTEMS

8

Major topics discussed in this chapter are the:

▲   *Differences between EDP and manual systems.*
▲   *Components and types of EDP systems.*
▲   *Impact of EDP on internal control structure.*
▲   *Nature and function of EDP general and application controls.*
▲   *Auditor's approach to considering internal control structure in EDP systems.*
▲   *Microcomputer applications in auditing.*

With the proliferation of mainframe, minicomputer, and microcomputer accounting information systems within the past decade, the complexion of financial statement audits has changed markedly. Although audit objectives are the same for all types of information processing systems — whether manual or electronic — the conduct of an audit in an EDP environment differs in many respects from audits of manual data processing systems.

This chapter addresses an auditor's consideration of internal control structure when accounting information is processed electronically. The chapter begins by explaining the major audit-related differences between EDP and manual systems and describes the components and types of EDP systems. In turn, the chapter discusses the impact of EDP on internal control structure, a series of EDP-based general and application controls often found in practice, and an auditor's approach to considering internal control structure in EDP systems. Finally, the chapter describes several microcomputer applications in auditing.

DISTINGUISHING EDP FROM MANUAL SYSTEMS

Electronic data processing systems serve exactly the same purposes as manual systems: to process accounting and other management information.

However, there are significant differences between EDP and manual systems, all of which affect an auditor's consideration of internal control structure.

Statement on Auditing Standards No. 48, "The Effects of Computer Processing on the Examination of Financial Statements," identifies several characteristics that distinguish EDP systems from manual systems, including:

▲ Elimination or distortion of audit trials.
▲ Uniform processing of transactions.
▲ Segregation of functions.
▲ Potential for errors and irregularities.

Audit trails — records and documents supporting executed transactions — can be eliminated or distorted in EDP systems. In some EDP systems, many records and documents common to manual systems are unnecessary and therefore are not prepared. For example, some entities use employee time clocks that are online with the computer. That is, employees "punch" in and out with magnetic identification cards, and the system automatically accumulates and transfers total hours worked to appropriate labor and payroll accounts. Because all information is stored within the system's computer, employee time cards — source documents common to manual payroll systems — are not used, thereby eliminating a segment of the audit trail otherwise available in manual systems. With audit trails eliminated or distorted, auditors are often unable to trace the flow of transactions explicitly. As a result, rather than focus upon audit trails in EDP systems, auditors focus upon management's controls over computer hardware and software. If controls are adequate, the system is likely to be reliable.

Computers *process like transactions uniformly,* thereby virtually eliminating the occurrence of clerical errors normally associated with manually processed transactions. However, computers also create a corresponding disadvantage, because transactions processed by poorly designed program commands will result in all like transactions being processed incorrectly, rather than just a few being processed incorrectly at random as is more likely in manual systems.

In Chapter 7, *segregation of duties* was described as a fundamental prerequisite to an effective internal control structure. However, some procedures performed by separate individuals in manual systems are performed by the computer in EDP systems. Thus, any employee who has access to the computer could potentially perform incompatible functions. In addition, the potential for individuals to gain unauthorized access to accounting records is much greater in EDP systems, since perpetrators need not be physically present to alter data, thereby increasing the *potential for error or irregularities.* As a result, other controls are necessary in EDP systems to achieve the control objectives accomplished by segregation of duties in manual systems. For example, other controls might include segregating incompatible functions within the EDP department or using secret passwords to prevent incompatible functions from being performed by employees who have access to both assets and accounting records through an online terminal.

COMPONENTS OF EDP SYSTEMS

EDP systems consist of computer hardware and software. Computer *hardware* is physical equipment comprising the input, processing, and output phases of an EDP system. Figure 8-1 illustrates the relationship among input, processing, and output equipment.

Input units read data and computer programs and may take the form of *magnetic tape drive* or *disk drive units*, though magnetic ink units, optical scan units, and data terminals are not uncommon. Punched cards are rarely seen in practice today, except as "turnaround" documents in billing systems

---

FIGURE 8-1
Computer Hardware

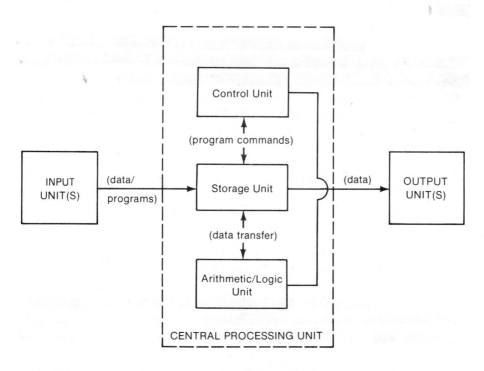

(e.g., remittance advices that are returned with payments). Magnetic tape drive and disk drive units record magnetized data in tracks on circular tapes or on disks. Tape drive and disk drive systems are considerably more efficient than the punched card systems popular in the 1960s. For example, a single reel of tape could contain data from several hundred thousand punched cards.

A *central processing unit* (CPU), or computer, operates all processing functions in an EDP system. Input media from data and program instructions are read by input units and stored in the CPU's storage unit. In turn, program instructions are interpreted by the control unit, triggering data transfer to the arithmetic or logic unit for processing. Results of arithmetic or logical processing are returned to storage, and appropriate output data are emitted.

Output units emit data and often take the form of high-speed printers, tape and disk drive units, or visual display devices. Many input units such as tape and disk drive also serve as output units, although output media can differ from input media.

Computer *software* includes all of the nonhardware components of an EDP system, most notably system programs and application programs. *System programs* perform generalized functions for more than one application and typically include "operating systems," which control and schedule hardware use, "data management systems," which perform multipurpose data handling functions, and "utility programs," which perform basic EDP operations. Generally, system programs are written and distributed by EDP hardware and software vendors.

In contrast, *application (user) programs* perform specialized functions, such as instructing a central processing unit to read input media, transfer data from storage for arithmetic or logical processing, and print output. Generally, application programs are written by users for specific data processing applications, though they are prepared and distributed by vendors as well.

TYPES OF EDP SYSTEMS

Although the components of most EDP systems are similar, the processing capabilities and physical form of selected systems differ markedly.

Online Real-Time Systems

In the term *online real-time*, "online" means that input and output units communicate directly with the CPU — the "mainframe" — and "real-time" means that input and processing are performed almost simultaneously, providing immediate output. Disk drive is a common form of input in online real-time systems.

Online real-time systems can be particularly useful when data are assembled from more than one location and must be updated immediately. For example, both major airlines and off-track betting sites process input from many locations and need updated information to monitor additional input. Airlines make reservations throughout the world and therefore must monitor flight bookings to control overbookings. Off-track betting sites accept wagers from several locations and therefore must monitor accumulated wagers to generate updated betting "odds." In these and other industries, online real-time information processing systems are indispensable, since information must be updated instantaneously.

Mini- and Microcomputer Systems

Minicomputers have become increasingly common in smaller entities. Generally, minicomputers are smaller and less costly and are designed for more specialized applications than larger systems. Several types of input media are common to minicomputers, including magnetic tape or disks, and data terminals. Minicomputers allow many smaller entities such as construction contractors to process contract costs, payroll, and billings more efficiently and more economically than in manual systems, yet without the higher costs of larger EDP systems. In comparison with larger systems, minicomputers have less storage space and process information more slowly. Thus, cost effectiveness is the primary advantage of minicomputers in comparison with larger systems.

Microcomputers are smaller, slower, and less costly than minicomputers, allowing many small entities, such as retail pharmacies and real estate brokerage firms, to enjoy the benefits of electronic data processing. Microcomputers have captured a significant share of the computer sales market and have become quite common, providing a cost effective information processing alternative for entities that might otherwise have been restricted to manual processing. Microcomputers are also used extensively by auditors, regardless of the type of EDP system used by clients. Microcomputer applications in auditing are discussed later in the chapter.

Service Bureaus

Service bureaus provide EDP services to entities that do not own or lease a computer and to entities wishing to supplement internal EDP capabilities. A single service bureau can process information for many entities, providing a cost effective alternative to owner- or lessee-operated computers and to manual data processing.

Generally, service bureaus require that entities provide input media according to predetermined specifications. Services can be tailored to an entity's specific internal information requirements or to more general requirements such as payroll and billings.

IMPACT OF EDP ON INTERNAL CONTROL STRUCTURE

The basic concepts and essential characteristics of internal control structure are similar regardless of whether accounting information is processed manually or by computer. However, the means of achieving control in EDP systems is apt to differ markedly from manual systems, since data are processed electronically rather than manually. Following is a discussion of the impact of EDP upon some aspects of internal control structure.

Quality Personnel

Whether data are processed manually or electronically, personnel must be competent. They must be independent of assigned functions and must understand their assigned responsibilities. Quality personnel are always essential to effective accounting systems. Although EDP systems typically operate with fewer employees, many of those employees require more specialized knowledge than would be necessary to process data manually. Thus, the effectiveness of an electronic accounting information system is centered in the hands of relatively few people, and the incompetence of a single employee could seriously impair the system's effectiveness.

Transaction Authorization, Execution, and Recording

Transaction flow from authorization to execution and recording can be quite different in EDP as opposed to manual accounting information systems. Transaction recording, however, usually represents the most striking change.

Authorization procedures are often similar in manual and EDP systems; general and specific authorization is given by management, not machines. Nevertheless, the terms of general authorization could be stored on tape or disk files for selected repetitive transactions, necessitating controls over automated authorizations. Likewise, transaction execution is similar in manual and EDP systems, since transaction execution results in the flow or exchange of resources, promises, or commitments.

In EDP systems, transactions are recorded by and processed within machines, not by humans and on manual records. Thus, specialized controls are necessary to monitor the transfer of source documents into machine-readable form, the initial recording, and the subsequent classification and summarization of accounting data. Importantly, EDP hardware and software can improve the reliability of recorded transactions, since the opportunity for human mistakes or carelessness is minimized.

Specific general and application controls over transaction authorization, execution, and recording are discussed later in this chapter.

Other Control Characteristics

In addition to quality personnel and controls over transaction authorization, execution, and recording, effective control requires limited access to assets, periodic accountability, and segregation of duties.

The control objective of safeguarding assets requires that access to physical assets and related accounting records be limited to authorized personnel. In an EDP environment, limited access to EDP hardware and software is critical to safeguarding assets.

Even though system reliability is potentially higher in EDP systems, the accuracy of transaction execution and recording processes should be assessed periodically by comparing recorded assets with actual assets. In EDP systems, periodic accountability is usually accomplished by specialized internal auditors called "control groups."

In EDP systems, many functions normally performed by employees are completed by computer hardware. As a result, EDP systems can improve control effectiveness by delegating incompatible — though programmable — functions to the central processing unit. Nevertheless, even though EDP can improve control effectiveness, functional responsibilities within the EDP department must be segregated in order to minimize the likelihood of EDP personnel processing unauthorized transactions or effecting unauthorized system changes.

Access controls, the role of control groups, and controls over segregation of duties are discussed more fully later in this chapter.

General and Application Controls

When significant accounting functions are processed electronically, an auditor's consideration of internal control structure should address the EDP applications, whether they are limited or extensive, including those operated by third parties (e.g., service bureaus). However, as noted earlier, EDP accounting applications typically eliminate or distort segments of an audit trail. Thus, in comparison with manual accounting applications, an auditor must place increased, if not complete, reliance upon the adequacy of controls; therefore, controls, rather than transactions, become the primary focus of an auditor's attention and approach. EDP controls can be categorized as: *general controls,* relating to all computerized accounting activities, and *application controls,* relating to specific accounting applications. Each category is discussed in detail below.

GENERAL CONTROLS

General controls pervade application controls and include:

▲ *Organization and operation controls:* the plan of organization and operation of an EDP activity.
▲ *Systems development and documentation controls:* procedures for documenting, reviewing, testing, and approving systems or programs and changes.
▲ *Hardware controls:* controls built into EDP equipment by manufacturers.
▲ *Access controls:* controls over access to equipment and data files.
▲ *Data and procedural controls:* other controls affecting overall EDP operations.

The AICPA Computer Services Executive Committee, in an Audit and Accounting Guide, "The Auditor's Study and Evaluation of Internal Control in EDP Systems," identifies a series of control techniques for each general control category listed. Several of these techniques are discussed in the following sections.

Organization and Operation Controls

In an effort to optimize system effectiveness and efficiency, the plan of organization for an entity's EDP operation should include the following controls:

▲ Segregation of functions between the EDP department and users.
▲ Provision for general authorization over the execution of transactions.
▲ Segregation of functions within the EDP department.

Segregation of the EDP Department and Users. The EDP department should be independent of all *user departments,* i.e., departments that provide input data for, or use output generated by, an automated accounting function.

Independence from non-EDP departments minimizes the likelihood of an EDP department employee manipulating input or output, since an independent employee would have no opportunity to influence non-EDP activities, short of collusion. Likewise, independent employees of non-EDP departments (e.g., billing, accounts payable, or payroll) would have no opportunity to influence EDP activities (e.g., coding payables listings to generate cash payments to vendors).

Transaction Authorization and Execution. The EDP department should neither authorize nor initiate transactions for processing. Rather, user departments should authorize and initiate transactions, and the EDP department should process transactions.

Occasionally, periodic and recurring transactions or entries are initiated in the EDP department rather than user departments. For example, EDP departments in some entities prepare purchase requisitions for economic-order-quantity calculations made automatically from automated perpetual inventory records. In these instances, the transaction is initiated within the central processing unit only to eliminate the possibility of non-EDP employees failing to monitor inventory quantities. Often, it is more efficient and economic to initiate requisitions automatically. Whenever transactions are initiated by computer, compensating controls should exist to assure that automatically initiated transactions are authorized, either generally or specifically.

Segregation of Functions within the EDP Department. Within an EDP department, functions should be segregated in order to maximize independence among functions and employees, thereby minimizing the likelihood of errors, irregularities, or illegal acts. The functions included within an EDP department depend upon the size and scope of EDP operations. An organization chart for a medium-size EDP department appears in Figure 8-2, and the general responsibilities of each function are summarized in Figure 8-3.

In general, if economically feasible, each of the functions should be segregated in order to maximize the number of checks and balances and minimize the likelihood of unauthorized revision of existing computer programs, preparation of unauthorized programs, and unauthorized access to data conversion or central processing equipment. However, in smaller EDP operations, some functions such as computer operators and librarians may be compressed into one function, thereby increasing the likelihood of unauthorized activities. If optimum segregation of functions is not practical, an auditor should either look for compensating controls or decide not to rely upon existing segregation controls.

FIGURE 8-2
Organization Chart: Medium-Size EDP Department *Report to*

V.P. of Finance

Should not report to controller

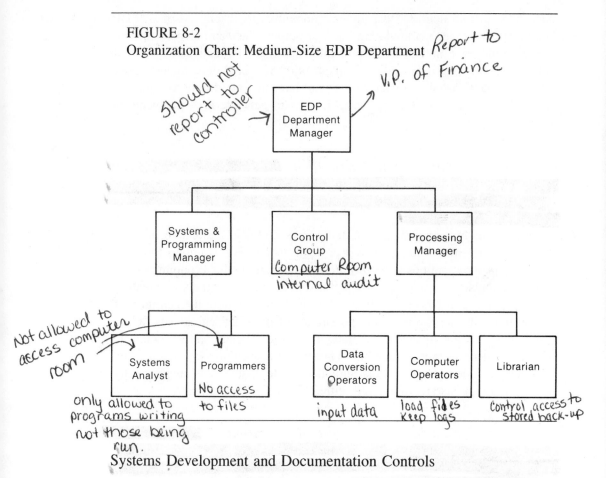

Computer Room internal audit

Not allowed to access computer room

No access to files

only allowed to programs writing not those being run.

input data

load files keep logs

Control access to stored back-up

Systems Development and Documentation Controls

Systems development and documentation controls are designed to monitor systems design, control over program changes, and documentation procedures and include:

▲ Participation by user departments, accounting personnel, and internal auditors, if appropriate, in systems design.
▲ Review and approval of written system specifications by appropriate management levels and user departments.
▲ Joint system testing by user department and EDP personnel.
▲ Final approval over new system applications.
▲ Control over master file and transaction file conversion.
▲ Approval of computer program changes.
▲ Formal procedures to create and maintain documentation.

Participation in Systems Design. At a minimum, a user department and systems analyst should each participate in the design of new EDP applica-

FIGURE 8-3
EDP Functions and Related Responsibilities

Function	General Responsibility
EDP Department Manager	Has overall responsibility for EDP activities.
• Systems and Programming Manager	Has overall operational responsibility for systems design and computer program preparation and maintenance.
• Systems Analysts	Analyze user information requirements; prepare computer program specifications.
• Programmers	Prepare computer program logic and coding (i.e., writing and editing machine-readable computer programs).
• Processing Manager	Has overall operational responsibility for data input, processing, and output.
• Data Conversion Operators	Prepare computer input (e.g., keypunch machine and optical-scan reading equipment).
• Computer Operators	Operate central processing unit.
• Librarian	Maintains library of system and program-support documentation. All computer programs are stored with librarian and can be retrieved by authorized personnel only.
• Control Group	Performs internal audit function for EDP department.

tions; the user department expresses specific departmental information needs, and the systems analyst prepares general specifications for computer programs. Communication at this stage is critical to the EDP department's effectively serving user departments.

Ideally, an entity's accountants and internal auditors should also be involved in systems design. Accountants should be involved because the system's output may have financial reporting implications, and internal auditors because they may wish to implement computer-assisted audit techniques.

Review and Approval of System Specifications. Before an EDP application is implemented, related system specifications should be reviewed and approved by both an appropriate level of management and the applicable user department. In turn, the application should be monitored periodically in light of changing user department information needs and updated when necessary.

Joint System Testing. To assure that an EDP application functions as designed, the application should be tested and modified as necessary by both EDP and user department personnel. An application should not be implemented unless testing and appropriate corrective procedures indicate that properly prepared input will yield desired output and that improper input will be detected.

Final Approval over New Applications. Prior to placing a new EDP application into operation, approval should be obtained from appropriate levels of management and from EDP and user department personnel. This final approval stage should consider the original program specifications, subsequent specification changes, and the results of testing and modification. Above all, the new application should not be approved and implemented unless resulting output clearly meets a user department's information needs. Approval is a critical stage in the system implementation process, since in many cases user departments are apt to ignore unusable output rather than request system modifications.

Control over Master File and Transaction File Conversion. Computer master files contain cumulative transaction data as of a particular date, and transaction files contain transaction data for a particular period or date. For example, the accounts receivable master file might include cumulative account balances and summary data as of November 27, and an accounts receivable transaction file might include receivable transactions for the week ended December 4. Of course, if data contained within either the November 27 master file or the December 4 transaction file are incorrect, the December 4 master file will also be incorrect.

To preclude errors in an updated master file, controls should be implemented to reconcile an updated file with the original file. Otherwise the integrity of updated files would be suspect and the accuracy of updated account balances questionable.

Program Change Approval. Much like new system applications, subsequent program changes should be authorized, tested, modified, and approved. Program changes can be initiated by appropriate levels of management, user departments, or EDP processing personnel. However, to assure independence and minimize the likelihood of errors, irregularities, and illegal acts, final approval should rest with personnel independent of EDP processing personnel.

Formal Procedures to Create and Maintain Documentation. Computer programs reveal very little about why a program was implemented, how it was designed, or how it should be implemented. As a result, program support documentation is necessary in order to facilitate subsequent program modifications or train computer processing personnel. A representative example of program support documentation appears in Figure 8-4.

FIGURE 8-4
Program-Support Documentation

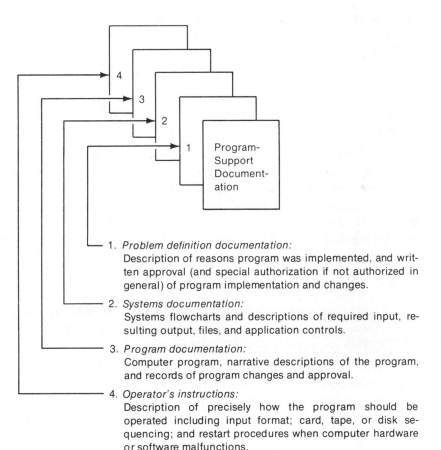

1. *Problem definition documentation:*
   Description of reasons program was implemented, and written approval (and special authorization if not authorized in general) of program implementation and changes.

2. *Systems documentation:*
   Systems flowcharts and descriptions of required input, resulting output, files, and application controls.

3. *Program documentation:*
   Computer program, narrative descriptions of the program, and records of program changes and approval.

4. *Operator's instructions:*
   Description of precisely how the program should be operated including input format; card, tape, or disk sequencing; and restart procedures when computer hardware or software malfunctions.

Program support documentation can be critical to an auditor's understanding of the design and function of accounting-related computer programs. Thus controls over program support documentation can be central to an auditor's consideration of internal control structure in EDP systems.

Hardware Controls

EDP hardware and software should produce accurate and reliable data. As a result, computer manufacturers build hardware controls into EDP equipment, and clients and program vendors build software controls into computer programs.

Hardware controls encompass controls built into computer equipment and designed to detect control override or malfunction. Two particularly common hardware controls are:

▲ *Echo check:* transmits or "echoes" data from output back to input for comparison, emitting error signals (exception listings) if necessary.

▲ *Parity check:* a check on negative (0) and positive (1) charged binary digits through arrays of internal computer bits designed to represent alpha or numeric data. A parity bit is added as necessary to an array of computer bits, yielding an odd- or even-summed array, depending upon the computer. Error signals are emitted if, for example, an odd-numbered digit results when an even number is expected.

In the overwhelming majority of cases, built-in hardware controls are adequate and reliable; they rarely pose a serious problem. Importantly, however, an entity must follow up and resolve any errors detected by hardware controls. As a result, an auditor's focus in hardware controls is typically toward the EDP department's response to errors detected, rather than toward the controls themselves.

Access Controls

Only authorized personnel should have access to EDP hardware, programs, data files, and program support documentation, thereby minimizing the likelihood of improper or unauthorized use.

Access to computer hardware can be restricted through physical security devices, such as door locks and security personnel, and processing schedules, which clearly indicate who is scheduled to process information at particular times. In general, access to data files, programs, and documentation can be limited through effective use of the library function; authorized documentation would be required to obtain any data file (e.g., accounts receivable master file), programs, or documentation from librarians.

Data and Procedural Controls

Data and procedural controls are general controls affecting overall EDP activity and include:

▲ Written manuals of procedures and general and specific authorization.
▲ Control groups to monitor processed data and to review and evaluate proposed EDP system changes.

Written Procedures and Authorization Manuals. In an effort to encourage efficiency and proper use, an EDP department should maintain written procedures manuals, including management's general or specific authorizations to process data. The manuals should clearly describe operations instructions, identifying necessary files, input, and output distribution. Aside from documenting prescribed procedures, manuals can also serve as an important source for training new staff.

Control Groups. A control group of EDP internal auditors should be responsible for receiving input data from user departments, investigating processing errors, and verifying output distribution. In general, a control group coordinates data communications between the EDP department and other user departments. In addition, the control group should review and evaluate proposed EDP systems changes at critical stages of development. Clearly, user departments and EDP department systems and programming personnel are responsible for designing program changes. The control group, however, is responsible for assuring that control criteria are functioning properly.

APPLICATION CONTROLS

Application controls relate to specific recording, processing, and reporting functions performed by EDP, and are usually categorized as input controls, processing controls, and output controls. The AICPA Computer Services Executive Committee's "The Auditor's Study and Evaluation of Internal Control in EDP Systems" identifies a series of application control techniques, several of which are discussed in the following sections.

Input Controls

EDP input controls are designed to provide reasonable assurance that data received for processing by EDP have been properly authorized, converted into machine-sensible form, and identified, and that data have not been lost, suppressed, added, duplicated, or otherwise improperly changed. Effective input controls are a fundamental prerequisite to valid and reliable output. Of course, valid and reliable input data do not necessarily guarantee valid and reliable output, although they do increase the likelihood, assuming effective processing and output controls. Five relevant input controls are:

▲ Input authorization and approval.
▲ Code verification.
▲ Data conversion control.
▲ Data movement control.
▲ Occurrence correction.

Input Authorization and Approval. Before input transactions are accepted for EDP processing, they should be properly authorized and approved in accordance with management's general or specific authorization. Evidence of authorization and approval might take the form of a signature or initials on a source document or batch of documents. In some systems, however, input is entered directly through a computer terminal located outside the EDP department. Terminal-entered input can be authorized or approved through a *user identification number* "punched" by a user prior to entering input; input can only be entered if the identification number is accepted by the central processing unit.

Code Verification. Identification codes are often used in EDP systems to represent data. For example, eight-digit code numbers could be used to represent customer accounts.

Identification codes also provide a vehicle for verifying the accuracy of input data. In many instances, *self-checking numbers* are added to identification codes and serve no purpose other than detecting transposition or clerical errors in codes or unauthorized use. For example, a three-digit self-checking number might be affixed to a customer identification code, representing the result of a predetermined mathematical formula applied to the first eight identification numbers; if the mathematical formula results in anything other than the self-checking digit, the identification code is rejected, thereby precluding data input for the incorrect identification code.

Data Conversion Controls. Input sources supplied by user departments must be converted into a form readable by the central processing unit. This data conversion process often represents the single most common source of input errors. Several data conversion control techniques are available, including the following:

▲ *Record counts:* The number of input documents are counted and compared with the number of converted records.

▲ *Batch totals:* Various totals associated with batches of input data are summed and compared after input conversion or after processing. Batch totals may relate to "meaningful" sums such as total dollars or to "meaningless" sums (called *hash totals*), such as totals of all customer identification numbers.

▲ *Key verification:* Keypunched input is repunched on a key verifier machine. "Punches" by the verifier which differ from the original keypunched input signal an error (e.g., key verifier machine locks).

▲ *Editing routines:* Input data are edited for accuracy or reasonableness. Editing routines include:

— *Character validity:* determines whether data fields correctly contain alpha or numeric data.

— *Limit tests:* determine the reasonableness of values by signaling an exception for data exceeding a predetermined amount.

— *Sequence tests:* determine whether data are processed in the proper sequence.

▲ *Anticipation routines:* Central processing unit "anticipates" the type of data forthcoming (e.g., credit terms for inventory received and recorded in perpetual records), printing a list of receiving reports for which the anticipated data are missing (i.e., an exception listing).

Data Movement Control. All data moved between or among departments or computer processes should be controlled against unauthorized additions, deletions, or alterations. Typically, data movement control is accomplished by comparing record counts and/or batch totals as data move from department to department and from computer run to computer run.

Occurrence Correction. Detecting occurrences (e.g., errors) through input authorization, code verification, data conversion, and data movement controls is not an end in itself. Rather, detecting occurrences is a means toward identifying problems that must be resolved and resubmitted for processing. In general, occurrences should be resolved within the department responsible for creating the occurrence, suggesting the EDP department is not responsible for resolving occurrences created by user departments.

Processing Controls

Unlike input and output controls, EDP processing controls are incorporated within computer programs and designed to provide reasonable assurances that electronic data processing has been performed as intended for the particular application, i.e., that all transactions are processed as authorized, that no authorized transactions are omitted, and that no unauthorized transactions are added. Three relevant processing controls are:

▲ Control totals.
▲ File labels.
▲ Limit (reasonableness) tests.

Control Totals. Record counts and batch totals calculated for input data can also be calculated during processing, thereby resulting in an additional control over data movement throughout the processing system. Control totals are compared from run to run, and differences are resolved.

File labels. In order to minimize the likelihood of processing the wrong files, a file's name and date and other relevant identification information should appear on internal and external file labels. Internal labels are checked against information anticipated by the computer program and external labels against program-support documentation by the computer operator.

Limit (Reasonableness) Tests. Limit, or reasonableness, tests can be conducted during processing by computer program commands just as they can be during input preparation. Several different types of limit tests can be conducted including comparisons to maximum values, ranges of values, or self-checking numbers.

Output Controls

EDP output controls are designed to assure that the processing result (such as account listings or displays, reports, magnetic files, invoices, or disbursement checks) is accurate and that only authorized personnel receive the output. Although potentially effective, output controls are less effective than input and processing controls in isolating specific detailed occurrences. Output controls cannot be relied upon to overcome an ineffective system of input and processing controls. Two relevant output controls are:

▲ Control totals comparisons.
▲ Output distribution.

Control Totals Comparisons. Record counts and batch totals calculated for input and during processing should be compared with similar totals printed on output. In addition, selected control totals can be compared with other internally stored data, such as the general ledger, as well as original source documents. Control totals comparisons can be made by the EDP control group, user departments, or both.

Output Distribution. The reason for processing data electronically, rather than manually, is to rapidly generate accurate, cost effective, and timely output. Modern computer equipment does generate accurate, cost effective output. However, the EDP control group must distribute the output to appropriate user personnel rapidly in order to assure timely output. As a result, controls should be implemented to assure that the control group plans and executes daily output distribution.

FILE RECONSTRUCTION

If magnetic tape drive or disk drive files are damaged or lost, filed information would also be lost, leaving no trail to reconstruct the file. As a result, controls are necessary to assure that files can be reconstructed if necessary.

The *grandfather-father-son* concept is a common approach to file reconstruction in tape drive systems. The concept recognizes that current master files consist of old (prior-period) master files updated with current-period transaction files. Therefore, after generating new master files, old master files and transaction files are saved and stored off-premises; if new master files are damaged or lost, the old master files and transaction files can be reprocessed, reconstructing the new master file. Figure 8-5 illustrates. Unlike magnetic tape drive systems, disk drive systems do not automatically produce a backup file. Thus, to produce a backup file for disk drive systems, the file can be created by copying the data to either another disk or another file medium as illustrated in Figure 8-6.

THE AUDITOR'S CONSIDERATION OF INTERNAL CONTROL STRUCTURE IN AN EDP SYSTEM

The rationale underlying an auditor's consideration of internal control structure in accordance with the second standard of field work is similar regardless of whether an entity processes accounting information manually or

FIGURE 8-5

Grandfather-Father-Son Backup for Magnetic Tape Files

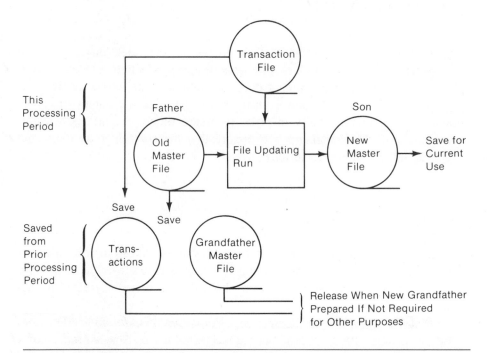

Source: G. B. Davis, D. L. Adams, and C. A. Schaller, *Auditing and EDP* (New York: AICPA, 2d. ed., 1983), p. 128.

electronically. In either case, an auditor's objective is to obtain a knowledge and understanding of internal control structure sufficient to plan the audit.

Auditing "Around" and "Through" the Computer

In general, two audit approaches are available when an entity functions in an EDP environment: auditing "around" and auditing "through" the computer. When auditing *around* the computer, an auditor ignores the EDP function, focusing solely upon (1) the source documents underlying EDP input and (2) EDP output. An auditor compares source documents with output (and vice versa), and data processing is ignored.

Auditing around the computer is appropriate when only minor segments of an audit trail are eliminated or distorted, for example, when the computer is used primarily to perform computational tasks. Advantages of auditing around the computer include lower direct audit costs and limited required technical

FIGURE 8-6
Backup and Recovery for Online Disk Files

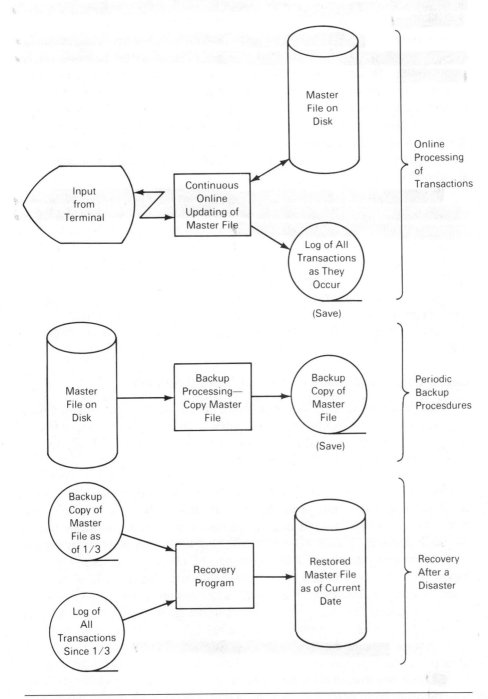

Source: G. B. Davis, D. L. Adams, and C. A. Schaller, *Auditing and EDP* (New York: AICPA, 2d ed., 1983), p. 130.

313

expertise. Disadvantages are that data may be too voluminous to examine manually and that no conclusions can be reached about data not examined specifically.

In contrast, auditing *through* the computer focuses upon all phases of the EDP function, including the processing phase ignored when auditing around the computer. Of course, regardless of the audit approach adopted, segments of the audit trail are still missing, reduced to electrical signals processed through the central processing unit. Rather than focus upon the flow of transactions or data, however — as in manual data processing systems — an auditor focuses upon EDP general and application controls when auditing through the computer. If controls are valid and reliable, electronically processed data are also likely to be valid and reliable.

Incorporated within auditing through the computer is the notion of auditing *with* the computer, the process of using a client's computer to aid in gathering substantive evidential matter. An auditor is perfectly justified in using a client's computer to generate audit evidence about transactions and account balances if — and only if — he or she is satisfied that general and application controls are effective.

When auditing through the computer, an auditor's consideration of internal control structure includes the same phases discussed in Chapter 7 and illustrated in Figure 7-4, although the auditor's approach differs as discussed below.

Obtain an Understanding of Internal Control Structure

The review of an EDP system consists of two components: a preliminary review, in which the auditor makes an initial evaluation about whether to rely on some EDP controls, and completion of the review, in which the auditor assesses an entity's general and application controls.

Preliminary Review of the System. In the preliminary review, an auditor develops an understanding of the flow of transactions through the system, the extent to which EDP is used in each significant accounting application, and the basic structure of control procedures. Ordinarily, the preliminary review is made through inquiries of EDP personnel, by observing personnel perform assigned duties, and by reviewing internal documentation such as the program-support documentation illustrated earlier in Figure 8-4.

Upon completing the preliminary review, the auditor must decide whether to continue the review, or discontinue the review and perform expanded substantive tests. An auditor would discontinue the review if:

▲ EDP controls are inadequate, or

▲ Reliance on EDP controls is not justified because alternative procedures for generating evidence are more effective or efficient or because compensating non-EDP accounting controls exist and are adequate.

If the preliminary review of the system indicates that EDP control procedures appear to provide a basis for reliance, then the auditor would complete the review by assessing the adequacy of general and application controls.

Complete Review: General Controls. In completing the review of general controls, an auditor expands on knowledge obtained during the preliminary review, attempting to identify major strengths and deficiencies to be considered subsequently when evaluating application controls. For example, as discussed earlier, an entity should implement general organization and operation controls which segregate the EDP department from user departments. However, if an employee works in both the EDP department and accounts payable, then that employee could have an opportunity to code payables listings to generate a fraudulent cash payment, and an auditor would have to consider that apparent deficiency when evaluating application controls over input authorization and approval.

To complete a review of general controls, an auditor reviews the corporate and EDP department organization structure, makes inquiries of EDP and user department personnel, and reviews the work of internal auditors, if any, to answer the following specific questions:

▲ Does the organization of the EDP department provide adequate supervision and segregation of functions within the EDP department and between EDP and user departments?

▲ Do procedures provide for control over systems development and access to systems documentation?

▲ Do procedures provide for control over program and systems maintenance?

▲ Do procedures provide control over computer operations, including access to data files and programs?

▲ Do procedures assure that file reconstruction and processing recoveries are complete?

▲ Do internal auditors, if any, provide adequate review and evaluation of EDP activities?

Following review of an entity's general controls, an auditor reviews specific application controls that he or she plans to rely on when designing and performing substantive tests of details.

Complete Review: Application Controls. To complete the review of application controls, an auditor builds on knowledge obtained during the preliminary review by making inquiries of systems analysts, programmers, users, and computer operators and, in some cases, by observing application controls as they function. The auditor's review should be designed to answer the following questions, which focus on the entity's specific controls over input, processing, and output:

▲ Do input controls provide reasonable assurance that data received for processing by the EDP department have been properly authorized and converted into machine-readable form and have not been lost, suppressed, added, duplicated, or otherwise altered?

▲ Do processing controls provide reasonable assurance that data processing has been performed as intended for the particular application, that no authorized transactions are omitted, and that no unauthorized transactions are added?

▲ Do output controls assure that the processing results are accurate and that only authorized personnel receive output?

After completing the review of application controls, an auditor decides whether to perform tests of the general and application controls to determine if they can be relied on. The auditor would decide not to test controls if:

▲ The review of controls disclosed deficiencies indicating that controls cannot be relied on, or

▲ Tests of specific controls would not be cost effective.

Tests of Controls

An auditor's tests of controls are intended to provide a reasonable degree of assurance that prescribed EDP general and application control procedures and methods are complied with and operating as planned. As discussed in Chapter 7, tests of controls are applied only to those controls on which the auditor intends to rely when designing substantive tests of account balances, and are concerned primarily with the questions: Were the necessary control procedures performed? How were they performed? By whom were they performed?

The nature of tests of controls depends upon whether EDP audit evidence is:

▲ External to the central processing unit, and therefore directly observable, or

▲ Internal to the central processing unit, and therefore not directly observable.

Tests of controls involving *external, directly observable EDP audit evidence* usually take the form of (1) corroborative inquiries, (2) observation, and (3) inspection of documentary evidence. Figure 8-7 illustrates tests for both general and application controls when audit evidence can be directly observed by the auditor. For example, the first general control listed in Figure 8-7 is: "Segregate EDP department and users," and the four tests listed for this control require corroborative inquiries of personnel, management, and operating employees; observation of actual operations; and inspection of documentary evidence such as management reports and organization charts.

FIGURE 8-7
Tests of EDP General and Application Controls

Controls	Tests of Controls

General Controls

Organization and Operation Controls:
• Segregate EDP department and users.

• Make inquiries of personnel and review organization charts and job descriptions for evidence of proper segregation of duties.
• Observe actual operations and note the degree of management supervision being exercised.
• Discuss with management and operating employees the extent and effectiveness of management supervision.
• Review available management reports, studies, or evaluations concerning the operations of the data processing system.

• Provide general authorization over the execution of transactions.

• Review the reconciliation of control totals maintained outside the EDP department with the results of computer processing.
• Examine available evidence indicating such reconciliations take place in the normal course of operations.
• Review preprocessing, processing, and postprocessing controls to determine if they provide for processing in accordance with management's authorization.

14   FIGURE 8-7 (*cont.*)

Controls	Tests of Controls
General Controls	
• Segregate functions within the EDP department.	• Observe EDP operations to determine that systems analysts and programmers do not have unrestricted access to hardware, files, or programs. • Review procedures for granting access to programs and data. • Observe the operation of the control group to determine whether it is independent of the systems and programming and processing groups.
Systems Development and Documentation Controls: • Participation by user departments, accounting personnel, and internal auditors in system design.	• Interview representatives of user departments for evidence of the level of their participation in systems design. • Review appropriate documents and related approvals for evidence that user departments adequately understand input and processing requirements, control requirements, and system output. • Review the extent of internal auditors' involvement in system design and review their related workpapers.
• Review and approval of system specifications.	• Review the EDP department's guidelines for systems design. • Review design specifications, seeking written evidence of approval. • Interview management, users, and EDP personnel to determine what approval procedures are used.
• Joint system testing by user department and EDP personnel.	• Review testing and modification standards, test data, and resulting output for adequacy. • Interview user and EDP department personnel to determine test procedures used during implementation.

- Final approval over new applications.

- Process independently prepared test data.
- Review evidence of the approval of significant EDP accounting applications.
- Interview management and user and EDP department personnel involved in the approval process, inquiring about their understanding of the system.

- Control over master file and transaction file conversion.

- Review the EDP department's procedures for reconciling files.
- Observe conversion procedures and controls.
- Test conversions by tracing detailed records from original to updated files and vice versa.

- Approval of computer program changes.

- Interview systems, programming, and processing personnel to determine the procedures for controlling program changes.
- Review documentation in support of program changes to determine if changes are properly approved.
- Review the results of tests made to verify system changes.

- Formal procedures to create and maintain documentation.

- Review documentation standards for adequacy.
- Review selected documentation for compliance with prescribed documentation standards.

Hardware Controls:
- Controls built into computers by manufacturers.

- Review the computer manufacturer's literature or other sources to determine the available hardware control capabilities.
- Review and evaluate available controls.
- Determine the internal accounting control weaknesses resulting from ignored control features.

Access Controls:
- Limit access to EDP hardware, programs, data files, and program-support documentation to authorized personnel.

- Review procedures for collecting and analyzing hardware utilization data.

FIGURE 8-7 *(cont.)*

Controls	Tests of Controls

General Controls

- Review selected available hardware utilization logs.
- On a test basis, compare hardware utilization logs and processing schedules.
- Review procedures for controlling access to programs, data files, and program support documentation.
- Review the librarian's method of controlling unauthorized access to programs, data files, and support documentation.

Data and Procedural Controls:
- Written procedures and authorization manuals.

- Review procedures manuals, determining whether they provide operators with an understanding of processing requirements.
- Observe operations on a test basis, determining whether prescribed procedures are followed.

- Control groups.

- Review the control group's organizational function.
- Interview users, EDP personnel, and control group personnel about control group activities.
- Review procedures for distributing output to determine that only authorized users receive output.
- Interview users, EDP personnel, and control group personnel about the extent of their involvement in systems design and implementation.
- Review control group working papers and reports to determine the extent and quality of the work.

Application Controls

Input Controls:
- Input authorization and approval.

- Obtain or prepare a list of input transaction sources along with required authorizations.

- Code verification.

- Data conversion control.

- Data movement control.

- Occurrence correction.

Processing Controls:
- Control Totals.

- On a test basis, examine evidence that transactions were properly authorized.
- Investigate significant authorization exceptions.
- Review procedures for verifying identification codes.
- On a test basis, trace identification codes to supporting source documents to assure that codes are accurate.
- Review the procedures and techniques for controlling data conversion.
- Observe the performance of verification procedures and the processing and disposition of exception listings.
- Trace batch totals to control logs on a test basis.
- Use a test deck (test data) to test the operations of specific controls.
- Review the adequacy of data movement controls.
- On a test basis, trace a representative group of transactions through the system from initiation to completion.
- Test the reconciliation of key department-to-department or run-to-run totals, reconciling any differences.
- Review and/or observe the adequacy of procedures for resolving occurrences.
- Determine if any occurrences remain unresolved for an unreason -able period of time.
- Test representative occurrences for resolution.

- Review the procedures for generating and reconciling control totals.
- Observe the reconciliation process.
- Trace control totals to related input totals.

FIGURE 8-7 (*cont.*)

Controls	Tests of Controls

Application Controls

• File labels.	• Review the adequacy of file controls.
	• Determine how selected occurrences were resolved.
• Limit (reasonableness) tests.	• Review program-support documentation for available limit tests.
	• Review representative output for evidence that limit tests are applied.
	• Use auditor-prepared test data to test the accuracy of limit tests.
Output Controls:	
• Control totals comparisons.	• Review the procedures for comparison.
	• Observe personnel making comparisons.
• Output distribution.	• Review procedures for controlling output distribution.
	• Observe output distribution.
	• Test the distribution of selected output, determining whether recipients are properly authorized.

Tests of controls involving *internal, nondirectly observable EDP audit evidence* require that an auditor use the computer to obtain a reasonable degree of assurance that general and application controls are operating as planned. Among the EDP techniques available to auditors, the following are particularly useful:

▲ Test data.
▲ Integrated test data.
▲ Parallel simulation.
▲ Generalized audit software.
▲ Program code and flowchart checking.
▲ Audit modules.
▲ Audit hooks.
▲ Controlled processing.

Each of these techniques can be used exclusively or in conjunction with other appropriate techniques. Each approaches tests of controls from a different perspective, though all are designed to provide a basis for determining whether prescribed controls are complied with and operating as planned. Each technique is described below.

Test Data. An entity's EDP function uses client-prepared computer programs to process client-prepared input on client-operated equipment; client personnel control all phases of the EDP function. The test data approach shifts control over EDP input and processing to the auditor by utilizing client-prepared programs to process auditor-prepared input (sometimes called a "test deck") under the auditor's supervision. If general and application controls are functioning properly, the client's program should detect all of the exceptions "planted" by auditors in the test data; if not, control overrides are possible. Like other EDP techniques, the test data approach can be applied to tape and disk drive input systems.

To be an effective and useful audit tool, test data must specifically test each control an auditor plans to rely upon. Thus, when preparing test data, an auditor must be technically proficient in designing erroneous data and imaginative in anticipating potential control overrides. However, despite an auditor's proficiency and imagination, the test data approach is totally ineffective if a client does not use the programs tested. As a result, an auditor should input test data on a surprise basis and/or throughout the year, if possible, thereby increasing the likelihood of observing the programs actually used.

Integrated Test Data. Integrated test data improve upon the test data approach by providing a vehicle for testing whether a client actually uses programs tested. Unlike test data, which are run independent of client data, integrated test data are merged (integrated) with actual client data in a dummy file (e.g., fictitious customer accounts), and removed from client records by journal entry or program commands prior to compiling financial reports. When processed throughout the year, integrated test data provide assurance that the programs tested are actually used to compile internal and external financial reports.

Parallel Simulation. Parallel simulation is roughly the opposite of the test data approach, shifting control over computer programs — rather than input — to the auditor. Thus, in parallel simulation, an auditor prepares programs to process client-prepared input under auditor supervision on the client's or auditor's computer. If an entity's general and application controls have been operating effectively, the client's program should have generated the same exceptions as the auditor's program. Potential control override is suggested when a client's program fails to yield exceptions noted by the auditor's program.

Importantly, parallel simulation provides auditors an independence from client EDP personnel, in that programs are prepared by the auditor rather than client. However, much like test data, parallel simulation provides no vehicle for determining whether actual computer programs are used throughout the year to process all input data. Thus, parallel simulation should be performed on a surprise basis and/or throughout the year, if possible.

Generalized Audit Software. Test data, integrated test data, and parallel simulation each require an auditor to prepare data or computer programs. Generalized audit software, in contrast, is similar to parallel simulation, except computer audit programs are designed and distributed by computer manufacturers, EDP consultants, and several large CPA firms for use by any public accounting firm. Generalized audit software packages shift program preparation responsibility away from auditors who lack either the technical expertise or time to prepare programs "from scratch." Since their development in the mid-1960s, generalized audit software packages have become quite popular, allowing some public accounting firms to accept and competently conduct EDP-based audit engagements, even though lacking high-level EDP expertise.

Most generalized software packages include easy-to-use coding or specification forms, computer program subroutines, and operating instructions. Generally, they function as follows:

▲ Complete software specification forms.
▲ Input specification (data conversion).
▲ Process input through central processing unit, accessing client data files for manipulation and summarization, as required.
▲ Review output reports and exception listings.

Preprinted *software specification forms* are used to specify an auditor's desired audit objectives, including the client data files to be accessed, tasks to be performed, and desired output format. For example, an auditor might access a payroll master file and select a random sample of employee names for further testing. Specific audit testing might include comparison of hourly wages and authorized deductions with stored personnel records, and recalculating gross pay and other deductions such as income tax withheld.

Information for software specification forms is converted into machine-readable form and compared back with specification forms for accuracy. Accurate input data, desired client data files, and the generalized audit software packages are then *processed.* During processing, the information of audit interest is extracted from client data files, manipulated (e.g., recalculations), and summarized in accordance with the auditor's specifications. Finally, output reports and exception listings are printed, providing audit evidence for *review* and evaluation per the auditor's specific audit objectives. Importantly, unlike client-generated output, generalized audit software output contains only information of audit interest and is in a form specified by the auditor.

As a practical matter, generalized audit software packages can be used in a variety of audit situations including the following:

▲ Calculate depreciation expense for automated fixed asset records.
▲ Apply statistical sampling techniques.
▲ Compile audit information from automated files in a form more conducive to conducting audit procedures.
▲ Compare physical inventory counts with perpetual records.
▲ Print accounts receivable confirmations.

Program Code and Flowchart Checking. Although actually separate techniques, program code checking and flowchart checking are similar in that each focuses upon the logic of program documentation. In program code checking an auditor examines each line of process code contained within a client's computer program. Thus, code checking requires a strong command of the program's computer language (e.g., COBOL, FORTRAN, PL-1) and extensive time for very long and complex programs.

Flowchart checking utilizes client computer programs as input for generalized automatic flowcharting packages that print detailed flowcharts of a program's internal logic. Although they provide less detailed information than program code checks, flowchart checks require somewhat less programming knowledge and considerably less time.

Audit Modules. In client EDP applications that involve rather large volumes of transactions, an auditor can place a generalized audit software module within an existing client application program for the purpose of selecting data for testing. Audit modules differ from integrated test facilities (ITF) in that an ITF actually performs audit tests on entity-prepared data, whereas audit modules are used to select data for subsequent testing and analysis. For example, an auditor could place a generalized accounts receivable confirmation module within an entity's monthly billing program. When desired, the audit module would be activated by the auditor, used to select customer accounts for confirmation, and commanded to print the confirmation wording directly on each selected customer's bill.

Audit Hooks. In general, audit hooks represent "exits" in an entity's programs that allow an auditor to insert commands for audit processing. That is, at appropriate exit points in an application program, audit hooks allow an auditor to modify the program by inserting specific commands to accumulate totals or otherwise manipulate data for audit proposes. Of course, the use of audit hooks depends on whether an entity's application programs include appropriate exit points, which are often built into software packages written by software vendors.

Controlled Processing. Rather than a test per se, controlled processing is an approach to applying other audit tests. In controlled processing, an auditor retains copies of tested client programs, applying them thereafter at critical times. For example, an auditor might use test data and flowchart checking to examine controls over the accounts receivable updating program, subsequently applying a copy of the program on the year-end date.

Control Risk

After testing controls, an auditor's final evaluation of EDP general and application controls continues as follows: (1) consider the types of errors that could occur, (2) determine the control procedures that should prevent or detect the errors, (3) determine whether the necessary controls are prescribed and being followed, and (4) evaluate any deficiencies. Based on the results of this evaluation, the auditor assesses control risk — i.e., determines whether to rely on general and application controls and therefore restrict substantive tests, or not to rely on controls and therefore perform expanded substantive tests.

MICROCOMPUTER APPLICATIONS IN AUDITING

Over the past several years, microcomputers have revolutionized both the working paper preparation process, as discussed in Chapter 6, and the mechanics of conducting an opinion audit. The following discussion addresses several microcomputer software tools for auditing and describes several typical microcomputer applications in auditing.

Software Tools

Many microcomputer (and mainframe) software packages are currently available for audit use, and each has its own capabilities, strengths, and weaknesses. Although the vernacular varies among competing software vendors, most microcomputer software packages can be categorized as applications software, generalized software, and utility programs.

Applications Software. In general, applications software is designed to perform a specific audit function, is easy to use, and does not require knowledge of programming languages. A wide variety of applications programs are available commercially, and most are reviewed in periodicals devoted to personal and small-business computers. For example, currently there are menu-driven, user-friendly applications programs designed to prepare trial balances, to prepare consolidated financial statements, to accomplish linear regression for analytical review, and to prepare lead schedules from automated trial balances.

Generalized Software. Generalized microcomputer software is quite similar to generalized audit software discussed earlier in the context of testing controls in an EDP system. Examples of microcomputer generalized software include electronic spreadsheet programs, word processing programs, and graphics programs.

  Electronic spreadsheets are programs that graphically display electronic representations of columnar worksheets, such as automated working papers. Most electronic spreadsheet programs include two levels of instructions: "commands" (e.g., print, copy, erase) and "functions" (e.g., add, subtract, multiply). Some include a third level called "macros," which represent combinations of commands and functions. *Word processing programs* allow the user to enter, format, and quickly edit written text, and are invaluable when preparing financial statements, which often require significant editing. *Graphics programs* convert tables of numerical information into summary graphs and charts, and are particularly useful for preparing special reports such as proposals for new client services.

Utility Programs. In general, utility programs, or "utilities," are programs that make other software easier to use. Three examples are print spoolers, keyboard definition software, and disk utility software.

  Print spoolers enable a microcomputer user to run programs and use the printer simultaneously, thereby eliminating the time-consuming disadvantage of waiting until the printer has completed a task before proceeding to the next program application. In turn, *keyboard definition software* speeds routine program operations by defining single keystrokes to combine commands and/or functions. For example, an auditor might use keyboard definition software to specify the dual keystroke "shift A" to represent the function "multiply" and the command "print." Finally, *disk utility software* allows the user to recover erased files, repair damaged files, and modify disks or diskettes. For example, disk utility programs are particularly useful to recall hours of work previously accomplished but erased through error or power failure.

Selecting Microcomputer Applications

Properly managed microcomputers can be powerful audit tools, but they can also be expensive and ineffective if used improperly. Under what conditions, then, are microcomputers most advantageous to auditors?

In general, microcomputers are most valuable when an auditor needs to perform repetitive tasks quickly and accurately, particularly where there are large volumes of data or where the analysis or situation is rather complex. For example, LIFO inventory calculations and capital lease amortization schedules often require repetitive, complex computations and are therefore well suited to microcomputers. Figure 8-8 includes other potential microcomputer applications related to specific audit areas and to engagement administration.

SUMMARY

Even though the essential characteristics of control are similar in EDP and manual systems, an auditor's focus in considering EDP controls differs, since audit trails are often eliminated or distorted. When auditing in an EDP environment, an auditor focuses upon the adequacy of controls over transactions, not upon the transactions themselves, as in manual systems.

EDP controls can be categorized as general controls or application controls. General controls relate to the organization and operation of EDP systems, system development and documentation, computer hardware, access to computer equipment and files, and control over data and procedures. Application controls relate to the input, processing, and output of EDP-based accounting information.

As in a manual accounting information system, an auditor's consideration of internal control structure in an EDP system includes obtaining an understanding of the system, performing tests of controls, and assessing control risk. Tests of controls are similar in focus to those applied in manual systems, but the method of testing is usually aided by EDP audit techniques such as test data, integrated test data, parallel simulation, generalized software, program code and flowchart checking, audit modules, audit hooks, and controlled processing.

FIGURE 8-8
Potential Microcomputer Applications

Cash
• Preparing cash lead schedules
• Preparing bank reconciliations or proofs of cash
Receivables
• Calculating estimated bad debt expense
• Calculating turnover statistics
• Preparing confirmation requests
• Preparing aging summaries
Inventory
• Calculating LIFO indexes, layers, and final balances
• Calculating turnover statistics
• Tracing inventory test counts to perpetual records
• Analyzing variances
Plant assets
• Depreciation calculations
• Computing capitalized interest
• Computing sale-leaseback gain deferral
Investments
• Determining portfolio valuation at the lower-of-cost-or-market
• Obtaining market prices at year-end from public data sources
Liabilities
• Warranty reserve calculations
• Determining debt covenant compliance
• Preparing loan amortization schedules
Income taxes
• Analyzing permanent and timing differences
• Reconciling pretax accounting and taxable income
• Computing deferred taxes
• Calculating effective tax rates
Equity
• Computing earnings per share
• Computing stock splits, preferred stock dividends
• Analyzing treasury stock
Engagement administration
• Controlling confirmations sent and responses received
• Controlling correspondence
• Monitoring time charged to engagements
• Controlling and monitoring client-prepared schedules
• Assigning staff to engagements

Microcomputers have altered the course of audit method by providing a valuable, cost effective tool for accomplishing repetitive and/or complex tasks on large volumes of data. Several software tools are now commonly available for audit use and include applications software, generalized software, and utility programs.

REFERENCES

Allen, B. "The Biggest Computer Frauds: Lessons for CPAs." *Journal of Accountancy* (May, 1977), pp. 52–62.

Burch, J. G., Jr., and J. L. Sardinas, Jr. *Computer Control and Audit: A Total Systems Approach.* New York: John Wiley & Sons, 1978.

Cash, J. I., Jr., A. D. Bailey, Jr., and A. B. Whinston. "A Survey of Techniques for Auditing EDP-Based Accounting Information Systems." *The Accounting Review* (October, 1977), pp. 813–832.

Cerullo, M. J., and J. C. Corliss. "Auditing Computer Systems." *The CPA Journal* (September, 1984), pp. 18–33.

Computer Services Executive Committee. *The Auditor's Study and Evaluation of Internal Control in EDP System.* New York: American Institute of Certified Public Accountants, 1977.

Computer Services Executive Committee. *Computer-Assisted Audit Techniques.* New York: American Institute of Certified Public Accountants, 1979.

Dascher, P. E., and W. K. Harmon. "Assessing Microcomputer Risks and Control for Clients." *The CPA Journal* (May, 1984), pp. 36–41.

Davis, G. B., D. L. Adams, and C. A. Schaller. *Auditing and EDP,* 2d ed. New York: American Institute of Certified Public Accountants, 1983.

Deloitte, Haskins & Sells. *Auditing with the Microcomputer: A Practical Guide.* New York: Deloitte, Haskins & Sells, 1984.

Loebbecke, J. K., J. F. Mullarkey, and G. R. Zuber. "Auditing in a Computer Environment." *Journal of Accountancy* (January, 1983), pp. 68–78.

Nottingham, C. "Conceptual Framework for Improved Computer Audits." *Accounting and Business Research* (Spring, 1976), pp. 140–148.

Porter, W. T., and W. E. Perry, *EDP Controls and Auditing* 4th. ed. Belmont, Calif.: Wadsworth Publishing Company, Inc., 1984.

Pound, G. D. "A Review of EDP Auditing." *Accounting and Business Research* (Spring, 1978), pp. 108–129.

Webb, R. D. "Audit Planning — EDP Considerations." *Journal of Accountancy* (May, 1979), pp. 65–75.

Weber, R. *EDP Auditing: Conceptual Foundations and Practice.* New York: McGraw-Hill, 1982.

QUESTIONS

1. Distinguish EDP from manual data processing systems.
2. Define and give three examples of computer hardware.

3. What is an "online real-time" EDP system?
4. How do microcomputers differ from batch processing and online real-time EDP systems?
5. Identify and briefly describe the major classifications of controls underlying general controls in an EDP system.
6. Why should the EDP department be independent of user departments?
7. In general, the EDP department should neither authorize nor initiate transactions. Discuss.
8. Identify the three major functions within an EDP department that should be separated.
9. Distinguish EDP systems analysts from programmers.
10. What are computer master files and transaction files?
11. Describe the purpose and usual components of program-support documentation.
12. What are hardware controls? Why do they rarely pose serious problems for auditors?
13. In order to minimize the likelihood of improper or unauthorized use of EDP facilities, only authorized personnel should have access to EDP hardware and software. How can access to hardware and software be restricted?
14. Describe the functions of an EDP control group.
15. Identify the purpose of EDP input controls.
16. What are self-checking numbers?
17. Distinguish record counts from batch totals.
18. Describe any two input editing routines.
19. What is the purpose of processing controls?
20. Identify the purpose of output controls.
21. Distinguish between auditing "through" and auditing "around" the computer.
22. Explain the test data approach to auditing "through" the computer.
23. How does integrated test data improve upon the test data approach to auditing "through" the computer?
24. Explain how controlled processing relates to other EDP testing techniques.

MULTIPLE CHOICE QUESTIONS

1. Accounting functions that are normally considered incompatible in a manual system are often combined in an electronic data processing system by using an electronic data processing program, or a series of programs. This necessitates an accounting control that prevents unapproved

   a. Access to the magnetic tape library.
   b. Revisions to existing computer programs.
   c. Usage of computer program tapes.
   d. Testing of modified computer programs.   (AICPA Adapted)

2. What is the computer process called when data processing is performed concurrently with a particular activity and the results are available soon enough to influence the particular course of action being taken or the decision being made?

   a. Real-time processing.
   b. Batch processing.

    c. Random access processing.

    d. Integrated data processing.   (AICPA Adapted)

3. Which of the following employees in a company's electronic data processing department should be responsible for designing new or improved data processing procedures?

    a. Flowchart editor.

    b. Programmer.

    c. Systems analyst.

    d. Control group supervisor.   (AICPA Adapted)

4. An auditor's investigation of a company's electronic data processing control procedures has disclosed the following four circumstances. Indicate which circumstances constitutes a deficiency in internal control.

    a. Machine operators do not have access to the complete run manual.

    b. Machine operators are closely supervised by programmers.

    c. Programmers do not have the authorization to operate equipment.

    d. Only one generation of backup files is stored in an off-premises location.

                                          (AICPA Adapted)

5. A control feature in an electronic data processing system requires the central processing unit (CPU) to send signals to the printer to activate the print mechanism for each character. The print mechanism, just prior to printing, sends a signal back to the CPU verifying that the proper print position has been activated. This type of hardware control is referred to as

    a. Echo control.

    b. Validity control.

    c. Signal control.

    d. Check digit control.   (AICPA Adapted)

6. In an electronic data processing system, hardware controls are designed to

    a. Arrange data in a logical sequential manner for processing purposes.

    b. Correct errors in the computer programs.

    c. Monitor and detect errors in source documents.

    d. Detect and control errors arising from use of equipment.   (AICPA Adapted)

7. Which of the following best describes a fundamental control weakness often associated with electronic data processing systems?

    a. Electronic data processing equipment is more subject to systems error than manual processing is subject to human error.

    b. Electronic data processing equipment processes and records similar transactions in a similar manner.

    c. Electronic data processing procedures for detection of invalid and unusual transactions are less effective than manual control procedures.

    d. Functions that would normally be separated in a manual system are combined in the electronic data processing system.   (AICPA Adapted)

8. Some electronic data processing control procedures relate to all electronic data processing activities (general controls), and some relate to specific tasks (application controls). General controls include

a. Controls designed to ascertain that all data submitted to electronic data processing for processing have been properly authorized.
b. Controls that relate to the correction and resubmission of data that were initially incorrect.
c. Controls for documenting and approving programs and changes to programs.
d. Controls designed to assure the accuracy of the processing results.

(AICPA Adapted)

9. Accounting control procedures within the EDP activity may leave no visible evidence indicating that the procedures were performed. In such instances, the auditor should test these accounting controls by

a. Making corroborative inquiries.
b. Observing the separation of duties of personnel.
c. Reviewing transactions submitted for processing and comparing them with related output.
d. Reviewing the run manual.   (AICPA Adapted)

10. After obtaining an understanding of a client's EDP controls, an auditor may decide not to perform tests of the control procedures within the EDP portion of the client's internal control structure. Which of the following would not be a valid reason for choosing to omit tests of controls?

a. The controls appear adequate.
b. The controls duplicate operative controls existing elsewhere in the system.
c. There appear to be major deficiencies that would preclude reliance on the stated procedure.
d. The time and dollar costs of testing exceed the time and dollar savings in substantive testing if the tests show the controls to be operative.

(AICPA Adapted)

11. Tests of controls in an advanced EDP system:

a. Can be performed using only actual transactions since testing of simulated transactions is of no consequence.
b. Can be performed using actual transactions or simulated transactions.
c. Is impractical since many procedures within the EDP activity leave no visible evidence of having been performed.
d. Is inadvisable because it may distort the evidence in master files.

(AICPA Adapted)

12. The grandfather-father-son approach to providing protection for important computer files is a concept that is most often found in

a. Online, real-time systems.
b. Punched card systems.
c. Magnetic tape systems.
d. Magnetic drum systems.   (AICPA Adapted)

PROBLEMS

8-1   When a company switches from a manual to an EDP accounting system, many records and documents become unnecessary and are therefore not prepared.

With the audit trail eliminated or distorted, the auditor must focus on controls over computer hardware and software.

Considering the following brief description of a manual cash disbursements system:

Purchase invoices are received in the accounting department from the various departments that have purchased goods and services. The accounts payable clerk matches the purchase invoices with supporting documents such as purchase orders, receiving reports, and inventory records. The clerk then prepares a journal voucher in order to record a liability for the amount of the purchase. Another clerk schedules the payments due in order to assure that all discounts for early payment are earned. Five days before the due date, this clerk prepares the input documents for a check and the check itself. These are submitted to the controller for review and final approval.

Required:
1. List and explain areas that could be automated in this manual system.
2. What controls should be present in the proposed automated system?

8-2   The following five topics are part of the relevant body of knowledge for CPAs having fieldwork or immediate supervisory responsibility in audits involving a computer:
a. Electronic data processing (EDP) equipment and its capabilities.
b. Organization and management of the data processing function.
c. Characteristics of computer-based systems.
d. Fundamentals of computer programming.
e. Computer center operations.

CPAs who are responsible for computer audits should possess certain general knowledge with respect to each of these five topics. For example, regarding topic a., EDP equipment and its capabilities, the auditor should have a general understanding of computer equipment and should be familiar with the uses and capabilities of the central processor and the peripheral equipment.

Required:
For each of the topics b. through e., describe the general knowledge that should be possessed by those CPAs who are responsible for computer audits.

(AICPA Adapted)

8-3   The audit of the financial statements of a client that utilizes the services of a computer for accounting functions compels the CPA to understand the operation of the client's electronic data processing (EDP) system.

Required:
The first requirement of an effective internal control structure is a satisfactory plan of organization. List the characteristics of a satisfactory plan of organization for an EDP department, including the relationship between the department and the rest of the organization.

(AICPA Adapted)

8-4   When auditing an electronic data processing (EDP) accounting system, the independent auditor should have a general familiarity with the effects of the use of

EDP on the various characteristics of control and on the auditor's consideration of the control structure. The independent auditor must be aware of those control procedures that are commonly referred to as "general" controls and those that are commonly referred to as "application" controls. General controls relate to all EDP activities and application controls relate to specific accounting tasks.

Required:
1. What are the general controls that should exist in EDP-based accounting systems?
2. What are the purposes of each of the following categories of application controls?
   a. Input controls.
   b. Processing controls.
   c. Output controls.

(AICPA Adapted)

8-5   Linder Company is completing the implementation of its new computerized inventory control and purchase order system. Linder's controller wants the controls incorporated into the programs of the new system to be reviewed and evaluated. This is to ensure that all necessary computer controls are included and functioning properly. The controller respects and has confidence in the system department's work and evaluation procedures, but would like a separate appraisal of the control procedures by the internal audit department. It is hoped that such a review would reveal any deficiencies in control procedures and lead to their immediate correction before the system becomes operational.

The internal audit department carefully reviews the input, processing, and output controls when evaluating a new system. When assessing the processing controls incorporated into the programs of new systems applications, the internal auditors regularly employ the technique commonly referred to as "auditing through the computer."

Required:
1. Identify the types of controls that should be incorporated in the programs of the new system.
2. Explain how the existence of the computer controls and their proper functioning are verified by the "auditing through the computer" technique.

(CMA Adapted)

8-6   When auditing an electronic data processing system, the CPA must be aware of the different types of controls built into the equipment.

Required:
1. Define and give the purpose of each of the following program checks and controls:
   a. Record counts.
   b. Limit check.
   c. Sequence check.
   d. Hash totals.
2. When computers are used, the CPA has to be familiar with the information stored on paper tape reels, magnetic tape reels, etc. A common form of magnetic tape record retention employs the grandfather-father-son principle.
   a. Define the grandfather-father-son principle.
   b. Why are grandfather-father-son tapes usually stored at different locations?

(AICPA Adapted)

8-7   Roger Peters, CPA, has examined the financial statements of the Solt Manufacturing Company for several years and is making preliminary plans for the audit for the year ended June 30, 1990. During this examination Peters plans to use a set of generalized computer audit programs. Solt's EDP manager has agreed to prepare special tapes of data from Solt's records for the CPA's use with the generalized programs.

The following information is applicable to Peters' examination of Solt's accounts payable and related procedures:

a. The formats of pertinent tapes are on the following page.
b. The following monthly runs are prepared:
1. Cash disbursements by check number.
2. Outstanding payables.
3. Purchase journals arranged (1) by account charged and (2) by vendor.
c. Vouchers and supporting invoices, receiving reports, and purchase order copies are filed by vendor code. Purchase orders and checks are filed numerically.
d. Company records are maintained on magnetic tapes. All tapes are stored in a restricted area within the computer room. A grandfather-father-son policy is followed for retaining and safeguarding tape files.

Required:
1. Discuss whether Solt's policies for retaining and safeguarding the tape files provide adequate protection against losses of data.
2. Describe the controls that the CPA should maintain over:
a. Preparing the special tape.
b. Processing the special tape with the generalized computer audit programs.
3. Prepare a schedule for the EDP manager outlining the data that should be included on the special tape for the CPA's examination of accounts payable and related procedures. This schedule should show the:
a. Client tape from which the item should be extracted.
b. Name of the item of data.

8-8   Talbert Corporation hired an independent computer programmer to develop a simplified payroll application for its newly purchased computer. The programmer developed an online, data-based microcomputer system that minimized the level of knowledge required by the operator. It was based upon typing answers to input cues that appeared on the terminal's viewing screen, examples of which follow:

a. Access routine:
1. Operator access number to payroll file?
2. Are there new employees?
b. New employees routine:
1. Employee name?
2. Employee number?
3. Social security number?
4. Rate per hour?
5. Single or married?
6. Number of dependents?
7. Account distribution?
c. Current payroll routine:
1. Employee number?
2. Regular hours worked?

Master File—Vendor Name

Master File—Vendor Address

Transaction File—Expense Detail

Transaction File—Payment Detail

3. Overtime hours worked?

4. Total employees this payroll period?

The independent auditor is attempting to verify that certain input validation (edit) checks exist to ensure that errors resulting from omissions, invalid entries, or other inaccuracies will be detected during the typing of answers to the input cues.

Required:

Identify the various types of input validation (edit) checks the independent aud-itor' would expect to find in the EDP system. Describe the assurances provided by each identified validation check.

(AICPA Adapted)

8-9   During your preliminary review of an entity's EDP system, you note the following:

a. Purchase orders initiated by line personnel within the manufacturing plant may be authorized and executed by EDP department personnel.

b. Software and data files are maintained in an unlocked filing cabinet within the EDP department. User department personnel are not denied access to the EDP department.

c. Transactions initiated by user departments are usually, but not always, processed, thereby requiring manual processing thereafter.

d. Line personnel sometimes receive weekly paychecks for amounts in excess of normal weekly pay. Overtime is not uncommon, particularly in peak production periods.

e. Transaction files may not be fully posted to updated master files.

Required:

For each of the above observations, indicate the specific, general, or application control violated and the test(s) most likely to detect errors resulting from the control.

8-10   CPAs may audit "around" or "through" computers in the examination of the financial statements of clients who utilize computers to process accounting data.

Required:

1. Describe the auditing approach referred to as auditing "around" the computer.

2. Under what conditions does the CPA decide to audit "through" the computer instead of "around" the computer?

3. In auditing "through" the computer, the CPA may use a "test deck."

   a. What is a "test deck"?

   b. Why does the CPA use a "test deck"?

4. How can the CPA determine that computer programs are actually being used by the client to process its accounting data?

(AICPA Adapted)

8-11   Shannon Bracken, CPA, is planning the consideration of internal control structure for the Rumford Company, a December 31 year-end company. Rumford's purchasing, billing, receivables, payables, and job-order cost accounting systems are fully automated on a magnetic tape drive mainframe computer.

Required:
Respond to each of the following:
1. Provide an overview of an auditor's consideration of internal control structure in an EDP environment.
2. From the facts in the case, is McDonald more likely to audit "around" or "through" the Trowbridge Company's EDP system? Why?
3. What is the purpose of an auditor's preliminary review of an EDP system?
4. Following the preliminary review of internal control structure, under what conditions would an auditor decide not to rely on EDP controls?
5. What is the purpose of tests of prescribed EDP controls, and what specific questions are addressed by tests of controls?

8-12   In the past, the records to be evaluated in an audit have been printed reports, listings, documents, and written papers, all of which are visible output. However, in fully computerized systems which employ daily updating of transaction files, output and files are frequently in machine-readable forms such as cards, tapes, or disks. Thus, they often present the auditor with an opportunity to use the computer in performing an audit.

Required:
Discuss how the computer can be used to aid the auditor in examining accounts receivable in such a fully computerized system.

(AICPA Adapted)

8-13   An auditor is conducting an examination of the financial statements of a wholesale cosmetics distributor with an inventory consisting of thousands of individual items. The distributor keeps its inventory in its own distribution center and in two public warehouses. An inventory computer file is maintained on a computer disk, and at the end of each business day the file is updated. Each record of the inventory file contains the following data:

Item number.
Location of item.
Description of item.
Quantity on hand.
Cost per item.
Date of last purchase.
Date of last sale.
Quantity sold during year.

The auditor is planning to observe the distributor's physical count of inventories as of a given date. The auditor will have available a computer tape of the data on the inventory file on the date of the physical count and a general-purpose computer software package.

Required:
The auditor is planning to perform basic inventory auditing procedures. Identify the basic inventory auditing procedures and describe how the use of the general purpose software package and the tape of the inventory file data might be helpful to the auditor in performing such auditing procedures.
Organize your answer as follows:

Basic inventory auditing procedure	How general purpose computer software package and tape of the inventory file data might be helpful
1. Observe the physical count, making and recording test counts where applicable.	Determining which items are to be test counted by selecting a random sample of a representative number of items from the inventory file as of the date of the physical count. (AICPA Adapted)

PART **III**   AUDIT METHOD

AUDIT SAMPLING IN
TESTS OF CONTROLS

9

Major topics discussed in this chapter are the:

▲   *Nature of attributes sampling in tests of controls.*

▲   *Role of audit risk, including sampling and nonsampling risk, and the risks of underreliance and overreliance in attributes sampling.*

▲   *Distinction between statistical and nonstatistical sampling.*

▲   *Components of a general audit sampling plan appropriate for tests of controls.*

▲   *Alternative audit sampling techniques used in practice:*
      —Attribute estimation
      —Sequential (stop-or-go) sampling
      —Discovery sampling
      —Nonstatistical sampling for attributes

There would be no market for audit services if the cost of an audit exceeded the benefits. As a result, audits are designed to generate reasonable rather than absolute assurance, and many if not most audit conclusions are based upon examining samples rather than entire populations.

This chapter addresses audit sampling plans applied to an auditor's consideration of internal control structure in general and to tests of controls in particular. The chapter begins by introducing the nature of audit sampling, discussing risk in the context of audit sampling, and addressing the difference between statistical and nonstatistical sampling. Thereafter, the chapter introduces a general sampling plan for accomplishing tests of controls and applies the plan to three important and frequently used audit sampling techniques: *attribute estimation, sequential (stop-or-go) sampling*, and *discovery sampling*. The discussion and illustrations throughout this chapter are consistent with SAS No. 39, "Audit Sampling," SAS No. 47, "Audit Risk and Materiality in Conducting an Audit," SAS No. 55, "Consideration of the Internal Control Structure in a Financial Statement Audit," and the AICPA Audit and Accounting Guide, *Audit Sampling* (New York: AICPA, 1983).

NATURE OF AUDIT SAMPLING

Audit sampling involves examining less than 100 percent of the items that constitute an audit population and is based on the premise that a sample can be sufficiently *representative* of an audit population to warrant valid and reliable conclusions without testing the entire population. An *audit population* may consist of all the items within a class of transactions, such as credit sales for a specified period, or all the items within an account balance, such as Accounts Receivable.

An *audit sampling plan* — that is, the procedures an auditor uses to accomplish a sampling application — aids an auditor in forming conclusions about one or more characteristics of either a particular class of transactions or a particular account balance. In any audit sampling plan, however, the characteristic of interest depends on whether the auditor is performing tests of controls or substantive tests. As discussed in Chapter 6, tests of controls are designed to obtain evidence about whether an entity is complying with the control procedures prescribed by management, and the auditor's characteristic of interest is called an *attribute*. *Attributes sampling plans* are most commonly used to test an entity's *rate of deviation* — also called *rate of occurrence* — from a prescribed control procedure. For example, an auditor might use an attributes sampling plan to test controls for voucher processing, billing systems, payroll and related personnel policy systems, inventory pricing, plant-asset additions, and depreciation computations, among other things.

In contrast, substantive tests, also discussed in Chapter 6, are designed to obtain evidence about whether monetary error exists within a class of transactions or an account balance, and the auditor's characteristic of interest is called a *variable*. *Variables sampling plans* are most commonly used to test whether recorded account balances are fairly stated. For example, an auditor might use a variables sampling plan to test recorded dollar amounts for receivables, inventory, payroll expense, and plant-asset additions among other things.

In summary, attributes sampling is generally used to reach a conclusion about a population in terms of a rate of deviation, and variables sampling is generally used to reach conclusions about a population in terms of a dollar amount. This chapter is devoted to attributes sampling, and Chapter 10 to variables sampling.

SAMPLING AND AUDIT RISK

Sampling and audit risk not only are well established in audit practice, but are implicitly recognized in the third standard of field work, which states in part that ". . . evidential matter is to be obtained . . . to afford a *reasonable basis* for an opinion" (emphasis provided). If an "absolute" basis were necessary to form an opinion, then entire populations rather than samples would have to be examined, thereby rendering opinion audits far too

FIGURE 9-1
Audit Risk in Tests of Controls

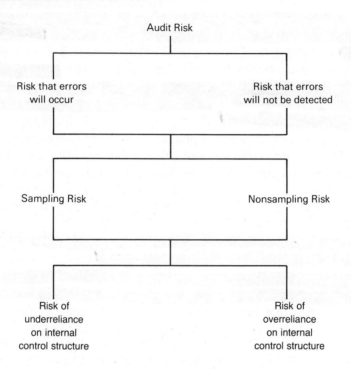

costly. Furthermore, audit risk cannot be totally eliminated by 100 percent examination, because risks not related to sampling would still exist. But what risks are sustained by an auditor in a typical financial statement audit, and how does sampling add to those risks? The following discussion focuses on the components of audit risk, which are summarized in Figure 9-1.

Components of Audit Risk

In Chapter 5, *audit risk* was defined as the likelihood that an auditor may unknowingly fail to modify his or her opinion on materially misstated financial statements. Audit risk is a combination of two components:

▲ The risk that material errors[1] *will occur* in the process by which financial statements are developed.
▲ The risk that any material errors that occur *will not be detected*.

---

[1] Throughout this chapter, the term "errors" is intended to include irregularities under SAS No. 53.

The first of these two components, the risk that errors or irregularities will occur, can be classified further into control risk and inherent risk, both of which were introduced in Chapter 5. *Control risk* represents the risk that errors could occur, and could be material when combined with errors in other accounts, but will not be prevented or detected by the entity's internal control structure. For example, control risk would be increased if an entity did not maintain effective physical controls over blank checks. *Inherent risk* represents the susceptibility of an account balance to errors that, when combined with errors in other accounts, could be material and that are not monitored by related control procedures. For example, inherent risk is higher for liquid assets, such as cash, than for nonliquid assets, such as property, plant, and equipment. Because neither control risk nor inherent risk is directly controllable by an auditor, the risk that material errors will occur — the first component of audit risk — is not directly controllable by the auditor. The auditor must therefore decide whether to rely on the entity's internal control structure to reduce the risk.

The second component of audit risk — the risk that material errors will not be detected — is referred to as *detection risk,* which was defined in Chapter 5 as the risk that errors could occur and could be material when combined with errors in other accounts, but will not be detected by the auditor's procedures. The risk that material errors will not be detected is directly controllable by the auditor through substantive tests of details and other substantive audit procedures.

Sampling Risk and Nonsampling Risk

The risk that material errors or irregularities may occur and remain undetected is influenced by two categories of uncertainties:

▲ Sampling risk, i.e., uncertainties due to sampling.
▲ Nonsampling risk, i.e., uncertainties arising from factors unrelated to sampling.

Sampling risk results from the fact that a particular audit sample may not be representative of the population tested. That is, the sample may contain disproportionately more or fewer control deviations or monetary differences than exist in the class of transactions or account balance as a whole, suggesting that the auditor's conclusions may be different if the entire population were tested. Since sampling risk can be reduced simply by increasing sample size, sampling risk varies inversely with sample size: the greater the sample size, the smaller the sampling risk. This relationship is quite logical, because if sample size were increased to include all the items in a population, there would be no sampling and therefore no sampling risk.

Nonsampling risk includes all aspects of audit risk not due to sampling. For example, nonsampling risk could result from human errors, such as failing to detect errors contained within sample items or overlooking or misinterpreting errors that are detected. Several factors can serve to reduce nonsampling risk, including proper planning and supervision and encouraging effective firm-wide quality control.

Risks of Underreliance and Overreliance on Internal Control Structure

Two aspects of sampling risk are critical in tests of controls:

▲ Risk of underreliance on internal control structure.
▲ Risk of overreliance on internal control structure.

The *risk of underreliance* is the risk that a sample does not support an auditor's planned degree of reliance on a control when, unknown to the auditor, the true deviation rate supports reliance. For example, underreliance would occur if, based on an unrepresentative sample, an auditor estimated a 5 percent rate of deviation but was willing to tolerate only 3 percent, and the true, but unknown, population rate of deviation was really 2 percent. In this example, the auditor would probably conclude that the control is not effective — and therefore would assess a higher level of control risk in determining the nature, timing, and extent of substantive tests — because the sample indicated a higher deviation rate (5 percent) than the auditor was willing to tolerate (3 percent). But, unknown to the auditor, he or she would actually be *underrelying* on the control because the true population deviation rate (2 percent) is less than the tolerable rate (3 percent).

The *risk of overreliance* on internal control structure is just the opposite of underreliance: it is the risk that a sample does support an auditor's planned degree of reliance on a control when, unknown to the auditor, the true deviation rate does not justify reliance. For example, overreliance would occur if, based on an unrepresentative sample, an auditor estimated a 4 percent rate of deviation but was willing to tolerate 6 percent, and the true, but unknown, population rate was really 7 percent. In this example, the auditor would conclude that the control is effective — and therefore would assess a lower level of control risk in determining the nature, timing, and extent of substantive tests — because the sample indicated fewer deviations (4 percent) than the auditor was willing to tolerate (6 percent). However, unknown to the auditor, he or she would actually be *overrelying* on the control since the true population rate (7 percent) exceeds the tolerable rate (6 percent).

The risk of underreliance relates to the efficiency of an audit, and the risk of overreliance relates to audit effectiveness. Underreliance results in *inefficiency* because when an auditor concludes that a control is ineffective and therefore that control risk is high, he or she ordinarily sets a lower acceptable detection risk and expands the scope of substantive tests to compensate for the perceived control deficiency. If the expanded scope of substantive tests is unjustified, the audit will be less efficient since more substantive tests will be performed than necessary. Overreliance, in contrast, results in *ineffectiveness*, because the scope of substantive tests will be restricted under the erroneous assumption that the control is effective and control risk is low. Thus, the substantive tests may be ineffective in detecting material misstatements.

Sampling risk, and more specifically the risk of overreliance, cannot be eliminated, but it can be controlled as illustrated in the sampling plans introduced later in the chapter.

STATISTICAL AND NONSTATISTICAL SAMPLING

Statistical sampling plans apply the laws of probability to aid an auditor in designing an efficient sample, in measuring the sufficiency of evidence obtained, and in evaluating the sample results. In contrast, *nonstatistical sampling plans* rely exclusively on subjective judgment to determine sample size and evaluate sample results. A properly designed nonstatistical sampling application can provide results as effective as those from a properly designed statistical sampling application. There is, however, one critical difference between a statistical and a nonstatistical sampling application: statistical sampling allows an auditor to *measure sampling risk.* That is, statistical sampling plans measure the risk that a sample is not representative of a population; nonstatistical sampling plans do not.

The choice between a statistical and a nonstatistical sampling plan is based primarily on the auditor's assessment of the relative costs and benefits. For example, an auditor might use nonstatistical sampling if the cost of selecting a statistical random sample was deemed too high. However, an auditor might consider the cost justifiable if the related controls were critical, and a measure of sampling risk was therefore deemed essential. Note that the choice between a statistical and nonstatistical sampling plan is made independently of the selection of audit procedures. Audit sampling, whether statistical or nonstatistical, is merely a means for accomplishing audit procedures.

In some instances, audit sampling — whether statistical or nonstatistical — is inappropriate, and the auditor must therefore test the entire population. For example, an auditor may not be willing to accept any degree of sampling risk with regard to a particular account balance or class of transactions, and would therefore test the entire population. Sampling is also inappropriate in tests of control procedures that depend primarily on segregation of duties or that otherwise provide no audit trail of documentary evidence. Audit evidence pertaining to these types of controls is gathered through observation and inquiry.

TESTS OF CONTROLS: AN ATTRIBUTES SAMPLING PLAN

A general sampling plan appropriate for tests of controls is presented in Figure 9-2 and discussed in the following sections. Subsequently, three specific methods of attributes sampling are explained and illustrated: attribute estimation, sequential (stop-or-go) sampling, and discovery sampling.

Determine the Objectives of the Test

As discussed earlier, tests of controls are designed to assess the effectiveness of control procedures in preventing or detecting material misstatements in the financial statements. Thus, in general terms, an auditor's objectives are stated in the context of determining whether the controls for a particular transaction cycle can be relied on in assessing control risk.

Auditors use sampling to conduct tests of controls more efficiently than might be accomplished otherwise. In practice, sampling is used when an entity's controls leave a trail of observable documentary evidence, such as approval initials on the face of a vendor's invoice, and when the controls are

---

FIGURE 9-2
Audit Sampling Plan: Tests of Controls

1. Determine the objectives of the test.
2. Define the attribute and deviation conditions.
3. Define the population. how many & for what period – (at least several 100 units)
4. Determine the method of sample selection.
5. Determine sample size.
6. Perform the sampling plan.
7. Evaluate the sample results.

Adapted from: *AICPA Audit and Accounting Guide,* ''Audit Sampling'' (New York: American Institute of Certified Public Accountants, 1983), pp. 21–22.

---

not dependent primarily on adequate segregation of duties, which is observable but not documentary. Sampling can be used when documentary evidence is not maintained, but requires that the sampling procedures be planned early in the engagement. For example, if an auditor wished to observe cash collection procedures at a theater, he or she would have to select the days for observation early in the engagement in order to allow each day in the period audited an equal chance of being selected for observation.

Define the Attribute and Deviation Conditions

Not all of a client's existing controls are tested: only those the auditor plans to rely on in planning and performing substantive tests, as discussed in Chapter 7. For each control to be tested, the auditor identifies attributes and deviations.

An *attribute* is a characteristic of a control, and a deviation is the absence of an attribute. To illustrate, assume an auditor's objective is to determine whether controls over sales returns can be relied on during substantive testing. The client prepared a credit memorandum to support each return. In this case, one attribute — that is, one characteristic of the control system — is that quantity and other data on the credit memorandum agree with the receiving report, a document prepared when the client receives returned goods. For this attribute, a deviation would occur each time an auditor found that the quantities or other data indicated on a credit memorandum disagreed with the related receiving report. Figure 9-4, page 362, to be discussed later in the context of a case illustration, gives additional examples of attributes related to controls over sales returns.

Define the Population

In attributes sampling, a *population* consists of all the items constituting a class of transactions, and because sample results can be projected only to the population from which the sample is selected, the defined population must be appropriate for the auditor's objectives. For example, if an auditor's objective is to test controls designed to assure that all shipped goods are billed, the population would be defined as all shipping documents issued during the period, not all billing invoices. Erroneously defining the population as all invoices issued during the period would ignore shipped goods that were not billed, which the test is intended to detect.

Period Covered. As discussed in Chapter 6, tests of controls are typically accomplished during the interim period of the engagement, which for a December 31 year-end client might be completed as early as the summer months or during the fall. Performing tests of controls prior to year-end creates an audit problem because, in order to design substantive tests, the auditor needs to reach a conclusion about the entire population of transactions covered by the year-end financial statements — for example, January 1 to December 31 — not just the months subjected to interim tests. Thus, when tests are conducted at interim, the auditor might define the population to include transactions through December 31, perform initial tests through the interim date, and complete the tests at year-end. Alternatively, the auditor might decide to define the population to include transactions through the interim date, and then consider the following factors in judging whether additional tests are necessary for the remaining period: (1) the results of interim tests, (2) responses to inquiries of management about the remaining period, (3) the length of the remaining period, (4) the nature and amount of the transactions completed during the remaining period, and (5) evidence of effective controls within the remaining period obtained through year-end substantive tests. The important point to recognize is that sample results can be generalized only to the population from which the sample items are selected. As a result, if interim tests are performed on transactions completed through October 31 for a December 31 year-end client, then the auditor's conclusions relate only to the ten-month period ended October 31.

Defining the Sampling Unit. A *sampling unit* is any of the individual elements constituting a population, and should be defined in the context of the control procedure to be tested and in light of audit efficiency. For example, if the audit objective is to test whether disbursements contain signatures authorizing payment, the sampling unit might be defined as a voucher, a summary form attached to purchase documents, such as a vendor's invoice. Alternatively, if one voucher pays several invoices from the same vendor, the sampling unit might be defined as a line item on a voucher, each line item representing an individual vendor invoice. Thus, a sampling unit might be a document, a line item on a document, or even a journal entry, among other things, depending on the auditor's objective.

Determine the Method of Sample Selection

The objective of audit sampling is to draw conclusions about one or more population characteristics without testing the entire population. Even with the most carefully designed sampling plan, there is still a degree of uncertainty about whether sample results are representative of the population.

Examining every item in the population is the only way to eliminate uncertainty arising from sampling risk. However, if a sample is selected at *random*, i.e., if each sampling unit is given an equal chance of being selected, the laws of probability can be applied to determine the likelihood that the sample is representative of the population from which it was drawn. A sample can be evaluated in terms of probability only if the sample is randomly selected and thus free from sampling bias. If each item in a population is not given an equal chance of selection, the sample would be biased toward the population items with the greater chance of selection.

Some commonly used methods of selecting a sample are:

▲ Random-number sampling.
▲ Systematic sampling.
▲ Block sampling.
▲ Haphazard sampling.

Each of these methods is discussed below.

Random-Number Sampling. Random-number sampling utilizes random-number tables or computer-generated random numbers to select sampling units from a population. Random-number tables contain columns and rows of randomly generated digits. An auditor begins at any digit in the table — a random start — and proceeds along a column or row or diagonally, selecting digits corresponding to identification numbers on the sampling units (e.g., invoice numbers or check numbers). If the sampling units do not have identifying numbers, the auditor could establish correspondence between population items and random digits by assigning numbers to each population item. To minimize potential bias in starting-point selection, an auditor could periodically proceed to a new starting (or continuing) point while selecting the sample. Random-number sampling is appropriate both for statistical sampling and for nonstatistical sampling.

Systematic Sampling. Systematic sampling involves selecting every n^{th} item from a population of sequentially ordered items. Systematic sampling eliminates the need to establish correspondence between population items and random digits, and therefore is useful when population items lack identification numbers. The number of sequential items to skip when selecting a sample systematically is determined by dividing population size by sample size. For example, assuming population and sample sizes of 5,000 and 200, respectively, an auditor would select a random starting point and proceed to select every 25th sampling unit ($5,000 \div 200$). Continuing points may be changed periodically to minimize any potential starting-point bias. Systematic selection is useful for nonstatistical sampling, and if the starting point is selected at random, it can be useful for statistical sampling.

Block Sampling. A block sample is a group of items arranged contiguously within a larger grouping of sampling units. For example, a block sample could consist of all vendor invoices processed on January 21, May 24, September 28, and November 13. In this case, if 75 invoices had been processed on these four days, then the sample would consist of 4 items, not 75, since the sampling unit is expressed in time — that is, in days — not transactions. Generally, so few blocks of sample items are insufficient to justify generalizing sample results to the population, suggesting that block sampling often results in excessively high sampling risk. Although a block sample could be designed with enough blocks to minimize sampling risk, testing large numbers of blocks could be inefficient. Thus, an auditor should not use block sampling, for either statistical or nonstatistical sampling, unless he or she exercises considerable care in controlling sampling risk.

Haphazard Sampling. A haphazard sample consists of sampling units selected without special reason, but also without conscious bias. For example, a haphazard sample could consist of 80 items selected simply by "pulling" vendor invoices from a file cabinet drawer. Like block sampling, haphazard sampling may fail to select samples that are wholly representative of the population tested. Although it may be useful for nonstatistical sampling, haphazard sampling cannot be used for statistical sampling.

Stratified Sampling. Stratified sampling involves subdividing populations into homogeneous subgroups or strata, and selecting (and evaluating) separate samples for each subgroup. The samples may be selected by random numbers, systematically, in blocks, or haphazardly. Stratified sampling is based on the assumption that items in some population strata are more similar to each other than to any other items in the population. For example, individual vendor invoices of less than $100 are apt to be more similar to each other than to invoices over $100,000. When compared, subgroups are apt to have strikingly dissimilar characteristics, such as different credit terms and different potential for material errors or irregularities. Thus, each group represents a stratum, and the variability of sampling units in each stratum is apt to be less than the variability of all population items.

Determine Sample Size

In order to determine required sample size for an attributes sampling plan, an auditor must first consider:

▲ Acceptable risk of overreliance.
▲ Tolerable rate of deviation.
▲ Expected population deviation rate.

Each of these elements is discussed below.

Acceptable risk of overreliance. As discussed earlier, an auditor is concerned with both the risk of underreliance and the risk of overreliance on internal control structure. However, attributes sampling plans usually quantify the risk of overreliance only, since overreliance relates to an audit's effectiveness — that is, to the likelihood of issuing an inappropriate audit report. Underreliance, on the other hand, relates to efficiency only.

Specifying an acceptable risk of overreliance is a matter of professional judgment and depends primarily on the extent to which an auditor wishes to rely on a client's internal control structure. Because there is an inverse relationship between sample size and the risk of overreliance — that is, as the acceptable risk of overreliance decreases, sample size increases — sample sizes are larger when an auditor specifies a lower acceptable risk of overreliance and smaller for higher acceptable risks. A lower acceptable risk of overreliance is appropriate when an auditor plans to rely heavily upon a control during substantive testing, and a higher risk is appropriate otherwise. In some engagements, an auditor might accept the same risk of overreliance for all tests of controls, and in other engagements vary the risk for individual controls, depending on the assessed level of control risk.

Auditors sometimes refer to their "reliability" or "confidence" levels when discussing or applying attributes sampling. *Reliability level* or *confidence level* is actually the complement of the risk of overreliance (i.e., one minus the risk of overreliance). Thus, for a 5 percent risk of overreliance, the reliability level would be 95 percent (i.e., 1.00-.05).

Tolerable Rate of Deviation. A tolerable rate of deviation (sometimes called a "tolerable rate of occurrence") is the maximum population rate of deviation from a prescribed control procedure that an auditor will tolerate without modifying the assessed level of control risk. Specifying a tolerable rate of deviation is a matter of professional judgment, and depends primarily on the auditor's assessment of control risk when planning the nature, timing, and extent of substantive tests. In general, a lower tolerable rate is appropriate when an auditor assesses a lower control risk.

After completing tests of controls, an auditor may find that the rate of deviation in the sample is close to or exceeds the tolerable rate. Under these conditions, an auditor could decide to increase the assessed level of control risk, since there is an unacceptably high sampling risk that the population deviation rate exceeds the tolerable rate.

Expected Population Deviation Rate. The expected population deviation rate can be estimated from either the prior year's results of testing the identical control attribute or from a pilot sample. The prior year's sample deviation rate can be used only if the related control procedures and client personnel have not changed since the prior year's sampling plan was conducted. If there have been changes, the prior year's results would not be applicable, since the rate of deviation would not reflect current conditions. When prior-year results are either nonexistent or inapplicable, an auditor can estimate the expected population deviation rate from a *pilot sample* drawn from the population of interest. Pilot sample items can be used as part of the audit sample, and typically are. For example, if 50 items are examined in a pilot sample and the audit sample size is 120, only 70 additional sample items need be selected and examined, since 50 had been selected and examined in the preliminary sample.

If an auditor judges that the expected population deviation rate equals or exceeds the tolerable rate, then the auditor expects to find more deviations than he or she is willing to tolerate, leading to the conclusion that the control is not effective. Under these conditions, the auditor would assess a higher control risk and, correspondingly, require extensive substantive tests to restrict detection risk.

Determine Sample Size. Once the auditor has specified both an acceptable risk of overreliance and tolerable and expected population rates of deviation, audit sample size can be determined from standard tables which are illustrated later in the chapter. In a nonstatistical sampling plan, sample size can be determined from tables, or it may be based solely on the auditor's professional judgment.

Importantly, increasing or decreasing any of the sample size parameters (i.e., acceptable risk of overreliance, tolerable rate of deviation, and expected population deviation rate) will have an impact on required sample size. Figure 9-3, page 356, illustrates the effect on sample size of changes in any one parameter; the effect of changes in more than one would depend on the magnitude and direction (increase or decrease) of each change.

In general, population size has very little effect on sample size, partic-

FIGURE 9-3
The Effect on Sample Size of Increasing or Decreasing Parameters:
Attributes Sampling

Parameter	Direction of Change	Effect on Sample Size Increase	Decrease
Acceptable risk of overreliance	Increase		X
	Decrease	X	
Tolerable rate of deviation	Increase		X
	Decrease	X	
Expected population deviation rate	Increase	X	
	Decrease		X

ularly for populations over 5,000 items. For example, the following table
illustrates the limited effect of population size on sample size, assuming a 5
percent acceptable risk of overreliance, 5 percent tolerable deviation rate, and
1 percent expected population deviation rate.[2]

Population Size	Required Sample Size
50	45
100	64
500	87
1,000	90
2,000	92
5,000	93
100,000	93

pop ↑ sample size ↓

Illustrations throughout this chapter assume a large population size.

Perform the Sampling Plan

Once selected, the sampling units should be examined for the attributes
of interest, and deviations should be documented in the working papers. Ex-

[2]*AICPA Audit and Accounting Guide,* "Audit Sampling" (New York: AICPA, 1983), p.
35.

amples of working paper documentation for attributes sampling appear later in the chapter.

In practice, auditors usually select more sampling units than required, thereby providing replacements for voided items and for documents that cannot be located. For example, an auditor might select 75 sampling units even though required sample size is 65, and then use the remaining 10 in the order selected if needed. If voided items are bona fide, they should not be considered deviations. However, missing items would ordinarily be considered deviations, since the auditor would have no basis to conclude that the tested controls were operating as prescribed by management.

Occasionally, an auditor might find a large number of deviations before completing tests of the entire sample. If the large number of deviations suggested that the sample deviation rate were likely to exceed the tolerable rate, the auditor would probably discontinue the sampling plan and conclude that the control could not be relied on in designing substantive tests. In this case, the benefits of continuing the sampling plan are not likely to exceed the cost.

Evaluate the Sample Results

After performing the sampling plan, an auditor summarizes and evaluates the results by:

▲ Determining the sample deviation rate.
▲ Determining the maximum population deviation rate, and allowance for sampling risk.
▲ Considering qualitative information.
▲ Reaching an overall conclusion.

Each aspect of sample evaluation is discussed below.

Sample Deviation Rate. The sample deviation rate is the auditor's estimate of the true but unknown population deviation rate, and is determined as follows:

$$\text{Sample Deviation Rate} = \frac{\text{Number of Deviations Observed}}{\text{Sample Size}}$$

For example, if an auditor observed 2 deviations in a sample of 100, the sample deviation rate would be 2 percent ($2 \div 100$).

Maximum Population Deviation Rate and Sampling Risk. An estimate of the maximum population deviation rate is represented by the following:

Maximum Population = Sample Deviation + Allowance for
Deviation Rate   —   Rate   =   Sampling Risk

In practice, the allowance for sampling risk is not calculated directly, but can be determined deductively from standard tables which yield maximum population deviation rates at specified risks of overreliance. For example, assuming a 10 percent acceptable risk of overreliance, sample size of 100, and 2 observed deviations, the maximum population deviation rate would be 5.3 percent, determined from tables that are illustrated later in the chapter. In this case, the sample deviation rate is 2 percent ($2 \div 100$), the maximum population deviation rate is 5.3 percent, and the allowance for sampling risk is therefore 3.3 percent (5.3 percent -2 percent). Summarizing, these results indicate that there is a 10 percent chance (the risk of overreliance) that the true but unknown population deviation rate exceeds 5.3 percent. Stated another way, the auditor would be 90 percent confident (recall that the level of confidence, or reliability, is the complement of the risk of overreliance) that the true population rate is less than or equal to 5.3 percent.

In a statistical sampling application, an auditor compares the maximum population deviation rate and the tolerable rate of deviation and evaluates the effectiveness of a control accordingly. The results suggest a control is effective when the tolerable rate equals or exceeds the maximum population rate. That is, the results would support assessing a low level of control risk only if the population is estimated to contain no more deviations than the auditor was willing to tolerate.

However, in a nonstatistical sampling application, sampling risk cannot be measured directly, as discussed earlier. Only the sample deviation rate can be determined. The results of a sampling plan would certainly not support assessing a low level of control risk if the sample deviation rate exceeds the auditor's tolerable rate. The results would also not support assessing a low level of control risk if the sample deviation rate exceeds the expected population deviation rate used initially to design the sampling plan. This is true because there is likely to be an unacceptably high risk that the true population rate exceeds the tolerable rate.

Considering Qualitative Information. When judging the results of a sampling plan, an auditor considers not only the frequency of deviations, but also the qualitative characteristics of the deviations, such as the nature and cause of the deviations and the possible relationship of the deviations to other phases of the audit. For example, if the observed deviations in a sample resulted from intentional acts (irregularities) rather than carelessness, an auditor would assess a higher control risk, even if the tolerable rate of deviation exceeded the maximum population deviation rate.

Reaching an overall conclusion. An auditor considers all available quantitative and qualitative information in assessing control risk. If the results support a low control risk — for example, if the maximum population rate does not exceed the tolerable rate and if all deviations result from unintended random errors — an auditor would judge the controls reliable and therefore would restrict substantive tests. However, if the results do not support a low control risk, the controls would not be relied on, and substantive tests would be expanded accordingly.

The following three sections of this chapter discuss and illustrate three commonly used attributes sampling techniques:

▲ Attribute estimation sampling.
▲ Sequential (stop-or-go) sampling.
▲ Discovery sampling.

The discussion and illustrations apply the steps identified in the general audit sampling plan in Figure 9-2.

ATTRIBUTE ESTIMATION SAMPLING: A CASE ILLUSTRATION

Attribute estimation, a statistical sampling plan for tests of controls, is appropriate when an auditor wishes to estimate a true but unknown population rate of deviation. To illustrate attribute estimation, and to apply the general attributes sampling plan in Figure 9-2, page 349, assume a first-year audit engagement is being planned for the Chandler Wire & Cable Company, a large supplier of synthetic-conductor cable for U.S. and foreign electronics manufacturers.

Determine the Objectives, Attributes, and Deviation Conditions

Although Chandler has been long respected for high-quality products, discussions with Chandler personnel indicate that quality control may have deteriorated recently, and this is supported by excessively large numbers of returns. The auditor's objective in this case is to determine whether control procedures for sales returns can be relied on during substantive tests of details.

Discussion with the predecessor auditor revealed that tests of sales returns in prior years had indicated relatively high deviation rates. Based on this information and interviews with client personnel, the auditor designs the following tests of controls, all of which are addressed more fully in Chapter 11.

Sales Returns

Step	Tests of Controls
1.	Obtain a random sample of credit memoranda from the files of the Customer Order Department.
2.	Test unit pricing and extensions on sampled credit memoranda.
3.	Trace details of sampled credit memoranda to: a. Receiving reports b. Perpetual inventory records c. Entries in Inventory and Cost of Goods Sold. d. Entries in Sales Returns and in the Accounts Receivable subsidiary ledger and general ledger.
4.	Review the credit register (Chandler's listing of credit memoranda) for unusual items such as credits for very large amounts or an unusually large number of credits for the same customer, and investigate.
5.	Document test results.

The auditor is now confronted with a very real and recurring question in auditing: Can any of these procedures be accomplished with statistical or nonstatistical sampling, thereby potentially saving audit time and cost? In this case, nonstatistical sampling is probably not appropriate, because the auditor has prior knowledge of potential problems and therefore will desire an estimate of sampling risk. Statistical sampling, though, can be useful, particularly since the population of credit memoranda is assumed to be too large to justify testing the entire population. But which of the tests of controls can be accomplished statistically?

Steps 4 and 5 of the tests of controls cannot be accomplished by statistical sampling: step 4 requires reviewing the entire population of credit register entries for attributes not clearly defined as either existing or not existing (a requirement of attribute estimation), and step 5 does not involve testing. Steps 1, 2, and 3, however, involve attributes that can be clearly defined as either existing or not existing. For example, the credit memoranda are either recorded properly in perpetual inventory records (step 3b), or they are not; there are no uncertainties about outcome. Thus, steps 1, 2, and 3 can be accomplished with attribute estimation.

Steps 1, 2, and 3 require one sampling unit and five attributes, as follows:

Sampling unit:
▲ Credit memorandum
Attributes of interest:
▲ Unit pricing and extensions on the credit memorandum are accurate.
▲ Quantity and other data on the credit memorandum agree with the receiving report.
▲ Quantity and other data on the credit memorandum agree with perpetual inventory records.
▲ Journal entry is properly recorded as a debit to Inventory and a credit to Cost of Goods Sold.
▲ Journal entry is properly recorded as a debit to Sales Returns and a credit to Accounts Receivable.

For each attribute, the deviation condition would be defined as the absence of the attribute. For example, for the first attribute, the deviation condition would be defined as: "Unit pricing and extensions on the credit memorandum are *not* accurate."

Define the Population

In this case, the population would be defined as all credit memoranda issued from the first day of the fiscal year, January 1, through the date that testing is performed. Assume that Chandler's balance sheet date is December 31, that interim testing of sales returns is being planned for October 19, and that the first sequentially numbered credit memorandum issued on January 1 was No. 4329 and the last issued on October 19 was No. 5948. From this information, the population would be represented by all credit memoranda numbered 4329 to 5948. The sampling unit in this case would be individual credit memoranda, and the auditor chooses random-number sampling as illustrated later in the chapter.

Determine Sample Size

The auditor's acceptable risk of overreliance, tolerable rate of deviation, and expected population deviation rate are indicated in Figure 9-4, page 370, for each of the five attributes of interest. (Note that the sample size, number of deviations, sample results, and audit conclusion are also indicated on the completed Figure 9-4, but are discussed later.) For example, for the first attribute — accurate unit pricing and extensions on credit memoranda —the auditor is willing to accept a 5 percent risk of overreliance, which, as discussed earlier, correlates with 95 percent reliability, the auditor's planned

FIGURE 9-4

Chandler Wire and Cable Co.
Attribute Estimation Worksheet – Sales Returns
December 31, 19A

B12
DM 10/21/19A

Attribute	1 Acceptable Risk of Overreliance	2 Tolerable Rate of Deviation	3 Expected Population Deviation Rate	4 Sample Size Table	Size Used	5 Number of Deviations	6 Sample Devia-tion Rate	Max. Pop'n Devia-tion Rate
1. Unit pricing and extensions on the credit memo are accurate	.05	.04	.0075	117	125	1 ✓	.008	.038
2. Quantity and other data on credit memo agree with receiving reports	.05	.05	.015	124	125	2 ✓	.016	.05
3. Quantity and description on credit memo agree with perpetual inventory	.10	.08	.02	48	50	1 ✓	.02	.076
4. Entry properly recorded as debit to inventory and credit to cost of goods sold	.05	.05	.01	93	100	0	0	.03
5. Entry properly recorded as debit to sales returns and credit to accounts rec.	.05	.05	.01	93	100	0	0	.03

(handwritten margin note: all yes & no situations)

✓ See analysis of deviations at B13

Audit Conclusion
Based on procedures performed, the tolerable rate of deviation equals or exceeds the maximum population deviation rate for all five attributes tested; therefore, controls over sales returns are considered effective in preventing or detecting misstatements.

level of confidence. The tolerable and expected rates of deviation for attribute 1 are .04 and .0075 respectively, indicating that the auditor is willing to tolerate more than four times the rate of deviation expected.

Sample size for each attribute is determined from Tables 9-1 or 9-2, pages 363 and 364, respectively. Table 9-1, used when the acceptable risk of overreliance is 5 percent, is appropriate for attributes 1, 2, 4, and 5. Table

TABLE 9-1
Attribute Estimation

Statistical Sample Sizes for Tests of Controls
Five-Percent Risk of Overreliance

Expected Population Deviation Rate	Tolerable Rate										
	2%	3%	4%	5%	6%	7%	8%	9%	10%	15%	20%
0.00%	149	99	74	59	49	42	36	32	29	19	14
.25	236	157	117	93	78	66	58	51	46	30	22
.50	*	157	117	93	78	66	58	51	46	30	22
.75	*	208	117	93	78	66	58	51	46	30	22
1.00	*	*	156	93	78	66	58	51	46	30	22
1.25	*	*	156	124	78	66	58	51	46	30	22
1.50	*	*	192	124	103	66	58	51	46	30	22
1.75	*	*	227	153	103	88	77	51	46	30	22
2.00	*	*	*	181	127	88	77	68	46	30	22
2.25	*	*	*	208	127	88	77	68	61	30	22
2.50	*	*	*	*	150	109	77	68	61	30	22
2.75	*	*	*	*	173	109	95	68	61	30	22
3.00	*	*	*	*	195	129	95	84	61	30	22
3.25	*	*	*	*	*	148	112	84	61	30	22
3.50	*	*	*	*	*	167	112	84	76	40	22
3.75	*	*	*	*	*	185	129	100	76	40	22
4.00	*	*	*	*	*	*	146	100	89	40	22
5.00	*	*	*	*	*	*	*	158	116	40	30
6.00	*	*	*	*	*	*	*	*	179	50	30
7.00	*	*	*	*	*	*	*	*	*	68	37

*Sample size is too large to be cost-effective for most audit applications.

Source: *AICPA Audit and Accounting Guide*, "Audit Sampling," p. 106. Copyright © 1983 by the American Institute of Certified Public Accountants, Inc. Reprinted with permission.

9-2, used when the acceptable risk of overreliance is 10 percent, is appropriate for attribute 3. Required sample size for each attribute is indicated in Figure 9-4. For example, for attribute 1, required sample size per Table 9-1 is 117, the intersection of the column associated with a 4 percent tolerable rate of deviation and the row associated with a .75 percent expected population deviation rate. Note that in Figure 9-4, the auditor has rounded sample size to 125 items. As noted previously, auditors frequently select more sampling units than required to compensate for any voided or missing items.

TABLE 9-2
Attribute Estimation

Statistical Sample Sizes for Tests of Controls
Ten-Percent Risk of Overreliance

Expected Population Deviation Rate	Tolerable Rate										
	2%	3%	4%	5%	6%	7%	8%	9%	10%	15%	20%
0.00%	114	76	57	45	38	32	28	25	22	15	11
.25	194	129	96	77	64	55	48	42	38	25	18
.50	194	129	96	77	64	55	48	42	38	25	18
.75	265	129	96	77	64	55	48	42	38	25	18
1.00	*	176	96	77	64	55	48	42	38	25	18
1.25	*	221	132	77	64	55	48	42	38	25·	18
1.50	*	*	132	105	64	55	48	42	38	25	18
1.75	*	*	166	105	88	55	48	42	38	25	18
2.00	*	*	198	132	88	75	48	42	38	25	18
2.25	*	*	*	132	88	75	65	42	38	25	18
2.50	*	*	*	158	110	75	65	58	38	25	18
2.75	*	*	*	209	132	94	65	58	52	25	18
3.00	*	*	*	*	132	94	65	58	52	25	18
3.25	*	*	*	*	153	113	82	58	52	25	18
3.50	*	*	*	*	194	113	82	73	52	25	18
3.75	*	*	*	*	*	131	98	73	52	25	18
4.00	*	*	*	*	*	149	98	73	65	25	18
5.00	*	*	*	*	*	*	160	115	78	34	18
6.00	*	*	*	*	*	*	*	182	116	43	25
7.00	*	*	*	*	*	*	*	*	199	52	25

*Sample size is too large to be cost-effective for most audit applications.

Source: *AICPA Audit and Accounting Guide,* ''Audit Sampling,'' p. 107. Copyright © 1983 by the American Institute of Certified Public Accountants, Inc. Reprinted with permission.

Perform the Sampling Plan

Selecting and testing sampling units is typically the most time-consuming phase of any sampling plan, since documents or other evidence must be gathered and then evaluated. As discussed earlier, either random-number sampling or systematic sampling is most appropriate for statistical sampling.

The auditor for Chandler selects random-number sampling, because the sequential four-digit credit memorandum numbers correspond readily to random-number tables. However, because sample size varies for the attributes tested — i.e., 50 for attribute 3, 100 for attributes 4 and 5, and 125 for attributes 1 and 2 — an initial sample of 50 can be selected for all attributes, an additional 50 for attributes 1, 2, 4 and 5, and another 25 for attributes 1 and 2. Figure 9-6 on page 367 illustrates how the auditor for Chandler selected the first 25 credit memoranda.

After selecting the necessary sampling units, the auditor examines them and documents any observed deviations for each attribute. Figure 9-4 indicates that one deviation was observed for attribute 1, two for attribute 2, and one for attribute 3; none were observed for attributes 4 and 5. Figure 9-5, page 366, is the auditor's analysis of each individual deviation. Note particularly the auditor's judgment expressed in Figure 9-5 about the effect of each deviation on substantive tests of details — in each case, no additional audit work was considered necessary for the reasons cited.

Evaluate the Sample Results

The results of the attribute estimation sampling plan are tabulated in the last two columns of Figure 9-4, page 362. The sample deviation rate for each attribute is calculated by dividing the number of deviations by the sample size used. For example, for attribute 1, the sample deviation rate is approximately .008 (1 deviation divided by 125 sampling units).

The maximum population deviation rate for each attribute is determined from Tables 9-3 and 9-4, pages 368 and 369, respectively. Table 9-3, used when the risk of overreliance is 5 percent, is appropriate for attributes 1, 2, 4, and 5. Table 9-4, used when the risk of overreliance is 10 percent, is appropriate for attribute 3. The maximum population deviation rate for each attribute is indicated in Figure 9-4. For example, for attribute 1, the maximum population deviation rate from Table 9-3 is .038, the intersection of the column associated with one deviation and the row associated with a sample size of 125. In statistical terms, the auditor's conclusion for attribute 1 could be expressed as follows:

> Based on procedures applied, the estimated population deviation rate is .008, and there is a 95 percent probability (i.e., 5 percent risk of overreliance) that the true but unknown population rate of deviation is less than or equal to .038.

A similar conclusion is reached for each attribute.

Based on the statistical conclusions, the auditor formulates an audit conclusion for the entire set of attributes tested (or for individual attributes, in

FIGURE 9-5

Chandler Wire and Cable Co.   B13
Analysis of Deviations: Sales Returns and Allowances
December 31, 19A

DM
10/21/19A

Attribute	Number of Deviations	Nature of Deviation	Effect on Substantive Detailed Testing
1	1	Cr memo #4823: $1,269 Although unit prices were correct, the extensions were incorrect, resulting in a $59. understatement.	No additional audit work is considered necessary at year-end because (1) the resulting error is immaterial and (2) the achieved upper precision limit (.032) is less than the tolerable rate (.04).
2	2	Cr. memo #4934: $2,528. Cr. memo #4687: $1,729. In both cases, the description of returned inventory is inaccurate.	No additional audit work is considered necessary at year-end because (1) both cr memos were recorded properly, despite the inaccurate descriptions, and (2) the achieved upper precision limit (.042) is less than the tolerable rate (.05).
3	1	Cr. memo #4731: $5,421. The quantity recorded within perpetual records was inaccurate.	No additional audit work is considered necessary at year-end because (1) journal entries were properly recorded for this credit memo (attributes 4 and 5), and (2) the achieved upper precision limit (.076) is less than the tolerable rate (.10).

FIGURE 9-6

Chandler Wire and Cable Co.   B-14
Random Number Sample Selection Sales Returns
December 31, 19A

7248	2987	⑥ 5392	7504	㉑ 4639	4302
8536	③ 4507	9502	7510	2094	㉓ 5646
4589	9076	⑦ 5647	9706	1039	8970
3905	0125	⑧ 4710	9626	2049	9574
9087	8965	8526	7524	2049	6859
2908	4075	7921	⑭ 4650	㉒ 5647	9706
start ⓪ 0012	1283	⑨ 4628	⑮ 4909	5960	㉔ 4657
↓ 1490	6904	6103	4310	3429	6720
4326	3209	3029	⑯ 5610	9706	㉕ 4382
① 5902	6520	2049	9706	6794	6857
3246	2840	⑩ 4900	⑰ 5820	8796	0978
7869	7512	⑪ 5930	7906	2538	0098
6793	④ 4629	⑫ 5291	⑱ 5647	6059	4039
7302	⑤ 5402	7946	8694	6721	8593
6739	8734	7501	⑲ 4910	8796	6758
② 4521	8053	⑬ 5342	⑳ 5768	6970	8079

Population: 4329 - 5948
Route: Select random start and proceed
vertically down column; continue with next
column at right.

DM
10/19/19A

---

the case of mixed results). Because the tolerable rate is greater than or equal to the maximum population deviation rate for all five attributes (see Figure 9-4), and no other qualitative evidence exists to the contrary, the audit conclusion would be that the control is effective in preventing or detecting misstatements. The auditor's conclusion for Chandler Wire & Cable Company appears in Figure 9-4.

TABLE 9-3
Attribute Estimation

Statistical Sample Results Evaluation
Table for Tests of Controls
Maximum Population Deviation Rates
at Five-Percent Risk of Overreliance

	Actual Number of Deviations Found										
Sample Size	0	1	2	3	4	5	6	7	8	9	10
25	11.3	17.6	*	*	*	*	*	*	*	*	*
30	9.5	14.9	19.6	*	*	*	*	*	*	*	*
35	8.3	12.9	17.0	*	*	*	*	*	*	*	*
40	7.3	11.4	15.0	18.3	*	*	*	*	*	*	*
45	6.5	10.2	13.4	16.4	19.2	*	*	*	*	*	*
50	5.9	9.2	12.1	14.8	17.4	19.9	*	*	*	*	*
55	5.4	8.4	11.1	13.5	15.9	18.2	*	*	*	*	*
60	4.9	7.7	10.2	12.5	14.7	16.8	18.8	*	*	*	*
65	4.6	7.1	9.4	11.5	13.6	15.5	17.4	19.3	*	*	*
70	4.2	6.6	8.8	10.8	12.6	14.5	16.3	18.0	19.7	*	*
75	4.0	6.2	8.2	10.1	11.8	13.6	15.2	16.9	18.5	20.0	*
80	3.7	5.8	7.7	9.5	11.1	12.7	14.3	15.9	17.4	18.9	*
90	3.3	5.2	6.9	8.4	9.9	11.4	12.8	14.2	15.5	16.8	18.2
100	3.0	4.7	6.2	7.6	9.0	10.3	11.5	12.8	14.0	15.2	16.4
125	2.4	3.8	5.0	6.1	7.2	8.3	9.3	10.3	11.3	12.3	13.2
150	2.0	3.2	4.2	5.1	6.0	6.9	7.8	8.6	9.5	10.3	11.1
200	1.5	2.4	3.2	3.9	4.6	5.2	5.9	6.5	7.2	7.8	8.4

*Over 20 percent.

NOTE: This table presents maximum population deviation rates as percentages. This table assumes a large population.
Source: *AICPA Audit and Accounting Guide*, "Audit Sampling," p. 108. Copyright © 1983 by the American Institute
   of Certified Public Accountants, Inc. Reprinted with permission.

Other Considerations

Three observations are in order about the results achieved and documented in Figure 9-4. First, the auditor's conclusions relate only to the period for which credit memoranda were available for testing — that is, January 1 through October 19. Thus, the conclusions do not apply to the period October 20 through December 31, in the absence of additional sampling procedures.

TABLE 9-4
Attribute Estimation

Statistical Sample Results Evaluation
Table for Tests of Controls
Maximum Population Deviation Rates
at Ten-Percent Risk of Overreliance

Sample Size	Actual Number of Deviations Found										
	0	1	2	3	4	5	6	7	8	9	10
20	10.9	18.1	*	*	*	*	*	*	*	*	*
25	8.8	14.7	19.9	*	*	*	*	*	*	*	*
30	7.4	12.4	16.8	*	*	*	*	*	*	*	*
35	6.4	10.7	14.5	18.1	*	*	*	*	*	*	*
40	5.6	9.4	12.8	16.0	19.0	*	*	*	*	*	*
45	5.0	8.4	11.4	14.3	17.0	19.7	*	*	*	*	*
50	4.6	7.6	10.3	12.9	15.4	17.8	*	*	*	*	*
55	4.1	6.9	9.4	11.8	14.1	16.3	18.4	*	*	*	*
60	3.8	6.4	8.7	10.8	12.9	15.0	16.9	18.9	*	*	*
70	3.3	5.5	7.5	9.3	11.1	12.9	14.6	16.3	17.9	19.6	*
80	2.9	4.8	6.6	8.2	9.8	11.3	12.8	14.3	15.8	17.2	18.6
90	2.6	4.3	5.9	7.3	8.7	10.1	11.5	12.8	14.1	15.4	16.6
100	2.3	3.9	5.3	6.6	7.9	9.1	10.3	11.5	12.7	13.9	15.0
120	2.0	3.3	4.4	5.5	6.6	7.6	8.7	9.7	10.7	11.6	12.6
160	1.5	2.5	3.3	4.2	5.0	5.8	6.5	7.3	8.0	8.8	9.5
200	1.2	2.0	2.7	3.4	4.0	4.6	5.3	5.9	6.5	7.1	7.6

*Over 20 percent.

NOTE: This table presents maximum population deviation rates as percentages. This table assumes a large population.

Source: *AICPA Audit and Accounting Guide*, ''Audit Sampling,'' p. 109. Copyright © 1983 by the American Institute
of Certified Public Accountants, Inc. Reprinted with permission.

Second, recall that the prior auditor experienced relatively high deviation rates
for tests of sales returns. However, the results in Figure 9-4 indicate otherwise for the current year, illustrating the very real phenomenon of changing
audit conditions from year to year.

Third, note that for attribute 2 in Figure 9-4 the maximum population
deviation rate, .05, is equal to the tolerable rate. Because the maximum population rate and tolerable rate are equal, the auditor might consider the control
questionable. On the other hand, the control attribute itself — credit memo

quantity and other data agree with receiving reports — may not be sufficiently critical to warrant not relying on the control, since there may be compensating controls and evidence exists that credit memoranda are recorded
properly in the accounts. The auditor's decision — that is, the assessed level
of control risk — would be based on weighing these two points of view, and
is an example of the types of trade-offs considered by auditors in practice.

SEQUENTIAL (STOP-OR-GO) SAMPLING

Audit sampling can be accomplished with either a fixed or a sequential
sampling plan. In a *fixed sampling plan,* such as attribute estimation, the
auditor tests a single sample. But in a *sequential sampling plan,* the sample
is performed in several steps, and following each step, an auditor decides
whether to stop testing or to go on to the next step, thus accounting for why
the plan is sometimes called *stop-or-go sampling.* Sequential sampling requires that the auditor test the first group of sampling units and, on the basis
of the sample results, decide whether to (1) assess a lower control risk, (2)
assess a higher control risk without further sampling, or (3) examine additional sampling units because the initial sample is insufficient to conclude
that planned reliance is warranted.

Sequential sampling can be used as an alternative to attribute estimation
when an auditor expects zero or very few deviations within an audit population. For example, for a continuing audit engagement, an auditor might decide to use sequential sampling if the prior year's attribute estimation sampling plans yielded very low maximum population deviation rates, the prior
year's observed deviations did not result in material misstatements, and there
was no reason to expect that deviations in the current year would result in
material misstatements. For this set of circumstances, an auditor could possibly minimize sample size using sequential sampling, thereby minimizing
audit time and improving audit efficiency.

Assuming that the objectives, attributes, deviation conditions, and population are defined properly and that the sample selection method is chosen,
an auditor would proceed through steps 5 through 7 of the general sampling
plan given in Figure 9-2, page 349, as discussed below.

Determine Sample Size

Determining required sample size in sequential sampling requires that an
auditor first specify the desired reliability and the tolerable rate of deviation.
As noted earlier, *desired reliability* is the complement of the risk of overre-

liance, which was needed to determine sample size in attribute estimation. As a result, desired reliability is also a matter of professional judgment and may be deduced from an auditor's acceptable risk of overreliance. That is, if an auditor intended to assess a low level of control risk and therefore decided on a rather low risk of overreliance, such as 2 percent, then desired reliability would be 98 percent (i.e., $1.00 - .02$). Note that because there is an inverse relationship between sample size and the risk of overreliance, there is a direct relationship between desired reliability and sample size: sample size is larger when an auditor specifies a higher desired reliability. In general, a higher desired reliability is appropriate when an auditor believes the internal control structure may be effective, resulting in a lower control risk; a lower reliability level is appropriate otherwise.

As in attribute estimation, *tolerable rate of deviation* is the maximum rate an auditor is willing to accept in the sample without deciding a control is ineffective. A lower tolerable rate of deviation is appropriate when an auditor plans to assess a low control risk.

Unlike attribute estimation, sequential sampling does not require an estimate of the expected population deviation rate, since sequential sampling is applied only when an auditor expects zero or very few deviations.

In sequential sampling, sample size can be determined from standard tables such as Table 9-5, pages 372 and 373, which is also used to evaluate results. Table 9-5 is appropriate for populations over 2,000 items and is used as follows:

▲ Locate the column associated with the tolerable rate of deviation (the %s in the table) and row associated with zero errors.

▲ Beginning with the smallest sample size (i.e., 50 at the extreme top left column of the table) and continuing for increasingly higher sample sizes, review the column and row (zero deviations) intersections until you locate the sample size which achieves the desired level of reliability.

For example, assume:

$$\text{Desired reliability} = .95$$
$$\text{Tolerable rate of deviation} = .05$$

In Table 9-5, the smallest sample size that achieves at least 95 percent reliability for zero expected deviations is 70.

Note that for a smaller sample size of 50, the intersection of 5 percent tolerable rate of deviation and zero expected deviations results in a reliability level of 92.31 percent, which is clearly below the desired reliability level of 95 percent. However, for sample size 70, the intersection of 5 percent toler-

TABLE 9-5
Sequential Sampling

Size of Sample Examined	No. of Deviations Found	Probability That Deviation Rate is Less Than:														
		1%	2%	3%	4%	5%	6%	7%	8%	9%	10%	12%	14%	16%	18%	20%
50	0	39.50	63.58	78.19	87.01	92.31	95.47	97.34	98.45	99.10	99.49	99.83	99.95	99.98	100.00	100.00
	1	8.94	26.42	44.47	59.95	72.06	81.00	87.35	91.73	94.68	96.62	98.69	99.52	99.83	99.94	99.98
	2	1.38	7.84	18.92	32.33	45.95	58.38	68.92	77.40	83.95	88.83	94.87	97.79	99.10	99.65	99.87
	3	0.16	1.78	6.28	13.91	23.96	35.27	46.73	57.47	66.97	74.97	86.55	93.30	96.88	98.64	99.43
	4	0.02	0.32	1.68	4.90	10.36	17.94	27.10	37.11	47.23	56.88	73.21	84.72	91.92	96.01	98.15
	5		0.05	0.37	1.44	3.78	7.76	13.51	20.81	29.28	38.39	56.47	71.86	83.23	90.71	95.20
	6		0.01	0.07	0.36	1.18	2.89	5.83	10.19	15.96	22.98	39.35	56.16	70.81	81.99	89.66
70	0	50.52	75.69	88.14	94.26	97.24	98.69	99.38	99.71	99.86	99.94	99.99	100.00	100.00	100.00	100.00
	1	15.53	40.96	62.47	77.51	87.03	92.81	96.10	97.93	98.92	99.45	99.86	99.97	99.99	100.00	100.00
	2	3.34	16.50	35.08	53.44	68.63	79.87	87.59	92.60	95.72	97.58	99.28	99.80	99.95	99.99	100.00
	3	0.54	5.19	15.87	30.71	46.61	61.15	73.07	82.10	88.53	92.88	97.48	99.19	99.76	99.93	99.98
	4	0.07	1.32	5.93	14.85	27.21	41.13	54.77	66.80	76.61	84.12	93.36	97.51	99.16	99.74	99.92
	5		0.28	1.86	6.12	13.72	24.27	36.58	49.24	61.06	71.28	85.94	93.92	97.64	99.17	99.73
	6		0.05	0.50	2.18	6.04	12.61	21.75	32.70	44.40	55.82	74.98	87.57	94.50	97.81	99.20
	7			0.12	0.68	2.34	5.80	11.54	19.54	29.33	40.12	61.33	78.13	89.04	95.08	98.00
	8			0.02	0.19	0.80	2.38	5.49	10.54	17.59	26.37	46.66	66.03	80.85	90.36	95.63
	9				0.05	0.25	0.88	2.36	5.14	9.60	15.86	32.88	52.46	70.10	83.23	91.55
100	0	63.40	86.74	95.25	98.31	99.41	99.80	99.93	99.98	99.99	100.00	100.00	100.00	100.00	100.00	100.00
	1	26.42	59.67	80.54	91.28	96.29	98.48	99.40	99.77	99.91	99.97	100.00	100.00	100.00	100.00	100.00
	2	7.94	32.33	58.02	76.79	88.17	94.34	97.42	98.87	99.52	99.81	99.97	100.00	100.00	100.00	100.00
	3	1.84	14.10	35.28	57.05	74.22	85.70	92.56	96.33	98.27	99.22	99.86	99.98	100.00	100.00	99.98
	4	0.34	5.08	18.22	37.11	56.40	72.32	83.68	90.97	95.26	97.63	99.47	99.90	99.98	100.00	100.00
	5	0.05	1.55	8.08	21.16	38.40	55.93	70.86	82.01	89.55	94.24	98.48	99.66	99.93	99.99	100.00
	6	0.01	0.41	3.12	10.64	23.40	39.37	55.57	69.68	80.60	88.28	96.33	99.03	99.78	99.96	99.99
	7		0.09	1.06	4.75	12.80	25.17	40.12	55.29	68.72	79.40	92.39	97.67	99.39	99.86	99.97
	8		0.02	0.32	1.90	6.31	14.63	26.60	40.74	55.06	67.91	86.14	95.08	98.53	99.62	99.91
	9			0.09	0.68	2.82	7.75	16.20	27.80	41.25	54.87	77.44	90.78	96.84	99.08	99.77
	10			0.02	0.22	1.15	3.76	9.08	17.57	28.82	41.68	66.63	84.40	93.93	98.00	99.43
	11				0.07	0.43	1.68	4.69	10.29	18.76	29.70	54.58	75.91	89.39	96.05	98.74
	12				0.02	0.15	0.69	2.24	5.59	11.38	19.82	42.39	65.66	82.97	92.89	97.47
	13					0.05	0.26	0.99	2.82	6.45	12.39	31.14	54.36	74.69	88.19	95.31
	14					0.01	0.09	0.41	1.33	3.41	7.26	21.60	42.94	64.90	81.77	91.96
	15						0.03	0.16	0.59	1.69	3.99	14.15	32.27	54.20	73.70	87.15

n = 120

#														
0	70.06	91.15	97.41	99.25	99.79	99.94	99.98	100.00	100.00	100.00	100.00	100.00	100.00	100.00	100.00
1	33.77	69.46	87.82	95.53	98.45	99.48	99.83	99.95	99.98	99.99	100.00	100.00	100.00	100.00	100.00
2	11.96	43.13	70.16	86.28	94.25	97.75	99.17	99.71	99.90	99.97	99.99	100.00	100.00	100.00	100.00
3	3.30	22.00	48.67	71.13	85.56	93.40	97.19	98.87	99.60	99.84	99.98	100.00	100.00	100.00	100.00
4	0.74	9.38	29.24	52.67	72.18	85.27	92.83	96.75	98.61	99.44	99.92				
5	0.14	3.41	15.29	34.83	55.85	73.23	85.23	92.47	96.42	98.40	99.72				
6	0.02	1.07	7.03	20.57	39.37	58.50	74.26	85.35	92.26	96.18	99.21				
7		0.30	2.86	10.90	25.24	43.20	60.81	75.25	85.57	92.16	98.08				
8		0.07	1.04	5.21	14.74	29.39	46.51	62.85	76.21	85.86	95.89	99.05	99.82	99.97	
9		0.02	0.34	2.26	7.86	18.43	33.12	49.44	64.70	77.14	92.18	97.89	99.53	99.91	
10			0.10	0.89	3.85	10.66	21.93	36.49	52.06	66.39	86.56	95.79	98.94	99.78	
11			0.03	0.32	1.73	5.70	13.50	25.23	39.56	54.45	78.90	92.39	97.80	99.48	
12			0.01	0.11	0.72	2.83	7.75	16.33	28.33	42.39	69.41	87.35	95.83	98.88	
13				0.03	0.28	1.31	4.15	9.91	19.11	31.27	58.66	80.53	92.71	97.78	99.44
14				0.01	0.10	0.56	2.07	5.64	12.13	21.82	47.45	72.05	88.17	95.95	98.86
15					0.03	0.23	0.97	3.01	7.26	14.40	36.66	62.30	82.06	93.10	97.82
16					0.01	0.09	0.43	1.51	4.10	8.99	26.99	51.88	74.42	89.00	96.12
17						0.03	0.18	0.72	2.18	5.31	18.93	41.50	65.52	83.49	93.53
18						0.01	0.07	0.32	1.10	2.97	12.64	31.84	55.82	76.57	89.81

n = 150

#														
0	77.86	95.17	98.96	99.78	99.95	99.99	100.00	100.00	100.00	100.00	100.00	100.00	100.00	100.00
1	44.30	80.39	94.15	98.41	99.60	99.90	99.98	100.00	100.00	100.00	100.00	100.00	100.00	100.00
2	19.05	57.91	83.07	94.16	98.19	99.48	99.86	99.96	99.99	100.00	100.00	100.00	100.00	100.00
3	6.47	35.28	66.16	85.42	94.52	98.14	99.42	99.83	99.95	99.99	100.00	100.00	100.00	100.00
4	1.80	18.30	46.93	72.04	87.44	95.01	98.20	99.40	99.81	99.95		100.00	100.00	100.00
5	0.42	8.19	29.57	55.76	76.56	89.17	95.52	98.31	99.41	99.81		100.00	100.00	100.00
6	0.08	3.20	16.60	39.37	62.71	80.16	90.66	96.03	98.45	99.44		100.00	100.00	100.00
7	0.02	1.11	8.34	25.32	47.72	68.34	83.12	91.94	96.50	98.60		100.00	100.00	100.00
8		0.34	3.78	14.85	33.62	54.84	72.98	85.58	93.04	96.93	99.52	99.94		100.00
9		0.10	1.55	7.97	21.91	41.26	60.93	76.85	87.65	94.00	98.89	99.84		100.00
10		0.02	0.58	3.93	13.22	29.03	48.15	66.16	80.13	89.40	97.66	99.61		100.00
11		0.01	0.20	1.79	7.40	19.09	35.90	54.32	70.66	82.91	95.54	99.14		100.00
12			0.06	0.75	3.85	11.74	25.23	42.40	59.82	74.55	92.19	98.25	99.96	100.00
13			0.02	0.29	1.87	6.77	16.70	31.39	48.43	64.70	87.34	96.70	99.90	100.00
14				0.11	0.85	3.66	10.42	22.03	37.41	53.98	80.86	94.25	99.77	100.00
15				0.04	0.36	1.86	6.13	14.64	27.53	43.18	72.85	90.62	99.52	100.00
16				0.01	0.14	0.89	3.40	9.22	19.28	33.06	63.64	85.63	99.05	
17					0.05	0.40	1.79	5.51	12.86	24.19	53.74	79.24	98.24	
18					0.02	0.17	0.89	3.13	8.16	16.92	43.76	71.54	96.92	
19					0.01	0.07	0.42	1.68	4.93	11.30	34.31	62.84	94.90	
20						0.03	0.19	0.86	2.84	7.21	25.87	53.56	92.01	97.76
21						0.01	0.08	0.42	1.56	4.40	18.74	44.22	88.08	96.28
22							0.03	0.20	0.82	2.56	13.04	35.29	83.02	94.10
23							0.01	0.09	0.41	1.43	8.72	27.20	76.84	91.07
24								0.04	0.20	0.76	5.60	20.24	69.66	87.06

Source: Ernst & Whinney, *Audit Sampling*, 1979, pp. 186–187. Copyright © 1979 by Ernst & Whinney. Reprinted with permission.

able rate and zero expected deviations results in a reliability level of 97.24 percent, a level that is acceptable — i.e., at least 95 percent for this example.

Perform the Sampling Plan and Evaluate Results

Sampling units are selected using, for example, random-number sampling or systematic sampling, as in attribute estimation. After examining the sampling units included within the initial sample selection, an auditor then decides from the sample results whether to "stop" or "go" on with the sampling plan. The decision to stop or go depends primarily on how many deviations are observed. If no deviations are observed, the auditor can conclude that the actual population deviation rate is within the predetermined tolerable rate, and therefore may stop the sampling plan. For the preceding example, no observed deviations would yield a conclusion as follows: *Based on procedures applied, there is a 97.24 percent probability that the actual population deviation rate is less than .05.*

However, if one or more deviations are observed within the original sample, the auditor could decide to increase sample size in an attempt to seek additional deviation-free sampling units and reevaluate the sample accordingly. In this situation, Table 9-5 would be used in essentially the same way as in determining initial sample size.

DISCOVERY SAMPLING

Discovery sampling for attributes is appropriate when the expected rate of deviation is near zero and is designed to find at least one deviation in a sample if the actual population deviation rate exceeds or equals a predetermined critical rate of deviation. In discovery sampling, a single deviation in a sample is sufficient to conclude that the population deviation rate exceeds the critical rate. The critical rate in discovery sampling is comparable to the tolerable rate in attribute estimation and sequential sampling.

Discovery sampling is used most often when no deviations would be expected and therefore even one would cause concern, e.g., suspected fraudulent cash payments. Thus, discovery sampling plans may be appropriate when the audit objective is to observe at least one deviation at a specified critical rate, the expected population deviation rate is near zero, and an auditor desires a specified probability of observing at least one deviation if the actual population rate exceeds the critical rate. Although discovery sampling is concerned with population rates of deviation, it does not specifically yield an estimated rate of deviation; rather, it generates sample sizes appropriate for finding at least one deviation for various size populations, various critical rates of deviation, and various probabilities of success.

Assuming that the objectives, attributes, deviation conditions, and population are defined properly, an auditor would proceed through the remaining phases as follows.

Determine Sample Size

Determining sample size in discovery sampling plans requires that an auditor first specify a critical rate of deviation and the desired probability of observing at least one deviation.

The *critical rate of deviation* is the minimum population deviation rate that must exist if one deviation is to be observed at a specified probability. Much like a tolerable rate in attribute estimation, the critical rate is a matter of professional judgment and depends partly on control risk and partly on materiality. The *desired probability* of observing at least one deviation is comparable to desired reliability in sequential sampling and is also a matter of professional judgment.

Increasing or decreasing the critical rate or desired probability can influence sample size. Increasing either will increase sample size; decreasing either will decrease sample size. The impact upon sample size of increasing one and decreasing the other would depend upon the magnitude of both the increase and the decrease.

Required sample sizes for discovery sampling plans can be determined from standard tables designed to yield the minimum sample size required to find at least one deviation with specified probability. Table 9-6, page 376, can be used to determine sample size for populations between 2,000 and 5,000, and Table 9-7, page 377, for populations between 5,000 and 10,000; other tables are required for populations over 10,000.

To determine sample size from the tables, identify the column associated with the critical rate of deviation, reading down the column to the desired probability. Required sample size is the number to the far left on the row containing the desired probability. For example, assume the following:

Population size   = 6,500 items
Critical rate of deviation = .0075 (.75%)
Desired probability   = .95 (95%)

From Table 9-7, used since population size is between 5,000 and 10,000, sample size would be obtained by reading down the column at .75 percent critical rate to 95 percent probability and left to required sample size of 400.

TABLE 9-6
Discovery Sampling

Probability in Percent of Including at
Least One Deviation in a Sample
For Populations Between 2,000 and 5,000

Upper Precision Limit: Critical Rate of Deviation

Sample Size	.3%	.4%	.5%	.6%	.8%	1%	1.5%	2%
50	14%	18%	22%	26%	33%	40%	53%	64%
60	17	21	26	30	38	45	60	70
70	19	25	30	35	43	51	66	76
80	22	28	33	38	48	56	70	80
90	24	31	37	42	52	60	75	84
100	26	33	40	46	56	64	78	87
120	31	39	46	52	62	70	84	91
140	35	43	51	57	68	76	88	94
160	39	48	56	62	73	80	91	96
200	46	56	64	71	81	87	95	98
240	52	63	71	77	86	92	98	99
300	61	71	79	84	92	96	99	99+
340	65	76	83	88	94	97	99+	99+
400	71	81	88	92	96	98	99+	99+
460	77	86	91	95	98	99	99+	99+
500	79	88	93	96	99	99	99+	99+
600	85	92	96	98	99	99+	99+	99+
700	90	95	98	99	99+	99+	99+	99+
800	93	97	99	99	99+	99+	99+	99+
900	95	98	99	99+	99+	99+	99+	99+
1,000	97	99	99+	99+	99+	99+	99+	99+

Perform the Sampling Plan and Evaluate the Sample Results

Sampling units should be selected at random and examined for the attribute of interest. If no deviations are observed, an auditor's conclusion would be stated in terms of the critical rate of deviation and desired probability.

TABLE 9-7
Discovery Sampling

Probability in Percent of Including at
Least One Deviation in a Sample
For Populations Between 5,000 and 10,000

Upper Precision Limit: Critical Rate of Deviation

Sample Size	.1%	.2%	.3%	.4%	.5%	.75%	1%	2%
50	5%	10%	14%	18%	22%	31%	40%	64%
60	6	11	17	21	26	36	45	70
70	7	13	19	25	30	41	51	76
80	8	15	21	28	33	45	55	80
90	9	17	24	30	36	49	60	84
100	10	18	26	33	40	53	64	87
120	11	21	30	38	45	60	70	91
140	13	25	35	43	51	65	76	94
160	15	28	38	48	55	70	80	96
200	18	33	45	56	64	78	87	98
240	22	39	52	62	70	84	91	99
300	26	46	60	70	78	90	95	99+
340	29	50	65	75	82	93	97	99+
400	34	56	71	81	87	95	98	99+
460	38	61	76	85	91	97	99	99+
500	40	64	79	87	92	98	99	99+
600	46	71	84	92	96	99	99+	99+
700	52	77	89	95	97	99+	99+	99+
800	57	81	92	96	98	99+	99+	99+
900	61	85	94	98	99	99+	99+	99+
1,000	65	88	96	99	99	99+	99+	99+
1,500	80	96	99	99+	99+	99+	99+	99+
2,000	89	99	99+	99+	99+	99+	99+	99+

Source: Ernst & Whinney, *Audit Sampling,* 1979, p. 169. Copyright © 1979 by Ernst & Whinney. Reprinted with permission.

Continuing the preceding example, assume no deviations are found. An auditor's statistical conclusion would be:

Based on procedures performed, there is a 95 percent probability that the population rate of deviation is less than or equal to the critical rate of deviation (.0075).

If an occurrence is observed, an auditor could use an attribute estimation evaluation table (e.g., Table 9-1) to estimate a maximum population deviation rate.

NONSTATISTICAL SAMPLING IN TESTS OF CONTROLS

Even though nonstatistical sampling plans do not measure sampling risk, they can provide results as effective as statistical plans, and are often chosen by auditors when the costs of generating statistical samples exceed the benefits. Generally, the steps in a nonstatistical sampling plan are the same as those of a statistical sampling plan — but the auditor's judgment is guided not by statistical theory, but by experience and by prior knowledge and current information about the client. The following discussion addresses some considerations in nonstatistical sampling not specifically covered earlier in the chapter.

Determine Sample Size

An auditor considers precisely the same parameters when determining nonstatistical sample size as when calculating statistical sample size: the risk of overreliance, tolerable rate of deviation, and expected population deviation rates. However, in nonstatistical sampling, the parameters may be expressed in relative terms, such as "low," "medium," "high," etc., rather than in quantitative terms. When determining sample size in nonstatistical sampling, the auditor should consider the impact on sample size of increasing or decreasing the acceptable risk of overreliance and the tolerable and expected rates of deviation, as illustrated earlier in Figure 9-3, page 356. For example, an auditor could justifiably consider decreasing sample size if his or her tolerable rate of deviation increased.

Alternatively, in a nonstatistical sampling plan the auditor could subjectively quantify each population parameter and then use standard tables (e.g., Table 9-1 or 9-2) to determine sample size. Calculated sample size could then either be used or be altered judgmentally to reflect the auditor's reconsideration of each parameter in Figure 9-3 and sampling risk.

As in statistical sampling, sampling units can be selected using random-number sampling or systematic sampling, either of which could achieve randomness, thereby improving the likelihood of selecting representative sample items. Two other selection methods are available — block sampling and haphazard sampling—both of which require extreme care by the auditor, as discussed earlier.

Evaluating Sample Results

Because nonstatistical sampling plans do not yield an estimate of sampling risk, the auditor must determine judgmentally whether the difference between his or her tolerable rate of deviation and the estimated population deviation rate is an adequate allowance for sampling risk. For example, assume that an auditor will tolerate 8 percent deviations, and observes 3 deviations in a sample of 50. In this case, the estimated population rate of deviation is the sample deviation rate of 6 percent ($3 \div 50$), and since the tolerable rate of deviation is 8 percent, then the auditor would be faced with the decision of whether 2 percent (8 percent tolerable rate minus 6 percent estimated population rate) is an adequate allowance for sampling risk.

SUMMARY

Audit sampling, whether statistical or nonstatistical, involves testing less than 100 percent of the items that compose an audit population, and is intended to aid an auditor in reaching cost-effective conclusions about audit populations. This chapter discussed audit sampling in tests of controls and Chapter 10 addresses audit sampling in substantive testing.

Attributes sampling plans focus on rates of deviation from prescribed internal control procedures, and are used to accomplish tests of controls during an auditor's consideration of internal control structure. However, attributes sampling does entail some risk, partly because the auditor is not certain that a sample is wholly representative of the population from which the sampling units were drawn, and therefore is not certain whether he or she is likely to underrely or overrely on internal control structure.

Attributes sampling plans may be either statistical or nonstatistical, and either approach can provide effective results if designed properly. A properly designed statistical or nonstatistical sampling plan should consider the following: the auditor's objectives; properly defined attributes, deviation conditions, and populations; a defendable method of sample selection; a rational means of determining sample size; and justifiable procedures for performing the sampling plan and evaluating the results. Three generally accepted statistical sampling plans commonly used in practice today are attribute estimation, sequential (stop-or-go) sampling, and discovery sampling, all of which were illustrated in detail in the chapter.

REFERENCES

AICPA Audit and Accounting Guide "Audit Sampling," New York: American Institute of Certified Public Accountants, 1983.

Akresh, A. D., and G. R. Zuber. "Exploring Statistical Sampling." *Journal of Accountancy* (February, 1981), pp. 50–56.

Bailey, A. D., Jr. *Statistical Auditing: Review, Concepts, and Problems*. New York: Harcourt Brace Jovanovich, Inc., 1981.

Elliott, R. K., and J. R. Rogers. "Relating Statistical Sampling to Audit Objectives." *Journal of Accountancy* (July, 1972), pp. 46–55.

Epstein, B. J. "Attributes Sampling: A Local Firm's Experience." *Journal of Accountancy* (January, 1986), pp. 130–135.

Ernst & Whinney. *Audit Sampling*. Cleveland: Ernst & Whinney, 1979.

Guy, D. M., and D. R. Carmichael. *Audit Sampling: An Introduction to Statistical Sampling in Auditing*. New York: John Wiley & Sons, 1986.

Myers, C. A. "Determining Nonstatistical (Judgmental) Sample Sizes." *The CPA Journal* (October, 1979), pp. 72–74.

Neter, J., and J. K. Loebbecke. *Behavior of Major Statistical Estimators in Sampling Accounting Populations*. New York: American Institute of Certified Public Accountants, 1975.

Roberts, D. M. *Statistical Auditing*. New York: American Institute of Certified Public Accountants, 1978.

Stringer, K. W. "Statistical Sampling in Auditing: The State of the Art." *Annual Accounting Review* (1979), pp. 113–127.

QUESTIONS

1. What is meant by the term *audit sampling?*
2. Distinguish between sampling for attributes and sampling for variables in an auditing context.
3. What is the purpose of attributes sampling in tests of controls?
4. Describe the nature and components of audit risk.
5. What is nonsampling risk and how can it be controlled?
6. Identify the sampling risks inherent in sampling for attributes.
7. Compare and contrast nonstatistical and statistical audit sampling plans.
8. Define *attribute* and *deviation* in the context of tests of controls.
9. Why is it important that audit populations be defined properly?
10. How can an auditor achieve randomness when selecting a statistical sample?
11. What is the purpose of stratifying audit populations?
12. Identify the three parameters necessary to determine sample size in attribute estimation sampling plans.
13. Briefly define *tolerable rate of deviation.*
14. Describe the alternative available to an auditor when an attributes sampling plan suggests that a control is not effective.
15. When is attribute estimation appropriate?
16. When is sequential sampling appropriate?

17. Under what conditions may discovery sampling be appropriate?
18. What is a *critical rate of deviation* in discovery sampling?

MULTIPLE CHOICE QUESTIONS

1. When using statistical sampling for tests of controls, an auditor's evaluation would include a statistical conclusion concerning whether:

   a. Procedural deviations in the population were within an acceptable range.
   b. Monetary precision is in excess of a certain predetermined amount.
   c. The population total is not in error by more than a fixed amount.
   d. Population characteristics occur at least once in the population.
                                                                 (AICPA Adapted)

2. The purpose of tests of controls is to provide reasonable assurance that the control procedures are being applied as prescribed. The sampling method that is most useful when testing for controls is:

   a. Nonstatistical sampling.
   b. Attribute estimation.
   c. Unrestricted random sampling with replacement.
   d. Stratified random sampling.   (AICPA Adapted)

3. Which of the following best describes the distinguishing feature of statistical sampling?

   a. It provides for measuring mathematically the degree of uncertainty that results from examining only a part of the data.
   b. It allows the auditor to have the same degree of confidence as with judgment sampling but with substantially less work.
   c. It allows the auditor to substitute sampling techniques for audit judgment.
   d. It provides for measuring the actual misstatements in financial statements in terms of reliability and precision.   (AICPA Adapted)

4. Discovery sampling should be used to estimate whether a population contains:

   a. Errors of any kind.
   b. Noncritical errors.
   c. Critical errors.
   d. No errors.   (AICPA Adapted)

5. Statistical sampling generally may be applied to test controls when the client's internal control procedures:

   a. Depend primarily on appropriate segregation of duties.
   b. Are carefully reduced to writing and are included in client accounting manuals.
   c. Leave an audit trail in the form of documentary evidence of compliance.
   d. Enable the detection of material irregularities in the accounting records.
                                                                 (AICPA Adapted)

6. In attribute estimation sampling, which one of the following must be known in order to appraise the results of the auditor's sample?

   a. Estimated dollar value of the population.
   b. Standard deviation of the values in the population.
   c. Actual occurrence rate of the attribute in the population.
   d. Sample size.   (AICPA Adapted)

7. If all other factors specified in a sampling plan remain constant, changing the estimated occurrence rate from 2% to 4% would cause the required sample size to:

   a. Increase.
   b. Remain the same.
   c. Decrease.
   d. Become indeterminate.   (AICPA Adapted)

8. Which of the following best illustrates the concept of sampling risk?

   a. A randomly chosen sample may *not* be representative of the population as a whole on the characteristic of interest.
   b. An auditor may select audit procedures that are *not* appropriate to achieve the specific objective.
   c. An auditor may fail to recognize errors in the documents examined for the chosen sample.
   d. The documents related to the chosen sample may *not* be available for inspection.   (AICPA Adapted)

9. If the auditor is concerned that a population may contain exceptions, the determination of a sample size sufficient to include at least one such exception is a characteristic of

   a. Discovery sampling.
   b. Variables sampling.
   c. Random sampling.
   d. Dollar-unit sampling.   (AICPA Adapted)

10. The tolerable rate of deviation for tests of controls is generally

   a. Lower than the expected rate of deviation in the population.
   b. Higher than the expected rate of deviation in the population.
   c. Identical to the expected rate of deviation in the population.
   d. Unrelated to the expected rate of deviation in the population.
                                                      (AICPA Adapted)

PROBLEMS

9-1   Auditors do not often have the luxury of testing 100 percent of the transactions and events underlying recorded account balances. More often, they rely on samples, thereby reducing audit costs, but also creating a risk that the samples selected will not be representative of the population.

Required:
1. What risks does an auditor sustain solely as a result of sampling?
2. Explain how an inefficient audit can increase audit risk.

9-2   The use of statistical sampling techniques in an audit of financial statements does not eliminate judgment.

Required:
Identify and explain four areas where judgment may be exercised by a CPA in planning a statistical sampling test.

(AICPA Adapted)

9-3   A sample of 80 accounts payable vouchers is to be selected from a population of 3,200. The vouchers are numbered consecutively from 1 to 3,200 and are listed, 40 to a page, in the voucher register.

Required:
Describe the techniques for selecting a random sample of vouchers for review.

(AICPA Adapted)

9-4   Within the chapter, three alternative statistical sampling plans were introduced and illustrated for use when conducting tests of controls under the second standard of field work: attribute estimation, sequential sampling, and discovery sampling. Importantly, no one of the three statistical sampling plans is necessarily appropriate for all tests. Rather, each is appropriate for particular audit circumstances, and blindly applying a sampling plan to inappropriate populations can lead to audit inefficiencies and, in some cases, ineffectiveness.

Required:
1. Explain the circumstances under which attribute estimation, sequential sampling, and discovery sampling are appropriate.
2. Explain the circumstances under which an auditor might justifiably decide to switch to attribute estimation after sequential sampling has already begun.

9-5   Assume that your audit objective is to estimate a true but unknown population rate of deviation. The risk of overreliance is .05, maximum tolerable rate of deviation .07, and the expected population deviation rate of .0325.

Required:
1. Determine sample size.
2. What would be your statistical conclusion if 4 deviations are observed?
3. How would the sample results be interpreted in forming an audit conclusion?

9-6   Walter Cole, CPA, has decided to use statistical, rather than nonstatistical, sampling to test a client's control over purchase transactions. Specifically, Cole is testing whether vendor invoices are properly approved for payment as evidenced by the initials of authorized personnel on the face of the invoice. Cole estimates that a sample size of more than 80 could prove uneconomical, since he simply does not have sufficient time to examine more than 80 documents. In addition, Cole believes that the expected population rate of deviation lies between 2 and 5 percent, and his tolerable rate of deviation cannot exceed 8 percent.

Required:
1. Given the parameters established by Cole, indicate the combination of tolerable and expected population rates of deviation that will achieve a sample size of 80 or less.
2. Can Cole justifiably alter the tolerable rate of deviation for the express purpose of limiting sample size? Why, or why not?

9-7   Robin Hamilton, a first-year staff accountant, is reviewing the following selected audit procedures scheduled for use during the consideration of Windham Manufacturing Company's internal control structure.

Step	Tests of Controls
1.	Review evidence of internal control procedures for: a. Reconciliation of daily sales summaries with sales journal totals by General Accounting personnel. b. Periodic reconciliation of accounts receivable trial balances with general ledger control balances.
2.	Scan sales journal for unusual transactions or unusually large amounts and follow up on any such items identified.
3.	Examine shipping documents to determine whether the document: a. Is accompanied by a sales order bearing Credit and Inventory Control authorization. b. Agrees with sales order as to description of goods, quantity, and destination.
4.	Trace details of sales invoices to entries in the sales journal and accounts receivable subsidiary ledger.

Required:
1. Indicate which of the above procedures could be accomplished with statistical sampling. Assume attribute estimation is to be used.
2. Identify the sampling unit you would use for each test of controls accomplished with statistical sampling.

9-8   Assume you are considering controls over a client's purchasing activities, and estimate the following for acceptable risk of overreliance, tolerable rate of deviation, and expected population deviation rate:

Attribute	Risk of Overreliance	Tolerable Rate	Expected Rate
	Auditor judgment	*Auditor judgment*	*last year or pilot sample*
1. Voucher package (e.g., purchase requisition, purchase order, receiving report, and invoice) is canceled after payment is made.	.05	.07	.01
2. Purchase is properly authorized.	.05	.05	.015
3. Details on purchase requisition, purchase order, receiving report, and invoice agree.	.05	.06	.0125

4. Purchase order in voucher package agrees with copy filed in Purchasing Department.   .10   .07   .035
5. Canceled checks contain appropriate signatures and endorsements.   .05   .08   .02
6. Details on voucher package agree with canceled check (e.g., check number, date, payee, and amount).   .05   .08   .03

The sampling results for each attribute follow:

			Attribute			
	1	2	3	4	5	6
Number of Deviations	2	2	1	4	2	2

Required:

· 1. Using Figure 9-4 as a guide, prepare a work sheet documenting the attribute estimation sampling results above. Your worksheet should indicate required sample size determined (and sample size used, if different), estimated population deviation rate, and maximum population deviation rate.

2. State a statistical conclusion and an audit conclusion for each attribute.

9-9   From prior audits of Bristol Inc. and recent discussions with management, an auditor believes that sales invoices agree in detail with related shipping documents, with very few exceptions. Therefore, zero or very few deviations are expected, and sequential sampling is selected as the statistical sampling plan. The auditor defines each relevant line item on the sales invoice as a separate sampling unit. Following are the auditor's desired reliability and tolerable rates of deviation for each attribute:

Attribute	Desired Reliability	Tolerable Rate of Deviation
1. Customer name	.90	.04
2. Description	.90	.05
3. Quantity	.95	.06
4. Unit price	.95	.05
5. Extensions	.95	.05

No deviations were observed for attributes 1 and 2, and one deviation was observed for attributes 3, 4, and 5, though not on the same sales invoices.

Required:
1. Determine initial sample size for each attribute.
2. How can the sales invoices be selected if sample size varies from attribute to attribute.
3. For each attribute, indicate whether to "stop" or "go," and why.

9-10   Assume your audit plan requires observing at least one deviation at a specified critical rate of deviation, and the expected rate of occurrence is zero. Population size is 7,750, the critical rate of deviation .01, and the desired probability of observing one deviation 98 percent.

Required:
1. Determine sample size.
2. What would be your statistical conclusion if no deviations are observed?

9-11   Statistical sampling is not a panacea and is not necessarily appropriate for all tests of controls and nonstatistical sampling is often applied by practicing auditors, and for good reason.

Required:
1. Describe three conditions under which nonstatistical sampling would probably be *in*appropriate.
2. What sample selection techniques are available in nonstatistical sampling? Do they differ from those used in statistical sampling? Why?

9-12   You are now conducting your third annual audit of the financial statements of Elite Corporation for the year ended December 31, 1988. You decide to employ a statistical sampling plan, using random-number selection, in testing the effectiveness of the company's control procedures relating to sales invoices, which are all serially numbered. In prior years, after selecting one representative two-week period during the year, you tested all invoices issued during that period and resolved all of the deviations to your satisfaction.

Required:
1. Explain the statistical procedures you would use to determine the size of the sample of sales invoices to be examined.
2. Once the sample size has been determined, how would you select the individual invoices to be included in the sample? Explain.
3. Would the use of statistical sampling procedures improve the examination of sales invoices as compared with the selection procedure used in prior years? Discuss.
4. Assume that the company issued 50,000 sales invoices during the year and the auditor specified an acceptable risk of overreliance of 5 percent and a tolerable rate of 5 percent and a precision limit of .05. Does this mean that the auditor would be willing to conclude a control is effective if errors are found on no more than 4 sales invoices out of every 95 invoices examined (i.e., a sample deviation rate of .0421)? Discuss.

(AICPA Adapted)

AUDIT SAMPLING IN SUBSTANTIVE TESTS OF ACCOUNT BALANCES

10

Major topics discussed in this chapter are the:

▲ *Risks of incorrect rejection and incorrect acceptance in variables sampling.*

▲ *Components of a general variables sampling plan appropriate for substantive testing.*

▲ *Alternative audit sampling plans used in practice:*
   —Difference estimation
   —Ratio estimation
   —Mean-per-unit estimation
   —Probability-proportional-to-size (PPS) sampling
   —Nonstatistical sampling for variables

C hapter 9 introduced several attributes sampling plans applicable to an auditor's tests of controls — that is, plans used to test an entity's rate of deviation from prescribed internal control procedures. This chapter, in contrast, introduces variables sampling plans often used by auditors to accomplish substantive tests of details and therefore to test whether an entity's recorded account balances are fairly stated. The chapter begins by discussing audit risk in the context of substantive testing and by introducing a general plan for accomplishing variables sampling. In turn, two classical variables sampling plans — *ratio estimation* and *difference estimation* — are presented, and *mean-per-unit estimation,* a variables sampling plans with narrow applicability, is introduced. Next, *probability-proportional-to-size* (dollar-unit) sampling, an increasingly popular plan for sampling both attributes and variables, is explained and illustrated. Finally, *stratified sampling* is discussed, and a nonstatistical sampling plan is presented as an alternative to traditional variables and probability-proportional-to-size sampling. The discussion and illustrations throughout this chapter are consistent with SAS No. 39, "Audit Sampling" (AU Sec. 350); SAS No. 47, "Audit Risk and Materiality in Conducting an Audit" (AU Sec. 312); and the AICPA Audit and Accounting Guide, *Audit Sampling.*

AUDIT RISK IN SUBSTANTIVE TESTING

As explained in Chapter 9, audit risk — the risk that an auditor may unknowingly fail to modify his or her opinion on materially misstated financial statements — consists of two components: (1) the uncontrollable risk that material errors will occur in financial statements, and (2) the controllable risk that material errors will not be detected. In turn, the risk that material errors will occur and remain undetected is influenced by two categories of uncertainties: (1) sampling risk, the risk that a sample may contain disproportionately more or less monetary error than exists within the population, and (2) nonsampling risk, those aspects of audit risk not attributable to sampling, such as human error.

As illustrated in Figure 10-1, two additional aspects of audit risk are critical in substantive tests of account balances:

▲ Risk of incorrect rejection.
▲ Risk of incorrect acceptance.

FIGURE 10-1
Audit Risk in Substantive Testing

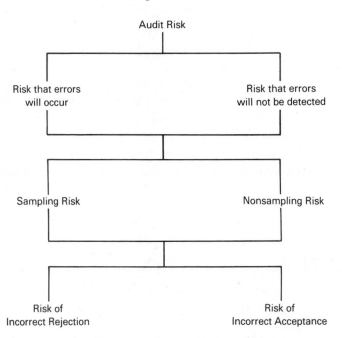

The *risk of incorrect rejection* is the risk that a sample supports the conclusion that a recorded account balance is materially misstated when, unknown to the auditor, the account is not materially misstated. Like the risk of underreliance on internal control structure in attributes sampling, the risk of incorrect rejection relates to the *efficiency* of an audit, because an initially erroneous conclusion that an account balance is misstated would ordinarily be revised when the auditor considers other evidence or performs additional audit procedures. For example, an auditor would ordinarily revise an initial conclusion that Cost of Goods Sold is misstated if a physical inventory observation and inventory price testing revealed that Inventory was not misstated, and other procedures revealed that Accounts Receivable and Sales were not misstated.

The *risk of incorrect acceptance,* in contrast, is the risk that a sample supports the conclusion that a recorded account balance is not materially misstated when, unknown to the auditor, the account is materially misstated. Like the risk of overreliance on internal control structure in attributes sampling, the risk of incorrect acceptance relates to audit *effectiveness,* and is particularly critical to an auditor, since incorrectly accepting a misstated account balance could result in financial statements that are materially misstated and therefore misleading.

When planning substantive tests, an auditor considers explicitly, and attempts to control, both the risk of incorrect rejection and the risk of incorrect acceptance. The following discussion presents a general variables sampling plan applicable to substantive testing and expands on the risks of incorrect rejection and acceptance.

SUBSTANTIVE TESTING: A VARIABLES SAMPLING PLAN

A variables sampling plan generally includes the steps outlined in Figure 10-2 and discussed in the following sections. Thereafter, four statistical sampling techniques are explained and illustrated: difference estimation, ratio estimation, mean-per-unit estimation, and probability-proportional-to-size (PPS) sampling.

Determine the Objectives of the Test

A sampling plan applied to substantive tests of details is designed either (1) to estimate an account balance that is not recorded within an entity's accounts, called dollar-value estimation, or (2) to test the reasonableness of a recorded account balance, called hypothesis testing.

Although a substantive test, *dollar-value estimation* is not actually an audit procedure, since its purpose is to "create" an account balance rather

FIGURE 10-2
Audit Sampling Plan: Substantive Tests

1. Determine the objectives of the test.
2. Define the population.
3. Choose an audit sampling technique.
4. Determine sample size.
5. Determine the method of sample selection.
6. Perform the sampling plan.
7. Evaluate the sample results.

Adapted from: *AICPA Audit and Accounting Guide,* "Audit Sampling" (New York: AICPA, 1983), pp. 41–42.

than to audit a recorded balance. For example, an auditor might be requested by management to convert a FIFO basis inventory to LIFO for purposes of external reporting. *Hypothesis testing,* however, is an audit procedure, since its purpose is to evaluate, not create, an account balance. For example, as part of a financial statement audit, an auditor might use sampling to test whether recorded accounts receivable are fairly stated at the balance sheet date. The sampling plan introduced in this chapter is used for hypothesis testing, not dollar-value estimation.

In general terms, an auditor's objectives in hypothesis testing are stated in the context of determining whether a recorded account balance is fairly stated. Once an objective is stated, the auditor must then identify the *characteristic of interest.* For example, if an auditor's objective is to determine whether an account is fairly stated, the characteristic might be defined as monetary error — that is, monetary differences between recorded and audited dollar amounts.

Define the Population

As explained in Chapter 9, an *audit population* consists of all the items constituting an account balance or class of transactions, and should be defined in the context of the auditor's characteristic of interest, since sample results can be generalized only to the population from which a sample is selected. For example, defining the population as all recorded payables would be inappropriate if an auditor's objective is to detect unrecorded liabilities, since the population would not include unrecorded accounts.

As in attributes sampling, the *sampling unit* is any of the individual elements constituting a population. For example, depending on the auditor's objective, a sampling unit in variables sampling might be a customer account balance, an individual transaction, or an individual entry within a transaction, among other things.

Choose an Audit Sampling Technique

Audit sampling is not used to accomplish all substantive tests of details, only those for which the auditor believes sampling is appropriate. For example, an auditor would not use sampling to accomplish the audit procedures of inquiry and observation, such as interviewing management and observing cash-handling procedures, or to accomplish analytical procedures, such as comparing current-period financial statement accounts with prior-period balances. However, when sampling is considered appropriate, auditors generally choose from among classical variables sampling techniques (e.g., difference, ratio, or mean-per-unit estimation), which use normal distribution theory to evaluate sample results; probability-proportional-to-size (PPS) sampling, which uses attributes sampling theory to evaluate results; and nonstatistical sampling. Thus, assuming variables sampling is appropriate in a given audit situation, an auditor first decides between statistical and nonstatistical sampling; if statistical sampling is chosen, the auditor then decides between classical variables sampling and probability-proportional-to-size sampling.

The choice between a statistical and a nonstatistical sampling plan is generally based on whether the auditor requires an estimate of sampling risk (which, as explained in Chapter 9, can only be accomplished with a statistical sampling plan) and the relative costs and effectiveness of each plan in the circumstances. In turn, the choice between classical variables sampling and probability-proportional-to-size sampling is based on the relative advantages and disadvantages (several of which are listed in Figure 10-3) of each plan in the circumstances.

Determine Sample Size

To determine sample size in a variables sampling plan, an auditor must generally consider:

▲ Variation within the population.
▲ Acceptable risk of incorrect rejection.
▲ Acceptable risk of incorrect acceptance.
▲ Tolerable error.

FIGURE 10-3

Relative Advantages and Disadvantages of Classical Variables
Sampling and Probability-Proportional-to-Size (PPS) Sampling

Classical Variables Sampling

Advantages:
- If there are many differences between recorded and audited amounts, classical
  variables sampling may result in a smaller sample size.
- Selection of zero or negative balances within a sample generally does not
  require special sample design considerations.
- If necessary, expanding classical variables samples may be easier than expanding probability-proportional-to-size samples.

Disadvantages:
- Classical variables sampling is more complex than probability-proportional-
  to-size sampling.
- To determine sample size, the auditor must have an estimate of the population
  standand deviation.
- Normal distribution theory, the basis underlying classical variables sampling,
  may not be appropriate when the sample size is not large and there are either
  very large items or very large differences between recorded and audited amounts
  in the population.

Probability-Proportional-to-Size (PPS) Sampling

Advantages:
- PPS sampling automatically results in a stratified sample, because items are
  selected in proportion to their dollar amounts.
- If no errors are expected, PPS sampling usually results in a smaller sample
  size than classical variables sampling.
- A PPS sample can be designed more easily and sample selection can begin
  before the complete population is available.

Disadvantages:
- If a PPS sample includes understatement errors, evaluation of the sample will
  require special design considerations.
- When errors are found, PPS evaluation may overstate the allowance for sampling risk.
- PPS sampling generally includes an assumption that the audited amount of a
  sampling unit should not be less than zero or greater than the recorded amount.

Adapted from: *AICPA Audit and Accounting Guide,* "Audit Sampling" (New York: AICPA,
    1983, pp. 68–70, 87–88.

Each of these elements is discussed in the sections that follow.

Variation within the Population. In general, the dollar amounts included within audit populations tend to vary significantly — that is, audit populations tend to include very few large-dollar-amount items, some moderately large items, and many small items. Because sample size varies in the same direction as the variation in population amounts — for example, as population variation increases, so does sample size — auditors require an estimate of the population variation.

In nonstatistical sampling, auditors subjectively consider population variation (e.g., ''high'' or ''low''), and in probability-proportional-to-size sampling, variation is considered indirectly. However, classical variables sampling requires an explicit estimate of population variation, which, in practice, is usually approximated by determining a *population standard deviation.* The standard deviation can be calculated by computer for an entire audit population or approximated manually from a *pilot sample,* an initial sample of 30 to 50 sampling units drawn from the population. Pilot sample items can be, and typically are, used as part of the audit sample. In some cases, auditors using classical variables sampling do not calculate a population standard deviation directly, but rely on the results of prior-year tests updated to reflect any changes in the current year that would affect population variation.

Acceptable Risk of Incorrect Rejection. As discussed in the chapter, the risk of incorrect rejection represents the risk of concluding that a recorded account balance is misstated when, in fact, material monetary error does not exist. Two alternative and undesirable outcomes can occur when an auditor incorrectly rejects a fairly stated account balance. First, the auditor might propose an unnecessary audit adjustment, thereby materially misstating an otherwise fairly stated account. Second, and more likely, the auditor could increase sample size or perform other audit procedures — both of which require additional work and therefore additional audit cost — thereby generating additional evidence necessary to conclude that the account is *not* materially misstated.

Generally, the risk of incorrect rejection is of greater concern to the auditor than the risk of underreliance on internal control structure, because incorrectly rejecting an account balance could result in an incorrect audit adjustment which, when recorded, would render the account misstated. The risk of incorrect rejection is of greater concern also because incorrect rejection is likely to be more costly than underreliance on internal control. For example, if an auditor increases sample size, the results could reverse an initially erroneous conclusion to reject an account balance. However, additional testing is costly, particularly when the sole purpose is to gather additional evidence about a previously rejected balance. The risk of underreliance on a client's internal control structure, in contrast, is usually not quite as costly. Rather than perform additional procedures at the end of the engagement, an auditor could plan ahead to rely on other controls or modify planned substantive tests — that is, consider an alternative audit approach, an alternative strategy.

Acceptable Risk of Incorrect Acceptance. As discussed earlier, the risk of incorrect acceptance represents the auditor's risk of concluding that an account balance is not materially misstated when, in fact, material monetary error exists. One predominant and undesirable outcome typically occurs when an auditor incorrectly accepts an account balance: a materially misstated account is believed to be fairly stated and therefore is not adjusted, rendering the audited financial statements potentially misleading.

In determining the acceptable risk of incorrect acceptance, an auditor considers the level of audit risk (*UR*) he or she is willing to sustain and the level of assurance provided by internal control (*IC*) and by analytical procedures and other tests (*AR*). The general relationship among these three factors and the auditor's risk of incorrect acceptance (*TD*) can be stated in the following model (AU Sec. 350.47).

$$TD = \frac{UR}{IC \times AR}$$

where:

TD = the acceptable risk of incorrect acceptance for the substantive tests of details.

UR = audit risk: the acceptable risk that an auditor may unknowingly fail to modify his or her opinion on materially misstated financial statements.

IC = the risk that the internal control structure fails to detect material errors that occur.

AR = the risk that analytical procedures and other tests fail to detect material errors that occur and that are not detected by the internal control structure.

Acceptable audit risk (*UR*) is often, but not always, set at 5 percent or 10 percent by those auditors who choose to use the preceding model. *IC,* in contrast, the auditor's assessment of the effectiveness of the internal control structure, and *AR,* the auditor's assessment of the effectiveness of analytical procedures and other tests, might be guided as follows:

Effectiveness of Internal Control Structure, Analytical Procedures, and Other Tests	AR Risk
Very effective	10–40 percent
Moderately effective	30–70 percent
Marginal or ineffective	60–100 percent

To illustrate, assume that an auditor is willing to accept 5 percent audit risk (UR), and subjectively judges IC to be 25 percent and AR to be 70 percent. The acceptable risk of incorrect acceptance would be:

$$TD = \frac{.05}{.25 \times .70}$$
$$= .29$$

Although seemingly precise, note carefully that the preceding risk model is neither authoritative nor intended as a mathematical formula. Rather, the model is a useful insight into how the risk of incorrect acceptance relates to other aspects of an audit. In short, the model is a decision aid, but not a decision.

Tolerable Error. When planning a variables sampling plan, an auditor considers tolerable error for the population — that is, the maximum monetary error that may exist in an account balance without causing the financial statements to be materially misstated. Tolerable error is closely related to an auditor's planned level of materiality in that the combined tolerable error for an entire audit should not exceed the auditor's preliminary estimate of materiality for the complete set of financial statements taken as a whole.

Effect on Sample Size. Increasing or decreasing any one of the three sample size determination parameters — risk of incorrect rejection, risk of incorrect acceptance, and tolerable error — has the opposite effect on sample size; increasing any one decreases sample size, and vice versa. In some circumstances, other aspects of the audit may be affected as well. For example, when an auditor decides to accept a higher risk of incorrect rejection, required sample size declines. But by decreasing sample size, the auditor simultaneously increases the risk of incurring additional costs to investigate differences between the sample results and the recorded account balance.

Determine the Method of Sample Selection

The four sample selection methods discussed for attributes sampling in Chapter 9 — random-number sampling, systematic sampling, block sampling, and haphazard sampling — are equally applicable to variables sampling. As in attributes sampling, an auditor should attempt to achieve randomness — that is, to assure that each sampling unit in a population is given an equal chance of selection, thereby not biasing either the sample selection or the sample results. In general, random-number sampling and systematic sampling are likely to achieve randomness if applied properly, whereas both block and haphazard sampling require extreme care by the auditor to avoid bias.

Perform the Sampling Plan

After a sample is selected, an auditor applies audit procedures to each sampling unit selected. However, in some instances, selected sampling units may be missing or lack supporting documentation, thereby creating uncertainty about whether the related transactions are recorded properly.

The treatment of missing or unsupported sampling units depends on how the related transactions would affect the auditor's overall evaluation of the sample. In general, if the auditor believed the overall sample evaluation would not change, even if the related transactions were misstated, he or she would not seek alternative evidence. However, if the auditor believed otherwise — i.e., that misstated sampling units would cause the account balance to be misstated — alternative procedures should be performed.

Evaluate the Sample Results

Upon completing audit procedures for the sampling units, an auditor summarizes and evaluates the results by:

▲ Projecting the sample error to the population.
▲ Considering sampling risk.
▲ Considering qualitative information.
▲ Reaching an overall conclusion.

Each aspect of the auditor's evaluation is discussed below.

Project Sample Error and Consider Sampling Risk. In a properly designed and executed sampling plan, an auditor draws conclusions about an audit population from the results of examining randomly selected samples; the intent is to reach defendable conclusions about a population without testing the entire population. As a result, auditors use the sample results to project detected monetary error to the population — that is, "generalize" the sample results to the population from which the sample was selected. However the projected error may not be a fair representation of true monetary error within the population. As a result, the auditor must also consider sampling risk, the risk that the auditor's conclusion about a population might be different if the entire population were examined.

All variables sampling techniques evaluate projected error and sampling risk, although the method of evaluation varies from one technique to another. Later in the chapter, the evaluation process is discussed for each specific sampling technique.

Consider Qualitative Information and Reach an Overall Conclusion. In variables sampling, an auditor considers not only the amount of misstatements, but also the qualitative characteristics of the misstatements, such as their nature and cause and the possible relationship of the misstatements to other phases of the audit. For example, in considering the nature and cause of misstatements, the auditor should consider whether the misstatements resulted from intentional acts (irregularities), which would require special procedures (see Chapter 3), or from carelessness and misunderstanding.

To reach an overall conclusion from a sampling plan, an auditor considers both quantitative and qualitative information. In some instances, however, the sample results may suggest that the auditor's assumptions in planning the variables sampling application were inappropriate, thereby requiring additional action. For example, if the frequency of misstatements observed in substantive testing exceeded the number expected given the presumed effectiveness of the internal control structure, the auditor should reconsider control risk and also judge whether to modify the substantive testing of related accounts.

The following sections of this chapter discuss and illustrate four commonly used variables sampling techniques:

▲ Difference estimation.
▲ Ratio estimation.
▲ Mean-per-unit estimation.
▲ Probability-proportional-to-size (PPS) sampling.

The discussion and illustrations apply the steps introduced in the general sampling plan outlined in Figure 10-2, page 390.

DIFFERENCE AND RATIO ESTIMATION

Difference estimation and ratio estimation are two similar classical variables sampling techniques that may be appropriate when the audit objective is to estimate a population's true but unknown monetary balance. Some general considerations in applying difference and ratio estimation are discussed below.

Conditions for Using Difference and Ratio Estimation

Three conditions must exist before either difference or ratio estimation can be applied:

▲ Each population item must have a recorded book value.
▲ Total population book value must be known and must correspond to the sum of all individual population items.
▲ Expected differences between audited and recorded book values must not be too rare.

The first and second conditions are related, and result because recorded book values are required in order to calculate either differences or ratios between audited and recorded book values.

The third condition — differences must not be too rare — results because sample size would be too large otherwise. If differences are rare, a relatively large number of sampling units would be required in order to observe representative population differences. Ordinarily, about thirty sample differences are sufficient to assure a reasonable estimate of the true but unknown population monetary balance.

Choosing between Difference and Ratio Estimation

When the three necessary conditions exist, an auditor may choose either difference or ratio estimation. However, one method may be more efficient than the other, depending upon the relationship between differences and recorded book values. In general, ratio estimation is more appropriate when the differences are nearly proportional to book values — that is, when the absolute amounts of the differences tend to increase as book values increase. Difference estimation, on the other hand, is more appropriate when there is little or no relationship between the absolute amounts of the differences and the book values. When differences are somewhat proportional but there is no strong tendency toward either proportionality or nonproportionality, ratio and difference estimation will yield similar results.

The Focus of Each Technique

Difference estimation focuses on the monetary difference between a sampling unit's audited and recorded book values. In contrast, ratio estimation focuses on the ratio between a sampling unit's audited and book values. Except for their focus on differences and ratios respectively, difference and ratio estimation sampling plans are identical in approach.

The application of either technique involves the steps outlined in the general variables sampling plan in Figure 10-2, page 390. The statistical aspects of the sampling plan — determining sample size, selecting the sample, and evaluating the results — are discussed in the following sections. Difference estimation is considered first, followed by ratio estimation.

DIFFERENCE ESTIMATION

In difference estimation, the strategy is to estimate the amount of monetary misstatement in the population — called the "difference estimate" — from misstatement observed in the sample, and then to calculate an "estimated audited value" for the population by netting the difference estimate with the recorded account balance. To determine a difference estimate, the auditor sums all sample differences between recorded and audited values to yield a net sample difference, divides the net sample difference by sample size, and then multiplies the result by population size. The difference estimate is then added to the recorded account balance if there is a net understatement (or subtracted if there is a net overstatement) to yield the estimated audited value. In turn, the auditor estimates an allowance for sampling risk.

The following example illustrates difference estimation, focusing on how an auditor defines the population (and sampling unit), determines sample size, chooses the method of sample selection, and evaluates the sample results.

Define the Population

In this illustration, assume that an auditor is applying difference estimation to the Dundee Corporation's trade accounts payable. Each payable has a recorded book value, the sum of all recorded payables agrees with the general ledger balance, and differences between audited and recorded book values are not rare. Thus, the necessary conditions for applying either difference or ratio estimation are met. The auditor has selected difference rather than ratio estimation because past experience indicates that differences are not proportional to recorded book value, and therefore that there is no discernible relationship between the absolute amounts of differences and the recorded book values.

The audit population consists of 4,100 individual payable accounts, each one of which represents a sampling unit. Recorded book value for all payables is $3,350,000.

Determine Sample Size

As discussed previously in the chapter, sample size requires estimates of:

▲ Variation within the population: the estimated population standard deviation.
▲ Acceptable risk of incorrect rejection.
▲ Acceptable risk of incorrect acceptance.
▲ Tolerable error.

In difference estimation, each can be determined as follows.

Estimated Population Standard Deviation. A pilot sample can be used to estimate a population standard deviation from the following formula:

$$S = \sqrt{\frac{\sum_{i=1}^{n} d_i^2 - n(\bar{d})^2}{n-1}}$$

where:
S = estimated population standard deviation.
d_i = difference between audited value (a_i) and book value (b_i) of the
      ith item.

n = sample size.
$\bar{d}$ = average difference between audited and book value for all pilot
sample items.

In this case, assume that the sum of all squared differences in the pilot sample, Σd_i^2, is \$765,000; the pilot sample size, n, is 50; and the average difference in the pilot sample, $\bar{d}$, is \$10. From these facts, the estimated population standard deviation would be:

$$S = \sqrt{\frac{\$765,000 - 50(10)^2}{49}}$$
$$= \$125 \text{ (rounded)}$$

Risk and Tolerable Error. Sample size calculations also require that the auditor specify the acceptable risk of incorrect rejection, the acceptable risk of incorrect acceptance, and tolerable error. Once these parameters have been established, the auditor then calculates the *desired allowance for sampling risk* (sometimes called "desired precision"), which is the auditor's allowance for the risk that the sample selected may contain disproportionately more or less monetary misstatement than exists within the population as a whole. The formula to calculate the allowance for sampling risk follows:

$$A = R \times TE$$

where:
A = desired allowance for sampling risk.
R = ratio of desired allowance for sampling risk to tolerable error.
TE = tolerable error.

The ratio of desired allowance for sampling risk to tolerable error (R) is determined from Table 10-1, page 402. For example, assume the auditor specifies the following parameters for the Dundee case:

▲ Acceptable risk of incorrect rejection   = .10
▲ Acceptable risk of incorrect acceptance = .05
▲ Tolerable error   = \$170,000

From Table 10-1, the ratio of desired allowance for sampling risk to tolerable error is .500, the intersect of the column associated with a 10 percent risk of incorrect rejection and the row associated with a 5 percent risk of incorrect acceptance. Desired allowance for sampling risk is then calculated as follows:

$$A = .500 \times \$170,000$$
$$= \$85,000$$

TABLE 10-1
Ratio of Desired Allowance for Sampling Risk to Tolerable Error

Risk of Incorrect Acceptance	Risk of Incorrect Rejection			
	.20	.10	.05	.01
.01	.355	.413	.457	.525
.025	.395	.456	.500	.568
.05	.437	.500	.543	.609
.075	.471	.532	.576	.641
.10	.500	.561	.605	.668
.15	.511	.612	.653	.712
.20	.603	.661	.700	.753
.25	.653	.708	.742	.791
.30	.707	.756	.787	.829
.35	.766	.808	.834	.868
.40	.831	.863	.883	.908
.45	.907	.926	.937	.952
.50	1.000	1.000	1.000	1.000

Source: *AICPA Audit and Accounting Guide,* "Audit Sampling," p. 115. Copyright © 1983 by the American Institute of Certified Public Accountants, Inc. Reprinted with permission.

Sample Size Calculation. Audit sample size can be determined by the following formula designed to generate the minimum number of observations required given population size and estimated variability, the acceptable risk of incorrect rejection, and the desired allowance for sampling risk:

$$n' = \left(\frac{S \times U \times N}{A}\right)^2$$

and

$$n = \frac{n'}{1 + \dfrac{n'}{N}}$$

where:
S = estimated population standard deviation.
U = acceptable risk of incorrect rejection.
N = population size.
A = desired allowance for sampling risk.
n' = uncorrected sample size.
n = sample size.

U, the standard normal deviate for the desired risk of incorrect rejection, is determined from Table 10-2 (below), a table of commonly used risk levels. In this case, the risk of incorrect rejection is .10, and from Table 10-2, the standard normal deviate is 1.65. Note that the risk levels in Table 10-2 vary from .01 to .30, the typical range of risk levels accepted by most practicing auditors.

The expression

$$1 + \frac{n'}{N}$$

is called a *finite population correction factor*, and is required when sampling without replacement, which is the typical case in auditing, since once a sampling unit is selected for examination, it is not returned to the population for possible reselection. A finite population correction factor is less important when n is less than 5 percent of population size, because the amount of correction is trivial, although it may still be used.

Based on the information given for the Dundee Corporation, sample size would be:

$$n' = \left(\frac{\$125 \times 1.65 \times 4,100}{\$85,000}\right)^2 = 99 \text{ rounded}$$

Since the uncorrected sample size (99) is less than 5 percent of population size (4,100), the finite population correction factor is not used. Thus, $n = 99$.

TABLE 10-2
Standard Normal Deviate for Selected Risks
of Incorrect Rejection

Risk of Incorrect Rejection	U Standard Normal Deviate
.01	2.58
.05	1.96
.10	1.65
.15	1.44
.20	1.28
.25	1.15
.30	1.04

Determine the Method of Sample Selection

As noted in Chapter 9, in a statistical sampling plan, sampling units must be selected at random. Otherwise, sampling risk cannot be measured, and the sampling plan would be nonstatistical. For this reason, random-number sampling and systematic sampling are commonly used in difference estimation.

Perform the Sampling Plan and Evaluate the Sample Results

Continuing the illustration, the auditor examines documentation supporting each of the 95 sampled payable accounts. An audited value is determined for each account, differences between audited and recorded book values are documented, and the following summary calculations are made:

$\hat{D}$ = the total projected monetary difference between the population value
and the recorded account balance.
$\hat{X}$ = the estimated population value.
A' = the achieved allowance for sampling risk.

In difference estimation, the total projected monetary difference between the population value and the recorded account balance ($\hat{D}$) is calculated as follows:

$$\hat{D} = N\bar{d}$$

where:

N = population size.
$\bar{d}$ = average difference, calculated by dividing the sum
of the differences by sample size.

To illustrate the evaluation of sample results for a difference estimation sampling plan, partial sample data for the Dundee Corporation are presented in Figure 10-4. Book and audited values are shown for the first through the tenth sample items and for the 99th item, with totals presented for all sample items. As shown in Figure 10-4, total book value for the 99 accounts examined was $74,416, and total audited value for these accounts was $76,000, a net understatement difference of $1,584.

The average difference ($\bar{d}$) is $16 ($1,584 ÷ 99), and the population size (N) is 4,100. Thus, the total projected monetary difference is:

$$\hat{D} = 4,100 \times \$16$$
$$= \$65,600$$

FIGURE 10-4
Dundee Corporation: Sample Data—Trade Accounts Payable

Sample Item (i)	Book Value (b_i)	Audited Value (a_i)	Difference $(d_i = a_i - b_i)$
1	$ 1,550	$ 1,550	$ 0
2	1,700	1,740	40
3	930	930	0
4	520	907	387
5	841	841	0
6	1,335	1,225	− 110
7	655	655	0
8	185	185	0
9	420	420	0
10	310	320	10
99	489	312	− 177
	$74,416	$76,000	$ − 1,584

The estimated population value $(\hat{X})$, sometimes referred to as the "point estimate," is calculated by adding the total projected difference $(\hat{D})$ to the recorded account balance (B):

$$\hat{X} = \hat{D} + B$$
$$= \$65,600 + \$3,350,000$$
$$= \$3,415,600$$

In order to determine the achieved allowance for sampling risk (A'), the auditor must first calculate the sample standard deviation from the formula used earlier to calculate the pilot sample standard deviation. Assume that for the 99 sampling units examined, the sample standard deviation was $120. The achieved allowance for sampling risk is calculated as follows:

$$A' = \frac{S \times U \times N}{\sqrt{n}} \sqrt{1 - \frac{n}{N}}$$

$$= \frac{\$120 \times 1.65 \times 4,100}{\sqrt{99}} \sqrt{1 - \frac{99}{4,100}}$$

$$= \$80,772 \text{ (rounded)}$$

A *precision interval*, determined from the estimated population value and achieved allowance for sampling risk, is calculated as follows:

$$\text{Precision Interval} = \hat{X} \pm A'$$
$$= \$3,415,600 \pm \$80,772$$
$$= \$3,334,828 \text{ to } \$3,496,372$$

From the sample results, the auditor would conclude that:

> Based on procedures applied, the estimated population value is $3,415,600, and there is a 95 percent probability (1 − risk of incorrect acceptance) that the true but unknown population value is included in the precision interval, $3,334,828 to $3,496,372. Conversely, there is a 5 percent risk that the true but unknown population value falls outside the precision interval.

In this case, the sample results support the conclusion that trade accounts payable for the Dundee Corporation are not materially misstated, since the precision interval ($3,334,828 to $3,496,372) includes the recorded account balance ($3,350,000), as illustrated below, and the desired allowance for sampling risk ($102,850) exceeds the achieved allowance ($80,772). Therefore, the auditor would accept the recorded account balance. However, what if the recorded account balance fell outside the precision interval and/or the achieved allowance for sampling risk exceeded the desired allowance for sampling risk? These conditions are discussed in the Appendix to this chapter.

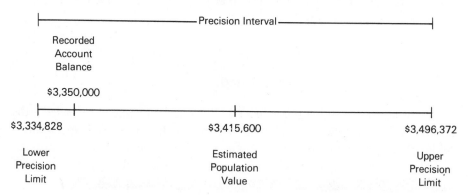

RATIO ESTIMATION

In ratio estimation, the strategy is to estimate the ratio between the population value and the recorded account balance — called the "ratio estimate" — from the ratio calculated for the sample, and then to calculate the

estimated population value by multiplying the ratio estimate times the recorded account balance. To determine a ratio estimate, the auditor divides
the sum of all audited values for the sample items by the sum of all recorded
values for the sample. The ratio is then multiplied by the recorded account
balance, yielding an estimated audited value, and the achieved allowance for
sampling risk is calculated.

Sample size is determined using exactly the same formula as in difference estimation, although the estimated population standard deviation, one of
the variables in the sample size formula, is computed somewhat differently.
Once the sampling units are selected and examined, an estimated audited
value $(\hat{X})$ is calculated by multiplying the ratio between audited and recorded
values in the sample $(\hat{R})$ times the recorded account balance (B). For example, using the data in Figure 10-4, the total audited value of the sampling
units in the Dundee Corporation accounts payable test is $76,000 and the
total recorded (book) value is $74,416. The ratio estimate would thus be 102
percent ($76,000 \div $74,416), and the estimated population value would be:

$$\hat{X} = \hat{R} \times B$$
$$= 1.02 \times \$3,350,000$$
$$= \$3,417,000$$

The auditor would next calculate the achieved allowance for sampling
risk from the same formula used in difference estimation, except that the
estimated population standard deviation, one of the variables in the sampling
risk formula, is calculated differently. The standard deviation formula is quite
cumbersome and, as a result, is usually calculated in practice with the aid of
a computer. Once the estimated audited value and achieved allowance for
sampling risk are calculated, a precision interval is determined and the results
evaluated as they are in difference estimation. If the recorded account balance
falls outside the precision interval and/or the achieved allowance for sampling
risk exceeds the desired allowance for sampling risk, the auditor evaluates
the sample results using the approach illustrated in the Appendix to this chapter.

MEAN-PER-UNIT ESTIMATION

Mean-per-unit (MPU) estimation (sometimes called "simple extension")
is similar to difference estimation, but is often less efficient than either difference or ratio estimation, both of which can usually achieve the same results with a smaller sample size. In general, MPU estimation is used only if
the necessary conditions for difference and ratio estimation are not present,

and particularly when (1) recorded amounts are not available for individual sampling units or (2) there are few expected differences between audited and recorded values.

In MPU estimation, the strategy is to estimate the average audited value for each population item from the average in the sample, and then to calculate "estimated audited value" for the account by multiplying the average audited value times population size. In turn, the auditor calculates an achieved allowance for sampling risk. The following illustrates MPU estimation, focusing on how an auditor defines the population (and sampling unit), determines sample size, chooses the method of sample selection, and evaluates the sample results.

Define the Population

In this illustration, assume an auditor is applying statistical sampling to the Dundee Corporation's inventory. Dundee does not maintain perpetual inventory records. Thus, there are no recorded amounts for individual sampling units in the population, and MPU estimation is chosen as the sampling technique. The audit population consists of 2,500 inventory items, each of which represents a sampling unit, and recorded book value is $850,000.

Determine Sample Size

As indicated in the variables sampling plan introduced earlier in the chapter, sample size calculations require estimates of variation in the population (estimated population standard deviation), acceptable risks of incorrect rejection and incorrect acceptance, and tolerable error.

The population standard deviation can be estimated from a pilot sample using a formula similar to the standard deviation formula for difference estimation, except that it focuses on the audited value of each sampling unit rather than the difference between audited and recorded values. The auditor draws a randomly selected pilot sample, examines each sampling unit, and calculates the estimated population standard deviation. In this case, assume the estimated population standard deviation is $185.

As in difference and ratio estimation, the auditor calculates a desired allowance for sampling risk after first specifying the acceptable risk of incorrect rejection, the acceptable risk of incorrect acceptance, and tolerable error. For example, assume the following:

> Acceptable risk of incorrect rejection   = .10
> Acceptable risk of incorrect acceptance = .05
> Tolerable error   = $150,000

From Table 10-1, page 402, the ratio of desired sampling risk to tolerable error is .500, and the desired allowance for sampling risk is:

$$A = R \times TE$$
$$= .500 \times \$150,000$$
$$= \$75,000$$

Once the population standard deviation is estimated and the allowance for sampling risk is determined, sample size can be calculated from the formula below, which assumes sampling without replacement, thereby accounting for the finite population correction factor.

$$n' = \left(\frac{S \times U \times N}{A} \right)^2$$

and

$$n = \frac{n'}{1 + \dfrac{n'}{N}}$$

where:
S = estimated population standard deviation.
U = acceptable risk of incorrect rejection.
N = population size.
A = desired allowance for sampling risk.
n' = uncorrected sample size.
n = sample size.

U, the standard normal deviate for the desired risk of incorrect rejection, is determined from Table 10-2, page 403. In this case, the risk of incorrect rejection is .10, and from Table 10-2, the standard normal deviate is 1.65. Thus, for the audit of Dundee Corporation's inventory, sample size would be:

$$n' = \left(\frac{\$185 \times 1.65 \times 2,500}{\$75,000} \right)^2$$
$$= 104 \text{ (rounded)}$$

Since the uncorrected sample size is less than 5 percent of population size, the finite population correction factor is not necessary. However, assume the auditor chooses to use the correction factor nevertheless.

$$n = \frac{104}{1 + \dfrac{104}{2,500}}$$
$$= 100 \text{ (rounded)}$$

Determine the Method of Sample Selection

As in other statistical sampling techniques, sampling units for MPU estimation must be selected at random, and random-number sampling and systematic sampling are used most often. After the sampling units are examined and audited amounts determined for each sampling unit, the results are evaluated and conclusions reached.

Evaluate the Sample Results

Evaluating results in MPU estimation requires calculations of:

$\hat{X}$, the estimated total audited value.
A', the achieved allowance for sampling risk.

The estimated total audited value $(\hat{X})$ is calculated by multiplying the average audited value for all sampling units $(\bar{x})$ times population size (N). In the inventory illustration for the Dundee Corporation, population size was 2,500. Assume that the total audited value for all 100 sampling units was \$32,500, and therefore that the average audited value is \$325 (\$32,500 ÷ 100). Thus, the estimated total audited value is:

$$\hat{X} = N\bar{x}$$
$$= 2,500 \times \$325$$
$$= \$812,500$$

Assuming the sample standard deviation is \$159, the achieved allowance for sampling risk is calculated from the following formula, which is the same as the formula used previously for difference estimation.

$$A' = \frac{S \times U \times N}{\sqrt{n}} \sqrt{1 - \frac{n}{N}}$$

$$= \frac{\$159 \times 1.65 \times 2,500}{\sqrt{100}} \sqrt{1 - \frac{100}{2,500}}$$

$$= \$64,262$$

Finally, the precision interval, determined from the estimated total audited value and the achieved allowance for sampling risk, is:

$$\text{Precision Interval} = \hat{X} \pm A'$$
$$= \$812,500 \pm \$64,262$$
$$= \$748,238 \text{ to } \$876,762$$

From these results, the auditor would conclude as follows:

> Based on procedures applied, the estimated population value is $812,500, and there is a 95 percent probability (1 − risk of incorrect acceptance) that the true but unknown population value is included in the precision interval, $748,238 to $876,762. Conversely, there is a 5% risk that the true but unknown population value falls outside the precision interval.

In this case, the sample results support the conclusion that inventory for the Dundee Corporation is not materially misstated, since the precision interval ($748,238 to $876,762) includes the recorded account balance ($850,000), and the desired allowance for sampling risk ($75,000) exceeds the achieved allowance ($64,262). The Appendix to this chapter discusses the auditor's course of action if the recorded account balance falls outside the precision interval and/or the achieved allowance for sampling risk exceeds the desired allowance.

PROBABILITY-PROPORTIONAL-TO-SIZE SAMPLING

Difference, ratio, and MPU estimation use classical variables sampling theory to compile and express sampling results in dollars. In contrast, probability-proportional-to-size (PPS)[1] sampling also expresses results in dollars but, like the sampling techniques introduced in Chapter 9, is derived from attributes sampling theory. Although appropriate when one or a few population errors are expected, PPS sampling is best applied when no errors are expected. When a larger number of errors is expected, required sample size may be much higher for PPS sampling than for difference, ratio, or MPU estimation.

In PPS sampling, the strategy is to randomly select individual dollars from a population and then to audit the balances, transactions, or documents — called *logical units* — that include the individual dollars selected. Each dollar in the population has an equal chance of being selected, but the likelihood of selecting any one logical unit for testing is directly proportional to its size, thereby accounting for the name "probability-proportional-to-size." For example, if the Dundee Corporation's trade accounts receivable balance is $1,750,000, then the population size is 1,750,000 and an individual customer account with a balance of $87,500 has a 5 percent ($87,500 ÷ $750,000) chance of being selected for testing. For this reason, PPS sampling has two unique properties. First PPS sampling automatically stratifies audit popula-

---

[1] Variations of PPS sampling include *dollar-unit sampling, cumulative monetary amount sampling,* and *combined attributes variables sampling.*

tions by monetary value, since larger-dollar-value balances or transactions have a higher probability of being selected. Second, because larger-dollar-value accounts have a higher probability of being selected, overstatements are more likely to be detected than understatements. As a result, PPS sampling is most appropriate when an auditor desires testing for material overstatements, since understated accounts have less chance of being selected for testing.

The following discussion illustrates PPS sampling, focusing on how an auditor defines the population, determines sample size, chooses the method of sample selection, and evaluates the sample results.

Define the Population

In PPS sampling, the population represents the class of transactions or account balance that an auditor intends to test, and may vary depending on the circumstances. For example, in testing trade accounts receivable, the audit population could consist of debit balances only or all customer balances, including debit balances, credit balances, and zero balances.

Negative balances in a population, such as credit balances in accounts receivable, usually require special consideration because they may contain properties not present in positive balances. For example, credit balances in accounts receivable may indicate overpayments or progress payments on revolving accounts. In practice, negative balances are often excluded from the sample selection process and are tested separately. In addition, zero balances may be treated separately, since they have no chance of being selected otherwise.

In this illustration, assume that an auditor's objective is to determine whether the trade accounts receivable of the Dundee Corporation are materially overstated. The population is defined as all customer accounts with debit balances, and the recorded book value of these accounts is $1,750,000.

Determine Sample Size

Sample size calculations in PPS sampling require that an auditor determine:

▲ A reliability factor for overstatement errors.
▲ Tolerable error.
▲ Anticipated error and an expansion factor.

Each is discussed below.

Reliability Factor for Overstatement Errors. The reliability factor for overstatement errors can be determined from tables after first specifying the expected number of overstatement errors and the risk of incorrect acceptance. In PPS sampling, the risk of incorrect acceptance is specifically incorporated into the sampling plan through the reliability factor for overstatement errors. However, the risk of incorrect rejection is not incorporated explicitly.

Since PPS sampling is most appropriate when no errors are expected, "zero" is the appropriate estimate for the *expected number of overstatement errors* (even when errors are expected). As was the case in variables sampling, the *risk of incorrect acceptance* is a matter of professional judgment and, in PPS sampling, represents an auditor's risk that book value is not materially overstated when, in fact, material monetary overstatement exists.

Table 10-3 can be used to determine a reliability factor at various risks of incorrect acceptance and for various numbers of overstatement errors. The reliability factor appears where the identified column and row intersect. For example, if the auditor's risk of incorrect acceptance is 15 percent for the Dundee Corporation's trade accounts receivable balance, the reliability factor

TABLE 10-3
PPS Sampling: Reliability Factors for Overstatement Errors

Number of Over-statement Errors	Risk of Incorrect Acceptance								
	1%	5%	10%	15%	20%	25%	30%	37%	50%
0	4.61	3.00	2.31	1.90	1.61	1.39	1.21	1.00	.70
1	6.64	4.75	3.89	3.38	3.00	2.70	2.44	2.14	1.68
2	8.41	6.30	5.33	4.72	4.28	3.93	3.62	3.25	2.68
3	10.05	7.76	6.69	6.02	5.52	5.11	4.77	4.34	3.68
4	11.61	9.16	8.00	7.27	6.73	6.28	5.90	5.43	4.68
5	13.11	10.52	9.28	8.50	7.91	7.43	7.01	6.49	5.68
6	14.57	11.85	10.54	9.71	9.08	8.56	8.12	7.56	6.67
7	16.00	13.15	11.78	10.90	10.24	9.69	9.21	8.63	7.67
8	17.41	14.44	13.00	12.08	11.38	10.81	10.31	9.68	8.67
9	18.79	15.71	14.21	13.25	12.52	11.92	11.39	10.74	9.67
10	20.15	16.97	15.41	14.42	13.66	13.02	12.47	11.79	10.67
11	21.49	18.21	16.60	15.57	14.78	14.13	13.55	12.84	11.67
12	22.83	19.45	17.79	16.72	15.90	15.22	14.63	13.89	12.67
13	24.14	20.67	18.96	17.86	17.02	16.32	15.70	14.93	13.67
14	25.45	21.89	20.13	19.00	18.13	17.40	16.77	15.97	14.67
15	26.75	23.10	21.30	20.13	19.24	18.49	17.84	17.02	15.67
16	28.03	24.31	22.46	21.26	20.34	19.58	18.90	18.06	16.67
17	29.31	25.50	23.61	22.39	21.44	20.66	19.97	19.10	17.67
18	30.59	26.70	24.76	23.51	22.54	21.74	21.03	20.14	18.67
19	31.85	27.88	25.91	24.63	23.64	22.81	22.09	21.18	19.67
20	33.11	29.07	27.05	25.74	24.73	23.89	23.15	22.22	20.67

Source: *AICPA Audit and Accounting Guide,* "Audit Sampling," p. 117. Copyright © 1983 by the American Institute of Certified Public Accountants, Inc. Reprinted with permission.

would be 1.90, the intersection of the column associated with a .15 risk of incorrect acceptance and the row associated with zero expected overstatement errors.

Tolerable Error. As in classical variables sampling, tolerable error in PPS sampling is closely related to an auditor's planned level of materiality, and represents the maximum monetary error that may exist in an account balance without causing the financial statements to be materially misstated. In the trade accounts receivable illustration for the Dundee Corporation, assume the auditor judges tolerable error to be $43,750.

Anticipated Error and Expansion Factor. As noted earlier, PPS sampling is best applied when no errors are expected, since sample size may be too high otherwise. However, if some errors are expected, the dollar value of anticipated error is explicitly incorporated into the sample size formula. For the Dundee case, assume anticipated error is $9,000, determined from the auditor's prior experience with the client.

An expansion factor is based on the auditor's risk of incorrect acceptance and is determined from Table 10-4. For the Dundee illustration, the risk of incorrect acceptance is 15 percent, and the expansion factor from Table 10-4 is 1.4. The expansion factor is multiplied by anticipated error, and the result is subtracted from the denominator in the sample size formula below, thereby serving to increase sample size. If no errors are anticipated in the sample, anticipated error and the expansion factor are not used.

Sample Size Calculation. Sample size for a PPS sampling plan can be calculated from the following formula:

$$n = \frac{RF \times B}{TE - (AE \times EF)}$$

where:

RF = reliability factor for overstatement errors.
B = recorded book value.
TE = tolerable error.
AE = anticipated error.
EF = expansion factor.

To illustrate, sample size in the accounts receivable application for the Dundee Corporation would be:

$$n = \frac{1.90 \times \$1,750,000}{\$43,750 - (\$9,000 \times 1.4)}$$
$$= 107 \text{ (rounded)}$$

TABLE 10-4
PPS Sampling: Expansion Factors for Expected Errors

				Risk of Incorrect Acceptance				
1%	5%	10%	15%	20%	25%	30%	37%	50%
Factor 1.9	1.6	1.5	1.4	1.3	1.25	1.2	1.15	1.0

Source: *AICPA Audit and Accounting Guide*, "Audit Sampling," p. 118. Copyright © 1983
   by the American Institute of Certified Public Accountants, Inc. Reprinted with permission.

Determine the Method of Sample Selection

In PPS sampling, logical units — the documents, transactions, or accounts selected for testing — may be selected using random-number sampling or systematic sampling. Assume that the auditor in the Dundee Corporation example has elected to use systematic sampling.

To facilitate sample selection, all population items are arrayed, and a cumulative listing of logical units is formed. Logical units are then selected from the cumulative listing. For example, in the Dundee accounts receivable illustration, sample size is 107 and population size is 1,750,000. As a result, the *sampling interval* is 16,355 (1,750,000/107), and, following a randomly selected start, every 16,355th dollar from the cumulative balance would be selected and the related customer account tested. Assuming a random start at the 5,000th cumulative dollar, the following customer accounts would be selected:

Customer No.	Book Value	Cumulative Dollars	Dollar Selected
1001	$ 6,500	1–6,500	5,000
1002	18,945	6,501–25,445	21,355
1003	2,210	25,446–27,655	
1004	12,500	27,656–40,155	37,710
1005	3,200	40,156–43,355	
.	.	.	.
.	.	.	.
.	.	.	.
	$1,750,000		

In the illustration, customer number 1001 would be selected for testing because 5,000, the random start, falls within the cumulative dollars 1 and 6,500; customer 1002 is selected because 21,355 (5,000 + 16,355, the sampling interval) falls within the cumulative dollars 6,501 and 25,445; and customer 1004 is selected because 37,710 [5,000 + (16,355 × 2)] falls within the cumulative balance 27,656 and 40,155. The selection process would continue until all logical units, in this case customer accounts, have been identified.

Evaluate the Sample

To evaluate the results of a PPS sample, an auditor estimates the *upper error limit,* which is the sum of the projected risk in the sample and the allowance for sampling risk. However, the procedure for evaluating results depends on whether overstatement errors are found in the sample.

No Errors in the Sample. If no errors are found in the sample, then the projected population error is zero, and the allowance for sampling risk is no more than tolerable error. As a result, when no errors are found in the sample, the upper error limit is less than or equal to tolerable error. The auditor can therefore conclude that the recorded book value in the population is not overstated by more than tolerable error at the specified risk of incorrect acceptance. For example, if no errors are found in the trade accounts receivable illustration for the Dundee Corporation, then the auditor could conclude that the recorded book value of the population, $1,750,000, is not overstated by more than $43,750 (tolerable error) with a 15 percent risk of incorrect acceptance.

Errors Found in the Sample. If overstatement errors are found, the auditor calculates the projected population error and the allowance for sampling risk, and sums the two to arrive at an estimate of the upper error limit. Understatement errors, in contrast, require special consideration, in part because PPS sampling is designed primarily for overstatements.[2]

The *projected population error* is calculated differently depending on whether logical units containing errors — for example, customer balances in the Dundee illustration — are recorded at (1) amounts less than the sampling interval or (2) greater than or equal to the sampling interval. The calculation is done separately for each logical unit containing error. For each logical unit recorded at less than the sampling interval, the error in the logical unit is

---

[2]Further discussion of understatement errors appears in *AICPA Audit and Accounting Guide,* "Audit Sampling," p. 77; Ernst & Whinney, *Audit Sampling,* pp. 43–44; Roberts, *Statistical Auditing,* p. 125.

projected to the population in the same proportion that the overstatement percentage — called a *tainting percentage* — bears to the sampling interval. For each logical unit recorded at an amount greater than or equal to the sampling interval, the projected error equals the overstatement error found. To illustrate, assume that overstatement errors are found in three customer receivable balances, the logical unit in the Dundee Corporation illustration. The projected error is calculated as follows:

	(a)	(b)	(c)	(d)	(e)	(f)
				Tainting		Projected
Error	Book	Audited	Difference	Percentage	Sampling	Error
Number	Value	Value	(a) − (b)	(c) ÷ (a)	Interval	(d) × (e)
Logical units recorded at less than sampling interval:						
1	$12,000	$ 9,000	$3,000	.25	$16,355	$4,089
2	10,000	9,500	500	.05	16,355	818
						$4,907
Logical unit greater than or equal to sampling interval:						
3	29,000	25,500	3,500	—	—	3,500
	$51,000	$44,000	$7,000			$8,407

The *allowance for sampling risk* requires calculation of two separate components: basic precision and an incremental allowance for sampling risk. *Basic precision* is determined by multiplying the sampling interval by the reliability factor is Table 10-3, page 413, associated with the auditor's risk of incorrect acceptance for zero errors. For example, for the Dundee illustration, basic precision is:

Sampling interval	$16,355
RF, reliability factor for	
.15 risk of incorrect acceptance	× 1.90
Basic precision	$31,075 (rounded)

The *incremental allowance* is determined from the projected error for each logical unit recorded at less than the sampling interval — for example, error numbers 1 and 2 in the Dundee illustration. An incremental allowance is not required for logical units recorded at amounts above or equal to the sampling interval, since they are always included in the sample and therefore do not contribute to sampling risk.

One approach to calculating the incremental allowance is to (1) rank the logical units containing errors in order of tainting percentage, (2) multiply the projected error for each logical unit by the incremental change in reliability factor at a specified risk of incorrect acceptance, and (3) subtract the projected error for the logical units recorded at less than the sampling interval from the summed result. This approach is illustrated for the Dundee Corporation accounts receivable example as follows:

Error No.	Projected Error	No. of Errors	Incremental Change in Reliability Factor		Projected Error × Increment
			Reliability Factor	Increment	
		0	1.90		
1	$4,089	1	3.38	1.48	$6,052
2	818	2	4.72	1.34	1,096
	$4,907				$7,148
			Projected error		(4,907)
			Incremental allowance		$2,241

handwritten annotations: "table 413" near Factor; "1.90−3.38" and "3.38 4.72" near Increment column

Thus, in the Dundee illustration, the allowance for sampling risk is:

Basic precision	$31,075
Incremental allowance	2,241
Allowance for sampling risk	$33,316

From these results, the auditor could conclude that there is a 15 percent risk (i.e., the risk of incorrect acceptance) that the recorded book value, $1,750,000, is overstated by $33,316 or more. If the upper error limit is less than tolerable error, the results support the conclusion that the recorded book value in the population is not overstated by more than tolerable error at the specified risk of incorrect acceptance. For example, in the Dundee case, the upper error limit, $33,316, is less than tolerable error, $43,750, and the auditor can therefore conclude that recorded book value, $1,750,000, is not overstated by more than $43,750 with a 15 percent risk of incorrect acceptance.

However, if the upper error limit exceeds tolerable error, recorded book value may be overstated. If this occurs, an auditor could (1) examine additional logical units from the population, (2) perform additional substantive tests directed toward the same audit objective, and, following these two steps, (3) have the client correct the errors found, reduce the upper error limit accordingly, and compare the revised upper error limit with tolerable error.

STRATIFIED SAMPLING

In any audit sampling plan, sample size is closely tied to the variability of population items — as the population variability increases, so will sample size. In an effort to control sample size without sacrificing reliability, an auditor can *stratify* a highly variable audit population into segments or strata, thereby minimizing variability within strata and eliminating variability between strata. As a result, total sample size for all strata combined will be less, since total variability will decrease.

Audit populations can be stratified on the basis of several different criteria, including the following for trade accounts receivable.

Criteria	Strata
Monetary values	• Accounts over $20,000 • Accounts between $10,000 and $20,000 • Accounts under $10,000
Time	• Accounts outstanding more than 90 days • Accounts outstanding from 60 to 90 days • Accounts outstanding from 30 to 59 days • Accounts outstanding less than 30 days

The emphasis in this chapter has been on understanding the nature of variables sampling applications in auditing. As a result, except for PPS sampling — an automatic stratification technique — the statistical plans discussed in the chapter have focused on unstratified rather than stratified sampling. Stratified sampling is based on the same logic as unstratified sampling, though the calculations are somewhat more involved and normally are not used in practice without the aid of a computer.

NONSTATISTICAL SAMPLING IN SUBSTANTIVE TESTS OF DETAILS

As noted in *Statement on Auditing Standards No. 39,* "Audit Sampling" (AU Sec. 350), there are two general approaches to audit sampling, statistical and nonstatistical, and either approach can provide sufficient evidential matter when applied properly. In short, a properly designed nonstatistical sampling plan can be just as effective as a properly designed statistical sampling plan, although, as discussed in Chapter 9, there is one critical difference: statistical plans provide a quantitative measure of sampling risk, and nonstatistical plans do not. Generally, auditors select a nonstatistical sampling plan when:

▲ There is no apparent need to quantify sampling risk.
▲ The cost of designing individual samples to meet statistical sampling requirements exceeds the benefits.
▲ The cost to randomly select sampling units exceeds the benefits.

Following is an example of a nonstatistical sampling plan. The discussion focuses on how an auditor might determine sample size and evaluate the sample results. Note carefully that the discussion addresses only one *example* of a nonstatistical sampling plan; others are also applied in practice.

Determine Sample Size

In a nonstatistical sampling plan, an auditor must first determine the following:

▲ The degree of audit assurance desired.
▲ An appropriate assurance factor.
▲ Estimated tolerable error.

Each of these considerations is explained below.

The Degree of Audit Assurance Desired. The degree of audit assurance desired is assessed judgmentally based on the auditor's assessment of the effectiveness of internal control structure (i.e., control risk) and on other procedures. For example, the degree of audit assurance could be assessed as follows:

Degree of Audit Assurance	Effectiveness of Internal Control Structure and Other Procedures
Substantial	Little or none
Moderate	Some
Little	Considerable

In general, the degree of audit assurance is determined after the auditor obtains an understanding of the internal control structure.

From the desired degree of audit assurance, the auditor next chooses a numerical factor based on the frequency and amount of errors expected in the population. For example, the assurance factor could be chosen as follows:

	Assurance Factor	
Audit Assurance Desired	Little Error Expected	Some Error Expected
Substantial	6	12
Moderate	4	8
Little	2	2

The numerical assurance factors listed above are illustrative only.

Estimate Tolerable Error and Key-Dollar Items. As in statistical sampling, *tolerable error* is the auditor's assessment of the maximum monetary error that may exist without causing the financial statements to be materially misstated. *Key-dollar items,* in contrast, are the items an auditor plans to test 100 percent. For example, assuming tolerable error of $8,000, the key-dollar items would at a minimum include all population items of $8,000 or more, since a misstatement item of $8,000 (or more) would alone consume the auditor's tolerable error for the entire account balance. As a result, the key-dollar items would be at least $8,000, and probably less.

Once an appropriate assurance factor is chosen and tolerable error and key-dollar items are estimated, preliminary sample size could be calculated as follows:

$$n = \left(\frac{B - KD}{TE}\right) \times AF$$

where:
B = recorded account balance.
KD = sum of key-dollar items.
TE = tolerable error.
AF = assurance factor.

To illustrate, assume the recorded account balance is $150,000, twelve key-dollar items sum to $70,000, tolerable error is $8,000, and the auditor desires moderate assurance and expects little error (i.e., assurance factor=4). From these data, preliminary sample size would be 52, represented by 12 key-dollar items and 40 sampling units calculated from the above formula:

$$n = \frac{\$150,000 - \$70,000}{\$8,000} \times 4$$
$$= 40$$

Alternatively, the auditor could use tables rather than a formula to determine sample size.

Unlike statistical sample sizes, preliminary nonstatistical sample sizes do not represent the minimum number of items necessary to achieve an auditor's acceptable risks of incorrect rejection and incorrect acceptance. Rather, the above nonstatistical sample size is preliminary and may be lowered judgmentally, for example, if the auditor decides to increase reliance on other substantive tests or expects smaller and less frequent errors, and may be raised judgmentally otherwise.

As in nonstatistical sampling for attributes (Chapter 9), an auditor can select the 40 sampling units with random-number sampling or systematic sampling, or select judgmentally with block or haphazard sampling.

Evaluate the Sample Results

An auditor completes the nonstatistical sampling plan by determining *known error*, the misstatement observed within the sampling units tested, and projecting *likely error*, the auditor's estimate of total population misstatement. An example follows.

For the preceding illustrative data above, assume that for the 12 key-dollar items, 2 overstatement errors are observed totaling $6,000, and for the 40 sampling units, 5 overstatement errors are observed totaling $1,000. Thus, known error is $7,000. Assume population size is 500 items.

Likely error can be estimated by adding the $6,000 overstatement error for the key-dollar items to the error projected for the 40 sampling units:

Key-dollar error	=$ 6,000
Sampling units:	
$\dfrac{\$1,000}{\left(\dfrac{40}{(500-12)}\right)}$	= 12,195
Total projected error	$18,195

In the above calculation, projected error for the 40 sampling units is estimated by dividing known error, $1,000, by the ratio of the number of sampling units to population size less the number of key-dollar items. In this case, likely error is $18,195, and the auditor has three alternative courses of action: (1) propose an audit adjustment, (2) perform additional substantive tests, or (3) request that the client revalue the entire population.

SUMMARY

Variables sampling plans focus upon population monetary balances rather than rates of deviation, the focus of attributes sampling plans. Difference and ratio estimation, two long-established statistical sampling plans for variables, can be applied when each population item has a recorded value, total recorded value is known and corresponds to the sum of all population items, and differences between audited and recorded values are not too rare. When the preconditions underlying difference and ratio estimation are not present, an auditor can apply mean-per-unit estimation.

Probability-proportional-to-size (PPS) sampling applies concepts from attributes sampling to reach conclusions about dollar amounts. The name "probability-proportional-to-size" derives from the fact that each sampling unit's likelihood of being selected for testing is directly proportional to its size. For this reason, PPS sampling automatically stratifies an audit population.

As an alternative to classical variables sampling and PPS sampling, an auditor could choose a nonstatistical sampling plan, and probably would if there was no apparent need to quantify sampling risk or if the cost of designing and selecting statistical samples exceeded the benefits of quantifying sampling risk.

APPENDIX
ADJUSTING RECORDED ACCOUNT BALANCES IN CLASSICAL VARIABLES SAMPLING

In the chapter illustrations of difference and mean-per-unit estimation, recorded account balances were accepted as fairly stated because (1) the precision interval included the recorded account balance and (2) the desired allowance for sampling risk exceeded the achieved allowance for sampling risk. But what if these conditions were not met? Each situation is discussed below.

Recorded Account Balance Falls outside Precision Interval

A recorded account balance falling outside the precision interval could still be accepted as fairly stated if tolerable error exceeds the difference between (1) the recorded account balance and (2) the furthest end of the preci-

FIGURE 10-5
Recorded Account Balance Falls Outside Precision Interval

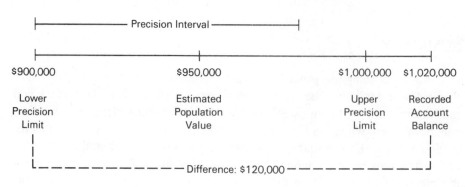

sion interval. For example, assume that the recorded account balance is $1,020,000, tolerable error is $125,000, estimated population value is $950,000, and the achieved allowance for sampling risk is $50,000, yielding a precision interval from $900,000 to $1,000,000, as illustrated in Figure 10-5.

From Figure 10-5 the difference between the recorded account balance ($1,020,000) and the furthest end of the precision interval (in this case, the lower precision limit, $900,000) is $120,000, which is less than the auditor's tolerable error ($125,000). As a result, the recorded account balance is accepted as fairly stated, since tolerable error exceeds the maximum likely error in the population. Incidentally, this situation typically occurs when the auditor's tolerable error greatly exceeds the achieved allowance for sampling risk, as in the illustration (i.e., tolerable error = $125,000; achieved allowance for sampling risk = $50,000).

In contrast, if tolerable error does not exceed the maximum likely error, an auditor could (1) increase sample size and reevaluate for all sampling units, (2) request that the client revalue the population, or (3) propose an audit adjustment, as illustrated below.

Achieved Allowance for Sampling Risk Exceeds Desired Allowance

If the achieved allowance for sampling risk (A') exceeds the desired allowance for sampling risk (A), the risk of incorrect acceptance becomes greater, because the precision interval, $\hat{X} \pm A'$, is larger than $\hat{X} \pm A$. Thus, for the larger $\hat{X} \pm A'$, there is a greater probability of accepting a materially misstated account balance — i.e., the risk of incorrect acceptance. The alternatives available to the auditor are the same as those identified in the preceding illustration, i.e., increase sample size, request that the client revalue the population, or propose an audit adjustment.

Altering the facts from the previous illustration, assume tolerable error is $60,000, and the desired allowance for sampling risk is $40,000. In this case, the recorded account balance could not be accepted as fairly stated, absent additional substantive tests, because (1) the recorded account balance ($1,020,000) falls outside the precision interval ($900,000 to $1,000,000), (2) the achieved allowance for sampling risk ($50,000) exceeds the desired allowance for sampling risk ($40,000), and (3) tolerable error ($60,000) does not exceed the difference between the recorded account balance ($1,020,000) and the lower precision limit ($900,000). As a result, an audit adjustment could be proposed. The adjusted book value would be $960,000, the lower precision limit ($900,000) plus tolerable error ($60,000), and the proposed audit adjustment would be $60,000, computed by subtracting the adjusted book balance from the recorded balance.

REFERENCES

AICPA Audit and Accounting Guide, "Audit Sampling." New York: AICPA, 1983.

Barnett, A. H., and W. J. Reed. "Sampling in Small Business Audits." *Journal of Accountancy* (January, 1986), pp. 78–88.

Ernst & Whinney. *Audit Sampling.* Cleveland: Ernst & Whinney, 1979.

Goodfellow, J. L., J. K. Loebbecke, and J. Neter. "Some Perspectives on CAV Sampling Plans (Part I)." *CA Magazine* (October, 1974).

————. "Some Perspectives on CAV Sampling Plans (Part II)." *CA Magazine* (November, 1974).

Guy, D. M. and D. R. Carmichael. *Audit Sampling: An Introduction to Statistical Sampling in Auditing.* New York: John Wiley & Sons, 1986.

Leslie, D. A., A. D. Teitlebaum, and R. J. Anderson. *Dollar-Unit Sampling: A Practical Guide for Auditors.* Toronto, Ontario: Copp, Clark, Pitman, 1979.

Roberts, D. M. *Statistical Auditing.* New York: AICPA, 1978.

QUESTIONS

1. Identify and briefly describe the two aspects of audit risk that are critical in an auditor's substantive tests of account balances.
2. Explain the difference between *dollar value estimation* and *hypothesis testing* in audit sampling. Which of the two is more common in auditing?
3. Define what is meant by an *audit population.* What is the importance of an auditor's *characteristic of interest* when defining an audit population?
4. What is a *sampling unit?*
5. Identify the relative advantages and disadvantages of classical variables sampling.

6. Identify the relative advantages and disadvantages of probability-proportional-to-size sampling.
7. Define *tolerable error*.
8. Identify three conditions which must exist before either difference or ratio estimation can be applied.
9. Under what condition is difference estimation more appropriate than ratio estimation?
10. Assume an auditor sets acceptable risks of incorrect rejection and incorrect acceptance at .10 and .05, respectively, applies ratio estimation, and obtains the following results: estimated population value, $250,000; achieved allowance for sampling risk, $32,500. Draft the auditor's conclusion.
11. Briefly describe the auditor's strategy when applying mean-per-unit (MPU) estimation.
12. Difference and ratio estimation, mean-per-unit estimation, and probability-proportional-to-size (PPS) sampling all express sampling results in dollars. How, though, does PPS sampling differ from the other three sampling techniques?
13. Briefly describe the auditor's strategy when applying probability-proportional-to-size sampling.
14. Why is probability-proportional-to-size sampling most appropriate when an auditor desires testing for material overstatements?
15. What is the auditor's objective when using stratified sampling?
16. Under what conditions would an auditor choose a nonstatistical sampling plan in substantive tests of details?

MULTIPLE CHOICE QUESTIONS

1. Tolerable error is a measure of the maximum monetary error that may exist in an account balance without causing the financial statements to be materially misstated, and is directly related to:

   a. Reliability of evidence.
   b. Audit risk.
   c. Materiality.
   d. Cost benefit analysis.   (AICPA adapted)

2. In variables sampling, which of the following must an auditor consider in order to estimate the appropriate sample size required to meet the auditor's needs in a given situation?

   a. The total amount of the population.
   b. Risk.
   c. The estimated rate of error in the population.
   d. Sample size used in the prior year audit.   (AICPA adapted)

3. Ratio estimation is inappropriate when:

   a. The total population book value is known and corresponds to the sum of all population items.

b. There are some observed differences between audited and recorded book values.

c. The audited values are nearly proportional to the recorded values.

d. There are no recorded values for some items in the population.

(AICPA adapted)

4. If all other factors specified in a variables sampling plan remain constant, increasing the acceptable risk of incorrect acceptance would cause the required sample size to:

a. Decrease.

b. Remain the same.

c. Increase.

d. Become indeterminate.   (AICPA adapted)

5. An accounts receivable aging schedule was prepared on 300 pages with each page containing the aging data for 50 accounts. The pages were numbered from 1 to 300 and the accounts listed on each were numbered from 1 to 50.

Godla, an auditor, selected accounts receivable for confirmation using a table of numbers as illustrated:

Procedures Performed by Godla

Select Column from Table of Numbers	Separate 5 Digits: First 3 Digits Last 2 Digits	
02011	020 — 11	x
85393	853 — 93	*
97265	972 — 65	*
61680	616 — 80	*
16656	166 — 56	*
42751	427 — 51	*
69994	699 — 94	*
07942	079 — 42	y
10231	102 — 31	z
53988	539 — 88	*

x Mailed confirmation to account 11 listed on page 20
y Mailed confirmation to account 42 listed on page 79
z Mailed confirmation to account 31 listed on page 102
* Rejected

This is an example of which of the following sampling methods?

a. Block sampling.

b. Systematic sampling.

c. Haphazard sampling.

d. Random number sampling.   (AICPA adapted)

6. In which sampling method is the probability of selection of an item proportional to the size of the value of the item (i.e., a $1,000 item is 10 times more likely to be selected than a $100 item)?

    a. Difference estimation.
    b. Mean-per-unit estimation.
    c. Probability-proportional-to-size sampling.
    d. Nonstatistical sampling for variables.   (IIA adapted)

7. Sample selection using probability-proportional-to-size sampling for inventory will most likely result in selection of a sample with characteristics roughly equivalent to one provided by:

    a. Nonstatistical sampling plans.
    b. Variables sampling plans with substantial stratification by dollar amount.
    c. Unstratified difference or ratio estimation sampling.
    d. Selection of inventory using a random starting point for record selection.
                                           (IIA adapted)

8. When an auditor uses probability-proportional-to-size sampling to examine invoices, each invoice:

    a. Has an equal probability of being selected.
    b. Can be represented by no more than one dollar unit.
    c. Has an unknown probability of being selected.
    d. Has a probability proportional to its dollar value of being selected.
                                           (IIA adapted)

9. Which of the following would be an improper technique when using probability-proportional-to-size sampling?

    a. Combining negative and positive dollar error item amounts in the appraisal of the sample.
    b. Using a sample selection technique in which the same account balance could be selected more than once.
    c. Selecting a random starting point and then sampling every nth dollar unit.
    d. Defining the sampling unit in the population as an individual dollar and not as an individual account balance.   (IIA adapted)

10. Assume you are the auditor for a department store, and want to estimate the dollar amount of errors on sales invoices using probability-proportional-to-size sampling. Such a plan means that:

    a. The risk of incorrect acceptance is greater than for a mean-per-unit sampling plan.
    b. Stratification by size of account is essential.
    c. An invoice with a large balance has a greater chance of being selected than one with a smaller balance.
    d. The estimate will be unreliable if the error rate is small.   (IIA adapted)

PROBLEMS

10-1   Assume you are the newly assigned senior accountant on a continuing audit engagement for the Ranson Corporation, and are meeting with Tom Porter, partner in charge of the audit. Interim field work is already complete, but was accomplished under another senior accountant's supervision, before you were assigned to the engagement. You have fully reviewed the interim working papers, and are discussing planned year-end audit risk with Porter.

Porter observes that in prior years few material audit adjustments were proposed, and that, in his judgment, management has integrity and Ranson is economically stable. Interim fieldwork revealed no significant deficiencies in the internal control structure, except that control over recorded credit sales transactions was deficient in one respect: credit approval documentation was missing for several material sales to new customers. In addition, Porter reminds you that in the prior year, the most significant audit adjustment related to accounts receivable — an account which usually represents about 25 percent of reported total assets — although, the adjustment was prompted by an unusual fluctuation in receivables turnover and the number-of-days-sales-in-accounts-receivable, rather than substantive tests of details.

Required:
1. From the information available, determine an acceptable risk that monetary errors greater than tolerable error might remain undetected after the audit team has completed all audit procedures deemed necessary. Justify the risk level determined.
2. Determine a risk that, should errors greater than tolerable error occur, the internal control structure fails to detect them. Justify the risk level determined.
3. Determine a risk that analytical and other procedures fail to detect errors greater than tolerable error. Justify the risk level determined.
4. Determine an acceptable risk of incorrect acceptance for this engagement. How should the quantified risk of incorrect acceptance be interpreted?

10-2   The risks of incorrect rejection and incorrect acceptance are related, but involve two entirely different outcomes: incorrect rejection means the risk of concluding that recorded book value is materially misstated when material monetary error does not exist, and incorrect acceptance means the risk of concluding that recorded book value is not materially misstated when in fact material monetary error does exist. Importantly, all three classical variables sampling plans — ratio estimation, difference estimation, and mean-per-unit estimation — require estimates of the risks of incorrect rejection and incorrect acceptance, and probability-proportional-to-size sampling requires an estimate of the risk of incorrect acceptance.

Required:
1. Explain why the risks of incorrect rejection and incorrect acceptance are competing risks — that is, why for example does increasing the risk of incorrect acceptance necessarily decrease the risk of incorrect rejection?
2. How can an auditor systematically reduce both the risk of incorrect rejection and the risk of incorrect acceptance simultaneously?

10-3   When applying a classical variables sampling plan — ratio or difference estimation, and MPU estimation — an auditor must estimate the risk of incorrect rejection, the risk of incorrect acceptance, and tolerable error, each of which is determined separately, but integrated before calculating sample size.

Required:
1. How are the risks of incorrect rejection and incorrect acceptance and tolerable error integrated in variables sampling plans?

2. Determine a desired allowance for sampling risk assuming:

- acceptable risk of incorrect rejection   = .20
- acceptable risk of incorrect acceptance = .10
- tolerable error   = $40,000

10-4   Because there is no discernible relationship between the absolute amount of differences (i.e., audited value v. recorded book value) and recorded book value for 50 preliminary sample items, an auditor decides to use difference estimation in the audit of accounts receivable. The following data are known:

- Population size   = 2,500
- Estimated population standard deviation   = $20
- Acceptable risk of incorrect rejection   = .05
- Desired allowance for sampling risk   = $10,000

After sample size is calculated and the sampling units selected and examined, the following summary data are available:

- Total recorded value for all sampling units   = $65,220
- Total audited value for all sampling units   = $64,380
- Net difference (i.e., between recorded and audited amounts)
  for all sampling units   = $250
- Squared differences for all sampling units   = $215,000
- Estimated population standard deviation   = $48.53

Required:
Assume difference estimation is applied, and total recorded book value is $500,000, determine:
a. sample size
b. total projected monetary difference
c. estimated population value
d. achieved allowance for sampling risk.
e. precision interval.

10-5   The following information is available for 50 sample items:

	Sample Item	Book Value	Audited Value
Subtotals, nondifference items	—	$55,265	$55,265
Difference items	5	670	720
	11	1,265	1,165
	18	1,980	1,800
	24	895	1,030
	29	725	912
	34	230	215
	38	415	490
		$61,445	$61,597

Population size is 2,100 items, recorded book value $1,235,000, the risk of incorrect rejection is .10, the risk of incorrect acceptance is .05, and the sample standard deviation is $46.

Required:
Formulate a conclusion for the above data assuming difference estimation is used. Show all work supporting your conclusion.

10-6   Following are data for four different audit populations to which variables sampling will be applied:

	Population			
	1	2	3	4
• acceptable risk of incorrect rejection	.10	.05	.05	.01
• acceptable risk of incorrect acceptance	.20	.10	.25	.05
• population size	2,500	3,000	2,750	2,100
• estimated population standard deviation	$20	$12	$10	$15
• tolerable error	$8,750	$6,200	$7,000	$9,000

Required:
1. Calculate sample size for each population. Assume sampling without replacement.
2. Assuming the actual sample standard deviation is 10 percent less than estimated, determine a precision interval for each population.

10-7   Following are data for four different audit populations. Mean-per-unit estimation will be applied to each population.

	Population			
	1	2	3	4
• Allowable risk that monetary error greater than tolerable error might remain undetected after the auditor has completed all audit procedures deemed necessary.	.05	.10	.07	.05
• The risk that, should errors greater than tolerable error occur, the internal control structure fails to detect them.	.20	.30	1.00	.50

	Population			
	1	2	3	4
• The risk that analytical procedures and other tests fail to detect errors greater than tolerable error that occur and are not detected by the internal control structure.	.50	.80	.70	.70

Required:
1. Calculate an acceptable risk of incorrect acceptance for each population.
2. For populations 1 and 3, calculate a desired allowance for sampling risk, assuming tolerable error is $100,000 and the risk of incorrect rejection is .10.

10-8   Because a client does not maintain perpetual records, an auditor elects to use mean-per-unit estimation to determine whether ending inventory is fairly stated. The following data are available:

• Acceptable risk of incorrect rejection	.05
• Acceptable risk of incorrect acceptance	.20
• Estimated population standard deviation	$70
• Tolerable error	$25,000
• Population size	1,800

After sample size is determined and sampling units selected and examined, the auditor compiles the following results:

• Total audited value for all sampling units	$25,060
• Sample standard deviation	$67

Required:
1. From the information available, what is the auditor's desired allowance for sampling risk?
2. Calculate sample size.
3. Determine the estimated population value.
4. Calculate the achieved allowance for sampling risk.
5. Determine the precision interval.
6. State a conclusion.

10-9   An auditor expects no errors in a particular audit population, but is concerned about potential monetary overstatement, and therefore elects to use probability-proportional-to-size sampling. Recorded book value is $1,200,000, maximum tolerable overstatement is $67,500, and the risk of incorrect acceptance is preset at 15 percent.
     After sample size is determined, and sampling units selected and examined, the following differences are noted:

Invoice No.	Recorded Value	Audited Value
1826	$15,000	$12,000
2041	16,000	15,050

―

Required:
1. Calculate sample size.
2. Calculate the allowance for sampling risk
3. Reach a conclusion.

10-10   Assume your audit objective is to estimate the upper error limit for an audit population and, therefore, you select probability-proportional-to-size (PPS) sampling. From prior year working papers and evidence accumulated during the consideration of internal control structure, you concluded that errors are expected and that the risk of incorrect acceptance is .10.

The following information is also known:
- Recorded book value $1,000,000
- Maximum tolerable overstatement $100,000
- Anticipated error $15,000

After testing logical units, three differences are observed, as follows:

Recorded Value	Audited Value	Difference
$20,000	$18,000	$2,000
15,000	14,250	750
40,000	38,000 over 33,333	2,000

Required:
From this information, determine the following:
1. The reliability factor for overstatement errors.
2. The expansion factor.
3. Sample size.
4. The sampling interval.
5. Basic precision.
6. The incremental allowance.
7. The allowance for sampling risk (the upper error limit).
8. The audit conclusion.

10-11   An auditor has no apparent need to quantify sampling risk, and therefore uses a nonstatistical sampling plan for inventory price testing. From prior experience with the client and current information regarding internal control structure, the auditor expects some pricing errors, but also desires moderate assurance that pricing of physical goods is fairly accurate. The auditor presets tolerable error at $12,000 and decides to test the fifteen highest dollar items, totalling $50,000, which represents forty percent of total recorded book value.

After determining sample size, selecting and examining the sampling units, the auditor compiles the following results:

	Number of Errors	Total Error
Key-dollar items	3	$5,000 overstatement
Sampled items	5	$1,500 overstatement

Population size is 600.

Required:
1. Determine an appropriate assurance factor.
2. Determine sample size.
3. Calculate likely error from the results indicated above.
4. Is recorded book value acceptable to the auditor? Why, or why not?

10-12   An auditor is selecting from among alternative variables sampling plans for accounts receivable, and gathers the following information.
The client, a midwestern manufacturer of high-technology electrical components, had been audited previously by a cross-town public accounting firm. In five prior engagements, the predecessor auditors had issued unqualified opinions except for last year when they issued a qualified opinion because of departures from generally accepted accounting principles. The client maintains subsidiary records for each individual customer account, and supporting documents are filed within the Accounts Receivable department. A review of selected sections of the predessor auditor's working papers indicates that differences between recorded and audited values for individual customer accounts tended to increase as recorded book value increased.

Required:
1. Is nonstatistical sampling appropriate in this case? Explain.
2. Explain why each of the following statistical sampling plans may be appropriate or inappropriate in this case:
    a. Ratio estimation
    b. Difference estimation
    c. Mean-per-unit estimation
    d. Probability-proportional-to-size sampling

*10-13   When completing a variables sampling plan, an auditor's evaluation is based on the relationship between and among a number of factors, including: recorded account balance, estimated total population value, tolerable error, the desired allowance for sampling risk, and the achieved allowance for sampling risk. The following table contains data for the above factors.

	Case			
	1	2	3	4
Recorded account balance	$260,000	$255,000	$217,000	$238,000
Estimated population value	$235,000	$235,000	$223,000	$220,000
Tolerable error	$ 20,000	$ 37,500	$ 18,000	$ 32,000
Desired allowance for sampling risk	$ 12,000	$ 18,000	$ 10,000	$ 22,000
Achieved allowance for sampling risk	$ 15,000	$ 15,000	$ 12,000	$ 20,000

Required:
For each case, indicate whether the recorded account balance can be accepted as fairly stated, or not accepted, and why. If an account balance is not accepted as fairly stated, determine the proper adjusted book value.

---

*Relates to Appendix.

TESTS OF CONTROLS OF THE REVENUE/RECEIPT CYCLE: SALES AND CASH RECEIPTS TRANSACTIONS

11

Major topics discussed in this chapter are the:

▲ *Nature of the revenue/receipt cycle, including the flow of documents throughout a company's customer order, credit, inventory control, shipping, billing, recording, and cash collection functions.*

▲ *Auditor's consideration of internal control structure in the revenue/ receipt cycle.*

▲ *Integration of EDP, audit sampling, and tests of controls within the revenue/receipt cycle (Chapter Appendix).*

Distilling auditing concepts and standards and available audit technology into a viable, cost-effective audit plan is more an art than a science. The specific plan adopted by an auditor for any one engagement depends on a variety of considerations, including tolerable error, audit risk, and the client's specific business, industry, and accounting principles. This and the following seven chapters focus on tests of controls and substantive tests within the revenue/receipt, expenditure/disbursement, conversion, and financing cycles. Each chapter should be viewed as one in a series of interrelated segments in a financial statement audit.

This chapter begins by describing the nature of the revenue/receipt cycle and representative internal controls over an entity's customer order, credit, inventory control, shipping, billing, and recording functions. Next, an auditor's consideration of internal control structure within the revenue/receipt cycle is discussed. Finally, an appendix to the chapter contains a case study which integrates material introduced in Chapter 8 (electronic data processing), Chapter 9 (audit sampling), and this chapter.

NATURE OF THE REVENUE/RECEIPT CYCLE

In general, the revenue/receipt cycle encompasses the sale of goods or services to customers and the collection of cash. The revenue/receipt cycle is directly or indirectly related to each of the other three cycles: in general, it receives resources and information provided by the financing and conversion cycles, and provides resources and information to the expenditure/disbursement cycle. For example, the revenue/receipt cycle might receive cash from the proceeds of capital stock sold through the financing cycle; receive finished goods produced by the conversion cycle to sell to customers; and provide cash to pay for raw materials purchased through the expenditure/disbursement cycle.

Figure 11-1 summarizes the scope of the revenue/receipt cycle, listing the primary business functions and activities, journal entries, and forms. As depicted in this figure, two major business functions are associated with the revenue/receipt cycle:

▲ Resources (goods or services) are sold to customers in exchange for promises for future payments.
▲ Cash is collected from customers for resources sold to them.

A series of internal activities relate to these functions. The cycle begins when a customer order is received and a decision is made to grant or deny credit. If credit is granted, the ordered goods are shipped, the customer is billed, and the sale is recorded. Cash is collected subsequently from the customer in accordance with the terms of sale.

Throughout the revenue/receipt cycle, journal entries are made for sales, including discounts and returns and allowances, cash receipts, allowances for potentially uncollectible accounts, and writeoffs of specific accounts identi-

---

FIGURE 11-1
The Scope of the Revenue/Receipt Cycle

Business Functions	Common Activities	Common Entries	Common Forms
• Resources are sold to customers in exchange for promises for future payments • Cash is collected from customers for resources sold to them	• Customer orders (order entry) • Credit approval • Inventory control • Shipping • Billing • Recording • Cash collection (and deposits) • Sales returns	• Sales • Sales discounts • Sales returns and allowances • Cash receipts • Allowance for uncollectible accounts • Writeoff of specific uncollectible accounts	• Customer order • Sales order • Shipping document • Sales invoice • Customer remittance advice

fied as uncollectible. Common forms and documents affecting the revenue/receipt cycle include:

▲ *Customer order:* a written (or unwritten, in the case of telephone orders) request from a customer to purchase goods.

▲ *Sales order:* a document describing goods ordered by a customer, including all relevant information regarding price, quantity, payment terms, etc.

▲ *Shipping document:* a document containing information about goods shipped, and representing a contract between the seller and carrier (e.g., trucking company); a shipping document is often in the form of a *bill of lading,* a Uniform Commercial Code document used by common carriers.

▲ *Sales invoice:* a document containing information about goods sold and representing formal notice to a customer about the amount and terms of payment.

▲ *Customer remittance advice:* a document that accompanies a sales invoice and is intended to be returned with a customer's cash payment (remittance); a returned remittance advice indicates the purpose of a cash payment and facilitates its handling and recording.

Specific revenue/receipt cycle activities and controls vary from one business to another, and are influenced by several factors, including the nature of a company's business, its size and organizational structure, and the extent to which electronic data processing is used. However, the activities of most businesses that sell goods are similar to those identified in Figure 11-1; of course, the activities would be modified somewhat for service enterprises. A company's credit sales activities and controls are explained below in the context of the following functional areas or departments:

▲ Customer order
▲ Credit
▲ Inventory control
▲ Shipping
▲ Billing
▲ Recording (general accounting, inventory accounting, and accounts receivable)

Cash collection is discussed separately later.

Credit Sales

Figure 11-2 is a flowchart of representative credit sales activities and common documents. In turn, Figure 11-3 summarizes the credit sales activities flowcharted in Figure 11-2. The following discussion explains each major activity and related documents.

When a customer order is received by telephone or in writing, a sales order form is completed by an employee of the Customer Order Department. A *sales order* describes the goods ordered, including catalog or stock numbers, prices, and payment terms. Copies of sales orders are sent to customers and distributed to the appropriate departments — Credit, Shipping, and Billing, as indicated in Figure 11-2. One copy is retained in the Customer Order Department in an unfilled order file until notice is received from Shipping that goods have been shipped.

Prior to any credit sale, a sales order should be reviewed and approved by Credit Department personnel. Credit review and approval is necessary to minimize the likelihood of granting credit to high-risk customers. Copies of sales orders bearing credit approval are forwarded to Inventory Control, where the goods are released for shipment. Goods transferred from Inventory Control to Shipping should be accompanied by a copy of the sales order bearing the initials of an Inventory Control employee authorized to release goods from inventory.

Shipping personnel should compare goods for shipment with sales orders and prepare the necessary *shipping documents.* When goods are shipped, Shipping personnel should obtain a receipt from the carrier. Receipts are often in the form of a copy of the "bill of lading," which describes the goods shipped and represents a contract between the seller and carrier. Notice of shipment should be sent to Customer Order for updating of unfilled order files.

After shipment, a copy of the shipping documents and a copy of the sales order approved by Credit and Inventory Control should be sent to the Billing Department. Billing personnel compare shipping documents and sales orders and prepare sales invoices, which are mailed to customers and distributed to the appropriate accounting departments for recording. A *sales invoice* describes the goods sold, and the customer's copy represents formal notice to the customer of the amount due and terms of payment. Some companies prepare a remittance advice to accompany customer sales invoices. A *remittance advice* is intended to be returned with a customer's payment (remittance) and facilitates handling and recording of cash receipts.

Copies of sales invoices prepared by Billing personnel, as well as sales orders and shipping documents are sent to Inventory Accounting. Billing employees also prepare *daily sales summaries* which are sent to General Accounting. Inventory Accounting personnel determine the cost of goods described in a sales invoice and update inventory records accordingly. The cost information is also recorded on the sales invoice, which is then sent to Gen-

FIGURE 11-2
Revenue/Receipt Cycle: Credit sales

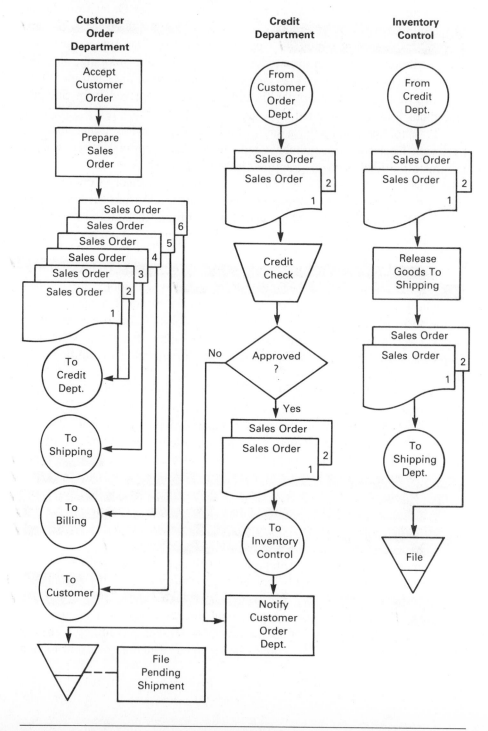

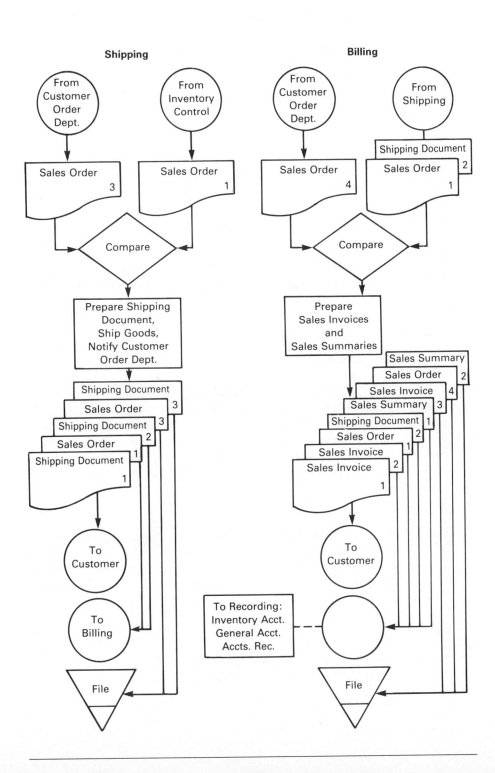

FIGURE 11-3
Summary of Credit Sales Activities

Customer Order Department:

• Accept customer order.
• Prepare sales order, distribute copies, and retain copy in unfilled order file.

Credit Department:

• Review sales order and investigate customer credit information.
• Initial copies of sales order if credit approved and forward to Inventory Control. If credit denied, notify Customer Order Department.

Inventory Control:

• Review sales order.
• Initial copies of sales order to authorize release of goods from warehouse.
• Forward goods and copy of sales order to Shipping, and retain file copy of sales order.

Shipping:

• Compare sales order from Inventory Control with sales order from Customer Order Department.
• Examine goods from warehouse and compare with sales orders.
• Prepare goods for shipment and complete shipping documents.
• Release goods to carrier and obtain receipt.
• Forward copy of sales order and shipping documents to Billing; retain file copy of sales order and shipping documents.
• Notify Customer Order Department that goods have been shipped.

Billing:

• Compare documents from shipping with sales order from Customer Order.
• Prepare sales invoice, send copy to customer and to Inventory Accounting, along with copy of sales order and shipping documents, and retain file copy.
• Prepare daily sales summary, send copy to General Accounting, and retain file copy.

Recording:

• Inventory Accounting: Enter cost information on sales invoice, update inventory records, and forward sales invoice and related documents to General Accounting.

- General Accounting: Record sale and forward sales invoice and related documents to Accounts Receivable.
- Accounts Receivable: Post sale to customer's account and file sales invoice and related documents.

---

eral Accounting where sales are recorded in the sales journal and posted to the general ledger. Daily totals of sales journal entries are compared with daily sales summaries prepared by Billing.

Finally, sales invoices are routed from General Accounting to Accounts Receivable, where sales are posted to individual accounts in the accounts receivable subsidiary ledger.

The various documents used throughout the revenue/receipt cycle are necessary for proper transaction authorization, execution, and recording. Importantly, these documents also provide an audit trail and are, therefore, a major source of audit evidence. The basic documents identified with the revenue/receipt cycle provide evidence that transactions are properly authorized, executed, and recorded. Note that a document is prepared by each execution function — sales orders by Customer Order, shipping documents by Shipping, and sales invoices by Billing. Authorization functions do not generate documents, but approve documents initiated elsewhere. Recording functions neither prepare nor approve documents, but transfer information from documents to accounting records.

All documents should be prenumbered consecutively, and any missing forms accounted for. Copies of documents should be distributed to appropriate functional areas. Multiple documentation provides important cross-checks which minimize possibilities for errors or irregularities.

Cash Collection

The revenue/receipt cycle for a particular transaction is completed when cash is collected for goods or services sold. Collection from customers and activities related to uncollected accounts are discussed in the following sections.

Cash Collection. As illustrated in Figure 11-4, incoming cash receipts (mailed remittances) should be listed immediately and checks should be endorsed restrictively (e.g., "for deposit to First National Bank account number _____") and deposited promptly. The list of incoming receipts (and returned remittance advices, if applicable) should be forwarded to Accounts Receivable for posting to individual customer accounts. Separate lists of totals should be forwarded to General Accounting for recording in the cash receipts journal and posting to the general ledger. The checks and a second list of receipts

FIGURE 11-4
Revenue/Receipt Cycle: Cash Collection on Credit Sales

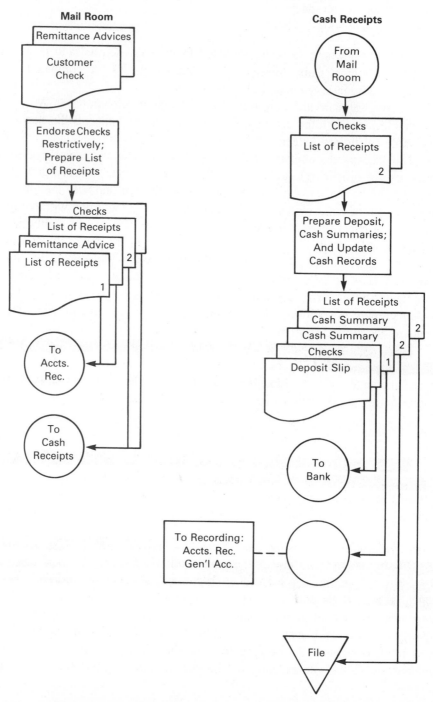

should be sent from the mailroom to Cash Receipts, where a bank deposit and cash summaries are prepared and cash records are updated.

Personnel involved in cash collection should be segregated from accounts receivable, general accounting, and billing. Combining cash collection with any of these functions provides opportunities to misappropriate cash.

Sales Returns and Allowances. Customer requests for adjustments for returned goods should be reviewed by personnel independent of cash collection and recording activities. For example, review of requests for adjustments may be handled by Customer Order personnel. An approved request is evidenced by a credit memorandum, copies of which are forwarded to Accounts Receivable for posting and to Inventory Control. Control totals should be forwarded to General Accounting for journalizing and posting. Returned goods should be handled through the Receiving Department, and returned to the warehouse along with a receiving report. Inventory Control personnel should match the receiving report with a copy of the credit memorandum. Credit memoranda should be prenumbered consecutively, and all missing forms accounted for.

Uncollected Accounts. Accounts Receivable should review individual customer accounts periodically as a check against authorized credit limits, and prepare monthly accounts receivable trial balances (i.e., summaries of unpaid balances) for reconciliation with general ledger control accounts. In addition, accounts receivable balances should be aged periodically and reviewed by personnel independent of the Credit Department.

Delinquent accounts should be reviewed periodically by personnel who report to the Treasurer and are independent of recording functions. When an individual customer account is determined to be uncollectible, written authorization to write off the account is sent to Accounts Receivable and General Accounting.

Internal Control Structure Objectives and Potential Errors or Irregularities

The following discussion focuses on internal control structure in the context of the revenue/receipt cycle. The discussion, summarized in Figure 11-5 (pages 446–450), identifies some specific control objectives, describes examples of potential errors or irregularities that may arise if an objective is not achieved, and provides examples of control procedures that are designed to prevent or detect the errors or irregularities. The specific objectives identified relate generally to transaction authorization, execution, and recording and access to assets.

FIGURE 11-5
Revenue/Receipt Cycle: Objectives, Potential Errors or Irregularities and Control Procedures

Objective	Types of Errors or Irregularities that Could Occur if Objective Is Not Met	Control Procedures Designed to Prevent or Detect Errors or Irregularities
Transaction Authorization		
◄ Customers' credit should be approved prior to shipping goods.	Shipments could be made to unauthorized parties, potentially resulting in uncollectible accounts receivable.	Perform a credit check for all new customers. Prepare and periodically update lists of authorized customers, indicating maximum credit limit for each customer.
◄ Unit prices and sales terms should be established for all products or services.	Orders could be accepted at unauthorized prices or unfavorable sales terms, potentially resulting in reduced revenues or inadequate cash flows.	Maintain updated lists of authorized prices and sales terms. Establish procedures for reviewing and approving prices and sales terms before sale.
	Unauthorized prices could be charged to customers, potentially resulting in violation of federal laws.	
◄ Sales-related deductions and adjustments should be made in accordance with management's authorization.	Unauthorized deductions or adjustments could be granted to underserving customers, potentially resulting in uncollectible receivables.	Establish written criteria and policies for granting sales deductions and adjustments. Prenumber and control credit memoranda.
	Otherwise collectible accounts receivable could be written off, potentially resulting in failure to realize the service potential of an asset.	

Execution

▲ Approved orders should be shipped in accordance with customer specifications and on a timely basis.	Shipments could be delivered to the wrong party, potentially resulting in uncollectible accounts receivable.	Verify that ordered products are in stock, and therefore can be shipped on a timely basis.
	Shipments could be delivered too late, potentially resulting in returned goods and canceled sales.	Limit access to shipping documents to authorized personnel.
	Incorrect shipments could be delivered, potentially resulting in returned goods and canceled sales.	Document policies and procedures for scheduling shipments.
▲ All shipments should be followed by prompt billing.	Shipments could go unbilled, potentially resulting in loss of revenue.	Prenumber bills of lading, and assure that related billings are made on a periodic (e.g., daily) basis.
	Shipments could be billed late, resulting in delayed cash payments from customers.	Establish procedures for prompt reporting and investigation of shipments not billed (and billings not shipped).
		Require prompt delivery of bills of lading (and related sales orders) to the Billing Department.

Recording

▲ Sales, cash receipts, and related transactions should be recorded at the	General ledger account balances may be inaccurate, potentially resulting in misstated financial statements.	Total input documents (e.g., number of documents, dollar amounts) and reconcile appropriate journals and ledgers.
		Establish processing and recording procedures.

FIGURE 11-5
Revenue/Receipt Cycle: Objectives, Potential Errors or Irregularities, and Control Procedures (*Continued*)

Objective	Types of Errors or Irregularities that Could Occur if Objective Is Not Met	Control Procedures Designed to Prevent or Detect Errors or Irregularities
Recording		
correct amounts and in the proper period, and should be properly classified.		Compare actual and planned (e.g., forecasted, budgeted) results, and analyze variances.
▲ Billings, collections, and related adjustment transactions (e.g., returns and allowances) should be posted accurately to individual customer accounts.	Summaries of detailed records may not agree with control accounts, potentially resulting in adjusting journal entries prompted by inaccurate information. Transactions may be posted to improper customer accounts, potentially resulting in improper billings.	Establish validation procedures to verify postings (e.g., check digits and key verification). Batch and reconcile input totals with processed and output totals. Reconcile total of individual customers accounts with control totals. Review customer statements for accuracy and follow up on discrepancies. Promptly investigate correspondence from customers.
▲ Recorded accounts receivable balances (and	Accounts may include errors or irregularities, potentially resulting in materially misstated financial statements.	Periodically substantiate and evaluate recorded account balances.

related transactions) should fairly reflect underlying transactions and events.

Management decisions may be based on erroneous data, potentially resulting in improper decisions.

Establish policy and procedures manuals, organization charts, and supporting documentation (e.g., compare selected customer balances with underlying documents).

Follow up promptly on customer complaints.

Reconcile subsidiary ledgers with general ledger control accounts.

Access to Assets

▲ Access to cash and cash-related records should be restricted to personnel authorized by management.

Cash receipts on credit sales could be lost or diverted, potentially resulting in overstated accounts receivable and unrecorded cash.

Cash receipts on noncredit sales could be unreported, potentially resulting in unrecorded cash.

Cash shortages could go undetected, potentially resulting in lost cash and overstated cash balances.

Establish the cash receipts function in a centralized location.

Require daily reconciliation of cash receipts records with bank deposit slips.

Prenumber and control cash remittance advices.

Prepare lists of cash receipts in the mail room.

Separate responsibility for handling and recording cash.

Establish periodic procedures for reconciling cash records with bank statements.

Establish physical barriers over cash and unused checks.

Maintain insurance and fidelity bonds for personnel handling cash.

FIGURE 11-5
Revenue/Receipt Cycle: Objectives, Potential Errors or Irregularities, and Control Procedures (*Continued*)

Objective	Types of Errors or Irregularities that Could Occur if Objective Is Not Met	Control Procedures Designed to Prevent or Detect Errors or Irregularities
Access to Assets		
▲ Access to shipping, billing, and inventory control, and accounting records should be restricted to personnel authorized by management.	Records or assets may be misused, potentially resulting in misappropriated assets.	Maintain listings — and signature samples — of authorized signatories.
		Inform the bank that no checks payable to the company are to be cashed (i.e., deposited only).
		Restrictively endorse checks received from customers.
		Segregate responsibilities for authorization, execution, and recording functions.
		Prenumber and control custody of forms and documents.

Transaction Authorization. Before accepting a customer's sales order, the customer's credit should be approved. Otherwise, shipments could be made to poor-credit-risk customers, potentially resulting in uncollectible receivables. Most companies perform a credit check for all new customers, and prepare (and periodically update) authorized-customer lists, indicating maximum credit limits for each customer.

In addition to authorizing credit limits, management should establish unit prices and sales terms that are consistent with the company's revenue objectives (prices) and cash flow needs (sales terms). Prices should also be set so that no customers are treated unfairly. Differential pricing could result in dissatisfaction among customers not offered favorable prices and could even lead to violations of federal antitrust laws. Management can remove the potential for differential pricing by maintaining updated price and sales-terms lists and by establishing procedures for reviewing and approving sales transactions before shipment.

Following shipment and delivery, customers may request allowances or adjustments for damaged, defective, or unwanted goods. All sales-related allowances and adjustments should be made only in accordance with policies and practices authorized by management, since unjustified allowances could result either in uncollectible receivables or in failure to realize the service potential of an asset. Management should establish written criteria and policies for sales-related deductions and adjustments, and forms, such as credit memoranda, should be numbered and controlled.

Transaction Execution. Once customer orders are approved, goods should be shipped on a timely basis and in accordance with the customer's specifications. Delayed or incorrect shipments would not only tie up resources (e.g., delay cash collection), but could result in returned goods, canceled orders, or uncollectible receivables. To encourage timely and accurate shipments, management should establish policies for scheduling prompt shipments and for verifying that ordered products are in stock.

Following shipment, customers should be billed promptly, thereby avoiding either losses arising from unbilled shipments or delayed cash collections. To avoid unbilled shipments, management should require prenumbered shipping documents periodically assuring that all sequentially numbered documents result in timely billing. Management should also establish procedures for the prompt investigation of unbilled shipments.

Recording. Because managerial decisions are made from recorded transactions, all sales, cash receipts, and related transactions should be recorded at the correct amounts, and in the proper period, and be classified properly within the accounts. Obviously, inaccurate recording can result in inaccurate account balances and misstated financial statements. Management can control the recording function by establishing written procedures, reconciling control totals (e.g., tracing the number of input documents to summarized output) and periodically comparing actual with budgeted results, if available.

Proper recording within general ledger control accounts, though, does not necessarily mean that billing, collection, and related adjustment transactions (e.g., returns and allowances) will be posted accurately to individual customer accounts. As a result, even if general ledger control accounts are accurate, summaries of detailed records may not agree to the control accounts, potentially resulting in improper billings or adjusting journal entries prompted by insufficient or inaccurate information. Several procedures are available to control inaccurate postings. These include promptly investigating customer complaints, implementing validation procedures to verify postings (e.g., check digits), and reconciling the total of individual customer account balances to control accounts.

Related to the accurate recording and posting of sales, billings, and receipts, management should also establish procedures to assure that recorded receivables balances fairly reflect underlying transactions and events. Otherwise, billings and management decisions may be based on improper data, or, equally compelling, recorded receivables may reflect material errors or irregularities. To control the recording of receivables, management could periodically substantiate and evaluate individual customer balances, and reconcile supporting detailed ledgers to the general ledger.

Access to Assets. Within the revenue/receipt cycle, management attempts to safeguard assets by restricting access to cash receipts and to cash-related records, thereby controlling against loss or diversion and, correspondingly, against understated cash balances. Access to assets is critical throughout a business organization, but particularly for cash since, unlike most types of inventory and plant assets, cash is liquid and therefore highly susceptible to theft or diversion. Normally, the cash receipts function is maintained in a centralized location that is off-limits to unauthorized personnel. As further controls over authorized personnel, however, management could establish procedures to prenumber and control remittance advices, prepare separate lists of incoming mail receipts, and periodically reconcile cash receipts records to deposit slips and bank statements.

Management should also limit access within shipping, billing, and inventory control, primarily to avoid the misappropriation of assets between or among related departments. For example, shipping personnel could be restricted from inventory control in order to minimize opportunities for unauthorized shipments. In many companies, however, access is not restricted, although employees are restricted from performing job functions outside of their own departments.

CONSIDERING INTERNAL CONTROL STRUCTURE

As explained in Chapter 7, an auditor's consideration of internal control structure involves obtaining an understanding of the structure, performing tests of controls, and assessing control risk. The following discussion focuses on an auditor's consideration of revenue/receipt cycle controls.

Obtain an Understanding

An auditor's objective in considering internal control structure is to obtain a knowledge and understanding of a client's prescribed policies and procedures sufficient to plan the audit. As discussed in Chapter 7, obtaining an understanding of the system includes: (1) performing a preliminary review, (2) documenting the system, (3) performing a transaction walk-through, and (4) determining whether existing control procedures are potentially reliable.

Preliminary Review. An auditor begins considering internal control structure by developing a general understanding of a client's control environment and the flow of credit sales and cash collection transactions. For example, an auditor could obtain an understanding by reviewing the client's procedures manuals and by interviewing employees in the Customer Order Department, Credit Department, Inventory Control, Shipping, Billing, and Cash Receipts. The purpose of the preliminary review is to determine whether further consideration is likely to justify relying on internal control structure and thus restricting substantive tests of Sales, Accounts Receivable, and Cash. If the preliminary review reveals that existing control procedures are inadequate to justify reliance (and thus inadequate to justify restricting substantive tests), then the auditor's documentation of the system would be limited to a memorandum describing the reasons for not deciding to continue considering the internal control structure. However, if existing control procedures appear potentially reliable, the auditor would continue by documenting the system.

System Documentation. Auditors typically document internal control structure with flowcharts, questionnaires, and/or written narratives. Flowcharts generally provide the most concise, informative, and unambiguous description of internal control structure, and are used when an entity's system is complex and processes large volumes of transactions. Although flowcharts vary in terms of physical layout, the format used earlier in Figures 11-2 and 11-4 is particularly useful to an auditor, since the activities are grouped by function or department, thereby clearly indicating responsibilities and providing the auditor with a basis for judging whether segregation of duties is adequate.

Questionnaires, in contrast, are designed to detect control deficiencies and, as explained in Chapter 7, typically require one of three responses for each individual question: "Yes," "No," or "N/A" (not applicable). "No" responses indicate potential deficiencies. Figure 11-6 illustrates a questionnaire for the customer·order, credit, shipping, billing, and cash receipts functions within the revenue/receipt cycle.

Written narratives describe, in prose, one or more phases of a control structure. Because narratives are more difficult to comprehend than flowcharts, they are used most often for a phase that is not complex or does not process material transactions, such as petty cash.

On many larger engagements, auditors use all three means of documentation. For example, in considering revenue/receipt cycle controls, an auditor might document the system as follows:

▲ Flowchart selling activities from customer order acceptance through recording of the sale and related receivable.
▲ Document cash collection activities with a questionnaire.
▲ Prepare a narrative description of activities related to sales returns and allowances and writeoffs of uncollectible accounts.

Regardless of the form of documentation, specific employee responsibilities and document flow should be clearly identified.

An auditor obtains information about a system through inquiry, observation, and review of written policies and procedures. In the case of a continuing engagement, an auditor should review the prior year's documentation and determine whether it accurately reflects current conditions. Prior documentation can be relied upon only if there have been no changes in assigned responsibilities and prescribed procedures.

Transaction Walk-Through. An auditor tests his or her understanding of a system by performing a transaction walk-through. For example, an auditor could select a sales transaction and trace it through the system from customer order acceptance through cash collection. If the tracing of one or a few transactions reveals deviations from the system as documented by the auditor, the

FIGURE 11-6
Questionnaire: Credit Sales and Cash Collection

Prepared by _____
Date _____

Question	Answer: Yes, No, or N/A	Remarks

Customer Order:

1. Are policies and procedures for accepting and approving customer orders clearly defined?
2. Are prenumbered sales orders prepared for all approved customers orders?
3. Is current information regarding prices, policies on discounts, sales taxes, freight, warranties, and returned goods available and communicated to Customer Order personnel?
4. Are copies of sales orders forwarded to Credits Shipping, and Billing?

Credit:

1. Are policies for approving credit established and clearly communicated to Credit personnel?
2. Is credit investigated before approval?
3. Are Credit personnel independent of Billing, Cash Collection, and Accounting personnel?
4. Is information about past due accounts communicated to Credit personnel?

Shipping:

1. Are goods shipped only in accordance with approved sales orders?
2. Are shipping documents prepared for all shipments?
3. Is access to Inventory Control restricted so that goods are released only in accordance with approved sales orders?

FIGURE 11-6 (*Continued*) Questionnaire: Credit Sales and Cash Collection	Prepared by _____	
Question	Answer: Yes, No, or N/A	Remarks

Shipping:

4. Are quantities of shipped goods verified either by double-counting or by independent counts (e.g., by the shipping company)?
5. Are shipping documents reviewed and compared with billings to assure that all shipped goods are billed?
6. Are Shipping personnel independent of billing, cash collection, and recording?

Billing and Recording:

1. Are prenumbered sales invoices prepared for all shipped goods?
2. Are sales invoices matched with approved sales orders and shipping documents, and checked for clerical accuracy?
3. Are prenumbered credit memos matched with receiving reports and recorded promptly?
4. Is the accounts receivable subsidiary ledger reconciled periodically with the general ledger?
5. Are monthly statements reviewed and mailed by personnel independent of Accounts Receivable and Cash Receipts?
6. Is an aging schedule of accounts receivable prepared monthly by personnel independent of Billing and Cash Receipts?
7. Does the credit manager review receivables balances and the aging analysis and investigate past-due accounts?
8. Is billing performed by personnel independent of Credit and Cash Receipts?

Cash Collection:

1. Are mail receipts opened by personnel independent of Shipping, Billing, and Accounting?

| | Answer: Yes, No, | |
| Question | or N/A | Remarks |

Cash Collection:

2. Are checks endorsed restrictively immediately upon opening the mail?
3. Are lists of receipts prepared when mail is opened?
4. Are checks forwarded promptly to personnel responsible for preparing bank deposits?
5. Are checks deposited daily?
6. Are cash summaries prepared and forwarded to Accounting?
7. Are all employees who handle cash bonded adequately?

reasons for the differences should be determined and documentation revised if necessary.

Identification of Control Procedures to Be Relied On. Once an auditor understands an entity's internal control structure and determines that controls are potentially reliable, he or she continues as follows:

▲ Identify the system's control objectives. The first column of Figure 11-5 identifies control objectives for credit sales and cash receipts transactions.
▲ Consider the potential errors or irregularities that might result if specific control objectives are not achieved. The second column of Figure 11-5 identifies examples of potential errors or irregularities.
▲ Determine what control procedures are used by the entity to prevent or detect potentially material errors or irregularities. The third column of Figure 11-5 identifies examples of control procedures.
▲ Design tests of controls for each control procedure to be relied on during substantive tests of account balances.

As explained in Chapter 7, only those control procedures that are to be relied on during substantive testing are subjected to tests of controls, which are discussed next.

Tests of Controls: Credit Sales and Cash Collections

Because of the scope of the revenue/receipt cycle, sales, receivables, and cash receipts often involve a large volume of transactions. As a result, auditors frequently attempt to rely on internal control structure fairly extensively when auditing the revenue/receipt cycle. But first, tests of controls are necessary in order to provide a reasonable degree of assurance that prescribed control procedures are complied with and operating as planned, and therefore that the controls are reliable.

Tests of an entity's selling activities focus on whether sales are properly authorized, executed, and recorded. Tests of cash collection activities focus on whether all cash receipts are recorded and deposited promptly. Tests of controls over sales returns and allowances and uncollectible accounts focus on proper authorization and recording.

Some representative tests of controls follow for the shipping, billing, recording, and cash collection (and deposit) functions illustrated in Figures 11-2 and 11-4, and for sales returns and allowances and uncollectible accounts. For each function, the discussion briefly introduces an auditor's major concerns, lists a series of representative tests of controls, and then describes the purpose of each test listed. The tests of controls are derived from the second column of Figure 11-5; that is, the auditor first considers what errors or irregularities are possible and then designs tests to determine whether the related control procedures are effective. An Appendix to the chapter describes further how an auditor documents some of the tests. At this point, the intent of the discussion is to introduce the purpose and role of a variety of tests used in testing controls of the revenue/receipt cycle.

Shipping. Weaknesses in Shipping Department controls present two major possibilities for errors or irregularities: goods may be shipped without authorization (e.g., to fictitious or related parties), or shipped goods may not be billed and recorded. Thus tests of controls for Shipping are intended to determine whether shipments are made only in accordance with approved sales orders and whether all shipments have been billed and recorded properly. Following are some illustrative tests for shipping.

Tests of Controls: Shipping

1. Randomly select a sample of shipping documents from Shipping Department files.
2. Examine each shipping document to determine whether the document:
   a. Is accompanied by a sales order bearing Credit and Inventory Control authorization.

     b. Agrees with sales order as to description of goods, quantity, destination, etc.
3. Trace details of sampled shipping documents to copies of shipping documents and related sales invoices in Billing Department files.
4. Trace details of related sales invoices (e.g., customer name, extended dollar amount) to entries in the sales journal and accounts receivable subsidiary ledger.
5. Trace sales invoices to inventory records in Inventory Accounting.
6. Document any deviations or discrepancies observed.

As suggested by step 1 of the tests of controls, shipping documents are the primary source from which the remaining tests of shipping are performed. That is, all further tests of shipping are derived from information contained on the shipping doucments. The tests are intended to determine whether all shipped goods are for bona fide sales and whether shipments are recorded and billed properly.

In step 2a, the auditor is testing two issues. First, by comparing shipping documents with related sales orders, the auditor is testing whether shipments are properly authorized and therefore whether goods may have been shipped without authorization for an employee's or management's benefit. Second, by comparing shipping documents with Inventory Control authorization on the sales order, the auditor is testing whether goods were actually transferred from the warehouse to shipping. In step 2b, the auditor tests whether clerical, mathematical, or other errors have been made in transcribing information from shipping documents to sales invoices. Step 3 is designed to determine that shipments are billed, and that customers are billed for the quantities shipped.

While steps 2 and 3 address transaction authorization and execution, steps 4 and 5 focus on recording of transactions. Step 4 tests whether the sales invoices related to sampled shipments are accurate and recorded properly in the sales journal and receivables ledger. Step 5 is intended to determine whether inventory records reflect the transfer of goods to shipping.

In step 6 the auditor documents any deviations and discrepancies observed, as illustrated, for example, in Figures 11-8 and 11-9, pages 470 and 471 (Appendix). This documentation is used to evaluate whether control procedures over shipping can be relied on, as explained in a case illustration in the Appendix in this chapter.

Billing. The preceding tests of controls address an entity's billing function from the standpoint of whether all shipments are billed. The following tests, in contrast, focus upon whether all billed goods have been shipped and whether bills (sales invoices) are accurate and have been prepared properly and recorded.

Tests of Controls: Billing

1. Randomly select a sample of sales invoices from Billing Department files.
2. For each sampled invoice, verify unit prices and clerical accuracy.
3. Trace details of sampled sales invoices to shipping documents.
4. Trace details of sampled sales invoices to entries in the sales journal and accounts receivable subsidiary ledger.
5. Trace sales invoices to inventory records in Inventory Accounting.
6. Document any deviations or discrepancies observed.

Just as shipping documents are the primary source document for tests of shipping, sales invoices are the primary source for tests of billings. Step 2 requires that an auditor compare unit prices and sales terms on sales invoices with lists of authorized prices and sales terms. Thus, step 2 tests whether goods are billed at appropriate prices and terms.

In step 3, the auditor traces sales invoices to shipping documents, and therefore focuses on whether goods listed on sales invoices were actually shipped. Step 3 is analogous to step 3 of the shipping tests; the shipping test addressed whether all shipments were billed, and the billing test addresses whether recorded sales are shipped.

Step 4 turns attention to the recording function, testing whether sales invoices are properly recorded in the sales journal and the accounts receivable subsidiary ledger. Step 5, also a test of recording, tests whether inventory records accurately reflect transfers of goods — i.e., for every sales entry, there should be a corresponding cost-of-sales entry. Step 6 requires that an auditor document any deviations or discrepancies.

Recording. The tests described for shipping and billing included tracing details of shipping documents and sales invoices to accounting records to verify recording of sampled transactions. Following are additional tests related specifically to the recording function.

Tests of Controls: Recording

1. Review evidence of internal procedures for:
   a. Reconciliation of daily sales summaries with sales journal totals by General Accounting personnel.
   b. Periodic reconciliation of accounts receivable trial balances with general ledger control balances.
2. Scan sales journal for unusual transactions or unusually large amounts and follow up on any such items identified.
3. Verify accuracy of sales journal (foot and cross-foot) for selected periods and trace totals to postings in general ledger.
4. Document any weaknesses or discrepancies observed.

The objective of all four tests for recording is to determine whether details are summarized, periodically reconciled, and — most important — accurately posted to sales journals, to the accounts receivable ledger, and finally to the general ledger. Steps 1a and 1b are not tests per se, but rather are intended to determine whether management has instituted procedures to reconcile sales summaries with sales journals (step 1a) and accounts receivable subsidiary records with the general ledger (step 1b). In short, sales summaries should agree with sales journals, and accounts receivable subsidiary records should agree with the general ledger. If all sales are made on credit, the sales journal should also agree with accounts receivable records.

In step 2, the auditor scans the sales journal for unusual transactions. For example, large sales to related parties — such as sales to, or for the indirect benefit of, officers, directors, or stockholders — may require special disclosure as discussed in Chapter 6. Step 3 tests the mathematical accuracy of the sales journal and traces totals to postings in the general ledger — that is, from details to the control accounts. Step 4 requires that the auditor document any weaknesses or discrepancies.

Cash Collection. An entity's cash collection activities are particularly susceptible to irregularities, since receipts in the form of checks are easily convertible into cash or easily deposited into improper accounts; only a forged endorsement is necessary. Representative tests of controls over cash collections and deposits follow.

Tests of Controls: Cash Collection and Deposits

Collection:
1. On a surprise basis, take control of bank deposits (deposit slip and checks) just prior to delivery by client personnel to the bank.
2. Compare total dollar amount of checks to total recorded on deposit slip.
3. Compare checks to details in cash receipts records and the accounts receivable subsidiary ledger (e.g., customer names, amounts), and determine that the lapse of time between cash receipt and deposit is reasonable.

Deposits:
4. For an interim month (or months):
   a. Compare entries in cash receipts journal with deposits listed on the monthly bank statement.
   b. Ascertain that cash receipts not listed on the bank statement are listed as deposits in transit in the bank reconciliation and are included with deposits in the subsequent month's bank statement.
5. Trace totals in cash receipts journal to postings in general ledger.
6. Document any weaknesses or discrepancies observed.

Steps 1 through 3 are designed to detect *lapping,* an irregularity that conceals cash shortages resulting from delays in recording cash collections. Lapping simultaneously involves both execution (cash collection) and recording (accounts receivable) functions and therefore is most likely to occur when one employee is responsible for both cash collections and receivables.

To accomplish lapping, an employee responsible for cash collections and accounts receivable simply retains a customer's payment for his or her personal use, covering up the shortage with a payment from a second customer; the first customer's receivable balance is credited when the second customer's check is received. In turn, the second customer's receivable balance is credited when a third customer's check is received, and so on. The lapping procedure may cease when the perpetrating employee replaces the cash shortage, may continue indefinitely, or may multiply in scope as a result of additional cash shortages.

Adequate and effective segregation of cash collections and accounts receivable is the best control against lapping. Mandatory vacations for all employees is a second, though less effective, control. However, even if collections and accounts receivable are segregated, an auditor should still test for lapping, in the event that two or more employees are in collusion. Steps 1, 2, and 3 in the program above address lapping by determining whether a customer's check is both deposited and recorded promptly. Of course, the tests should be performed on a surprise basis to minimize the likelihood of an employee (or employees) temporarily correcting a cash shortage in anticipation of an audit.

Steps 4 and 5 are concerned with whether recorded cash collections are deposited in total and promptly. Step 4a traces entries from the cash receipts journal to deposits listed on bank statements, thereby testing whether recorded receipts are deposited. Step 4b relates to cash receipts received and deposited too late to appear on the next bank statement — the receipts are traced to a bank reconciliation (deposits in transit) and to subsequent bank statements when available. Step 5 traces cash receipts totals to the general ledger in order to assure that detailed records agree in total with the control accounts. In step 6 the auditor documents any weaknesses or discrepancies noted in any of the tests.

Sales Returns and Allowances. An auditor's tests of controls for sales returns and allowances focus upon whether credit memoranda are approved and recorded properly. Selected tests follows.

Tests of Controls: Sales Returns and Allowances

1. Obtain a random sample of credit memoranda from the files of the issuing department (e.g., Customer Order).
2. Trace details of sampled credit memoranda to:
   a. Receiving reports.
   b. Perpetual inventory records.
   c. Entries in the accounts receivable subsidiary ledger and general ledger.
3. Review the credit register (or other listing of approved credit memoranda) for unusual items such as credits for very large amounts or an unusually large number of credits for the same customer, and investigate any such items.
4. Document any weaknesses or discrepancies observed.

In step 1, credit memoranda, the primary source document used for tests of sales returns and allowances, are obtained from the issuing department, often the Customer Order Department. Step 2 addresses whether goods were actually returned, by tracing credit memoranda details to receiving reports and to entries in perpetual inventory and accounts receivable records; this step also traces totals from accounts receivable to the general ledger, thereby testing the accuracy of postings. Step 3 is designed to detect unusual credits. For example, credits for very large amounts could signal future large returns, indicating that material receivables may not be collectible. In step 4, the auditor documents any weaknesses or discrepancies.

Uncollectible Accounts. An auditor's compliance tests of controls over uncollectible accounts focus upon whether writeoffs are properly authorized and recorded. Some representative compliance tests follow.

Tests of Controls: Uncollectible Accounts

1. Select a sample of writeoff entries (100 percent testing may be elected by an auditor if writeoffs are infrequent).
2. Trace each entry to the related writeoff authorization memo; examine memo for appropriate authorization and compare authorized amount with recorded amount.
3. Trace each entry to posting in the general ledger.
4. Review all writeoff entries for unusual items such as very large amounts or multiple writeoffs for the same customer, and investigate any such items discovered.
5. Document any weaknesses or discrepancies observed.

Tests of controls over uncollectible accounts start from recorded writeoff entries, rather than a source document as in the compliance tests discussed previously. In step 2, the auditor tests whether writeoffs are authorized, usually by examining writeoff authorization memoranda and related correspondence between the company and customer. Step 3 traces writeoff entries to the general ledger, thereby testing controls over posting. Assuming writeoffs are sampled rather than tested 100 percent, step 4 reviews writeoff entries for unusual items, such as multiple writeoffs for one customer, which could suggest an error or irregularity, since orders generally should not be accepted for previously uncollectible accounts. In step 5, the auditor documents any weaknesses or discrepancies.

Assess Control Risk

To complete the consideration of internal control structure within the revenue/receipt cycle, an auditor reviews system documentation and the results of tests of controls, and determines whether existing controls can be relied on to restrict substantive tests of sales, receivables, and cash (low control risk), or whether expanded substantive tests are required (high control risk). The evaluation is based on the types of errors or irregularities that could occur, necessary control procedures that should prevent the errors or irregularities, a determination of whether the necessary procedures exist and are followed, and any weaknesses detected in the internal control structure. Substantive tests applicable to revenue/receipt cycle accounts are introduced in Chapter 12.

SUMMARY

The revenue/receipt cycle encompasses an entity's selling and collection activities and involves two major business functions: distribution of resources to outsiders and subsequent collection for resources distributed. Internal activities typically associated with the selling or distribution function include customer order, credit, inventory control, shipping, billing, and recording. Basic documentation associated with selling activities, including sales orders, shipping documents, and sales invoices, provides both a basis for recording sales transactions and an audit trial. Effective control over selling activities requries proper transaction authorization, execution, and recording and appropriate access of duties.

Incoming cash receipts should be listed and deposited promptly by an employee independent from the recording function. Transactions relating to intervening activities, such as sales returns and writeoffs of uncollectible accounts, should be properly authorized and documented.

An auditor tests controls within the revenue/receipt cycle after documenting the system and identifying control procedures to be relied on. Substantive tests of accounts receivable, sales, and cash balances are conducted as necessary to satisfy the audit objectives of existence or occurrence, rights, valuation, completeness, and presentation or disclosure, and are discussed in the next chapter, Chapter 12.

APPENDIX
CASE ILLUSTRATION: EDP AND AUDIT SAMPLING IN TESTS OF CONTROLS IN THE REVENUE/RECEIPT CYCLE

To illustrate the material introduced in this chapter and, equally important, to integrate with material presented on EDP (Chapter 8) and audit sampling (Chapter 9), assume a continuing audit engagement for a December 31 year-end client, the Letts Corporation, a medium-sized supplier of hand-held power tools. The specific objective in this case is to determine whether Letts' controls over billing can be relied on during year-end substantive tests of details.

FIGURE 11-7
Letts Corporation: Flowchart of Billing, Data Entry, and Computer Processing

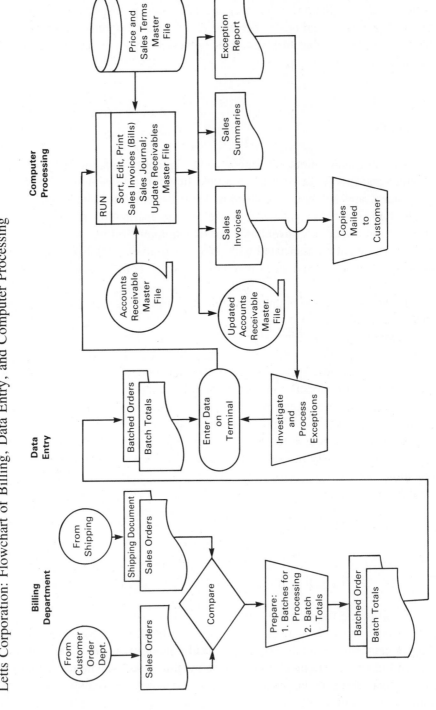

EDP System: Billing, Data Entry, and Computer Processing

Early this year, Letts automated the billing function, resulting in the billing, data entry, and computer processing system partially flowcharted in Figure 11-7. As shown in Figure 11-7, the Billing Department's activities are similar to those illustrated in Figure 11-2, page 440. Here, however, sales invoices and sales summaries, which were prepared manually in Figure 11-2, are prepared using data entry and computer processing, as illustrated at Figure 11-7. In data entry, batched orders and batch control totals are entered on input terminals, and in computer processing, the data entry input is sorted, compared with the price and sales terms master file, and merged with the accounts receivable master file to yield an updated accounts receivable master file, sales invoices, sales summaries, and an exception report. Even though the system shown in Figure 11-7 is processed by computer, the auditor's objectives in considering Letts' internal control structure are no different than when information is processed manually.

Consideration of Internal Control Structure

The auditor's understanding of the system, tests of controls, and evaluation of Letts Corporation's billing function follow.

Understanding the System

Because Letts' billing system has not been reviewed previously, the auditor decides to document the system by flowcharting and by using a questionnaire. The flowchart appears in Figure 11-7, and a transaction walkthrough indicates that the flowchart is accurate. The questionnaire consists of the seven billing and cash collection questions from the questionnaire shown in Figure 11-6, page 455, and questions 4 and 5 received "No" responses, indicating the following deficiencies:

▲ The accounts receivable subsidiary ledger is not reconciled periodically with the general ledger.
▲ Monthly statements and bills are not reviewed by personnel independent of accounts receivable.

Despite these weaknesses, the auditor decides to continue considering internal control structure since the Billing Department processes large volumes of transactions, and the weaknesses relate to manual output controls only, not to EDP processing controls.

Tests of Controls

Because of the deficiencies, the auditor elects a twofold strategy for testing controls. First, test data (explained in Chapter 8) will be used to test the effectiveness of EDP application controls over data entry and computer processing. Second, sampling will be used to test transactions processed during the year. Thus, the test data will focus on the effectiveness of controls when the system processes error-packed auditor-prepared "dummy" data, and the sampling plan will focus on "live" data previously processed by the system.

The auditor is satisfied that EDP general controls are adequate, and prepares a file of test data that is "planted" with errors intended to test the following input and processing controls.

Control	Potential Errors
Input Controls:	
• Code verification	• There are false user identification codes.
• Data entry controls	• Batch totals are inaccurate.
Processing Controls:	
• Control totals	• Processed records do not agree with record counts.
• Limit test	• Transactions exceed authorized maximum dollar amount.

The test data are processed on Letts' computer under the auditor's supervision, and no exceptions are found.

Given the deficiencies noted per the questionnaire, two types of errors or irregularities could occur. The first appears at objective 6 of Figure 11-5 (middle column) and the second at objective 7:

Potential Errors or Irregularities

▲ General ledger account balances may be inaccurate, potentially resulting in misstated financial statements.
▲ Transactions may be posted to improper customer accounts, potentially resulting in improper billings.

After considering the above potential errors or irregularities and other evidence gathered, the auditor decides to focus tests of controls on the posting of sales information from detailed records to control accounts, and therefore drafts the following tests, all of which were explained earlier in the chapter.

Billing

Step	Tests of Controls
1.	Randomly select a sample of sales invoices from Billing Department files.
2.	For each sampled sales invoice verify unit prices and clerical accuracy.
3.	Trace details of sampled sales invoices to shipping documents.
4.	Trace details of sampled sales invoices to entries in the sales journal and accounts receivable subsidiary ledger.
5.	Trace sales invoices to inventory records in inventory accounting.
6.	Document any deviations or discrepancies observed.

As discussed in Chapter 9, the auditor next determines whether the above steps can be accomplished by sampling and, in turn, whether to use statistical or nonstatistical sampling. In this case, steps 2 through 5 can be accomplished with sampling. In addition, the auditor decides to sample statistically, since the EDP billing system had not previously been tested (a newly implemented system), and, therefore, the auditor desires a quantified estimate of sampling risk. Because the auditor has no reason to expect low deviation rates, attributes estimation is chosen as the statistical sampling plan. The results of the attributes estimation sampling plan are summarized in Figure 11-8, an attributes estimation worksheet, and Figure 11-9, an analysis of deviations.

Control Risk

The auditor's assessment of control risk for Letts Corporation's controls over billing would be based on the following quantitative and qualitative factors:

▲ No exceptions were noted when test data were run with client-prepared programs.
▲ The tolerable rate of deviation exceeded the maximum population deviation rate for all five billing-related attributes tested.
▲ The internal control structure questionnaire revealed two weaknesses in internal accounting control.

In this case, the auditor's decision would probably be to rely on the client's controls over billing (low control risk), since test data and audit sampling indicate that the two deficiencies are not likely to produce aggregate error in excess of tolerable error.

FIGURE 11-8

B15

KR
11/20/90

Letts Corporation
Attributes Estimation Worksheet – Billing
December 31, 1990

| | 1 | 2 | 3 | 4 Sample Size | | 5 | | 6 |
Attribute	Risk of Overreliance	Tolerable Rate	Expected Rate	Table *	Used	Number of Deviations	Sample Rate	Max Population Deviation Rate
1. Unit pricing and extensions on the sales invoice are accurate.	.05	.05	.01	93	100	1**	.01	.047
2. Details on sales invoice agree with bill of lading.	.05	.04	.005	117	125	1**	.008	.038
3. Details on sales invoice tie to sales journal and accounts receivable postings.	.05	.05	.0125	124	125	0	0	.024
4. Details on sales invoice tie to inventory records.	.05	.07	.01	66	65	0	0	.046

*Tables 9-1, 9-2
**See analysis of deviations at B16

Audit Conclusion

Based on procedures performed, the tolerable rate of deviation exceeds the maximum population deviation rate for all four attributes tested. Therefore, controls over billing can be relied on during substantive tests of details.

FIGURE 11-9

Letts Corporation
Analysis of Deviations _ Billing
December 31, 1990

Attribute	Number of Deviations	Nature of Deviations	Effect on Substantive Tests of Details
1	1	Sales Invoice #12267, August 23, $10,657; unit prices did not reflect August 22 price increase.	No additional audit work is necessary because (1) the price and sales terms master file disk was updated on August 23, and (2) the maximum population deviation rate (.047) is less than the tolerable rate (.05).
3	1	Sales Invoice #17631, November 15, $7,650; shipping documents indicate 170 units were shipped, but the sales invoice bills for only 165 units.	No additional audit work is necessary because (1) the client's November 15 exception report noted the difference and customer was re-billed, and (2) the maximum population deviation rate (.038) is less than the tolerable rate (.04).

QUESTIONS

1. What are the major business functions and activities common to the revenue/receipt cycle?
2. How does a transaction cycle create an "audit trail"?
3. Explain why the billing function should be segregated from credit granting, cash collection, and accounting.
4. What potential errors or irregularities could occur if customer credit were not approved by authorized personnel? Identify controls that management could implement to assure that a customer is creditworthy.
5. How can management assure that all shipped goods are billed?
6. Accurate recording within general ledger control accounts does not necessarily mean that billing, collection, and adjustment transactions will be posted accurately to individual customer accounts. What controls can management implement to mitigate the probability of inaccurate postings to individual customer accounts?
7. In most circumstances, management is more concerned with restricting employee access to cash than restricting access to inventory. But shouldn't management be more concerned with inventory, since inventory is usually a more material item on the financial statements than cash? Explain your answer.
8. Why is the physical layout of the system flowcharts in Figures 11-2 and 11-4 particularly applicable to auditing?
9. What is the primary focus of the tests of controls performed on an entity's selling and cash receipts activities?
10. Identify the two major errors or irregularities that could result from weaknesses in shipping controls.
11. What is the primary source document from which most shipping-related compliance tests evolve?
12. In performing tests of controls, why would an auditor compare shipping documents with approved sales orders?
13. What is the focus of an auditor's tests of billing, and how do the tests complement tests of shipping controls?
14. What is the primary source document for an auditor's tests of billing?
15. What is the role of tests performed on an entity's recording function within the revenue/receipt cycle?
16. "Lapping" is an irregularity that conceals cash shortages by delaying the recording of cash receipts. How can management control against lapping?
17. What is the focus of an auditor's tests of sales returns and allowances?
18. If a credit memorandum were issued for returned goods, how might an auditor determine whether the goods were actually returned?
19. How does an auditor evaluate the effectiveness and reliability of a client's control procedures over revenue/receipt cycle activities?

MULTIPLE CHOICE QUESTIONS

1. For effective control when there is no Billing Department, the billing function should be performed by the

a. Accounting Department.
b. Sales Department.
c. Shipping Department.
d. Credit and Collection Department   (AICPA Adapted)

2. To verify that all sales transactions have been recorded, a test of controls should be completed on a representative sample drawn from

   a. Entries in the sales journal.
   b. The filling clerk's file of sales orders.
   c. A file of duplicate copies of sales invoices for which all prenumbered forms in the series have been accounted for.
   d. The shipping clerk's file of duplicate copies of bills of lading.
                                                        (AICPA Adapted)

3. Tracing copies of sales invoices to shipping documents will provide evidence that all

   a. Shipments to customers were recorded as receivables.
   b. Billed sales were shipped.
   c. Debits to the subsidiary accounts receivable ledger are for sales shipped.
   d. Shipments to customers were billed.   (AICPA Adapted)

4. Which one of the following would the auditor consider to be an incompatible operation if the cashier receives remittances from the mail room?

   a. The cashier prepares the daily deposit.
   b. The cashier makes the daily deposit at a local bank.
   c. The cashier posts the receipts to the accounts receivable subsidiary ledger cards.
   d. The cashier endorses the checks.   (AICPA Adapted)

5. When a customer fails to include a remittance advice with a payment, it is a common practice for the person opening the mail to prepare one. Consequently, mail should be opened by which of the following four company employees?

   a. Credit manager.
   b. Receptionist.
   c. Sales manager.
   d. Accounts receivable clerk.   (AICPA Adapted)

6. Which of the following internal control procedures will most likely prevent the concealment of a cash shortage resulting from the improper writeoff of a trade account receivable?

   a. Writeoffs must be approved by a responsible officer after review of Credit Department recommendations and supporting evidence.
   b. Writeoffs must be supported by an aging schedule showing that only receivables overdue several months have been written off.
   c. Writeoffs must be approved by the cashier who is in a position to know if the receivables have, in fact, been collected.
   d. Writeoffs must be authorized by company field sales employees who are in a position to determine the financial standing of the customers.
                                                        (AICPA Adapted)

7. Which of the following is **not** a universal rule for achieving effective control over cash?

   a. Separate the cash-handling and record-keeping functions.
   b. Decentralize the receiving of cash as much as possible.
   c. Deposit each day's cash receipts by the end of the day.
   d. Have bank reconciliations performed by employees independent with respect to handling cash.   (AICPA Adapted)

8. The **least** crucial element of control over cash is

   a. Separation of cash record-keeping from custody of cash.
   b. Preparation of the monthly bank reconciliation.
   c. Batch processing of checks.
   d. Separation of cash receipts from cash disbursements.   (AICPA Adapted)

9. Which of the following would be the best protection for a company that wishes to prevent the "lapping" of trade accounts receivable?

   a. Segregate duties so that the bookkeeper in charge of the general ledger has no access to incoming mail.
   b. Segregate duties so that no employee has access to both checks from customers and currency from daily cash receipts.
   c. Have customers send payments directly to the company's depository bank.
   d. Request that customers' payment checks be made payable to the company and addressed to the treasurer.   (AICPA Adapted)

10. At which point in an ordinary sales transaction of a wholesaling business would a lack of specific authorization be of **least** concern to the auditor in the conduct of an audit?

   a. Granting of credit.
   b. Shipment of goods.
   c. Determination of discounts.
   d. Selling of goods for cash.   (AICPA Adapted)

11. A sales cutoff test of billings complements the verification of

   a. Sales returns.
   b. Cash.
   c. Accounts receivable.
   d. Sales allowances.   (AICPA Adapted)

PROBLEMS

11-1   Within the revenue/receipt cycle, several forms and documents are typically used to create an accounting system and, correspondingly, an audit trail for credit sales and cash collections. Among these forms and documents are:
- Sales orders
- Shipping documents
- Sales invoices

Required:
1. Explain how approved sales orders can be used to test credit sales for understatements.
2. Explain how shipping documents can be used to verify that all sales transactions that should be recorded are actually recorded.
3. Explain how an auditor can use sales invoices to test whether billed sales were actually shipped.

11-2   Assume you are considering an entity's internal control structure over credit sales and cash collection. System documentation was accomplished through a questionnaire and written narratives and, in conjunction with a transaction walk-through, revealed the following potential weaknesses in internal control:
a. New customers are not approved before ordered goods are shipped.
b. Sales prices vary from customer to customer.
c. No approval is required for returned goods from customers.
d. Subsidiary accounts receivable records do not always agree with the general ledger control account.
e. Blank checks are left unprotected in an unlocked, open safe.

Required:
For each potential weakness, indicate a control or controls that management could implement to reduce the likelihood of errors or irregularities.

11-3   In connection with your examination of Cheever and Company's December 31, 1990 financial statements, you become aware of the following controls or procedures over Cheever's credit sales and cash collection activities:
a. Sales terms are approved by supervisory personnel before shipment.
b. All credit memoranda are prenumbered sequentially and controlled.
c. Shipping documents are prenumbered sequentially and controlled.
d. Copies of shipping documents are hand-carried to the Billing Department within one hour after shipment.
e. Sales invoices are compared with sales journals and with customers' individual subsidiary records.
f. In contrast with prior years, noncredit cash sales are handled in one centralized location, rather than throughout all departments.
g. Unused checks are prenumbered and locked in a fireproof vault accessible only to the treasurer, one of two endorsers on customers' checks.

Required:
For each control or procedure, indicate (1) a potential error or irregularity that might be circumvented as a result of the control or procedure, and (2) the internal control objective that is served by the control or procedure. Organize your answer as follows.

Control or Procedure	Potential Error or Irregularity That Might Be Circumvented	Related Internal Control Objective
1.		

11-4   George Beemster, CPA, is auditing the financial statements of the Louisville Sales Corporation, which recently installed an off-line electronic computer. The following comments have been extracted from Mr. Beemster's notes on computer operations and the processing and control of shipping notices and customer invoices:

- To minimize inconvenience Louisville converted without change its existing data processing system, which utilized tabulating equipment. The computer company supervised the conversion and has provided training to all Computer Department employees (except keypunch operators) in systems design, operations, and programming.
- Each computer run is assigned to a specific employee, who is responsible for making program changes, running the program, and answering questions. This procedure has the advantage of eliminating the need for records of computer operations because each employee is responsible for his or her own computer runs.
- At least one Computer Department employee remains in the computer room during office hours, and only Computer Department employees have keys to the computer room.
- System documentation consists of those materials furnished by the computer company — a set of record formats and program listings. These and the tape library are kept in a corner of the Computer Department.
- Louisville Sales considered the desirability of programmed controls but decided to retain the manual controls from its existing system.
- The company products are shipped directly from public warehouses which forward shipping notices to General Accounting. There a billing clerk enters the price of the item and accounts for the numerical sequence of shipping notices from each warehouse. The billing clerk also prepares daily adding machine tapes ("control tapes") of the units shipped and the unit prices.
- Shipping notices and control tapes are forwarded to the Computer Department for keypunching and processing. Extensions are made on the computer. Output consists of invoices (in six copies) and a daily sales register. The daily sales register shows the aggregate totals of units shipped and unit prices which the computer operator compares with the control tapes.
- All copies of the invoice are returned to the billing clerk. The clerk mails three copies to the customer, forwards one copy to the warehouse, maintains one copy in a numerical file, and retains one copy in an open invoice file that serves as a detail accounts receivable record.

Required:

Describe weaknesses in the internal control structure over information and data flows and the procedures for processing shipping notices and customer invoices and recommend improvements in these controls and processing procedures. Organize your answer sheets as follows:

Weakness	Recommended Improvement

(AICPA Adapted).

11-5 A partially completed credit sales system flowchart is presented on page 478. The flowchart depicts the charge sales activities of the Bottom Manufacturing Corporation.

A customer's order is received, and a six-part sales order is prepared. The six copies are initially distributed as follows:

Copy No. 1 — Billing Copy — to Billing Department.
Copy No. 2 — Shipping copy — to Shipping Department.

Copy No. 3 — Credit copy — to Credit Department.

Copy No. 4 — Stock request copy — to Credit Department.

Copy No. 5 — Customer copy — to customer.

Copy No. 6 — Sales order copy — file in Customer Order Department.

When each copy of the sales order reaches the applicable department or destination, specific internal control procedures and related documents are required. Some of the procedures and related documents are indicated on the flowchart. Other procedures and documents are labeled letters a to r.

Required:

List the procedures or the internal documents that are labeled letters c to r in the flowchart of Bottom Manufacturing Corporation's credit sales system.

Organize your answer as follows (note that an explanation of the letters a and b which appear in the flowchart are entered as examples):

Flowchart Symbol Letter	Procedures or Internal Document
a.	Prepare six-part sales order.
b.	File by order number.

(AICPA Adapted)

11-6   Jiblum, CPA, is planning to use attribute sampling in order to determine the degree of reliance to be placed on an audit client's control procedures over sales. Jiblum has begun to develop an outline of the main steps in the sampling plan as follows:

a. State the objectives of the audit test (e.g., to test the reliability of controls over sales).

b. Define the population (define the period covered by the test: define the sampling unit; define the completeness of the population).

c. Define the sampling unit (e.g., client copies of sales invoices).

Required:

1. What are the remaining steps which Jiblum should include in the statistical test of sales invoices? Do not present a detailed analysis of tasks which must be performed to carry out the objectives of each step.

2. How does statistical methodology help the auditor to develop a satisfactory sampling plan?   (AICPA Adapted)

11-7   You are reviewing the trade accounts receivable for a retail organization as of the end of the second quarter of the fiscal year. The receivables are maintained on disk on the organization's minicomputer. You are particularly interested in the validity, accuracy, and age of the receivables. You have a computer programmer available to develop a computer program for extracting data from the receivables files and desire to use the computer to the maximum extent feasible in your audit.

Required:

With respect to substantiating the (a) validity, (b) accuracy, and (c) age of the receivables, specify for each:

1. The audit procedures you want the programmer to write up in a computer language.

2. The reports, schedules, and lists for each you want printed out for your review.

(continued)

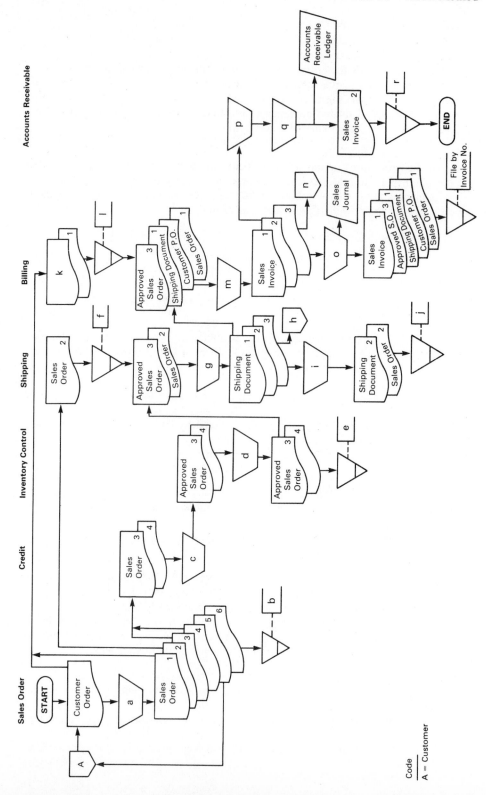

For example:

Procedures — Identify all accounts with credit balances.

Reports — Print out list of accounts with credit balances.

Present your answers for a, b, and c, listing the procedures you want the programmer to write up and any reports, schedules, and lists you expect.   (IIA Adapted)

11-8   The Art Appreciation Society operates a museum for the benefit and enjoyment of the community. During hours when the museum is open to the public, two clerks who are positioned at the entrance collect a $5 admission fee from each non-member patron. Members of the Art Appreciation Society are permitted to enter free of charge upon presentation of their membership cards.

At the end of each day one of the clerks delivers the proceeds to the treasurer. The treasurer counts the cash in the presence of the clerk and places it in a safe. Each Friday afternoon the treasurer and one of the clerks deliver all cash held in the safe to the bank, and receive an authenticated deposit slip which provides the basis for the weekly entry in the cash receipts journal.

The Board of Directors of the Art Appreciation Society has identified a need to improve the system of internal control over cash admission fees. The Board has determined that the cost of installing turnstiles or sales booths or otherwise altering the physical layout of the museum will greatly exceed any benefits which may be derived. However, the Board has agreed that the sale of admission tickets must be an integral part of its improvement efforts.

Smith has been asked by the Board of Directors of the Art Appreciation Society to review the internal control over cash admission fees and provide suggestions for improvement.

Required:
Indicate weaknesses in the existing system of internal control over cash admission fees, which Smith should identify, and recommend one improvement for each of the weaknesses identified.

Organize the answer as indicated in the following illustrative example:

Weakness	Recommendation
1. There is no basis for establishing the documentation of the number of paying patrons.	1. Prenumbered admission tickets should be issued upon payment of the admission fee.

(AICPA Adapted)

11-9   You are auditing the Alaska Branch of Far Distributing Co. This branch has substantial annual sales which are billed and collected locally. As a part of your audit you find that the procedures for handling cash receipts are as follows:

Cash collections on over-the-counter sales and COD sales are received from the customer or delivery service by the cashier. Upon receipt of cash the cashier stamps the sales ticket "paid" and files a copy for future reference. The only record of COD sales is a copy of the sales ticket, which is given to the cashier to hold until the cash is received from the delivery service.

Mail is opened by the secretary to the credit manager, and remittances are given to the credit manager for review. The credit manager than places the remittances in a tray on the cashier's desk. At the daily deposit cutoff time the cashier delivers the checks and cash on hand to the assistant credit manager, who prepares remittance lists, makes up the bank deposit, and takes the deposit to the bank. The assistant credit manager also posts remittances to the accounts receivable ledger cards and verifies the cash discount allowable.

You also ascertain that the credit manager obtains approval from the executive office of Far Distributing Co., located in Chicago, to write off uncollectible accounts, and that as of the end of the fiscal year, some remittances that were received on various days during the last month have been retained in the custody of the credit manager.

Required:
1. Describe the irregularities that might occur under the procedures now in effect for handling cash collections and remittances.
2. Give procedures that you would recommend to strengthen control over cash collections and remittances.   (AICPA Adapted)

11-10   Assume you are auditing the financial statements of Fashionation, Inc., a retail clothing store. The following narrative description is available for Fashionation's cash sales procedures:

All sales are for cash; no credit cards are accepted. Each individual sale is rung up by the sales clerk on a cash register which ejects a sales slip. The sales slip is given to the customer, and a copy of the sales slip is made by the cash register on a continuous tape locked inside the machine. At the end of the day, the sales clerk presses a "total" key and the machine prints the total sales for the day on the continuous tape. The clerk then unlocks the cash register, removes the day's tape, makes an entry in the cash receipts book, counts the cash in the drawer, retains a change fund of $100, and turns the rest of the cash over to the cashier. The sales clerk then files the cash register tape and is ready for the next day.

Required
From the narrative description of Fashionation's cash sales procedures, indicate specific recommendations to improve controls over cash.

11-11   Trapan Retailing, Inc., has decided to diversify operations by selling through vending machines. Trapan's plans call for the purchase of 312 vending machines which will be situated at 78 different locations, within one city, and the rental of a warehouse to store merchandise. Trapan intends to sell only canned beverages at a standard price.

Management has hired an inventory control clerk to oversee the warehousing functions, and two truck drivers who will periodically fill the machines with merchandise, and who will deposit cash collected at a designated bank. Drivers will be required to report to the warehouse daily.

Required:
What internal controls will assure the integrity of the cash receipts and warehousing functions?   (AICPA Adapted)

11-12   Following are selected questions from internal control questionnaires relating to a company's customer order, credit, shipping, billing, and cash receipts functions. A "Yes" response to any question would indicate a potential strength, and a "No" response a potential weakness of the system.

a. Are sales orders prepared for all approved customer orders?
b. Are copies of sales orders forwarded to the credit, shipping, and billing departments?
c. Is credit investigated before customer is approved?
d. Are goods shipped only in accordance with approved sales orders?
e. Are shipping documents reviewed and compared with billings to assure that all shipped goods are billed?
f. Are all credit memos prenumbered, matched with approved sales orders and shipping documents, and checked for clerical accuracy?
g. Is the accounts receivable subsidiary ledger reconciled periodically with the general ledger?
h. Are mail receipts opened by personnel independent of shipping, billing, sales invoice processing, and recording?

Required:
Assume that inquiries indicate the answer is "Yes" to each question. Draft a compliance test you believe would provide persuasive evidence that controls are reliable.

11-13   You are the in-charge accountant examining the financial statements of the Gutzler Company for the year ending December 31, 1990. During late October, 1990, you, with the help of Gutzler's controller, completed an internal control structure questionnaire and prepared the appropriate memoranda describing Gutzler's accounting procedures. Your comments relative to cash receipts are as follows.

All cash receipts are sent directly to the accounts receivable clerk with no processing by the Mail Department. The accounts receivable clerk keeps the cash receipts journal; prepares the bank deposit slip in duplicate; posts from the deposit slip to the subsidiary accounts receivable ledger; and mails the deposit to the bank.

The controller receives the validated deposit slips directly (unopened) from the bank and also receives the monthly bank statement directly (unopened) from the bank and promptly reconciles it.

At the end of each month, the accounts receivable clerk sends the general ledger clerk the monthly totals of the cash receipts journal for posting to the general ledger.

Each month, with regard to the general ledger cash account, the general ledger clerk makes an entry to record the total debits to cash from the cash receipts journal. In addition, the general ledger clerk on occasion makes debit entries in the general ledger cash account from sources other than the cash receipts journal, e.g., funds borrowed from the bank.

The following standard auditing procedures have already been performed by you in the audit of cash receipts.
a. Total and cross-total all columns in the cash receipts journal.
b. Trace postings from the cash receipts journal to the general ledger.
c. Examine remittance advices and related correspondence to support entries in the cash receipts journal.

Required:
Considering Gutzler's control over cash receipts and standard auditing procedures already performed, list all other auditing procedures and reasons therefore which should be performed to obtain sufficient audit evidence regarding cash receipts. Do not discuss the procedures for cash disbursements and cash balances. Also do not discuss the extent to which any of the procedures are to be performed. Assume that

adequate controls exist to assure that all sales transactions are recorded. Organize
your answer sheet as follows:

Other audit procedures	Reason for other audit procedures

(AICPA Adapted)

11-14   During the year Strang Corporation began to encounter cash flow difficulties, and a cursory review by management revealed receivable collection problems.
Strang's management engaged Stanley, CPA, to perform a special investigation. Stanley
studied the billing and collection functions of the revenue/receipt cycle and noted the
following:

The accounting department employs one bookkeeper who receives and opens all
incoming mail. This bookkeeper is also responsible for depositing receipts, filing
remittance advices on a daily basis, recording receipts in the cash receipts journal,
and posting receipts in the individual customer accounts and the general ledger accounts. There are no cash sales. The bookkeeper prepares and controls the mailing
of monthly statements to customers.

The concentration of functions and the receivable collection problems caused
Stanley to suspect that a systematic defalcation of customers' payments through a
delayed posting of remittances (lapping of accounts receivable) is present. Stanley
was surprised to find that no customers complained about receiving erroneous monthly
statements.

Required:

Identify the procedures which Stanley should perform to determine whether lapping
exists. Do not discuss deficiencies in the internal control structure.

(AICPA Adapted)

11-15   Within the revenue/receipt cycle, controls must be implemented not only
for sales and shipments, but also for sales returns and allowances. Otherwise, sales
could be overstated and the financial statements significantly misstated.

Required:

1. Design and explain the journal entry an employee could make to commit an irregularity with sales returns and allowances.
2. In tests of controls over credit memoranda, how can an auditor test whether goods
   related to sales returns and allowances were actually returned?

11-16   The president of a large utility has requested that you audit the customer
payment system with special emphasis on the data entry and data transmission functions at local branch offices. Customers may send their payments to the central office
or pay in person at any of the company's twenty-four branch offices. When a customer pays a utility bill at a branch office, the payment data are immediately entered
into the branch payment system by an employee via a terminal which is connected
to the company's central computer.

In auditing the branch payment system, the internal auditor divided the process
into the following three segments:

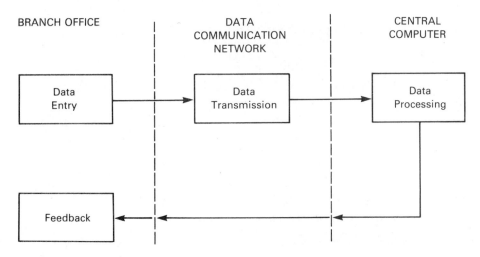

BRANCH OFFICE | **DATA COMMUNICATION NETWORK** | **CENTRAL COMPUTER**

Data Entry → Data Transmission → Data Processing

Feedback ←

Required:
1. List the major data entry control objectives that the auditor should identify.
2. For *each* of the data entry control objectives listed in your answer to (1), briefly describe the control techniques to accomplish each objective.

(IIA Adapted)

SUBSTANTIVE TESTS OF THE REVENUE/RECEIPT CYCLE: SALES, ACCOUNTS RECEIVABLE, AND CASH

12

Major topics discussed in this chapter are the:

▲ *Relationship among financial statement assertions, audit objectives, and audit procedures within the revenue/receipt cycle.*

▲ *Audit objectives and substantive tests applicable to sales, accounts receivable, and cash balances.*

▲ *Application of audit sampling in substantive tests of accounts receivable (Appendix A).*

▲ *Computer-assisted audit techniques applicable to accounts receivable (Appendix B).*

B ased on the assessed level of control risk in the revenue/receipt cycle, an auditor determines the acceptable level of detection risk and then designs substantive tests of the accounts related to the cycle: sales, accounts receivable, and cash. This chapter focuses on substantive tests of details for these accounts.

The chapter begins by discussing how each of the financial statement assertions introduced in Chapter 6 — existence or occurrence, completeness, rights and obligations, valuation or allocation, and presentation and disclosure — is tested for audits of sales, accounts receivable, and cash, the major financial statement accounts within the revenue/receipt cycle. In turn, the chapter relates the assertions to specific substantive tests for these accounts, and then describes and illustrates each test. Two appendices appear at the end of the chapter. Appendix A, a case study, illustrates how audit sampling, introduced in Chapter 10, can be used in substantive tests of receivables balances. Finally, Appendix B discusses computer-assisted audit procedures applicable to the revenue/receipt cycle.

FINANCIAL STATEMENT ASSERTIONS, OBJECTIVES, AND AUDIT PROCEDURES

As explained in Chapter 6, much of an auditor's work during a financial statement audit consists of obtaining and evaluating evidence relating to the assertions within an entity's financial statements. For example, management asserts that recorded receivables and cash balances:

▲ Exist
▲ Represent all transactions that should be presented
▲ Represent rights of the entity
▲ Are valued appropriately
▲ Are presented and disclosed properly within the financial statements.

From each assertion, an auditor develops audit objectives, and then selects appropriate audit procedures to test each objective. For example, management's assertion that cash and receivables exist creates a corresponding audit objective to determine whether each asset actually does exist, and auditors generally use confirmation procedures to test their existence.

The preceding discussion links assertions, objectives, and audit procedures. But, specifically, what procedures do practicing auditors commonly use to address these audit objectives? The following discussion relates each audit objective to specific audit procedures that are commonly used in auditing revenue/receipt cycle accounts. The objectives and related procedures are summarized in Figure 12-1.

Existence or Occurrence

Within the revenue/receipt cycle, the existence or occurrence objective addresses whether all recorded sales, receivables, and cash balances actually exist and whether all recorded transactions actually occurred. Existence is normally tested by physical observation or confirmation with outside parties. For receivables, existence is tested by confirming balances with debtors (customers). For cash on deposit existence is tested by confirming bank balances with banks, while cash on hand can be physically observed and counted. In addition, cutoff testing is used to determine whether recorded sales transactions and related receivables and cash transactions are recorded in the proper period.

Completeness

The completeness objective addresses whether all receivables, sales, and cash transactions and accounts that should be included in the financial state-

FIGURE 12-1

Relating Audit Objectives and Audit Procedures: Sales, Receivables, and Cash Balances

Audit Objectives	Audit Procedures		
	Sales	Receivables	Cash Balances
Existence or occurrence	Test cutoff.	Confirm with debtors. Test cutoff.	Confirm with banks. Test cutoff.
Completeness	Perform analytical procedures. Test cutoff.	Perform analytical procedures. Test cutoff.	Test cutoff. Examine bank reconciliations or proofs of cash. Examine intercompany and interbank transfers.
Rights and obligations		Confirm with debtors. Review collectibility.	Confirm with banks.
Valuation or allocation	Perform analytical procedures.	Confirm with debtors. Review collectibility. Verify accuracy of aged trial balance.	Confirm with banks. Verify mathematical accuracy of recorded cash balances. Test cutoff.
Presentation and disclosure.	Compare statement presentation and disclosures with those required by GAAP.	Compare statement presentation and disclosures with those required by GAAP.	Compare statement presentation and disclosures with those required by GAAP.

ments are actually presented. Generally, completeness is tested by examining documentation and by making comparisons among related accounts. For sales and receivables, completeness is tested by performing analytical procedures, which helps determine whether recorded receivables and sales balances are reasonable at the balance sheet date, and by testing cutoff, which determines whether transactions are recorded in the proper accounting period. Auditors typically test completeness for cash balances by (a) examining cutoff bank statements to assure that all receipts and disbursements are recorded in the proper period, and (2) examining bank reconciliations (or proofs of cash) and records of intercompany and interbank transfers.

Rights and Obligations

Within the revenue/receipt cycle, the rights and obligations objective addresses whether a company has property rights — e.g., claims against third parties — for recorded receivables and cash balances. That is, does the company have legally binding claims against customers for receivables balances and against commercial banks and other depositories for recorded cash balances? Generally, an auditor tests rights by examining documentation and by confirmations and inquiries. Rights to receivables are typically tested by confirming balances with debtors and by reviewing the collectibility of confirmed and unconfirmed customer balances. In turn, rights to cash are tested primarily by confirming balances and deposit terms (e.g., demand deposits and compensating balances) with banks.

Valuation or Allocation

The valuation objective addresses whether receivables, sales, and cash balances are reported in the financial statements at appropriate amounts. That is, are they valued in accordance with generally accepted accounting principles? In general, auditors test valuation by examining documentation, confirmation, observation, mechanical tests, and inquiries. More specifically, the carrying value of receivables is tested by confirming balances with debtors and reviewing collectibility — both of which also addressed rights and obligations — and by verifying the accuracy of management's aged trial balance. Recorded values for cash are tested by confirming balances with banks, by verifying the mathematical accuracy of recorded cash balances, and by examining the details within cutoff bank statements.

Presentation and Disclosure

The presentation and disclosure objective addresses whether recorded transactions and balances are properly classified, described, and disclosed. Generally, auditors address this objective by comparing a client's financial statement presentation and disclosures with those required by generally accepted accounting principles. Presentation and disclosure guidelines, such as the AICPA's annually updated *Accounting and Audit Manual*, are often used by practicing auditors in accomplishing this objective.

SUBSTANTIVE TESTS IN THE REVENUE/RECEIPT CYCLE

As explained in Chapter 6, interim audit work concludes with the drafting of preliminary year-end audit programs — detailed lists of substantive procedures for each audit area. Prior to performing substantive tests, an auditor should review and evaluate any significant changes occurring since the interim assessment of control risk was performed and revise year-end audit programs as necessary. If controls or their method of application have changed, an auditor must either perform additional tests of controls and reevaluate the system, or increase the assessed level of control risk and extend the scope of substantive testing to control detection risk.

Substantive testing of revenue/receipt cycle accounts involves obtaining and evaluating evidence about transactions and events related to a company's sales and collection activities. However, because the revenue/receipt cycle varies in scope from one company to another, an auditor does not apply the same procedures on all engagements: business activities, functional organization, internal control structures, and materiality and audit risk all vary from one engagement to the next. In an effort to blend the conceptual and procedural aspects of substantive tests for receivables, sales, and cash balances, the audit programs presented are keyed to and discussed in the context of the audit objectives presented earlier:

▲ Existence or occurrence.
▲ Completeness.
▲ Rights and obligations.
▲ Valuation or allocation.
▲ Presentation and disclosure.

ACCOUNTS RECEIVABLE AND SALES

A program of representative year-end substantive tests applicable to accounts receivable and sales is presented in Figure 12-2. Each of the procedures identified and the related audit objectives are discussed in the following sections. Not all of these procedures would be performed in every audit. Rather, the nature, timing, and extent of the procedures performed in an engagement depend on the auditor's assessed level of control risk and the resulting detection risk he or she accepts for each assertion. For example, a minimum level of control risk would result in a higher acceptable detection risk and, therefore, in less extensive substantive tests.

Verify Mathematical Accuracy

The audit objective of valuation is satisfied in part by testing the mathematical (clerical) accuracy of reported amounts. Recomputation of client-

FIGURE 12-2
Substantive Tests: Accounts Receivable and Sales

Audit Objectives	Procedures

Valuation	1. Verify mathematical accuracy of accounts receivable.
	     a. Obtain an accounts receivable aged trial balance from Accounts Receivable Department personnel.
	     b. Foot (add columns) and cross-foot (add column totals across) the trial balance.
	     c. Compare total accounts receivable per the trial balance to accounts receivable in the general ledger.

Existence Rights Valuation	2. Confirm year-end accounts and notes receivable balances with debtors. *Even ⏀ balance accounts*
Existence or occurrence Completeness	3. Test cutoff to determine whether sales and receivables are recorded in the proper accounting period.
Valuation Rights	4. Review the collectibility of receivables, and determine the adequacy of the allowance for doubtful accounts.
Existence or occurrence Completeness Valuation	5. Perform analytical procedures to determine whether recorded sales and receivables balances appear reasonable.

Presentation and
 disclosure
	6. Review financial statements to determine whether:
	     a. Accounts and notes receivable and sales are properly classified and described.
	     b. Disclosures are adequate.

computed amounts is a commonly used procedure for determining mathematical accuracy. In verifying the accuracy of accounts receivable, an aged trial balance similar to the one illustrated in Figure 12-3 is obtained from Accounts Receivable personnel and footed and cross-footed by the auditor. The resulting total should be compared and reconciled with the general ledger balance.

The mathematical accuracy of a client's aged trial balance is particularly critical, since the trial balance is also used as the basic source for other tests of receivables. For example, the aged trial balance is typically used to select individual customer balances for confirmation, discussed next in the chapter,

FIGURE 12-3
Accounts Receivable Aged Trial Balance

(Schedule prepared
by client)

Woodard Company
Accounts Receivable Aged Trial Balance
December 31, 1990

Account Number	Customer Name	Balance Dec. 31, 1990	0-30 Days	31-60 Days	61-90 Days	Over 90 Days
0103	Andrie Supplies	$ 6,319.07	$ 6,319.07			
0107	Alpine Roofing	1,754.00	1,754.00			
0108	Atwells, Inc.	5,629.83	5,629.83			
0110	Bennington & Co.	10,743.76		$10,243.76	$ 500.00	
0112	Blakely & Schuster	8,250.00	7,250.00	1,000.00		
0115	Burns & Alec	1,805.00				$1,805.00
. . .	. . .	. . .	. . .	. . .	. . .	. . .
0960	Van Allen Sales	2,500.00	1,250.00		1,250.00	
0961	Victor Company, Inc.	16,000.00	16,000.00			
0967	Webster Corporation	1,724.30	1,724.30			
0968	Wellington & Shine	6,225.40	6,225.40			
0971	Yellowstone Stores	5,280.50	5,280.50			
0974	Zelanie & Aveno	17,250.00	17,250.00			
		$232,228.57	$190,922.50	$21,222.42	$14,462.15	$5,621.50

and to identify credit balances which, under generally accepted accounting principles, should be reclassified to accounts payable.

If discrepancies are observed, or if tests of controls revealed deficiencies in controls over receivables, additional tests may be performed. For example, an auditor might select a sample of customer accounts from the aged trial balance and examine details in the subsidiary ledger for the selected accounts.

Confirm Receivables Balances

The *Codification of Statements on Auditing Standards* (Sec. 331) specifically states that an auditor sustains the burden of justifying his or her opinion on financial statements when receivables are not confirmed. In general, failing to confirm receivables is justifiable only when confirmation is impractical and an auditor is satisfied by other procedures that receivables are fairly presented. Receivables are sometimes confirmed at interim, but interim confirmation is appropriate only when an auditor is satisfied that the internal control structure is effective and balances in receivables and sales accounts can be reconciled from the interim confirmation date to year-end. Otherwise, receivables are confirmed at year-end.

Confirming receivables balances requires direct communication with customers through positive or negative confirmation requests. *Positive confirmations* request that a customer review the account balance indicated and respond to the auditor whether the balance is correct or incorrect, as illustrated in Figure 12-4. In contrast, *negative confirmations* request that a debtor respond to the auditor only if the balance in an attached statement is incorrect, as illustrated in Figure 12-5. In general, positive confirmations are appropriate when individual account balances are relatively large or when substantial numbers of inaccuracies or irregularities are expected in individual account balances. Negative confirmations are generally appropriate when internal control is adequate, balances are small, and the auditor has no reason to believe that debtors will not return the confirmation request. Both types of confirmations may be appropriate in any one audit, for example, positive requests could be used for larger account balances, and negative requests for smaller balances.

When positive confirmations are used, an auditor should mail second (and perhaps even third) requests, attempting to maximize the number of responses. If a statistical sampling plan is used to select and evaluate confirmations, a poor response rate could affect sampling risk, requiring that an auditor alter or abandon the sampling plan. However, despite the efforts expended to maximize response rates, a number of customers invariably will fail to respond, thereby requiring alternative audit procedures for those ac-

FIGURE 12-4
Positive Accounts Receivable Confirmation

January 4, 1991

Woodard Company
100 Western Avenue
Boston, MA 02134

Wellington Products, Inc.
6540 Lincolnway Road
Los Angeles, CA 90041

Please confirm the correctness of your December 31, 1990 account balance of $15,652 directly to our auditors:

John J. Schubert & Co., CPAs

who are auditing our financial statements. This is not a request for payment.

An envelope addressed to our auditors is enclosed.

Paula Maronti

Paula Maronti
Controller

The above balance is correct ☐.

The above balance is incorrect as noted below ☐.

_____

_____

By: _____

Date: _____

FIGURE 12-5
Negative Accounts Receivable Confirmation

Please examine the attached statement. If the statement disagrees with your records, respond directly to our auditors:

John J. Schubert & Co., CPAs

who are auditing our financial statements. An envelope addressed to our auditors is enclosed.

THIS IS NOT A REQUEST FOR PAYMENT

counts. In the absence of a returned confirmation an auditor could examine other evidence, such as:

▲ Subsequent cash collections.
▲ Sales invoices.
▲ Shipping documents.

Notes receivable confirmation requests are similar in substance to positive accounts receivable requests, although negative notes receivable confirmations are not commonly used in practice.

Importantly, confirmation procedures provide evidence to fulfill no less than three audit objectives:

▲ Existence — recorded receivables exist at the balance sheet date.
▲ Rights — recorded receivables are the rights of the audited entity (e.g., receivables have not been assigned or sold).
▲ Valuation — receivables are reported at appropriate amounts.

Test Cutoff

Additional evidence of existence or occurrence and of completeness is generated in tests of sales cutoff.

An auditor tests sales cutoff to determine whether sales entries are recorded in the period in which title to goods passed to the customer. Cutoff tests involve examining a sample of sales entries recorded at or near the year-end date. For example, assuming a December 31 year-end, an auditor might examine a sample of sales transactions recorded from December 20 through January 10. Shipping documents are obtained and examined for each sampled sales entry to determine whether sales have been recorded in the proper period. Sales should be included for the current year under audit if shipping terms are (1) FOB (free-on-board) shipping point and goods were shipped on or before the year-end date or (2) FOB destination and goods were received by the customer on or before year-end.

Review Collectibility of Receivables

Despite policies and procedures for reviewing and approving customer requests for credit, an entity cannot eliminate the risk that some accounts will not be paid. As a result, the appropriate valuation or carrying value of receivables is usually less than the sum of all outstanding balances. An auditor evaluates the carrying value of receivables by reviewing their collectibility and determining the adequacy of an entity's allowance for uncollectible accounts.

Evidence of collectibility as obtained through examination of an accounts receivable aged trial balance, discussions with Credit Department personnel, review of post-balance-sheet-date collections, review of any available correspondence with delinquent debtors, and examination of credit ratings with recognized bureaus such as Dun & Bradstreet, Inc. All relevant evidence should be evaluated by the auditor in assessing the reasonableness of the entity's allowance for uncollectible accounts.

Perform Analytical Procedures

In general, the role of analytical procedures is to direct an auditor's attention to accounts or balances which appear unusual or unreasonable, and therefore may require additional substantive tests of details. Thus, within the revenue/receipt cycle, analytical procedures can be used (1) to identify accounts which appear reasonable — that is, appear to be "behaving" as expected — and therefore do not require additional testing and (2) to identify accounts which appear unreasonable or unusual — that is, do not appear to be "behaving" as expected — and therefore require additional testing beyond the extent of procedures planned. For example, if a client's number-of-days-sales in receivables was at or around 30 days for four successive years, this would suggest that sales, receivables, and collection activity were behaving similarly for the four-year period, and would not signal the need for additional substantive tests of details. However, if the number-of-days-sales were at or around 30 days for the three preceding years and 45 days for the current year, then this variation would indicate the need for additional tests of collectibility.

For sales and receivables, an auditor might use any or all of the following analytical procedures among others.

▲ Compare product-line sales and gross margin percentages by month and by year to identify potential overstatements or understatements of sales.

▲ Compare receivables aging categories (e.g., 0–30 days, 31–60 days, 61–90 days, etc.) and uncollectible accounts as percentages of accounts receivable for a series of years to test the reasonableness of the allowance for uncollectible accounts.

▲ Compare actual bad debt writeoffs with recorded bad debt expense for prior years to test the reasonableness of the provision for bad bebts in the current year.

Of course, no one of the preceding analytical procedures will necessarily detect material misstatements. Rather, the procedures will direct an auditor's attention to accounts or balances requiring additional inquiries or substantive tests of details.

Review Financial Statement Presentation and Disclosure

The audit program in Figure 12-2 concludes with the auditor's review of financial statement presentation and disclosure of revenue/receipt cycle accounts. An auditor should determine whether accounts, notes, and other receivables and related sales accounts are classified, described, and disclosed in accordance with generally accepted accounting principles.

Accounts and notes receivable are usually classified as current or non-current assets, depending on the terms of payment, and carried at net realizable value, i.e., net of an allowance for uncollectible accounts, unearned discounts, interest, and finance charges. Trade notes and accounts receivable should be segregated from nontrade receivables, such as employee or officer receivables. All material information should be disclosed in the financial statements or in the notes to the financial statements. Disclosures should include, for example, information pertaining to the pledge or assignment of receivables.

CASH BALANCES

Figure 12-6 presents a program of representative year-end substantive tests applicable to cash balances, and identifies related audit objectives. Each of the procedures is discussed in the following sections.

Confirm Cash Balances

Cash balances representing deposits with banks (e.g., checking accounts and certificates of deposit) and other depositaries (e.g., money funds) are

FIGURE 12-6
Substantive Tests: Cash Balances

Audit Objectives	Procedures
Existence Rights Valuation	1. Confirm year-end cash balances with all banks and other depositaries.

Valuation	2. Verify mathematical accuracy of recorded cash balances.
	  a. Foot cash journals.
	  b. Trace totals to general ledger and to year-end bank reconciliations prepared by client.
	  c. Test cash on hand as necessary.

Existence
Completeness
Valuation
	3. Test cutoff.
	  a. Obtain cutoff bank statements (including canceled checks, deposit slips, and other debit/credit memoranda) directly from banks.
	    (1) Verify accuracy of cutoff bank statements by comparing canceled checks, deposit slips, and memoranda with debits and credits listed on statement.
	    (2) Examine information (e.g., dates and amounts) on cutoff bank statement and trace to reconciling items in year-end bank reconciliation and to entries in cash journals.
	    (3) Consider necessity of preparing a proof of cash.
	  b. Reconcile recorded cash balances with returned bank confirmations.
	  c. Examine intercompany and interbank transfers near year-end.

Presentation and Disclosure	4. Review financial statements to determine whether:
	  a. Cash balances are properly classified and described.
	  b. Disclosures are adequate.

confirmed by auditors in essentially the same manner as accounts receivable. However, an auditor confirms all, rather than a sample of, cash accounts. An example of a completed AICPA standard bank confirmation form with audit working paper references is presented in Figure 12-7. In addition to cash

FIGURE 12-7
Bank Confirmation

STANDARD BANK CONFIRMATION INQUIRY
Approved 1966 by
AMERICAN INSTITUTE OF CERTIFIED PUBLIC ACCOUNTANTS
and
BANK ADMINISTRATION INSTITUTE (FORMERLY NABAC)

O R I G I N A L
To be mailed to accountant   A6

December 31 19 90

Your completion of the following report will be sincerely appreciated. IF THE ANSWER TO ANY ITEM IS "NONE," PLEASE SO STATE. Kindly mail it in the enclosed stamped, addressed envelope *direct* to the accountant named below.

Report from   Yours truly,   **Woodard Company**

(ACCOUNT NAME PER BANK RECORDS)

(Bank)   Peoples Bank & Trust   By *Paula Maronti*
                                                Authorized Signature
          5100 Peoples Bank Bldg.
                                        Bank customer should check here if confirma-
          New York, New York 10010   tion of bank balances only (item 1) is desired. ☐

                                        NOTE—If the space provided is inadequate,
                                        please enter totals hereon and attach a state-
Accountant   John J. Schubert & Co., CPA's   ment giving full details as called for by the
             New York, New York 10010   columnar headings below.

1. At the close of business on ___December 31,___ 19 __90__ our records showed the following balance(s) to the **credit** of the above named customer. In the event that we could readily ascertain whether there were any balances to the credit of the customer not designated in this request, the appropriate information is given below.

AMOUNT	ACCOUNT NAME	ACCOUNT NUMBER	Subject to With-drawal by Check?	Interest Bearing? Give Rate
$175,517.10 (A5)	General Account	158-6798-321	Yes	No

2. The customer was directly liable to us in respect of loans, acceptances, etc., at the close of business on that date in the total amount of $ __150,000__ , as follows:

AMOUNT	DATE OF LOAN OR DISCOUNT	DUE DATE	INTEREST Rate	INTEREST Paid to	DESCRIPTION OF LIABILITY, COLLATERAL, SECURITY INTERESTS, LIENS, ENDORSERS, ETC.
$150,000	6-10-82	6-10-92	9.5	12-01-90	Mortgage on warehouse

3. The customer was contingently liable as endorser of notes discounted and/or as guarantor at the close of business on that date in the total amount of $ __None__ , as below:

AMOUNT	NAME OF MAKER	DATE OF NOTE	DUE DATE	REMARKS
$				

4. Other direct or contingent liabilities, open letters of credit, and relative collateral, were

   None

5. Security agreements under the Uniform Commercial Code or any other agreements providing for restrictions, not noted above, were as follows (if officially recorded, indicate date and office in which filed):

   None

                                Yours truly, (Bank) Peoples Bank & Trust
Date __January 7,__ 19 __91__   By *John Menichello*
                                            Authorized Signature

Additional copies of this form are available from the American Institute of CPAs, 1211 Avenue of the Americas, New York, N.Y. 10036

Goes to auditor outside of clients office

balances, information pertaining to loans outstanding and contingent liabilities is requested in a standard bank confirmation.

Verify Mathematical Accuracy

To test the valuation of recorded cash balances in terms of mathematical accuracy, an auditor recomputes (foots) client-computed totals in cash journals and year-end bank reconciliations (and other client-prepared supporting schedules if any). Journal totals are compared with bank reconciliation totals and traced to postings in the general ledger.

Even though usually immaterial in relation to financial statements taken as a whole, petty cash and other cash funds on hand are tested on many audits since cash is highly susceptible to misappropriation. In general, an auditor counts cash in the presence of the fund custodian and examines the undeposited receipts and paid vouchers that reconcile cash on hand to the imprest balance. For example, if a petty cash fund imprest balance is $500, and $175 is on hand, undeposited receipts and paid vouchers should total $325.

Test Cutoff

Tests of cash cutoff are most directly related to the audit objectives of existence and completeness. Generally, these tests involve the reconciliation of all internal and external documentation relating to cash balances, such as:

▲ *Internal documentation:* cash journals, the general ledger, and bank reconciliations.
▲ *External documentation:* year-end bank statements, cutoff bank statements, and returned bank confirmations.

Item 3a of the audit program in Figure 12-6 requires that cutoff statements for each bank account be obtained by the auditor directly from the bank (or banks). *Cutoff bank statements* do not represent a full month's transactions, as do most bank statements. Rather, they represent transactions (cleared checks, deposits, and miscellaneous debits and credits) for a short period after year-end (e.g., seven to ten days) and are used to verify reconciling items appearing on year-end bank reconciliations prepared by client personnel. For example, December 31 year-end bank reconciliations usually include deposits in transit and outstanding checks that could not otherwise be verified until January bank statements are received in early February. Adding to their persuasiveness as audit evidence, cutoff bank statements are sent directly to the auditor by a bank, thereby representing external evidence received directly from third parties rather than external evidence received and held by a client.

Individual canceled checks, deposit slips, and debit/credit memoranda accompanying each cutoff statement should be compared with debits and credits listed on the statement to verify the statement's accuracy. Each item on the cutoff statement should then be traced to the client-prepared year-end bank reconciliation and to cash journals. Dates of entries in cash journals, as well as amounts, should be examined to verify that receipts and disbursements near year-end are recorded in the proper period. These tests are intended to detect such practices as delays in recording cash disbursements in order to present a more favorable cash position on the balance sheet. Also, checks may be written and recorded as disbursements prior to year-end, but not mailed until after the balance sheet date, thus understating liabilities.

Copies of client-prepared bank reconciliations are typically included in audit working papers as evidence of tests of cutoff. Figure 12-8 presents an illustrative year-end bank reconciliation with appropriate working paper indexes, tick marks, and explanations. Note that the reconciliation adjusts both bank and book balances, yielding a "true" cash balance as of a particular date.

Internal auditors typically prepare a form of reconciliation called a *proof of cash* at one or more times during the year to verify the reliability of monthly bank reconciliations. However, if the client lacks a strong internal audit function or if discrepancies are observed in client-prepared year-end bank reconciliations, the independent auditor may decide to prepare a proof of cash for one or more periods.

Routine monthly bank reconciliations focus upon cash balances, while a proof of cash focuses upon both balances and transactions. Figure 12-9 depicts a four-column proof of cash for two successive months, November and December, 1990. Like the bank reconciliation in Figure 12-8, the proof of cash adjusts both the bank and book balances, yielding a "true" cash balance, although for two successive months rather than one particular date.

The procedures described in item 3a of Figure 12-6 are applicable to checking account (demand deposit) balances. Items 3b and 3c, however, relate to all recorded cash balances, including interest-bearing time deposits and money fund balances. Returned bank confirmations (item 3b) are a persuasive form of external evidence and should be reconciled with recorded amounts. Item 3c is a particularly effective cutoff test applicable when an entity engages in intercompany transactions or maintains more than one bank account.

Intercompany cash transfers at or near year-end should be tested to determine whether they are recorded properly as both a receipt by one entity and disbursement by another in the same accounting period; if not, cash balances for the consolidated group of entities could be overstated (or understated, though this is rarely the case). For example, if a subsidiary records a $10,000 cash receipt from a parent on December 31, but the parent defers recording the disbursement until January 1, consolidated December 31 financial statements would overstate cash by $10,000, since the related receipt and

FIGURE 12-8
Bank Reconciliation

```
(Schedule                                                      A5
prepared                                                  Dec. 31, 1990
by Client)                       Woodard Company
                        Bank Reconciliation as of 12-31-90      bank stmt
                           Acct. 1001: Peoples Bank          bank conf.

Balance per bank, 12-31-90                                 $17,551,710 b
   Add: Deposits in transit, 12-31-90  $1,578,143 c
   Check drawn by Martin Davis Co.
     charged to Marc David, Inc.,
     by bank in error                       275,000 d    1,853,143
   Deduct outstanding checks:
          No. 5775  12-24  $1,431,000 e
              5776  12-26     156,050 e
              5779  12-26     181,021 e
              5780  12-27   2,169,540 e
              5781  12-29   1,589,176 e
              5785  12-30   1,191,240 e              <6,718,027>
Adjusted bank balance, 12-31-90                          $12,686,826
                                                              a

Balance per books, 12-31-90                              $13,241,386 f
   Deduct: December bank service
     charge                              $    28,500 b
     Check from Apex Services, Inc.,
       deposited 12-15 returned for
       insufficient funds, 12-18             526,060 b    <554,560>
Adjusted book balance, 12-31-90                          $12,686,826
                                                              a


a Footed.
b Agreed to 12-31-90 bank statement.
c Agreed to cutoff bank statement and to cash receipts
  journal.
d Agreed to cutoff bank statement.
e Agreed to cutoff bank statement and to cash disburse-
  ments journal.
f Agreed to general ledger.
                              SC
                          1-18-90
```

disbursement are recorded in different accounting periods. Intercompany transfers can be tested by reviewing all transfers between related entities for a period, e.g., five days, before and after year-end; corresponding receipt and disbursement entries should accompany each transfer and should be recorded in the same accounting period.

FIGURE 12-9
Proof of Cash

(Prepared by Client)

A10
Dec. 31, 1990

FM
1-15-91

Woodard Company
Proof of Cash
Acct. 101: Old Stone Bank

	11-30-90	December Receipts	December Disbursements	12-31-90
Balance per bank	$8,576,110 b	$41,954,430 b	<$41,694,175>b	$8,836,365 b
Deposits in transit: 11-30	2,462,590 c	<2,462,590>		
12-31		2,170,050 d		2,170,050
Outstanding checks: 11-30	<3,156,129>e		<279,547>	<279,547>
12-31			<1,933,212>f	<1,933,212>
Adjusted bank balance:	$7,882,571 a	$41,661,890 a	<$40,750,805> a	$8,793,656 a
Balance per books	$7,905,571 g	$41,661,890 h	<$40,748,805>i	$8,818,656 g
Bank service charge: 11-30	<23,000>j		23,000	
12-31			<25,000>b	<25,000>
Adjusted book balance	$7,882,571 a	$41,661,890 a	<$40,750,805> a	$8,793,656 a

a Footed.
b Agreed to December bank statement.
c Agreed to December bank statement and cash receipts journal.
d Agreed to cutoff bank statement and to cash receipts journal.
e Agreed to December bank statement and to cash disbursements journal.
f Agreed to cutoff bank statement and cash disbursements journal.
g Agreed to general ledger.
h Agreed to cash receipts journal.
i Agreed to cash disbursements journal.
j Agreed to November bank statement.

Interbank transfers, similar in nature to intercompany transfers, can also be tested by examining transactions near the year-end date. For each transfer of funds between banks, a receipt and corresponding disbursement should be recorded in the same period; otherwise cash will be misstated on the balance sheet. While tests of interbank transfers may reveal understatements of cash (i.e., a disbursement recorded on or before year-end and corresponding receipt after year-end), such tests are primarily designed to detect overstatements of cash. For example, concealment of a cash shortage could be attempted by transferring funds from one bank account to another and recording the receipt on or before year-end and the disbursement after year-end. Overstating cash through interbank transfers is called *kiting*.

Figure 12-10 illustrates a working paper schedule of intercompany and interbank transfers.

Review Financial Statement Presentation and Disclosure

The audit program in Figure 12-6 (page 496) concludes with the auditor's review of financial statement presentation and disclosure of cash balances. An auditor should determine whether cash balances are classified, described, and disclosed in accordance with generally accepted accounting principles.

Amounts presented as "Cash" in the current assets section of a balance sheet should represent cash on hand and unrestricted deposits. Special-purpose funds, such as cash set aside for plant expansion, should be reported separately from "Cash." Balances subject to withdrawal restrictions, such as compensating balances and certificates of deposit, should be reported as separate components of cash or adequately described and disclosed in the balance sheet or in notes to the financial statements.

SUMMARY

As discussed in Chapter 11, the revenue/receipt cycle encompasses two major business functions — selling resources to customers and, subsequently, collecting cash for resources sold. In turn, these functions are reflected in three major financial statements accounts, sales, accounts receivable, and cash, each of which is discussed in this chapter in the context of substantive tests. When performing substantive tests of sales, receivables, and cash balances, an auditor's objectives are to determine that each account balance exists, represents all transactions that should be presented, represents rights of the entity, is valued appropriately, and is presented and disclosed properly in the financial statements.

FIGURE 12-10

A9
KC
1/21/91

Woodard Company
Schedule of Interbank and
Intercompany Transfers
December 31, 1990

Check No.	Transferred: From	To	Amount	Disbursement Date Per Books	Disbursement Date Per Bank	Receipt Date Per Books	Receipt Date Per Bank
Interbank Transfers							
6721	First Nat'l Bk	Union Trust	$25,000 a	12/30 b	1/2 c	12/30 d	1/2 c
6741	First Nat'l Bk	People's Bk	35,500 a	12/31 b	1/3 c	12/31 d	1/2 c
6743	First Nat'l General Account	First Nat'l Payroll Account	75,000 a	12/31 b	1/2 c	12/31 d	1/2 c
Intercompany Transfers							
6742	Woodard (Union Trust)	Westco (subsidiary)	25,000 a	12/31 b	1/2 c	12/31 d	1/2 e

a Agreed check number, payee, payor, and amount to cash disbursements journal.
b Per cash disbursements journal.
c Agreed to Woodard cutoff bank statement.
d Per cash receipts journal.
e Agreed to Westco cutoff bank statement.

Importantly, the material presented in Chapter 8 on EDP and in Chapter 10 on audit sampling is directly applicable to substantive tests of sales, receivables, and cash because: (1) many U.S. companies now process some, if not most, revenue/receipt cycle transactions electronically, and (2) sampling is used frequently in auditing the revenue/receipt cycle because of the large volume of transactions involved. Applications of audit sampling and EDP are discussed and illustrated in Appendix A and Appendix B, respectively.

APPENDIX A
CASE ILLUSTRATION: APPLYING STATISTICAL SAMPLING IN SUBSTANTIVE TESTS OF ACCOUNTS RECEIVABLE

To integrate material presented in this chapter with the statistical sampling applications introduced in Chapter 10 and with the tests of revenue/receipt cycle controls introduced in Chapter 11, assume a continuing audit engagement for the Madison Corporation, a relatively large manufacturer and supplier of health-care equipment, whose financial year ends December 31. Madison is a publicly held corporation and has been an industry leader for over two decades. The specific objective in this case is to determine whether recorded trade accounts receivable are fairly stated at December 31 — that is, program step 2, Figure 12-2, page 489.

Updating the Interim Assessment of Control Risk

Assume the interim tests of controls were accomplished during September and revealed that control procedures over customer order, credit, shipping, billing, recording, and cash collection — Madison's major revenue/receipt cycle activities — were adequate and reliable and that undetected control deficiencies were not likely to produce aggregate error in excess of tolerable error. The auditor assesses a minimum level of control risk. However, because of employee turnover and to assure that controls were reliable at year-end, the auditor:

▲ Updated tests of controls through December 31 by applying nonstatistical sampling to transactions recorded in October, November, and December.
▲ Made inquiries of management regarding any significant changes to revenue/receipt cycle controls.

In contrast to the interim tests of controls, the auditor's updated tests for October through December revealed a significant number of inaccuracies in recorded receivables. Inquiries indicated that two key employees were re-placed on October 1, thereby explaining the markedly higher rate of clerical and posting errors in October, November, and December. No other personnel or procedures had changed since September 30.

Planning the Receivables Confirmation and Selecting a Sampling Plan

In this case, the auditor would probably elect to use positive confirma-tions to control detection risk since the updated tests of controls suggest that inaccurate balances are likely. The likelihood of inaccurate balances also sug-gests that differences between audited and recorded amounts are not apt to be rare, indicating that ratio or difference estimation may be the most effec-tive statistical sampling plan, particularly since Madison maintains subsidiary records for each customer account. Ratio estimation is selected by the auditor because in prior years — and for October through December — differences between audited and book values tended to increase as book values increased, indicating differences were highly proportional to book values.

The auditor's confirmation of Madison Corporation's receivables balance is accomplished by ratio estimation, which was introduced in Chapter 10 and is illustrated below.

Population, Sampling Unit, and Estimated Standard Deviation

The audit population consists of 1,550 customer accounts, each repre-sented by detailed subsidiary records totaling $1,250,000 at December 31. An aged trial balance is obtained from accounts receivable personnel, footed, cross-footed, traced in part to detailed subsidiary records, and agreed in total with the general ledger. The sampling unit is represented by individual cus-tomer accounts, not invoices, since account balances rather than invoice terms will be confirmed.

In this case, the auditor would not use a preliminary sample to estimate the population standard deviation, since audited amounts could only be ob-tained by confirmation, which is time consuming and therefore not efficient. As a result, the auditor estimates the standard deviation to be $175 because (1) in three successive years, the population standard deviation was approxi-mately $150 and (2) changes in conditions since September 30 suggest greater error is likely.

Risk and Tolerable Error

To continue the sampling plan, the auditor requires estimates of the risk of incorrect rejection, the risk of incorrect acceptance, and tolerable error, all three of which are used to determine the allowance for sampling risk, the remaining variable needed to calculate sample size.

The risks of incorrect rejection and incorrect acceptance are both set at .05, a relatively low level, because (1) updated tests of controls revealed clerical inaccuracies and mispostings and (2) no other procedures within the audit program in Figure 12-2, page 489, can be relied on to address directly whether trade receivables exist at December 31. Tolerable error, the maximum monetary error that may exist without causing the financial statements to be materially misstated, is judged to be $90,000 by the auditor.

From Table 10-1, page 402, R, the ratio of desired sampling risk to tolerable error, is .543, the intersect of the column associated with a .05 risk of incorrect rejection and the row associated with a .05 risk of incorrect acceptance. Since TE, tolerable error, is $90,000, then A, the desired allowance for sampling risk, is:

$$
\begin{aligned}
A &= R \times TE \\
&= .543 \times \$90,000 \\
&= \$48,870
\end{aligned}
$$

SAMPLE SIZE

Recapping, the following variables are known or have been estimated:

▲ Population size $(N) = 1,550$
▲ Estimated standard deviation $(S) = \$175$
▲ Risk of incorrect rejection $(U) = .05$ (i.e., 1.96 standard deviations)
▲ Desired allowance for sampling risk $(A) = \$48,870$

From this information, sample size would be calculated as follows:

$$
\begin{aligned}
n' &= \left(\frac{S \times U \times N}{A} \right)^2 \\
&= \left(\frac{\$175 \times 1.96 \times 1,550}{\$48,870} \right)^2 \\
&= 118
\end{aligned}
$$

and

$$
n = \frac{n'}{1 + \dfrac{n'}{N}}
$$

$$= \frac{118}{1 + \frac{118}{1,550}}$$
$$= 110$$

Thus, given the auditor's acceptable risks and tolerable error, 110 randomly selected account balances must be confirmed in order to generate evidence bearing on whether the 1,550 customer accounts are fairly stated at December 31.

Method of Sample Selection

To select the 110 sample accounts, the auditor assigns sequential numbers from 0001 through 1550 to the client's alphabetically arrayed aged trial balance. A random number table or computer-generated random number list is used to select individual customer accounts for confirmation.

All confirmations are mailed in early-January, and second requests are sent to nonrespondents within ten days. For disputed balances and for nonrespondents, the auditor applies alternative procedures including (1) determining whether the account was paid subsequent to year-end, and therefore was collectible at December 31, (2) examining copies of sales invoices to determine if and when billing occurred, and (3) examining shipping documents to determine if and when goods were shipped.

Evaluate Sample Results

Assume that from compiled confirmation responses and alternative procedures for disputed accounts and nonrespondents, the sampling plan indicates the audited value for all 110 sampled accounts is $89,000 while book value is $92,710, yielding $\hat{R}$, the ratio of audited value to book value, of .96 (i.e., $89,000 \div $92,710$). The estimated total population value, $\hat{X}$, is determined by multiplying total book value, B, times $\hat{R}$:

$$\hat{X} = \hat{R} \times B$$
$$= .96 \times \$1,250,000$$
$$= \$1,200,000$$

Assume the population standard deviation, calculated from sample data, is $167.

The achieved allowance for sampling risk, A', is calculated next as follows:

$$A' = \frac{S \times U \times N}{\sqrt{n}} \sqrt{1 - \frac{n}{N}}$$

$$= \frac{\$167 \times 1.96 \times 1,550}{\sqrt{110}} \sqrt{1 - \frac{110}{1,550}}$$

$$= 46,580$$

Finally, the auditor determines a precision interval from the estimated population audited value, $\hat{X}$, and the achieved allowance for sampling risk, A'.

Precision interval $= \hat{X} \pm A'$
$= \$1,200,000 \pm \$46,580$
$= \$1,153,420$ to $\$1,246,580$

The precision interval leads to the following statistical conclusion:

Based upon procedures applied, the estimated population value is $1,200,000, and there is a 95 percent probability (1.0 minus the risk of incorrect acceptance, .05) that the true but unknown population value is included in the precision interval, $1,153,420 to $1,246,580.

In this case, even though the desired allowance for sampling risk, $48,870 exceeds the achieved allowance for sampling risk, $46,580, an audit adjustment could be proposed because:

▲ Recorded book value, $1,250,000, falls outside the precision interval, $1,153,420 to $1,246,580.
▲ Tolerable error, $90,000, does not exceed the difference between recorded book value, $1,250,000, and the furthest end of the precision interval away from book value, $1,153,420. That is, $90,000 is less than $96,580 ($1,250,000 − $1,153,420).

As a result, using the methodology introduced in the Appendix to Chapter 10, the auditor could propose an adjustment in the amount of $6,475, calculated as follows:

$$\text{Adjustment} = \frac{\text{Recorded}}{\text{book value}} - \left(\frac{\text{Lower}}{\text{precision}} + \frac{\text{Tolerable}}{\text{error}} \right)$$

$$= \$1,250,000 - (1,153,525 + \$90,000)$$
$$= \$6,475$$

Of course, as indicated in Chapter 10, the auditor need not necessarily propose an audit adjustment. Rather, he or she could increase sample size and reevaluate for all sampling units, or request that the client revalue the entire population. In this case, given the relatively low dollar magnitude of the proposed adjustment, the auditor's most likely course of action would be to propose an audit adjustment, reducing recorded book value, $1,250,000, to the adjusted value, $1,243,420 (i.e., the lower precision limit, $1,153,420, plus tolerable error, $90,000).

Assuming that the audit adjustment is booked by the client and that no other evidence surfaces to the contrary, the auditor's audit conclusion would be:

> *Based on audit procedures applied, I am satisfied that Accounts Receivable — Trade, excluding the allowance for uncollectibles, is fairly stated at December 31.*

APPENDIX B
COMPUTER-ASSISTED SUBSTANTIVE TESTS OF ACCOUNTS RECEIVABLE

Regardless of whether a client's revenue/receipt cycle activities are accomplished manually or by computer, an auditor's objectives are identical. However, when part or all of the cycle is recorded, classified, or summarized electronically, an auditor's substantive tests of details can be accomplished in part by computer-assisted procedures. Figure 12-11 lists several computer-assisted techniques for a series of audit procedures common to audits of accounts receivable.

To illustrate the application of computer-assisted procedures, assume an auditor wishes to accomplish portions of the following three substantive tests (included in Figure 12–11) with the aid of a computer:

▲ Verify mathematical accuracy of the accounts receivable subsidiary records.
▲ Age receivables according to computer-stored invoice dates.
▲ List credit balances in accounts receivable for reclassification to accounts payable.

The auditor may either design a computer program to accomplish these procedures or use generalized audit software. As discussed in Chapter 8, generalized software is available from outside vendors, including some of the larger public accounting firms. Auditor-prepared programs, in contrast, are designed for each client application, and require that the auditor accomplish all of the

FIGURE 12-11

Computer-Assisted Substantive Tests: Accounts Receivable

Audit Procedure	Computer-Assisted Substantive Test
Test mathematical accuracy.	• Verify footings, cross-footings, and extensions of the accounts receivable aged trial balance and/or the subsidiary records.
Summarize data for further testing or analysis.	• Age receivables according to computer-stored invoice dates. • List credit balances in accounts receivable for reclassification to accounts payable. • Print accounts receivable confirmations.
Test accuracy of recorded data.	• Trace details in computer-stored subsidiary records with machine-readable source documents.
Select samples.	• Select audit samples from internally stored random number generators and aged trial balances (or subsidiary records).
Compare similar data files.	• Compare aged trial balance with accounts receivable subsidiary records.

tasks normally associated with computer program preparation, including developing systems flowcharts and program specifications, coding, testing, and debugging, before the program is applied in a specific audit engagement.

Figure 12-12 flowcharts the tasks necessary to accomplish the three substantive tests and would be identical whether the auditor used a generalized software package or prepared a tailored computer program.

As illustrated in Figure 12-12 the computer-assisted tests require three separate tapes: the client's accounts receivable master file and sales journal and the auditor's computer program. The program would be designed to perform the following tasks for each substantive test:

Substantive Test	Computer Software Task
Verify mathematical accuracy.	• Foot and cross-foot the amounts recorded in each customer account within the accounts receivable master file. • Total the balances of all customer accounts, leading to a total for all receivables. • Print exceptions

FIGURE 12-12

Flowchart of Computer-Assisted Tests of Accounts Receivable

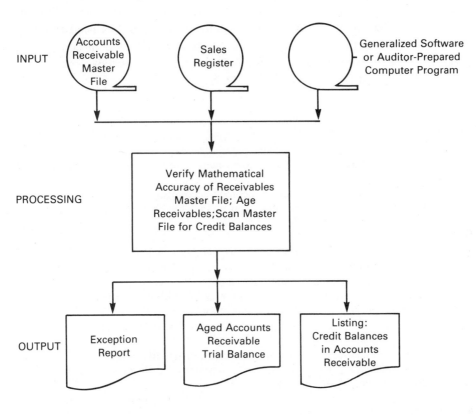

Age receivables.	• Trace individual customer balances on the accounts receivable master file to related sales entries in the sales journal.
	• For each customer, print balances by invoice dates, i.e., 0–30 days, 31–60 days, 61–90 days, 91–120 days, and over 120 days.
	• Print aged trial balances.
List credit balances in receivables.	• Scan the accounts receivable master file for net credit balances.
	• Print listing of credit balance accounts.

The program would be run on the client's computer, either directly by the auditor or by client personnel under the auditor's supervision. The printed exception report, aged trial balance, and credit balance listing — the output documents depicted in Figure 12-12 — would be obtained by the auditor directly from the client's printer. The output and computer-assisted tests are then documented in the auditor's working papers, and used in conjunction with other audit evidence to help form conclusions about whether receivables are fairly stated at the balance sheet date.

QUESTIONS

1. What are financial statement assertions, audit objectives and audit procedures? How are they related?
2. How does an auditor test whether recorded accounts receivable exist?
3. Why does an auditor perform analytical procedures on receivables?
4. How does an auditor test whether recorded receivables represent bona fide rights of the client?
5. How does an auditor test the valuation of accounts receivable and sales?
6. Receivables confirmation is a ''generally accepted procedure of auditing.'' Explain the significance of this statement.
7. Describe and distinguish between positive and negative confirmation requests.
8. Explain the purpose and nature of sales cutoff tests.
9. How is the audit objective of presentation and disclosure accomplished for receivables and sales?
10. How does an auditor test whether cash balances actually exist?
11. List the audit tests available to determine whether all cash transactions that should be recorded actually are recorded.
12. Aside from cash balances, what other information is requested by an AICPA standard bank confirmation?
13. Identify the internal and external documentation available to an auditor to test cutoff.
14. How does an auditor test the valuation of cash balances?
15. Explain the purpose and nature of cutoff tests of cash balances.
16. How does a proof of cash differ from an ordinary bank reconciliation?
17. How and why does an auditor test intercompany and interbank transfers?
18. Describe some computer-assisted substantive tests an auditor might apply to accounts receivable.

MULTIPLE CHOICE QUESTIONS

1. The audit working papers often include a client-prepared, aged trial balance of accounts receivable as of the balance sheet date. This aging is best used by the auditor to

   a. Evaluate control procedures over credit sales.
   b. Test the accuracy of recorded charge sales.

c. Estimate credit losses.
d. Verify the validity of the recorded receivables.   (AICPA Adapted)

2. Once a CPA has determined that accounts receivable have increased due to slow collections in a "tight money" environment, the CPA would be likely to

   a. Increase the balance in the allowance for bad debts account.
   b. Review the going concern ramifications.
   c. Review the credit and collection policy.
   d. Expand tests of collectibility.   (AICPA Adapted)

3. If accounts receivable turned over 7.1 times in 1989 as compared with only 5.6 times in 1990, it is possible that there were

   a. Unrecorded credit sales in 1990.
   b. Unrecorded cash receipts in 1989.
   c. More thorough credit investigations made by the company late in 1989.
   d. Fictitious sales in 1990.   (AICPA Adapted)

4. Which of the following might be detected by an auditor's cutoff review and examination of sales journal entries for several days prior to and subsequent to the balance sheet date?

   a. Lapping year-end accounts receivable.
   b. Inflating sales for the year.
   c. Kiting bank balances.
   d. Misappropriating merchandise.   (AICPA Adapted)

5. To verify that all sales transactions have been recorded, a test of transactions should be completed on a representative sample drawn from

   a. Entries in the sales journal.
   b. The billing clerk's file of sales orders.
   c. A file of duplicate copies of sales invoices for which all prenumbered forms in the series have been accounted for.
   d. The shipping clerk's file of duplicate copies of bills of lading.
          (AICPA Adapted)

6. In determining the adequacy of the allowance for uncollectible accounts, the least reliance should be placed upon which of the following?

   a. The credit manager's opinion.
   b. An aging schedule of past due accounts.
   c. Collection experience of the client's collection agency.
   d. Ratios calculated showing the past relationship of the valuation allowance to net credit sales.   (AICPA Adapted)

7. In determining validity of accounts receivable, which of the following would the auditor consider most reliable?

   a. Documentary evidence that supports the accounts receivable balance.
   b. Credits to accounts receivable from the cash receipts book after the close of business at year-end.
   c. Direct telephone communication between auditor and debtor.
   d. Confirmation replies received directly from customers.   (AICPA Adapted)

8. An auditor confirms a representative number of open accounts receivable as of December 31, and investigates respondents' exceptions and comments. By this procedure the auditor would be most likely to learn of which of the following?

   a. One of the cashiers has been covering a personal embezzlement by lapping.
   b. One of the sales clerks has not been preparing charge slips for credit sales to family and friends.
   c. One of the EDP control clerks has been removing all sales invoices applicable to his account from the data file.
   d. The credit manager has misappropriated remittances from customers whose accounts have been written off.   (AICPA Adapted)

9. The auditor should ordinarily mail confirmation requests to all banks with which the client has conducted any business during the year, regardless of the year-end balance, since

   a. The confirmation form also seeks informtion about indebtedness to the bank.
   b. This procedure will detect kiting activities which would otherwise not be detected.
   c. The mailing of confirmation forms to all such banks is required by generally accepted auditing standards.
   d. This procedure relieves the auditor of any responsibility with respect to non-detection of forged checks.   (AICPA Adapted)

10. Customers having substantial year-end past due balances fail to reply after second request forms have been mailed directly to them. Which of the following is the most appropriate audit procedure?

    a. Examine shipping documents.
    b. Review collections during the year being examined.
    c. Intensify the study of the client's internal control structure with respect to receivables.
    d. Increase the balance in the accounts receivable allowance (contra) account.
                                                              (AICPA Adapted)

11. The negative form of accounts receivable confirmation request is particularly useful except when

    a. Internal control structure surrounding accounts receivable is considered to be effective.
    b. A large number of small balances are involved.
    c. The auditor has reason to believe the persons receiving the requests are likely to give them consideration.
    d. Individual account balances are relatively large.   (AICPA Adapted)

12. The auditor should ordinarily mail confirmation requests to all banks with which the client has conducted any business during the year, regardless of the year-end balance, since

    a. The confirmation form also seeks information about indebtedness to the bank.
    b. This procedure will detect kiting activities which would otherwise not be detected.
    c. The mailing of confirmation forms to all such banks is required by generally accepted auditing standards.

    d. This procedure relieves the auditor of any responsibility with respect to non-detection of forged checks.   (AICPA Adapted)

13. An auditor who is engaged to examine the financial statements of a business enterprise will request a cutoff bank statement primarily in order to

    a. Verify the cash balance reported on the bank confirmation inquiry form.

    b. Verify reconciling items on the client's bank reconciliation.

    c. Detect lapping.

    d. Detect kiting.   (AICPA Adapted)

PROBLEMS

12-1   Following are errors, irregularities, or other circumstances that an auditor might encounter as a result of applying year-end substantive tests to accounts receivable as of December 31, 1990:

a. Sales totaling $12,500 were shipped on January 2, 1991 and recorded on December 31, 1990.

b. Balances in selected individual customer accounts do not reconcile with supporting documentation (e.g., sales invoices, cash receipts).

c. Not all sales transactions are recorded.

d. The aged trial balance prepared by the client includes a customer account within the 30 to 60-day category that is actually 120 days old.

e. Positive confirmations were not returned by 27 of 100 mailed receivables confirmations.

f. Actual writeoffs during 1990 of receivables arising from 1989 sales were greater than the December 31, 1990 allowance for doubtful accounts.

Required:
For each of the preceding items indicate (1) specific procedures that might address the error, irregularity, or circumstance and (2) the audit objective addressed by each procedure.

12-2   Dodge, CPA is examining the financial statements of a manufacturing company with a significant amount of trade accounts receivable. Dodge is satisfied that the accounts are properly summarized and classified and that allocations, reclassifications, and valuations are made in accordance with generally accepted accounting principles. Dodge is planning to use accounts receivable confirmation requests to satisfy the third standard of fieldwork as to trade accounts receivable.

Required:
1. Identify and describe the two forms of accounts receivable confirmation requests and indicate what factors Dodge will consider in determining when to use each.
2. What alternative procedures could Dodge use to verify unconfirmed accounts?
                    (AICPA Adapted)

12-3   You have examined the financial statements of the Heft Company for several years. The internal control structure for accounts receivable is very satisfactory. The Heft Company is on a calendar year basis. An interim audit, which included confirmation of the accounts receivable, was performed on August 31 and indicated that the accounting for receivables was very reliable.

The company's sales are principally to manufacturing concerns. There are about 1,500 active trade accounts receivable, of which about 35% represent 65% of the total dollar amount. The accounts receivable are maintained alphabetically in five subsidiary ledgers which are controlled by one general ledger account.

Sales are machine-posted in the subledgers by an operation that simultaneously updates the customer's ledger card and monthly statement, and records the transaction in the sales journal. All cash receipts are in the form of customers' checks and are machine-posted, simultaneously updating the customer's ledger card, monthly statement, and the cash receipts journal. Information for posting cash receipts is obtained from the remittance advice returned with of the customers' checks. The bookkeeping machine operator compares the remittance advices with the list of checks that was prepared by another person when the mail was received.

Summary totals are produced monthly by the bookkeeping machine operations for posting to the appropriate general ledger accounts such as cash, sales, and accounts receivable. An aged trial balances for each subsidiary is prepared monthly.

Sales returns and allowances and bad debt writeoffs are summarized periodically and recorded in the general journal. Supporting documents for these journal entries are available. The usual documents arising from billing and shipping are also available.

Required:

Prepare in detail an audit program of substantive tests for Heft Company's year-end balance in trade accounts receivable. The program should be tailored specifically to the audit of Heft Company. Therefore, the representative substantive tests listed and discussed within the chapter should be used as a guide, but not as a final and complete answer.   (AICPA Adapted)

12-4   Martin Kline, CPA, is auditing the RCT Manufacturing Company as of February 28, 1990. As with all engagements, one of Kline's initial procedures is to make overall checks of the client's financial data by reviewing significant ratios and trends to gain a better understanding of the business and to determine where audit efforts should be concentrated.

The financial statements prepared by the client with audited 1989 figures and preliminary 1990 figures are presented below in condensed form.

RCT Manufacturing Company
Condensed Balance Sheets
February 28, 1990 and 1989

Assets	1990	1989
Cash	$ 12,000	$ 15,000
Accounts receivable, net	93,000	50,000
Inventory	72,000	67,000
Other current assets	5,000	6,000
Plant and equipment, net of depreciation	60,000	80,000
Total assets	$242,000	$218,000

Liabilities and Equities

Accounts payable.........................	$ 38,000	$ 41,000
Federal income tax payable................	30,000	14,400
Long-term liabilities	20,000	40,000
Common stock	70,000	70,000
Retained earnings........................	84,000	52,600
Total liabilities and equities	$242,000	$218,000

RCT Manufacturing Company
Condensed Income Statements
Years Ended February 28, 1990 and 1989

	1990	1989
Net sales	$1,684,000	$1,250,000
Cost of goods sold	927,000	710,000
Gross margin on sales................	$ 757,000	$ 540,000
Selling and administrative expenses......	682,000	504,000
Income before federal income taxes......	$ 75,000	$ 36,000
Income tax expense..................	30,000	14,400
Net income	$ 45,000	$ 21,600

Additional information:

a. The company has only an insignificant amount of cash sales.

b. The end-of-year figures are comparable to the average for each respective year.

Required:

For each year compute a turnover ratio for accounts receivable. On the basis of these ratios, identify and discuss audit procedures that should be included in Kline's audit of accounts receivable.   (AICPA Adapted)

12-5   In designing an audit program for accounts receivable, an auditor should include procedures for determining the adequacy of the allowance for uncollectible accounts.

Required:

Cite various procedures that an auditor employs that might lead to detection of an inadequate allowance for uncollectible accounts receivable.

(AICPA Adapted)

12-6   In connection with an examination of the financial statements of Houston Wholesalers, Inc., for the year ended June 30, 1990, a CPA performs several cutoff tests.

Required:

1. What is a cutoff test and why must cutoff tests be performed?
2. The CPA wishes to test Houston's sales cutoff at June 30, 1988. Describe the steps that should be included in this test.   (AICPA Adapted)

12-7   In connection with year-end substantive procedures related to cash balances as of June 30, 1990, a CPA obtains a July 10, 1990 bank statement directly from a bank.

Required:
Explain how the CPA will use the "cutoff" bank statement:
1. When reviewing the June 30, 1990 bank reconciliation.
2. To obtain other audit information.   (AICPA Adapted)

12-8   Following are errors, irregularities, or other circumstances that an auditor might encounter as a result of applying substantive detailed tests to cash balances as of December 31.
a. The petty cash fund is short $75.
b. Cash in banks is overstated by $1,500.
c. Several checks were issued on December 31, but were postdated January 2.
d. Outstanding checks per the bank reconciliation do not agree with the cash disbursements journal.
e. On December 31, the sum of $15,000 was transferred from an account in the First National Bank to an account in Tower Savings Bank.
f. The December 31 bank reconciliation contains several discrepancies.
g. On December 31, the client transferred $25,000 to a wholly owned subsidiary.

Required:
Indicate a specific procedure(s) that might detect each error, irregularity, or circumstance and identify the audit objective(s) addressed by each procedure.

12-9   Finney, CPA, was engaged to conduct an audit of the financial statements of Clayton Realty Corporation for the month ending January 31, 1990. The examination of monthly rent reconciliations is a vital portion of the audit engagement.

The following rent reconciliation was prepared by the controller of Clayton Realty Corporation and was presented to Finney, who subjected it to various audit procedures:

Clayton Realty Corporation
RENT RECONCILIATION
For the month ended
January 31, 1990

Gross apartment rents (Schedule A)	$1,600,800*
Less vacancies (Schedule B)	20,500*
Net apartment rentals	$1,580,300
Less unpaid January rents (Schedule C)	7,800*
Total	$1,572,500
Add prepaid rent collected (Apartment 116)	500*
Total cash collected	$1,573,000*

Schedules A, B, and C are available to Finney but have not been illustrated. Finney has conducted a study and evaluation of the system of internal control and found that it could be relied upon to produce reliable accounting information. Cash receipts from rental operations are deposited in a special bank account.

Required:
What substantive audit procedures should Finney employ during the audit in order to substantiate the validity of each of the amounts marked by an asterisk (*)?

(AICPA Adapted)

12-10   The following client-prepared bank reconciliation is being examined by Kautz, CPA, during an examination of the financial statements of Cynthia Company:

Cynthia Company
BANK RECONCILIATION
VILLAGE BANK ACCOUNT 2
December 31, 1990

Bank per bank (a)		$18,375.91
Deposits in transit (b)		
12/30	1,471.10	
12/31	2,840.69	4,311.79
Subtotal		22,687.70
Outstanding checks (c)		
837	6,000.00	
1941	671.80	
1966	320.00	
1984	1,855.42	
1985	3,621.22	
1987	2,576.89	
1991	4,420.88	(19,466.21)
Subtotal		3,221.49
NSF check returned		
12/29 (d)		200.00
Bank charges		5.50
Error Check No. 1932		148.10
Customer note collected by		
the bank ($2,750 plus		
$275 interest) (e)		(3,025.00)
Balance per books (f)		$ 550.09

Required:
Indicate one or more audit procedures that should be performed by Kautz in gathering evidence in support of each of the items (a) through (f).   (AICPA Adapted)

12-11   You have completed your examination of the cash on hand and in banks in your audit of the Hoosier Company's financial statements for the year ended December 31, 1990, and noted the following:

a. The company maintains a general bank account at the National Bank and an imprest payroll bank account at The City Bank. All checks are signed by the company president, Deidre Hoosier.

b. Data and reconciliations prepared by Donald Hume, the company bookkeeper, on November 30, 1990, indicated that the payroll account had a $1,000 general ledger and bank balance with no in-transit or outstanding items, and the general bank account had a $12,405 general ledger balance with checks outstanding aggregating $918 (No. 1202 for $575 and No. 1205 for $343) and one deposit of $492 in transit.

c. Your surprise cash count on Tuesday, January 2, 1991, revealed customers' checks totaling $540 and a National Bank deposit slip for that amount dated December 29, 1990 were in the company safe and that no cash was in transit to the bank at that time. Your examination of the general account checkbook revealed check No. 1216 to be the first unused check.

d. Company general ledger accounts are prepared on a posting machine, and all transactions are posted in chronological sequence. The ledger card for the general bank account is reproduced on the next page.

e. The December statements from both banks were delivered unopened to you. The City Bank statement contained deposits for $1,675; $1706; $1,845; and $2,597 and 72 paid checks totaling $7,823. The National Bank statement is reproduced below:

The National Bank
Account: Hoosier Commpany (General Account)

Date	Charges		Credits	Balance
Nov. 30				12,831
Dec. 1			492	13,323
Dec. 5	1,675	267 RT	496	11,877
Dec. 8	575		832	12,134
Dec. 11	1,706	654	975	10,749
Dec. 14	1,987 D	2,062	8,045	14,745
Dec. 18	6,237	1,845	9,949	16,612
Dec. 21	241 RT	546 RT	546 CM	16,371
Dec. 22	2,072 D		1,513	15,812
Dec. 26	2,597			13,215
Dec. 28	362	4 DM	1,010 CM	13,859
Dec. 29	12 DM		362	14,209
	Total charges — $22,842		Total Cr. — $24,220	

Legend:	OD: Overdraft	RT: Returned check	DM: Debit memo
	CM: Credit memo	D: Draft	

f. Cutoff statements were secured by you personally from both banks on January 8, 1991, and The National Bank statement is reproduced below:

The National Bank
Account: Hoosier Company (General Account)

Date	Charges		Credits	Balance
Dec. 29, 1990				14,209
Jan. 2, 1991	1,739	3,945	540	9,065
Jan. 5	350		942	9,657

g. You determine that the bank statements are correct except that The National Bank incorrectly charged a returned check on December 21 but credited the account the same day.

General Ledger
General Bank Account
(The National Bank)

Ref.	Debits	Credits	Balance
Bal.			12,405
12-1	496		12,901
1206		1,675	11,226
1207		645	10,581
12-6	832		11,413
1208		1,706	9,707
12-8	975		10,682
1209		2,062	8,620
1210		3,945	4,675
1211		6,237	1,562*
12-12	8,045		6,483
12-15	9,549		16,032
1212		1,845	14,187
RT		241	13,946
1213		350	13,596
D		2,072	11,524
12-22	1,513		13,037
1214		2,597	10,440
1215		1,739	8,701
12-29	540		9,241
12-31	942		10,183
1216		1,120	9,063
	22,892	26,234	

h. The $362 check charged by The National Bank on December 28 was check No. 2000 drawn payable to Hoosier Company and indorsed "Hoosier Company by Donald Hume." Your investigation showed that the amount credited by The National Bank on December 29 was an unauthorized transfer from The City Bank Payroll Account to The National Bank General Account which had been made by the company's bookkeeper who made no related entry in the company's records. The check was charged to Hoosier Company on January 2, 1991, on the cutoff statement from The City Bank.

i. Drafts charged against The National Bank account were for trade acceptances which were signed by Deidre Hoosier and issued to a supplier.

j. On December 28 a 60-day, 14 percent $1,000 note was collected by The National Bank for Hoosier for a $4 collection fee.

k. The $12 debit memo from The National Bank was a charge for printed checks.

l. Check No. 1213 was issued to replace check No. 1205 when the latter was reported not received by a vendor. Because of the delay in paying this account Hoosier Company was no longer entitled to the 2 percent cash discount it had taken in preparing the original check.

Required:

Prepare a proof of cash for December for Hoosier's General Bank Account in The National Bank. Your proof of cash should show the computation of the adjusted balances for both the bank statement and the general ledger account of The National Bank for cash in bank November 30, December receipts, December disbursements, and cash in bank December 31.   (AICPA Adapted)

12-12   After determining that computer controls are valid, Hastings is reviewing the sales system of Rosco Corporation in order to determine how a computerized audit program may be used to assist in performing tests of Rosco's sales records.

Rosco sells crude oil from one central location. All orders are received by mail and indicate the preassigned customer identification number, desired quantity, proposed delivery date, method of payment, and shipping terms. Since price fluctuates daily, orders do not indicate a price. Price sheets ate printed daily, and details are stored in a permanent disk file. The details of orders are also maintained in a permanent disk file.

Each morning the shipping clerk receives a computer printout which indicates details of customers' orders to be shipped that day. After the orders have been shipped, the shipping details are inputted in the computer, which simultaneously updates the sales journal, perpetual inventory records, accounts receivable, and sales accounts.

The details of all transactions, as well as daily updates, are maintained on disks which are available for use by Hastings in the performance of the audit.

Required:

1. How may a computerized audit program be used by Hastings to perform substantive tests of Rosco's sales records in their machine-readable form? Do not discuss amounts receivable and inventory.

2. After having performed these tests with the assistance of the computer, what other auditing procedures should Hastings perform in order to complete the examination of Rosco's sales records?   (AICPA Adapted)

TESTS OF CONTROLS OF THE EXPENDITURE/DISBURSEMENT CYCLE: PURCHASES AND CASH DISBURSEMENTS

13

Major topics discussed in this chapter are the:

▲ *Nature of the expenditure/disbursement cycle, including the flow of documents throughout a company's purchasing, receiving, accounts payable, and cash disbursements functions.*

▲ *Auditor's consideration of internal control structure in the expenditure/disbursement cycle.*

▲ *Case illustration integrating EDP, audit sampling, and tests of controls within the expenditure/disbursement cycle (Appendix).*

Returning to the discussion of internal control structure, this chapter begins by describing the nature of the expenditure/disbursement cycle and controls over an entity's purchasing, receiving, and cash disbursements functions. In turn, an auditor's consideration of internal control structure is discussed, and in the Appendix at the end of the chapter, a case illustration is developed to integrate material introduced in Chapter 8 (EDP), Chapter 9 (audit sampling), and this chapter.

THE NATURE OF THE EXPENDITURE/DISBURSEMENT CYCLE

In general, the expenditure/disbursement cycle encompasses the activities related to acquiring and paying for resources. That is, the cycle focuses on the exchange of cash for noncash resources, such as inventory or services. The expenditure/disbursement cycle is directly related to each of the other three cycles: it uses resources and information provided by the revenue/receipt cycle and provides resources and information for the financing and conversion cycles. For example, the expenditure/disbursement cycle might use cash provided from the sale of finished goods inventory (revenue/receipt cycle), disburse cash to meet principal and interest payments on funds borrowed through the investors in exchange for capital stock financing cycle, and disburse cash to employees involved in manufacturing finished goods (conversion cycle).

Figure 13-1 summarizes the scope of the expenditure/disbursement cycle, listing the primary business functions and representative activities, journal entries, and forms. Two major business functions are associated with the expenditure/disbursement cycle:

▲ Resources (goods and services) are acquired from vendors and employees in exchange for obligations to pay.
▲ Obligations to vendors and employees are paid.

Each of these business functions relates to both vendors and employees. However, employees, personnel, and payroll are discussed separately in Chapter 15.

An entity purchases raw materials and supplies, utilities, insurance, and advertising, among other things, from a vendor, who is selected by purchasing department personnel after a purchase requisition is approved. In turn, a purchase order is sent to the vendor, goods are received (and a receiving report prepared), and a liability (accounts payable) is recorded. The expenditure/disbursement cycle continues when a vendor's invoice arrives and is matched with copies of the receiving report, purchase requisition, and purchase order. From these documents a voucher is prepared, and all five are attached, forming a voucher package, the basis for making a cash payment to a vendor. The voucher package is "canceled," usually by perforation, when payment is made.

Throughout the expenditure/disbursement cycle, journal entries are made for a variety of transactions and events, including purchases, prepaid and accrued expenses, cash disbursements, adjustments, and account distributions. Common forms and documents include:

▲ *Purchase requisition:* a written request to internal supervisory personnel from an employee or department requesting that goods be purchased.
▲ *Purchase order:* a written request to a vendor to purchase goods.
▲ *Receiving report:* a document containing information about goods received from a vendor.
▲ *Vendor's invoice:* a document containing information about goods purchased, representing formal notice about the terms and due date of payment.
▲ *Voucher package:* a set of documents (purchase requisition, purchase order, receiving report, voucher, and invoice) relating to a purchase transaction.

As indicated in Chapter 11, organizational structure and control procedures vary from one company to another, although the expenditure/disbursement

FIGURE 13-1
Scope of the Expenditure/Disbursement Cycle

Related Business Functions	Common Activities	Common Entries	Common Forms
• Resources (goods and services) are acquired from vendors (and employees) in exchange for obligations to pay. • Obligations to vendors (and employees) are paid.	• Purchasing • Receiving • Recording • Payment (including authorizing and preparing checks)	• Purchases • Account distribution • Prepaid and accrued expenses • Adjustments • Cash disbursements	• Purchase requisitions • Purchase orders • Receiving reports • Vendors' invoices • Vouchers

cycle activities identified in Figure 13-1 are relatively common. Controls within the expenditure/disbursement cycle are explained below in the context of two functional areas common to the cycle: the purchasing function, including ordering, receiving, and accounts payable, and the cash disbursements function. Personnel and payroll, also related to the expenditure/disbursement cycle, are discussed in Chapter 15.

Figure 13-2 on pages 528–529 is a flowchart of representative purchasing and cash disbursement activities. In turn, Figure 13-3 on page 530, derived from Figure 13-2, lists the purchasing and cash disbursement activities common to the expenditure/disbursement cycle. The following discussion explains each major activity illustrated.

Purchasing and Related Activities

Purchasing relates to all acquisitions of goods and services from external vendors. *Goods* include any form of tangible resource, such as raw materials, supplies, and equipment. *Services* include all nontangible resources, such as advertising, repairs and maintenance, utilities, and insurance. Goods and services may be acquired for the use or benefit of any department or operational area within a company. Regardless of the ultimate use, however, the initial purchase, subsequent payment, and other intervening activities are processed through the expenditure/disbursement cycle.

Acquisition of Resources from Vendors

Any department within a company may initiate a request to purchase goods or services from outside vendors. An employee of the requesting department (user department) prepares a *purchase requisition*, which must be submitted to an appropriate level of management for approval.

Approved purchase requisitions are forwarded to Purchasing, where the request is reviewed, a vendor selected, and a purchase order prepared. A *purchase order* describes the goods (or services) requested, specifying price, quantity, and other appropriate information, such as catalog numbers. Copies of purchase orders are sent to vendors and distributed internally to appropriate departments, such as the requisitioning department, Receiving, and Accounts Payable, as depicted in Figure 13-2.

Goods ordered from vendors are delivered to the Receiving Department, where goods are compared with the purchase order and a *receiving report* is prepared. Receiving Department personnel should also maintain a receiving log cross-referenced to related receiving reports. A copy of the receiving report should be forwarded to Purchasing and to Accounts Payable. Similar procedures are required in the case of purchasing services; i.e., appropriate documentation should be completed to indicate that services have been rendered or "received."

Accounts Payable personnel file receiving reports with purchase requisitions and purchase orders pending receipt of a *vendor's invoice* or "bill." Many companies employ some form of voucher system for recording and controlling payables. Typically, a *voucher* is prepared by Accounts Payable (or Vouchers Payable) personnel upon receipt of a vendor's invoice. A *voucher package* consisting of the voucher, vendor's invoice, receiving report, purchase order, and purchase requisition is filed in an unpaid vouchers file by due date, and a copy of the daily summary of vouchers, prepared in Accounts Payable, is forwarded to General Accounting for recording in a voucher register. Column totals in the voucher register are posted (usually daily) to general ledger accounts.

Cash Disbursements

Cash disbursements should be authorized and executed by personnel who report to the Treasurer and are independent of purchasing and recording, as illustrated in Figure 13-2. Voucher packages in the unpaid voucher file are forwarded to the Treasurer's Department — usually prior to the date payment is due. Personnel in the Treasurer's Department should review voucher packages for accuracy and authenticity before approving vouchers for payment. For vouchers involving new or unfamiliar vendors, special precautions should be taken to assure that the transaction is bona fide, since employees are more apt to perpetrate disbursement irregularities with fictitious company names than with established vendors.

To minimize opportunities for unauthorized use, blank checks should be prenumbered, and all voided checks should be retained and accounted for. Unused checks should be physically controlled (preferably under lock and key) to limit access to authorized personnel only. Drawn checks (i.e., checks completed as to payee, date, and amount) and approved supporting vouchers should be forwarded to authorized check signers who are not otherwise involved in either processing or recording payables. Checks drawn in amounts above specified limits may require dual signatures of two authorized and independent officials. In no circumstances should checks be signed blank (without payee, date, and amount) or drawn to "Cash."

Checks may be prepared by EDP equipment and/or signed with a facsimile signature stamp or check-signing machine. In these instances, controls should be instituted that limit access to check preparation and signing media and earmark for further approval (e.g., dual signatures) any checks drawn in amounts above a specified limit. Electronic or mechanical check preparation and signing media can be highly efficient and economical, particularly in

FIGURE 13-2
Expenditure/Disbursement Cycle: Purchases and Cash Disbursements

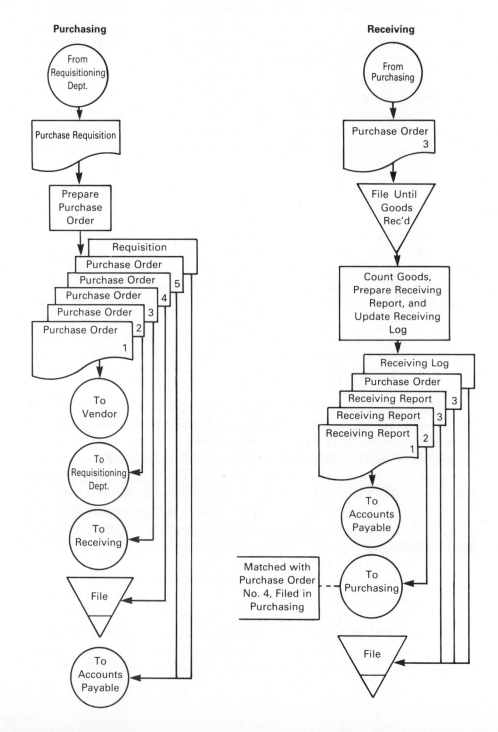

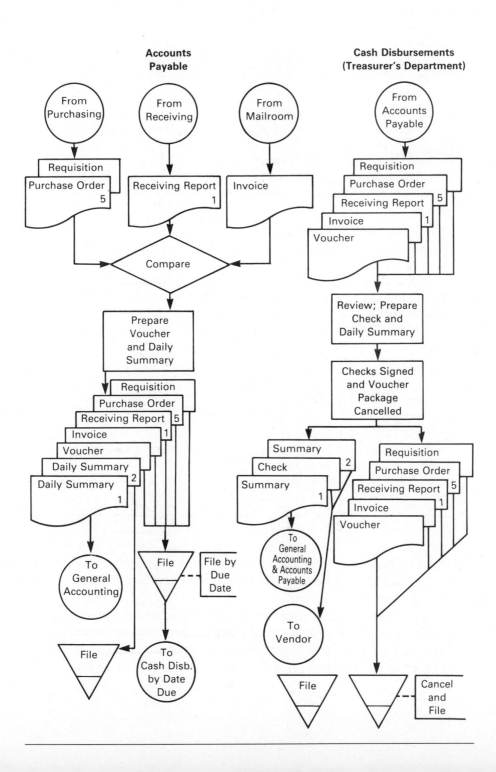

FIGURE 13-3
Summary of Purchasing and Cash Disbursement Activities

Purchasing:
• Accept approved purchase requisitions from user departments.
• Prepare purchase order, distribute copies, and retain file copy.

Receiving:
• File purchase orders until goods are received.
• Upon receipt of goods, count quantities and compare with purchase order.
• Prepare receiving report.
• Forward goods to Inventory Control.
• Forward copies of receiving report to Accounts Payable and to Purchasing; retain file copy of receiving report, purchase order, and updated receiving log.

Accounts Payable:
• Compare purchase requisition, purchase order, receiving report, and vendor's invoice.
• Prepare voucher and daily summary; assemble voucher package.
• File voucher package by due date; forward to cash disbursements (Treasurer's Department) on date due.
• Forward daily summary to General Accounting for recording; retain file copy.

Cash Disbursements (Treasurer's Department):
• Review voucher packages received from Accounts Payable on due date.
• Prepare checks and daily summary.
• Have checks signed by authorized signatories.
• Forward checks to vendors.
• Forward summary to General Accounting and Inventory Accounting for recording; retain file copy of summary.
• Cancel and file voucher packages.

companies which process a large number of cash payments. However, they provide increased opportunities for errors or irregularities, thereby requiring additional controls.

Signed checks should be mailed directly to the vendor without intervention by personnel responsible for approving, recording, or processing the transaction. Paid voucher packages should be canceled immediately, preferably by or in the presence of check signers. Cancellation is necessary to prevent duplicate payments and is often accomplished by perforating the voucher package.

Canceled voucher packages, with check numbers entered on the vouchers, should be filed. A daily summary of all remittances should be prepared and forwarded to Accounts Payable for posting to the subsidiary payables ledger and to General Accounting for recording in the voucher register. In a voucher system, the voucher register replaces the cash disbursements journal.

Payments are sometimes made prior to the receipt of goods or services. Examples include deposits with vendors for goods ordered and prepayments for items such as insurance, rent, and advertising. Such payments should be made only in accordance with appropriate authorization and supporting documentation. Prepayments should be carefully reviewed by accounting personnel to determine the appropriate account classification. At the end of an accounting period, all such expenditures should be reviewed by designated personnel and adjusting entries made as necessary to reflect expenses in the proper period.

Internal Control Structure Objectives and Potential Errors or Irregularities

The following discussion focuses on internal control structure in the context of purchasing and cash disbursements. The discussion, summarized in Figure 13-4, identifies some specific control objectives, describes examples of potential errors or irregularities that may arise if an objective is not achieved, and provides examples of control procedures that are designed to prevent or detect the errors or irregularities. The specific objectives identified relate generally to transaction authorization, execution, and recording and access to assets.

Transaction Authorization. Effective control over a company's purchasing activities requires that purchases be made only in accordance with general or specific authorization. All purchases should be initiated by user departments and approved by appropriate supervisory personnel. Goods or services should not be ordered in the absence of properly authorized purchase requisitions. Required authorization procedures may vary with the cost or nature of the goods or services requested, and company authorization policies should be clearly specified in written procedures.

Prior to purchasing goods and services, vendors should be approved in accordance with management's policies. Otherwise, for example, purchases

FIGURE 13-4
Purchasing and Cash Disbursements: Objectives, Potential Errors or Irregularities, and Control Procedures

Objective	Types of Errors or Irregularities That Could Occur If Objective Not Met	Control Procedures Designed to Prevent or Detect Errors or Irregularities
TRANSACTION AUTHORIZATION:		
• Vendors should be approved prior to purchasing goods.	Purchases could be made from unauthorized vendors, potentially resulting in purchasing from related parties without senior management's knowledge or from foreign vendors in violation of import quotas.	Prepare lists of authorized vendors. Establish criteria for adding to, changing, or deleting from the vendor list.
• Types, quantities, terms, and prices should be approved for all products and services.	Unnecessary goods may be ordered, potentially resulting in write-downs of unusable or unsaleable inventory. Goods may be purchased at noncompetitive prices or unfavorable terms, resulting in reduced earnings.	Maintain updated guidelines for purchase transactions (e.g., competitive bids, specific authorization for all purchases exceeding minimum dollar amounts). Establish procedures for reviewing and approving purchase prices and terms prior to purchase.
EXECUTION:		
• Received goods should be counted and inspected for quality.	Damaged or unordered goods could be accepted, potentially creating delays in receiving the goods desired.	Establish procedures for inspecting and counting goods received before releasing the carrier.
• All cash disbursements for goods and services should be based on a bona fide liability.	Cash could be disbursed to unauthorized parties, for goods or services not received, or as a duplicate payment.	Prenumber and control vouchers and checks. Cancel voucher packages immediately upon payment.

RECORDING:		
• All goods and services received should be accurately and promptly reported.	Goods may be received but not reported, potentially resulting in understated inventory and liabilities.	Require manual dual signatories for all checks over a prespecified amount. Prenumber receiving reports, and subsequently review for prompt recording.
• Purchases and cash disbursement transactions should be recorded properly and in the proper accounting period.	Account balances may be inaccurate, potentially resulting in misstated financial statements.	Total input documents (e.g., number of documents, dollar amounts) and reconcile journals and ledgers. Establish processing and recording procedures.
• Purchase and cash disbursement transactions should be posted accurately to individual vendor accounts.	Summaries of detailed records may not agree with control accounts. Transactions may be posted to improper vendor accounts, potentially resulting in improper payments.	Establish validation procedures to verify postings (e.g., check digits). Batch and reconcile input totals to processed and output controls. Promptly investigate correspondence from vendors (e.g., collection notices).
ACCESS TO ASSETS:		
• Access to purchasing and cash disbursement records and to forms and documents should be restricted to personnel authorized by management.	Records, forms or documents may be misused by unauthorized personnel, potentially resulting in misstated payables or diversion for personal use.	Establish physical controls over unused forms and documents. Segregate responsibilities for authorization, execution, and recording functions. Maintain listings and samples of authorized signatories.

could be made from related parties without management's knowledge or from foreign vendors in violation of regulated import quotas, among other things. To control against purchasing from unauthorized vendors, many companies prepare lists of authorized vendors and establish criteria for adding to, changing, or deleting from the list.

In addition to authorizing vendor lists, management should also establish policies relating to the types, quantities, payment terms, and prices of goods and services purchased. Failure to establish the types of goods and services authorized for purchase could result in reduced earnings caused by write-downs of unusable or unsaleable inventory or, equally important, unnecessary purchases made for the benefit of employees or related parties. In turn, authorizing quantities, payment terms, and prices protects against excessive warehousing costs (i.e., for unnecessary inventory), unfavorable payment terms, and noncompetitive prices. As a result, management should maintain current price lists and actively seek suppliers whose goods and services optimize the relationship between price and quality. Where applicable, competitive bids or formal price quotations should be obtained from suppliers, particularly for purchases involving high priced items, large quantities, or infrequently requested items.

Transaction Execution. When goods are received, they should be inspected for quality, and the quantities should be verified by physical count and compared with the purchase order. If not inspected, counted, and compared with the purchase order, a company could experience significant delays as a result of returning damaged or unordered goods and awaiting delivery of the goods ordered. To avoid delays, management should require that receiving personnel inspect and count all received goods before releasing the carrier.

After goods or services are received, a liability is incurred and, subsequently, cash is disbursed. Management should institute policies to assure that cash is disbursed only for bona fide liabilities, thereby protecting against disbursements for goods not received, payment to unauthorized parties, and duplicate payments. To control against improper disbursements, management could prenumber and control vouchers and checks, require dual signatures for all checks exceeding prespecified dollar amounts, and cancel all paid voucher packages immediately upon payment.

Recording. After purchase transactions are executed, all goods and services received should be accurately and promptly reported to accounts payable, indicating title has passed, and to purchasing, indicating ordered goods have been received. Otherwise, goods and services may be received and used, but not recorded, thereby resulting in understated inventory and liabilities. Many companies control the receipt of goods and services by prenumbering receiving reports — and subsequently reviewing for prompt recording — and maintaining a receiving log which lists sequentially each receiving report processed.

To protect against inaccurate account balances, and therefore against misstated financial statements, management should institute policies to assure that all purchases and cash disbursements are recorded properly and in the proper period. Management could control the recording function by preparing input totals (e.g., batch totals, hash totals) and reconciling journals and subsidiary ledgers, and by establishing processing and recording procedures.

However, proper recording within general ledger control accounts does not necessarily indicate that transactions are posted to individual vendor subsidiary accounts. That is, summaries of detailed records may not agree with control accounts. To control against inaccurate vendor accounts, management could establish validation procedures to verify postings (e.g., check digits), and batch and reconcile input totals to processed and output totals. In addition, authorized personnel should investigate correspondence from vendors, particularly collection notices.

Access to Assets. Management should establish procedures to safeguard assets by restricting access to purchase and cash disbursements records and forms. Otherwise, records or forms may be misused by unauthorized personnel, potentially resulting in misstated payables or diversion of cash or other assets for personal use. Many companies control access to purchasing and cash disbursements by prenumbering and controlling forms and documents, maintaining lists and samples of authorized signatories, and segregating responsibility for authorizing, executing, and recording.

CONSIDERING INTERNAL CONTROL STRUCTURE

As introduced in Chapter 7 and illustrated for the revenue/receipt cycle in Chapter 11, considering internal control structure involves obtaining an understanding of the structure, performing tests of controls, and assessing control risk. The following discussion addresses an auditor's consideration of internal control structure within the expenditure/disbursement cycle, and focuses on purchasing, receiving, and cash disbursements.

Obtain an Understanding

In a review of the internal control structure, an auditor's predominant concern is to obtain a knowledge and understanding of a client's prescribed policies and procedures sufficient to plan the audit. That is, how is the system supposed to work, and what control procedures have been prescribed by management to assure that the system is functioning as planned? Obtaining an understanding consists of four components: (1) making a preliminary review, (2) documenting the system, (3) performing a transaction walk-through, and (4) determining whether existing control procedures are potentially reliable.

Preliminary Review. To begin considering internal control structure, an auditor develops a general understanding of a client's control environment and the flow of purchase and cash disbursement transactions throughout the expenditure/disbursement cycle. The purpose of the preliminary review is to determine whether further consideration is likely to justify restricting substantive tests of accounts payable. If the preliminary review reveals that existing controls are inadequate, then the auditor would not be justified in restricting substantive tests, and working paper documentation would be limited to a memorandum describing the reasons for not continuing to consider the internal control structure.

System Documentation. A company's expenditure/disbursement cycle can be documented with flowcharts, questionnaires, and/or narratives. Figure 13-2, discussed earlier, illustrates a flowchart for purchases and cash disbursements.

Figure 13-5 illustrates a questionnaire for purchasing, receiving, accounts payable, and cash disbursements. As in Chapter 11, the questionnaire is designed to elicit a ''No'' response when a potential deficiency is apparent. That is, a ''No'' response would indicate a commonly used control is not used, and therefore that, lacking compensating controls, a material weakness might exist.

Alternatively, or in conjunction with a flowchart and/or questionnaire, an auditor could describe the system — or segments of the system — in a written narrative. For example, a narrative could be used to describe the distribution of documents and reports outside of the predominant areas of concern — that is, outside of purchasing, receiving, accounts payable, and cash disbursements. These four areas are typically of most interest to the auditor.

Transaction Walk-Through. To confirm his or her understanding of the system flowcharted in Figure 13-2, the auditor could select a canceled voucher package at random from files maintained in the Treasurer's Department. The purchase requisition, purchase order, receiving report, invoice, and voucher would be examined for compliance with company policies, and compared with documents filed in Purchasing, Receiving, and Accounts Payable.

Identification of Controls To Be Relied On. Following system documentation, and assuming that controls are potentially reliable, an auditor continues as follows:

▲ Identify the system's control objectives. The first column of Figure 13-4 identifies control objectives for purchases and cash disbursements transactions.
▲ Consider the potential errors or irregularities that might result if specific control objectives are not met. The second column of Figure 13-4 identifies examples of potential errors or irregularities.
▲ Determine what control procedures are used by the entity to prevent or detect potentially material errors or irregularities. The third column of Figure 13-4 identifies examples of potential controls.
▲ Design tests of controls for each control procedure to be relied on during substantive testing.

Tests for purchases and cash disbursements are described next.

Tests of Controls: Purchasing and Cash Disbursements

Like sales and cash collections (Chapter 11), purchasing and cash disbursements usually represent large volumes of transactions; each purchase of goods and services on credit must be recorded as a payable and each must ultimately be paid. As a result, sheer volume alone often precludes an auditor from relying exclusively on substantive tests. Rather, an auditor is more apt to perform tests of controls, thereby attempting to obtain a reasonable degree of assurance that prescribed control procedures are complied with, operating as planned, and reliable.

Tests for the purchasing, receiving, and cash disbursement system flowcharted in Figure 13-2 are presented in the following sections. The Appendix at the end of the chapter provides a case illustrating how an auditor can use sampling to accomplish tests of controls of the expenditure/disbursement cycle.

Purchasing. Given the significant resources often expended for goods and services, purchases made at anything other than authorized and competitive prices can spell the difference between successful and unsuccessful enterprises. As a result, tests of controls of a company's purchasing activities focus on whether all purchases are properly authorized. Representative tests follow on page 540.

FIGURE 13-5

Questionnaire: Purchases and Cash Disbursement

Question	Answer: Yes, No, or N/A	Remarks

PURCHASING:

1. Are policies and procedures for reviewing and processing purchase requisitions clearly defined?
2. Are prenumbered purchase orders prepared for all approved purchase requisitions?
3. Are competitive bids or price quotations obtained for purchased goods and services?
4. Are price lists maintained for repetitive transactions that do not require competitive bids or price quotations?
5. Are purchase transactions reviewed periodically by personnel independent of purchasing?
6. Are copies of purchase orders forwarded to the requisitioning department and to receiving and accounts payable?
7. Are lists of previously authorized vendors maintained by purchasing?

RECEIVING:

1. Are prenumbered receiving reports prepared for all goods received?
2. Is a receiving log maintained for all receiving reports processed?
3. Are all received goods inspected, counted, and compared with copies of purchase orders?
4. Are receiving personnel independent of purchasing, accounts payable, and cash disbursements?

Question	Answer: Yes, No, or N/A	Remarks

CASH DISBURSEMENT AND
RECORDING:

1. Are voucher packages reviewed before being approved for payment?
2. Are steps taken to assure that unfamiliar payees (vendors) are bona fide?
3. Are voucher packages and checks reviewed by signatories before they sign checks (or before submitting vouchers to EDP for check preparation)?
4. Are voucher packages canceled when or immediately after checks are signed?
5. Are signed checks delivered directly to the mail room without intervention by other personnel?
6. Are cash disbursements personnel (e.g., Treasurer's Department) independent of purchasing, receiving, and accounts payable?
7. Is account distribution indicated on the purchase requisition by the requisitioning department?
8. Are vouchers prepared from requisitions and purchase orders received from Purchasing, from receiving reports received from Receiving, and from invoices received from the mail room?
9. Are daily summaries of processed vouchers forwarded by accounts payable to general accounting for summary entries?

Tests of Controls: Purchasing

1. Randomly select a sample of paid voucher packages.
   a. Review each voucher package for appropriate cancellation (e.g., perforation).
   b. Review documents in each sampled voucher package for appropriate authorization.
   c. Compare details on purchase requisitions, purchase orders, receiving reports, vendors' invoices, and voucher, and verify mathematical accuracy.
2. For each sampled voucher package, obtain a copy of the related purchase order and requisition from Purchasing Department files.
   a. Compare purchase orders in voucher packages with copies of purchase orders in Purchasing Department files.
   b. Trace prices on purchase orders to competitive bids, formal price quotations, or other pricing sources.
   c. Examine periodic reports by personnel independent of the Purchasing Department regarding prices and vendor selection practices.
3. Document any deviations or discrepancies observed.

As suggested by step 1, a paid voucher package is the primary source from which the tests of purchasing are performed. In step 1a, the auditor tests whether paid voucher packages are canceled, thereby addressing whether duplicate payments could occur. However, the test does not assure that cancellation occurred simultaneously with (or immediately after) payment — only direct observation by the auditor could assess whether the time span between payment and cancellation is reasonable.

Step 1b addresses transaction authorization and requires that the auditor examine signatures or initials on the (1) purchase order, indicating an authorized transaction, (2) receiving report, indicating responsibility for incoming goods, and (3) voucher, indicating an authorized cash payment. In step 1c, the auditor tests whether all documents agree, and therefore that goods were received and paid for at the price quoted and in the quantity ordered.

In step 2a, the auditor compares sampled voucher packages with copies of purchase orders and requisitions filed in the Purchasing Department, as shown in Figure 13-2. Here, the intent is to determine if all paid vouchers resulted from authorized purchases. Steps 2b and 2c, in contrast, address whether prices paid are competitive. That is, evidence of competitive bids or price quotations would suggest management is conscientiously attempting to safeguard assets — in particular, cash — by seeking the best prices available.

Receiving. The receipt of goods is the first step in readying inventory for conversion and in recognizing a liability. Since little can be done after-the-fact to determine if receiving procedures are applied appropriately, an auditor could consider visiting the Receiving Department on a surprise basis, determining whether received goods are conscientiously counted and compared with purchase orders. Some additional tests follow.

Tests of Controls: Receiving

1. For each sampled voucher package, obtain the related copy of the receiving report from Receiving Department files.
   a. Compare receiving reports in voucher packages with copies of receiving reports in Receiving Department files.
   b. Review receiving reports for evidence that received goods have been inspected, counted, and compared with packing slips and purchase orders.
   c. Trace receiving reports to entries in the receiving log.
2. Document any deviations or discrepancies observed.

In addition to observing the Receiving Department on a surprise basis, an auditor can design tests that address whether goods received according to the voucher packages used to test Purchasing agree with Receiving Department files, such as the copy of the receiving report filed in Receiving and the receiving log, a chronological listing of goods received. In step 1a, the auditor compares the receiving report in Accounts Payable with the copy filed in Receiving, and therefore tests whether the copy used by Accounts Payable to prepare a voucher is in error. Step 1b addresses the accuracy of quantities received by examining evidence that received goods are inspected, counted, and agreed with a packing slip, the vendor's list of goods shipped that is normally found on or within shipping cartons. In step 1c, the auditor further tests for discrepancies in reported quantities by comparing receiving reports to entries in the company's receiving log.

Cash Disbursement and Recording. Cash payment activities are particularly susceptible to irregularities, since cash is liquid and only an unauthorized payee and forged endorsement are necessary to misappropriate funds. As a result, an auditor's tests of controls over payments to vendors focus on approvals for payment, proper entries, and, to the extent possible, the authenticity of signatures and endorsements.

The recording function for purchases and cash disbursements encompasses entries to accounts payable, requiring that an auditor determine whether details recorded within a voucher register are recorded in the proper vendor accounts and agree in total with the general ledger. Representative tests follow.

Tests of Controls: Cash Disbursement and Recording

1. For each sampled voucher package, obtain the canceled check.
   a. Examine canceled checks for appropriate signatures and endorsements.
   b. Compare details of the voucher package with the canceled check — check number, date, payee, and amount.
   c. Trace voucher packages and canceled checks to postings in the accounts payable subsidiary ledger and to entries in the voucher register.
      (1) Review entries in the voucher register for appropriate account distribution (classification).
      (2) Verify the accuracy of the voucher register (foot and cross-foot) for selected periods and trace totals to entries in the general ledger.
      (3) Scan the voucher register for unusual items (e.g., unfamiliar vendor names) and unusually large amounts, and investigate any such items identified.
2. Document any deviations or discrepancies observed.

The tests of controls discussed thus far address whether purchases are authorized, executed, and recorded properly. But they ignore the possibility that authorized transactions might be executed with unauthorized or fictitious vendors. Thus, the tests for cash disbursements and recording focus on canceled checks, the primary evidence that vendors were paid and bona fide.

In step 1a, the auditor examines the signatures and endorsements on canceled checks, looking specifically for unusual items. For example, a manually signed check would be unusual for a company that normally processes disbursements by computer. On one hand, the check might have been for an amount exceeding limits authorized, thereby legitimately requiring manual signatures. On the other hand, the manual signature might indicate an error or irregularity.

Step 1b compares details of the canceled check with the related voucher package, thereby assuring the amount paid was the amount owed. In step 1c, the auditor traces the voucher package to entries in accounts payable and in the voucher register. The entries are tested for appropriate account distribution — e.g., expense classification for financial reporting and tax purposes — and the voucher register is tested for mathematical accuracy and unusual items.

Assess Control Risk

To complete the consideration of internal control structure within the expenditure/disbursement cycle, an auditor reviews system documentation and the results of tests of controls, and determines whether existing controls can be relied on to restrict year-end substantive tests of accounts payable (low control risk), or whether expanded substantive tests are necessary (high control risk). The evaluation is based on the types of errors or irregularities that could occur; necessary control procedures that should prevent the errors or irregularities; whether the necessary procedures exist and are followed; and any deficiencies in the internal control structure. Substantive tests applicable to the expenditure/disbursement cycle in general and to accounts payable in particular are introduced in Chapter 14.

SUMMARY

The expenditure/disbursement cycle encompasses the acquisition of resources from vendors (and employees) and subsequent payments for resources acquired. Common vendor-related activities include purchasing, receiving, recording, and cash payment. Documents evidencing appropriate transaction authorization and execution typically include purchase requisitions, purchase orders, receiving reports, vendors' invoices, and vouchers. Together these documents form a voucher package which serves as a basis for making payments to vendors.

Cash disbursements should be authorized and executed by personnel independent of the recording function. Access to unused checks and check preparation and signing equipment should be limited to authorized personnel.

Tests of controls of an entity's purchasing activities focus upon whether purchases and related disbursements are properly authorized, executed, and recorded. Substantive tests are performed as necessary to fulfill audit objectives, and are discussed in Chapter 14.

APPENDIX
CASE ILLUSTRATION: INTEGRATING EDP, AUDIT SAMPLING, AND TESTS OF CONTROLS WITHIN THE EXPENDITURE/DISBURSEMENT CYCLE

To illustrate the material introduced in this chapter and to integrate with material presented on EDP (Chapter 8) and audit sampling (Chapter 9), assume a continuing audit engagement for the Gorham Corporation, a medium-sized manufacturer of paper products, whose fiscal year ends June 30. The specific objective in this case is to determine whether Gorham's controls over cash disbursements can be relied on during substantive tests of details.

EDP System: Accounts Payable, Data Entry, and Computer Processing

For the past two years, Gorham has used the accounts payable, data entry and computer processing system flowcharted in Figure 13-6. The accounts payable system is manual, but data entry and processing are accomplished with the computer. The vouchers and batched totals are entered on input terminals. In Computer Processing, which accomplishes the cash disbursements functions depicted in the manual system in Figure 13-2, inputted data are sorted and edited, checks and the voucher register are printed, and all processed master files are updated.

Consideration of Internal Control Structure

The following sections discuss the review of the system, tests of controls, and control risk for Gorham Corporation's payables and disbursements function.

Understanding the System

The auditor decides to document the system with both a flowchart and a questionnaire. The flowchart appears in Figure 13-6. Assume a transaction walk-through indicates that the flowchart is accurate. The questionnaire consists of the nine disbursement and recording questions given in Figure 13-5, page 538–539. Questions 1, 3, 5, 6, 8, and 9 result in "Yes" responses, but questions 2, 4, and 7 receive "No" responses, indicating the following deficiencies:

▲ No procedures exist to assure that unfamiliar payees are bona fide.
▲ Voucher packages are not canceled when or immediately after checks are signed.
▲ Account distribution is not indicated on the purchase requisition by the requisitioning department.

Although significant, the auditor believes no one or combination of these deficiencies is sufficient to render the system completely unreliable. In this case, the auditor reaches this conclusion for three reasons. First, even though no procedures are taken to assure that unfamiliar payees are bona fide, inspection of the check register indicates that vendors unfamiliar to the auditor accounted for less than one percent of cash payments during the year. Thus,

FIGURE 13-6
Gorham Corporation: Flowchart of Accounts Payable, Data Entry and Computer Processing

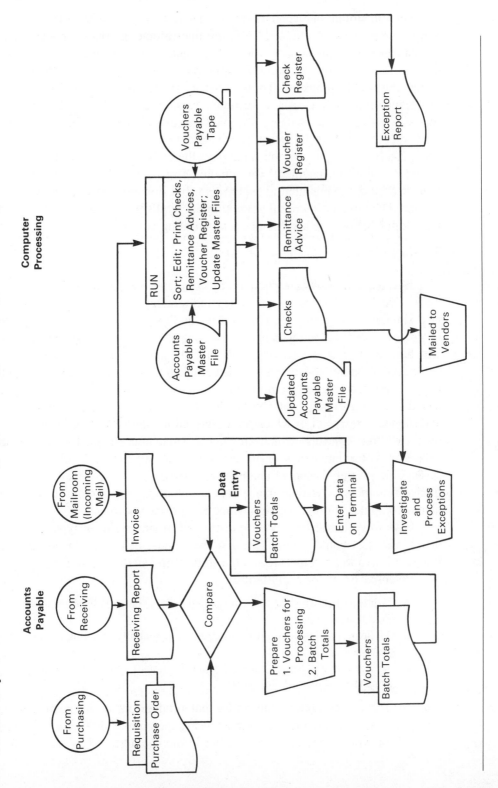

payments to unfamiliar vendors are immaterial, and therefore of little audit consequence. Second, inquiries indicate that, although voucher packages are not canceled simultaneously when or immediately after checks are signed, they are canceled by Accounts Payable personnel at the end of the day on which checks are prepared. To assure that cancellation does in fact occur at day's end, the auditor visited Accounts Payable unannounced at the end of two successive business days, observed the cancellation process, and noted no discrepancies or deficiencies. Since checks are prepared only once per day and cancellation occurs on the same day, the auditor concluded that the likelihood of duplicate payment was remote. Third, account distribution is not indicated by the requisitioning department, but it is indicated by the Accounts Payable Department in consultation with the requisitioning department, which the auditor believes is a sufficient compensating control.

Tests of Controls

Because all checks are prepared by computer and payables are processed manually, the auditor elects the following strategy for testing controls. Parallel simulation — which requires that the auditor prepare computer programs to process client-prepared input under controlled conditions (Chapter 8) — will be used to test the effectiveness of EDP application controls over data entry and computer processing. To accomplish parallel simulation, the auditor prepares a computer program which focuses on code verification and selected data conversion controls: batch totals, character validity, limit tests, and sequence tests, all of which are described in Chapter 8. All of these tests relate to input controls, which are of particular concern in this case, since data entry is accomplished on off-site terminals (see Figure 13-6), which are susceptible to irregularities if unauthorized personnel gain access to user identification numbers. Assume that parallel simulation is accomplished on Gorham's computer and that no significant exceptions are found.

Given the deficiencies noted per the questionnaire, three types of errors or irregularities could occur. The first two appear at the fourth objective of Figure 13-4 (middle column), and the third at the sixth objective:

Potential Errors or Irregularities:

▲ Cash may be disbursed to unauthorized parties, potentially resulting in fraudulent payments.
▲ Duplicate payments could be inaccurate, potentially resulting in misspent cash.
▲ General ledger account balances could be made, potentially resulting in misstated financial statements.

Following consideration of the above potential errors or irregularities and other evidence gathered during interim tests, the auditor drafts the following tests, all of which were explained earlier in the chapter.

Cash Disbursements and Recording

Step	Tests of Controls

1.   For each sampled voucher package, obtain the canceled check.
      a. Examine canceled checks for appropriate signatures and endorsements.
      b. Compare details of the voucher package with the canceled check—check number, date, payee, and amount.
      c. Trace voucher packages and canceled checks to postings in the accounts payable subsidiary ledger and to entries in the voucher register.
         (1) Review entries in the voucher register for appropriate distribution (classification).
         (2) Verify the accuracy of the voucher register (foot and crossfoot) for selected periods and trace totals to entries in the general ledger.
         (3) Scan the voucher register for unusual items (e.g., unfamiliar vendor names) and unusually large amounts, and investigate any such items identified.
2.   Document any deviations or discrepancies.

Cash Disbursements and Recording

As discussed in Chapter 9, the auditor next determines which if any of the tests can be accomplished by sampling and whether to use statistical or nonstatistical sampling. For Gorham Corporation's cash disbursements system, steps 1a, 1b, and 1c(1) can be accomplished using sampling. Further, the auditor decides to use statistical sampling, since the system processes very large numbers of checks (i.e., large population sizes). Because interim tests of controls in prior years revealed very few errors, the auditor selects sequential sampling as the statistical sampling plan. The results of the sequential sampling plan are summarized in Figure 13-7, a sequential sampling worksheet, and Figure 13-8, an analysis of deviations.

Two observations about Figure 13-7 are noteworthy. First, note that for attribute 2 the achieved probability, 80.54 percent, is *less* than desired reliability, 95.0 percent, suggesting the auditor should increase sample size — that is, the auditor should go on with the sequential (stop-or-go) sampling plan for attribute 2. However, note that in the explanation in Figure 13-7 (tick mark $\sqrt{}$) and the analysis of deviations in Figure 13-8, the deviation

FIGURE 13-7

A10
RJW
5/12/90

Gorham Corporation
Sampling Worksheet – Cash Disbursements
June 30, 1990

Attribute	Desired Reliability	Tolerable Rate	Sample Size*	Number of Deviations	Achieved Probability*
1. Signatures on checks are appropriate	.98	.04	100	0	98.31
2. Endorsements on checks are appropriate	.95	.03	100	1√	80.54
3. Details of voucher pkg. agree with cancelled check	.95	.05	70	0	97.24
4. Details of voucher tie to entries	.95	.05	70	0	97.24
5. Account distribution is appropriate	.90	.08	50	1√	91.73

*Table 9-5
√As noted at A11, failure to endorse was an oversight by Elston employees. Therefore, there is no need to increase sample size.
√See analysis of occurrences at A11

Audit Conclusion

Based upon procedures performed, the achieved probability exceeds desired reliability for 4 of 5 attributes, and the one deviation for attribute no. 2 resulted from a vendor's oversight. Therefore, controls over cash disbursements can be relied on during substantive testing.

FIGURE 13-8

Gorham Corporation
Analysis of Deviations: Cash Disbursements
June 30, 1990

Attribute	Number of Deviations	Nature of Deviations	Effect on Substantive Detailed Testing
1	1	ck no. 3267, $5,320; Elston Corp. Check was accepted for deposit by Elston's bank, but not endorsed.	No add'l audit work is necessary because alternate procedures (i.e., review of Dun & Bradstreet reports; and telephone conversation with Elston Corp. officials indicate failure to endorse was an oversight by Elston employees.)
5	1	ck no. 9861, $2,319, Davis Co. Purchase was charged to travel & entertainment expense, rather than advertising expense	No add'l audit work is necessary because (1) achieved probability (91.73) exceeds desired reliability (.90) and (2) the error does not affect income, and neither expense affects overhead in inventory. (The client corrected the error).

resulted from an oversight by the payee's employees. As a result, the auditor does not believe that Gorham's failure to investigate the matter is sufficiently compelling to warrant increasing sample size. Second, even though attribute 5 resulted in one deviation, the achieved probability from Table 9-5 (Chapter 9), 91.73 percent, still exceeds desired reliability, 90.0 percent. As a result, the auditor does not need to increase sample size. Steps 1c(2) and 1c(3) are performed by the auditor, and no exceptions are noted.

Control Risk

The auditor's assessments of control risk for Gorham Corporation's controls over cash disbursements would be based on the following quantitative and qualitative factors:

▲ No exceptions were noted when parallel simulation was run with actual or "live" client data.

▲ Achieved probability exceeded desired reliability for four of five attributes tested, and for one attribute, the deviation observed was (1) the result of a vendor's oversight and (2) not deemed sufficiently compelling to warrant additional testing.

▲ The questionnaire revealed three control deficiencies.

In this case, the auditor's decision would probably be to rely on Gorham's controls over cash disbursement (low control risk), since parallel simulation and audit sampling indicate that the three deficiencies are not likely to produce aggregate error in excess of tolerable error.

QUESTIONS

1. Identify the major business functions and activities common to the expenditure/disbursement cycle.
2. Why should purchasing policies assure that vendors are approved before purchasing goods and services from them?
3. How can management control against unauthorized or duplicate cash payments?
4. Proper recording within general ledger control accounts does not necessarily mean that transactions are posted accurately to individual vendor accounts. What controls can management institute to assure that detailed records agree with control accounts?
5. Why should Receiving Department functions be segregated from inventory control and, if possible, from shipping?
6. Explain how an auditor could perform a "transaction walk-through" for purchases and cash disbursements.
7. Why do auditors not usually rely on substantive tests alone when auditing accounts payable that result from credit purchase transactions?
8. What is the primary focus of an auditor's tests of controls over purchasing?

9. How does an auditor test whether purchase transactions are authorized in accordance with management's prespecified criteria?
10. Explain the primary focus of an auditor's tests of cash disbursements to vendors.
11. As a normal part of tests of controls for cash disbursements, an auditor examines signatures and endorsements on canceled checks, looking specifically for unusual items. Give two examples of unusual items an auditor might confront.

MULTIPLE CHOICE QUESTIONS

1. A client's expenditure/disbursement cycle begins with requisitions from user departments and ends with the receipt of materials and the recognition of a liability. An auditor's primary objective in reviewing this cycle is to:

   a. Evaluate the reliability of information generated as a result of the purchasing process.
   b. Investigate the physical handling and recording of unusual acquisitions of materials.
   c. Consider the need to be on hand for the annual physical count if this system is not functioning properly.
   d. Ascertain that materials said to be ordered, received, and paid for are on hand.   (AICPA Adapted)

2. When considering internal control structure for purchasing and disbursement procedures, the auditor will be least influenced by:

   a. The availability of a company manual describing purchasing and disbursement procedures.
   b. The scope and results of audit work by the company's internal auditor.
   c. The existence within the purchasing and disbursement area of compensating controls that offset deficiencies.
   d. The strength or weakness of internal control structure in other areas, e.g., sales and accounts receivable.   (AICPA Adapted)

3. Which of the following is a primary function of the Purchasing Department?

   a. Authorizing the acquisition of goods.
   b. Ensuring the acquisition of goods of a specified quality.
   c. Verifying the propriety of goods acquired.
   d. Reducing expenditures for goods acquired.

4. On the basis of observations made during an audit, the independent auditor should discuss with management the effectiveness of the company's control procedures that protect against the purchase of:

   a. Required supplies provided by a vendor who offers no trade or cash discounts.
   b. Inventory items acquired based on an economic order quantity (EOQ) inventory management concept.

c. New equipment that is needed but does not qualify for investment tax credit treatment.

d. Supplies individually ordered, without considering possible volume discounts. (AICPA Adapted)

5. Effective internal control over the purchasing of raw materials should usually include all of the following procedures except:

   a. Systematic reporting of product changes which will affect raw materials.
   b. Determining the need for the raw materials prior to preparing the purchase order.
   c. Obtaining third-party written quality and quantity reports prior to payment for the raw materials.
   d. Obtaining financial approval prior to making a commitment.

(AICPA Adapted)

6. To strengthen control over the purchase of merchandise, a company's Receiving Department should:

   a. Accept merchandise only if a purchase order or approval granted by the Purchasing Department is on hand.
   b. Accept and count all merchandise received from the usual company vendors.
   c. Rely on shipping documents for the preparation of receiving reports.
   d. Be responsible for the physical handling of merchandise but not the preparation of receiving reports. (AICPA Adapted)

7. To avoid potential errors and irregularities, a well-designed system of control procedures in the accounts payable area should include separation of which of the following functions?

   a. Cash disbursements and invoice verification.
   b. Invoice verification and merchandise ordering.
   c. Physical handling of merchandise received and preparation of receiving reports.
   d. Check signing and cancellation of payment documentation.

(AICPA Adapted)

8. An internal control structure questionnaire indicates that an approved receiving report is required to accompany every check request for payment of merchandise. Which of the following audit procedures provides the greatest assurance that this control is operating effectively?

   a. Select and examine receiving reports and ascertain that the related canceled checks are dated no earlier than the receiving reports.
   b. Select and examine receiving reports and ascertain that the related canceled checks are dated no later than the receiving reports.
   c. Select and examine canceled checks and ascertain that the related receiving reports are dated no earlier than the checks.
   d. Select and examine canceled checks and ascertain that the related receiving reports are dated no later than the checks. (AICPA Adapted)

9. An effective control procedure that protects against the preparation of improper or inaccurate disbursements would be to require that all checks be:

a. Signed by an officer after necessary supporting evidence has been examined.
b. Reviewed by the treasurer before mailing.
c. Sequentially numbered and accounted for by internal auditors.
d. Perforated or otherwise effectively canceled when they are returned with the
   bank statement.   (AICPA Adapted)

10. An auditor plans to examine a sample of twenty checks for countersignatures as
    prescribed by the client's internal control procedures. One of the checks in the
    chosen sample of twenty cannot be found. The auditor should consider the rea-
    sons for this limitation and

    a. Evaluate the results as if the sample size had been nineteen.
    b. Treat the missing check as a deviation for the purpose of evaluating the sam-
       ple.
    c. Treat the missing check in the same manner as the majority of the other
       nineteen checks, i.e., countersigned or not.
    d. Choose another check to replace the missing check in the sample.
                                                                 (AICPA Adapted)

11. Which of the following is an internal control procedure that would prevent a
    paid disbursement voucher from being presented for payment a second time?

    a. Vouchers should be prepared by individuals who are responsible for signing
       disbursement checks.
    b. Disbursement vouchers should be approved by at least two responsible man-
       agement officials.
    c. The date on a disbursement voucher should be within a few days of the date
       the voucher is presented for payment.
    d. The official signing the check should compare the check with the voucher
       and should deface the voucher documents.   (AICPA Adapted)

PROBLEMS

13-1   Assume you are considering a client's controls over purchases and cash
disbursements. System documentation was accomplished through flowcharts and narratives and, in conjunction with a transaction walk-through, revealed the following
potential deficiencies:
a. Carrying costs of inventory have increased significantly since the prior year.
b. Prices for purchases are sometimes unusually high or fluctuate significantly from
   month to month.
c. Purchase discounts are frequently not taken.
d. During lunch, the controller commented to you that on two occasions during the
   year duplicate payments had been made for a single transaction.
e. Cash disbursements records do not always reconcile with general ledger control
   accounts.

Required:
For each potential deficiency, indicate a control or controls that management could
implement to reduce the likelihood of errors or irregularities.

13-2   In connection with your examination of Dundee Corporation's financial statements, you become aware of the following control procedures for Dundee's purchasing and cash disbursements activities:

1. Purchases are made only from companies that warrant products for workmanship and related damages.
2. Competitive bids are required for all purchases in excess of $12,000.
3. A written memoranda is required for each purchase discount not taken.
4. Receiving reports are prenumbered sequentially and controlled.
5. Voucher packages are canceled immediately after payment.
6. A procedures manual is maintained for all job functions related to processing purchases and cash disbursements transactions.
7. Postings are verified by check digits.

Required:

For each control procedure, indicate (a) a potential error or irregularity that might be prevented or detected as a result of the control procedure and (b) the objective served by the control procedure. Organize your answer as follows.

Control Procedure	Potential Error or Irregularity That Might Be Prevented or Detected	Related Objective
1.	(a)	(b)

13-3   Lecimore Company has a centralized purchasing department which is managed by Joan Jones. Jones has established policies and procedures to guide the clerical staff and purchasing agents in the day-to-day operation of the department. She is satisfied that these policies and procedures are in conformity with company objectives and believes that are no major problems in the regular operations of the Purchasing Department.

- All significant purchases are made on a competitive bid basis. The probability of timely delivery, reliability of vendor, etc., are taken into consideration on a subjective basis.
- Detailed specifications of the minimum acceptable quality for all goods purchased are provided to vendors.
- Vendor's adherence to the quality specifications is the responsibility of the Materials Manager of the Inventory Control Department and not the Purchasing Department. The Materials Manager inspects the goods as they arrive to be sure the quality meets the minimum standards and then sees that the goods are transferred from the receiving dock to the storeroom.
- All purchase requests are prepared by the Materials Manager on the basis of the production schedule for a four-month period.
- One vendor provides 90% of a critical raw material. This vendor has a good delivery record and is very reliable. Furthermore, this vendor has been the low bidder over the past few years.
- As production plans change, rush and expedite orders are made by production directly to the Purchasing Department. Materials ordered for canceled production runs are stored for future use. The costs of these special requests are borne by the Purchasing Department. Jones considers the additional costs associated with these special requests as "costs of being a good member of the corporate team."

- Materials to accomplish engineering changes are ordered by the Purchasing Department as soon as the changes are made by the Engineering Department. Jones is very proud of the quick response by the purchasing staff to product changes. Materials on hand are not reviewed before any orders are placed.
- Partial shipments and advance shipments (i.e., those received before the requested data of delivery) are accepted by the Materials Manager, who notifies the Purchasing Department of the receipt. The Purchasing Department is responsible for follow-up on partial shipments. No action is taken to discourage advance shipments.

Required:
On the basis of the Purchasing Department's policies and procedures and your findings,
1. Identify weaknesses and/or inefficiencies in Lecimore Company's purchasing function.
2. Make recommendations for those weaknesses/inefficiencies which you identify.

Use the following format in preparing your response:

Weaknesses/Inefficiencies   Recommendations
1.   1.

(CMA Adapted)

13-4   The flowchart on page 556 illustrates a manual system for executing purchases and cash disbursement transactions.

Required:
Indicate what each of the letters (A) through (L) represents. Do not discuss adequacies or inadequacies in the internal control structure.   (AICPA Adapted)

13-5   Dunbar Camera Manufacturing, Inc., is a manufacturer of high-priced precision motion picture cameras in which the specifications of component parts are vital to the manufacturing process. Dunbar buys valuable camera lenses and large quantities of sheet metal and screws. Screws and lenses are ordered by Dunbar and are billed by the vendors on a unit basis. Sheet metal is ordered by Dunbar and is billed by the vendors on the basis of weight. The receiving clerk is responsible for documenting the quality and quantity of merchandise received.

A preliminary review of the internal control structure indicates that the following procedures are being followed:

Receiving Report
1. Properly approved purchase orders, which are prenumbered, are filed numerically. The copy sent to the receiving clerk is an exact duplicate of the copy sent to the vendor. Receipts of merchandise are recorded on the duplicate copy by the receiving clerk.

Sheet metal
2. The company receives sheet metal by railroad. The railroad independently weighs the sheet metal and reports the weight and date of receipt on a bill of lading (waybill), which accompanies all deliveries. The receiving clerk only checks the weight on the waybill against the purchase order.

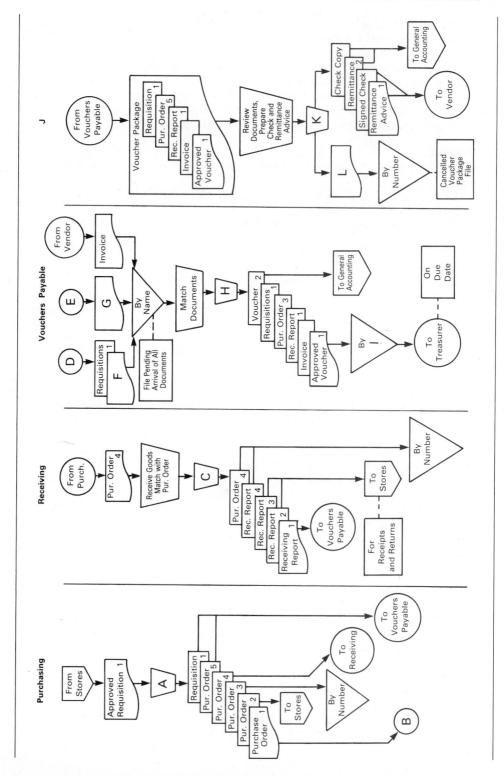

Screws

3. The receiving clerk opens cartons containing screws and then inspects and weighs the contents. The weight is converted to number of units by means of conversion charts. The receiving clerk then checks the computed quantity against the purchase order.

Camera lenses

4. Each camera lens is delivered in a separate corrugated carton. Cartons are counted as they are received by the receiving clerk and the number of cartons are checked against purchase orders.

Required:

(1) Explain why the control procedures as they apply individually to receiving reports and the receipt of sheet metal, screws, and camera lenses are adequate or inadequate. Do not discuss recommendations for improvements.

(2) What financial statement distortions may arise because of the inadequacies in Dunbar's internal control structure and how may they occur? (AICPA Adapted)

13-6   Long, CPA, has been engaged to examine and report on the financial statements of Maylou Corporation. In considering Maylou's controls over purchases, Long was given the following document flowchart for purchases.

MAYLOU CORPORATION
Document Flowchart for Purchases

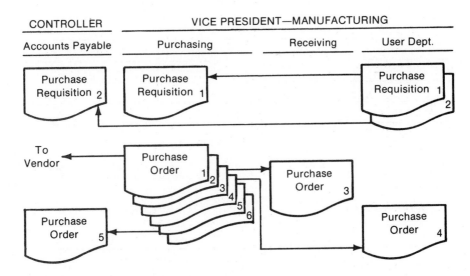

Required:

Identify the procedures, relating to purchase requisitions and purchase orders, that Long would expect to find if Maylou's controls over purchases are effective. For example, purchase orders are prepared only after giving proper consideration to the time to order and to the quantity to order. Do not comment on the effectiveness of the flow of documents as presented in the flowchart or on separation of duties.

(AICPA Adapted)

13-7   Properly designed and utilized forms facilitate adherence to prescribed control policies and procedures. One such form might be a multicopy purchase order, with one copy intended to be mailed to the vendor. The remaining copies would ordinarily be distributed to the stores and to the Purchasing, Receiving, and Accounting Departments.

The following purchase order is currently being used by National Industrial Corporation:

                                                            PURCHASE ORDER

SEND INVOICE ONLY TO:

297 HARDINGTEN DR., BX., NY 10461

TO _____   SHIP TO _____

     _____   _____

     _____   _____

DATE TO BE SHIPPED	SHIP VIA	DISC. TERMS	FREIGHT TERMS	ADV. ALLOWANCE	SPECIAL ALLOWANCE
QUANTITY		DESCRIPTION			

PURCHASE CONDITIONS

1. Supplier will be responsible for extra freight cost on partial shipment, unless prior permission is obtained.

2. Please acknowledge this order.

3. Please notify us immediately if you are unable to complete order.

4. All items must be individually packed.

Required:

(1) In addition to the name of the company, what other necessary information would an auditor recommend be included in the illustrative purchase order?

(2) What control objectives are served by the purchase order copies that are distributed to the stores and to the Purchasing, Receiving, and Accounting Departments?

13-8   Taylor, a CPA, has been engaged to audit the financial statements of University Books, Incorporated. University Books maintains a large imprest cash fund exclusively for the purpose of buying used books from students for cash. The cash fund is active all year because the nearby university offers a large variety of courses with varying starting and completion dates throughout the year.

Receipts are prepared for each purchase, and reimbursement vouchers are periodically submitted.

Required:
Construct a questionnaire to be used in documenting University Book's controls over the imprest cash fund for purchasing used books. The questionnaire should elicit a ''Yes'' or ''No'' response.   (AICPA Adapted)

13-9   Following are selected questions from a questionnaire relating to a company's purchasing, receiving, cash disbursements, and recording functions. A ''Yes'' response to any question would indicate a potential strength of the system, and a ''No'' a potential weakness.
a. Are prenumbered purchase orders prepared for all approved purchase requisitions?
b. Are competitive bids or price quotations obtained for purchased goods and services?
c. Are price lists maintained for repetitive transactions that do not require competitive bids or price quotations?
d. Are copies of purchase orders forwarded to the requisitioning department and to receiving?
e. Are all goods received, inspected, counted, and compared with copies of purchase orders?
f. Are voucher packages reviewed before being approved for payment?
g. Are voucher packages and checks reviewed by signatories before signing checks?

Required:
Assume that inquiries indicate the answer is ''Yes'' to each question. For each question, draft a test of controls that you believe would provide persuasive evidence that the answer is correct.

13-10   Following are several compliance tests of controls introduced in the chapter. For each test, indicate the expenditure/disbursement cycle activity tested and the purpose of the test.

Tests of Controls:
(1) Examine periodic reports by non-Purchasing Department personnel regarding purchase prices and practices.
(2) Observe Receiving Department procedures, determining whether received goods are counted and compared with quantities and descriptions on purchase orders.
(3) Foot the voucher register for a selected period and compare the total with postings in the general ledger.
(4) Observe voucher cancellation procedures, determining whether vouchers are canceled by or in the presence of check signers.

SUBSTANTIVE TESTS OF THE EXPENDITURE/DISBURSEMENT CYCLE: ACCOUNTS PAYABLE, PREPAID EXPENSES, AND ACCRUED LIABILITIES

14

Major topics discussed in this chapter are the:

▲ *Relationships among financial statement assertions, audit objectives, and audit procedures within the expenditure/disbursement cycle.*

▲ *Audit objectives and substantive tests applicable to accounts payable.*

▲ *Substantive tests applicable to prepaid expenses and accrued liabilities.*

▲ *Application of audit sampling to accounts payable (Appendix A).*

▲ *Computer-assisted audit techniques applicable to accounts payable (Appendix B).*

This chapter begins by discussing how each of the audit objectives introduced in Chapter 6 — existence or occurrence, completeness, rights and obligations, valuation or allocation, and presentation and disclosure — is accomplished for audits of accounts payable, a major financial statement account within the expenditure/disbursement cycle. The chapter then relates the objectives to specific substantive tests of accounts payable. In turn, the chapter addresses the audit of prepaid expenses and accrued liabilities. Finally, two appendices at the end of the chapter illustrate the application of nonstatistical sampling to accounts payable (Appendix A) and computer-assisted audit techniques applicable to accounts payable (Appendix B).

FINANCIAL STATEMENT ASSERTIONS, OBJECTIVES, AND AUDIT PROCEDURES

Within the expenditure/disbursement cycle, purchases and accounts payable are usually the highest-volume financial statement accounts and often represent the most material account balances processed by the cycle. The expenditure/disbursement cycle affects other financial statement accounts —

FIGURE 14-1
Relating Audit Objectives and Audit Procedures: Purchases and
Accounts Payable

Audit Objective	Audit Procedure
Existence or occurrence	Confirm with creditors. Test cutoff.
Completeness	Test for unrecorded liabilities. Perform analytical procedures. Test cutoff.
Rights and obligations	Confirm with creditors. Test for unrecorded liabilities.
Valuation or allocation	Verify accounts payable trial balance. Confirm with creditors. Test for unrecorded liabilities.
Presentation and disclosure	Compare statement presentation and disclosure with those required by GAAP.

for example, prepaid expenses and accrued liabilities, both of which are discussed in this chapter — but the transactions in these accounts are not typically voluminous. As a result, the audit of purchases and payables is emphasized in this chapter and discussed below in the context of specific audit objectives. Figure 14-1 relates each objective to specific audit procedures and summarizes the following discussion.

Existence or Occurrence

Within the expenditure/disbursement cycle, the existence or occurrence objective addresses whether all recorded payables exist at the balance sheet date and whether all recorded purchase transactions occurred during the period. The existence of accounts payable balances may be tested by confirming balances with creditors, although payables confirmations are used less frequently than receivables confirmations and generally are not used when the auditor suspects understatements. When confirmations are not used, the auditor can test existence by examining documentation — for example, purchase orders, receiving reports, and invoices — supporting recorded payables. The occurrence objective is accomplished by testing cutoff to determine whether purchases are recorded in the proper accounting period.

Completeness

The completeness objective addresses whether all purchase transactions and payables balances that should be presented in the financial statements are actually presented. That is, were all transactions recorded?

Completeness is tested by reviewing post-balance sheet date cash disbursements for payments made on previously unrecorded payables, and by examining unmatched receiving reports (filed in unpaid vouchers file) to assure that liabilities have been recorded at the balance sheet date. In addition, analytical procedures are used to detect any unusual relationships which might suggest unrecorded liabilities, not to detect unrecorded liabilities directly. Testing cutoff also addresses completeness.

Rights and Obligations

Within the expenditure/disbursement cycle, the rights and obligations objective addresses whether payables and other liabilities are bona fide obligations of the entity. Payables obligations may be tested by confirming payables balances with creditors and by searching for unrecorded liabilities as discussed in the preceding section, i.e., examining cash disbursements for the period subsequent to the balance sheet date.

Valuation or Allocation

The valuation objective addresses whether existing payables are reported in the financial statements at appropriate dollar amounts. The value of payables is tested by verifying the mathematical accuracy of the accounts payable aged trial balance, by confirming payables with creditors, and by testing for unrecorded liabilities.

Presentation and Disclosure

The presentation and disclosure objective addresses whether recorded payables are properly classified, described, and disclosed in financial statements. To test presentation and disclosure, an auditor compares a client's financial statement disclosures with those required by generally accepted accounting principles. Disclosure guidelines, such as the AICPA's annually updated *Accounting and Audit Manual,* are frequently used by practicing auditors.

SUBSTANTIVE TESTS OF ACCOUNTS PAYABLE

Substantive testing of expenditure/disbursement cycle accounts involves obtaining and evaluating evidence about a company's acquisition of resources and related obligations. Although cash disbursements are encompassed by the expenditure/disbursement cycle, substantive tests of cash balances were discussed and illustrated in Chapter 12 in the context of the revenue/receipt cycle (see Figure 12-6, page 496).

Like the revenue/receipt cycle, the expenditure/disbursement cycle varies in scope from one company to another and therefore so do the audit procedures applied to the cycle. Thus, the substantive tests discussed in this chapter are representative, not definitive. The nature, timing, and extent of procedures applied in an engagement depend on the assessed level of control risk and the resulting detection risk the auditor is willing to accept for each assertion. The audit programs presented are keyed to, and discussed in the context of, the audit objectives presented in Chapter 6 and discussed in this chapter.

▲ Existence or occurrence
▲ Completeness
▲ Rights and obligations
▲ Valuation or allocation
▲ Presentation and disclosure

A program of substantive tests and audit objectives applicable to purchases and accounts payable is presented in Figure 14-2. As discussed in Chapter 12, if controls or their method of application has changed since the interim assessment of control risk, an auditor should either perform additional tests of controls and reevaluate the system or increase the assessed level of control risk and extend the scope of substantive testing.

Verify Mathematical Accuracy

Verification of the mathematical or clerical accuracy of recorded payables is a first step in satisfying the valuation objective. A client-prepared listing of individual accounts payable, in the form of an aged trial balance similar to Figure 14-3, is obtained from client personnel and footed and cross-footed by the auditor. The trial balance may be prepared from unpaid vouchers on file, from a voucher register, or from an accounts payable subsidiary ledger. The recomputed total should be traced to the general ledger balance, and any difference should be reconciled.

If discrepancies are observed, or if deficiencies were detected in tests of controls, the auditor may conduct additional tests of mathematical accuracy. For example, the auditor may select a sample of accounts from the trial bal-

FIGURE 14-2
Substantive Tests: Purchases and Accounts Payable

Audit Objectives	Procedures

Valuation	1. Verify mathematical accuracy of accounts payable.
	  a. Obtain an accounts payable aged trial balance from Accounts Payable Department personnel.
	  b. Foot and cross-foot the trial balance.
	  c. Compare total accounts payable per the trial balance with accounts payable in the general ledger.
	  d. Trace sampled vendor accounts to voucher packages, and examine supporting documents.

Existence Obligations Valuation	2. Consider the need to confirm year-end accounts payable directly with creditors.
Existence or Occurrence Completeness	3. Test cutoff to determine whether purchases and payables are recorded in the proper accounting period.
Completeness Valuation Obligations	4. Test for unrecorded liabilities.
Existence or Occurrence Completeness Valuation	5. Perform analytical procedures.

Presentation and
Disclosure
	6. Review financial statements to determine whether:
	  a. Accounts and notes payable and other liabilities are properly classified and described.
	  b. Disclosures are adequate.

FIGURE 14-3
Accounts Payable Aged Trial Balance

(Schedule prepared
by client)

Christopher Supply Company
Accounts Payable Aged Trial Balance
December 31, 1990

Account Number	Vendor Name	Balance Dec. 31, 1990	0-30 Days	31-60 Days	Over 60 Days
0001	Adams Supply	$ 7,859.76	$ 7,859.76		
0002	Andrews & Company	17,621.40	17,621.40		
0003	Art Design Inc.	784.50	784.50		
0004	Ashton Mfg.	10,005.00	9,000.00	$ 1,005.00	
0005	Attleboro Bindings	1,147.61	1,147.61		
0006	Bates Motel	123.49	123.49		
0007	Faunce & Co.	1,456.90			$1,456.90
.	.	.	.	.	.
.	.	.	.	.	.
.	.	.	.	.	.
0162	Van Nuys & Co.	6,724.82	6,724.82		
0163	Wallace's	12,654.09	12,654.09		
0164	Western Electric	1,164.21	1,164.21		
0165	Yantze Inc.	550.00		550.00	
		$238,858.89	$225,282.64	$10,125.50	$3,450.75

ance and trace each account to the voucher package in the unpaid vouchers file and to the voucher register and accounts payable subsidiary ledger.

Confirm Payables

Unlike the confirmation of receivables (Chapter 12), an auditor is not required to justify his or her opinion on financial statements when payables are not confirmed. In fact, payables confirmations are not ordinarily used in practice, unless internal control is inadequate and other forms of evidence, such as detailed vendors' invoices, are unavailable or an auditor is concerned that liabilities are overstated.

A predominant concern in auditing receivables is the detection of overstatements, and confirmation is an effective procedure for verifying the existence, rights, and valuation of recorded accounts receivable. In auditing payables, however, an auditor is usually concerned with the possibility of understatement — specifically, unrecorded obligations to vendors and inadequate accruals for various operating expenses. Confirming recorded payables with vendors is not an effective means for detecting unrecorded liabilities; if a payable is unrecorded, its existence would not be known, and thus a confirmation request would not be sent.

This does not mean that auditors are never concerned with overstated liabilities, only that understatement is more common. An auditor may suspect overstatement, for example, if he or she has reason to believe that a client motivated by tax avoidance has overstated liabilities and thus understated income. Also, if a client's income is significantly lower than in preceding years and liabilities significantly higher, an auditor may suspect that liabilities are overstated if there is no other apparent cause for the reduction in income.

When confirmation of payables is considered necessary by an auditor, balances are usually confirmed as of the balance sheet date rather than at interim. Confirming payables balances requires direct communication with vendors, requesting that an itemized statement of account be sent directly to the auditor. Unlike positive and negative receivables confirmations, payables confirmation requests usually do not reveal the audited entity's recorded balance; rather, they request a statement reflecting the vendor's records. A sample payables confirmation request appears in Figure 14-4.

As in the case of receivables confirmations, an auditor should mail second (and perhaps even third) requests to vendors who have failed to respond. For accounts that are not confirmed, an auditor could examine subsequent cash payments, vendors' invoices, and receiving documents.

FIGURE 14-4
Accounts Payable Confirmation

CHRISTOPHER SUPPLY COMPANY
653 Broadway
New York, New York 01284

January 7, 1991

Frank Raftis Co., Inc.
305 Columbus Avenue
Pawtucket, R.I. 02861

Our auditors, Cermak & Willingham, CPAs, are examining our financial statements for 1990. Will you please furnish them with the following information as of December 31, 1990:

 • An itemized statement of amounts owed to you by us.

 • An itemized statement of any merchandise consigned to us by you.

 • An itemized list of any notes, acceptances, or other obligations owed to you by us.

A prompt reply to our auditors will be appreciated. An envelope addressed to our auditors is enclosed.

Molly Gilmore
Molly Gilmore
Controller
Christopher Supply Company

Test Cutoff

Purchases cutoff tests are very similar in nature and logic to sales cutoff tests, discussed in Chapter 12. An auditor tests purchases cutoff to determine whether purchases and corresponding payables are recorded in the appropriate period — i.e., whether purchases of goods are recorded in the period that title to the goods passed to the company that received the goods, and whether services are recorded in the period rendered. Cutoff tests relate most directly to the audit objectives of existence and completeness.

Cutoff tests of purchase transactions involve selecting and examining a sample of purchase entries on or near year-end (e.g., ten days before to ten days after year-end). Receiving reports are examined for each sampled purchase entry. A purchase of goods and a related payable should have been recorded to the year under audit if shipping terms are (1) FOB shipping point (origin) and goods were shipped by the seller on or before year-end, or (2) FOB destination and goods were received on or before the year-end date. Transactions relating to services should be reflected in the year under audit if the services were received by the entity on or before the year-end date.

Another aspect of cutoff relates to prepayments and accruals. An auditor should review the client's year-end entries relating to prepaid and accrued expenses to determine whether expenses are recognized in the appropriate accounting period. Prepayments and accruals are discussed more fully later in the chapter.

Test for Unrecorded Liabilities

As noted above, auditors are often concerned that liabilities may be understated as a result of unrecorded payables. This does not suggest, however, that an auditor is never concerned with overstated liabilities, only that understatement is more common, since understating liabilities can result in overstated income. Figure 14-5 depicts the sources for testing accounts payable balances for both understatements and overstatements. Testing for understatements, or unrecorded liabilities, is discussed first.

A search for unrecorded liabilities is closely related to tests of cutoff and, in fact, may result in detection of items recorded in the wrong accounting period. Similarly, cutoff tests may reveal unrecorded liabilities. However, auditors usually conduct an investigation specifically designed to detect unrecorded liabilities, and thus specifically related to the audit objectives of completeness, valuation, and obligations.

Four basic sources are used to search for unrecorded payables:

▲ A year-end accounts payable trial balance.
▲ The cash disbursements journal.
▲ Canceled (paid) voucher packages.
▲ The file of unmatched receiving reports (filed in the unpaid vouchers file).

Assuming a December 31 year-end, an auditor would trace a sample of disbursements for January to receiving reports contained in canceled voucher packages; if goods were received or title to the goods passed on or before December 31, the accounts payable trial balance should reflect a liability. Likewise, since many accounting systems require a completed voucher package — purchase requisition, purchase order, receiving report, and vendor's

FIGURE 14-5
Auditing Accounts Payable Balances

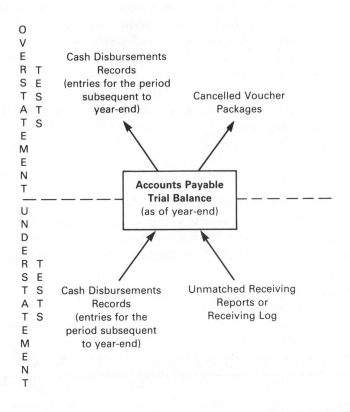

invoice — before a payable is recorded, an auditor would examine un-matched (unprocessed) receiving reports; again, if goods were received or title passed on or before December 31, the accounts payable trial balance should reflect the liability. The search for unrecorded liabilities is completed by inquiring of management personnel about whether they are aware of any significant payables not recorded and not detected by the above tests.

Even though payables understatement is often an overriding concern, an auditor cannot ignore the potential for overstatement, since particular clients may have incentives to overstate expenses (e.g., to avoid income taxes). Three basic sources are used to test for overstated payables:

▲ A year-end accounts payable trial balance.
▲ The cash disbursements journal.
▲ Canceled (paid) voucher packages.

Assuming a December 31 year-end, an auditor would trace sample items from the accounts payable trial balance to receiving reports and shipping terms contained in canceled voucher packages; title should have passed on or before December 31. In addition, sampled items would be traced to subsequent payments in the cash disbursements book, assuring that the liability was paid, and therefore that documentation for returned goods was not concealed. For example, a payable recorded on or before December 31 with payment terms of 2/10, net 30, should have been paid no later than January 10 to take advantage of the two percent discount, and no later than January 30 if the discount were not taken. If not paid, an auditor would obtain an explanation from management; nonpayment could suggest the liability did not exist as of December 31, despite documentation to the contrary.

Perform Analytical Procedures

As in tests of receivables balances (Chapter 12), the role of year-end analytical procedures for payables is to direct attention to unusual, unreasonable, or otherwise unexplainable relationships among accounts or account components. That is, analytical procedures can be used to identify accounts which:

▲ Appear reasonable in relation to other accounts and therefore do not require additional substantive testing.
▲ Appear unusual or unreasonable and therefore require additional substantive testing.

For accounts payable, an auditor might use any of the following analytical procedures, among others, to assess the reasonableness of recorded balances.

▲ Compare the average number of days purchases in accounts payable at the end of the current year with prior years.
▲ Compare purchases divided by payables for the current and prior years.
▲ Compare payables divided by total current liabilities for the current and prior years.
▲ Compare both purchases and payables with budgeted or forecasted amounts.

An auditor should investigate any unusual relationships among accounts or account components, and design additional substantive tests of details if warranted. For example, if payables divided by current liabilities appear low in comparison with prior years, the auditor might increase the scope of testing for unrecorded liabilities, as discussed earlier in the chapter.

Presentation and Disclosure

Item 6 of the program for substantive testing of purchases and payables requires that an auditor assess whether expenditure/disbursement cycle accounts such as payables, accrued liabilities, and related purchase and expense accounts are classified and disclosed in accordance with generally accepted accounting principles. Payables and accrued liabilities are usually classified as current if due within one year or expected to be paid either with existing current assets or by incurring additional current liabilities. Depending upon materiality, liabilities such as trade accounts payable, advances (for example, from officers), customer credit balances, dividends payable, interest payable, and liabilities for product warranties should all be disclosed separately.

PREPAID EXPENSES AND ACCRUED LIABILITIES

For most business entities, the accounts payable balance summarizes a large volume of recurring transactions, is material, and, therefore, is often the most time-consuming audit area within the expenditure/disbursement cycle. However, two other expenditure/disbursement cycle accounts, prepaid expenses and accrued liabilities, are also important to an audit but they're important because they result from timing differences between when cash is expended and an asset or liability is recorded, not because of volume or even materiality necessarily. In fact, the volume of transactions underlying prepaid expenses and accrued liabilities is often small. As a result, auditors usually either test 100 percent of the transactions and events underlying individual prepaid expense and accrued liability accounts or rely on analytical procedures. Note, though, that regardless of the audit procedures performed, an auditor's objectives are identical to those applied to all other balance sheet accounts.

Prepaid Expenses

Prepaid expenses normally result because the future service potential of assets may extend beyond the period in which payment is made. Common examples include prepaid insurance, prepaid rent, accumulated income tax prepayments, and other deferred charges. For illustration purposes, the following discussion focuses on a specific prepaid expense account, prepaid insurance, but the audit issues discussed apply to other prepaid expense accounts.

Controls. In general, an auditor is concerned with three predominant controls in the audit of prepaid insurance — control procedures over the:

▲ Acquisition of new insurance policies.
▲ Disbursement of cash for premiums.
▲ Recording of expense and premium disbursements.

The acquisition of new insurance coverage should be authorized by the board of directors, and the specific insurance company and policy selected should be approved by authorized personnel. As in other cash payments within the expenditure/disbursement cycle, disbursements for premiums and the recording of insurance expense and disbursements should be segregated, thereby separating the execution and recording functions. As a further control over recording, an *insurance register* should be maintained to compile detailed information about coverage, terms, and payment due dates.

Substantive Tests. Figure 14-6 illustrates an audit working paper for prepaid insurance, and indicates how each of an auditor's objectives is addressed. To test existence, the auditor examines current insurance policies and may, as indicated in Figure 14-6, confirm the coverage, terms, due dates, and unexpired premiums directly with insurance companies.

Completeness is tested two ways, though neither is apt to reveal errors or irregularities since all transactions in Figure 14-6 have been tested 100 percent. First, the auditor assures that total insurance coverage exceeds the replacement cost of all tangible assets. In addition, cutoff testing is used, but not directly on the prepaid insurance working paper. Rather, cutoff testing is addressed during substantive tests of accounts payable and the auditor's search for unrecorded liabilities, both of which were discussed earlier in the chapter.

Rights and obligations are tested by examining the insurance policies and, as in Figure 14-6, confirming the policy with insurance carriers. In turn, an auditor tests valuation by recalculating unexpired premiums through evidence obtained from the prior year's unexpired insurance and from current premiums. In addition, to address clerical accuracy, the auditor reconciles premium payments with cash disbursements records, and total expense and unexpired premiums with the general ledger.

Finally, the objective of presentation and disclosure is not particularly problematic, except in one area: the adequacy of insurance coverage. An auditor should determine whether total insurance coverage exceeds his or her best estimate of the replacement cost for all tangible assets, insured or otherwise. If replacement cost exceeds insurance coverage, the client is partially self-insured. In this case, the excess of replacement cost over insurance should be disclosed in a note to the financial statements, though not accrued, since the conditions for accruing loss contingencies in FASB *Statement of Financial Accounting Standards No. 5*, ''Accounting for Contingencies,'' — that is, (1) the loss is probable, and (2) the amount of the loss can be estimated reasonably — would not have been met.

Accrued Liabilities

Accrued liabilities result because some unpaid obligations for services may have been incurred before the balance sheet date. Common examples include accrued property taxes, accrued payroll taxes, accrued product war-

FIGURE 14-6
Analysis of Prepaid Insurance

D4
SEB
1/15/91

Christopher Supply Company
Prepaid Insurance
December 31, 1990

Insurer Policy Number	Coverage	Period	Premium	Year Paid	Unexpired Premium 12-31-89	Additions	Expense	Unexpired Premium 12-31-90
Provident Casualty AE-1067-48139 d	Automobiles-collision, comprehensive, uninsured motorist; covers all autos operated	Jan 1, 89- Dec 31, 91	$9,000 e	87	$6,000 f	-	$3,000 g	$3,000 a,h
Washington Ins. Co PBL-462-1982-63 d	Casualty-buildings, covers all buildings and equipment	July 1, 90- June 30, 95	$7,000	88	-	$7,000 i	1,750 g	5,250 a,h
New York Equitable NY 743-96218 d	Business interruption	Oct 1, 89- Sept 30, 91	$3,000 e	87	2,625 f	-	1,500 g	1,125 a,h
					$8,625	$7,000	$6,250	$9,375 h
					c	c	b,c,j	b,c,j

Note: Total coverage exceeds the replacement cost of all insured assets.

a Cross footed
b Agreed to general ledger
c Footed
d Examined insurance policy, agreeing policy number, terms, period covered and premium.
e Examined premium notice in company files, and traced to prior year's working papers which indicated payment was agreed to cash disbursement records in the year paid. (1989)
f Agreed to 12-31-89 general ledger, and last year's working papers.
g .Calculated
h Confirmed with insurance company. See insurance confirmation file.
i Examined premium notice and traced to cash disbursements; policy is for five years, but premiums are paid two years in advance during the first four years, and the fifth year is paid one year in advance.
j Agreed to trial balance.

ranty costs, accrued rent, accrued interest, and accrued income taxes. The discussion focuses on accrued property taxes, although the audit issues discussed are common to other accrued liabilities.

Controls. In the audit of property taxes, an auditor is concerned with a company's controls over three activities:

▲ Recognition of accrued taxes.
▲ Recording of expense for taxes owed.
▲ Disbursement of cash for taxes.

When a company conducts business in several locations, particularly across state or national borders, management should institute policies to assure that liabilities for property taxes in all relevant municipalities, states, or countries are accrued at the balance sheet date. The recording of property tax expense should be based on bills actually received or estimated from prior years adjusted for tax rate changes, if any. As with other cash payments processed through the expenditure/disbursement cycle, responsibility for disbursing cash and for recording disbursements should be segregated. If property taxes are paid in several localities, a separate property tax ledger should be maintained to compile and control both accruals and payments.

Substantive Tests. Figure 14-7 illustrates an audit working paper for accrued property taxes and indicates how each relevant audit objective is addressed. To test occurrence, obligations, and valuation, an auditor examines receipted property tax bills for the current year, if available, or, as in Figure 14-7, compares the current provision for property tax expense with prior-year payments for reasonableness. In testing reasonableness, though, the auditor should consider plant asset additions/disposals and tax rate changes, since either or both could alter the amount owed for the current year. In turn, reasonableness tests also address completeness, since unusual fluctuations in accrued property taxes from one year to the next could signal underaccruals or overaccruals.

SUMMARY

The expenditure/disbursement cycle encompasses two major business functions — acquiring resources from vendors and employees and paying obligations to vendors and employees. These business functions lead to one major balance sheet account: accounts payable. The functions also result in

FIGURE 14-7
Analysis of Accrued Property Taxes   *D7*

SEB

1/16/91

Christopher Supply Company
Accrued Property Taxes
December 31, 1990

Balance, Dec 31, 1989		$34,230 a
Provision for property tax expense		35,000 d
Payments:		
State of Missouri	$15,473 b	
State of Illinois	12,696 b	
City of St. Louis	3,210 b	
City of Chicago	2,842 b	(34,221)
Balance, Dec 31, 1990		$35,009
		c,e

a Agreed to prior year working papers and financial statements

b Traced to receipted tax bill and cash disbursements records

c Footed

d Provision for property tax expense appears reasonable, since the provision reasonably approximates 1990 actual payments adjusted for plant asset additions less retirements (See E1)

e Agreed to trial balance

prepaid expenses and accrued liabilities. When performing substantive tests of payables, an auditor's major objectives are to determine that each account exists, represents all transactions that should be presented, represents rights or obligations of the entity, is valued properly, and is presented and disclosed properly within the financial statements.

APPENDIX A
CASE ILLUSTRATION: APPLYING NONSTATISTICAL SAMPLING IN SUBSTANTIVE TESTS OF ACCOUNTS PAYABLE

To integrate material presented in this chapter with the nonstatistical sampling applications introduced in Chapter 10 assume a continuing audit engagement for the Skynob Corporation, a wholesaler of college- and high-school supplies, whose fiscal year ends December 31. The specific purpose in this case is to determine whether recorded accounts payable are fairly stated at December 31.

Assessment of Control Risk

Assume consideration of internal control structure was accomplished as of October 31 and revealed that controls over payables were adequate, reliable, and not likely to produce aggregate error in excess of tolerable error. The auditor assesses a minimum level of control risk. However, these tests did reveal delays of 36 to 48 hours in recording disbursements, thereby suggesting potential year-end cutoff problems that could result in overstated payables and overstated cash at December 31, the balance sheet date. At year-end, the auditor made inquiries of management which indicated that neither the controls nor responsible personnel had changed since interim. Thus, the auditor has no reason to perform additional tests of controls for the period November 1 to December 31 although the delay in recording disbursements would affect planned audit procedures.

Selecting a Sampling Plan

Although Skynob's cash disbursements volume is high, payables represent only five percent of total liabilities — an amount the auditor judges material, but not highly material. Rather, long-term debt, leaseholds, and equity are far more material to the Skynob audit, and, further, tests of controls suggest debt and leaseholds may entail more audit risk than payables.

For the Skynob engagement, the auditor now has three important pieces of information:

▲ Controls over payables are adequate and reliable.
▲ Disbursement recording is sometimes delayed, suggesting the possibility of overstated payables and overstated cash at the balance sheet date.
▲ Payables are material, but neither as material nor as risky as long-term debt and leaseholds.

From this information, the auditor decides to confirm a sample of accounts payable balances, since year-end balances could be overstated and in this case the auditor believes confirmations would be less costly than extensive cutoff tests. The auditor elects to use a nonstatistical sampling plan, since there is no apparent reason to quantify audit risk.

The auditor's confirmation of Skynob Corporation's payables balances is accomplished by the nonstatistical sampling for variables plan introduced in Chapter 10 and illustrated below.

Population, Sampling Unit, and Determination of Sample Size

At December 31, the audit population consists of 253 vendor accounts, totaling $475,000. The accounts payable trial balance, the source for selecting accounts for confirmation, is clerically accurate and agrees in total with the general ledger. Each vendor account represents a sampling unit. To choose an appropriate sample size, the auditor must next classify the degree of audit assurance desired, choose an appropriate assurance factor, and estimate tolerable error and key-dollar items, all of which appear in the nonstatistical sampling plan in Chapter 10, pages 419–423.

Because the auditor plans some reliance on internal control structure and on cutoff tests, the auditor requires a moderate degree of audit assurance (see the decision aid on page 421, Chapter 10). Because some error is anticipated, the auditor's assurance factor is 8.

The auditor decides to set tolerable error, the maximum monetary error that may exist without causing the financial statements to be misleading, at $25,000, which is a little over five percent of Skynob's recorded book value. The amount of key-dollar items is set at $8,000, and 28 of the 253 account balances in the population are $8,000 or more, and in total sum to $275,000.

Recapping, the following information is known:

$$
\begin{aligned}
B &= \text{Recorded book value} = \$475,000 \\
KD &= \text{Key-dollar items} \quad = \$275,000 \\
TE &= \text{Tolerable error} \quad\;\; = \$\ 25,000 \\
AF &= \text{Assurance factor} \quad = 8
\end{aligned}
$$

From these data, sample size can be calculated using the method introduced in Chapter 10, page 421.

$$
\begin{aligned}
n &= \frac{B - KD}{TE} \times AF \\
&= \frac{\$475,000 - \$275,000}{\$25,000} \times 8 \\
&= 64
\end{aligned}
$$

Ninety-two confirmations are mailed on January 3: 28 to vendors with balances of $8,000 or more (the key-dollar items) and 64 to vendors whose accounts were selected randomly from the 225 remaining accounts (i.e., 253 accounts less 28 key items).

Evaluating Results

Assume confirmations are received from 24 of the key-dollar accounts and from 61 of the 64 randomly selected accounts. For nonresponding vendors, the auditor examines subsequent payments and voucher packages. The confirmations and other procedures reveal $5,975 of known error:

Known error:
Key-dollar items $3,625 overstatement
Randomly selected items   2,350 overstatement
                                               $5,975 overstatement

From this information, likely error, the auditor's estimate of total population error, is a $12,018 overstatement, calculated as follows:

Likely error:
  Key-dollar error $3,625
  Other error:

$$\left[\frac{\$2,350}{\left(\frac{64}{253-28}\right)}\right] = \frac{8,393}{\$12,018} \text{ overstatement}$$

In this case, since tolerable error ($25,000) exceeds likely error ($12,018), the auditor could propose adjusting known error only — that is, propose an audit adjustment reducing payables by $5,975.

APPENDIX B
COMPUTER-ASSISTED SUBSTANTIVE TESTS OF ACCOUNTS PAYABLE

When a client's accounting information system processes data by computer rather than manually, some of an auditor's substantive tests of details can be accomplished with the computer. Figure 14-8 lists several computer-

FIGURE 14-8
Computer-Assisted Substantive Tests: Accounts Payable

Audit Procedure	Computer-Assisted Substantive Tests
Test mathematical accuracy.	Verify footings, cross-footings, and extensions of the accounts payable aged trial balance and/or detailed subsidiary records.
Summarize data for further testing or analysis.	Age payables according to computer-stored due dates.
	List debit balances in accounts payable for reclassification to accounts receivable.
	Print accounts payable confirmations.
Test accuracy of recorded data.	Compare details in accounts payable trial balance with detailed subsidiary records.
	Compare details in subsidiary records with machine-readable source documents (e.g., voucher packages).
Sample selection.	Select accounts for testing from internally stored random number generators and the aged accounts payable trial balance.
Compare similar data files.	Compare charges/credits in detailed subsidiary records with the purchases/cash disbursements master files.

assisted techniques for a series of audit procedures common to accounts payable. These procedures can be accomplished through computer programs prepared by the auditor or through generalized audit software available from outside vendors.

QUESTIONS

1. How can an auditor test whether all payables transactions that should be recorded are actually recorded?
2. Explain how an auditor determines whether all recorded payables actually represent bona fide obligations of the entity.

3. What procedures might an auditor use in satisfying the valuation objective for purchases and payables?

4. Under what conditions are payables most likely to be confirmed by an auditor?

5. Why is confirmation ineffective in detecting understatement of liabilities?

6. How and why does an auditor test purchases cutoff?

7. Describe how an auditor searches for unrecorded liabilities.

8. What major sources does an auditor use to test for overstated accounts payable, and how are those major sources used?

9. In testing prepaid insurance, how does an auditor address the audit objectives of rights and obligations?

10. What are the major internal controls an auditor considers when designing substantive tests of accrued property taxes?

MULTIPLE CHOICE QUESTIONS

1. Which of the following procedures relating to the examination of accounts payable could the auditor delegate entirely to the client's employees?

   a. Test footings in the accounts payable ledger.
   b. Reconcile unpaid invoices to vendors' statements.
   c. Prepare a schedule of accounts payable.
   d. Mail confirmations for selected account balances.   (AICPA Adapted)

2. In order to efficiently establish the correctness of the accounts payable cutoff, an auditor will be most likely to

   a. Coordinate cutoff tests with physical inventory observation.
   b. Compare cutoff reports with purchase orders.
   c. Compare vendors' invoices with vendors' statements.
   d. Coordinate mailing of confirmations with cutoff tests.   (AICPA Adapted)

3. An examination of the balance in the accounts payable account is ordinarily not designed to

   a. Detect accounts payable which are substantially past due.
   b. Verify that accounts payable were properly authorized.
   c. Ascertain the reasonableness of recorded liabilities.
   d. Determine that all existing liabilities at the balance sheet date have been recorded.   (AICPA Adapted)

4. When an auditor selects a sample of items from the vouchers payable register for the last month of the period under audit and traces these items to underlying documents, the auditor is gathering evidence primarily in support of the assertion that

   a. Recorded obligations were paid.
   b. Incurred obligations were recorded in the correct period.
   c. Recorded obligations were valid.
   d. Cash disbursements were recorded as incurred obligations.

                                                                 (AICPA Adapted)

5. Which of the following is the most efficient audit procedure for the detection of unrecorded liabilities at the balance sheet date?

   a. Confirm large accounts payable balances at the balance sheet date.
   b. Compare cash disbursements in the subsequent period with the accounts payable trial balance at year-end.
   c. Examine purchase orders issued for several days prior to the close of the year.
   d. Obtain an attorney's letter from the client's attorney.   (AICPA Adapted)

6. Which of the following audit procedures is least likely to detect an unrecorded liability?

   a. Analysis and recomputation of interest expense.
   b. Analysis and recomputation of depreciation expense.
   c. Mailing of standard bank confirmation form.
   d. Reading of the minutes of meetings of the board of directors.
                                                                     (AICPA Adapted)

7. A company sells a particular product only in the last month of its fiscal year. The company uses commission agents for such sales and pays them 6% of their net sales 30 days after the sales are made. The agents' sales were $10,000,000. Experience indicates that 10% of the sales are usually not collected and 2% are returned in the first month of the new year. The auditor would expect the year-end balance in the accrued commissions payable account to be:

   a. $528,000.
   b. $540,000.
   c. $588,000.
   d. $600,000.   (AICPA Adapted)

PROBLEMS

14-1   Following are errors, irregularities, or other circumstances that an auditor might encounter as a result of applying year-end substantive tests of details to accounts payable as of December 31, 1990:
   a. The aged trial balance does not agree with individual accounts payable ledger records.
   b. The auditor suspects that accounts payable may be overstated.
   c. Several shipments were received from an overseas FOB shipping point on January 2, 1991.
   d. The December 31, 1990, accounts payable balance appears low in comparison with the prior two years.
   e. The Accounts Payable Department maintains a file of unmatched receiving reports, i.e., receiving reports for which an invoice had not yet been received.
   f. Payables are not usually recorded until two days following the date that goods are received.

Required:
For each of the above, indicate (1) a specific detailed test or tests that might address the error, irregularity, or circumstance and (2) the audit objective addressed by each test.

14-2   Mincin, CPA, is the auditor of the Raleigh Corporation. Mincin is considering the audit work to be performed in the accounts payable area for the current year's engagement.

The prior year's working papers show that confirmation requests were mailed to 100 of Raleigh's 1,000 suppliers. The selected suppliers were based on Mincin's sample that was designed to select accounts with large dollar balances. A substantial number of hours were spent by Raleigh and Mincin resolving relatively minor differences between the confirmation replies and Raleigh's accounting records. Alternative audit procedures were used for those suppliers who did not respond to the confirmation requests.

Required:
(1) Identify the accounts payable audit objectives that Mincin must consider in determining the audit procedures to be followed.
(2) Identify situations when Mincin should use accounts payable confirmations and discuss whether Mincin is required to use them.
(3) Discuss why the use of large dollar balances as the basis for selecting accounts payable for confirmation might not be the most efficient approach and indicate what more efficient procedures could be followed when selecting accounts payable for confirmation.
                                                                                    (AICPA Adapted)

14-3   Taylor, CPA, is engaged in the audit of Rex Wholesaling for the year ended December 31, 1990. Taylor performed a proper study of internal control structure relating to the purchasing, receiving, trade accounts payable, and cash disbursement cycles and has decided not to proceed with tests of controls. On the basis of analytical procedures Taylor believes that the trade accounts payable balance on the balance sheet as of December 31, 1990 may be understated.

Taylor requested and obtained a client-prepared trade accounts payable schedule listing the total amount owed to each vendor.

Required:
What additional substantive audit procedures should Taylor apply in examining the trade accounts payable?

14-4   Compare the confirmation of accounts receivable with the confirmation of accounts payable under the following headings:
(a) Generally accepted auditing procedures. (Justify the differences revealed by your comparison.)
(b) Form of confirmation requests. (You need not supply examples.)
                                                                                    (AICPA Adapted)

14-5   Partly to address the audit objectives of existence and completeness, auditors typically test purchase cutoff at the balance sheet date, thereby addressing whether purchase transactions are recorded in the proper accounting period. Your audit supervisor has asked that you perform a purchase cutoff test for the Ridgeview Corporation, a December 31, 1990 year-end client. The supervisor suggests you test all purchase transactions over $5,000 for the period December 25, 1990 through January 5, 1991. Audit working papers compiled during the December 31 physical inventory observation indicate that the last receiving report used on December 31 was No. 13402. The following schedule is available for your use.

Receiving Report No.	Amount	Date Shipped	Date Received	Shipping Terms
13398	$13,500**	Dec. 26	Dec. 28	FOB: Origin ✓
13399	7,560*	Dec. 27	Dec. 27	FOB: Destination ✓
13400	24,000*	Dec. 29	Dec. 29	FOB: Origin ✓
13401	5,000**	Dec. 31	Dec. 31	FOB: Origin ✓
13402	15,980*	Dec. 29	Dec. 31	FOB: Destination ✓
13404	9,765*	Dec. 30	Jan. 2	FOB: Destination ✗
13405	45,000**	Jan. 1	Jan. 3	FOB: Destination ✗
13406	10,855**	Dec. 31	Jan. 2	FOB: Origin ✓

origin – shipp on or before 12-31-90
dest. – rec. before 12-31

Note: * indicates the item was included in December 31 payables.
      ** indicates the item was not included in December 31 payables.

Required:
For the items included in the above schedule, indicate whether the item is treated properly in December 31 accounts payable and provide adjusting journal entries for those not treated properly.

14-6   Auditors are often concerned that liabilities may be understated as a result of unrecorded payables. On the other hand, auditors may be concerned that liabilities are overstated as a result of payables recorded in the wrong accounting period, among other things.

Required:
(1) Give several reasons why an entity may want to *understate* payables.
(2) Give several reasons why an entity may want to *overstate* payables.

14-7   Auditors typically perform a search for unrecorded payables during year-end substantive testing.

Required:
Prepare an audit program to search for unrecorded payables.

14-8   You were in the final stages of your examination of the financial statements of Ozine Corporation for the year ended December 31, 1990, when you were consulted by the corporation's president, Gordon Sumner, who believes there is no point to your examining the 1991 voucher register and testing data in support of 1991 entries. He stated that (a) bills pertaining to 1990 that were received too late to be included in the December voucher register were recorded as of the year-end by the corporation by journal entry, (b) the internal auditor made tests after the year-end, and (c) he would furnish you with a letter certifying that there were no unrecorded liabilities.

Required:
a. Should a CPA's test for unrecorded liabilities be affected by the fact that the client made a journal entry to record 1990 bills that were received late? Explain.
b. Should a CPA's test for unrecorded liabilities be affected by the fact that a letter is obtained in which a responsible management official certifies that to the best of his knowledge all liabilities have been recorded? Explain.
c. Should a CPA's test for unrecorded liabilities be eliminated or reduced because of the internal audit tests? Explain.
d. Assume that the corporation, which handled some government contracts, had no internal auditor but that an auditor for a federal agency spent three weeks auditing the records and was just completing his work at the time. How would the CPA's unrecorded liability test be affected by the work of the auditor for a federal agency?
e. What sources in addition to the 1991 voucher register should the CPA consider to locate possible unrecorded liabilities?   (AICPA Adapted)

14-9   During an audit engagement Harper, CPA, has satisfactorily completed an examination of accounts payable and other liabilities and now plans to determine whether there are any loss contingencies arising from litigation, claims, or assessments.

Required:
What are the audit procedures that Harper should follow with respect to the existence of loss contingencies arising from litigation, claims, and assessments?

(AICPA Adapted)

14-10   During your examination of the financial statements of the John Delaney Manufacturing Company for the year ended December 31, 1990, you find that at January 1, 1990, the company had installed the following punched-card processing system for recording raw material purchases and related accounts payable:
(a) Vendors' invoices are sent directly to the Accounts Payable Department by the Mail Department.
(b) All supporting documents to the invoices are accumulated in the Accounts Payable Department and attached to the invoices. After being checked and cash discounts computed, the invoices are accumulated in batches and adding machine tapes prepared of the net invoice amounts to provide predetermined totals. Then the batches of invoices and tapes are sent to the Tabulating Department.
(c) In the Tabulating Department, keypunch operators prepare for each invoice an accounts payable punched card and one or more punched cards for the related debit distribution to several departmental inventories.
(d) The invoice register is prepared by tab runs of the distribution cards and accounts payable cards. In this run, totals of distribution cards are compared by the tabulating machine with the amounts punched for the related accounts payable cards.

Tab run subtotals by invoice batches are taken for checking to the predetermined totals.

(e) The general ledger control account is posted monthly from the totals shown in the invoice register and all other journals.

(f) By sorting, the distribution and accounts payable cards are separated. The distribution cards are filed for further processing. The accounts payable cards are sorted by due dates, and tab runs are prepared to determine cash requirements.

(g) On the due dates the accounts payable cards are processed to prepare combined check and remittance statements.

(h) At the end of the month the accounts payable cards in the unpaid file are tabulated for comparison with the general ledger control account.

Required:
What audit procedures would you employ to satisfy yourself about the reasonableness of the accounts payable balance at December 31, 1990?   (AICPA Adapted)

14-11   Robbins, CPA, during an examination of the financial statements of Gole Inc., requested and received a client-prepared property casualty insurance schedule which included appropriate premium information.

Required:
(1) Identify the type of information, in addition to the appropriate premium information, that would ordinarily be expected to be included in a property casualty insurance schedule.

(2) What are the basic audit procedures which Robbins should perform in examining the client-prepared property casualty insurance schedule?   (AICPA Adapted)

TESTS OF CONTROLS AND SUBSTANTIVE TESTS OF PERSONNEL AND PAYROLL

15

Major topics discussed in this chapter are the:

▲ *Nature of the personnel and payroll-related aspects of the expenditure/disbursement cycle.*

▲ *Controls over personnel and payroll activities.*

▲ *Auditor's consideration of controls over personnel and payroll.*

▲ *Audit objectives and substantive tests applicable to payroll accounts.*

The previous two chapters focused on tests of controls and substantive tests of purchases and accounts payable, both of which are processed through the expenditure/disbursement cycle. This chapter continues the discussion of the expenditure/disbursement cycle, focusing on tests of controls and substantive tests related to personnel and payroll. The chapter begins by reviewing the nature of the expenditure/disbursement cycle and by discussing the activities and controls common to the personnel and payroll functions. In turn, an auditor's consideration of control over personnel, payroll preparation, and payroll-related cash disbursements are explained. Finally, substantive tests of payroll account balances are introduced.

THE NATURE OF THE EXPENDITURE/DISBURSEMENT CYCLE: PERSONNEL AND PAYROLL

As discussed in Chapter 13, the expenditure/disbursement cycle encompasses the acquisition of and payment for resources acquired from vendors and from employees. Figure 15-1 summarizes the scope of the cycle as it relates to personnel and payroll, and indicates the two major business functions encompassed by the personnel and payroll aspects of the cycle:

▲ Resources (services) are acquired from employees in exchange for obligations to pay.

▲ Obligations to employees are paid.

FIGURE 15-1
The Scope of the Expenditure/Disbursement Cycle: Personnel and Payroll

Related Business Functions	Common Activities	Common Entries	Common Forms
• Resources (services) are acquired from employees in exchange for obligations to pay. • Obligations to employees are paid.	• Prepare and update personnel records • Prepare and record payroll • Distribute paychecks to employees.	• Payments to employees (cash disbursements) • Account distribution • Accrued payroll	• Personnel records • Time cards • Payroll register • Employee earnings records

The personnel and payroll aspects of the expenditure/disbursement cycle are particularly critical to most companies for at least three reasons. First, salaries and wages are usually a major expenditure for most manufacturing and service-oriented companies. Second, in manufacturing companies, labor is an important component in valuing inventory and, if misclassified, could result in the material misstatement of inventory and cost of goods sold. Third, personnel and payroll activities typically involve several categories of employee compensation, including salaries, hourly wages, incentive compensation and bonuses, overtime, vacation pay, and employee benefits such as health insurance, pensions, and profit sharing.

Personnel and payroll activities within the expenditure/disbursement cycle include hiring and terminations, payroll preparation and recording, and distribution of payroll checks. Journal entries are made for payments of wages and salaries, account distribution, and end-of-period adjustments for accrued payroll. Common forms and documents include:

▲ *Personnel records:* Documents maintained for each employee by the Personnel Department which provide a permanent record of all essential information pertaining to the employee including: date of employment, job classification, salary or hourly pay rate, promotions, payroll deductions, terminations, etc.
▲ *Time card:* Record of hours worked by an employee during a particular pay period (e.g., weekly, biweekly, or monthly).
▲ *Payroll register:* A record prepared each pay period, listing all employees and indicating the gross pay, withholdings, deductions and net pay for each employee for the period. The payroll register serves as the basis for preparation of paychecks, for recording the payroll, and for updating employee earnings records.
▲ *Employee earnings record:* A record maintained for each employee that provides a cumulative, year-to-date summary of total earnings, withholdings, and deductions.

A company acquires resources from employees in exchange for obligations (salaries and wages) which are subsequently paid. Initial hirings, cash payments to employees, and other employee-related activities are processed through the expenditure/disbursement cycle. Internal activities relating to personnel and payroll are discussed in the following sections.

Figure 15-2 is a flowchart of representative personnel and payroll activities within the expenditure/disbursement cycle. In turn, Figure 15-3 is derived from Figure 15-2, and briefly summarizes the flow of documents and activities common to personnel and payroll. The following discussion explains each major activity illustrated.

FIGURE 15-2
Flowchart of Expenditure/Disbursement Cycle: Personnel and Payroll

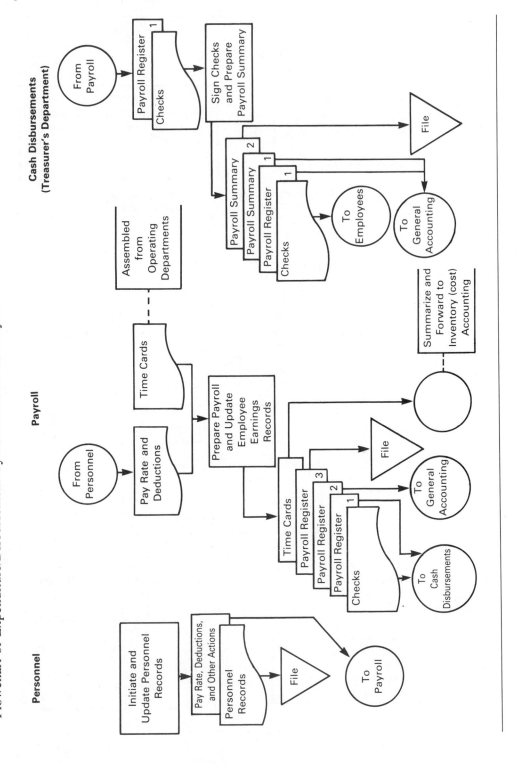

FIGURE 15-3
Personnel and Payroll: Document Flow

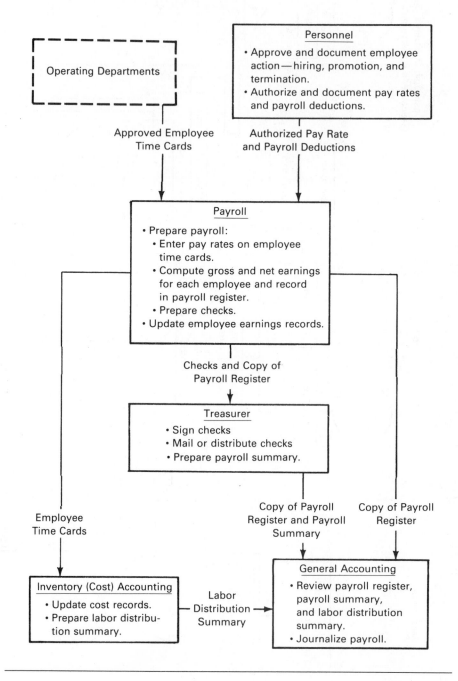

Personnel

Without exception, all personnel action taken with regard to an employee — including hiring, promotion, transfer, and termination — should be approved both by operating department supervisors and by the Personnel Department and documented in an employee's permanent personnel records. Personnel records should also include documentation related to:

▲ Salary or wage rates.
▲ Payroll deductions.
▲ Employee signatures.
▲ Job classification.
▲ Performance evaluation reports.

To minimize the likelihood of irregularities, personnel records should not be accessible to employees responsible for preparing, approving, or distributing payroll. If an individual maintained personnel records and prepared payroll, an employee's wage rate could be inflated, resulting in overstated paychecks; if an individual maintained personnel records and distributed payroll checks, he or she could destroy documentation related to a salaried employee's termination and retain (and forge endorsements for) subsequent paychecks.

When employees are terminated, the Personnel Department should clearly determine the nature and terms of any related cash or other termination settlement (e.g., accrued vacation pay). Immediately thereafter, the Payroll Department should be advised of the termination settlement and notified that further work-related compensation has ceased.

Payroll Preparation and Distribution

Payroll Department personnel prepare payrolls based on pay rate and payroll deduction information approved and provided by Personnel. For hourly (nonsalaried) employees, time reports indicating hours worked for the payroll period are also necessary for payroll preparation. Time cards, the traditional manually prepared form of labor hour records, are a basis for accumulating hours worked by hourly wage earning employees. In addition, hours worked may also be documented by production project on other time reports (e.g., accumulated departmental labor charge reports), thereby providing a basis for charging direct labor hours to specific items of work-in-process inventory. Employee time cards should be approved by operating department supervisors, who, to minimize the likelihood of irregularities, should not also be involved in payroll preparation.

Gross and net earnings are computed by Payroll Department personnel for each employee and entered in a payroll register. For hourly employees, pay rates are entered on time cards and multiplied by hours worked to determine gross earnings for the payroll period. Time cards are subsequently forwarded to Inventory (Cost) Accounting.

From the information in the payroll register, checks are prepared by Payroll Department personnel and forwarded to the Treasurer's Department along with a copy of the payroll register. A copy of the payroll register is also sent to General Accounting. As a control over payroll accuracy, the payroll register should be checked in detail by an employee not otherwise involved in payroll preparation. The payroll should also be reviewed for reasonableness by a higher level of management.

Each pay period, after the payroll has been prepared, employee earnings records are updated by Payroll Department personnel. These records provide a cumulative, year-to-date summary of total earnings, taxes withheld, and deductions (e.g., for union dues, health insurance, savings, etc.).

Payroll checks forwarded to the Treasurer's Department should be compared with listings in the payroll register and signed by authorized personnel. Signed checks should be delivered to operating department supervisors for distribution to individual employees. The payroll register and a copy of the payroll summary prepared by Treasurer's Department personnel should be sent to General Accounting.

To obtain reasonable assurance that payroll checks are distributed to bona fide employees only, an employee independent of payroll preparation should compare, on a test basis, endorsements on canceled payroll checks with employee signatures maintained within personnel records. Differences could suggest irregularities and should be investigated. At the end of the year, employee W-2 forms should be prepared from internally stored EDP records, or by employees not otherwise responsible for payroll preparation or distribution, and mailed to employees. Mailed W-2 forms that are returned by the postal service as undeliverable should be followed up; returned W-2 forms could signal either incorrect addresses or, more seriously, nonexistent employees.

A separate bank account (or accounts) should be maintained exclusively for payroll disbursements. As indicated in Chapter 13, controls are necessary to limit access to blank checks and to check preparation and signing equipment and to ensure that checks are signed by one or more authorized officials.

Internal Control Structure Objectives and Potential Errors or Irregularities: Personnel and Payroll

In Chapter 13, also devoted to the expenditure/disbursement cycle, control objectives relating to transaction authorization, execution, recording, and access to assets were discussed in the context of purchasing and cash disbursements. The following discussion focuses on internal control structure in the context of personnel and payroll. The discussion identifies specific control objectives, describes examples of potential errors or irregularities that may arise if an objective is not achieved, and provides examples of control procedures designed to prevent or detect errors or irregularities. Figure 15-4 summarizes the discussion.

FIGURE 15-4

Personnel and Payroll: Objectives, Potential Errors or Irregularies, and Control Procedures

Objective	Types of Errors or Irregularities that Could Occur if Objective Not Met	Control Procedures Designed to Prevent or Detect Errors or Irregularities
TRANSACTION AUTHORIZATION: • Employees should be hired according to criteria authorized by management.	Unqualified employees may be hired, potentially resulting in excessive training costs, unnecessary relocation costs, or penalties for violating equal opportunity laws.	Establish clear statements of hiring policies and procedures. Maintain updated personnel records for all employees. Verify employment applications.
• Compensation and payroll deductions should be made in accordance with management's authorization.	Employees may be paid unauthorized amounts, potentially resulting in excessive labor costs or violation of union contracts. Accruals for pensions, vacations, or bonuses may be calculated from inaccurate information, potentially resulting in misstated accruals.	Maintain updated listings of authorized pay rates and deductions. Establish procedures for reviewing and approving pay rates and deductions.

FIGURE 15-4 (*Continued*)

Objective	Types of Errors or Irregularities that Could Occur if Objective Not Met	Control Procedures Designed to Prevent or Detect Errors or Irregularities
TRANSACTION AUTHORIZATION:		
• Adjustments to payroll or personnel records should be made in accordance with management's authorization.	Unauthorized adjustments may be processed to increase an employee's pay, potentially misappropriating cash and overstating labor costs.	Establish clear statements of adjustment policies and procedures.
EXECUTION:		
• Payroll and personnel procedures should be established in accordance with management's authorization.	Employees could process paychecks for terminated or fictitious employees, potentially resulting in misappropriated cash.	Establish personnel and payroll procedures manuals. Periodically verify employee reassignments and personnel action reports.
• All payroll cash disbursements should be based upon a recognized liability.	Cash may be disbursed for services not performed, potentially resulting in misappropriated cash and overstated labor costs.	Prenumber and control time records, paychecks, and adjustment forms. Require manual dual signatories for all pay over a prespecified dollar amount.
RECORDING:		
• Amounts due to employees should be recorded at the proper amounts, be recorded in the proper period and be properly classified.	Payroll costs, labor costs, and related liabilities (e.g., federal tax withheld) may be inaccurate, potentially resulting in misstated expenses and liabilities.	Establish and document account distribution procedures. Reconcile appropriate ledgers and journals.

Objective	Types of Errors or Irregularities that Could Occur if Objective Not Met	Control Procedures Designed to Prevent or Detect Errors or Irregularities
RECORDING:	Summaries of detail records (e.g., payroll register and summary of labor costs) may not agree, potentially resulting in miscalculated payroll or missapplied labor costs.	
ACCESS TO ASSETS: • Access to personnel and payroll records and to forms and documents should be restricted to personnel authorized by management.	Records, forms, or documents may be misused by unauthorized personnel, potentially resulting in misapplied cash and labor costs.	Establish physical barriers over unused documents and forms. Prenumber and control forms and documents. Segregate responsibilities for authorizing, executing, and recording payroll and personnel transactions. Maintain listing—and samples—of authorized signatories.

Transaction Authorization. Much as vendors should be approved in accordance with management's authorization, management should also establish criteria for hiring line and staff employees. Otherwise, unqualified employees may be hired, potentially resulting in excessive training costs, unnecessary relocation costs, or penalties for violating equal opportunity laws, among other things. To control against unauthorized hiring, management should establish written hiring policies and procedures and maintain updated personnel records for all employees. In addition, management should verify all relevant information included in employment applications.

Likewise, compensation and payroll deductions should be made in accordance with management's authorization, thereby protecting against excessive labor costs, violation of union contracts, and inaccurate accruals for pensions, vacations, or bonuses. Many companies control compensation and deductions by establishing procedures for reviewing and approving pay rates and deductions and by maintaining updated listings of authorized rates by job classification.

Although entry-level pay rates may be determined by authorized pay rate listings, subsequent adjustments — for example, for promotions, transfers, and merit increases — should also be made only in accordance with management's authorization. Otherwise, unauthorized pay increases could be processed. Management could control unauthorized pay increases by establishing written policies for pay rate adjustments and communicating the policies to the Personnel Department and operating department supervisors.

Execution. In labor-intensive businesses, such as companies that utilize non-automated assembly lines, labor costs can be extensive, suggesting the need for effective controls over payroll and personnel. Otherwise, employees could process paychecks for terminated or fictitious employees. As a result, most medium- to large-sized companies usually establish personnel and payroll procedures manuals, and communicate all available job openings widely within the company.

To control against disbursements for services not performed, all payroll-related cash disbursements should be based upon a recognized liability; paychecks should reflect adequate and fair compensation for services actually rendered, just as disbursements to vendors should be based on goods and services actually received. Management can control unauthorized payroll disbursements by forms and by requiring dual manual signatures for all unusual or excessive paychecks.

Recording. All amounts due to employees should be recorded at the proper amounts, be recorded in the proper period, and be properly classified. Otherwise, payroll and labor costs and related liabilities (e.g., taxes withheld) may be inaccurate, potentially resulting in misstated expenses, labor costs, and liabilities. In addition, summaries of detailed records, such as payroll summaries and registers, may not agree, which could result in miscalculated payroll or misapplied labor costs. In short, accurately calculated paychecks do not necessarily result in proper account distribution or properly applied labor costs. To control against improper recording, management could establish account distribution and labor cost allocation procedures, and reconcile appropriate ledgers, journals, and summaries.

Access to Assets. To control against misapplied cash and unauthorized labor costs, management should institute policies to restrict access to personnel and payroll records, and to forms and documents, to authorized personnel only. For example, management could establish physical barriers over unused documents and forms (e.g., safes), prenumber documents, maintain listings of authorized signatories, and segregate responsibility for authorizing, executing, and recording payroll and personnel transactions — the same controls listed in Chapter 13 for purchases and cash disbursements.

Segregation of Duties. To assure adequate segregation of duties, Personnel Department responsibilities should be separated from payroll preparation, and both should be separated from cash disbursements and operating departments. Otherwise, an authorization function, personnel, would be combined with an execution function, payroll, thereby increasing opportunities for unauthorized employee action and for inflated pay rates. In addition, combining payroll with operating departments, such as production or inventory control, increases opportunities for unauthorized disbursements, since an employee would be responsible both for reporting hours worked and for calculating gross pay.

CONSIDERING INTERNAL CONTROL STRUCTURE

Chapter 13 discussed the auditor's consideration of controls over three expenditure/disbursement cycle functions: purchasing, receiving, and cash disbursement. The following discussion focuses on consideration of controls over the personnel and payroll activities within the expenditure/disbursement cycle.

Obtain an Understanding

In the initial phase of considering internal control structure, an auditor attempts to determine how the system is supposed to work and whether control procedures have been prescribed by management to assure that the system is functioning as planned. Obtaining an understanding consists of four components: performing a preliminary review, documenting the system, performing a transaction walk-through, and determining whether existing controls are potentially reliable.

Preliminary Review. In performing a preliminary review, an auditor develops a general understanding of a client's control environment, the flow of personnel and payroll transactions and records through the accounting system, and control procedures designed to prevent or detect errors or irregularities. Assuming the preliminary review suggests that further consideration of the internal control structure is likely to justify relying on control procedures and thus restricting substantive tests of payroll balances, an auditor would proceed as follows.

System Documentation. Figure 15-2, discussed earlier, illustrates a flow-chart for personnel and payroll activities within the expenditure/disbursement cycle. In turn, Figure 15-5 on pages 600–601 illustrates a questionnaire, a second method for obtaining system documentation, for personnel and payroll and for distributing payroll checks.

Alternatively, an auditor could use a narrative to describe the payroll system either in whole or in part. For example, an auditor might use flow-charts and questionnaires to document payroll procedures for hourly employees, and prepare a narrative description of the executive payroll, which typically involves far fewer personnel and therefore far fewer payroll checks.

Transaction Walk-Through. To confirm his or her understanding of the system flowcharted in Figure 15-2, the auditor could select a line item from a processed payroll register filed in the Cash Disbursements Department, and trace the information to time reports summarized in the Payroll Department and filed in the Inventory Accounting Department and to records maintained in the Personnel Department. The purpose of the walk-through, however, is not necessarily to test control procedures, but to confirm the flowchart and completed questionnaire.

Identification of Controls to Be Relied On. An auditor completes the system documentation, and continues the consideration of internal control structure in the same manner as outlined in Chapter 13 for purchases and cash disbursements:

▲ Identify the system's control objectives. The first column of Figure 15-4 identifies control objectives for personnel and payroll.
▲ Consider the potential errors or irregularities that might result if specific control objectives are not met. The second column of Figure 15-4 identifies examples of potential errors or irregularities.
▲ Determine what control procedures are used by the entity to prevent or detect potentially material errors or irregularities. The third column of Figure 15-4 identifies examples of such controls.
▲ Design tests of controls for each control procedure to be relied on during substantive tests of account balances.

Tests of Controls: Personnel and Payroll

Generally, internal evidence prepared by the client is the only persuasive audit evidence available for testing payroll accounts. As a result, auditors often rely predominantly, if not exclusively, on tests of controls rather than substantive procedures when auditing payroll. If the results of tests of controls indicate that control procedures can be relied on, substantive testing focuses on analytical procedures such as ratio analysis.

Tests of controls must be sufficiently detailed and comprehensive to justify extensive reliance on the controls. Thus, tests of controls over personnel and payroll activities typically include procedures usually associated with substantive tests. Some representative tests of controls for personnel and payroll and for distribution of payroll checks are discussed below in the context of the system flowcharted in Figure 15-2.

Personnel and Payroll. The payroll register is an entity's continuing record of compensation and provides the basis for preparation, distribution, and recording of periodic payroll. Tests of controls follow.

Tests of Controls: Personnel and Payroll

1. Obtain payroll register for a selected period (or periods) from Payroll Department files and verify mathematical accuracy (foot and cross-foot).
2. Obtain related payroll summary and labor distribution summary.
   a. Verify mathematical accuracy of payroll and labor distribution summaries and compare with totals in payroll register.
   b. Trace totals to postings in general ledger and cost accounting records.
3. Select a random sample of employees from the payroll register and obtain the personnel file for each selected employee.
   a. Examine files for completeness and review employee action reports for appropriate authorization.
   b. Compare pay rates and payroll deduction information in personnel records with entries in payroll register; for hourly employees, obtain time reports and recompute gross earnings for the payroll period.
   c. Trace sampled entries in payroll register to postings in individual employee cumulative earnings records.
   d. Trace selected employee names to a payroll register for a prior period and to a payroll register for a subsequent period; examine employee action reports for newly hired or terminated personnel.
4. Document any discrepancies or deviations observed.

As indicated in step 1, the payroll register is the starting point for an auditor in tests of personnel and payroll activities. In step 2, the auditor addresses mathematical accuracy and postings by footing and cross-footing the payroll register and reconciling totals with related summary schedules and

FIGURE 15-5
Questionnaire: Personnel and Payroll

Question	Answer: Yes, No, or N/A	Remarks

PERSONNEL AND PAYROLL:

1. Are all employee changes—hiring, promotions, transfers, terminations—approved by operating department supervisors and by the Personnel Department?

2. Are all employee changes documented in personnel records?

3. Are all employee changes communicated promptly to the Payroll Department?

4. Do employee personnel records include authorizations for all deductions and withholdings?

5. Are guidelines established for determining account distribution for labor charges?

6. Are employees who prepare or process payroll independent of hiring and terminations and excluded from distributing paychecks to employees?

7. Is payroll approved by a responsible official independent of payroll preparation and processing?

8. Is the preparation of employee time reports supervised to assure that hours reported are accurate?

Page 2

	Answer: Yes, No, or N/A	Remarks
Question		

CASH DISBURSEMENT:

1. Are paychecks distributed by personnel independent of the Personnel and Payroll Departments?
2. Is the payroll bank account reconciled monthly by an employee independent of payroll preparation, processing, and distribution?
3. Are employees required to provide identification before receiving a paycheck?
4. Are unclaimed paychecks returned to an employee independent of payroll preparation, processing, and distribution?
5. Are W-2 forms compared with payroll records and mailed by employees independent of payroll preparation, processing, and distribution?
6. Are returned W-2 forms (e.g., marked "return to sender" by the U.S. Postal Service) investigated by employees who are independent of payroll?

---

with the general ledger and inventory accounting records. Payroll accuracy and appropriate account distribution are of major concern to an auditor because of the significant impact of payroll on no less than seven financial statement accounts, including:

▲ Payroll expense
▲ Payroll taxes
▲ Work-in-process inventory
▲ Finished goods inventory
▲ Cost of sales

▲ Accrued payroll
▲ Accrued payroll taxes

In step 3, an auditor selects a sample of entries in the payroll register as a basis for testing personnel records for completeness and proper authorization and for determining whether employee compensation accurately reflects authorized pay rates, payroll deductions, and hours worked. In addition, the auditor examines postings to individual employee cumulative earnings records, since these records provide the basis for preparing W-2 forms and for figuring payroll tax expense.

Distribution of Employee Paychecks. Tests of payments to employees focus upon the existence and authenticity of employees to whom disbursements are made, rather than cash disbursements per se. Representative tests of controls follow.

Tests of Controls: Distribution of Paychecks

1. Obtain a sample of canceled payroll checks.
   a. Trace details of sampled checks (payee name, date, amount, and check number) to entries in the payroll register.
   b. Compare endorsements on checks with signatures maintained in employee personnel records.
2. Take control of payroll checks just prior to distribution by operating department supervisors and personally distribute checks to properly identified employees.
3. Document any discrepancies or deviations observed.

In step la, the auditor traces details of sampled paychecks to entries in the payroll register, thereby addressing whether checks are properly recorded. Step 1b, in contrast, focuses on the authenticity of employees, by comparing endorsements on canceled checks with signatures maintained in employee personnel records. The auditor also addresses the authenticity of employees in step 2 by personally distributing paychecks to employees during work hours. This procedure normally requires that the auditor first examine an employee identification card with photo, if available, to assure that the employee is actually who he or she purports to be.

Assess Control Risk

To complete the consideration of internal control structure for personnel and payroll, an auditor reviews system documentation and the results of tests of controls and determines whether existing controls can be relied on to restrict substantive tests of payroll (low control risk), or whether expanded substantive tests are necessary (high control risk). The evaluation is based on the types of errors or irregularities that could occur, control procedures that should prevent the errors or irregularities, a determination of whether the necessary procedures exist and are followed, and any deficiencies in the internal control structure.

Assuming control procedures can be relied on, auditors normally restrict year-end substantive tests of payroll to analytical procedures. If analytical procedures then suggest that payroll-related balances are not reasonable, an auditor would increase the scope of year-end testing by performing expanded substantive tests of details. The analytical procedures applied to payroll are discussed next.

SUBSTANTIVE TESTS: PAYROLL

As noted previously, substantive tests related to payroll usually focus primarily or exclusively on analytical procedures. Representative year-end procedures and related audit objectives are presented in Figure 15-6. If results of tests of controls indicated that the planned degree of reliance on internal control was not justified, substantive procedures would have to be expanded accordingly. Also, if significant changes in control procedures or their method of application occurred subsequent to testing controls, the auditor would have to either reconsider control structure or not rely on the controls.

FIGURE 15-6
Substantive Tests: Payroll

Audit Objectives	Procedures
Occurrence Valuation	1. Determine by analytical procedures the reasonableness of payroll expense and account distribution.
Obligations Valuation Completeness	2. Determine the reasonableness of accruals for wages, salaries, and related accounts.

Presentation/
Disclosure
	3. Review financial statements to determine whether:
	    a. Payroll and related accruals are properly classified and described.
	    b. Disclosures are adequate.

Stock Options, Deferred Pension, GAAP

Analytical Procedures: Payroll Expense and Accruals

In assessing the overall reasonableness of payroll expense and distribution, an auditor might develop and analyze relationships among data. Selected items can be compared with corresponding items from prior years and/or with other items in the same period. Ratios are often useful in making comparisons, since relationships between accounts generally should not vary significantly over time in the absence of changes in the nature of an entity's business, production process, accounting methods, or other factors. Ratios can be calculated by an auditor to determine whether accounts relate to each other in the manner expected. For example, if total direct labor has been approximately thirty-five percent of cost of sales for the previous two years, an auditor would expect the percentage for the current year to be close to thirty-five percent, unless changes have occurred which would be expected to alter the relationship. If relationships vary significantly from expected results, an auditor might conclude that additional substantive tests of account balances are necessary.

The reasonableness of payroll-related accruals can usually be determined with little detailed testing. For example, if employees are paid biweekly and one week's payroll is accrued at the end of the year, an auditor could simply determine whether the accrual is approximately equal to fifty percent of the total payroll for the most recent complete pay period. If different categories of employees are paid at different intervals, an auditor might recalculate the accrual and examine subsequent payroll disbursements.

Financial Statement Disclosures

Finally, an auditor should review financial statements to determine that payroll and related accounts are properly classified and described and that all material information is disclosed. For example, information relating to compensatory stock options or executive deferred compensation plans should be included in the notes to the financial statements.

SUMMARY

In addition to purchases and cash disbursement transactions, the expenditure/disbursement cycle also processes transactions and events related to personnel and payroll. Activities typically associated with personnel and payroll include the maintenance of personnel records and labor records, payroll preparation and account distribution, and cash disbursements to employees.

Common documentation for personnel and payroll includes personnel records — the evidence supporting employee hirings, promotions, and terminations — and employee time cards.

Audit tests of payroll usually focus on interim tests of controls although, unlike most other audit areas, interim testing also includes procedures normally associated with year-end substantive tests of account balances. As a result, year-end testing of payroll often focuses on analytical procedures designed to assess the reasonableness of recorded payroll expense and accruals. If the consideration of internal control structure indicates control procedures are unreliable, or if analytical procedures suggest that payroll and payroll-related accounts appear unreasonable, an auditor would increase the scope of year-end testing to include substantive tests of details.

QUESTIONS

1. Identify the major activities associated with a company's Payroll, Personnel, and Treasury Departments.
2. How can management assure that payroll checks are distributed only to bona fide employees?
3. How can management mitigate the likelihood of department managers processing payroll checks for terminated employees or processing unauthorized promotions and transfers?
4. Explain why Personnel Department employees should be separated from payroll preparation, and why Personnel and Payroll Department employees should be separated from cash disbursements.
5. How might an auditor perform a transaction walk-through when considering controls over personnel and payroll?
6. What source does an auditor use as the starting point for tests of personnel and payroll activities?
7. Why are payroll preparation accuracy and appropriate account distribution of major concern to an auditor?
8. How does an auditor test whether employees whose names appear on payroll registers are bona fide, i.e. actually employed by the company?
9. How can management control against paychecks being prepared for unauthorized or fictitious employees?
10. How can an auditor test the authenticity of employees to whom payroll checks are disbursed?

MULTIPLE CHOICE QUESTIONS

1. Effective controls over the payroll function would include which of the following?

a. Total time recorded on time clock punch cards should be reconciled with job reports by employees responsible for those specific jobs.

b. Payroll Department employees should be supervised by the management of the Personnel Department.

c. Payroll Department employees should be responsible for maintaining employee personnel records.

(d) Total time spent on jobs should be compared with total time indicated on time clock punch cards.   (AICPA Adapted)

2. Hitech, Inc., has changed from a conventional to a computerized payroll clock card system. Factory employees now record time in and out with magnetic cards, and the EDP system automatically updates all payroll records. Because of this change

   a. The auditor must audit through the computer.
   b. Internal control has improved.
   (c) Part of the audit trail has been lost.
   d. The potential for payroll-related fraud has been diminished.

                                                                    (AICPA Adapted)

3. In the weekly computer run to prepare payroll checks, a check was printed for an employee who had been terminated the previous week. Which of the following controls, if properly utilized, would have been most effective in preventing the error or ensuring its prompt detection?

   (a) A control total for hours worked, prepared from time cards collected by the Timekeeping Department.

   b. Requiring the Treasurer's Office to account for the numbers of the prenumbered checks issued to the EDP Department for the processing of the payroll.

   c) Use of a check digit for employee numbers.

   d. Use of a header label for the payroll input sheet.   (AICPA Adapted)

4. For control purposes, which of the following individuals should preferably be responsible for the distribution of payroll checks?

   a. Bookkeeper.
   b. Payroll clerk.
   c. Cashier.
   (d) Receptionist.   (AICPA Adapted)

5. One of the auditor's objectives in observing the actual distribution of payroll checks is to determine that every name on the payroll is that of a bona fide employee. The payroll observation is an auditing procedure that is generally performed for which of the following reasons?

   a. The professional standards that are generally accepted require the auditor to perform the payroll observation.

   (b) The various phases of payroll work are not sufficiently segregated to afford effective internal accounting control.

   c. The independent auditor uses personal judgment and decides to observe the payroll distribution on a particular audit.

   d. The standards that are generally accepted by the profession are interpreted to mean that payroll observation is expected on an audit unless circumstances dictate otherwise.   (AICPA Adapted)

6. A common audit procedure in the audit of payroll transactions involves tracing selected items from the payroll register to employee time cards that have been approved by supervisory personnel. This procedure is designed to provide evidence in support of the audit proposition that

   a. Only bona fide employees worked and their pay was properly computed.
   b. Jobs on which employees worked were charged with the appropriate labor cost.
   c. Internal controls relating to payroll disbursements are operating effectively.
   d. All employees worked the number of hours for which their pay was computed.   (AICPA Adapted)

7. A large retail enterprise has established a policy which requires that the paymaster deliver all unclaimed payroll checks to the Internal Auditing Department at the end of each payroll distribution day. This policy was most likely adopted in order to

   a. Assure that employees who were absent on a payroll distribution day are not paid for that day.
   b. Prevent the paymaster from cashing checks which are unclaimed for several weeks.
   c. Prevent a bona fide employee's check from being claimed by another employee.
   d. Detect any fictitious employee who may have been placed on the payroll.
                                                                      (AICPA Adapted)

PROBLEMS

15-1   You are considering the controls over a client's personnel and payroll activities. System documentation was accomplished with a questionnaire and a narrative memorandum and, in conjunction with a transaction walk-through, indicated that the following potential errors or irregularities may exist:
a. Several recent hirings violated equal opportunity laws.
b. A pay raise to employees in Department A was effected but not approved by management.
c. An unauthorized, unapproved, and excessively high paycheck was cashed by a bona fide employee, but the check was for hours neither authorized nor worked.
d. Detailed payroll records sometimes do not agree with labor summaries or payroll tax accruals, and go unnoticed.
e. When an employee's time card is not available, the employee obtains a new time card from an open bin outside the payroll office.

Required:
For each potential error or irregularity, indicate a control procedure(s) that management could implement to prevent or detect the error or irregularity.

15-2   A CPA's audit working papers contain the following narrative description of a segment of the Croyden, Inc. factory payroll system and an accompanying flowchart presented on pages 608 and 609.

Factory Employees   **Factory Foreman**   **Personnel**

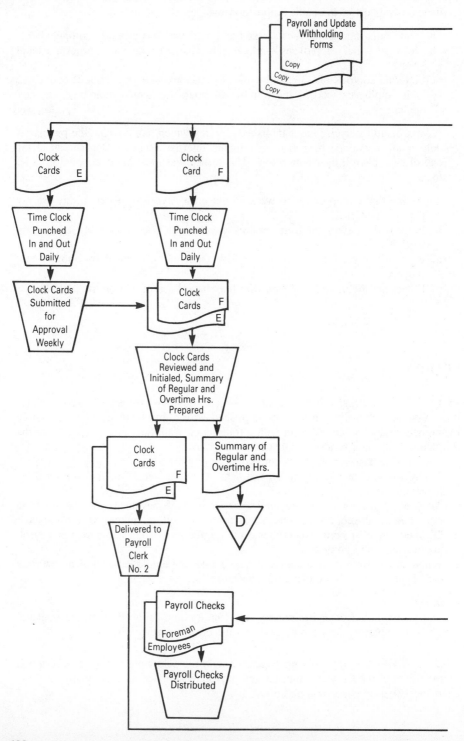

608

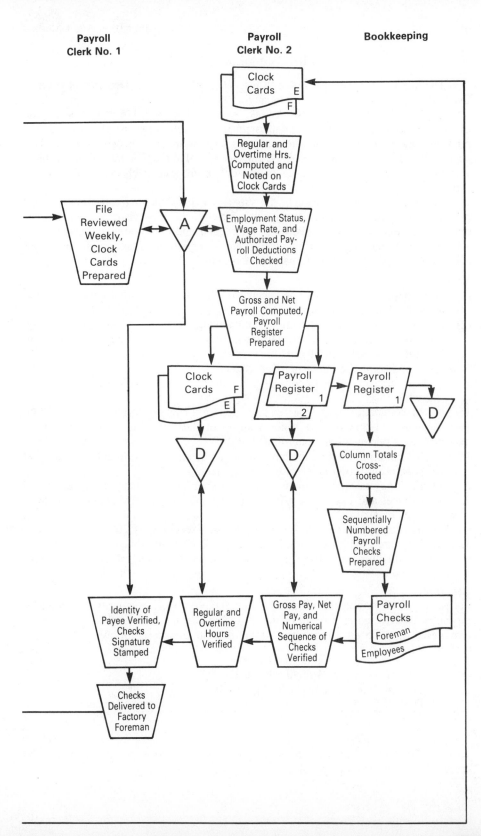

**Payroll
Clerk No. 1**

**Payroll
Clerk No. 2**

Bookkeeping

Clock
Cards E
F

Regular and
Overtime Hrs.
Computed and
Noted on
Clock Cards

File
Reviewed
Weekly,
Clock
Cards
Prepared

A

Employment Status,
Wage Rate, and
Authorized Pay-
roll Deductions
Checked

Gross and Net
Payroll Computed,
Payroll
Register
Prepared

Clock
Cards F
E

Payroll
Register 1
2

Payroll
Register 1

D

D

D

Column Totals
Cross-
footed

Sequentially
Numbered
Payroll
Checks
Prepared

Identity of
Payee Verified,
Checks
Signature
Stamped

Regular and
Overtime
Hours
Verified

Gross Pay, Net
Pay, and
Numerical
Sequence of
Checks
Verified

Payroll
Checks
Foreman
Employees

Checks
Delivered to
Factory
Foreman

NARRATIVE MEMORANDUM

The internal control structure with respect to the Personnel Department is effective and is not included in the accompanying flowchart.

At the beginning of each workweek, payroll clerk No. 1 reviews the Payroll Department files to determine the employment status of factory employees and then prepares time cards and distributes them as each individual arrives at work. This payroll clerk, who is also responsible for custody of the signature stamp machine, verifies the identity of each payee before delivering signed checks to the factory supervisor.

At the end of each workweek, the supervisor distributes payroll checks for the preceding workweek. Concurrent with this activity, the supervisor reviews the current week's employee time cards, notes the regular and overtime hours worked on a summary form, and initials the time cards. The supervisor then delivers all time cards and unclaimed payroll checks to payroll clerk No. 2.

Required:
(1) On the basis of the narrative and accompanying flowchart, what are the deficiencies in the internal control structure?
(2) On the basis of the narrative and accompanying flowchart, what inquiries should be made with respect to clarifying the existence of possible additional deficiencies in the internal control structure?

Note: Do not discuss the Personnel Department.

(AICPA Adapted)

15-3   In connection with your examination of Fletcher Corporation's June 30, 1990 financial statements, you become aware of the following control procedures over Fletcher's personnel and payroll activities:
1. All substantive information in employment applications is thoroughly checked and verified before offering an employment contract.
2. Authorized pay rates are maintained in personnel files for each employee.
3. All Personnel and Payroll Department procedures are clearly written in updated procedures manuals.
4. Dual signatories are required for all paychecks exceeding $1,200.
5. Procedures are established for charging direct labor hours to appropriate jobs.
6. Responsibility for authorizing, executing, and recording payroll is vested in separate personnel.

Required:
For each control procedure, indicate (a) a potential error or irregularity that might be prevented or detected as a result of the control procedure, and (b) the control objective served by the control procedure. Organize your answer as follows:

Control Procedure	Potential Error or Irregularity That Might Be Prevented or Detected	Control Objective
1.	(a)	(b)

15-4   The Kowal Manufacturing Company employs about fifty production workers and has the following payroll procedures.

The factory supervisor interviews applicants and on the basis of the interview either hires or rejects the applicants. When the applicant is hired, he or she prepares a W-4 form (Employee's Withholding Exemption Certificate) and gives it to the supervisor. The supervisor writes the hourly rate of pay for the new employee in the corner of the W-4 form and then gives the form to a payroll clerk as notice that the worker has been employed. The supervisor verbally advises the Payroll Department of rate adjustments.

A supply of blank time cards is kept in a box near the entrance of the factory. Each worker takes a time card on Monday morning, fills in his or her name, and notes daily arrival and departure times in pencil on the time card. At the end of the week the workers drop the time cards in a box near the door to the factory.

The completed time cards are taken from the box on Monday morning by a payroll clerk. Two payroll clerks divide the cards alphabetically between them, one taking the A to L section of the payroll and the other taking the M to Z section. Each clerk is fully responsible for his or her section of the payroll. The clerks compute gross pay, deductions, and net pay, post the details to each employee's earnings records, and prepare and number the payroll checks. Employees are automatically removed from the payroll when they fail to turn in a time card.

The payroll checks are manually signed by the chief accountant and given to the supervisor. The supervisor distributes the checks to the workers in the factory and arranges for the delivery of the checks to the workers who are absent. The payroll bank account is reconciled by the chief accountant who also prepares the various quarterly and annual payroll tax reports.

Required:
List your suggestions for improving the Kowal Manufacturing Company's internal control structure for the factory hiring practices and payroll procedures.

(AICPA Adapted)

15-5   Early in your examination of the Kimberly Corporation you note that the factory supervisor approved time cards for hours worked and hourly rates and also distributed the factory payroll checks.

Required:
(1) Describe the compensating controls you would look for before concluding that an internal control structure deficiency does in fact exist.
(2) If you find that no compensating controls are in effect for the factory payroll, what steps in your factory payroll audit program would serve as a test for possible errors or irregularities? List only the procedures which would be of benefit in testing for this specific deficiency.   (AICPA Adapted)

15-6   When auditing within the expenditure/disbursement cycle, auditors often rely predominantly on interim tests of controls rather than year-end substantive tests of details. In fact, in many cases, year-end procedures consist primarily of updating the auditor's understanding of the system and tests of payroll-related activities and performing analytical procedures to test the reasonableness of reported payroll balances.

Required:
Explain why an auditor might rely predominantly on tests of controls, rather than substantive tests of details in auditing payroll.

15-7   Following are selected questions from an internal control questionnaire relating to a company's personnel and payroll functions. A "Yes" response would indicate a potential strength of the system, and a "No" a potential weakness.

a. Are all employee changes — e.g., hirings, transfers, promotions, terminations — approved by operating department supervisors and by the Personnel Department?

b. Do employee personnel records include authorizations for all deductions and withholdings?

c. Are employees who prepare payroll independent of payroll processing?

d. Is payroll approved by a responsible official independent of payroll preparation and processing?

e. Is the payroll bank account reconciled monthly by an employee independent of payroll preparation, processing, and distribution?

f. Are returned W-2 forms forwarded for investigation by employees independent of the Payroll Department?

Required:

Assume that inquiries indicate the answer is "Yes" to each question. Design tests of controls that you believe would provide persuasive evidence that controls are reliable.

15-8   An internal auditor is preparing an audit program for a computerized payroll operation and is developing the portion of the program relating to payroll preparation, labor cost distribution, and paycheck distribution.

Required:

List numbers 1 through 8 on your answer sheet. Indicate by each number whether the proposed audit step should ("Yes") or should not ("No") be included in this portion of the audit program. Justify each "No" response that you recorded.

1. Review the computer programming related to payroll computation.

2. Determine whether checks are delivered to department timekeepers for distribution.

3. Perform a review of worker's compensation claims.

4. Perform a reconciliation of time card hours to hours recorded on production job cards.

5. Distribute checks to employees on a sample basis.

6. Obtain a certificate from the timekeeper for employees who were absent when the auditor distributed paychecks and who are to be paid later in the usual manner.

7. Review personnel files to verify documents in payroll files.

8. Review procedures related to payroll check signing.   (IIA Adapted)

15-9   Many organizations maintain separate bank accounts for payroll, thereby segregating all payroll disbursements from general disbursements, such as payments for purchases, inventory, plant assets, and investments, among other things.

Required:

Explain why a separate bank account should be maintained for payroll and why one general bank account can be used for all other disbursements.

15-10   James, who was engaged to examine the financial statements of Talbert Corporation, is about to audit payroll. Talbert uses a computer service center to process weekly payroll as follows:

Talbert Corporation Payroll Input — Week Ending Friday, Nov. 23, 1990

Name	Social Security	W-4 Information	Hourly Rate	Reg	OT	Bonds	Union	Other
	—Employee Data—Permanent File—			—Current Week's Payroll Data—				
				Hours		Special Deductions		
A. Bell	999-99-9991	M-1	10.00	35	5	18.75		
B. Carr	999-99-9992	M-2	10.00	35	4			
C. Dawn	999-99-9993	S-1	10.00	35	6	18.75	4.00	
D. Ellis	999-99-9994	S-1	10.00	35	2		4.00	50.00
E. Frank	999-99-9995	M-4	10.00	35	1		4.00	
F. Gillis	999-99-9996	M-4	10.00	35			4.00	
G. Hugh	999-99-9997	M-1	7.00	35	2	18.75	4.00	
H. Jones	999-99-9998	M-2	7.00	35			4.00	25.00
I. King	999-99-9999	S-1	7.00	35	4		4.00	
New Employee								
J. Smith	999-99-9990	M-3	7.00	35				

Talbert Corporation Payroll Register — Nov. 23, 1990

Employee	Social Security	Hours		Payroll		Gross Payroll	Taxes Withheld			Other Withheld	Net Pay	Check No.
		Reg.	OT	Reg.	OT		FICA	Fed	State			
A. Bell	999-99-9991	35	5	350.00	75.00	425.00	26.05	76.00	27.40	18.75	276.80	1499
B. Carr	999-99-9992	35	4	350.00	60.00	410.00	25.13	65.00	23.60		296.27	1500
C. Dawn	999-99-9993	35	6	350.00	90.00	440.00	26.97	100.90	28.60	22.75	260.78	1501
D. Ellis	999-99-9994	35	2	350.00	30.00	380.00	23.29	80.50	21.70	54.00	200.51	1502
E. Frank	999-99-9995	35	1	350.00	15.00	365.00	22.37	43.50	15.90	4.00	279.23	1503
F. Gillis	999-99-9996	35		350.00		350.00	21.46	41.40	15.00	4.00	268.14	1504
G. Hugh	999-99-9997	35	2	245.00	21.00	266.00	16.31	34.80	10.90	22.75	181.24	1505
H. Jones	999-99-9998	35		245.00		245.00	15.02	26.40	8.70	29.00	165.88	1506
I. King	999-99-9999	35	4	245.00	42.00	287.00	17.59	49.40	12.20	4.00	203.81	1507
J. Smith	999-99-9990	35		245.00		245.00	15.02	23.00	7.80		199.18	1508
Totals		350	24	3,080.00	333.00	3,413.00	209.21	540.90	171.80	159.25	2,331.84	

Each Monday Talbert's payroll clerk inserts data in appropriate spaces on the preprinted service-center-prepared input form, and sends it to the service center via messenger. The service center extracts new permanent data from the input form and updates master files. The weekly payroll data are then processed. The weekly payroll register and payroll checks are printed and delivered by messenger to Talbert on Thursday.

Part of the sample selected for audit by James includes the following input form and payroll register:

Required:
(1) Describe how James should verify the information in the payroll input form shown above.
(2) Describe the procedures that James should follow in the examination of the November 23, 1990 payroll register shown above.   (AICPA Adapted)

TESTS OF CONTROLS AND SUBSTANTIVE TESTS OF THE CONVERSION CYCLE: INVENTORY AND PLANT ASSETS

16

Major topics discussed in this chapter are the:

▲ *Nature of the conversion cycle.*

▲ *Auditor's consideration of internal control structure in the conversion cycle.*

▲ *Audit objectives and substantive tests applicable to inventory and plant assets.*

▲ *Computer-assisted audit techniques applicable to inventory and plant assets.*

Continuing the discussion of audit method, this chapter introduces tests of controls and substantive tests applicable to two major conversion cycle accounts: inventory and plant assets. Internal control structure is discussed first, and substantive tests of account balances are discussed thereafter.

The chapter begins by summarizing the nature of the conversion cycle and introducing controls over a company's inventory, inventory accounting, and plant asset transactions. In turn, an auditor's consideration of internal control structure within the conversion cycle is addressed. Next, the chapter explains specific substantive tests of details applicable to inventory and plant assets. Finally, some computer-assisted substantive tests relevant to inventory and plant assets are presented in an appendix to the chapter.

THE NATURE OF THE CONVERSION CYCLE

In general, the conversion cycle encompasses a company's business functions and other activities related to producing finished products for sale. The conversion cycle is directly related to two of the other cycles: it uses resources and information provided by the expenditure/disbursement cycle and provides resources and information to the revenue/receipt cycle. For example, the conversion cycle uses raw materials purchased from vendors through the expenditure/disbursement cycle and produces finished goods that are sold to customers through the revenue/receipt cycle.

Figure 16-1 summarizes the scope of the conversion cycle, listing the primary business functions and related activities, journal entries, and forms. One major business function is associated with the conversion cycle:

▲ Resources are held, used, or transformed.

Although stated simply, this one business function can be quite significant, since it relates to both inventory and plant assets, frequently the two most significant assets in capital-intensive manufacturing companies.

Inventory

As noted in Chapter 13, when a company purchases raw materials inventory, a purchase order is sent to the vendor, goods are received, and a liability is recorded. Assuming a perpetual rather than periodic inventory system, the activities included in the conversion cycle include recording purchases in perpetual records, processing accumulated costs through a cost accounting system, and physically controlling the inventory.

Throughout the conversion cycle, journal entries are made to process inventory costs through production, to record costs of goods sold, and to write down obsolete or damaged inventory. Common forms and documents include:

▲ *Labor charge report:* A summary of labor costs to be applied to work-in-process inventory.
▲ *Materials requisition:* A formal request for materials by an operating department.
▲ *Perpetual inventory record:* A cumulative record of quantities on hand for a particular item or class of inventory.

Plant Assets

Property, plant, and equipment — plant assets — are used both directly and indirectly to transform raw materials into finished products. For example, equipment might be used directly to extrude wire from copper, while a building would be used indirectly in the sense that wire extrusion equipment is housed within a manufacturing plant. As a result, plant assets are related to both the conversion cycle and to inventory: to the conversion cycle because plant assets transform inventory, and to inventory because some plant asset depreciation is applied to products as overhead.

Throughout the conversion cycle, journal entries are made to record de-

FIGURE 16-1
The Scope of the Conversion Cycle

Primary Business Function	Common Activities	Common Entries	Common Forms
• Resources are held, used, or transformed.	**Inventory** • Maintaining perpetual inventory records • Recording (cost accounting) • Physically controlling inventory	• Processing inventory costs through production (raw materials, work in process, finished goods) • Cost of goods sold • Writedown of obsolete or damaged inventory	• Labor charge reports • Materials requisition forms
	Plant Assets • Additions • Disposals and retirements • Recording • Depreciation allocations	• Depreciation • Overhead applied • Additions, disposals, and retirements	• Depreciation schedules • Overhead application reports

preciation and apply overhead to inventory. Common forms and documents include:

▲ *Depreciation schedule:* A work sheet computing and summarizing depreciation.

▲ *Overhead application report:* A summary of overhead applied to work-in-process inventory.

The following section discusses the nature of the conversion cycle and related internal control structure considerations. The major activities and controls related to inventory — inventory control and inventory accounting — are discussed first, followed by the major activities and controls related to plant assets — records, additions, disposals, and depreciation.

INVENTORY

In general, the term *inventory* relates to all goods intended for sale to customers in the ordinary course of business. In the case of a nonmanufacturing entity (wholesaler or retailer), goods are acquired from vendors and sold to customers without alteration. Thus, the conversion cycle of a non-manufacturing entity involves activities related to holding and physically controlling inventory prior to sale.

For a manufacturing concern, however, the conversion cycle is more complex: raw materials acquired from vendors must be transformed prior to sale, and the costs of transformation (direct labor and manufacturing overhead) must be accumulated and classified. Thus, conversion cycle controls focus upon physical control of assets and recorded accountability. The functional areas associated with physical control and recording are inventory control and inventory accounting, respectively.

Inventory Control

Figure 16-2 illustrates the flow of inventory within a manufacturing company. The acquisition of inventory is part of the expenditure/disbursement cycle, and the distribution of finished goods is part of the revenue/receipt cycle. The conversion cycle encompasses activities related to the movement of goods through the production process.

A *materials requisition* form is prepared by production personnel to request materials and supplies for use in production. Requisitions should be approved at an appropriate supervisory level and forwarded to inventory control. Materials and supplies should not be released by inventory control personnel in the absence of an approved requisition.

FIGURE 16-2
Inventory Flow

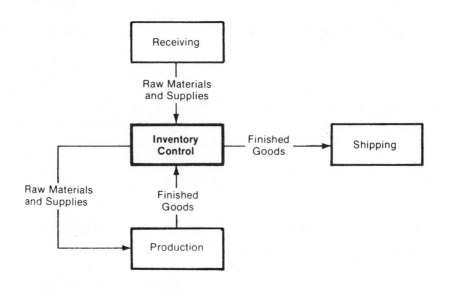

Raw materials and finished goods should be controlled by inventory control personnel not involved in purchasing, receiving, shipping, production, or recording. Access to storage areas should be limited to authorized personnel. Physical safeguards within each production department are necessary to protect work in process.

Inventory control personnel should be responsible not only for controlling transfers of inventory in and out of storage areas, but also for monitoring inventory levels and reporting slow-moving or damaged items. Inventory levels should be monitored to assure that they are neither too large, which would result in needlessly high carrying costs, nor too low, which would risk insufficient quantities on hand. Many companies monitor inventory levels through quantitative techniques such as economic-order-quantity models, which optimize the relationship between carrying costs and the risk of shortages. As a means for determining whether inventory is obsolete or otherwise unusable, slow-moving or damaged items should be reported to responsible officials and, if appropriate, removed from inventory; salable items should be written down to net realizable value and sold as scrap.

Inventory Accounting

Throughout the conversion cycle, entries are made to record the movement of inventory through production. Inventory accounting (or cost accounting) systems vary widely among entities due to variations in the nature and complexity of production processes. Generally, however, an inventory accounting system involves two major sets of records: perpetual inventory records and cost records.

Perpetual Inventory Records. Inventory quantities, physical locations, and selected unit cost information usually are accumulated on perpetual records maintained for a variety of major inventory classifications, including supplies, raw materials, and finished goods. Work-in-process inventory should also be controlled on perpetual records, though the records may take the form of progress reports, such as job-cost summaries.

As inventory flows through the production process, perpetual records should be continually updated, thereby providing a cumulative up-to-date record of quantities, physical location, and selected unit cost information. Updated information should be generated from formal source documents, such as requisitions, invoices, production reports, and shipping documents, which themselves should be controlled through prenumbering and formal indications (e.g., initials) of approval or specific authorization, as discussed in Chapter 13.

In many businesses, significant segments of inventory are stored off-premises in public warehouses or transferred either to customers on consignment or to outside companies for processing. Off-premises inventory should be accounted for and controlled by the outside parties holding the goods. Periodically, a company should confirm off-premises inventory, physically count quantities at off-premise locations, and reconcile confirmed or counted quantities with internal perpetual records.

Cost Records. Perpetual inventory records are used predominantly to account for inventory quantities throughout the production process. An inventory accounting system, however, must also account for inventory costs, which may be allocated on a fifo, lifo, average cost, or other acceptable basis. Whatever the cost-flow approach used, an inventory accounting system should be designed to account for and control inventory costs as they flow through the accounts illustrated in Figure 16-3.

Like perpetual inventory records, cost accounting records and reports should be updated continually, thereby providing a cumulative up-to-date re-

FIGURE 16-3
Inventory Cost Flow

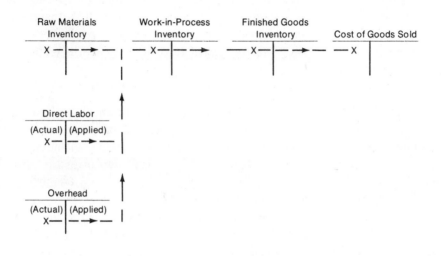

cord of accumulated costs. The updated information should be communicated to general accounting personnel for summarization and appropriate entries in general ledger control accounts. If updated information is not communicated to accounting, accounts such as raw materials, work in process, and finished goods could be misstated. For example, if units of a particular raw material are physically transferred to production, the related inventory costs (for raw materials) should be transferred from raw materials to work-in-process inventory; otherwise raw materials inventory would be overstated and work-in-process inventory understated, although total inventory would not be misstated. Thus, cost accounting records should be updated continually and "tied" to — and periodically reconciled with — general ledger control accounts. To maintain effective segregation of duties, cost accounting records should be maintained by personnel independent of perpetual records, general accounting, purchasing, production, and inventory control.

Internal Control Structure Objectives and Potential Errors or Irregularities: Inventory

The following discussion focuses on internal control structure in the context of inventory. The discussion, summarized in Figure 16-4, identifies some specific control objectives, describes examples of potential errors or irregularities that may arise if an objective is not achieved, and provides examples of control procedures that are designed to prevent or detect the errors or irregularities. The specific objectives identified relate generally to transaction authorization, execution, and recording and access to assets.

FIGURE 16-4
Inventory: Objectives, Potential Errors or Irregularities, and Control Procedures

Objective	Types of Errors or Irregularities that Could Occur if Objective Is Not Met	Control Procedures Designed to Prevent or Detect Errors or Irregularities
TRANSACTION AUTHORIZATION: • Production should be authorized in accordance with management's criteria.	Unauthorized quantities or products may be produced, potentially resulting both in obsolete, excess, or otherwise unusable inventory and excess carrying costs.	Prepare statements of criteria for determining which products are to be produced and in what quantities.
EXECUTION: • Procedures for using and physically transferring inventory should be established in accordance with management's authorization.	Unauthorized personnel may circumvent existing procedures, potentially resulting in stolen or misused inventory. Inventory may be misplaced, potentially resulting in unused assets.	Prepare inventory processing manuals, including procedures for controlling all inventory movement. Restrict access to inventory.
RECORDING: • Inventory used or transferred should be recorded at the correct amounts, be recorded in the proper period, and be properly classified.	Inventory placed in production may not be recorded, potentially resulting in misstated inventory and cost of sales.	Establish processing and recording procedures. Prenumber and control materials release forms and production orders. Maintain logs of inventory movement into and

FIGURE 16-4 (*Continued*)

Objective	Types of Errors or Irregularities that Could Occur if Objective Is Not Met	Control Procedures Designed to Prevent or Detect Errors or Irregularities
		out of storerooms and production stages.
		Conduct periodic inventory counts, and investigate differences between recorded and actual quantities.
		Limit access to inventory and unused forms.
• Inventory-related adjustments (e.g., to adjust recorded inventory to physical counts; to write down obsolete or unusable inventory) should be authorized in accordance with management's criteria.	Unauthorized adjustments may be recorded to conceal physical shortages, potentially resulting in misused and misstated inventory.	Establish policies for approving and recording adjustments. Prenumber and control inventory adjustment forms.
ACCESS TO ASSETS: • Access to inventory should be restricted to personnel authorized by management.	Inventory could be stolen, lost, or diverted, potentially resulting in misapplied assets and misstated accounts.	Establish physical controls over inventory (e.g., fences, locks, inventory control clerks). Maintain insurance and fidelity bonds for personnel handling valuable inventory. Maintain adequate insurance coverage. Segregate responsibility for handling inventory from inventory record-

Objective	Types of Errors or Irregularities that Could Occur if Objective Is Not Met	Control Procedures Designed to Prevent or Detect Errors or Irregularities
		ing, cost accounting, and general accounting.
• Access to production, cost accounting, and perpetual inventory records should be restricted to personnel authorized by management.	Inventory records could be misused, destroyed, or lost, potentially resulting in misstated and misused inventory.	Establish physical controls over unused forms and records. Maintain files of authorized signatures. Perform periodic compliance audits.

Transaction Authorization. Before goods are produced, production should be authorized in accordance with management's criteria. That is, no goods should be produced which are not specifically authorized by management. Otherwise, unauthorized products or quantities may be produced — perhaps, for example, for the express benefit of employees, rather than the company — potentially resulting both in obsolete, excess, or otherwise unusable inventory and in excess carrying costs. To control against unauthorized production, management could prepare clear statements of criteria for determining which products are to be produced and in what quantities. For example, management could require that no inventory be produced unless quantities on hand have declined to a predetermined quantity.

Execution. In order to avoid lost and misused inventory, procedures for using and physically transferring inventory should be established in accordance with management's authorization. For example, management could prepare inventory processing manuals, including procedures for controlling all inventory movement, and restrict access to inventory to authorized personnel.

Recording. Procedures for using and transferring inventory, though, do not necessarily mean that inventory transfers and use will be recorded properly. Therefore, to avoid misplaced or misstated inventory, used or transferred inventory should be recorded at the correct amounts, be recorded in the proper period, and be properly classified. To control inventory recording, management could establish processing and recording procedures, prenumber and control materials release forms and production orders, and maintain logs of inventory movement into and out of storerooms and production stages.

Throughout, but most often at the end of, an accounting period, companies make journal entries to adjust recorded inventory to physical counts or to adjust carrying value for obsolete or unusable inventory. To avoid unauthorized adjustments — for example, adjustments to conceal physical shortages — management should require that all inventory-related adjustments be authorized in accordance with management's criteria. For example, management could establish policies for approving and recording adjustments and, in large companies, prenumber and control inventory adjustments documentation.

Access to Assets. Inventory — particularly inventories of valuable consumer products, such as portable electric appliances — can be stolen, lost, or diverted, potentially resulting in misapplied assets and misstated accounts. As a result, access to inventory should be restricted to personnel authorized by management. In practice, a variety of techniques are available to control inventory. For example, management could establish physical control over inventory (e.g., fences, locks, inventory control clerks), maintain insurance — both for inventory and for inventory personnel (i.e., fidelity bonds) — and segregate responsibility for handling inventory from inventory recording, cost accounting, and general accounting.

In turn, management should also restrict access to production, cost accounting, and perpetual inventory records, thereby preventing misused, destroyed, or lost inventory or inventory records. For example, management could establish physical controls over unused forms and records, maintain files of authorized signatures, and perform periodic compliance audits to assure that controls are being complied with.

PLANT ASSETS

In some companies, a separate cycle may exist for processing transactions relating to the acquisition, use, and disposition of plant assets — land, buildings, machinery, and equipment. In others, plant asset additions may be processed through the expenditure/disbursement cycle, and disposals through the revenue/receipt cycle, with the conversion cycle encompassing the transactions and events relating to the use of plant assets. The latter situation is assumed in the following discussion, which focuses on specific controls applicable to plant assets.

Plant Asset Records

Land, buildings, machinery, and equipment should be documented in detailed records for each individual asset. For example, the detailed records might include purchase dates, historical cost, depreciation methods, estimated useful lives, salvage values, and accumulated depreciation. The records should be maintained by personnel not responsible for physically controlling plant assets.

Periodically, but no less than annually, detailed records should be reconciled with plant asset general ledger control accounts. Also, responsible personnel independent of plant asset recording and physical control should periodically determine that recorded assets actually exist, by physically observing machinery and equipment, comparing identification numbers and general descriptions with detailed records.

Plant assets should be insured against fire or other potential casualties. As a result, assets should be appraised periodically to determine that insurance coverage reasonably approximates replacement cost. If coverage is inadequate, an entity could risk serious losses through both business interruption and an inability to replace productive assets. Clearly, the consequences of underinsurance can be devastating.

Additions

Unlike many other purchases, individual plant asset additions are often material, necessitating specific authorization by the board of directors or members of senior management. In many companies, formal authorization is also required for major repairs or improvements; since the expenditures may be large, management should assess the desirability of replacing, rather than repairing or improving, existing assets. Authorizations should be documented and sufficiently detailed to provide operational employees a basis for executing plant asset transactions in accordance with senior management's specific authorization. On a related note, additions should be reported to insurance companies, and coverage increased accordingly.

Unforeseen circumstances such as vendor price increases could raise the purchase price of an asset above amounts originally authorized, thereby requiring additional authorization (or approval). As a result, procedures should require that actual costs be compared with amounts authorized, and cost overruns reported to senior management for authorization. An entity should also assure that authorized additions are actually received and functioning as expected.

In addition to purchasing plant assets, a company might hire outside contractors to construct (or modify existing) buildings, machinery, or equipment. Constructed additions should also be authorized, and additional controls should be implemented to require both inspection and approval privileges at various stages of production, and detailed cost records as construction progresses. Inspection and approval privileges and cost records allow an entity to continually monitor progress, assuring that the project will meet specifications and cost ceilings authorized by senior management.

Disposals

Plant asset disposals such as sales or retirements should be authorized by senior management. Authorizations should be documented, and copies forwarded to accounting personnel to assure that assets disposed of are subsequently removed from plant asset accounts.

Since insurance premiums are usually determined by the appraisal value of assets carried, asset disposals should be reported to insurance companies and premiums adjusted accordingly. Disposal of assets may result in gains or losses, measured by the difference between the asset's net book value and proceeds from the disposition. Controls should be established to assure that proceeds are deposited and gains or losses are recorded.

Depreciation

Over time and through use, the future service potential of plant assets (other than land) expires and is recognized as depreciation expense. Depreciation expense for plant assets used in production is assigned to work-in-process inventory as applied overhead and, as a result, flows through the conversion cycle. When finished goods are sold, depreciation expense is charged against revenue as part of the cost of sales.

Because of the significant impact that depreciation expense can have upon reported net income, a company should maintain formal policies for determining depreciation methods, estimated useful lives, and salvage values. Periodically, the policies should be reviewed to determine whether they reasonably approximate actual experience. For example, if a particular type of machinery is depreciated over five years but normally lasts ten years, useful lives should be reconsidered.

Internal Control Structure Objectives and Potential Errors or Irregularities: Plant Assets

Earlier, control objectives relating to transaction authorization, execution, and recording and access to assets were discussed in the context of inventory. The following discusses control objectives in the context of plant assets. The discussion identifies specific control objectives, describes examples of potential errors or irregularities that may arise if an objective is not achieved, and provides examples of controls often used by management to prevent or detect errors or irregularities. Figure 16-5 summarizes the discussion.

FIGURE 16-5
Plant Assets: Objectives, Potential Errors or Irregularities, and Control Procedures

Objective	Types of Errors or Irregularities That Could Occur if Objective Is Not Met	Control Procedures Designed to Prevent or Detect Errors or Irregularities
TRANSACTION AUTHORIZATION: • Plant additions, disposals, and retirements should be authorized in accordance with management's criteria.	Assets may be purchased or sold without management's knowledge, potentially resulting in misapplied cash and misstated plant asset records. Assets may be disposed of at unfavorable prices, potentially resulting in lost resources.	Prepare written procedures for all additions, disposals, and retirements. Periodically compare prices received for scrap with published prices.
EXECUTION: • Procedures for operating, using, and physically moving plant assets should be established in accordance with management's authorization.	Unauthorized personnel may circumvent existing procedures, potentially resulting in stolen or misused equipment. Equipment may be misplaced, potentially resulting in unused assets.	Establish procedures for operating, using, moving, and controlling plant assets. Restrict access to moveable plant assets.
RECORDING: • Plant assets added, disposed, or retired should be recorded at the correct amounts,	Plant asset transactions may go unreported, potentially resulting in misstated balances.	Establish procedures for processing and recording plant asset transactions.

FIGURE 16-5 (*Continued*)

Objective	Types of Errors or Irregularities That Could Occur if Objective Is Not Met	Control Procedures Designed to Prevent or Detect Errors or Irregularities
be recorded in the proper period, and be properly classified.		Establish procedures for identifying plant assets eligible for disposal (e.g., sell as scrap) and retirement. Maintain detailed plant asset records. Periodically reconcile plant asset records with existing assets and investigate differences.
• Depreciation and amortization should be calculated in accordance with management's authorization, and recorded in the proper period and be properly classified.	Depreciation could be miscalculated or recognized on plant assets not in service, potentially resulting in misstated depreciation expense and asset book values.	Establish policies for determining depreciation methods and for calculating depreciation on all categories of plant assets.
ACCESS TO ASSETS: • Access to plant assets should be restricted to personnel authorized by management.	Plant assets (e.g., equipment) could be stolen or lost, potentially resulting in misapplied assets and misstated accounts.	Establish physical controls over unused plant assets (e.g., garages, secured fences). Maintain adequate insurance coverage. Segregate physical custody of plant assets from plant asset records and general accounting.

Objective	Types of Errors or Irregularities That Could Occur if Objective Is Not Met	Control Procedures Designed to Prevent or Detect Errors or Irregularities
• Access to asset and depreciation records should be restricted to personnel authorized by management.	Plant asset and depreciation records could be misused, destroyed, or lost, potentially resulting in misstated assets.	Establish physical controls over unused forms and records. Perform periodic compliance audits.

Transaction Authorization. Just as production should be authorized, plant asset additions, disposals, and retirements should be authorized in accordance with management's criteria. Otherwise, assets such as machinery and equipment may be purchased or sold without management's knowledge, or assets may be disposed of at unfavorable prices, thereby sacrificing otherwise attainable resources. To control unauthorized transactions, management could develop written procedures for all additions, disposals, and retirements, and periodically compare scrap sale prices with published price lists.

Execution. Optimum operating capacity simply cannot be attained unless all plant assets are accounted for, operating properly, and protected from misuse. For this reason, procedures for operating, using, and physically moving plant assets should be established in accordance with management's authorization. Without such procedures, plant assets could be stolen or misplaced. To prevent these outcomes, management could establish procedures for operating, using, moving, and controlling plant assets, and restrict access to movable plant assets.

Recording. To avoid unreported plant asset transactions, additions, disposals, and retirements should be recorded at the correct amounts, be recorded in the proper period, and be properly classified. Unrecorded or improperly recorded transactions could result in misstated plant asset accounts, and therefore in misstated financial statements. Management can control the recording function by establishing procedures for processing and recording plant asset transactions and for identifying plant assets eligible for sale or retirement. In addition, detailed plant asset records should be maintained and periodically reconciled with existing assets.

The expiration of future service potential — depreciation and amortization — should be calculated in accordance with management's authorization, and recorded in the proper period. Otherwise, depreciation could be miscalculated or recognized on plant assets not actually in service, either of which could result in misstated depreciation expense. As a result, management should establish policies for determining depreciation methods and for calculating depreciation on all plant assets.

Access to Assets. To control against stolen or lost plant assets, access should be restricted only to personnel authorized by management. Likewise, access to manufacturing areas and to production sites should be restricted, thereby reducing the likelihood of misused assets and, correspondingly, misstated accounts. Management should establish physical controls over unused assets — for example, garages, secured fences — maintain adequate insurance coverage, and segregate the physical custody of plant assets from recording and general accounting.

Just as access to plant assets should be restricted, so should access to plant asset records be restricted. Otherwise, plant asset records could be altered to conceal shortages or be destroyed or lost, potentially resulting in misstated accounts. To control plant asset records, management should establish controls over unused forms and records (e.g., locked cabinets or safes) or could perform periodic compliance audits, reconciling recorded assets with existing assets.

CONSIDERING INTERNAL CONTROL STRUCTURE: INVENTORY

As introduced in Chapter 7 and illustrated for the revenue/receipt and expenditure/disbursement cycles in Chapters 11, 13, and 15, an auditor's consideration of internal control structure involves obtaining an understanding of the structure, testing controls, and assessing control risk. The following discussion focuses on an auditor's consideration of conversion cycle controls. Controls over inventory are addressed first, followed by controls over plant assets.

Obtain an Understanding

An auditor's objective is to obtain a knowledge and understanding of a client's internal control structure — an impression of how the system is supposed to work and what controls have been prescribed by management to assure that the system is functioning as planned. As discussed in Chapter 7, obtaining an understanding consists of (1) performing a preliminary review, (2) documenting the system, (3) performing a transaction walk-through, and (4) determining whether existing controls are potentially reliable.

Preliminary Review. The purpose of the preliminary review is to determine whether further consideration of the internal control structure is likely to justify restricting substantive tests of inventory. An auditor performs the preliminary review for inventory by reviewing the client's procedures manuals and by interviewing client personnel who are responsible for perpetual inventory records, cost records, and inventory accounting. Assuming that existing controls appear potentially reliable, an auditor proceeds by documenting the system.

System Documentation. An entity's inventory control and inventory accounting procedures can be documented with flowcharts, questionnaires, and/ or narratives, although detailed flowcharts are less common in practice, particularly for small to medium-size companies. Figure 16-6 illustrates an internal control structure questionnaire for inventory, focusing on physical control, perpetual inventory records, and cost records, three primary areas of interest to an auditor when considering controls over inventory. A "No" response to any question would indicate a control procedure is not used, and therefore that, lacking compensating controls, a material error could result. Alternatively, or in conjunction with a flowchart or questionnaire, an auditor could use a narrative memorandum, for example to document materials transfer and recording procedures.

Transaction Walk-Through. To confirm his or her understanding of the system, the auditor could trace one or several materials transfers from raw materials to work-in-process to finished goods perpetual records, and to entries and postings in cost records, inventory accounting, and general accounting. Several transfers — rather than a single transfer — are often used for transaction walk-through, since individual units transferred (for example, from raw materials to work in process) are not likely to be directly identifiable as the same units transferred from work in process to finished goods.

Identification of Controls to be Relied On. An auditor identifies controls to be relied on and designs tests of controls using the same methodology

FIGURE 16-6   Performed by: _____
Questionnaire: Inventory   Date: _____

Question	Answer: Yes, No, or N/A	Remarks

Inventory Control:

1. Is inventory reasonably protected from physical deterioration and theft (e.g., fenced areas, restricted access storerooms)?
2. Are materials requisition forms required to obtain materials and supplies for use in production?
3. Are inventory control personnel segregated from purchasing, receiving, shipping, production, and recording?
4. Are inventory control personnel responsible for controlling transfers in and out of storage areas?
5. Are inventory control or other personnel responsible for monitoring inventory levels and reporting slow-moving or damaged items?
6. Is access to inventory restricted to authorized personnel?
7. Are physical inventory counts taken at least once a year for all inventories?
8. Is insurance coverage maintained and periodically reviewed for all inventory?

Perpetual Inventory Records:

1. Are perpetual inventory records continually updated on a timely basis?
2. Are perpetual records maintained by employees independent of shipping, receiving, cost accounting, production, inventory control, and general accounting?
3. Are perpetual records reconciled with general ledger control accounts on a regular basis?
4. Are source documents (e.g., invoices, requisitions, bills of lading, etc.) that are related to perpetual records prenumbered, approved and sent to general accounting for entry in control accounts?

Question	Answer: Yes, No, or N/A	Remarks

5. Are periodic inventory counts reconciled with perpetual records?

Cost Records:

1. Are cost records continually updated on a timely basis?
2. Are cost records maintained independent of perpetual records, production, inventory control, and general accounting?
3. Are cost records reconciled with general ledger control accounts on a regular basis?
4. Are cost accountants familiar with and continually updated about production processes?
5. Are direct and indirect production costs accumulated in sufficient detail to enable accurate charges to work-in-process or finished goods inventory?
6. Are all inventory transfers reported and recorded on a timely basis?
7. Are production personnel required to explain price and volume variances?

---

outlined in Chapter 11 for the revenue/receipt cycle and in Chapters 13 and 15 for the expenditure/disbursement cycle:

▲ Identify the system's control objectives. The first column of Figure 16-4 identifies control objectives for inventory.
▲ Consider the potential errors or irregularities that might result if specific control objectives are not met. The second column of Figure 16-4 identifies examples of potential errors or irregularities.
▲ Determine which control procedures are used by the entity to prevent or detect potentially material errors or irregularities. The third column of Figure 16-4 identifies examples of potential controls.
▲ Design tests of controls for each control procedure to be relied on during substantive tests of account balances.

Tests of controls for inventory are described next.

Tests of Controls: Inventory

Tests of controls over inventory focus on whether transfers of inventory through the production process are properly authorized and recorded. However, since tests of purchasing and selling activities may include tests of inventory records, an auditor should carefully coordinate tests to avoid duplication of effort.

Perpetual Records. Tests of controls an entity's perpetual records focus on physical transfers of inventory to and from raw materials, work in process and finished goods. The integrity and accuracy of transfers are important for at least two reasons. First, inaccurate recording of transfers could suggest that prescribed control procedures and methods are neither complied with nor operating as planned, further suggesting that the records cannot be relied on. Second, inaccurate recording could suggest the possibility of ''double-counted'' inventory quantities. For example, if 100 units of raw materials inventory is transferred to work in process, perpetual records should reflect a 100-unit reduction in raw materials and a 100-unit increase in work in process; if, however, only the increase in work in process is recorded, raw materials would be overstated by 100 units, resulting in double counting. Correspondingly, if only the decrease in raw materials is recorded, work in process would be understated by 100 units. Some representative tests for perpetual records are presented below.

Tests of Controls: Perpetual Records

1. For sampled purchases of raw materials, compare quantities and unit costs from vendors' invoices with perpetual records, coordinating with compliance tests of purchases in the expenditure/disbursement cycle.
2. For sampled transfers of raw materials from inventory control trace to:
   a. Approved materials requisitions.
   b. Transfers to work-in-process perpetual records, comparing quantities and unit costs.
   c. Summary transfer entries in general ledger control accounts.
3. For sampled transfers from work in process, trace to:
   a. Transfers to finished goods perpetual records, comparing quantities and unit costs.
   b. Summary transfer entries in general ledger control accounts.
4. For sampled transfers from finished goods, trace to:

>   a. Shipping documents comparing quantities and unit costs, coordinating with compliance tests for sales in the revenue/receipt cycle.
>   b. Summary of cost of goods sold and sales entries.
> 5. Document any weaknesses or deviations observed.

In step 1, the auditor is testing whether raw materials quantities and unit costs per the perpetual inventory records reflect actual purchases made during the period. Step 2, in contrast, tests transfers from raw materials to work-in-process perpetual records, but from three different perspectives. First, in step 2a, the auditor tests whether transfers were prompted by approved materials requisitions. That is, transfers to work in process should result only when authorized production personnel request raw materials for specific jobs. Second, step 2b tests whether quantities and unit costs on materials requisitions are accurately reflected on work-in-process perpetual records. Third, in step 2c, the auditor's focus shifts to the integrity of accounting records by tracing summary transfer entries from work-in-process perpetual records to raw materials and work-in-process inventory, two general ledger control accounts.

In step 3, the auditor focuses on transfers from work-in-process to finished goods perpetual records. The logic and intent of steps 3a and 3b are identical to those of steps 2b and 2c, respectively.

Step 4, the logical follow-up to steps 2 and 3, focuses on transfers from finished goods perpetual records. Since transfers from finished goods inventory should result only from shipments, the auditor in step 4a traces transfers out of finished goods perpetual records to shipping documents filed in the Shipping Department (see Figure 11-2, pages 448–449). In step 4b, sampled finished goods transfers are traced to cost of goods sold and sales entries, thereby assuring that the cost of finished goods shipped is matched with realized sales revenues.

Cost Records. Perpetual records are an important element of an entity's inventory accounting system. However, perpetual records are intended primarily as a control over the location and flow of inventory quantities. Tests of controls must also be performed for the flow of inventory costs from raw materials to work in process, finished goods, and cost of goods sold.

Cost accounting systems differ significantly from entity to entity, depending upon the specific products manufactured or processed. As a result, tests of controls also vary significantly from engagement to engagement. In many audit engagements, though, an auditor focuses upon accumulated labor and overhead charges to work-in-process inventory. Several appropriate tests follow.

> **Tests of Controls: Cost Records**
>
> 1. Obtain summaries of charges to work-in-process inventory.
> 2. Test accumulated direct labor and overhead charges:
>   a. For sampled direct labor charges, reconcile amounts with:
>   (1) Departmental labor charge reports, coordinating with compliance tests of labor records in the expenditure/disbursement cycle, and
>   (2) Work-in-process perpetual records.
>   b. For sampled overhead charges, reconcile rates with authorized standard costs, assuring that the basis for application (e.g., direct labor hours) is appropriate.
> 3. Review the basis for determining standard overhead rates, determining that:
>   a. Expenses charged to overhead are reasonable and consistent with the prior period, and
>   b. Standard rates reasonably approximate actual costs.
> 4. Determine the disposition of overabsorbed and underabsorbed overhead.
> 5. Document any weaknesses or deviations observed.

As indicated in step 1, tests of cost records stem from a client's summary of charges (debits) to work-in-process inventory and, as suggested by steps 2 through 4, focus on direct labor and overhead charges.

In step 2a, the auditor traces direct labor charges to two independent sources: departmental labor charge reports and work-in-process perpetual records (assuming labor charges are included in perpetual records, which in some companies may not be). Step 2b addresses whether overhead charges agree with authorized standard costs, and whether the basis for applying overhead — for example, direct labor hours, units of production, etc. — is appropriate. In turn, step 3 further addresses standard overhead costs, but from the viewpoint of whether overhead is applied consistently with the prior period and reasonably approximates actual costs.

Step 4 addresses how a client disposes of overabsorbed and underabsorbed overhead. Under generally accepted accounting principles, normal variances between actual and standard costs — the basis for determining overabsorbed and underabsorbed overhead — are period costs, and therefore should be charged to current operations, usually through cost of sales. Abnormal variances, in contrast, should be charged to the cost of products — that is, to inventory — and expensed in the period of the related sales, again through cost of sales, but in the period of sale rather than the period incurred.

Assess Control Risk

An auditor reviews system documentation and the results of tests of controls to determine whether existing control procedures can be relied on to restrict substantive tests of inventory (low control risk) or whether expanded substantive tests are required (high control risk). The evaluation is based on four issues: (1) the types of errors or irregularities that could occur, (2) necessary control procedures that should prevent or detect the errors or irregularities, (3) whether the necessary procedures exist and are followed, and (4) any deficiencies in the internal control structure. Substantive tests applicable to inventory are discussed later in the chapter.

CONSIDERING INTERNAL CONTROL STRUCTURE: PLANT ASSETS

The following discussion addresses the auditor's consideration of controls over plant assets.

Obtain an Understanding

In comparison with inventory, plant asset transactions are considerably less numerous, and individual transactions usually involve considerably larger dollar amounts. Thus, the components of a review of the system are identical (preliminary review, system documentation, transaction walk-through, and evaluation), but an auditor's focus is different, since any one transaction alone could exceed the auditor's tolerable error for plant assets.

Preliminary Review. As with inventory, the preliminary review is conducted by reviewing the client's procedures manuals and by interviewing client personnel responsible for plant asset additions, disposals and retirements, and recording. Assuming controls are potentially reliable, an auditor would proceed as follows.

System Documentation. Flowcharts are not often used to document an entity's plant asset system, primarily because the number of transactions is not likely to justify extensive flowcharting. Rather, internal control structure questionnaires similar to Figure 16-7 are more likely to be used to identify apparent deficiencies, and narratives are likely to be used to document procedures for plant asset additions, disposals and retirements and recording.

FIGURE 16-7   Prepared by: _____
Questionnaire: Plant Assets   Date: _____
                                         Answer:
                                         Yes, No,
              Question   or N/A   Remarks

Plant Asset Records:

1. Are detailed records maintained for each
   class of plant assets (e.g., land, buildings,
   machinery, equipment)?
2. Is responsibility for maintaining plant asset
   records segregated from responsibility for
   physically controlling plant assets and from
   general accounting?
3. Are detailed records reconciled periodically
   with general ledger control accounts?
4. Are procedures followed to determine
   whether recorded plant assets actually exist?
5. Is access to and the use of plant assets
   restricted only to authorized personnel?
6. Is insurance coverage maintained and
   reviewed for all plant assets?
7. Are plant assets physically safeguarded from
   deterioration or theft?

Additions:

1. Do procedures require authorization by the
   board of directors or senior management for
   plant asset additions?
2. Are actual expenditures for plant assets
   compared with amounts authorized?
3. Are procedures established to assure that
   plant assets purchased are delivered in
   accordance with orders placed?
4. Are plant asset additions promptly recorded
   in plant asset records?
5. Are plant asset additions promptly reported
   to general accounting?
6. Are insurance companies notified of plant
   asset additions in order to increase insurance
   coverage?
7. Is construction in progress — whether
   internal or externally contracted —
   authorized and periodically inspected?

	Answer:	
	Yes, No,	
Question	or N/A	Remarks

Disposals and Retirements:

1. Do procedures require authorization by the board of directors or senior management for plant asset disposals and retirements?
2. Are procedures established to assure that the proceeds from plant asset disposals are recorded properly and deposited?
3. Are plant asset disposals and retirements promptly recorded in plant asset records?
4. Are plant asset disposals and retirements promptly reported to general accounting for recording gains or losses?
5. Are insurance companies notified to assure that insurance coverage is altered accordingly?

Depreciation:

1. Are procedures established to assure that additions are added to depreciation records and that disposals/retirements are deleted?
2. Are procedures established to assure that depreciation is recorded only for those plant assets actually in service during the period?
3. Are procedures established for determining depreciation methods, estimated useful lives, and salvage values?

Transaction Walk-Through. To confirm her or his understanding of an entity's plant asset system, an auditor could trace an addition transaction, a disposal transaction, and a retirement through the accounting system, and examine depreciation schedules for conformity with prescribed procedures. Alternatively, some auditors ignore transaction walk-through altogether, electing instead to perform substantive tests of details on all plant asset transactions at year-end. In that case, tests of controls would also be ignored.

Identification of Controls to Be Relied On. Following system documentation, an auditor continues considering the internal control structure exactly as outlined earlier in the chapter for inventory. Figure 16-5 identifies control objectives (column one), potential errors or irregularities (column two), and control procedures (column three).

Tests of Controls: Plant Assets

For many entities, the volume of plant asset transactions is likely to be much lower than for other major financial statement accounts. When the number of plant asset transactions is limited, an auditor may forego or limit tests of controls, electing instead to rely solely or predominantly on year-end substantive tests. However, if the number of transactions is large, an auditor may elect to rely on the internal control structure and, as a result, to perform tests of controls over an entity's recording, addition, disposal, and depreciation activities.

Plant Asset Records. Tests of an entity's plant asset records focus on the relationship between detailed records and the general ledger and on the existence and insurance coverage of recorded assets. Some representative tests follow.

Tests of Controls: Plant Asset Records

1. Reconcile total plant assets per detailed records with the general ledger, and investigate any differences.
2. Physically inspect sampled plant assets.
3. Review the adequacy of insurance coverage on recorded assets.

A company's detailed plant asset records may take the form of a computer printout or a ledger, and as indicated in step 1 should be reconciled in total with the general ledger. In step 2, the auditor assures that the plant assets (particularly additions for the current year) physically exist and have not been disposed of or otherwise retired. In step 3, the auditor reviews the adequacy of plant asset insurance coverage, since inadequate coverage may require additional financial statement disclosure.

Additions. An auditor's predominant concern in tests of plant asset additions is that the related transactions are authorized and properly recorded. Several appropriate tests follow.

Tests of Controls: Additions

1. Obtain a summary of plant asset additions from accounting personnel.
2. Foot the summary and reconcile total additions with total additions per the general ledger.
3. Randomly select a sample of additions, and for each sampled addition:
   a. Examine authorizations, purchase orders (or contracts), receiving reports, vendors' invoices, and other supporting documents.
   b. Examine evidence of cash payment (e.g., canceled checks) and trace to entries in voucher register (or other cash disbursements records).
   c. Examine evidence of obligations for payment (e.g., notes payable) and trace to subsidiary and general ledger accounts.
   d. Determine that classification as plant assets, rather than repairs and maintenance expense, is consistent with policy.

The company's summary of plant asset additions is the basis for testing additions, and may take the form of a computer printout or a detailed work sheet among other things. Step 2 determines whether the summary is mathematically accurate, and reconciles the summary with the general ledger, which is the source for preparing financial statements; the general ledger must accurately represent detailed records.

Step 3 addresses the substance of recorded plant asset addition transactions. Additions can be sampled, as suggested, or tested entirely, the typical case when additions are not numerous.

In step 3a, the auditor examines evidence that an addition was authorized and an asset received. Evidence of authorization could appear within the board of directors' minutes, particularly for substantial additions such as buildings, or could take the form of a division manager's memorandum. Receiving reports and invoices would indicate that the additions arrived and were billed by independent vendors.

Step 3b, in contrast, determines whether the addition was paid for and was recorded properly as a cash disbursement. If a note or other obligation exists, the auditor would examine the document in step 3c, reconciling details with the subsidiary records and general ledger. Step 3d assures that additions are properly classified as plant assets rather than as repairs and maintenance expense. In addition, the step also assures that classification as an asset or expense is consistent with company policy. For example, in some companies, additions of less than a predetermined dollar amount, say $500, might be charged to expense regardless of useful life, since the burden of record keeping (e.g., depreciation) is not necessarily justified for immaterial amounts.

Disposals. As is the case with additions, an auditor is concerned that plant asset disposals are authorized and properly recorded. Some representative tests follow.

Tests of Controls: Disposals

1. Obtain a summary of plant asset disposals and retirements from accounting personnel.
2. Foot the summary and reconcile total disposals with total disposals per the general ledger.
3. Randomly select a sample of disposals, and for each sampled disposal:
   a. Examine authorizations, contracts, sales invoices, and other supporting documents.
   b. Examine entries in cash receipt records.
   c. Examine any notes receivable and trace to subsidiary and general ledger accounts.
   d. Calculate any gain or loss and trace to general ledger.

The company's summary of plant asset disposals and retirements — again, for example, a printout or work sheet — is obtained in step 1, tested for mathematical accuracy in step 2, and agreed with the general ledger. As with additions, disposals and retirements may be sampled or tested entirely.

In step 3a, the auditor examines evidence that the transaction is authorized, for example, by reading the board of directors' minutes, and that the transaction occurred, as would be suggested by signed contracts and sales invoices. Step 3b examines entries in cash receipts records, thereby further supporting whether a transaction occurred. If a note was received for a disposed asset, the auditor should examine the instrument and reconcile the transaction with the general ledger, as indicated in step 3c. In step 3d, the auditor recalculates any gain or loss resulting from the disposal transaction, reconciling the amount with entries in the general ledger.

Depreciation. Tests of depreciation involve calculations and reviewing methods, recorded amounts, useful lives, and salvage values. These tests would be substantially similar for the amortization of intangible assets and depletion of wasting assets. Several appropriate tests of depreciation follow.

Tests of Controls: Depreciation

1. Review depreciation methods by asset class and policies regarding useful lives and salvage values.
2. Randomly select a sample of plant assets, and for each sampled asset:
   a. Determine whether useful lives and salvage values are consistent with policies.
   b. Recalculate depreciation expense and accumulated depreciation.

In step 1, the auditor reviews methods and policies to assure that depreciation is calculated as planned. Step 2 tests sampled assets, but could also be performed for all assets. Step 2a determines whether each asset's useful life and salvage value are consistent with company policy (step 1), and step 2b recalculates depreciation expense and accumulated depreciation.

Assess Control Risk

The auditor assesses control risk for plant assets in the same manner as discussed earlier for inventory.

FINANCIAL STATEMENT ASSERTIONS, OBJECTIVES, AND AUDIT PROCEDURES

Inventory and plant assets represent the most significant financial statement accounts processed through the conversion cycle. The following provides an overview of how practicing auditors typically test each of the audit objectives introduced in Chapter 6: existence or occurrence, completeness, rights and obligations, valuation or allocation, and presentation and disclosure. Figure 16-8 summarizes the discussion by relating each objective to specific audit procedures.

Existence or Occurrence

Within the conversion cycle, the existence or occurrence objective addresses whether all recorded inventory and plant assets existed at the balance sheet date and whether all recorded inventory and plant asset transactions occurred during the period.

FIGURE 16-8
Relating Audit Objectives and Audit Procedures:
Inventory and Plant Assets

Audit Objective	Audit Procedures	
	Inventory	Plant Assets
Existence or Occurrence	Observe physical inventory Confirm inventory off-premises. Test cutoff.	Observe asset additions. Test cutoff.
Completeness	Observe physical inventory. Confirm inventory off-premises. Perform analytical procedures.	Observe asset additions. Test cutoff. Perform analytical procedures.
Rights and Obligations	Confirm inventory off-premises. Test cutoff. Review consignment and purchase commitments.	Test additions. Test cutoff. Examine contracts and other documentation.
Valuation or Allocation	Test final priced inventory.	Verify accuracy of recorded plant assets and depreciation expense. Test additions and disposals.
Presentation and Disclosure	Compare statement presentation and disclosures with those required by GAAP	Compare statement presentation and disclosures with those required by GAAP.

For inventory, existence or occurrence is tested by three separate but related procedures. First, and foremost, the auditor observes the client's physical count of inventory, often at the balance sheet date, thereby assuring that recorded inventory exists. Second, for off-premises inventory, the auditor confirms recorded quantities with consignees or public warehouses. Finally, inventory cutoff is tested to assure that inventory-related transactions, such as purchases and sales, are recorded in the proper accounting period.

The existence of plant asset balances and occurrence of transactions are tested by observing additions and perhaps some previously existing assets, and by testing cutoff, to assure that additions and disposals are recorded in the proper accounting period.

Completeness

The completeness objective addresses whether all inventory and plant asset transactions that should be presented in the financial statements are actually presented. That is, were all transactions recorded?

To test completeness for inventory, an auditor observes the physical inventory and confirms off-premises inventory, to assure that all inventory is recorded. Cutoff testing assures that the recording of year-end transactions is not postponed to the next accounting period. Analytical procedures also address completeness by testing whether recorded balances appear reasonable in relation to other accounts.

Completeness for plant assets is addressed by testing additions to assure that all additions are recorded, by testing cutoff, and by performing analytical procedures.

Rights and Obligations

Within the conversion cycle, the rights objective addresses whether an entity has property rights to inventory and plant assets. Rights to inventory are tested by confirming off-premises inventory quantities and by testing cutoff, which assures that rights to recorded inventory exist as of the balance sheet date. In addition, auditors also test current obligations for future commitments by reviewing any outstanding consignment or purchase agreements.

For plant assets, rights are examined by testing additions (and disposals), testing cutoff to determine whether rights exist at the balance sheet date, and examining contracts or other supporting documentation, such as invoices for purchased assets and cost records for internally manufactured equipment.

Valuation or Allocation

The valuation objective addresses whether existing inventory and plant assets are carried in the financial statements at appropriate amounts. For inventory, an auditor addresses carrying value primarily by testing the client's final priced inventory, but also by reviewing during the physical inventory observations for obsolete, slow-moving, or otherwise nonsalable goods. The carrying value of plant assets is tested by verifying the mathematical accuracy of recorded plant assets and of the client's recorded depreciation expense. Valuation is also addressed when an auditor tests additions and disposals, since added plant assets should be included in current financial statements and disposed assets should not.

Presentation and Disclosure

The presentation and disclosure objective addresses whether recorded inventory and plant assets are properly classified, described, and disclosed in external financial statements. Presentation and disclosure are tested by comparing a client's financial statement disclosures with generally accepted accounting principles for each reported account. Disclosure guidelines, such as the AICPA's annually updated *Accounting and Audit Manual* among others, are used frequently by practicing auditors.

The following sections expand on this discussion by illustrating and further explaining each audit procedure. Substantive tests of inventory are discussed first, followed thereafter by tests of plant assets.

SUBSTANTIVE TESTS OF INVENTORY

Substantive tests of inventory center on observing the physical counting of inventory by the client's personnel (and confirming off-premises inventory not observed), testing priced inventory, testing cutoff, and performing analytical procedures. A program of substantive tests appears in Figure 16-9 and is keyed to, and discussed in the context of, the audit objectives presented earlier.

Observe Physical Inventory

As discussed in Chapter 6, knowledge obtained directly by an auditor through observation can provide a highly persuasive form of evidence, and nowhere is observation more relevant than in testing inventory. Observation of a client's procedures for physically counting inventories contributes to the fulfillment of no less than two audit objectives:

▲ *Existence:* Do inventories reported on the balance sheet physically exist?

FIGURE 16-9
Substantive Tests: Inventory

Audit Objective	Procedures
Existence Completeness	1. Observe physical inventory.
Existence Completeness Rights	2. Confirm inventory at off-premises locations.

Valuation	3. Obtain the final-priced inventory records.
	    a. Extend, foot, and cross-foot the final priced inventory.
	    b. Test unit prices.
	    c. Agree total inventory per the final-priced inventory with the general ledger.

Existence or Occurrence Completeness Rights	4. Test cutoff, coordinating with tests performed for sales and receivables and for purchases and payables.
Existence or Occurrence Completeness Valuation	5. Perform analytical procedures.

Presentation/
  Disclosure
	6. Review financial statements to determine whether:
	    a. Inventories and cost of sales are properly classified and described.
	    b. Disclosures are adequate.

▲ *Completeness:* Do inventories reported on the balance sheet include all materials, work in process, and finished goods?

Planning Inventory Counts. An auditor does not physically count inventory for a client, nor does the auditor physically participate as a counter. Rather, client personnel count and document inventory quantities, and an auditor observes the client's procedures. For periodic inventory systems, the physical counts serve as the only measure of quantities on hand; for perpetual systems, the counts serve as both a measure of quantities on hand and a test of perpetual records.

Inventory quantities may be counted at interim rather than year-end. From an auditor's point of view, the appropriate timing of inventory counts depends upon the type of inventory system — periodic or perpetual — and the effectiveness of internal control. Interim counts are more appropriate when well-kept perpetual records are maintained, internal control (including physical control) is effective, and perpetual records and financial statement accounts can be reconciled with year-end balances. Otherwise, counts on or near the year-end balance sheet date are more appropriate — for example, when a periodic inventory system is used, when perpetual records are not well kept, or when the internal control structure is ineffective.

Some time in advance of the count date, an auditor should plan for the inventory observation by reviewing the client's proposed inventory counting procedures and instructions for the employees who will count the inventory. The procedures should be well planned and among other things might provide for:

▲ Controlling or eliminating stock movement on the count date.
▲ Stocking or arranging inventory in a manner convenient for counting (e.g., like-sized rows, clear separations between inventory classes).
▲ Pretesting counting devices such as weight scales.
▲ Segregating stock not to be included in count, such as inventory held on consignment from suppliers.
▲ Identifying off-premises stock to be included in count, such as inventory out on consignment with customers.
▲ Preparing preprinted count media, such as multipart tags, count sheets, or punched cards.
▲ Documenting damaged or obsolete inventory.

The employees who count inventory should be given written instructions which include such information as the:

▲ Count date and times.
▲ Names of supervisors and count teams by location.
▲ Count media.
▲ Procedures for counting and documenting quantities.
▲ Procedures for controlling and accounting for count media before, during, and after the physical counts.

The procedures and instructions should be complete, explicit, and reasonably adequate to facilitate accurate and reliable counts.

Observing Client Inventory Counts. Prior to or on the inventory count date, the in-charge auditor should coordinate with audit staff members assigned to the observation, providing them with specific duties, detailed instructions, and copies of the clients' instructions. In general, most staff members' duties will include:

▲ Observing count teams.
▲ Making and documenting test counts.
▲ Noting damaged or slow-moving inventory.

An auditor observes client count teams in order to determine whether counters are adhering to the client's instructions and are counting and documenting quantities accurately. Count teams should proceed systematically, taking precautions to cover all — but not more than — their assigned areas; counting outside assigned areas could result in double counting, thereby potentially overstating inventory.

In conjunction with observing count teams, an auditor should make and document test counts of selected inventory items, agreeing quantities with count media compiled by client personnel. Test counts should be documented on working papers and indicate all details necessary to agree quantities subsequently with the final priced inventory, as illustrated in Figure 16-10. Documented details might include count media numbers (e.g., tag number), inventory stock numbers and descriptions, and quantities. In addition, an auditor should document any damaged or slow-moving goods, since these items may need to be adjusted in the accounts to net realizable value.

Information should be documented for goods shipped and received on the inventory count date. Assuming title passes on the count date, inventory shipments should be excluded from physical counts, and receipts included. Information documented for shipments and receipts on the count date is used in conjunction with other information in tests of cutoff.

Some goods on hand may represent consignments from suppliers, and therefore are the supplier's inventory. An auditor should ascertain that all goods held on consignment are segregated from inventory prior to physical counts. An auditor can further test for consignments by reviewing consignment agreements and making inquiries of client personnel.

Following completion of all inventory observation procedures, each audit staff member should prepare a working paper memorandum summarizing his or her observations, any significant departures from the client's preplanned instructions, and a specific conclusion about the accuracy of client counts.

Confirm Off-Premise Inventory

Inventory held off-premises by consignees or in public warehouses need not necessarily be examined by an auditor, but should be confirmed. An

FIGURE 16-10   C19
Inventory Test Counts

                                                                         DN
                                                                         1/27/91

                            Christopher Supply Co.
                            Inventory Test Counts
                             December 31, 1990

Inventory Ticket Number	Location & Description	Count per:			Difference: Over (Under)	
		Client	Audit			
	Warehouse A					
0462	Part A24-Copper Cable	870 ft	820 ft	a	50 ft	b
0163	Part A98-Rubber Tubing	565 ft	565 ft	a	–	
0241	Part A99-Synthetic Tubing	405 ft	400 ft	a	5 ft	b
0328	Solder	125 lb	125 lb	a	–	
0612	3/8" Wire Binding	600 ft	600 ft	a	–	
0761	3/4" Wire Binding	298 ft	295 ft	a	3 ft	b
0824	298 Engine Oil	125 qts	125 qts	a	–	
0822	Bushings, 5/8"	625 in	625 in	a	–	
	Department A-Finishing					
0014	Plating Fluid	405 gals	410 gals	a	(5 gals)	b
0129	Electrolite Solution	75 gals	75 gals	a	–	
0146	Oaklite 32	127 gals	127 gals	a	–	

a Reconciled with client's final priced inventory (work done 1/17/91-See C20-C24)
b Difference confirmed by client recount, and inventory tag corrected

                                 Conclusion

  Based on test counts and observations, I am satisfied that the client's count procedures
were reasonable, that counts were reasonably accurate, and that neither Warehouse A nor
Dept A-Finishing contain significant quantities of obsolete, slow-moving, or otherwise
nonsaleable inventory.

example of a typical off-premises inventory confirmation appears in Figure
16-11. The *Codification of Statements on Auditing Standards* (AU Sec. 331.14)
provides that, if inventory in public warehouses is significant in relation to
current or total assets, an auditor should also make supplemental inquiries,
such as:

▲ Discussion about the client's control procedures for investigating
  warehouse managers, and tests of related evidence.
▲ Review of the client's control procedures concerning performance of
  the warehouse managers, and tests of related evidence.
▲ Observation of physical counts whenever practicable and reasonable.
▲ Confirmation (on a test basis, where appropriate) from lenders as to
  pertinent details of warehouse receipts pledged as collateral.

FIGURE 16-11
Confirmation of Off-Premises Inventory

CHRISTOPHER SUPPLY COMPANY
653 Broadway
New York, New York 01284

January 7, 1991

McGowen Warehousing
12456 Dartmouth Road
Indianapolis, IN 46298

Our auditors, Cermak & Willingham, CPAs, are examining our financial state-
ments for 1990. Will you please furnish them with the following information
regarding merchandise held in your custody for us as of December 31, 1990.
• Quantities on hand, including:
    Lot number
    Date received
    Description of merchandise
• A statement about whether the quantities were determined by physical count
  or represent your recorded amounts only.
• A list of negotiable or nonnegotiable warehouse receipts issued, if any.
• A statement of any known liens against this merchandise
• Indication of any damaged, spoiled, or deteriorated merchandise.
A prompt reply to our auditors will be appreciated. An envelope addressed to
our auditors is enclosed.

Molly Gilmore
Controller

Final Priced Inventory

Physical inventory counts provide information about quantities, but not
about carrying values. Thus, after completed count media are summarized,
employees not otherwise responsible for inventory record keeping or control
should extend quantities by unit costs, resulting in a final priced inventory by
item number, product line, and inventory classification. To facilitate follow-
up, each line item on the final priced inventory should identify the count
media from which quantities were compiled. Quantities and the final priced
inventory should be reconciled by client personnel with perpetual records and
control accounts, respectively, and necessary adjustments recorded.

As part of year-end substantive procedures, an auditor obtains the client's final priced inventory and performs tests of clerical accuracy. The auditor should extend (multiply quantities by unit costs), foot, and cross-foot the priced inventory, agreeing test counts with priced quantities, as illustrated in Figure 16-10 (tickmark b), dollar amounts to control accounts, and required adjustments to general ledger entries. On a sample basis, unit prices per the final priced inventory should be agreed with source documents, with appropriate consideration for prescribed cost flow methods. For example, if raw materials costs are assigned to production on a first-in, first-out basis, unit costs should be agreed with the latest vendor invoices available for a period prior to the inventory count date, since the latest prices would be assigned to raw materials inventory and earlier costs would have been charged to work in process.

Test Cutoff

As noted earlier, an auditor compiles inventory cutoff documentation during the physical inventory observation. The documentation may include shipping documents and receiving reports and is used to test sales cutoff in conjunction with substantive tests for revenue/receipt cycle accounts (sales and accounts receivable) and purchase cutoff in conjunction with expenditure/disbursement cycle accounts (purchases and accounts payable).

The cutoff information, however, cannot necessarily be agreed with inventory account balances. For example, if goods are received (and title passes) on the count date, tracing related receiving reports to subsequent purchase and payable entries does not assure that the received goods were counted in inventory. Likewise, if goods are shipped (and title passes) on the count date, tracing related shipping documents to subsequent sales and receivables entries does not assure that the shipped goods were not counted in inventory. As a result, during the physical inventory observation, an auditor must assure that shipped and received goods are controlled to avoid both double counting as in the case of counting shipped goods in inventory and undercounting as in the case of failing to count received goods.

Perform Analytical Procedures

An auditor uses analytical procedures — for example, comparing relationships between and among accounts — to address completeness and to determine whether conclusions drawn from substantive tests of details are reasonable. For example, inventory price tests might indicate that a client's inventory is priced accurately. But an auditor would not likely conclude that the priced sample was representative if other tests indicated that quantities at year-end had dropped sharply since the prior year and yet the general ledger book value of inventory had not.

For inventory, an auditor might use any of the following analytical tests, among others.

▲ Compare cost of goods sold divided by average inventory — inventory turnover — for the current year with that for prior years, thereby testing whether reduced turnover suggests slow-moving or obsolete inventory.

▲ Compare the number-of-days sales in inventory for the current year with that for prior years, again testing turnover.

▲ Compare gross profit margin for the current year with that for prior years, thereby testing whether inventory might possibly be understated or overstated.

▲ Compare volume-adjusted manufacturing costs for the current year with those for prior years, thereby testing whether unit costs might possibly be understated or overstated.

If any of the preceding tests reveal unusual relationships, an auditor would first make inquiries of management and then design additional detailed substantive tests or extend sample sizes if necessary. For example, in the above testing illustration, the auditor might increase sample size, thereby performing additional price tests and attempting to control the risk of incorrect acceptance.

Review Financial Statements

An auditor reviews financial statements to assess whether inventory and costs of sales are properly classified, described, and disclosed in accordance with generally accepted accounting principles. Inventories are usually stated at the lower of cost or market, according to a specific cost flow assumption (e.g., first-in, first-out), and may be classified as supplies, raw materials, work in process, and finished goods. Accrued losses should be disclosed for any firm purchase commitments made at unfavorable prices.

SUBSTANTIVE TESTS OF PLANT ASSETS

Plant assets are less susceptible to irregularities than some other assets, such as cash, securities, and some types of inventories. As a result, auditors often address some year-end audit objectives at interim, during the consideration of internal control structure. For example, an auditor addresses existence when physically inspecting plant assets in conjunction with tests of controls over records. Thus, some substantive procedures are performed at interim, and follow-up or additional tests are conducted at year-end for the intervening period since interim. Figure 16-12 represents a program of representative year-end substantive tests for plant assets, and is keyed to the audit objectives discussed earlier.

Verify Accuracy of Recorded Plant Assets

To test the valuation of plant assets from the standpoint of mathematical accuracy, an auditor obtains a client-prepared schedule summarizing detailed asset records. The schedule should include beginning balances, additions, disposals, and ending balances by plant asset class, as illustrated in Figure 16-13. The auditor should reconcile beginning balances per the schedule with the prior year's financial statements. The accuracy of the summary schedule is checked by footing and cross-footing and agreeing totals with general ledger accounts. Details for selected assets are then traced to the underlying detailed records.

Test Additions and Disposals Since Interim

Additions and disposals since interim are tested in the same manner as earlier additions and disposals (see tests of controls of additions and disposals). If relatively few plant assets have been acquired since interim, an auditor may physically inspect all recorded additions. Otherwise, a randomly selected sample of additions should be observed.

While physically inspecting recorded additions, an auditor should also be cognizant of other assets that appear new and therefore may represent unrecorded additions. Likewise, he or she should be cognizant of areas where plant assets may recently have been removed, suggesting the possibility of unrecorded disposals. For example, an area within a manufacturing plant may appear unusually clean and contain obvious floor markings that could suggest a machine was removed. Of course, the presence of any of these conditions does not necessarily suggest irregularities; such conditions merely suggest than an auditor should determine whether any related transactions are recorded.

In addition, and closely related to the existence and rights objectives, an auditor also examines documentation supporting plant additions, and traces to entries in the accounting records. Documentation may take several forms, depending on the nature of the asset. Several examples are presented in Figure 16-12.

Supporting documentation also addresses asset valuation, since supporting documents such as contracts, invoices, and canceled checks also represent evidence of an asset's historical cost.

FIGURE 16-12

Substantive Tests: Plant Assets and Depreciation

Audit Objectives	Procedures
Valuation	1. Verify mathematical accuracy of recorded plant assets. a. Obtain a year-end summary schedule of plant asset detailed records; foot and cross-foot the schedule. b. Agree total plant assets per the summary schedule with the general ledger. c. Randomly select a sample of plant assets from the summary schedule and trace to plant asset detailed records.
Existence/ Occurrence Completeness Rights Valuation	2. Test additions and disposals since interim. a. Examine supporting documentation and trace to entries in accounting records. b. Observe (physically inspect) additions.
Existence/ Occurrence Completeness Rights Completeness	3. Test cutoff to determine whether plant asset additions and disposals near year-end are recorded in the appropriate accounting period.
Valuation	4. Verify mathematical accuracy of depreciation expense. a. Obtain summary schedules of depreciation expense by asset class from accounting personnel; foot and cross-foot schedules. b. Trace totals per summary schedules to totals in general ledger. c. Randomly select a sample of plant assets from the summary schedules and recalculate depreciation expense.
Existence or Occurrence Valuation Completeness	5. Perform analytical procedures.
Presentation/ Disclosure	6. Review financial statements to determine whether: a. Plant assets, accumulated depreciation, and depreciation expense are properly classified and described. b. Disclosures are adequate.

FIGURE 16-13
Schedule of Plant Assets and Accumulated Depreciation

E1

JB

1-18-91

Singer Company
Plant Assets and Accumulated Depreciation
December 31, 1990

(Schedule prepared
by client)

Plant Assets

	Final Bal. 12-31-89	Additions	Retirements/ Disposals	Balance 12-31-90	Adjustments/ Reclass	Adjusted Balance 12-31-90
Land	$ 257,650 c	$ 15,200 E2		$ 272,850		$ 272,850 b
Buildings	3,461,520 c		$90,000 E2	3,371,520		3,371,520 b
Machinery & Equipment	1,590,850 c	175,000 E2		1,765,850		1,765,850 b
Furniture & Fixtures	621,420 c			621,420	$37,400	658,820 b
Automobiles	105,000 c			105,000		105,000 b
	$6,036,440 c	$190,200	$90,000	$6,136,640	$37,400	$6,174,040 b
	a	a	a	a,TB	a	a

Accumulated Depreciation

	Final Bal. 12-31-89	Expense	Retirements/ Disposals	Balance 12-31-90	Adjustments/ Reclass	Adjusted Balance 12-31-90
Land	$ 128,000 c	$ 13,200 d		$ 141,200		$ 141,200 b
Buildings	1,461,850 c	138,000 d	$48,000 E2	1,551,850	$24,000	1,575,850 b
Machinery & Equipment	825,500 c	81,500 d		907,000		907,000 b
Furniture & Fixtures	242,100 c	26,500 d		268,600		268,600 b
Automobiles	68,250 c	13,200 d		81,450		81,450 b
	$2,725,700 c	$272,400 d	$48,000	$2,950,100	$24,000	$2,974,100 b
	a	a	a	a,TB	a	a

a Footed
b Crossfooted
c Agreed to 12-31-89 general ledger and financial statements
d Recalculated for reasonableness
TB Agreed to trial balance

Test Cutoff

Cutoff tests for plant assets relate to whether additions and disposals near year-end are recorded in the proper accounting period. Since acquisitions are processed through the expenditure/disbursement cycle and disposals through the revenue/receipt cycle, plant asset cutoff can be tested in conjunction with cutoff tests for purchases and payables and for sales and receivables. Retired assets which are not sold, however, should be tested separately.

Verify Accuracy of Depreciation Expense

As part of an auditor's tests of valuation, he or she tests depreciation expense, since plant assets are reported net of accumulated depreciation. Year-end detailed tests may not be necessary, however, if interim tests of controls indicate that control over depreciation is adequate. Rather, an auditor might test the reasonableness of depreciation instead through analytical procedures.

If an auditor decides to perform detailed substantive tests of depreciation expense at year-end, a summary schedule of depreciation by asset class should be obtained from accounting personnel. The schedule should include beginning accumulated depreciation balances (which should be agreed with prior year's financial statements), current-year depreciation expense, reversals of accumulated depreciation for disposed assets, and ending accumulated depreciation balances, as illustrated in Figure 6-13. The auditor would test the schedule's accuracy by footing and cross-footing and agreeing totals with general ledger accounts. Depreciation expense for selected assets should be recalculated.

Perform Analytical Procedures

To address completeness, an auditor uses analytical procedures such as ratio and trend analysis and comparison of relationships between and among related accounts or account components. For plant assets, an auditor might use any of the following analytical tests, among others.

▲ Compare repairs and maintenance costs for the current and prior years, thereby testing whether unusually large expenses signal potentially capitalizable assets.

▲ Compare repairs and maintenance costs for the current year with budgeted amounts, again testing for signals of potentially capitalizable assets.

▲ Compare depreciation expense divided by total depreciable assets for the current and prior years, thereby testing whether depreciable assets might possibly be miscalculated.

▲ Compare units of production divided by total productive assets, thereby testing whether assets may have been retired or disposed of without proper recording.

As in other analytical procedures, unusual items should be investigated by inquiries of management and then by substantive testing if necessary. For example, an auditor would likely recalculate depreciation completely if depreciation expense divided by productive assets declined significantly without a corresponding decline in total productive assets.

Review Financial Statements

The balance sheet should be reviewed to determine whether plant assets and related accumulated depreciation balances are properly classified and described. When a single net book value is reported for plant assets in a condensed balance sheet, details should be included in the notes to the financial statements. Disclosures should include depreciation methods used (including any differences between methods for tax purposes and financial reporting purposes), useful lives employed for major asset categories, and other significant policies, such as policies for capitalizing major repairs and reporting gains and losses.

An entity may possess significant leasehold rights, though not ownership, to property and, as a result, may be required to capitalize the related asset. For example, a lease that transfers substantially all of the benefits and risks incident to property ownership should be accounted for as (1) the acquisition of an asset and incurrence of an obligation by a lessee, and (2) the sale or financing arrangement by a lessor. An auditor should examine all lease agreements, assuring that the transactions are accounted for properly under the Financial Accounting Standards Board's (FASB) *Statement of Financial Accounting Standards No. 13,* "Accounting for Leases," and other FASB lease-related statements and interpretations. All leased assets requiring capitalization under generally accepted accounting principles should be properly classified and described in the balance sheet, and details of lease agreements disclosed in notes to financial statements.

The income statement should be reviewed to determine whether depreciation expense is properly reported. Depreciation expense included in cost of sales should be disclosed separately in the income statement or in notes to the statements.

SUMMARY

The conversion cycle relates to the holding, use, or transformation of resources such as inventory and plant assets. Internal controls over inventory focus primarily upon the physical safeguarding of inventory and recorded accountability. Thus, tests of controls over inventory focus upon whether transfers of inventory through production are properly authorized and recorded in perpetual records and cost records. Substantive tests of inventory and cost of sales include physical inventory observation, confirmation of off-premises inventory, verification of the accuracy of final priced inventory records, cutoff tests, analytical procedures, and review of financial statement presentation and disclosures.

Controls over plant assets and tests of the controls focus on detailed asset records and proper authorization and recording of asset additions and disposals. Tests of controls over depreciation involve recalculations and reviewing depreciation methods, useful lives, and salvage values. Substantive tests of plant assets and depreciation include verifying mathematical accuracy, testing additions and disposals, testing cutoff, analytical procedures, and reviewing financial statement presentation and disclosures.

APPENDIX
COMPUTER-ASSISTED SUBSTANTIVE TESTS OF INVENTORY AND PLANT ASSETS

Although audit procedures can be performed effectively on manual accounting information systems, electronic data processing (EDP) systems allow an auditor to be just as effective though more reliable, since some audit tests can often be applied to entire audit populations rather than to samples, and since human processing errors are less likely. Thus, when part or all of a company's conversion cycle activities are recorded, classified, or summarized electronically, an auditor's year-end procedures can be accomplished by computer-assisted substantive and other tests of details. Figure 16-14 lists several computer-assisted techniques for a series of audit procedures common to audits of inventory and plant assets.

To illustrate computer-assisted substantive tests, assume an auditor wishes to accomplish portions of the substantive tests listed in Figure 16-9 for inventory:

▲ Verify mathematical accuracy of the final priced inventory and perpetual records.
▲ Compare details in the final priced inventory with perpetual records.
▲ Perform price tests.
▲ Merge physical inventory counts with perpetual inventory records.

Any or all of these procedures can be accomplished using either generalized audit software or auditor-prepared computer programs, although in either case the auditor's methodology would be identical to the procedures flowcharted in Figure 16-15.

As illustrated in Figure 16-15, the computer-assisted tests require four data files: the perpetual inventory master file, the physical inventory quantities master file, the final priced inventory master file, and the invoice price

FIGURE 16-14

Computer-Assisted Audit Tests: Accounts Payable, Inventory, and
Plant Assets

Audit Procedure	Computer-Assisted Substantive Test	
	Inventory	Plant Assets
Test mathematical accuracy.	Verify footings, cross-footings, and extensions of the final priced inventory and/or perpetual records.	Verify footings, cross-footings, and extensions of detailed plant asset records. Recompute depreciation.
Summarize data for further testing or analysis.	Print listing of off-premises inventory for confirmation, and print confirmations. Array perpetual inventory records in descending order of dollar amounts to select target items for test counting. Access and print year-end receipts and shipments for agreement with cutoff information obtained during the physical inventory observation.	Print plant asset additions for observation. Print plant asset disposals for agreement with recorded gain or loss.
Test accuracy of recorded data.	Trace details in final priced inventory to perpetual records. Perform price tests. Trace details in perpetual records to machine-readable source documents (e.g., receiving reports, production records).	Trace details in plant asset records to machine-readable source documents.

Audit Procedure	Computer-Assisted Substantive Test	
	Inventory	Plant Assets
Make sample selection.	Select inventory items for price testing using internally stored random-number generators and perpetual records.	Select additions for testing (or observation) from internally stored random-number generators and detailed plant asset records.
Compare similar data files.	Compare charges/credits in perpetual inventory records with the purchases/sales master files. Merge physical inventory counts with perpetual inventory records.	Agree plant asset additions/disposals with the cash disbursements/ cash receipts master files.

and terms master file. The audit software would be designed to perform the following tasks for each of the above-listed substantive tests:

Substantive Test	Computer Software Task
Verify mathematical accuracy	Foot, crossfoot, and test extensions for the details constituting each stock number item within the perpetual inventory master file. Foot, crossfoot, and test extensions for each line item in the final priced inventory master file. Print exceptions.
Compare details.	Compare quantities listed in the final priced inventory master file with quantities listed in the perpetual inventory master file. Print exceptions.
Perform price tests.	Compare prices listed in the final priced inventory with appropriate invoice prices

FIGURE 16-14 (*Continued*)

Substantive Test	Computer Software Task
	contained within the invoice price and terms master file. Print exceptions.
Merge physical counts with perpetual records.	Update quantities within the perpetual inventory master file for quantities counted on the physical inventory date and contained within the physical inventory quantities master file. Print exceptions.

To perform the tests listed above and illustrated in Figure 16-15, the auditor would arrange with client EDP personnel to load and run the computer program on the client's computer. The program could be run either directly by the auditor or be run by client personnel under the auditor's supervision. Exception reports would be obtained by the auditor directly from the client's printer. In turn, the output and computer-assisted tests would be documented within the audit working papers, and used in conjunction with other audit evidence to form judgments about whether the client's inventory is fairly stated at the balance sheet date.

QUESTIONS

1. Identify the major business functions and activities common to the conversion cycle.
2. How does the conversion cycle of a manufacturing entity differ from that of a retailer or wholesaler?
3. Describe the internal activities and controls relating to inventories from the time raw materials are acquired until finished goods are sold.
4. Briefly describe the nature and purpose of perpetual inventory records and cost records.
5. Describe the flow of inventory costs through the accounts of a manufacturing entity.
6. What is the major focus of tests of controls of perpetual records and cost records?
7. How can management control against misplaced or misused inventory?
8. What procedure does an auditor use to determine whether recorded inventory exists?

FIGURE 16-15
Flowchart of Computer-Assisted Tests

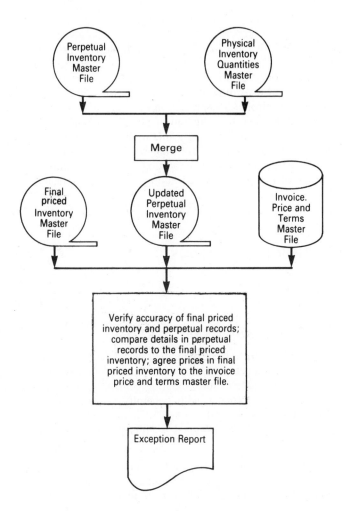

9. For what reason does an auditor test a client's final priced inventory?
10. Give examples of analytical procedures applicable to inventory, and indicate what each procedure could signal to an auditor.
11. Identify and briefly describe the audit objectives associated with physical inventory observation.
12. Under what conditions are interim, as opposed to year-end, physical inventory counts appropriate?
13. Explain an auditor's role during a physical inventory observation.

14. How does an auditor test the valuation of inventory.
15. Why should plant assets be appraised periodically?
16. How can management assure that all plant asset transactions are recorded properly?
17. Describe the nature and purpose of plant asset detailed records.
18. Identify some control procedures for plant asset additions and disposals.
19. Why might an auditor elect to perform only limited or no tests of controls for plant assets?
20. What is the focus of tests of controls for plant asset records?
21. What is the focus of tests of controls for plant asset additions and disposals?
22. What do tests of controls for depreciation involve?
23. How does an auditor test the valuation of plant assets and depreciation?
24. Describe some substantive tests applicable to plant asset additions and disposals.
25. Why would an auditor test cutoff for plant asset transactions?
26. Give examples of documentation supporting plant asset additions.
27. Give examples of computer-assisted audit techniques applicable to the conversion cycle.

MULTIPLE CHOICE QUESTIONS

Inventory

1. When an auditor tests a client's cost accounting system, the auditor's tests are primarily designed to determine that

   a. Quantities on hand have been computed based on acceptable cost accounting techniques that reasonably approximate actual quantities on hand.
   b. Physical inventories are in substantial agreement with book inventories.
   c. The system is in accordance with generally accepted accounting principles and is functioning as planned.
   d. Costs have been properly assigned to finished goods, work in process, and cost of goods sold.   (AICPA Adapted)

2. Sanbor Corporation has an inventory of parts consisting of thousands of different items of small value individually, but significant in total. Sanbor could establish effective internal accounting control over the parts by requiring

   a. Approval of requisitions for inventory parts by a company officer.
   b. Maintenance of inventory records for all parts included in the inventory.
   c. Physical counts of the parts on a cycle basis rather than at year-end.
   d. Separation of the store-keeping function from the production and inventory record-keeping functions.   (AICPA Adapted)

3. When verifying debits to the perpetual inventory records of a nonmanufacturing company, an auditor would be most interested in examining a sample of purchase

   a. Approvals.
   b. Requisitions.

c) Invoices.
d) Orders.   (AICPA Adapted)

4. To best ascertain that a company has properly included merchandise that it owns in its ending inventory, the auditor should review and test the

   a. Terms of the open purchase orders.
   b. Purchase cutoff procedures.
   c. Contractual commitments made by the Purchasing Department.
   d. Purchase invoices received on or around year-end.   (AICPA Adapted)

5. From which of the following evidence-gathering audit procedures would an auditor obtain most assurance concerning the existence of inventories?

   a. Observation of physical inventory counts.
   b. Written inventory representations from management.
   c. Confirmation of inventories in a public warehouse.
   d. Auditor's recomputation of inventory extensions.   (AICPA Adapted)

6. The audit of year-end physical inventories should include steps to verify that the client's purchases and sales cutoffs were adequate. The audit steps should be designed to detect whether merchandise included in the physical count at year-end was not recorded as a

   a. Sale in the subsequent period.
   b. Purchase in the current period.
   c. Sale in the current period.
   d. Purchase return in the subsequent period.   (AICPA Adapted)

7. A client's physical count of inventories was higher than the inventory quantities per the perpetual records. This situation could be the result of the failure to record

   a. Sales.
   b. Sales discounts.
   c. Purchases.
   d. Purchase returns.   (AICPA Adapted)

8. An auditor will usually trace the details of the test counts made during the observation of the physical inventory taking to a final inventory schedule. This audit procedure is undertaken to provide evidence that items physically present and observed by the auditor at the time of the physical inventory count are

   a. Owned by the client.
   b. Not obsolete.
   c. Physically present at the time of the preparation of the final inventory schedule.
   d. Included in the final inventory schedule.   (AICPA Adapted)

9. An auditor would be most likely to learn of slow-moving inventory through

   a. Inquiry of sales personnel.
   b. Inquiry of stores personnel.

    c. Physical observation of inventory.
    d. Review of perpetual inventory records.   (AICPA Adapted)

10. When an outside specialist has assumed full responsibility for taking the client's physical inventory, reliance on the specialist's report is acceptable if

    a. The auditor is satisfied through application of appropriate procedures as to the reputation and competence of the specialist.
    b. Circumstances made it impracticable or impossible for the auditor either to do the work personally or to observe the work done by the inventory firm.
    c. The auditor conducted the same audit tests and procedures as would have been applicable if the client employees took the physical inventory.
    d. The auditor's report contains a reference to the assumption of full responsibility.   (AICPA Adapted)

Plant Assets

11. To achieve effective control over plant asset additions, a company should establish control procedures that require

    a. Capitalization of the cost of plant asset additions in excess of a specific dollar amount.
    b. Performance of recurring plant asset maintenance work solely by Maintenance Department employees.
    c. Classification as investments those plant asset additions that are not used in the business.
    d. Authorization and approval of major plant asset additions. (AICPA Adapted)

12. With respect to a control procedure that will assure accountability for plant asset retirements, management should implement a system that includes

    a. Continuous analysis of miscellaneous revenue to locate any cash proceeds from sale of plant assets.
    b. Periodic inquiry of plant executives by internal auditors as to whether any plant assets have been retired.
    c. Continuous utilization of serially numbered retirement work orders.
    d. Periodic observation of plant assets by the internal auditors.
                             (AICPA Adapted)

13. Which of the following is an internal control structure deficiency related to factory equipment?

    a. Checks issued in payment of purchases of equipment are not signed by the controller.
    b. All purchases of factory equipment are required to be made by the department in need of the equipment.
    c. Factory equipment replacements are generally made when estimated useful lives, as indicated in depreciation schedules, have expired.
    d. Proceeds from sales of fully depreciated equipment are credited to other income.   (AICPA Adapted)

14. A company has additional temporary funds to invest. The board of directors decided to purchase marketable securities and assigned the future purchase and

sale decisions to a responsible financial executive. The best person(s) to make periodic reviews of the investment activity should be

a. The investment committee of the board of directors.
b. The treasurer.
c. The corporate controller.
d. The chief operating officer.   (AICPA Adapted)

15. In the examination of property, plant, and equipment, the auditor tries to determine all of the following except the

a. Adequacy of internal control.
b. Extent of property abandoned during the year.
c. Adequacy of replacement funds.
d. Reasonableness of the depreciation.   (AICPA Adapted)

16. Which of the following is the best evidence of real estate ownership at the balance sheet date?

a. Title insurance policy.
b. Original deed held in the client's safe.
c. Paid real estate tax bills.
d. Closing statement.   (AICPA Adapted)

17. Which of the following audit procedures would be least likely to lead the auditor to find unrecorded plant asset disposals?

a. Examination of insurance policies.
b. Review of repairs and maintenance expense.
c. Review of property tax files.
d. Scanning of invoices for plant asset additions.   (AICPA Adapted)

18. Which of the following explanations might satisfy an auditor who discovers significant debits to an accumulated depreciation account?

a. Extraordinary repairs have lengthened the life of an asset.
b. Prior years' depreciation charges were erroneously understated.
c. A reserve for possible loss on retirement has been recorded.
d. An asset has been recorded at its fair value.   (AICPA Adapted)

19. The auditor may conclude that depreciation charges are insufficient by noting

a. Insured values greatly in excess of book values.
b. Large amounts of fully depreciated assets.
c. Continuous trade-ins of relatively new assets.
d. Excessive recurring losses on assets retired.   (AICPA Adapted)

20. In violation of company policy, Lowell Company erroneously capitalized the cost of painting its warehouse. The auditor examining Lowell's financial statements would most likely detect this when

a. Discussing capitalization policies with Lowell's controller.
b. Examining maintenance expense accounts.

c. Observing, during the physical inventory observation, that the warehouse had
   been painted.
d. Examining the construction work orders supporting items capitalized during
   the year.   (AICPA Adapted)

PROBLEMS

16-1   Assume you are considering internal control structure in the context of a
client's inventory and plant asset records. System documentation was accomplished
with a flowchart and questionnaire and, in conjunction with a transaction walk-through,
revealed the following potential deficiencies in internal control:
a. Although immaterial in relation to the financial statements taken as a whole, employees sometimes use company assets and tools to build products for home use.
b. Inventory is sometimes misplaced, resulting in potentially time-consuming production delays.
c. During an interim month, the controller observed that inventory containing precious metals was stolen.
d. Delivery trucks were sold during the year without management's knowledge.
e. Scrap sales are sometimes executed but not recorded.
f. Depreciation for the first quarter was inaccurate although not materially misstated.
g. Cash receipts personnel were observed making notations in plant asset records.

Required:
For each potential deficiency, indicate a control procedure(s) that management could
implement to reduce the likelihood of errors or irregularities.

16-2   In connection with your examination of Trowbridge Corporation's June 30,
1990 financial statements, you become aware of the following controls or procedures
over Trowbridge's inventory control and inventory accounting activities.
1. No new products are produced without management's express written authorization.
2. Access to the warehouses is restricted to personnel named in a memorandum
   dated August 10, 1989.
3. Inventory movement into and out of storerooms and production sites is logged in
   journals maintained by inventory control personnel.
4. All personnel named in the August 10, 1989 memorandum (item 2) are bonded
   for loss or theft.
5. Responsibility for handling inventory is segregated from inventory recording, cost
   accounting, and general accounting.
6. All materials release and production forms are maintained under lock and key,
   and are distributed only to authorized personnel.

Required:
For each control procedure, indicate (a) a potential error or irregularity that might be
prevented or detected as a result of the control procedure, and (b) the control objective served by the control procedure. Organize your answer as follows.

Control Procedure	Potential Error or Irregularity That Might Be Prevented or Detected	Control Objective
1.	(a)	(b)

16-3   In connection with the audit of Preston Corporation, Denise Marino, CPA, is drafting an audit program for testing controls over the cost records.

Required:
(1) Explain the importance of determining the disposition of overapplied and under-applied overhead. In your explanation, describe how the overhead should be treated.
(2) List and explain some items that should be included in the overhead. What should not be included?

16-4   Following are selected questions from an internal control questionnaire relating to a company's inventory control, perpetual inventory, and cost records functions. A "Yes" response would indicate a potential strength of the system, and a "No" a potential weakness.
a. Is inventory reasonably protected from physical deterioration and theft?
b. Are materials requisition forms required to request materials and supplies for use in production?
c. Are physical inventory counts taken at least once per year for all inventories?
d. Are perpetual inventory records continually updated on a timely basis?
e. Are perpetual records reconciled with general ledger control accounts on a regular basis?
f. Are all inventory transfers reported and recorded on a timely basis?
g. Are production personnel required to explain price and volume variances?

Required:
Assume that inquiries indicate the answer is "Yes" to each question. Draft tests of controls that you believe would provide persuasive evidence that the answer to each question, *a* through *g,* is correct.

16-5   You are reviewing the inventory control function of a large maintenance operation for city-owned vehicles. At this point, the following information has been discovered:
a. Vehicle maintenance records indicate that the number of inoperative trucks waiting for spare parts is increasing, even though the total number of trucks is decreasing.
b. Stockroom employees have been unable to find some parts, even though the perpetual inventory system shows them as being on hand.
c. The investment in spare-parts inventory has remained at about the same level since the last audit three years ago.
d. Many of the spare parts can be used for passenger cars.
e. The perpetual inventory is maintained on inventory record cards by a clerk in the parts warehouse office.

Required:
Draft tests of controls for each of the five items listed.   (IIA Adapted)

16-6   Following are errors, irregularities, or other circumstances that an auditor might encounter as a result of applying year-end substantive tests of details to inventory as of December 31, 1989:
a. Perpetual inventory records for selected products are not accurate.
b. A material amount of inventory is held in several public warehouses throughout the midwest.
c. Unit prices for selected products on the final-priced inventory appear low; the client uses the first-in, first-out cost flow assumption.
d. The final priced inventory reflects quantities from the perpetual inventory records.
e. Goods were received on December 31, but not recorded until January 2, 1990.
f. The client has begun to lag behind competitors in market share; the client is in the computer components industry.

Required:
For each of the above items, indicate (1) a specific substantive test or tests that might address the error, irregularity, or circumstance, and (2) the audit objective addressed by each test.

16-7   During your examination of the financial statements of The Gary Manufacturing Company for the year ended December 31, 1990, you find that at January 1, 1990, the company had installed the following processing system for recording raw material purchases and related accounts payable:
(a) Vendors' invoices are sent directly to the Accounts Payable Department by the Mail Department.
(b) All supporting documents to the invoices are accumulated in the Accounts Payable Department and attached to the invoices. After being checked and cash discounts computed, the invoices are accumulated in batches and adding machine tapes prepared of the net invoice amounts to provide predetermined totals. Then the batches of invoices and tapes are sent to the Tabulating Department.
(c) In the Tabulating Department keypunch operators prepare for each invoice an accounts payable punched card and one or more punched cards for the related debit distribution to several departmental inventories.
(d) The invoice register is prepared by tab runs of the distribution cards and accounts payable cards. In this run, totals of distribution cards are compared by the tabulating machine with the amounts punched for the related accounts payable cards. Tab run subtotals by invoice batches are taken for checking to the predetermined totals.
(e) The general ledger control account is posted monthly from the totals shown in the invoice register and all other journals.
(f) By sorting, the distribution and accounts payable cards are separated. The distribution cards are filed for further processing. The accounts payable cards are sorted by due dates, and tab runs are prepared to determine cash requirements.
(g) On the due dates the accounts payable cards are processed to prepare combined check and remittance statements.
(h) At the end of the month the accounts payable cards in the unpaid file are tabulated for comparison with the general ledger control account.

Required:
List the audit procedures you would employ in the audit of raw material purchases. Limit your discussion to procedures up to and including the preparation of punched cards.

16-8   Decker, CPA, is performing an examination of the financial statements of Allright Wholesale Sales, Inc., for the year ended December 31, 1990. Allright has been in business for many years and has never had its financial statements audited. Decker has gained satisfaction with respect to the ending inventory and is considering alternative audit procedures to gain satisfaction with respect to management's representations concerning the beginning inventory which was not observed.

Allright sells only one product (bottled brand X beer), and maintains perpetual inventory records. In addition, Allright takes physical inventory counts monthly. Decker has already confirmed purchases with the manufacturer and has decided to concentrate on evaluating the reliability of perpetual inventory records and performing analytical review procedures to the extent that prior years' unaudited records will enable such procedures to be performed.

Required:
What are the audit tests, including analytical procedures, which Decker should apply in evaluating the reliability of perpetual inventory records and gaining satisfaction with respect to the January 1, 1990, inventory?   (AICPA Adapted)

16-9   In connection with his examination of the financial statements of Knutson Products Co., an assembler of home appliances, for the year ended May 31, 1990, Ray Mendez, CPA, is reviewing with Knutson's controller the plans for a physical inventory at the company warehouse on May 31, 1990. *Note:* In answering the two parts of this question do not discuss procedures for the physical inventory of work in process, inventory pricing, or other audit steps not directly related to the physical inventory taking.

Part A. Finished appliances, unassembled parts, and supplies are stored in the warehouse, which is attached to Knutson's assembly plant. The plant will operate during the count. On May 30 the warehouse will deliver to the plant the estimated quantities of unassembled parts and supplies required for May 31 production, but there may be emergency requisitions on May 31. During the count the warehouse will continue to receive parts and supplies and to ship finished appliances. However, appliances completed on May 31 will be held in the plant until after the physical inventory.

Required:
What procedures should the company establish to ensure that the inventory count includes all items that should be included and that nothing is counted twice?

Part B. Warehouse employees will join with Accounting Department employees in counting the inventory. The inventory takers will use a tag system.

Required:
What instructions should the company give to the inventory takers?
                                                                 (AICPA Adapted)

16-10   Late in December 1990, your CPA firm accepted an audit engagement at Fine Jewelers, Inc., a corporation which deals largely in diamonds. The corporation has retail jewelry stores in several Eastern cities and a diamond wholesale store in New York City. The wholesale store also sets the diamonds in rings and in other quality jewelry.

The retail stores place orders for diamond jewelry with the wholesale store in New York City. A buyer employed by the wholesale store purchases diamonds in the New York diamond market, and the wholesale store then fills orders from the retail stores and from independent customers and maintains a substantial inventory of diamonds. The corporation values its inventory by the specific identification cost method.

Required:

Assume that at the inventory date you are satisfied that Fine Jewelers, Inc., has no items left by customers for repair or sale on consignment and that no inventory owned by the corporation is in the possession of outsiders.

(1) Discuss the problems the auditor should anticipate in planning for the observation of the physical inventory on this engagement because of the
  (a) Different locations of the inventories.
  (b) Nature of the inventory.
(2) (a) Explain how your audit program for this inventory would be different from that used for most other inventories.
  (b) Prepare an audit program for the verification of the corporation's diamond and diamond jewelry inventories, identifying any steps which you would apply only to the retail stores or to the wholesale store.
(3) Assume that a shipment of diamond rings was in transit by corporation messenger from the wholesale store to a retail store on the inventory date. What additional audit steps would you take to satisfy yourself as to the gems which were in transit from the wholesale store on the inventory date?   (AICPA Adapted)

16-11   Your audit client, Household Appliances, Inc., operates a retail store in the center of town. Because of lack of storage space, Household keeps inventory that is not on display in a public warehouse outside of town. The warehouse receives inventory from suppliers and, on request from your client by a shipping advice or telephone call, delivers merchandise to customers or to the retail outlet.

The accounts are maintained at the retail store by a bookkeeper. Each month the warehouse sends to the bookkeeper a quantity report indicating opening balance, receipts, deliveries, and ending balance. The bookkeeper compares book quantities on hand at month-end with the warehouse report and adjusts the books to agree with the report. No physical counts of the merchandise at the warehouse were made by your client during the year.

You are now preparing for your examination of the current year's financial statements in this recurring engagement. Last year you rendered an unqualified opinion.

Required:

(1) Prepare an audit program for the observation of the physical inventory of Household Appliances, Inc., (a) at the retail outlet and (b) at the warehouse.
(2) As part of your examination would you verify inventory quantities at the warehouse by means of
  (a) A warehouse confirmation? Why?

(b) Test counts of inventory at the warehouse? Why?

(3) Since the bookkeeper adjusts books to quantities shown on the warehouse report each month, what significance would you attach to the year-end adjustments if they were substantial? Discuss.

(4) Assume you are unable to satisfy yourself as to the inventory at the audit date of Household Appliances, Inc. Could you render an unqualified opinion? Why?

(AICPA Adapted)

16-12   The year-end physical inventory of a large wholesaler of automotive parts has just been completed. The auditor reviewed the inventory-taking instructions before the start of the physical inventory, made and recorded test counts, and observed the controls over the inventory-taking process. No significant exceptions to the process were observed. Subsequent comparisons by the auditor of the quantities shown on the count sheets with those listed on the perpetual inventory cards disclosed numerous discrepancies.

Required:
Other than theft, what are the likely causes of such discrepancies?   (IIA Adapted)

16-13   Following the observation of a physical inventory, the auditor compared the physical inventory counts with the perpetual inventory records and noted that there were apparent shortages. These shortages were materially greater than those found at the end of the previous year.

Required:
a. Identify possible causes, other than theft, for the differences between the physical counts and the perpetual inventory records.
b. Briefly describe potential adverse effects on the organization which could be caused by the differences.
c. Assuming that the cause of the differences was theft, give recommendations to prevent theft.   (IIA Adapted)

16-14   Donna Anderson, CPA, is engaged in the examination of the financial statements of Redondo Manufacturing Corporation for the year ended June 30, 1990. Redondo's inventories at year-end include finished merchandise on consignment with consignees, and finished merchandise held in public warehouses. The merchandise held in public warehouses is pledged as collateral for outstanding debt.

Required:
Normal inventory and notes payable auditing procedures have been satisfactorily completed. Describe the specific additional auditing procedures that Anderson should undertake with respect to:
(1) Consignments out.
(2) Finished merchandise in public warehouses pledged as collateral for outstanding debt.   (AICPA Adapted)

16-15   Ace Corporation does not conduct a complete annual physical count of purchased parts and supplies in its principal warehouse but uses statistical sampling instead to estimate the year-end inventory. Ace maintains a perpetual inventory record of parts and supplies and believes that statistical sampling is highly effective in determining inventory values and is sufficiently reliable to make a physical count of each item of inventory unnecessary.

Required:

(1) Identify the audit procedures that should be used by the independent auditor that change or are in addition to normal required audit procedures when a client utilizes statistical sampling to determine inventory value and does not conduct a 100 percent annual physical count of inventory items.

(2) List at least ten normal audit procedures that should be performed to verify physical quantities whenever a client conducts a periodic physical count of all or part of its inventory.   (AICPA Adapted)

16-16   LOC Container Corporation is in the process of preparing its annual financial statements for the fiscal year ended April 30, 1990. Because all of LOC Container's shares are traded intrastate, the company does not have to file any reports with the Securities and Exchange Commission. The company manufactures plastic, glass, and paper containers for sale to food and drink manufacturers and distributors. LOC Container Corporation maintains separate control accounts for its raw materials, work-in-process, and finished goods inventories for each of the three types of containers. The inventories are valued at the lower of cost or market.

The company's plant assets are classified into the following major classes: land, office buildings, furniture and fixtures, manufacturing facilities, manufacturing equipment, and leasehold improvements. All plant assets are carried at cost. The depreciation methods employed depend upon the type of asset (its classification) and when it was acquired.

LOC Container Corporation plans to present the inventory and plant asset amounts in its April 30, 1990, balance sheet as follows.

Inventories $1,659,609
Property, plant, and equipment (net of depreciation) $3,578,475

Required:

What information regarding inventories and plant assets must be disclosed by LOC Container Corporation in the audited financial statements issued to stockholders in either the body or the notes, for the 1989–90 fiscal year?   (CMA Adapted)

16-17   In connection with your examination of Gatehouse & Company's financial statements, you became aware of the following control procedures for Gatehouse's plant asset activities:

1. All scrapped assets are agreed with published price lists before being offered for sale, and are never sold for amounts significantly below established prices.

2. Procedures for operating, using, moving, and controlling plant assets are firmly established in periodically updated procedures manuals.

3. Procedures are established for identifying assets as potential scrap sale items, although actual sales must first be approved by division managers.

4. Physical custody over plant assets is segregated from recording.

5. Plant assets on the floor are periodically reconciled with plant asset records, and vice versa.

Required:
For each control procedure, indicate (a) a potential error or irregularity that might be prevented as a result of the control/procedure, and (b) the control objective served by the control procedure. Organize your answer as follows:

Control Procedure	Potential Error or Irregularity That Might Be Prevented	Control Objective
1.	(a)	(b)

16-18   A preliminary survey of a maintenance service operation for office machines and equipment produced the following information:
1. The manager of the maintenance service operation stated that, in his opinion, the objective of the organization was to respond to calls for service in a minimum time.
2. When a backlog of service calls accumulated, a contract was issued to a local repair organization to assist in covering the overload.
3. The manager assured the auditor that the maintenance service operation was very efficient.
4. More experienced repairmen were used to respond to second calls when the original repairs were not effective.
5. A comprehensive perpetual inventory system was maintained for all repair parts and supplies.

Required:
For *each* of the *five* items above, list *two* key questions relating to this operation that the auditor would attempt to answer in performing the audit.   (IIA Adapted)

16-19   Following are selected questions from an internal control questionnaire relating to a company's plant asset records, additions, disposals, retirements, and depreciation functions. A "Yes" response would indicate a potential strength of the system, and a "No" a potential weakness.
a. Are procedures followed to determine whether recorded plant assets actually exist?
b. Is insurance coverage maintained and reviewed for all plant assets?
c. Do procedures require authorization by the board of directors or senior management for plant asset additions?
d. Are actual expenditures for plant assets compared with amounts authorized?
e. Are procedures established to assure that the proceeds from plant asset disposals are recorded properly and deposited?
f. Are plant asset disposals and retirements promptly reported to general accounting for recording gains and losses?
g. Are procedures established to assure that additions are added to depreciation records and disposals/retirements deleted?

Required:
Assume that inquiries indicate the answer is "Yes" to each question. Draft a test of controls that you believe would provide persuasive evidence that the answer to each question, *a* through *g*, is correct.

16-20   Following are errors, irregularities, or other circumstances that an auditor might encounter as a result of applying year-end substantive tests of details to plant assets as of December 31, 1990:

a. During the physical inventory observation, the auditor sees machinery not present during the December 31, 1989 physical inventory.
b. Separate detailed records are now maintained for all plant assets.
c. New equipment was installed during late December and early January.
d. Depreciation expense is lower than in 1989, and yet additions far exceeded disposals and retirements in 1990.
e. Equipment may have been disposed of, but the disposal was not recorded.

Required:

For each of the above items, indicate (1) a specific substantive test or tests that might address the error, irregularity, or circumstance, and (2) the audit objective addressed by each test.

16-21   In connection with a recurring examination of the financial statements of the Louis Manufacturing Company for the year ended December 31, you have been assigned the audit of these accounts: manufacturing equipment, manufacturing equipment — accumulated depreciation, and repairs to manufacturing equipment. Your review of Louis's policies and procedures has disclosed the following pertinent information:

(a) The manufacturing equipment account includes the net invoice price plus related freight and installation costs for all of the equipment in Louis's manufacturing plant.
(b) The manufacturing equipment and accumulated depreciation accounts are supported by a subsidiary ledger which shows the cost and accumulated depreciation for each piece of equipment.
(c) An annual budget for capital expenditures of $1,000 or more is prepared by the budget committee and approved by the board of directors. Capital expenditures over $1,000 which are not included in this budget must be approved by the board of directors, and variations of 20% or more must be explained to the board. Approval by the supervisor of production is required for capital expenditures under $1,000.
(d) Company employees handle installation, removal, repair, and rebuilding of the machinery. Work orders are prepared for these activities and are subject to the same budgetary control as other expenditures. Work orders are not required for internal expenditures.

Required:

(1) Cite the major objectives of your audit of the manufacturing equipment, manufacturing equipment — accumulated depreciation, and repairs of manufacturing equipment accounts. Do not include in this listing the auditing procedures designed to accomplish these objectives.
(2) Prepare the portion of your audit program applicable to the review of current year additions to the manufacturing equipment account.   (AICPA Adapted)

16-22   Rivers, CPA, is the auditor for a manufacturing company with a balance sheet that includes the caption "Property, Plant, and Equipment." Rivers has been asked by the company's management if audit adjustments or reclassifications are required for the following material items that have been included or excluded from "Property, Plant and Equipment."

(a) A tract of land was acquired during the year. The land is the future site of the client's new headquarters which will be constructed in the following year. Commissions were paid to the real estate agent used to acquire the land, and expenditures were made to relocate the previous owner's equipment. These commissions and expenditures were expensed and are excluded from "Property, Plant and Equipment."

(b) Clearing costs were incurred to make the land ready for construction. These costs were included in "Property, Plant and Equipment."

(c) During the land clearing process, timber and gravel were recovered and sold. The proceeds from the sale were recorded as other income and are excluded from "Property, Plant and Equipment."

(d) A group of machines was purchased under a royalty agreement which provides royalty payments based on units of production from the machines. The cost of the machines, freight costs, unloading charges, and royalty payments were capitalized and are included in "Property, Plant and Equipment."

Required:

(1) Describe the general characteristics of assets, such as land, buildings, improvements, machinery, equipment, fixtures, etc., that should normally be classified as "Property, Plant and Equipment," and identify audit objectives (i.e., how an auditor can obtain audit satisfaction) in connection with the examination of "Property, Plant and Equipment." Do not discuss specific audit procedures.

(2) Indicate whether each of the items (a) to (d) requires one or more audit adjustments or reclassifications, and explain why such adjustments or reclassifications are required or not required.

Organize your answer as follows:

Item Number	Is Audit Adjustment or Reclassification Required? Yes or No	Reasons Why Audit Adjustment or Reclassification Is Required or Not Required

(AICPA Adapted)

16-23   Terra Land Development Corporation is a closely held family corporation engaged in the business of purchasing large tracts of land, subdividing the tracts, and installing paved streets and utilities. The corporation does not construct buildings for the buyers of the land and does not have any affiliated construction companies. Undeveloped land is usually leased for farming until the corporation is ready to begin developing it.

The corporation finances its land acquisitions by mortgages; the mortgagees require audited financial statements. This is your first audit of the company, and you have now begun the examination of the financial statements for the year ended December 31, 1990.

Your preliminary review of the accounts has indicated that the corporation would have had a highly profitable year except that the corporate officers — all members of the family owning the corporation — were reimbursed for exceptionally large travel and entertainment expenses.

Required:

The corporation has three tracts of land in various stages of development. List the audit procedures to be employed in the verification of the physical existence of and title to the corporation's three landholdings.　　　　　　　　(AICPA Adapted)

16-24　　You are engaged in the examination of the financial statements of the Ute Corp. for the year ended December 31, 1990. The following schedules for plant assets and related allowance for depreciation accounts have been prepared by the client. You have checked the opening balances with your prior year's audit working papers.

Ute Corp.
Analysis of Plant Assets and
Related Allowance for Depreciation Accounts
Year Ended December 31, 1990

Description	Final 12/31/89	Additions	Retirements	Per Book 12/31/90
Land	$ 22,500	$ 15,000		$ 37,500
Buildings	120,000	175,000		295,000
Machinery and equipment . . .	385,000	40,400	$26,000	399,400
	$527,500	$230,400	$26,000	$731,900

Allowance for Depreciation

Description	Final 12/31/89	Additions*	Retirements	Per Books 12/31/90
Buildings	$ 60,000	$ 8,300		$ 68,300
Machinery and equipment . . .	173,250	39,220		212,470
	$233,250	$47,520		$280,770

*Depreciation expense for the year.

Your examination reveals the following information:
(a) All equipment is depreciated on the straight-line basis (no salvage value taken into consideration) based on the following estimated lives: buildings, 25 years; all other items, 10 years. The company's policy is to take one-half year's depreciation on all asset acquisitions and disposals during the year.
(b) On April 1 the company entered into a ten-year lease contract for a die casting machine with annual rentals of $5,000 payable in advance every April 1. The lease is cancelable by either party (sixty days written notice is required), and

there is no option to renew the lease or buy the equipment at the end of the lease. The estimated useful life of the machine is ten years with no salvage value. The company recorded the die casting machine in the machinery and equipment account at $40,400, the discounted present value at the date of the lease, and $2,020, applicable to the machine, has been included in depreciation expense for the year.

(c) The company completed the construction of a wing on the factory building on June 30. The useful life of the building was not extended by this addition. The lowest construction bid received was $175,000 — the amount recorded in the buildings account. Company personnel were used to construct the addition at a cost of $160,000 (materials, $75,000; labor, $55,000; and overhead, $30,000).

(d) On August 18, $15,000 was paid for paving and fencing a portion of land owned by the company and used as a parking lot for employees. The expenditure was charged to the land account.

(e) The amount shown in the machinery and equipment asset retirement column represents cash received on September 5 upon disposal of a machine purchased in July, 1986, for $48,000. The bookkeeper recorded depreciation expense of $3,500 on this machine in 1990.

(f) Crux City donated land and building appraised at $100,000 and $400,000, respectively, to the Ute Corporation for a plant. On September 1 the company began operating the plant. Since no costs were involved, the bookkeeper made no entry for the transaction.

Required:
Prepare the formal adjusting journal entries that you would suggest at December 31, 1990, to adjust the accounts for transactions (a) to (f). Disregard income tax implications. The books have not been closed. Computations should be rounded to the nearest dollar.   (AICPA Adapted)

16-25   In connection with the annual examination of Johnson Corp., a manufacturer of janitorial supplies, you have been assigned to audit the plant assets. The company maintains a detailed property ledger for all plant assets. You prepare an audit program for the asset balances, but have yet to prepare one for accumulated depreciation and depreciation expense.

Required:
Prepare a separate comprehensive audit program for the accumulated depreciation and depreciation expense accounts.   (AICPA Adapted)

16-26   During an examination of the financial statements of Gole Inc., Robbins, CPA, requested and received a client-prepared property casualty insurance schedule which included appropriate premium information.

Required:
(1) Identify the type of information, in addition to the appropriate premium information, that would ordinarily be expected to be included in a property casualty insurance schedule.

(2) What are the basic audit procedures which Robbins should perform in examining the client-prepared property casualty insurance schedule?

TESTS OF CONTROLS AND SUBSTANTIVE TESTS OF THE FINANCING CYCLE: INVESTMENTS, DEBT, AND EQUITY

17

Major topics discussed in this chapter are the:

▲ *Nature of the financing cycle.*

▲ *Controls over the custody, recording, valuation, acquisition, and sale of investments and over the issuance and retirement of long-term debt and equity securities.*

▲ *An auditor's consideration of internal control structure in the financing cycle.*

▲ *Audit objectives and substantive tests of investments, long-term debt, and equity balances.*

This chapter introduces tests of controls and substantive tests applicable to three major financing cycle accounts: investments, long-term debt, and equity. The chapter begins by summarizing the nature of the financing cycle and by introducing controls over the custody, recording, acquisition, and sale of investments and over the issuance and retirement of debt instruments and equity securities. In turn, the nature of an auditor's consideration of internal control structure in the financing cycle is introduced, and detailed substantive tests are explained.

THE NATURE OF THE FINANCING CYCLE

In general, the financing cycle encompasses an entity's business functions and activities related to generating capital funds. The financing cycle is directly related to two of the other cycles: it uses resources and information provided by the expenditure/disbursement cycle, and provides resources and information to the revenue/receipt cycle. For example, the financing cycle might cause a cash disbursement (expenditure/disbursement cycle) to retire long-term debt and a cash receipt (revenue/receipt cycle) from the sale of capital stock.

Figure 17-1 summarizes the scope of the financing cycle, listing the cycle's primary business functions and common activities, journal entries,

682

FIGURE 17-1
The Scope of the Financing Cycle

Primary Business Functions	Common Activities	Common Entries	Common Forms
	Investments		
• Capital funds are received from investors and creditors.	• Custody • Recording • Valuation • Acquisitions and sales • Income	• Investment acquisitions • Investment sales • Interest income • Dividend income	• Bond certificates • Commercial paper • Stock certificates • Treasury bills
	Debt		
• Capital funds are used for operations or temporarily invested until needed for operations.	• Recording • Incurrence and retirement • Interest	• Debt incurrence • Debt retirement • Interest expense	• Bond certificates • Notes
	Equity		
	• Recording • Issuance and retirement • Dividends	• Stock issuance • Stock retirement • Dividends	• Stock certificates

and forms. Two major business functions are associated with the financing cycle:

▲ Capital funds are received from investors and creditors.
▲ Capital funds are used for operations or temporarily invested until needed for operations.

Several internal activities relate to these two functions. The cycle begins with management decisions about the optimum sources of capital funds from debt and equity financing, and optimum allocation of funds between internal operations and external investments. In turn, the cycle encompasses payment of dividends on capital stock and interest on debt, and the redemption of capital stock (treasury stock transactions) and retirement of debt.

Throughout the financing cycle, journal entries are made for the issuance and retirement of debt and capital stock, and the acquisition and sale of investments. Common forms and documents include:

▲ *Bond certificate:* A document (debt security) representing a stated amount of corporate debt. Bond certificates are frequently issued in denominations of $1,000.

▲ *Commercial paper:* A general category of commercial loan instruments, due and payable in accordance with terms described on the instrument.

▲ *Stock certificate:* A document (equity security) representing ownership of a stated number of shares of capital stock.

▲ *Treasury bill:* A debt instrument issued by the U.S. Treasury Department.

Following are internal control structure considerations for the three major groups of transactions underlying the financing cycle: investments in marketable securities, the issuance of long-term debt securities, and the issuance of equity securities. Investments are discussed first, followed thereafter by debt, and in turn by equity.

Investments

Depending on cash position and operating cash requirements, a company may invest resources in (1) marketable debt instruments and marketable equity securities, such as instruments representing ownership (e.g., common and preferred stock) or rights to acquire ownership (e.g., warrants, rights, and call options) or dispose of ownership (e.g., put options), or (2) government obligations such as U.S. Treasury bills. The financing cycle processes current and noncurrent investments, directing resources into other private- and public-sector equity and debt instruments, with the objective of optimizing financial return on idle cash. In short, the financing cycle processes transactions which convert internal resources into external investments, liquidating when necessary to convert external investments into cash either for internal working capital needs or for alternative investments.

The major functions and controls related to investments are discussed in the following sections. Custody, recording, and valuation are addressed first, followed by acquisitions, sales, and income.

Custody, Recording, and Valuation. Generally, a company's investment securities are maintained in the custody of either internal officials or independent external custodians, such as stock brokerage firms. If securities are maintained internally, at least two officials should be held jointly responsible, thereby minimizing the likelihood of unauthorized sales in the absence of collusion. Securities maintained by internal parties should be counted periodically on a surprise basis by employees who do not otherwise have custody or access.

An employee independent of the custodial function should maintain detailed records for securities held, compiling information such as certificate numbers and quantities. Detailed records provide a control over securities that should be in the custody of either external custodians or internal officials. If maintained externally, securities listings should be prepared by the custodian at least monthly, mailed to the company, and reconciled with detailed internal records.

According to Financial Accounting Standards Board *Statement of Financial Accounting Standards No. 12,* ''Accounting for Certain Marketable Securities,'' marketable securities should be grouped into separate portfolios according to current and noncurrent classifications, and each portfolio should be reported at the lower of its aggregate cost or market value. As a result, information about security values must be obtained at the balance sheet date, preferably by employees independent of both custodians and officials responsible for acquisitions and sales.

Acquisitions, Sales, and Income. All acquisitions and sales of current and noncurrent securities should be authorized by the board of directors or an appropriately authorized investment committee. Periodically, recorded acquisition and selling prices should be compared with published price quotations, assuring that transactions were recorded at accurate prices.

Debt and equity securities yield income in the form of interest and dividends, respectively, and result in gains or losses when sold. Dividend income should be recognized when declared, interest income accrued when earned, and gains and losses recorded when the securities are sold. Periodically, recorded income, gains, and losses should be recalculated by employees not otherwise responsible for the custody, acquisition, or sale of securities.

Debt

Long-term debt, such as bonds and loans, is incurred to generate capital funds for internal or external investment potentially yielding a rate of return greater than the cost of debt financing. For example, an entity would issue ten percent, ten-year bonds only if the internal rate of return, for example, is higher than ten percent; otherwise, the debt issuance would not be economically feasible.

Generally, debt incurrence and retirement transactions are relatively few in number, but are usually accompanied by extensive supporting documentation (e.g., SEC filings, bond issuance authorizations from shareholders and the board of directors). The financing cycle processes debt incurrence and retirement transactions, directing resources through the revenue/receipt and expenditure/disbursement cycles, respectively. Following are specific control techniques related to several of the more common debt-related financing cycle activities: recording, incurrence, retirement, and interest.

All long-term debt, such as bonds and loans should be authorized by the board of directors. Authorizations should be expressly documented in the board's minutes, clearly indicating maximum indebtedness and the names of officers authorized to negotiate the transaction.

Typically, debt instruments such as loan agreements contain restrictive covenants which, if violated by a debtor, could result in the debt becoming due immediately. For example, a restrictive covenant might cause a loan to become due if a debtor's current ratio falls below a predetermined level. Interestingly, even if a debtor violates a restrictive covenant, the creditor is not likely to know without investigating. As a result, creditors often require that debtors submit periodic compliance reports, thereby providing a formal, though unaudited, barometer of debt covenant compliance.

Bonds and notes present additional control problems, since unissued instruments are held by the entity and are therefore susceptible to errors or irregularities. Unissued bonds and notes should be prenumbered consecutively and controlled by an employee who neither maintains detailed debt records nor has access to general accounting records. Periodically, an independent employee should physically inspect unissued debt instruments and account for the numerical sequence.

When retired, debt instruments should either be canceled — for example, by perforation — or be destroyed. Records should be kept for canceled instruments, and affidavits from witnesses kept for destroyed instruments.

All debt instruments should be accounted for in detailed records often called *bond* or *note registers*. The registers should be maintained by an employee not otherwise responsible for the custody, incurrence, or redemption of long-term debt. Periodically, an independent employee should reconcile the registers with the general ledger. An authorized employee should calculate interest expense in accordance with the terms of each instrument, and the resulting payments should be processed through the expenditure/disbursement cycle.

Equity

Equity securities (common and preferred stock) are issued by a company in order to generate capital funds for internal investment. Like long-term debt incurrence and retirement, equity issuance and retirement transactions are generally not numerous, but are usually supported by extensive documentation (e.g., authorizations, SEC registration statements). The financing cycle processes equity issuance and retirement transactions, directing resources through the revenue/receipt and expenditure/disbursement cycles, respectively. Following are specific control techniques related to several of the more common equity-related financing cycle activities: recording, issuance, retirement, and dividends.

All transactions relating to equity securities — including issuance, retirement, and dividend distributions — should be formally authorized by the board of directors and documented. Some transactions may also require stockholder approval in accordance with state laws or corporation bylaws. All issuances and retirements should be approved in both price and quantity by the board of directors either specifically or generally, as in the case of authorized stock option plans.

Stock certificates should be prenumbered consecutively, signed by authorized officers when issued, and promptly canceled when surrendered for retirement. Unissued certificates should be physically safeguarded and access limited to authorized individuals. Treasury shares which have not been retired and canceled should be adequately accounted for and controlled.

Many companies enhance control over equity securities by utilizing independent external *registrars* and *transfer agents* (e.g., investment bankers) to assure that securities are properly issued, recorded, and transferred. In other companies, however, detailed equity securities records are maintained internally by employees, necessitating particularly effective internal controls, since in many cases securities can be easily converted into cash. If maintained internally, the custody of stock certificates, processing of stock transactions, and detailed record keeping should each be performed by separate officials or employees.

Depending on the materiality and volume of stock transactions, a company's detailed records might include a *stockholder's ledger* to account for outstanding shares and owners, a *transfer journal* to record shares transferred, and *certificate control records* to account for the numbers of issued and unissued shares. The stockholders' ledger should be up to date, particularly as of dividend record dates, and periodically reconciled with the transfer journal and certificate control records. The reconciliations should be performed by an employee not otherwise responsible for the records. If an entity has stock option plans or convertible securities (e.g., convertible preferred stock or bonds) outstanding, adequate records of equity shares reserved for potential issuance should also be maintained. A company should maintain adequate procedures and policies to assure that all applicable SEC filing requirements are met, and that stock exchange regulations and security laws are not violated. Some of these filing requirements, regulations, and laws are discussed in Chapter 4.

Unlike interest on long-term debt which must be paid in accordance with debt instruments outstanding, dividends on capital stock are paid only if declared by the board of directors. Cash dividends to individual shareholders should be computed from record-date information in the stockholders' ledger and paid from a special bank account reserved for dividend payments. The dividend bank account should be reconciled periodically by an independent employee not otherwise responsible for maintaining stockholder records or processing dividend payments. Although not usually a significant problem, unclaimed dividend checks, resulting for example from incorrect stockholder mailing addresses, should be returned to an independent official and controlled until resolved.

Internal Control Structure Objectives and Potential Errors or Irregularities: Investments, Debt, and Equity

The following discussion focuses on internal control structure in the context of investments, debt, and equity. As in previous chapters, the discussion identifies control objectives related to transaction authorization, execution, and recording and access to assets. Examples of potential errors or irregularities are described, along with examples of control procedures often used to prevent or detect the errors or irregularities. Figure 17-2 summarizes the discussion.

Transaction Authorization. Before trading securities on the capital markets, all investment acquisitions and sales should be authorized in accordance with management's criteria, as discussed earlier. Likewise, the sources of capital funds — debt and capital stock — should be authorized. Lacking authorization, investments could be made in violation of company policies. For example, bonds could be purchased without regard for the fact that the board of directors resolved to restrict investment in non-AAA bonds to five percent of the total investment portfolio. In addition, capital funds could be obtained at excessive interest rates or overly restrictive debt covenants, resulting in uneconomical financing. To control these potential errors, management could establish policies for selecting and approving investment transactions and for obtaining capital funds, and prepare lists of authorized investments if necessary.

Journal entries that adjust investment carrying values and debt obligations should be authorized in accordance with management's criteria; otherwise, unauthorized or incorrect adjustments could be made, potentially re-

FIGURE 17-2

Investments, Debt, and Equity: Objectives, Potential Errors or Irregularities, and Control Procedures

Objective	Types of Errors or Irregularities That Could Occur if Objective Is Not Met	Control Procedures That Should Prevent or Detect Errors or Irregularities
TRANSACTION AUTHORIZATION AND EXECUTION:		
• Investment transactions (marketable securities, long-term debt, and equity investments) should be made in accordance with management's authorization.	Investments could be made in violation of company policies (e.g., an investment portfolio that includes more debt instruments than allowed by the board of directors), potentially resulting in more risk on investments than desired.	Establish policies for selecting and approving investment transactions. Prepare lists of authorized investments.
• Sources of capital funds—debt and equity—should be authorized in accordance with management's criteria.	Capital funds could be obtained at unfavorable terms/cost or overly restrictive covenants, potentially resulting in uneconomical financing.	Establish policies for obtaining capital funds.
• Adjustment of investments (e.g., adjustment of carrying values), debt (e.g., adjustment of debt obligations after renegotiation), and equity (e.g., changes to par or stated value of stock) should be authorized in accordance with management's criteria.	Unauthorized or incorrect adjustments could be made, potentially resulting in misstated accounts and violations of loan covenants.	Establish policies for approving investment, debt, and equity adjustments. Prenumber and control adjustment forms. Require specific authorization for adjustments exceeding preestablished dollar amounts.

FIGURE 17-2 (*Continued*)

Objective	Types of Errors or Irregularities That Could Occur if Objective Is Not Met	Control Procedures That should Prevent or Detect Errors of Irregularities
RECORDING: • Investment, debt, and equity transactions should be recorded at the correct amounts, be recorded in the proper period, and be properly classified.	Detailed or subsidiary records may be inaccurate, potentially resulting in inaccurate account balances and misstated financial statements.	Establish processing and recording procedures. Review board minutes regularly for directives related to dividend, long-term debt, and treasury transactions. Prepare schedules of interest and loan payment due dates.
ACCESS TO ASSETS: • Access to securities should be restricted to personnel authorized by management.	Securities may be lost, stolen, destroyed, or diverted, potentially resulting in misapplied resources and misstated accounts.	Establish physical barriers over investment securities (e.g., locked safes), or place them with independent parties, such as brokers. Carry insurance and fidelity bonds. Maintain files of authorized signatures. Segregate investment approval from accounting and from custody of securities.
• Access to investment-, debt-, and equity-related records and forms should be restricted	Records may be lost or stolen, potentially resulting in an inability to prepare accurate carrying values.	Establish physical barriers over forms and records. Prenumber critical forms.

Objective	Types of Errors or Irregularities That Could Occur if Objective Is Not Met	Control Procedures That Should Prevent or Detect Errors or Irregularities
to personnel authorized by management.	Forms could be used to sell securities and divert the cash proceeds, potentially resulting in misappropriated assets and misstated financial statements.	Carry insurance and fidelity bonds. Account for all unissued, issued, and retired securities, by an official independent of physically controlling securities, accounting, and cash activities.

sulting in misstated accounts and violations of loan covenants. To control adjustments, management could establish processing procedures, prenumber and control adjustment forms, and require specific authorization for adjustments exceeding preestablished amounts.

Recording. If detailed or subsidiary records are inaccurate, then account balances may be inaccurate and financial statements misstated. As a result, all investment, debt, and equity transactions should be recorded at the correct amounts, be recorded in the proper period, and be classified properly. Management could control against inaccurate records by establishing processing and recording procedures, regularly reviewing board minutes for financing cycle resolutions, and preparing schedules of interest and loan payment due dates.

Access to Assets. Apart from cash, no other asset is more susceptible to irregularities than investment securities — there is a ready market for them, and as a result, they can be converted into cash easily. Therefore, access to securities should be restricted to personnel authorized by management. Otherwise, securities may be lost or stolen, potentially resulting in misapplied resources and misstated accounts. Management can help control securities by establishing physical barriers, such as fireproof safes. Alternatively, securities can be held by independent custodians such as brokerage houses. In addition, personnel responsible for approving investments should not also be responsible for recording or for maintaining custody of the securities.

To protect capital funds, access to investment-, debt-, and equity-related records and forms should be restricted to personnel authorized by management. If access is not restricted, records may be lost or stolen, or forms could be used to sell securities and divert the cash proceeds. Management could control access by establishing physical barriers over prenumbered forms and records, and by carrying insurance and fidelity bonds. Also, officials responsible for accounting for unissued, issued, and retired securities should not also be responsible for physically controlling securities or for performing accounting and cash activities.

CONSIDERING INTERNAL CONTROL STRUCTURE IN THE FINANCING CYCLE

As discussed in Chapter 7, an auditor considers an entity's internal control structure as a basis for assessing control risk and thus determining the nature, timing, and extent of substantive tests. However, in some instances, an auditor may conclude that the volume of transactions is not sufficiently large to justify the cost of performing tests of controls for selected transactions or transaction cycles. In these instances, the auditor normally would not rely on the internal control structure. Rather, the auditor would omit tests of controls, electing instead to obtain an understanding of the system sufficient for planning the audit and, therefore, to rely exclusively or primarily on substantive tests of account balances.

Except in some large publicly traded corporations, the volume of transactions relating to marketable securities, long-term debt, and equity is not often sufficient to justify a complete consideration of internal control structure as described in Chapter 7. At a minimum, however, the auditor should review the system to obtain sufficient knowledge and understanding of the system to design and implement effective substantive tests. The following discussion briefly describes an auditor's review of the system for investments, debt, and equity.

Investments

If an entity's investments are maintained by an independent external custodian such as a broker, the auditor's review of the system will consist primarily of obtaining an understanding of how investment transactions are authorized and how documentation from the custodian is recorded in the general ledger. As a result, when custodians are used, transaction execution — that is, the purchase and sale of securities — and access to assets are of less concern to the auditor, since they are handled by independent external parties. In contrast, if securities are maintained by internal officials such as a corporate secretary, the auditor must be concerned with transaction authorization, execution, recording, and access to assets, since all aspects of investment transactions are handled internally, and inadequate segregation of duties can lead to irregularities.

Flowcharts are not often used to document an entity's investment system, unless investment transactions are numerous and entail significant dollar amounts. More often, auditors use questionnaires similar to Figure 17-3 to identify deficiencies, and narratives to document procedures for the custody, recording, valuation, acquisition, and sale of investments.

Long-Term Debt and Equity

As with investments, the auditor's review of a client's debt and equity issuance and retirement procedures is crucial, since the auditor will require an understanding of the procedures in order to design substantive tests. Unless debt and equity transactions are numerous, though, auditors typically use questionnaires similar to Figure 17-4 for debt and Figure 17-5 for equity rather than flowcharting the system.

The following discussion focuses on substantive tests for investments, debt, and equity. The discussion assumes that a complete consideration of internal control structure has not been performed.

FINANCIAL STATEMENT ASSERTIONS, OBJECTIVES, AND AUDIT PROCEDURES

Within the financing cycle, investments, long-term debt, and capital stock are typically the most material financial statement account balances. Each account is discussed below in the context of the audit procedures commonly used by auditors to address each of the audit objectives introduced in Chapter 6: existence or occurrence, completeness, rights and obligations, valuation or allocation, and presentation and disclosure. Figure 17-6 relates each objective to specific audit procedures, and summarizes the discussion that follows.

Existence or Occurrence

Within the financing cycle, the existence or occurrence objective addresses whether all recorded investments, debt, and capital stock exist at the

FIGURE 17-3   Performed by: _____

Questionnaire: Investments   Date: _____

                                           Answer:
                                           Yes, No,
                    Question   or N/A   Remarks

Custody, Recording, and Valuation

   1. Are securities and other negotiable instru-
      ments in the custody of an independent cus-
      todian? If not, are they adequately secured
      (e.g., locked safe)?
   2. Are at least two officials responsible for in-
      ternally held securities?
   3. Is a detailed record of securities maintained
      by an offical independent of officials respon-
      sible for custody?
   4. Is the listing of investments periodically rec-
      onciled with investment records?
   5. Are securities in the name of the client (or
      restrictively endorsed in the name of the
      client)?
   6. Are independent officials responsible for re-
      viewing and reporting changing securities'
      values?
   7. Are adequately detailed investment records
      and general ledger control accounts main-
      tained for the various investment classifica-
      tions?

Acquisitions, Sales, and Income

   1. Are acquisitions and sales of investment se-
      curities authorized by the board of directors
      or a duly authorized investment committee?
   2. Are brokers, custodians, or other intermedi-
      aries authorized or designated by the board
      of directors?
   3. Are broker's advices promptly compared
      with documented acquisition and sales au-
      thorizations?
   4. Is an independent check made to determine
      whether acquisition or sale prices are fair
      and objective?
   5. Is investment income (e.g., interest, divi-
      dends) periodically recalculated and veri-
      fied?

FIGURE 17-4   Prepared by: _____

Questionnaire: Debt   Date: _____

Question	Answer: Yes, No, or N/A	Remarks
1. Are all long-term debt and other borrowings authorized by the board of directors?		
2. Is an officer responsible for determining whether all debt covenants are complied with?		
3. Are unissued bonds and notes prenumbered consecutively and controlled by an official independent of recording?		
4. Are all retired debt instruments canceled or destroyed?		
5. Are adequately detailed bond and note registers and general ledger accounts maintained for the various debt classifications?		
6. Are interest payments and accruals periodically recalculated?		

balance sheet date and whether all recorded investment, debt, and capital stock transactions occurred during the period.

Testing the existence or occurrence objective for investments depends on whether securities are maintained externally by an independent trustee/broker or internally by authorized personnel. If securities are maintained externally, the auditor would confirm balances with the independent trustee or broker; if held internally, the auditor would physically inspect and count all securities on hand. In turn, cutoff testing also addresses existence or occurrence by assuring that all investment-related transactions are recorded in the proper accounting period.

The existence or occurrence of long-term debt can be tested three ways. First, all recorded loans and other notes payable — including terms, due dates, and accrued interest — are confirmed with creditors. Second, to support the results of confirmation procedures, the auditor physically examines all bond indentures and other long-term indebtedness agreements, thereby determining whether all outstanding debt was confirmed. Third, the auditor physically inspects unissued instruments, thereby testing whether all issued securities are

---

FIGURE 17-5   Prepared by: _____
Questionnaire: Equity   Date: _____

                                          Answer:
                                          Yes, No,
               Question   or N/A   Remarks
               _____   _____   _____

1. Are all capital stock issuances, retirements,
   and dividend distributions authorized by the
   board of directors?
2. Are capital stock transactions authorized by
   stockholder vote, where required by state
   law?
3. Are unissued stock certificates prenumbered
   consecutively and safeguarded?
4. Are independent registrars and transfer
   agents authorized by the board of directors?
5. Are detailed capital stock records such as a
   stockholders' ledger, transfer journal, and
   certificate control records and general ledger
   control accounts maintained for the various
   capital stock classifications?
6. Are detailed capital stock records maintained by officials independent of the custody for securities?
7. Are treasury shares adequately controlled
   and accounted for?
8. Are procedures established to assure that the
   entity is complying with stock exchange and
   securities laws?
9. Are dividend payments and accruals periodically recalculated?

---

recorded as long-term debt. That is, long-term debt could be understated if a debt instrument were neither on hand nor recorded.

For capital stock, an auditor tests existence or occurrence by verifying recorded stockholders' equity balances. That is, the auditor would foot and cross-foot the client's schedule of changes in stockholders' equity balances, account for unissued or retired shares, and, if detailed records and stock certificates are maintained externally, confirm shares outstanding with registrars and transfer agents. In addition, the auditor would also examine supporting documentation and authorizations for any stock issuances, stock dividends, and stock splits occurring during the year. Of course, if securities transactions are executed by independent registrars or transfer agents, the auditor would confirm capital stock transactions and balances directly with the registrar or agent.

Completeness

The completeness objective addresses whether all investments, long-term debt, and capital stock that should be presented in the financial statements are actually presented. That is, were all transactions recorded?

For investments, completeness is addressed by testing cutoff, which tests whether otherwise bona fide transactions are recorded in the proper accounting period, and by analytical procedures, which help determine whether recorded investment transactions are reasonable or, in contrast, whether unusual balances may require inquiries of management and/or additional substantive tests.

Analytical procedures also constitute a primary test of completeness for long-term debt and capital stock, since unusual relationships — for example, widely varying ratios in comparison with prior years — may signal unrecorded or improperly recorded transactions. However, for long-term debt, the auditor should also inspect and account for unissued instruments; and for capital stock, the auditor would also verify recorded shareholders' equity balances.

Rights and Obligations

Within the financing cycle, the rights objective addresses whether an entity has property rights to investments, and the obligations objective addresses whether long-term debt and capital stock represent bona fide obligations.

Rights to investments are tested by confirming securities held by external trustees/brokers and/or by physically inspecting securities on hand, depending on whether securities are maintained internally or externally.

For long-term debt, obligations are tested by confirming loans and other notes with creditors, by examining bond indentures and other indebtedness agreements, and by confirming bond and serial note balances and interest with trustees. In turn, since issued capital stock is held by many and varied stockholders, auditors typically test obligations by verifying recorded stockholders' equity balances as discussed earlier, rather than confirm with stockholders.

FIGURE 17-6
Relating Audit Objectives and Audit Procedures:
Investments, Long-Term Debt, and Capital Stock

Audit Objective	Audit Procedures		
	Investments	Long-Term Debt	Capital Stock
Existence or Occurrence	Confirm securities held by trustees. Physically inspect securities. Test cutoff.	Confirm loans and other notes payable with creditors. Examine bond indentures and other long-term indebtedness agreements. Physically inspect unissued instruments.	Verify recorded stockholders' equity balances. Examine supporting documentation and authorizations for stock issuances, stock dividends, and stock splits.
Completeness	Test cutoff. Perform analytical procedures.	Perform analytical procedures. Physically inspect and account for unissued instruments.	Perform analytical procedures. Verify recorded stockholders' equity balances.
Rights and Obligations	Confirm securities held by trustees.	Confirm loans and other notes payable with creditors.	Verify recorded stockholders' equity balances.

	Physically inspect securities.	Examine bond indentures and other long-term indebtedness agreements. Confirm bond and serial note balances and interest payments directly with trustees.	Verify recorded stockholders' equity balances.
Valuation	Verify securities transactions. Confirm securities held by trustees. Check quoted securities prices.	Verify debt-related transactions. Confirm loans and other notes payable with creditors. Recalculate interest and premium/discount amortizations.	
Presentation and Disclosure	Compare statement presentation and disclosures with those required by GAAP.	Compare statement presentation and disclosures with those required by GAAP.	Compare statement presentation and disclosures with those required by GAAP.

Valuation

The valuation objective addresses whether investments, debt, and capital stock balances are carried in the financial statements at appropriate dollar amounts.

For investments, valuation is addressed by verifying securities transactions and unit prices, i.e., market values, at the balance sheet date and by confirming securities held by trustees. For debt, auditors test valuation by verifying debt-related transactions, by confirming loans and other notes payable with creditors, and by recalculating interest and amortizations of premiums and discounts. The carrying value of capital stock is tested by verifying recorded stockholders' equity balances, which was also a primary test of existence or occurrence, completeness, and rights and obligations.

Presentation and Disclosure

The presentation and disclosure objective addresses whether recorded investments, debt, and capital stock are properly classified, described, and disclosed in the financial statements. As indicated in earlier chapters, presentation and disclosure are tested by comparing a client's financial statement disclosures with generally accepted accounting principles for each reported account. Disclosure guidelines, such as the AICPA's annually updated *Accounting and Audit Manual,* are often used by practicing auditors to assure that disclosures are complete.

INVESTMENTS IN MARKETABLE SECURITIES

A program of representative substantive tests applicable to investments is presented in Figure 17-7 along with the related audit objectives. The following discusses each procedure.

Verify Mathematical Accuracy and Examine Documentation

An auditor's tests of clerical accuracy relate primarily to a schedule of securities transactions that summarizes investment activity for the entire year, as illustrated in Figure 17-8. The working paper for securities trading activity is the auditor's primary source for testing acquisitions, sales, and the recognition of dividend and interest income. Because the schedule is the primary source for testing, the auditor tests the schedule's mathematical accuracy and reconciles balances with the general ledger, thereby assuring that detailed

FIGURE 17-7
Substantive Tests: Investments and Investment Revenue

Audit Objectives	Procedures
Valuation	1. Obtain a schedule of securities transactions from client personnel and verify mathematical accuracy 　a. Foot and cross-foot the schedule. 　b. Reconcile security balances with the general ledger. 2. For sampled (or all) transactions: 　a. Examine board of directors' or other appropriate authorization. 　b. Examine broker's advice or other documentation. 　c. Compare price with published market quotations. 　d. Test calculations for dividend and interest income and accruals, for premium and discount amortizations, and for gains and losses on sales.
Existence Valuation Rights	3. Confirm securities held by trustees or physically inspect and count securities on hand.
Existence Completeness	4. Test cutoff to determine whether acquisitions, sales, and investment revenue are recorded in the proper accounting period.
Valuation	5. Review the valuation of securities.
Completeness	6. Perform analytical procedures.
Presentation/ Disclosure	7. Review financial statements to determine whether: 　a. Investments, gains and losses, and investment revenue are properly classified and described. 　b. Disclosures are adequate.

records accurately represent the investment account's recorded general ledger balance.

In step 2, the auditor samples or tests all investment transactions for board of directors' or other (e.g., an investment committee) appropriate au-

FIGURE 17-8
Investments: Marketable Equity Securities

D2

AP
1/10/91

Ingstrom Corporation
Investments: Marketable Equity Securities
December 31, 1990

Description	Date Acquired/Sold	No. Shs	Price per Share	Balance 12-31-89	Acquired	<Sold>	Balance 12-31-90	Realized Gain <Loss>	Dividend Income	Market Value 12/31/90 Per Share	Market Value 12/31/90 Total
Current											
ABC Corp- Common	5/20/87	700	$23	$16,100 a			$16,100 d,j		$ 725 f	$25.50 g	$17,850 h
Albion Co- Common	6/30/88	800	32	25,600 a			32,400 d,j		1,050 f	35.00 g	35,000 h
	7/15/90	200	34		$6,800 b						
Elston Inc.- Common	8/12/89	500	19	9,500 a			3,800 d,j	$<600> e	550 f	16.00 g	3,200 h
	9/30/90	300	17			$<5,700> c					
Merton Inc.- Common	11/15/86	800	18	14,400 a			14,400 d,j		1,100 f	23.00 g	18,400 h
				$65,600 a	$6,800	$<5,700>	$66,700 d,j	$<600>	$3,425		$74,450
Noncurrent											
Carter, Rice- Common	12/1/85	1000	28	$28,000 a			$28,000 d,j		$2,050 f	33.00 g	$33,000 h
Ling Inc- Common	10/9/87	1500	13	19,500 a			19,500 d,j		875 f	18.00 g	27,000 h
Winston Corp- Common	5/10/87	800	15	12,000 a			-	$1,600 e		-	-
	12/30/90	800	17			$<12,000> c					
				$59,500 a	-	$<12,000>	$47,500	$1,600	$2,925		$60,000

a Traced to general ledger and prior year working papers.
b Agreed with broker's advice, cash disbursements records, and board of directors' authorization.
c Agreed with broker's advice, cash receipts records, and board of directors' authorization.
d Traced to general ledger.
e Calculated and agreed with general ledger.
f Agreed with dividend rates in Standard & Poors and calculated; traced proceeds to cash receipts records.
g Agreed with 12/31/90 market quotations in 1/2/91 Wall Street Journal.
h Calculated.
i Footed.
j Cross-footed.

thorization, for brokers' advices, for published market quotations, and for properly calculated dividend and interest accruals, premium and discount amortization, and gains and losses on sales. Thus, the focus of step 2 is on whether recorded transactions are authorized and, equally important, whether they actually occurred.

Confirm or Physically Inspect Securities

For securities held externally, an auditor confirms details with the external custodian and compares confirmation responses with internally maintained records. The auditor should also determine whether the external custodian is trustworthy, and therefore whether a client's investments are secure. Normally, though, this procedure is not performed when the custodian is well known and insured, such as national or regional brokerage houses.

For securities held internally, an auditor should physically inspect and count securities on hand, and compare the certificate numbers, quantity, and description of securities with detailed records. In addition, an auditor should determine if a client's balance sheet valuation procedures for infrequently traded securities are reasonable and reliable. Infrequently traded securities are of particular concern to the auditor, since there may not be objective balance-sheet-date price quotations for the securities, thereby necessitating that the auditor consult an investee's audited financial statements and credit ratings in order to assess the reasonableness of carrying values.

Test Cutoff

Cutoff tests are performed to determine that securities transactions near the balance sheet date are recorded in the proper accounting period. Supporting documentation may be examined for all, or a sample of, acquisitions and sales shortly before and after the balance sheet date. Transaction dates and amounts for each transaction reviewed should be agreed with detailed records and entries in the general ledger. The auditor should recalculate gains and losses for each sales transaction examined and agree with recorded amounts. Tests of cutoff should also be performed for investment revenue transactions near the balance sheet date, and accruals for interest revenue should be reviewed for reasonableness.

Review Valuation

An auditor tests valuation by examining documentation supporting transactions recorded and by recalculating dividend and interest income. Examining supporting documentation, however, substantiates historical cost only.

Thus, an auditor examines market quotations to assure that marketable equity securities are reported at the lower of aggregate cost or market, and that marketable debt securities are reported at the lower of cost or cost less permanent declines in market value. According to *FASB Statement of Financial Accounting Standards No. 12,* "Accounting for Certain Marketable Securities," marketable equity securities should be grouped into separate portfolios according to current and noncurrent classifications, and each portfolio reported at the lower of its aggregate cost or market value.

Perform Analytical Procedures

An auditor can use analytical procedures to test completeness and to determine whether conclusions drawn from substantive tests are reasonable. Several representative analytical procedures follow:

▲ Compare current-year purchase and sales transactions to those of prior years and to the entity's stated investment plans.
▲ Compare current-year dividends, interest, and other investment income with those of prior years.
▲ Calculate the percentage of accrued investment income to total investments, and estimate total accrued income based on current investments.

Any unusual or unexpected relationships should be investigated further through inquiries of management and additional substantive tests of details.

Review Financial Statements

Financial statements are reviewed to determine that investments are properly classified and described in the balance sheet and that gains and losses and investment revenue are properly presented in the income statement. Current and noncurrent securities, as defined in FASB Statement No. 12, should be reported separately in the balance sheet. For each classification, disclosures should include market declines, unrealized gains and losses, and realized gains and losses, and any other information necessary for adequate disclosure.

SUBSTANTIVE TESTS OF LONG-TERM DEBT

For most companies, long-term debt transactions are likely to be relatively infrequent but highly material, resulting in extensive or exclusive reliance on substantive procedures. A representative program of substantive tests applicable to debt is presented in Figure 17-9 and is tied to audit objectives.

FIGURE 17-9
Substantive Tests: Debt and Interest Expense

Audit Objectives	Procedures
Existence/ Occurrence Valuation Completeness Obligations	1. Obtain a schedule of bonds, notes, and other long-term indebtedness from accounting personnel and verify mathematical accuracy. a. Foot and cross-foot the schedule. b. Reconcile totals with balances in the general ledger. c. Examine documentation supporting debt-related transactions. d. If applicable, review a sample of entries in detailed bond records, and physically inspect and account for unissued instruments.
Existence Obligations Valuation	2. Confirm bonds outstanding and interest payments directly with trustees, and loans and notes payable directly with creditors, coordinating with bank confirmations where appropriate (Chapter 14).
Existence/ Occurrence Obligations	3. Obtain bond indentures and other long-term indebtedness agreements. a. Examine documentation and board of directors' authorizations. b. Determine that proceeds are recorded properly and used as intended by the board. c. Review for compliance with restrictive covenants.
Valuation	4. Recalculate interest paid or accrued and amortizations of premiums or discounts.
Existence or Occurrence Completeness	5. Perform analytical procedures.
Presentation/ Disclosure	6. Review financial statements to determine whether: a. Debt obligations are properly classified and described in the balance sheet and interest expense is properly reported in the income statement. b. Disclosures are adequate.

Verify Mathematical Accuracy and Examine Documentation

To test mathematical accuracy, an auditor examines a schedule that summarizes debt transactions for the year. Figure 17-10 illustrates.

The auditor foots and cross-foots the schedule, reconciling totals with balances in the general ledger, and, as illustrated in Figure 17-10, examines documentation supporting each debt-related transaction. For example, new debt would be reconciled with cash receipts records and with the board of directors' authorization, and the auditor would examine the debt instrument, determining which assets, if any, had been pledged as collateral. In turn, payments would be reconciled in amount with bonds or notes and with cash disbursement records. If debt instruments are maintained internally, an auditor would review a sample of entries in detailed bond records, and physically inspect and account for unissued instruments. Otherwise — that is, if debt is handled by independent trustees — the auditor would confirm, as indicated next.

Confirm Bonds, Loans, and Notes Payable

Bonds, notes payable balances, and interest payments should be confirmed directly with trustees, thereby determining whether the debt exists, is valued properly, and represents a bona fide obligation. In turn, loans and other notes payable are confirmed directly with creditors and coordinated with standard bank confirmations (illustrated in Chapter 12) which request indebtedness information in addition to cash balances. All returned confirmations should be examined in detail and agreed with recorded balances, and differences should be investigated.

Examine Bond Indentures and Other Long-Term Indebtedness Agreements

All long-term indebtedness agreements should be examined by the auditor to determine that transactions were executed in accordance with board of directors' authorizations, including the subsequent use of borrowed funds. If funds are not used as stipulated in indebtedness agreements, the company may be in violation of state or federal laws, since monies would have been expended in violation of agreements with creditors. When examining debt instruments, the auditor should note any and all restrictive covenants, and determine that the company is in compliance for the current period. For example, if a long-term note in the amount of $1,000,000 carries a debt covenant specifying that the borrower's current ratio may not fall below 3 to 2, lack of compliance at the balance sheet date could result in the creditor call-

FIGURE 17-10
Long-Term Debt, Bonds, and Related Interest

E1
GS
1/12/91

Ingstrom Corporation
Long-Term Debt: Bonds: Notes Payable, and Related Interest
December 31, 1990

Description	Balance 12/31/89	Principal Additions	Principal Payments	Balance 12/31/90	Interest Balance 12/31/89	Interest Expense	Interest Payments	Interest Balance 12/31/90
8% bonds, due 12/31/97; due $100,000 per year; 10 yr. bond; issued 1/1/88; face- $1,000,000; qtrly interest.	$ 800,000	—	$100,000	$ 700,000 d,e	$20,000 a	$ 80,000 f	$ 80,000 g	$20,000 d,e
9% note to First Nat'l Bank; due 12/31/92; 3 yr. note; incurred 1/1/90; face $360,000; semiannual interest; due $60,000 every six months.		$360,000 b,k	120,000 c	240,000 d,e	—	32,400 f	—	32,400 d,e
10% note to Nat'l Bank; due 6/30/92; 3 yr. note; incurred 7/1/89; face- $300,000; qtrly interest; due $50,000 every six months.	250,200 a,j	—	100,000 c	150,000 d,e	15,000 a	30,000 f	30,000 g	15,000 d,e
	$1,050,000 a	$360,000	$320,000	$1,090,000 d,e	$35,000 a	$142,400	$110,000	$67,400 d,e
	h	h	h	h	h	h	h	h

a Traced to general ledger and prior-year working papers.
b Examined note, agreed with cash receipts records and board of directors' authorization.
c Agreed amount with bond/note, and agreed with cash disbursements records.
d Traced to general ledger.
e Cross-footed.
f Calculated.
g Calculated and agreed with cash disbursement records.
h Footed.
i Land and buildings at 1001 Dexter St. pledged as collateral.
j Investment in Carter, Rice (see D2) pledged as collateral.
k Land and building at 131 Japonaca Street pledged as collateral.

ing the loan immediately, thereby requiring that the auditor propose a journal entry to reclassify the principal from a long-term to a current liability.

Recalculate Interest and Amortizations

Interest paid or accrued for the year should be recalculated by the auditor and reconciled with the general ledger, as illustrated in Figure 17-10. In addition, any related interest payments should be reconciled with cash disbursements records. If outstanding bonds were issued originally at more or less than face value, the related premium or discount amortization should be recalculated by the auditor and compared with entries in the general ledger.

Perform Analytical Procedures

To test existence or occurrence and completeness and to confirm the results of detailed substantive tests of details, the auditor performs analytical procedures such as ratio analysis and comparisons of relationships among related accounts or transactions. For example, analytical procedures for long-term debt could include any or all of the following tests:

▲ Compare current amortization amounts with prior actual and current budgeted amounts.
▲ Compare current interest costs with prior actual and current budgeted amounts.
▲ Compare current and noncurrent debt obligations with prior actual and current budgeted amounts.
▲ Compare debt issue costs and premiums/discounts to prospectuses and other internal debt reports.

Although no one of the above analytical procedures will necessarily detect misstatements, they will direct an auditor's attention to accounts or balances requiring additional tests of details or inquiries.

Review Financial Statements

Financial statement classifications, descriptions, and disclosures relating to debt and interest expense should be reviewed by the auditor. The currently maturing portion of long-term debt should generally be classified as a current liability in the absence of refinancing agreements. Disclosures should include information regarding maturities, interest rates, and other terms and conditions; assets pledged as collateral; debt conversion features; and troubled debt restructurings.

SUBSTANTIVE TESTS OF CAPITAL STOCK, RETAINED EARNINGS, AND EARNINGS PER SHARE

Figure 17-11, pages 710-711, presents a program of substantive tests for capital stock, retained earnings, and earnings per share, and, like other audit programs, is tied to the audit objectives introduced earlier. The procedures listed in Figure 17-11 encompass all the major types of transactions which normally affect stockholders' equity. However, it is unlikely that all these transactions would occur within a single year for any given audit client. In fact, in many cases, changes in stockholders' equity are attributable solely to changes in retained earnings resulting from net earnings or losses and from dividend payments.

Verify Stockholders' Equity Balances

In order to address the valuation of stockholders' equity from the standpoint of mathematical accuracy, an auditor should obtain a client-prepared schedule summarizing changes in stockholders' equity accounts, including: capital stock and related premium accounts for each class of stock outstanding, treasury stock accounts, and retained earnings. The schedule is footed and cross-footed by the auditor and totals reconciled with the general ledger, as illustrated in Figure 17-12. Other procedures for verifying stockholders' equity depend upon whether equity transactions are executed through independent external parties or internally.

FIGURE 17-12   J2
Capital Stock and Additional Paid-In Capital

Ingstrom Corporation   AP

Capital Stock and Add'l Paid-In Capital   1/12/91

December 31, 1990

	Authorized	Issued & Outstanding	Amount (at Par)	Additional Paid-In Capital
Balance, Dec. 31, 1989, $5 par. Issued 6/1/88 at par (proceeds in cash)	15,000 Shs a	12,000 Shs b 2,000 Shs c	$60,000 b 10,000 d	$5,000 b -
Balance, Dec. 31, 1990	15,000 Shs	14,000 Shs	$70,000	$5,000
		e	e	

a Agreed with corporate charter.
b Traced to general ledger and prior-year working papers.
c Agreed with board of directors' authorization.
d Agreed with cash receipts records.
e Footed.

FIGURE 17-11
Substantive Tests: Capital Stock, Retained Earnings, and Earnings
per Share

Audit Objectives	Procedures
Existence/ Occurrence Valuation Completeness Obligations	1. Verify recorded stockholders' equity balances. 　a. Obtain a schedule of changes in stockholders' equity accounts from accounting personnel. 　b. Foot and cross-foot the schedule, reconciling balances with the general ledger. 　c. If detailed records and stock certificates are maintained internally: 　　(1) Examine a sample of entries in stockholders' ledger, transfer journal, and certificate control records. 　　(2) Foot stockholders' ledger and reconcile with general ledger. 　　(3) Account for unissued certificates, examine retired shares for evidence of cancellation, and count treasury shares on hand. 　d. If detailed records and stock certificates are maintained externally, confirm shares outstanding, unissued shares, and treasury shares directly with registrars and transfer agents.
Occurrence Valuation	2. Review stock issuances, stock dividends, and stock splits. 　a. Examine supporting documentation and authorizations. 　b. For issuances, compare the authorized number of shares and price per share with entries in the general ledger and compare proceeds from issuance with cash records. 　c. For stock dividends, compare the authorized number of shares and value per share with entries in general ledger, and determine that stock dividends are recorded in accordance with GAAP. 　d. For stock splits, examine memorandum entries and compare with authorized number of shares and assigned value per share.
Occurrence Valuation	3. Review stock transactions. 　a. Examine supporting documentation and authorizations. 　b. Compare authorized number of shares and price per share with entries in general ledger.

Audit Objectives	Procedures

c. Compare disbursements for purchases and receipts for sales with cash records.

d. Determine that basis of accounting is appropriate.

Occurrence
Valuation

4. Verify recorded dividends.
   a. Examine supporting documentation and authorization.
   b. Recalculate dividends and agree with entries in general ledger.
   c. Reconcile recorded dividends with cash records.

Valuation

5. Recalculate earnings per share.

Existence or
Occurrence
Completeness

6. Perform analytical procedures.

Presentation/
Disclosure

7. Review financial statements to determine whether:
   a. Capital stock, retained earnings, and earnings per share are properly classified and described.
   b. Disclosures are adequate.

Review Stock Issuances, Stock Dividends, and Splits

If the number of shares outstanding has increased during the year as a result of stock issuances, stock dividends, or stock splits, the supporting documentation and authorizations should be examined for each transaction. For stock issuances (sales of previously unissued stock), an auditor should determine through recalculation that the general ledger entries accurately reflect the number of shares and selling price per share authorized by the board of directors. In the case of par or stated value stock, the auditor should determine that the selling price is properly allocated to capital stock and related premium accounts. Proceeds from the issuance of stock should be traced to cash receipt records.

When dividends are issued to shareholders in the form of additional shares of stock, an auditor should determine that entries in the general ledger reflect the number of shares and value per share authorized by the board of directors. The auditor should also review the assigned value per share to ascertain whether the value is appropriate in light of the number of shares issued.

Although stock splits have no effect on total stockholders' equity, they do increase the number of shares outstanding. An auditor should review underlying documentation and related memorandum entries to determine that stock splits were properly authorized and that the change in shares outstanding is properly recorded.

Review Treasury Stock Transactions

Many entities, particularly large publicly traded corporations, frequently buy and sell shares of their own stock. Shares may be acquired directly from stockholder in a stock redemption, or may be bought and sold on the open market. Treasury stock transactions may be undertaken for a variety of reasons including, for example, the acquisition of shares needed for distribution to employees under employee stock option plans. An auditor should review documentation and authorizations for treasury stock transactions and examine related entries in the general ledger and cash records. The auditor should determine that the accounting method used to record treasury stock transactions is in accordance with generally accepted accounting principles and that general ledger entries accurately reflect the method used by the company.

Verify Recorded Dividends

Supporting documentation and authorizations should be reviewed by an auditor for all dividends declared during the year under audit. The mathematical accuracy of dividends should be verified through recalculation and totals compared with the general ledger and cash records.

Recalculate Earnings Per Share

An auditor should recalculate earnings per share to ascertain that all increases and decreases in shares outstanding are properly reflected in the earnings per share figure. In some cases, entities with complex capital structures are required to report several separate earnings per share amounts. An auditor should review the terms of all outstanding stock rights, warrants, options, and convertible securities to determine whether reported earnings per share are consistent with generally accepted accounting principles.

Perform Analytical Procedures

Analytical procedures are not typically used for equity accounts unless the volume and breadth of transactions are extensive. When transactions are extensive, any or all of the following analytical procedures, among others, may be informative:

▲ For the current year, compute the return on stockholders' equity, the book value per share, and the dividend payout ratio, and compare with those of prior years.

▲ Compare current-year dividend amounts with those of prior years.

▲ Compare current-year balances for common and preferred stock and additional paid-in capital, and compare with those of prior years.

▲ Compare current-year treasury shares with those of prior years.

Of course, the auditor would investigate any unusual or unexpected relationships.

Review Financial Statements

A company's financial statements should be reviewed to determine whether all stockholders' equity balances are properly classified and described in the balance sheet and whether earnings per share are properly reported in the income statement. Notes to the financial statements should be reviewed to determine that disclosures are adequate. Frequently, disclosures relating to stockholders' equity are fairly extensive and include detailed schedules of changes in capital stock balances and retained earnings.

SUMMARY

The financing cycle involves an entity's business functions related to generating capital funds and investing funds not currently needed for operations. Common activities related to equity and debt financing include the issuance and retirement of equity and debt securities, payment of dividends and interest to investors and creditors, and recording of equity and debt transactions. In turn, these functions lead to three major balance sheet accounts, investments, long-term debt, and capital stock, each of which is discussed in this chapter in the context of substantive tests of details. When performing substantive tests of investments, long-term debt, and capital stock, an auditor's major objectives are to determine that each account exists, represents all transactions that should be presented, represents rights and obligations of the entity, is valued properly, and is presented and disclosed properly within the financial statements.

QUESTIONS

1. Identify the business functions associated with the financing cycle.
2. Describe some control procedures applicable to capital stock.
3. What is a restrictive debt covenant?
4. Why should unissued bonds be consecutively prenumbered?
5. Explain how an auditor tests the existence of investments recorded within a client's financial statements.
6. How does an auditor test the valuation of investment securities?
7. Why does an auditor typically examine market quotations for a client's investments?
8. What procedures can be used to determine whether all transactions that should be recorded are recorded?
9. Briefly describe the procedures an auditor might employ in testing long-term debt and interest expense at year-end.
10. Why do auditors frequently rely predominantly or exclusively on substantive tests in auditing stockholders' equity and long-term debt?
11. How does an auditor verify recorded stockholders' equity balances?
12. Identify the specific types of transactions relating to stockholders' equity that are tested by an auditor at year-end.
13. How and why does an auditor test earnings per share?

MULTIPLE CHOICE QUESTIONS

1. Jones was engaged to examine the financial statements of Gamma Corporation for the year ended June 30, 1989. Having completed an examination of the investment securities, which of the following is the best method of verifying the accuracy of recorded dividend income?

   a. Tracing recorded dividend income to cash receipts records and validated deposit slips.
   b. Utilizing analytical review techniques and statistical sampling.
   c. Comparing recorded dividends with amounts appearing on federal information forms 1099.
   d. Comparing recorded dividends with a standard financial reporting service's record of dividends.   (AICPA Adapted)

2. Which of the following is **not** one of the auditor's primary objectives in an examination of marketable securities?

   a. To determine whether securities are authentic.
   b. To determine whether securities are the property of the client.
   c. To determine whether securities actually exist.

d. To determine whether securities are properly classified on the balance sheet.

(AICPA Adapted)

3. The auditor's program for the examination of long-term debt should include steps that require the

a. Verification of the existence of the bondholders.
b. Examination of any bond trust indenture.
c. Inspection of the accounts payable subsidiary ledger.
d. Investigation of credits to the bond interest income account.

(AICPA Adapted)

4. During its fiscal year, a company issued, at a discount, a substantial amount of first-mortgage bonds. When performing audit work in connection with the bond issue, the independent auditor should

a. Confirm the existence of the bondholders.
b. Review the minutes for authorization.
c. Trace the net cash received from the issuance to the bond payable account.
d. Inspect the records maintained by the bond trustee.   (AICPA Adapted)

5. During the year under audit, a company has completed a private placement of a substantial amount of bonds. Which of the following is the **most** important step in the auditor's program for testing existence?

a. Confirming the amount issued with the bond trustee.
b. Tracing the cash received from the issue to the accounting records.
c. Examining the bond records maintained by the transfer agent.
d. Recomputing the annual interest cost and the effective yield.

(AICPA Adapted)

6. During the course of an audit, a CPA observes that the recorded interest expense seems to be excessive in relation to the balance in the long-term debt account. This observation could lead the auditor to suspect that

a. Long-term debt is understated.
b. Discount on bonds payable is overstated.
c. Long-term debt is overstated.
d. Premium on bonds payable is understated.   (AICPA Adapted)

7. Which of the following is the most important consideration of an auditor when examining the stockholders' equity section of a client's balance sheet?

a. Changes in the capital stock account are verified by an independent stock transfer agent.
b. Stock dividends and/or stock splits during the year under audit were approved by the stockholders.
c. Stock dividends are capitalized at par or stated value on the dividend declaration date.
d. Entries in the capital stock account can be traced to a resolution in the minutes of the board of directors' meetings.   (AICPA Adapted)

8. All corporate capital stock transactions should ultimately be traced to the

a. Minutes of the board of directors.
b. Cash receipts journal.

c. Cash disbursements journal.
d. Numbered stock certificates.   (AICPA Adapted)

9. Where no independent stock transfer agents are employed and the corporation issues its own stocks and maintains stock records, canceled stock certificates should

  a. Be defaced to prevent reissuance and attached to their corresponding stubs.
  b. Not be defaced, but segregated from other stock certificates and retained in a canceled certificates file.
  c. Be destroyed to prevent fraudulent reissuance.
  d. Be defaced and sent to the secretary of state.   (AICPA Adapted)

PROBLEMS

17-1   In connection with your examination of the Whitestable Company's December 31, 1990 financial statements, you become aware of the following controls or procedures over Whitestable's investment, debt, and equity activities:

1. On June 15, 1988, the board of directors established criteria for selecting debt and equity investments.
2. Policies have been established for selecting debt or equity financing.
3. On a monthly basis, interest and loan payment amounts are prepared or updated.
4. All internally held securities are maintained under lock and key in a fireproof vault within the treasurer's office.
5. All unissued securities are maintained and periodically checked by personnel independent of cash activities.

Required:
For each control procedure, indicate (a) a potential error or irregularity that might be prevented or detected as a result of the control procedure, and (b) what control objective is served by the control procedure. Organize your answer as follows:

Control Procedure	Potential Error or Irregularity That Might Be Prevented or Detected	Control Objective
1.	(a)	(b)

17-2   Following are selected questions from an internal control questionnaire relating to a company's investment transactions. The questions relate to the custody, recording, and valuation of investments, and to acquisitions, sales, and income. A "Yes" response to any question would indicate a potential strength of the system, and a "No" a potential weakness.

a. Is a detailed record of securities maintained by an official who is independent of officials responsible for custody?
b. Is the listing of investments periodically reconciled with investment records?
c. Are securities in the name of the entity (or restrictively endorsed in the name of the entity)?
d. Are acquisitions and sales of investment securities authorized by the board of directors or a duly authorized investment committee?

e. Are broker's advices promptly compared with documented acquisition and sales authorizations?

f. Is an independent check made to determine whether acquisition or sale prices are fair and objective?

g. Is investment income periodically recalculated and verified?

Required:
Assume that inquiries indicate no apparent weaknesses in the internal control structure. Draft a test of controls you believe would provide persuasive evidence that no deficiencies exist.

17-3   Following are errors, irregularities, or other circumstances that an auditor might encounter as a result of applying audit tests to investments as of the balance sheet date:

a. The client does not maintain detailed records for investments.

b. All debt securities are maintained in a locked, fireproof vault in the treasurer's office.

c. All equity securities are held by independent brokers.

d. The client traded heavily in marketable securities near the end of the year.

e. The market value of selected equity securities fluctuated widely throughout the year.

Required:
For each of the above, indicate (1) a specific substantive test or tests that might address the error, irregularity, or circumstance, and (2) the audit objective addressed by each test.

17-4   As auditor for a corporation which has assets approximating $250,000,000, you are planning an initial audit of the corporation's financing function.

Required:
With regard to the custodianship of securities, list several key internal control questions that should be answered during your audit.   (IIA Adapted)

17-5   In connection with her examination of the financial statements of Belasco Chemicals, Inc., Karen Mack, CPA, is considering the necessity of inspecting marketable securities on the balance sheet date, May 31, 1990, or at some other date. The marketable securities held by Belasco include negotiable bearer bonds, which are kept in a safe in the treasurer's office, and miscellaneous stocks and bonds, which are kept in a safe deposit box at The Merchants Bank. Both the negotiable bearer bonds and the miscellaneous stocks and bonds are material to proper presentation of Belasco's financial position.

Required:
(1) What are the factors that Mack should consider in determining the necessity for inspecting these securities on May 31, 1990, as opposed to other dates?

(2) Assume that Mack plans to send a member of her staff to Belasco's offices and The Merchants Bank on May 31, 1990, to make the security inspection. What instructions should she give to this staff member as to the conduct of the inspection and the evidence to be included in the audit working papers? (*Note:* Do not

discuss the valuation of securities, the income from securities, or the examination of information contained in the books and records of the company.)

(3) Assume that Mack finds it impracticable to send a member of her staff to Belasco's offices and The Merchants Bank on May 31, 1990. What alternative procedures may she employ to assure herself that the company had physical possession of its marketable securities on May 31, 1990, if the securities are inspected (a) May 28, 1990? (b) June 5, 1990?   (AICPA Adapted)

17-6   As a result of highly profitable operations over a number of years, Eastern Manufacturing Corporation accumulated a substantial investment portfolio. In examining the financial statements for the year ended December 31, 1990, the following information came to the attention of the corporation's CPA:

(a) The manufacturing operations of the corporation resulted in an operating loss for the year.

(b) In 1990, the corporation placed the securities making up the investment portfolio with a financial institution which will serve as custodian of the securities. Formerly the securities were kept in the corporation's safe deposit box in the local bank.

(c) On December 22, 1990, the corporation sold and then repurchased on the same day a number of securities that had appreciated greatly in value. Management stated that the purpose of the sale and repurchases was to establish a higher cost and book value for the securities and to avoid the reporting of a loss for the year.

Required:

(1) List the objectives of the CPA's examination of the investment account.

(2) Under what conditions would the CPA accept a confirmation of the securities on hand from the custodian in lieu of personally inspecting and counting the securities?

(3) What disclosure, if any, of the sale and repurchase of securities would the CPA recommend for the financial statements? What impact, if any, would the sale and repurchase have upon the CPA's opinion on the financial statements if the client accepts the CPA's disclosure recommendations? Discuss.   (AICPA Adapted)

17-7   The schedule on page 719 was prepared by the controller of World Manufacturing, Inc., for use by the independent auditors during their examination of World's year-end financial statements. All procedures performed by the audit assistant were noted at the bottom "Legend" section, and it was properly initialed, dated and indexed, and then submitted to a senior member of the audit staff for review. Internal control structure was reviewed and is considered to be effective.

Required:

(1) What information that is essential to the audit of marketable securities is missing from this schedule?

(2) What are the essential audit procedures that were not noted as having been performed by the audit assistant?

17-8   You have been engaged to examine the financial statements of the Elliott Company for the year ended December 31, 1990. You performed a similar examination as of December 31, 1989.

World Manufacturing, Inc.
MARKETABLE SECURITIES
Year Ended December 31, 1990

Description of Security	%	Yr. Due	Serial No.	Face value of bonds	Gen. ledger 1/1	Purch. in 1990	Sold in 1990	Cost	Gen. ledger 12/31	12/31 market	Pay date(s)	Amt. rec.	Accruals 12/31
Corp. Bonds													
A	6	97	21-7	10000	9400a				9400	9100	1/15	300 b,d	275
											7/15	300 b,d	
D	4	91	73-0	30000	27500a				27500	26220	12/1	1200 b,d	100
G	9	98	16-4	5000	4000a				4000	5080	8/1	450 b,d	188
Rc	5	93	08-2	70000	66000a		57000b	66000					
Sc	10	99	07-4	100000		100000e			100000	101250	7/1	5000 b,d	5000
				100000	106900	100000	57000	66000	140900	141650		7250	5563
					a,f	f	f	f	f,g	f		f	f
Stocks													
P 1,000 shs. Common			1044		7500a				7500	7600	3/1	750 b,d	250
											6/1	750 b,d	
											9/1	750 b,d	
											12/1	750 b,d	
U 50 shs. Common			8530		9700a				9700	9800	2/1	800 b,d	667
											8/1	800 b,d	
					17200				17200	17400		4600	917
					a,f				f,g	f		f	f

Legends and comments relative to above

a = Beginning balances reconciled with 1989 working papers
b = Traced to cash receipts
c = Minutes examined (purchase and sales approved by the board of directors)
d = Reconciled with 1099
e = Confirmed by tracing to broker's advice
f = Total footed
g = Reconciled with general ledger

Following is the trial balance for the company as of December 31, 1990:

	Dr.(Cr.)
Cash	$128,000
Interest Receivable	47,450
Dividends Receivable	1,750
14% Secured Note Receivable	730,000
Investments at Cost:	
Bowen Common Stock	322,000
Investments at equity:	
Woods Common Stock	284,000
Land	185,000
Accounts Payable	(31,000)
Interest Payable	(6,500)
16% Secured Note Payable to Bank	(275,000)
Common Stock	(480,000)
Paid-In Capital in Excess of Par	(800,000)
Retained Earnings	(100,500)
Dividend Revenue	(3,750)
Interest Revenue	(47,450)
Equity in Earnings of Investments Carried at Equity	(40,000)
Interest Expense	26,000
General and Administrative Expense	60,000

You have obtained the following data concerning certain accounts:

(a) The 14% note receivable is due from Tysinger Corporation and is secured by a first mortgage on land sold to Tysinger by Elliott on December 21, 1989. The note was to have been paid in 20 equal quarterly payments beginning March 31, 1990, plus interest. Tysinger, however, is in very poor financial condition and has not made any principal or interest payments to date.

(b) The Bowen common stock was purchased on September 21, 1989, for cash in the market where it is actively traded. It is used as security for the note payable and held by the bank. Elliott's investment in Bowen represents approximately 1% of the total outstanding shares of Bowen.

(c) Elliott's investment in Woods represents 40% of the outstanding common stock which is actively traded. Woods is audited by another CPA and has a December 31 year-end.

(d) Elliott neither purchased nor sold any stock investments during the year other than that noted above.

Required:

For the following account balances, discuss (1) the types of evidential matter you should obtain and (2) the audit procedures you should perform during your examination.

(a) 14% Secured Note Receivable.
(b) Bowen Common Stock.
(c) Woods Common Stock.
(d) Dividend Revenue.

(AICPA Adapted)

17-9   Kent, CPA, who is engaged in the audit of the financial statements of Bass Corporation for the year ended December 31, 1990, is about to commence on audit

of the noncurrent investment securities. Bass' records indicate that the company owns various bearer bonds, as well as 25% of the outstanding common stock of Commercial Industrial Inc. Kent is satisfied with evidence that supports the presumption of significant influence over Commercial Industrial Inc. The various securities are at two locations as follows:
- Recently acquired securities are in the company's safe in the custody of the treasurer.
- All other securities are in the company's bank safe deposit box.

All the securities in Bass' portfolio are actively traded in a broad market.

Required:
(1) Assuming that control procedures for securities are satisfactory and may be relied upon, what are the objectives of the examination of these noncurrent investment securities?
(2) What audit procedures should be undertaken by Kent with respect to the examination of Bass' noncurrent investment securities?   (AICPA Adapted)

17-10   Following are selected questions from an internal control questionnaire relating to a company's debt and equity transactions. A "Yes" response to any question indicates a potential strength of the system, and a "No" response indicates a potential weakness.
a. Are all long-term debt and other borrowings authorized by the board of directors?
b. Is an officer responsible for determining whether all debt covenants are complied with?
c. Are unissued bonds and notes prenumbered consecutively and controlled by an official independent of recording?
d. Are interest payments and accruals periodically recalculated?
e. Are unissued stock certificates prenumbered consecutively and safeguarded?
f. Are treasury shares adequately controlled and accounted for?
g. Are dividend payments and accruals periodically recalculated?

Required:
Assume that inquiries indicate no apparent deficiencies in the internal control structure. Draft tests of controls that you believe would provide persuasive evidence that no deficiencies exist.

17-11   Following are errors, irregularities, or other circumstances that an auditor might encounter as a result of applying audit tests to long-term debt as of the balance sheet date:
a. Detailed long-term debt records may not be accurate.
b. All debt instruments are held by banks.
c. There is no documentation supporting a bond indenture.
d. Proceeds from the bond issuance have all been expended.
e. Interest on various debt instruments required interest payments on the last day of all but two months.

Required:
For each of the above, indicate (1) a specific substantive test or tests that might address the error, irregularity, or circumstance, and (2) the audit objective addressed by each test.

17-12   Ronald Ondeyko, CPA, is considering the internal control structure of River Commons, Inc. in the context of investments, long-term debt, and capital stock activities. System documentation was accomplished with a questionnaire and a narrative memorandum and, in conjunction with a transaction walkthrough, revealed the following potential deficiencies in internal control structure:

a. The historical cost of all long term debt exceeds company policies for debt to equity ratios.
b. The company entered into a long term debt agreement requiring a 2 to 1 current ratio at year end, yet the current ratio when the agreement was signed was approximately 1.5 to 1.
c. Internally held securities are occasionally misplaced, though in all cases the securities were recovered.
d. In an open letter to the board of directors, a group of stockholders criticized the company for investing in a domestic corporation alleged to have violated human rights in a foreign country.
e. Signatures on investment authorizations vary from the chairman of the board's investment committee, to the treasurer and controller.

Required:
For each potential deficiency indicate a control procedure or procedures that management could implement to reduce the likelihood of errors or irregularities.

17-13   The following covenants are extracted from the indenture of a bond issue. The indenture provides that failure to comply with its terms in any respect automatically advances the due date of the loan to the date of noncompliance (the regular due date is twenty years hence):

(a) "The debtor company shall endeavor to maintain a working capital ratio of 2 to 1 at all times, and, in any fiscal year following a failure to maintain said ratio, the company shall restrict compensation of officers to a total of $250,000. Officers for this purpose shall include chairman of the board of directors, president, all vice presidents, secretary, and treasurer."
(b) "The debtor company shall keep all property which is security for this debt insured against loss by fire to the extent of 100 percent of its actual value. Policies of insurance constituting this protection shall be filed with the trustee."
(c) "The debtor company shall pay all taxes legally assessed against property which is security for this debt within the time provided by law for payment without penalty, and shall deposit receipted tax bills or equally acceptable evidence of payment of same with the trustee."
(d) "A sinking fund shall be deposited with the trustee by semiannual payments of $300,000, from which the trustee shall, at his discretion, purchase bonds of this issue."

Required:
(1) Indicate the audit procedures you would perform for each covenant.
(2) Comment on any disclosure requirements that you believe are necessary.

(AICPA Adapted)

17-14   You were engaged to examine the financial statements of Ronlyn Corporation for the year ended June 30, 1990.

On May 1, 1990, the corporation borrowed $500,000 from Second National

Bank to finance plant expansion. The long-term note agreement provided for the annual payment of principal and interest over five years. The existing plant was pledged as security for the loan.

Due to unexpected difficulties in acquiring the building site, the plant expansion had not begun at June 30, 1990. To make use of the borrowed funds, management decided to invest in stocks and bonds, and on May 16, 1990, the $500,000 was invested in securities.

Required:
(1) What are the audit objectives in the examination of long-term debt?
(2) Prepare an audit program for the examination of the long-term note agreement between Ronlyn and Second National Bank.
(3) How could you verify the security position of Ronlyn at June 30, 1990?
(4) In your audit of investments, how would you
   (a) Verify the dividend or interest income recorded?
   (b) Determine market value?
   (c) Establish the authority for security purchases?   (AICPA Adapted)

17-15   Andrews, CPA, has been engaged to audit the financial statements of Broadwall Corporation for the year ended December 31, 1990. During the year, Broadwall obtained a long-term loan from a local bank pursuant to a financing agreement which provided that the:
1. Loan was to be secured by the company's inventory and accounts receivable.
2. Company was to maintain a debt to equity ratio not to exceed two to one.
3. Company was not to pay dividends without permission from the bank.
4. Monthly installment payments were to commence July 1, 1990.

In addition, during the year the company also borrowed, on a short-term basis, from the president of the company, including substantial amounts just prior to the year-end.

Required:
(1) For purposes of Andrews' audit of the financial statements of Broadwall Corporation, what substantive tests should Andrews apply in auditing the described loans.
(2) What are the financial statement disclosures that Andrews should expect to find with respect to the loans from the president?   (AICPA Adapted)

17-16   Following are errors, irregularities, or other circumstances that an auditor might encounter as a result of applying audit tests to capital stock as of the balance sheet date:
a. Stockholders equity accounts are not accurate.
b. Stock dividends were issued during the year.
c. Treasury stock was purchased in December.
d. Dividends were declared and paid before the end of the year.
e. The client's common stock is traded actively on a national stock exchange.

Required:
For each of the above, indicate (1) a specific substantive test or tests that might address the error, irregularity, or circumstance, and (2) the audit objective addressed by each test.

17-17   You were engaged on May 1, 1990, by a committee of stockholders to perform a special audit as of December 31, 1989, of the stockholders' equity of the Major Corporation, whose stock is actively traded on a stock exchange. The stockholders who engage you believe that the information contained in the stockholders' equity section of the published annual report for the year ended December 31, 1989, is not correct. If your examination confirms their suspicions, they intend to use the report in a proxy fight.

Management agrees to permit your audit but refuses to permit any direct confirmation with stockholders. To secure cooperation in the audit, the committee of stockholders has agreed to this limitation, and you have been instructed to limit your audit in this respect. You have been instructed also to exclude the audit of revenue and expense accounts for the year.

Required:
(1) Prepare a general audit program for the initial examination of the stockholders' equity section of a corporation's balance sheet, assuming no limitation on the scope of your examination. Exclude the audit of revenue and expense accounts.
(2) Describe any special auditing procedures you would undertake in view of the limitations and other special circumstances of your examination of the Major Corporation's stockholders' equity accounts.
(3) Discuss the content of your auditor's report for the special engagement including comments on the opinion that you would render. Do not prepare your auditor's report.   (AICPA Adapted)

17-18   You are a CPA engaged in an audit of the financial statements of Pate Corporation for the year ended December 31, 1990. The financial statements and records of Pate Corporation have not been audited by a CPA in prior years.

The stockholders' equity section of Pate Corporation's balance sheet at December 31, 1990, follows:

Stockholders' equity:

Capital stock — 10,000 shares of $10 par value authorized; 5,000 shares issued and outstanding	$ 50,000
Capital contributed in excess of par value of capital stock	32,580
Retained earnings	47,320
Total stockholders' equity	$129,900

Pate Corporation was founded in 1988. The corporation has ten stockholders and serves as its own registrar and transfer agent. There are no capital stock subscription contracts in effect.

Required:
(1) Prepare a detailed audit program for the audit of the three accounts constituting the stockholders' equity section of Pate Corporation's balance sheet. (Do not include in the audit program the verification of the results of the current year's operations.)
(2) After every other figure on the balance sheet has been audited by the CPA, it might appear that the retained earnings figure is a balancing figure and requires no further verification. Why does the CPA verify retained earnings as he or she does the other figures on the balance sheet? Discuss.   (AICPA Adapted)

17-19   The Eaton Company was incorporated July 10, 1990, with an authorized capital as follows:
(a) Common stock, Class A, 20,000 shares, par value $25 per share.
(b) Common stock, Class B, 100,000 shares, par value $5 per share.

The capital stock account in the general ledger is credited with only one item in the year 1990. This represents capital stock sold for cash, at par, as follows:
(a) Class A, 12,000 shares.
(b) Class B, 60,000 shares.

The sum of open certificate stubs in the stock certificate books at December 31, 1990, indicates that 82,000 shares of stock were outstanding.

Required:
(1) State possible explanations for this apparent discrepancy.
(2) State the procedures you would perform to determine the cause of the discrepancy.   (AICPA Adapted)

COMPLETING AN AUDIT

18

Major topics discussed in this chapter are the:

▲   *Substantive tests of revenue and expense accounts.*

▲   *Review for subsequent events.*

▲   *Procedures for auditing accounting estimates, including loss contingencies.*

▲   *Inquiries necessary of a client's legal counsel.*

▲   *Nature and content of a management representation letter.*

▲   *Process of forming an opinion on financial statements.*

▲   *Auditor's responsibility for communication with audit committees.*

▲   *Subsequent discovery of facts existing at the date of the auditor's report.*

▲   *Consideration of omitted procedures after the report date.*

Completing the discussion of detailed audit procedures, this chapter introduces procedures normally conducted when completing an audit engagement. The chapter begins by describing and illustrating tests of details and reasonableness tests for revenue and expense accounts. Many tests of revenues and expenses have been introduced in earlier chapters; the purpose here is to distinguish between two types of substantive tests for revenue and expense accounts: tests of details and analytical procedures. Next, the chapter addresses procedures for auditing accounting estimates and other procedures designed to "wrap up" an audit engagement: the review for events occurring subsequent to the balance sheet date, making inquiries of a client's lawyer, and obtaining a management representation letter.

In turn, the chapter discusses how and why an auditor performs overall analytical procedures on the financial statements, why an auditor reviews working papers in detail, and why the auditor arranges for an independent technical review of working papers by an audit partner not assigned to the engagement. Each of these procedures is an integral part of the auditor's process of formulating an opinion on the client's financial statements taken as a whole. Finally, the chapter discusses current requirements for an auditor to communicate with the audit committee, and two issues related to the period after the auditor issues an audit report: the subsequent discovery of facts existing at the report date, and the consideration of procedures unknowingly omitted during the engagement.

SUBSTANTIVE TESTS OF REVENUE
AND EXPENSE ACCOUNTS

A financial statement audit under generally accepted auditing standards encompasses all the basic financial statements, not just the balance sheet. Yet the discussion of substantive procedures in Chapters 11 through 17 has focused primarily on balance sheet accounts, and only secondarily on income statement accounts. Although focusing on the balance sheet is not uncommon in practice, an auditor must also perform substantive tests of revenue and expense accounts, since (1) an audit report extends not only to balance sheet accounts, but also to income statement accounts, and (2) some financial statement users are equally if not more interested in results of operations, which are measured by the income statement, than in financial position, which is measured in part by the balance sheet.

Not all of the audit objectives introduced in Chapter 6 are necessarily relevant to revenue and expense accounts. Rather, the most relevant objectives are occurrence, valuation and allocation, completeness, and presentation and disclosure, and each can be tested either by direct tests of details or by analytical procedures, or both. The following discussion describes and illustrates each type of test.

Tests of Details

In general, tests of details rather than analytical procedures are appropriate when:

▲ Internal control structure is not reliable.
▲ Transaction volume is not high.
▲ Analytical procedures reveal unusual or unexpected results, or
▲ An account(s) requires special attention.

Analytical procedures, tests of reasonableness, are highly dependent on the reliability of internal control structure, since poorly designed or unreliable control precedures could result in misstated accounts and, therefore, in unusual or unexpected relationships. Thus, when control procedures are not reliable, an auditor should apply direct tests of details rather than risk misleading analytical tests.

Although analytical procedures are appropriate regardless of transaction volume, very low volume accounts are better tested by direct tests of details, since all transactions can be tested, thereby minimizing uncertainty about whether an account is fairly stated. Further, analytical procedures are not particularly informative for low-volume accounts because the information content of minor account balance fluctuations is often trivial.

As indicated previously in the chapter — and throughout the book — tests of details are particularly appropriate when analytical procedures reveal unusual or unexpected results. For example, declining receivables balances coupled with steady collections *and* rising sales could signal overstated sales, and would prompt an auditor to design detailed tests of recorded sales.

Some income statement accounts require special attention, thereby rendering analytical procedures inappropriate. For example, charitable contributions must be listed in detail for income tax returns, and executive compensation must be disclosed separately in Securities and Exchange Commission filings. Thus, for these among other accounts, auditors typically opt for direct tests of details rather than rely exclusively on analytical procedures.

The nature and extent of direct tests of details for revenue and expense accounts will vary depending on the circumstances, but in all cases the auditor must address the audit objectives listed earlier. For example, an auditor might address occurrence, i.e., determine whether recorded revenue and expense transactions actually occurred, by comparing recorded revenue with underlying documents such as deposits and contracts, as illustrated in the analysis of other income in Figure 18-1, or by physically examining evidence of expenditures such as advertising copy in a local newspaper, as illustrated in Figure 18-2. Typically, valuation is tested by extending, footing, and cross-footing detail schedules prepared by the client in support of recorded revenues and expenses and reconciling totals with balances in the general ledger. In addition, an auditor might trace recorded amounts for a sample of transactions to supporting documents such as deposit records and canceled checks. In turn, an auditor can test completeness by performing tests of cutoff for transactions occurring near the balance sheet date.

The occurrence, valuation, and completeness of revenue that has been earned but not yet received or expenses incurred but not yet paid could be tested by recalculations that match incurred costs with earned revenue in accordance with the accounting concept of matching.

Analytical Procedures

If tests of details are not necessary, or in addition to tests of details, an auditor can test the reasonableness of recorded revenue and expense balances by analytical procedures that focus on relationships over time and between accounts. Relationships over time provide evidence about the fluctuation of account balances from one period to the next. For example, an auditor might compare the balances of current-year revenue and expense accounts with balances for the prior year, obtaining explanations from management for unusual fluctuations. In turn, relationships between accounts provide evidence about

FIGURE 18-1   BB6
Direct Tests of Details: Other Income

```
                         Ingstrom Corporation                    AP
                         Analysis of Other Income               1/10/91
                            December 31, 1990

     Date          Received From            Description          Amount


 April 30      Weil & White, Inc.      Royalty Income:
               Los Angeles, Calif.       Annual royalty due by
                                         April 30 of each year
                                         for Weil & White's
                                         use of Ingstrom pat-
                                         ents on centrifuge
                                         machines. Royalty
                                         based on Weil & White
                                         production through
                                         March 31                $7430 a
 December 31   Sansibar & Company      Rent Income:
               Denver, Colorado.         Initial month's rent
                                         for property at 6204
                                         Mitchell Street,
                                         Denver, rented for 12
                                         months to Sansibar        850 b
                                                                 $8280

                                                                   c
```

a Reconciled with royalty report (see workpaper BB9), with royalty contract, and with cash receipts journal.
b Reconciled with rent agreement and with cash receipts journal; agreement
  expires November 30, 1991
c Footed and reconciled with general ledger.

whether the balance of one account is reasonable in relation to another account or to the same account for the preceding year.

An example of analytical procedures for payroll appears in the audit program in Figure 15-6, page 603, and the related discussion. Note that the payroll tests emphasize analytical procedures and, therefore, assume that controls over payroll are reliable and that transaction volume is relatively high; otherwise, direct tests of details would have been more appropriate.

AUDITING ACCOUNTING ESTIMATES

Most transactions and events can be readily tested by an auditor because the audit population is known with certainty, supporting documentation generally exists, and there are no uncertainties about the existence of an asset, liability, income, or expense. However, auditors must also apply audit procedures to financial statement elements, items, or accounts that have been

FIGURE 18-2   BB12

Direct Tests of Details: Advertising Expense

Ingstrom Corporation   AP
Analysis of Advertising Expense   1/13/91
December 31, 1990

Date	Payee	Description	Amount
March 30	Wire & Cable Monthly Chicago, Illinois	Full-page advertisement for cable Intruding machinery	$ 950 a
May 15	Chemical Weekly New York, New York	Half-page advertisement for recently introduced chemical centrifuge machinery. Ad ran for six weekly issues, beginning June 1.	1500 b
August 10	St. Louis Post-Dispatch St. Louis, Missouri	Full-page color ad in Sunday Supplement (newspaper) advertising Ingstrom's support and involvement in youth job-training program.	400 a
			$2850
			c

a Examined ad copy and invoice; traced to cash disbursements journal.
b Examined ad copy and contract; traced to cash disbursements journal.
c Footed and reconciled with general ledger.

approximated by management — that is, *accounting estimates* that measure either the effects of past transactions or events or the present status of assets or liabilities in order to disclose them in the accounting period that gave rise to their economic substance. Accounting estimates are often necessary because the measurement of some amounts or the valuation of some accounts may be uncertain pending the outcome of future events or because data concerning past events cannot be accumulated on a timely cost-effective basis. Examples include:

▲ Allowance for uncollectible receivables
▲ Obsolete inventory
▲ Depreciation and amortization
▲ Warranty claims
▲ Accrued property taxes
▲ Pension costs
▲ Airline passenger revenue

▲ Subscription income
▲ Percentage of completion income on construction contracts

Although management is responsible for making the accounting estimates, auditors under *Statement on Auditing Standards No. 57*, "Auditing Accounting Estimates," are responsible for evaluating the reasonableness of management's estimates in the context of the financial statements taken as a whole.

Evaluating Accounting Estimates. Accounting estimates are generally more susceptible to material misstatement than factual data, partly because they involve uncertainty and subjectivity, and partly because controls over estimates are more difficult for management to establish than controls over factual data. An auditor's objectives in evaluating accounting estimates are to:

▲ Provide reasonable assurance that all material estimates have been developed by management.
▲ Assure that the estimates are reasonable and are presented in the financial statements in accordance with GAAP.

Generally, the risk of material misstatement of accounting estimates will vary depending on the controls established by management, the complexity and subjectivity of the estimation process, the availability and reliability of relevant data, and the nature and uncertainty of assumptions made by management. In evaluating the reasonableness of accounting estimates, an auditor should obtain an understanding of how management developed the estimate and then, based on his or her understanding, consider:

▲ Reviewing and testing the process used by management,
▲ Developing an independent estimate for comparison, and/or,
▲ Reviewing transactions or events that occurred subsequent to the balance sheet date.

Loss Contingencies. One among these accounting estimates is a *contingency*, defined in *Statement of Financial Accounting Standards No. 5* as ". . . an existing condition, situation, or set of circumstances involving uncertainty as to possible gain or loss to an enterprise that will ultimately be resolved when one or more future events occur or fail to occur." When completing an engagement, auditors are particularly concerned with the existence of unrecorded *loss contingencies,* since failure to recognize a material loss contingency would result in overstated income and understated liabilities and, therefore, in materially misstated financial statements. As a result, one of the normal procedures performed when completing an audit is a review for potential contingent liabilities. Examples of loss contingencies include the following:

▲ Pending or threatened litigation for patent infringements, product warranties, or product defects.

▲ Guarantees of third-party obligations.

▲ Discounted notes receivable or factored accounts receivable.

▲ Disputed income tax deductions.

Generally, loss contingencies should be recognized and a liability recorded in the accounts if (a) it is *probable* that a liability had been incurred at the balance sheet date and (b) the amount of the loss can be *reasonably esti-mated*. However, if the loss is either probable or estimable — that is, either (a) or (b) but not both — or if there is a *reasonable possibility* that a liability may have been incurred, then the financial statements should include a foot-note explaining the nature of the contingency and an estimate of the possible loss, or range of loss, or a statement that an estimate cannot be made.

Audit Procedures. Searching for potential loss contingencies requires that auditors exercise not only keen judgment but significant creativity, since the existence of contingent liabilities is not always readily apparent. At a mini-mum, an auditor should perform the following procedures to search for un-recorded loss contingencies.

▲ Inquire of management about the possibility of unrecorded contingen-cies. (This inquiry is also made in the management representation let-ter illustrated later in the chapter.)

▲ Read minutes of the board of directors' and stockholders' meetings, and follow up on any indications of potential contingencies.

▲ Read contracts, loan agreements, lease agreements, and similar docu-ments.

▲ Review reports prepared by agents of the Internal Revenue Service and other taxing authorities.

▲ Analyze the legal expenses for the year, and examine documentation (e.g., invoices) from attorneys that may suggest litigation is pending or in progress.

▲ Review current-year working papers for indications of potential con-tingencies. (For example, the standard AICPA bank confirmation il-lustrated in Figure 12-7, page 497, specifically requests information on contingencies.)

Importantly, auditors are also responsible for loss contingencies that occur or are discovered after the balance sheet date, since they could be material sub-sequent events, discussed next in the chapter.

COMPLETING AN AUDIT

After completing the audit procedures discussed in Chapters 11 through 17 and in this chapter, an auditor performs procedures designed to ''wrap up'' the audit and to generate additional evidence that may affect audit conclusions for individual accounts and the auditor's opinion on the financial statements taken as a whole. These procedures are:

▲ Review for subsequent events.
▲ Make inquiries of a client's legal counsel.
▲ Obtain a management representation letter.
▲ Form an opinion on the financial statements.

Importantly, an auditor's responsibility for audited financial statements does not end either on the report date or when an audit report is physically communicated to the client. Rather, an auditor continues to be responsible for the:

▲ Communication with audit committees.
▲ Subsequent discovery of facts existing at the date of the auditor's report.
▲ Consideration of omitted procedures after the report date.

All these procedures and responsibilities are discussed below.

Subsequent Events Review

An auditor is primarily concerned with the balance sheet as of a particular date, such as December 31, 1990, and related statements of income, retained earnings, and cash flows for a particular period, such as January 1 through December 31, 1990. However, events sometimes occur or become known subsequent to the balance sheet date and before issuance of the audit report — the subsequent period — that have an effect upon financial statement disclosures. An independent auditor's responsibility for subsequent events and related audit procedures are addressed in AU Sections 560 and 561 of the *Codification of Statements on Auditing Standards*.

Subsequent events are classified into two major types:

▲ *Type I Events:* Subsequent events that disclose or confirm conditions existing at or before the balance sheet date and require adjustment to the financial statements.
▲ *Type II Events:* Subsequent events that disclose conditions arising after the balance sheet date and require disclosure, but not financial statement adjustment.

Type I Events. Type I events relate to conditions existing at or before the balance sheet date which affect estimates inherent in the process of preparing financial statements. Accordingly, the financial statements should be adjusted for any material changes in estimates. Examples include:

▲ Collection of receivables or settlement of liabilities in amounts substantially different from amounts recorded in financial statements at the balance sheet date.

▲ Realization of a loss on the sale of investments, inventories, or properties held for sale when the subsequent sale merely confirms a previously existing unrecognized loss.

▲ Discontinuance, at an estimated loss, of operations of a subsidiary where the contributing circumstances developed over a period of time prior to the balance sheet date.

Some Type I subsequent events require only a ''reclassification'' of amounts, rather than adjustment, and therefore do not affect recorded net income or loss. A common example is reclassifying long-term liabilities to short-term when an expected refinancing did not occur before the liabilities became due.

Type II Events. Type II events relate to conditions which did not exist at or before the balance sheet date, yet are disclosed because they may be of such significance that the financial statements would be misleading if the events are not disclosed. Normally, financial statements are supplemented with proforma information giving retroactive effect to Type II events. Examples include:

▲ Business combinations.

▲ Issuing of new notes, bonds, or other indebtedness.

▲ Changes in capital structure.

▲ Declaration of unusual cash or stock dividends or omission of a regular dividend.

▲ Damage from fire, flood, or other casualty.

Borderline Cases. In some cases, classifying an event as either Type I or Type II is questionable. For example, the sale or abandonment of significant manufacturing facilities typically results from careful management studies which, if not documented, are at least substantially contemplated over a somewhat lengthy period of time. Even if not ''contemplated,'' certainly the conditions leading to the motive for sale or abandonment (e.g., significant losses over several periods) would have arisen prior to the balance sheet date. Thus, in the case of a sale or abandonment, an argument could be made for either Type I or Type II treatment: Type I because conditions giving rise to the event probably occurred before year-end, and Type II because the economic impact of the event did not occur until after year-end.

A related question is the decision about whether adjustment or disclosure is really necessary at all. For example, declaring a regular quarterly dividend after year-end may not be considered worthy of disclosure if the entity has paid similar dividends for several years. That is, if a dividend is normally paid, disclosure may not be useful. On the other hand, however, a "first time" dividend declared after year-end certainly would represent useful information and should be disclosed.

Audit Procedures in the Subsequent Period. During the subsequent period, an auditor performs the majority of, if not all, year-end substantive tests, but is also responsible to detect and, if warranted, disclose material subsequent events. Some year-end substantive procedures, such as cutoff testing, partly address subsequent events, but are insufficient to discharge an auditor's responsibility for detecting and disclosing subsequent events. As a result, the *Codification of Statements on Auditing Standards* (AU Sec. 560.12) requires that the following procedures be performed at or near the completion of field work:

▲ Read the latest available interim financial statements and
  — Compare them with the financial statements being reported upon, and make any other comparisons considered appropriate in the circumstances.
  — Inquire of management whether the interim statements have been prepared on the same basis as the statements being audited.
▲ Inquire of and discuss with management
  — Whether any substantial contingent liabilities or commitments existed at the date of the balance sheet.
  — Whether there was any significant change in the capital stock, long-term debt, or working capital to the date of inquiry.
  — Whether there were any significant changes in estimates with respect to amounts included or disclosed in the financial statements.
  — Whether any unusual adjustments were made during the period from the balance sheet date to the date of inquiry.
▲ Read the available minutes of meetings of stockholders, directors, and appropriate committees, such as the finance committee.
▲ Assemble pertinent findings resulting from inquiries of legal counsel (discussed later in the chapter) and other auditing procedures concerning litigation, claims, and assessments
▲ Obtain a letter of representation (discussed later in the chapter), dated as of the date of the auditor's report, from management.

In addition, the auditor would make any additional inquiries or design and perform additional procedures to address any questions or uncertainties arising from the above procedures. Any necessary disclosures would be handled as follows.

Disclosure. Although they require adjustments to financial statements, Type I subsequent events generally need not also be disclosed by notes to the financial statements or other method. Type II events should be fully disclosed in any of the following alternative forms:

▲ Explanatory note.
▲ Parenthetical explanation.
▲ Reference in the financial statements to pro-forma information.
▲ If warranted by the circumstances, issuance of qualified opinion, adverse opinion, or disclaimer of opinion.

The use of an explanatory note can be illustrated by the following example. Assume X Company incurred a contingent liability on February 5, 1990 and the auditor's report is dated February 7, 1990. The information could be disclosed in an explanatory note as follows:

Note 12: Contingent liabilities.

On February 5, 1990 the management of X Company was advised by the U.S. Attorney located in New York City that a federal grand jury in New York had indicted the company on charges of conspiracy and fraud in the 1988 sale of the company's common stock to Y Investment Company. The management has not had sufficient time to properly evaluate the effect this indictment will have upon the company; however, we understand that the fine, if any, that could be levied against the company if found guilty of the actions charged, would not exceed $225,000.

Parenthetical explanations simply represent a comment next to the accounts affected in the financial statements. For example, liquidation of a material note payable after year-end could be disclosed in parentheses with Notes Payable on the balance sheet.

Pro-forma information, i.e., disclosing what the financial statements would have "looked like" if the event had occurred on or before year-end, may be appropriate if any Type II subsequent events are so material that historical financial statements alone would be misleading. Pro-forma statements, however, can be misleading themselves if certain events are included in the pro-forma statements and other significant events are excluded.

Issuing a qualified or adverse opinion or disclaiming an opinion is typically done only as a last resort, when all other efforts to persuade the client to use alternative disclosure methods have failed. The wording of these types of reports is discussed in Chapter 19.

Inquiry of Client's Legal Counsel

Occasionally, an economic event can impact financial position more heavily than a transaction. The most prominent illustration of such a significant event is loss contingencies, discussed above. A loss contingency arising from litigation, claims, and assessments, however, is not only an accounting and disclosure matter, but also a legal matter, since, as discussed earlier, a liability must be recorded when (a) the loss is probable and (b) the amount of the loss can be estimated reasonably. That is, determining the existence of a loss contingency is often a legal question, requiring that an auditor communicate directly with a client's attorney about liabilities arising from litigation, claims, and assessments.

Because of their own potential legal exposure for providing incorrect or confidential information, many attorneys had been reluctant to furnish auditors with letters divulging legal matters — sometimes called "legal letters." The most controversial issue underscoring most attorneys' reluctance involved "unasserted claims," claims for which a plaintiff may have a legal right but has not yet taken action. For example, an attorney may be aware of a client's exposure for infringing upon another entity's patent, even though no suit has been brought by the other entity. Obviously, if the attorney discloses the unasserted claim, the disclosure may well result in a claim being asserted against the client.

Following extensive correspondence between the AICPA and the American Bar Association, *Statement on Auditing Standards No. 12*, "Inquiry of a Client's Lawyer Concerning Litigation, Claims, and Assessments" (AU Sec. 337), was issued. SAS No. 12 requires that a list of legal issues be prepared by management and sent to the client's attorney, requesting information about (a) pending or threatened litigation, claims, and assessments and (b) unasserted claims and assessments. The attorney is requested to respond to each of the listed items.

As illustrated in Figure 18-3, the attorney is requested to furnish the following information for each pending or threatened litigation, claim, and assessment, and comment on differences between the attorney's and management's views (AU Sec. 337.09):

▲ A description of the nature of the matter, the case's progress to date, and action the client intends to take.
▲ An evaluation of the likelihood of an unfavorable outcome and an estimate, if one can be made, of the amount or range of potential loss.
▲ A statement that management's list of pending or threatened claims is complete, or identification of any omissions.

As also illustrated in Figure 18-3, for unasserted claims, an attorney is requested to identify any differences between management's and his or her views. Thus, SAS No. 12 requires that an attorney respond to management's representations regarding pending or threatened litigation and unasserted claims; it does not require that the attorney prepare a list. If an attorney fails to respond or responds insufficiently, a significant uncertainty may exist about

FIGURE 18-3
Inquiry Letter to Legal Counsel

INGSTROM CORPORATION
1710 Fawn Valley Drive
St. Louis, Missouri 63136

January 21, 1991

Benjamin & Nichols
Attorneys at Law
126 East 57th Street
New York, New York 10025

Dear Ms. Nichols:

In connection with an examination of our financial statements at December 31, 1990 and for the period then ended, management of the company has prepared, and furnished to our auditors (name and address of auditors), a description and evaluation of certain contingencies, including those set forth below involving matters with respect to which you have been engaged and to which you have devoted substantive attention on behalf of the company in the form of legal consultation or representation. These contingencies are regarded by management of the company as material for this purpose. Your response should include matters that existed at December 31, 1990 and during the period from that date to the date of your response.

Pending or Threatened Litigation

[In this section, management would list all pending or threatened litigation, including the following information for each: (1) the nature of the litigation, (2) the progress of the case, (3) the way management is responding or intends to respond, and (4) an evaluation of the likelihood of an unfavorable outcome and an estimate, if one can be made, of the amount or range of potential loss.]

Please furnish to our auditors such explanation, if any, that you consider necessary to supplement the foregoing information, including an explanation of those matters about which your views may differ from those stated and an indication of the omission of any pending or threatened litigation, claims, and assessments or a statement that the list of such matters is complete.

Unasserted Claims and Assessments

[In this section, management would list all probable unasserted claims and assessments, including the following for each: (1) the nature of the matter, (2) the way management intends to respond if the claim is asserted, and (3) an evaluation of the likelihood of an unfavorable outcome and an estimate, if one can be made, of the amount or range of potential loss.]

Please furnish to our auditors such explanation, if any, that you consider necessary to supplement the foregoing information, including an explanation of those matters as to which your views may differ from those stated.

We understand that whenever, in the course of performing legal services for us with respect to a matter recognized to involve an unasserted possible claim that may call for financial statement disclosure, you have formed a professional conclusion that we should disclose or consider disclosure concerning such possible claim or assessment, as a matter of professional responsibility to us, you will so advise us and will consult with us concerning the question of such disclosure and the applicable requirements of *Statement of Financial Accounting Standards No. 5*. Please specifically confirm to our auditors that our understanding is correct.

Please specifically identify the nature of and reasons for any limitation on your response.

Very truly yours,
Ingstrom Corporation

Charles Donnelly
President

---

the recording and disclosure of loss contingencies, requiring that an auditor modify the audit report, as discussed in Chapter 19.

Management Representation Letter

Throughout an audit engagement, an auditor obtains numerous representations from management. In fact, much of the evidence obtained during an audit consists of management's oral representations — for example, inquiries about errors, irregularities, and related parties — and written representations — for example, journals, ledgers, and other documentation. Although written representations are tangible, oral representations are not, thereby requiring that an auditor obtain a *management representation letter* documenting management's most significant representations.

In accordance with *Statement on Auditing Standards No. 19*, "Client Representations" (AU Sec. 333), the letter should be addressed to the auditor and dated as of the audit report date, since the auditor is concerned with events occurring through that date (AU Sec. 333.09). The letter should be signed by appropriate members of management, normally the chief executive officer and the chief financial officer, and should specifically state management's understanding that (1) financial statements are management's representations and primary responsibility, and (2) the auditors relied upon management's representations in forming an opinion on the financial statements.

The specific representations obtained for an audit engagement vary depending upon the circumstances, but ordinarily include the following matters (AU Sec. 333.04):

▲ Management's acknowledgment of its responsibility for the fair presentation in the financial statements of financial position, results of operations, and cash flows in conformity with generally accepted accounting principles or other comprehensive basis of accounting.
▲ Availability of all financial records and related data.
▲ Completeness and availability of all minutes of meetings of stockholders, directors, and committees of directors.
▲ Absence of errors in financial statements and unrecorded transactions.
▲ Information concerning related party transactions and related amounts receivable or payable.
▲ Information concerning subsequent events.
▲ Irregularities involving management or employees.
▲ Plans or intentions that may affect the carrying value or classification of assets or liabilities.
▲ Satisfactory title to assets, liens on assets, and assets pledged as collateral.

A management representation letter is so critical to an audit that management's refusal to furnish a written representation would preclude an auditor from issuing an unqualified opinion, regardless of the audit results otherwise. A sample representation letter appears in Figure 18-4.

FORMING AN OPINION

In a public accounting firm, an audit partner is responsible for reaching an overall opinion on financial statements taken as a whole after:

▲ Performing an overall analytical review of the financial statements through analytical procedures.
▲ Reviewing audit working papers in detail.
▲ Obtaining a technical review of the working papers by an audit partner not assigned to the engagement.

Each of these is discussed below.

FIGURE 18-4
Management Representation Letter

(From Client)

(To Independent Auditor)

In connection with your audit of the (identification of financial statements) of (name of client) as of (date) and for the (period of examination) for the purpose of expressing an opinion about whether the (consolidated) financial statements present fairly the financial position, results of operations, and cash flows of (name of client) in conformity with generally accepted accounting principles, we confirm, to the best of our knowledge and belief, the following representations made to you during your audit.

1. We are responsible for the fair presentation in the (consolidated) financial statements of financial position, results of operations, and cash flows in conformity with generally accepted accounting principles (other comprehensive basis of accounting).

2. We have made available to you all —
   a. Financial records and related data.
   b. Minutes of the meetings of stockholders, directors, and committees of directors, or summaries of actions of recent meetings for which minutes have not yet been prepared.

3. There have been no —
   a. Irregularities involving management or employees who have significant roles in the internal control structure.
   b. Irregularities involving other employees that could have a material effect on the financial statements.
   c. Communications from regulatory agencies concerning noncompliance with, or deficiencies in, financial reporting practices that could have a material effect on the financial statements.

4. We have no plans or intentions that may materially affect the carrying value or classification of assets and liabilities.

5. The following have been properly recorded or disclosed in the financial statements:
   a. Related party transactions and related amounts receivable or payable, including sales, purchases, loans, transfers, leasing arrangements, and guarantees.
   b. Capital stock repurchase options or agreements or capital stock reserved for options, warrants, conversions, or other requirements.
   c. Arrangements with financial institutions involving compensating balances or other arrangements involving restrictions on cash balances and line-of-credit or similar arrangements.
   d. Agreements to repurchase assets previously sold.

6. There are no —
   a. Violations or possible violations of laws or regulations whose ef-

FIGURE 18-4 (*continued*)

fects should be considered for disclosure in the financial statements or as a basis for recording a loss contingency.

b. Other material liabilities or gain or loss contingencies that are required to be accrued or disclosed by *Statement of Financial Accounting Standards No. 5.*

7. There are no unasserted claims or assessments that our lawyer has advised us are probable of assertion and must be disclosed in accordance with *Statement of Financial Accounting Standards No. 5.*

8. There are no material transactions that have not been properly recorded in the accounting records underlying the financial statements.

9. Provision, when material, has been made to reduce excess or obsolete inventories to their estimated net realizable value.

10. The company has satisfactory title to all owned assets, and there are no liens or encumbrances on such assets nor has any asset been pledged.

11. Provision has been made for any material loss to be sustained in the fulfillment of, or from inability to fulfill, any sales commitments.

12. Provision has been made for any material loss to be sustained as a result of purchase commitments for inventory quantities in excess of normal requirements or at prices in excess of the prevailing market prices.

13. We have complied with all aspects of contractual agreements that would have a material effect on the financial statements in the event of non-compliance.

14. No events have occurred subsequent to the balance sheet date that would require adjusment to, or disclosure in, the financial statements.

Analytical Procedures as an Overall Review

Statement on Auditing Standards No. 56, "Analytical Procedures," requires that, when completing an audit, an auditor apply analytical procedures encompassing the overall reasonableness of the financial statement accounts in an effort to identify issues that might otherwise have gone undetected during detailed testing. In short, at the completion of the audit, analytical procedures, such as ratio analysis, can be used to study and evaluate relationships among data that yield evidence about the reasonableness of reported financial information.

For example, analytical procedures applied to the relationship between recorded sales and accounts receivable does not provide evidence that the accounts may be misstated, but if sales were to decrease in the current period by fifty percent, an auditor might reasonably expect receivables to decrease by a comparable percentage. However, if receivables did not decrease significantly, the auditor might consider several potential explanations, among them:

▲ The allowance for doubtful accounts might be understated.
▲ Accounts receivable might be overstated.
▲ Sales might be understated.

If changes in relationships between account balances appear unreasonable, as in this illustration, the auditor should make suitable inquiries of management and then (a) evaluate the reasonableness of management's replies in relation to the auditor's knowledge of the client's business and other information obtained during the audit, and (b) consider the need to corroborate management's replies through additional procedures, such as further substantive tests of sales, receivables, and/or the allowance for doubtful accounts.

Working Paper Review

After documenting audit procedures for an individual financial statement account, an auditor documents his or her conclusion about the account in the audit working papers. The conclusion should state whether, in the auditor's judgment, (a) the account is presented fairly, (b) the account is not presented fairly, or (c) evidence is insufficient or inadequate to reach a conclusion. For example, a conclusion that an account is presented fairly might be worded:

> Based upon audit procedures performed, I am satisfied that *(name of the account)* is presented fairly at December 31, 1990.

A conclusion should be included on the lead schedule of each major financial statement account examined. Thereafter — typically on or about the last day of field work — the audit partner reviews the entire set of working papers, all of which should have been reviewed previously by the manager and senior accountants who acted in a supervisory capacity during the engagement. The partner's review is intended to determine whether the working papers demonstrate and document compliance with generally accepted auditing standards and the firm's standards of performance. Figure 18-5 outlines the partner's review process, indicating the major issues addressed in the review.

The audit partner reaches an overall opinion on the financial statements taken as a whole by considering the propriety of all audit conclusions documented within the working papers. If all the conclusions are favorable, the partner would issue an unqualified opinion. However, if any are unfavorable or if a conclusion is not reached for a specific account, the partner would consider the need to issue a qualified opinion, an adverse opinion, or a disclaimer of opinion, all of which are discussed in detail and illustrated in Chapter 19.

Obtain an Independent Technical Review

Before an audit report is communicated to a client, an audit partner or partners not otherwise assigned to the engagement should perform a technical review of the audit working papers, determining whether generally accepted auditing standards were followed and whether the working papers support the conclusions and opinion reached. The technical review represents the final step in the process of reviewing audit working papers, and therefore is the final check before an audit report and other documents, including financial statements, are delivered.

FIGURE 18-5
Working Paper Review Checklist

Mechanical Accuracy

- Trace supporting balances on individual working paper schedules to lead schedules.
- Trace lead schedule balances to working trial balances.
- Trace trial balance amounts to the financial statements.
- Review compliance with restrictive loan covenants.
- Review indexing of working papers.
- Review cross-referencing within the working papers.
- Test significant calculations in the working papers, for example:
  - Accruals for interest income and expense.
  - Accruals for state, local, and federal income taxes.
  - Accruals for pension and profit-sharing plans.
  - Depreciation.
  - Inventory price testing.
  - Lease calculations.
  - Earnings per share.
- Determine that all audit working papers are complete, properly headed, and dated.

Audit Scope

- Determine that the consideration of internal control structure is adequate and that the scope of year-end substantive tests of details is justified given the level of control risk.
- Determine that audit programs were appropriate for the circumstances.
- Determine that audit procedures adequately addressed the audit objectives of existence or occurrence, completeness, rights and obligations, valuation or allocation, and presentation and disclosure.

- Determine that the scope and results of the accounts receivable confirmations were reasonable.
- Determine that the physical inventory observation procedures were adequate.
- Determine that management representation letters are accurate, complete, and signed by management.
- Determine that legal letters are appropriate and signed.
- Determine that related party transactions are disclosed as necessary.
- Review all proposed adjusting journal entries.
- Determine that the audited financial statements are properly presented in accordance with generally accepted accounting principles.
- Determine that the opinion expressed in the audit report (unqualified, qualified, adverse, or disclaimer of opinion) is justified by evidence documented within the working papers.
- Determine that all exceptions and review notes within the working papers have been cleared.

COMMUNICATION WITH AUDIT COMMITTEES

Throughout an independent audit, auditors acquire information that does not necessarily require disclosure in the financial statements, but that may be helpful to the board of director's audit committee in discharging their responsibility for overseeing the entity's financial reporting function. Certain professional pronouncements require that auditors communicate specific matters to the audit committee, among them SAS No. 60, "The Communication of Internal Control Structure Related Matters Noted in an Audit," discussed in Chapter 7, and SAS No. 53, "The Auditor's Responsibility to Detect and Report Errors and Irregularities," and SAS No. 54, "Illegal Acts by Clients," both discussed in Chapter 3. Given the increasing responsibility assumed by audit committees as the sole intermediary between external auditors and the full board of directors, the Auditing Standards Board in 1988 issued *Statement on Auditing Standards No. 61*, "Communication with Audit Committees," which requires that auditors communicate to the audit committee additional information not specifically addressed otherwise in professional pronouncements but that may assist the committee in overseeing the financial reporting and disclosure process for which management is responsible.

The statement requires communication with the audit committee, but does not preclude communication with management or others within the entity who may benefit from the information. The matters to be communicated are:

▲ The auditor's responsibility under generally accepted auditing standards.

▲ Significant accounting policies.

▲ Management judgments and accounting estimates.

▲ Significant audit adjustments.

▲ Other information in documents containing audited financial statements.

▲ Disagreements with management.

▲ Consultation made by management with other accountants about accounting and auditing matters.

▲ Major issues discussed with management prior to retaining the auditor for the next audit.

▲ Difficulties encountered in performing the audit.

The communications specified are typically incidental to the audit and therefore need not be made before issuance of the audit report. In addition, the communication may either be oral or written, although if oral, should be documented by written memoranda in the working papers.

SUBSEQUENT DISCOVERY OF FACTS EXISTING AT REPORT DATE

After an audit report has been issued, an auditor is under no obligation to make any further or continuing inquiries or to perform any additional audit procedures. However, sometimes new information may surface which bears on one or more of an auditor's objectives, and which would have impacted the audited financial statements or audit report had the information come to the auditor's attention before or on the report date. For example, the auditor may become aware that inventory had become obsolete, indicating that inventory valuation is overstated, or that an essential footnote was omitted, indicating presentation and disclosure is incomplete. Regardless of whether the new information could or should have been known by the auditor as of the report date, he or she is responsible to discuss the matter with appropriate levels of management, including the board of directors, and to take additional action if:

▲ The information is reliable,

▲ The facts existed at the report date,

▲ The audit report would have been affected if the information had been known, and

▲ Persons are currently relying or are likely to rely on the financial statements and would attach importance to the information.

The additional action taken by an auditor would depend on whether the client makes appropriate disclosure of the newly discovered information, as discussed below. However, in either case — that is, whether the client makes additional disclosures, or refuses — the auditor's overriding concern is to assure that current and potential financial statement users no longer place reliance on the originally issued audit report.

Client Makes Disclosure

When a client agrees to make appropriate disclosure, the method and form of disclosure will depend on the circumstances. If the effect of the newly discovered information can be determined promptly, disclosure would consist of revised financial statements and a revised audit report. The reasons for revision should be described in a note to the financial statements and referred to in the auditor's report. Further, the revised statements and report should be communicated to all persons known to be, or likely to be, relying on them. However, if the effect of the newly discovered information cannot be determined without a prolonged investigation, the issuance of revised statements and a revised report would be necessarily delayed. In this case, appropriate disclosure would consist of the client notifying all persons known to be or likely to be relying on the originally issued statements that the report should no longer be relied on and that revised financial statements and a revised audit report are forthcoming.

Client Refuses Disclosure

In contrast, if the client refuses to make appropriate disclosure, the auditor should notify each member of the board of directors about management's refusal. In addition, unless the auditor's attorney recommends a different course of action, the auditor should formally notify management, the regulatory agencies having jurisdiction over the client, and each person known to be relying on the financial statements that the originally issued auditor's report should no longer be relied upon. For publicly traded clients, notification to each person known to be relying on the report is an ominous, time-consuming task. As a result, notification to the regulatory agencies will usually be the only practicable method for the auditor to provide appropriate disclosure.

CONSIDERATION OF OMITTED PROCEDURES
AFTER THE REPORT DATE

The previous section dealt with the subsequent discovery of *facts* existing at the report date. But what if a public accounting firm's peer review or internal quality-control inspection reveals that a client's previously issued financial statements are fairly stated but that one or more necessary *auditing procedures* were omitted during the audit engagement? This situation is addressed in *Statement on Auditing Standards No. 46,* "Consideration of Omitted Procedures after the Report Date" (AU Sec. 390).

As in the subsequent discovery of facts, an auditor is under no obligation either to perform audit procedures after the report is issued or to conduct any retrospective review of previously completed audit work. However, because of potential legal liability for due diligence, an auditor should consider consulting an attorney and, with the attorney's advice and assistance, determine an appropriate course of action.

In most cases, the auditor would assess the importance of the omitted procedures to the financial statements taken as a whole by reviewing the completed working papers, discussing the circumstances with assigned audit staff, and, from this information, reevaluating overall audit scope. That is, was the extent of audit scope adequate even in the absence of the procedures omitted? For example, an auditor might conclude that confirming loans and other long-term notes payable was adequate to partially address the objectives of existence, obligations, and valuation even though the audit program reveals that bond indentures and other long-term indebtedness agreements were not examined. However, if the auditor believes that a previously issued report is no longer supported absent the procedures, and that persons are either relying or likely to rely on the report, he or she should promptly undertake to apply the omitted procedures. If as a result of applying the omitted procedures the auditor concludes that the previously issued report is no longer supported, he or she should assure that current and potential financial statement users no longer place reliance on the previously issued report by following the procedures discussed in the previous section of this chapter.

SUMMARY

This chapter, which concludes the discussion of detailed audit procedures, addressed substantive tests of revenue and expense accounts and introduced procedures necessary to complete a financial statement audit. In general, substantive tests of revenue and expense accounts take the form of detailed tests or reasonableness tests (analytical procedures), both of which can be used to provide complete or partial support for the audit objectives of occurrence, valuation or allocation, completeness, and presentation and disclosure.

When completing an audit, an auditor must review for both material subsequent events and for contingent liabilities. Each requires considerable judgment because, unlike many other audit areas, neither is recorded in the financial statements. An auditor must also make inquiries of a client's legal counsel about pending or threatened litigation and unasserted claims, and obtain a representation letter from management about assertions made during the engagement.

To form an overall opinion on the financial statements taken as a whole, auditors review the entire set of working papers and perform overall analytical procedures. In turn, before an audit report is issued, an independent review should be performed by an audit partner not otherwise assigned to the engagement. The purpose of the independent review is to provide assurance that members of the audit team — most of whom have been involved in the details of the engagement — have not overlooked an issue central to either the audited financial statements or the audit report.

Even after communicating with the audit committee and after an audit report is issued, the auditor maintains responsibility for the subsequent discovery of facts existing at the date of the auditor's report, and for consideration of the omission of procedures during the engagement, both of which are critical to an auditor's potential legal liability.

QUESTIONS

1. Identify and briefly discuss the two types of substantive tests an auditor performs for revenue and expense accounts.
2. "Subsequent events" occur after the last day of an entity's fiscal year and on or before the report date. Why would an auditor be concerned about transactions and events occurring in this time period?
3. What is the difference between Type I and Type II subsequent events?
4. Identify the alternative types of disclosure appropriate for Type II subsequent events.
5. What is the purpose of a management representation letter?
6. What information should an auditor request from a client's legal counsel in a letter of audit inquiry?
7. What is the relationship between audit conclusions reached for individual financial statement accounts and an auditor's overall opinion on financial statements taken as a whole?
8. In general, what auditing procedures does an auditor apply during the subsequent period in order to isolate significant subsequent events?
9. Under what conditions would an auditor take action for the subsequent discovery of facts existing at the report date?
10. How should an auditor proceed if a client refuses to disclose the subsequent discovery of facts existing at the report date?

11. How should an auditor proceed in the event he or she becomes aware after the report date that audit procedures were omitted during the engagement?

MULTIPLE CHOICE QUESTIONS

1. An auditor compares revenues and expenses of the current year with those of the prior year and investigates all changes exceeding 10%. By this procedure the auditor would be most likely to learn that

   a. An increase in property tax rates has not been recognized in the client's accrual.
   b. The current year provision for uncollectible accounts is inadequate, because of worsening economic conditions.
   c. Fourth-quarter payroll taxes were not paid.
   d. The client changed its capitalization policy for small tools in the current year.
                                                                      (AICPA Adapted)

2. "Subsequent events" for reporting purposes are defined as events which occur subsequent to the

   a. Balance sheet date.
   b. Date of the auditor's report.
   c. Balance sheet date but prior to the date of the auditor's report.
   d. Date of the auditor's report and concern contingencies which are not reflected in the financial statements.   (AICPA Adapted)

3. Under which of the following circumstances may audited financial statements contain a note disclosing a subsequent event which is labeled unaudited?

   a. When the subsequent event does not require adjustment of the financial statements.
   b. When the event occurs after completion of field work and before issuance of the auditor's report.
   c. When audit procedures with respect to the subsequent event were not performed by the auditor.
   d. When the event occurs between the date of the auditor's original report and the date of the reissuance of the report.   (AICPA Adapted)

4. Which event that occurred after the end of the fiscal year under audit but prior to issuance of the auditor's report would not require disclosure in the financial statements?

   a. Sale of a bond or capital stock issue.
   b. Loss of plant or inventories as a result of fire or flood.
   c. A major drop in the quoted market price of the stock of the corporation.
   d. Settlement of litigation when the event giving rise to the claim took place after the balance sheet date.   (AICPA Adapted)

5. Auditors often request that the audit client send a letter of inquiry to those attorneys who have been consulted with respect to litigation, claims, or assessments. The primary reason for this request is to provide the auditor with

   a. An estimate of the dollar amount of the probable loss.
   b. An expert opinion as to whether a loss is possible, probable, or remote.
   c. Information concerning the progress of cases to date.
   d. Corroborative evidential matter.   (AICPA Adapted)

6. A CPA has received an attorney's letter in which no significant disagreements with the client's assessments of contingent liabilities were noted. The resignation of the client's lawyer shortly after receipt of the letter should alert the auditor that

   a. Undisclosed unasserted claims may have arisen.
   b. The attorney was unable to form a conclusion with respect to the significance of litigation, claims, and assessments.
   c. The auditor must begin a completely new examination of contingent liabilities.
   d. An adverse opinion will be necessary.   (AICPA Adapted)

7. A lawyer's response to an auditor's request for information concerning litigation, claims, and assessments will ordinarily contain which of the following?

   a. An explanation regarding limitations on the scope of the response.
   b. A statement of concurrence with the client's determination of which unasserted possible claims warrant specification.
   c. Confidential information which would be prejudicial to the client's defense if publicized.
   d. An assertion that the list of unasserted possible claims identified by the client represents all such claims of which the lawyer may be aware.
                                                               (AICPA Adapted)

8. A lawyer's response to a letter of audit inquiry may be limited to matters that are considered individually or collectively material to the financial statements if

   a. The auditor has instructed the lawyer regarding the limits of materiality in financial statements.
   b. The client and the auditor have agreed on the limits of materiality and the lawyer has been notified.
   c. The lawyer and auditor have reached an understanding on the limits of materiality for this purpose.
   d. The lawyer's response to the inquiry explains the legal meaning of materiality limits and establishes quantitative parameters.   (AICPA Adapted)

9. An attorney is responding to an independent auditor as a result of the audit client's letter of inquiry. The attorney may appropriately limit the response to

   a. Asserted claims and litigation.
   b. Matters to which the attorney has given substantive attention in the form of legal consultation or representation.

    c. Asserted, overtly threatened, or pending claims and litigation.

    d. Items which have an extremely high probability of being resolved to the client's detriment. (AICPA Adapted)

10. A representation letter issued by a client

    a. Is essential for the preparation of the audit program.

    b. Is a substitute for testing.

    c. Does not reduce the auditor's responsibility.

    d. Reduces the auditor's responsibility only to the extent that it is relied upon. (AICPA Adapted)

11. The date of the management representation letter should coincide with the

    a. Date of the auditor's report.

    b. Balance sheet date.

    c. Date of the latest subsequent event referred to in the notes to the financial statements.

    d. Date of the engagement agreement. (AICPA Adapted)

12. Management's refusal to furnish a written representation on a matter which the auditor considers essential constitutes

    a. Prima facie evidence that the financial statements are not presented fairly.

    b. A violation of the Foreign Corrupt Practices Act.

    c. An uncertainty sufficient to preclude an unqualified opinion.

    d. A scope limitation sufficient to preclude an unqualified opinion. (AICPA Adapted)

PROBLEMS

18-1   In a properly planned audit of financial statements, the auditor coordinates his or her reviews of specific balance sheet and income statement accounts.

Required:
Discuss the reasons for coordinating the examinations and illustrate by examples.
(AICPA Adapted)

18-2   Michele Avery, a partner in a regional CPA firm, is conducting the independent technical review of working papers for the December 31, 1990 year-end audit of Singer Corporation. In 1987, two years before Avery was admitted to the partnership, she was the audit manager on the Singer engagement.

    One of the working papers, a schedule of ratios and an analysis of account balance changes from 1989 to 1990, indicates that advertising expense, stated at $150,000 on December 31, 1989, rose to $180,000 in 1990, an increase of $30,000, or 20 percent. Sales and cost of goods sold in both years were relatively stable. Avery reviews a working paper schedule, ''Analysis of Advertising Expense,'' which reveals that for $20,000 of the 1990 advertising expense balance the audit staff examined advertising copy and invoices, and traced payments to the cash disbursements records. Interim tests of controls indicated that control procedures over advertising transactions are not particularly reliable. The working papers provide no explanation of the $30,000 increase in advertising.

Required:
(1) Explain the purpose of an independent technical review of working papers.
(2) Is Avery a reasonable choice to perform the 1990 independent technical review given that she was the manager on the 1987 Singer Corporation audit? Explain.
(3) In your judgment, were the nature and scope of the audit of advertising expense reasonable? Explain.

18-3   Michael, CPA, is examining the financial statements of the Diannah Corporation as of and for the period ended September 30, 1990. Michael plans to complete the field work and sign the auditor's report on November 15, 1990. Michael's audit work is primarily designed to obtain evidence that will provide a reasonable degree of assurance that the Diannah Corporation's September 30, 1990 financial statements present fairly the financial position, results of operations, and cash flows of that enterprise in accordance with generally accepted accounting principles. Michael is concerned, however, about events and transactions of Diannah Corporation that occur after September 30, 1990, since Michael does not have the same degree of assurance for such events as for those that occurred in the period ending September 30, 1990.

Required:
Define what is commonly referred to in auditing as a "subsequent event" and describe the two general types of subsequent events that require consideration by the management of Diannah Corporation and evaluation by Michael. (AICPA Adapted)

18-4   Although an auditor reaches an opinion on financial statements as of the last day of a client's fiscal year, e.g. December 31, the auditor is also responsible for material transactions or events occuring through the last day of field work that provide additional evidence regarding financial statement disclosures as of the balance sheet date.

Required:
Describe the specific procedures an auditor should apply at or near the completion of field work to transactions occurring in the subsequent period.

18-5   In connection with his audit of Flowmeter, Inc., for the year ended December 31, 1989, Jason Hirsch, CPA, is aware that certain events and transactions that took place after December 31, 1989, but before he issues his report dated February 28, 1990, may affect the company's financial statements.
     The following material events or transactions have come to his attention.
(a) On January 3, 1990, Flowmeter Inc., received a shipment of raw materials from Canada. The materials had been ordered in October, 1989, and shipped FOB shipping point in November, 1989.
(b) On January 15, 1990, the company settled and paid a personal injury claim of a former employee as the result of an accident which occurred in March 1985. The company had not previously recorded a liability for the claim.
(c) On January 25, 1990, the company agreed to purchase for cash the outstanding

stock of Porter Electrical Co. The acquisition is likely to double the sales volume of Flowmeter, Inc.

(d) On February 1, 1990, a plant owned by Flowmeter, Inc., was damaged by a flood, resulting in an uninsured loss of inventory.

(e) On February 5, 1990, Flowmeter, Inc., issued and sold to the general public $2,000,000 in convertible bonds.

Required:

For each of the above events or transactions, indicate the audit procedures that should have brought the item to the attention of the auditor, and the form of disclosure in the financial statements including the reasons for such disclosures.

Arrange your answer in the following format:

Item	Audit Procedures	Required Disclosure and Reasons

(AICPA Adapted)

18-6   Windek, a CPA, is nearing the completion of an examination of the financial statements of Jubilee, Inc., for the year ended December 31, 1990. Windek is currently concerned with ascertaining the occurrence of subsequent events that may require adjustment or disclosure essential to a fair presentation in conformity with generally accepted accounting principles.

Required:

(1) Briefly explain what is meant by the phrase "subsequent event."
(2) How do those subsequent events which require financial statement adjustment differ from those that require financial statements disclosure?
(3) What are the procedures which should be performed in order to ascertain the occurrence of subsequent events?   (AICPA Adapted)

18-7   During an audit engagement, Harper, CPA, has satisfactorily completed an examination of accounts payable and other liabilities and now plans to determine whether there are any loss contingencies arising from litigation, claims, or assessments.

Required:

What are the audit procedures that Harper should follow with respect to the existence of loss contingencies arising from litigation, claims, and assessments? Do not discuss reporting requirements.   (AICPA Adapted)

18-8   Statement on Auditing Standards No. 19, "Client Representations," establishes a requirement that the independent auditor obtain certain written representations from management as a part of an audit made in accordance with generally accepted auditing standards.

Required:

(a) What are the objectives of obtaining management representation letters?
(b) Who should prepare and sign the representation letters?

(c) When should the representation letters be obtained?

(d) Why should the representation letters be prepared for each examination?

(AICPA Adapted)

18-9   Oscar Morales, CPA, is completing the June 30, 1990 audit of Carter, Rice, Storrs & Bement, a manufacturer and supplier of paper products. The company has operated successfully since 1948 when it was founded by Charles Carter, still the chief executive officer. The last day of field work is August 2, 1990.

During the engagement, Morales received numerous oral representations, but is particularly concerned with representations relating to:

• Potential irregularities involving management and employees.

• Related party transactions.

• Compensating balances involving restrictions on cash balances.

• Possible violations of state law.

• Loss contingencies.

• Potential unasserted claims or assessments.

Morales has no evidence to suggest that any of the items listed is necessarily a problem in the Carter, Rice engagement, but is concerned that the client may not sign a management representation letter because of the potential legal implications if some of the items listed were to occur without management's knowledge.

Required:

(1) Draft a management representation letter, including the proper date, addressee, and signatory. The letter should cover only the items listed.

(2) How should Morales proceed if management fails to sign the representation letter?

18-10   During the audit of the annual financial statements of Amis Manufacturing, Inc., the company's president, R. Alderman, and Luddy, the auditor, reviewed matters that were supposed to be included in a written representation letter. Upon receipt of the following client representation letter, Luddy contacted Alderman to state that it was incomplete.

To. E. K. Luddy, CPA

In connection with your audit of the balance sheet of Amis Manufacturing, Inc. as of December 31, 1989, and the related statements of income, retained earnings, and cash flows for the year then ended, for the purpose of expressing an opinion as to whether the financial statements present fairly the financial position, results of operations, and cash flows of Amis Manufacturing, Inc., in conformity with generally accepted accounting principles, we confirm, to the best of our knowledge and belief, the following representations made to you during your examination. There were no:

• Plans or intentions that may materially affect the carrying value or classification of assets and liabilities.

• Communications from regulatory agencies concerning noncompliance with, or deficiencies in, financial reporting practices.

• Agreements to repurchase assets previously sold.

• Violations or possible violations of laws or regulations whose effects should be considered for disclosure in the financial statements or as a basis for recording a loss contingency.

- Unasserted claims or assessments that our lawyer has advised are probable of assertion and must be disclosed in accordance with *Statement of Financial Accounting Standards No. 5.*
- Capital stock repurchase options or agreements or capital stock reserved for options, warrants, conversions, or other requirements.
- Compensating balance or other arrangements involving restrictions on cash balances.

R. Alderman, President
Amis Manufacturing, Inc.

March 14, 1990

Required:

Identify the other matters that Alderman's representation letter should specifically confirm.   (AICPA Adapted)

PART **IV** REPORTING

IV

REPORTS ON AUDITED
FINANCIAL STATEMENTS

19

Major topics discussed in this chapter are the:

▲ *Historical evolution of audit reports.*
▲ *Major components of a standard audit report.*
▲ *Types of opinions: unqualified, qualified, adverse, and disclaimer of opinion.*
▲ *Meaning, required circumstances, and wording for modifications to standard audit reports.*
▲ *Reporting requirements for comparative financial statements.*
▲ *Auditor's responsibility for information accompanying or derived from audited financial statements, including supplementary information required by the FASB, segment information, information in auditor-submitted documents, condensed financial statements, and selected financial data.*
▲ *Auditor's responsibility for reporting on financial statements prepared for use in foreign countries.*

The *attest function* is the process of communicating an opinion (or disclaiming an opinion) on financial statements, and the *audit report* is the auditor's means of communication. The language of audit reports is fairly uniform, and depending on the circumstances, a report may be three or more paragraphs in length. A *standard audit report* contains three paragraphs and states that the financial statements present fairly, in all material respects, financial position, results of operations, and cash flows in conformity with generally accepted accounting principles.

This chapter begins with a discussion of the evolution of audit reports, followed by an overview of the major elements of a standard report. In turn, the types of opinions — unqualified, qualified, adverse, and disclaimer — are described, and modifications to standard reports are discussed and illustrated. The chapter continues with discussions of comparative financial statements, and an auditor's responsibility for information accompanying or derived from audited financial statements.

EVOLUTION OF AUDIT REPORTS

Auditing in the United States evolved from Scotland and Great Britain in general and in particular from the English Joint Stock Companies Act of 1844. The Act required that an auditor be appointed to report on the fairness of a listed company's financial statements. Prior to that time, auditors' reports on published financial statements were rare.

As Scottish and British investments came to the U.S. in the late nineteenth century, so too did Scottish and British accountants. Prominent among them was George O. May, senior partner of Price Waterhouse & Co., who, as chairman of an American Institute of Accountants committee on cooperation with stock exchanges, first drafted the wording of a standard audit report. The report appeared in a 1934 pamphlet entitled "Audits of Corporate Reports." Audit reports prior to that time were not uniform in either form or content. In 1949, the American Institute of CPAs adopted standard report wording that incorporated a reference to GAAS and that contained language which would not change appreciably until 1988.

Although the standard audit report remained essentially unchanged from 1949 to 1988, it was not without critics. For example, in 1978, the Commission on Auditors' Responsibilities in its *Report, Conclusions, and Recommendations* criticized the clarity of audit reports, concluding that the language of the standard report was somewhat confusing and unsatisfactory as a means for communicating information to the financial markets. Also in 1978, proposed Congressional legislation (the Public Accountancy Regulation Act) and the Securities and Exchange Commission both suggested that the auditor's standard report be revised.

The Auditing Standards Board addressed criticisms of the standard report over a three-year period from 1978 to 1980, and proposed major revisions to the content of standard audit reports. The changes were intended to provide the users of audit reports with a clearer indication of the character of an audit — and the degree of responsibility an auditor assumes — by incorporating concepts from authoritative professional literature that were only implied rather than expressed in the standard wording. In 1980, the Board issued a proposed Statement on Auditing Standards. But, as a result of opposition expressed in public hearings and in comment letters (over 450 letters were submitted, an unprecedented number), the Auditing Standards Board voted in 1981 to rescind the proposed SAS, allowing the standard wording to remain intact.

Partly in response to hearings conducted by the House Subcommittee on Oversight and Investigations in the 1980s, and as part of the expectation gap agenda, the Auditing Standards Board reconsidered the standard audit report and in 1988 issued SAS No. 58, "Reports on Audited Financial Statements."

SAS No. 58 made sweeping changes to the standard report. Significant among the changes were the addition of an introductory paragraph that differentiates management's responsibility for the financial statements from the auditor's role in issuing an opinion on them, and a scope paragraph which acknowledges that an audit provides reasonable assurance, within the context of materiality, and adds a brief explanation of what an audit entails.

An example of today's standard report on comparative financial statements follows:

Independent Auditor's Report

(Introductory Paragraph)

We have audited the accompanying balance sheets of X Company as of December 31, 19X2 and 19X1, and the related statements of income, retained earnings, and cash flows for the years then ended. These financial statements are the responsibility of the Company's management. Our responsibility is to express an opinion on these financial statements based on our audits.

(Scope Paragraph)

We conducted our audits in accordance with generally accepted auditing standards. Those standards require that we plan and perform the audit to obtain reasonable assurance about whether the financial statements are free of material misstatement. An audit includes examining, on a test basis, evidence supporting the amounts and disclosures in the financial statements. An audit also includes assessing the accounting principles used and significant estimates made by management, as well as evaluating the overall financial statement presentation. We believe that our audits provide a reasonable basis for our opinion.

(Opinion Paragraph)

In our opinion, the financial statements referred to above present fairly, in all material respects, the financial position of X Company as of December 31, 19X2 and 19X1, and the results of its operations and its cash flows for the years then ended in conformity with generally accepted accounting principles.

The above three-paragraph, standard report includes several basic elements:

▲ A title that includes the word "independent."
▲ A statement that the financial statements were audited.
▲ A statement that the financial statements are management's responsi-

bility, and that the auditor's responsibility is to express an opinion on
them.

▲ A statement that the audit was conducted in accordance with generally
accepted auditing standards.

▲ A statement that generally accepted auditing standards require planning and performing the audit to obtain reasonable assurance about
whether the financial statements are free of material misstatement.

▲ A statement that an audit includes (1) examining evidence on a test
basis, (2) evaluating the accounting principles and significant estimates
used by management, and (3) evaluating the overall financial statement presentation.

TYPES OF OPINIONS

An independent auditor forms an opinion on financial statements by reviewing the conclusions reached about each financial statement amount and
disclosure. The process of forming an opinion is similar to the decision making process illustrated in Chapter 3, Figure 3-1, and begins when the audit is
planned, continues during the engagement's interim phase, and concludes
during the year-end phase.

An audit under generally accepted auditing standards may result in any
one of four types of opinions, which were introduced and briefly described
in Chapter 1:

▲ Unqualified Opinion
▲ Qualified Opinion
▲ Adverse Opinion
▲ Disclaimer of Opinion

Unqualified Opinion

An *unqualified opinion* communicates a favorable signal and means the
financial statements present financial position, results of operations, and cash
flows in conformity with generally accepted accounting principles. This type
of report cannot be issued if any of the generally accepted auditing standards
is violated. In most cases, a report that expresses an unqualified opinion contains the standard introductory, scope, and opinion paragraphs illustrated earlier. However, when an opinion is based partly on the report of another auditor or when an auditor emphasizes a particular matter within the report, an
explanatory paragraph may be added to the standard report without distorting
or detracting from the meaning of an unqualified opinion.

Qualified Opinion

A *qualified opinion* means that "except for" the effects of a particular matter, the financial statements present financial position, results of operations, and cash flows in conformity with generally accepted accounting principles. Only the term "except for" or some variation — like "except," "exception," or "with the exception of" — may be used to qualify an opinion. Qualified opinions are issued when there is a lack of evidence or restrictions on the scope of an audit, or the auditor believes the financial statements contain a material departure from generally accepted accounting principles.

Adverse Opinion

An *adverse opinion* means the financial statements do not present the financial position, results of operations, and cash flows in conformity with generally accepted accounting principles. Adverse opinions are issued when the effect of a departure from generally accepted accounting principles is so material that a qualified opinion is unwarranted.

Disclaimer of Opinion

A *disclaimer of opinion* means an auditor does not express an opinion on the financial statements. Generally, a disclaimer of opinion is issued when the auditor has not performed an audit sufficient in scope to provide a basis for an opinion on the financial statements. As suggested, the difference between a qualified opinion and an adverse opinion is the auditor's professional judgment about the materiality of the effects on financial statements. In turn, the essential difference between a disclaimer of opinion and an adverse opinion is that an auditor disclaims when there is insufficient evidence to reach an opinion — for example, when the scope of an audit is limited by the client. In an adverse opinion, sufficient evidence *is* available.

THE STANDARD REPORT: AN OVERVIEW

The specific content of a standard report is determined by the extent and results of an audit. However, a standard audit report normally includes a date, addressee, introductory paragraph, scope paragraph, opinion paragraph, and auditor's signature, all of which are illustrated in the following report for the Randolph International Corporation. Note that the Randolph report differs somewhat from the sample report presented on page 761. The Randolph report relates to consolidated financial statements, as opposed to statements for a single company, and identifies a statement of stockholders' equity rather than retained earnings. Also, the Randolph report applies to statements of income, equity, and cash flows for three years rather than two. Publicly held companies are required by the SEC to present these statements for a three-year period. In all other respects, the Randolph report and the sample report presented earlier are the same. Both are examples of an auditor's standard report. The major components of the Randolph report are discussed below.

November 6, 1990

Independent Auditor's Report

To the Directors and Stockholders of
Randolph International Corporation:

We have audited the consolidated balance sheets of Randolph International Corporation as of September 30, 1990 and 1989, and the related consolidated statements of income, stockholders' equity, and cash flows for each of the three years in the period ended September 30, 1990. These financial statements are the responsibility of the Company's management. Our responsibility is to express an opinion on these financial statements based on our audits.

We conducted our audits in accordance with generally accepted auditing standards. Those standards require that we plan and perform the audit to obtain reasonable assurance about whether the financial statements are free of material misstatement. An audit includes examining, on a test basis, evidence supporting the amounts and disclosures in the financial statements. An audit also includes assessing the accounting principles used and significant estimates made by management, as well as evaluating the overall financial statement presentation. We believe that our audits provide a reasonable basis for our opinion.

In our opinion, the consolidated financial statements referred to above present fairly, in all material respects, the financial position of Randolph International Corporation as of September 30, 1990 and 1989, and the results of its operations and its cash flows for each of the three years in the period ended September 30, 1990, in conformity with generally accepted accounting principles.

Correnti & Saunders, CPAs
One PPG Place
Pittsburgh, Pennsylvania 15222

Date of Report

A report is dated as of the day audit work is completed in the client's office, i.e., the last day of field work. For example, the Randolph report is dated November 6, 1990 because field work for the September 30, 1990 year-end audit was completed on November 6.

The date of a report is quite significant because it identifies the end of the period for which an auditor is responsible to search for material events occurring after the balance sheet date which may affect the audited financial statements. For example, since the Randolph report is dated November 6, 1990, the auditors are responsible for any material events occurring between October 1, 1990 and November 6, 1990 that would require disclosure in the financial statements for September 30, 1990 (the balance sheet date). These subsequent events were discussed in Chapter 18.

On occasion, a material subsequent event may occur and come to an auditor's attention after the last day of field work but before the report is released. If the financial statements are revised to include disclosure of the subsequent event, the auditor has two alternatives for dating the report:

▲ Date the report as of the date of the subsequent event, for example, "November 15, 1990."
▲ Dual date the report, for example, "November 6, 1990 except for Note X, November 15, 1990."

Dual dating extends an auditor's responsibility beyond the last day of field work, but only for the specific subsequent event disclosed. Dating the entire report as of the later date extends an auditor's responsibility beyond the last day of field work (e.g., from November 6 to November 15), even to events neither discovered nor disclosed.

Addressee

An auditor's report for a corporation may be addressed to the company whose financial statements have been audited or to the board of directors, stockholders, or both. Note that the Randolph report is addressed to both the directors and the stockholders. A report for an unincorporated entity may be addressed to the partners, the general partner, or the proprietor. Occasionally, an auditor is engaged by one entity to audit the financial statements of another entity. In such cases, the auditor's report is generally addressed to the client rather than the company whose statements were audited.

Introductory Paragraph

The introductory paragraph states that the financial statements were audited; that the statements are management's, not the auditor's, responsibility; and that the auditor is responsible only to express an opinion on the statements, not for the amounts and disclosures included within the statements.

The role of the introductory paragraph is to differentiate management's responsibility (for the financial statements) from the auditor's responsibility (to express an opinion on management's financial statements).

Scope Paragraph

The scope paragraph states that the audit was performed in accordance with generally accepted auditing standards and describes what an audit is. The paragraph is typically worded as illustrated in the Randolph report. This standard wording implies compliance with the three general standards and the three standards of field work, discussed in Chapter 5. Thus, a standard scope paragraph can be interpreted as follows:

Compliance with General Standards
▲ The examination was performed by a person or persons having adequate technical training and proficiency as an auditor.
▲ An independence in mental attitude was maintained by the auditor.
▲ Due professional care was exercised in the performance of the audit and preparation of the report.

Compliance with Field Work Standards
▲ The work was adequately planned and assistants were properly supervised.
▲ A sufficient understanding of internal control structure was obtained to plan the audit and to determine the nature, timing, and extent of tests to be performed.
▲ Sufficient competent evidential matter was obtained to afford a reasonable basis for an opinion on the financial statements.

Each of these statements must be true without qualification for an auditor to use the wording of a standard scope paragraph. Otherwise, the scope paragraph must be changed. Examples of departures from the wording of a standard scope paragraph are presented later in this chapter.

Opinion Paragraph

The opinion paragraph follows the scope paragraph in a standard report and states that the financial statements present fairly, in all material respects, financial position, results of operations, and cash flows. A standard opinion paragraph is illustrated in the Randolph report. Just as the wording of a standard scope paragraph implies compliance with the general and field standards, the wording of a standard opinion paragraph implies compliance with the four standards of reporting. Thus, a standard opinion paragraph can be interpreted as follows:

Compliance with Reporting Standards

▲ The financial statements are presented in accordance with generally
  accepted accounting principles.
▲ Accounting principles have been applied consistently.
▲ Informative disclosures are reasonably adequate.
▲ The opinion relates to the financial statements taken as a whole.

Each of these statements must be true without qualification for an auditor
to use the wording of a standard opinion paragraph; otherwise an explanation
is required. Examples of departures from the wording of a standard opinion
paragraph are presented later in this chapter.

An auditor's opinion extends only to the financial statements named and
for the dates indicated. The opinion is neither a casual impression nor a statement of fact; it is a reasoned and deliberate professional judgment that is
based on the quality and quantity of audit evidence obtained. When financial
statements for one or more prior periods are presented on a comparative basis
with statements for the current period, both the scope and opinion paragraphs
should include a reference to the prior-period statements, as in the Randolph
report.

Although not specifically mentioned in the opinion paragraph, financial
statements include footnotes and, therefore, the auditor's opinion extends to
the information contained in the notes. Reference to financial statements also
implies that it is the financial statements that are audited, not the books and
records. Audit evidence to corroborate financial statements is gathered from
many sources, including the underlying books and records.

Prior to 1975, auditors sometimes issued opinions on certain identified
accounts and disclaimed an opinion on the overall financial statements. These
"piecemeal" opinions were usually issued when scope limitations precluded
auditing certain accounts, such as inventory or accounts receivable. However,
an inherent deficiency of piecemeal opinions is that many accounts affect
other accounts in the financial statements, and few if any are wholly independent. As a result, SAS No. 58, "Reports on Audited Financial Statements,"
includes a provision that prohibits the issuance of piecemeal opinions under
any circumstances.

Signature

Every report must be signed by an independent auditor in the name of
his or her public accounting firm, whether a professional service corporation,
partnership, or sole proprietorship. Only in the case of a sole proprietorship
should an auditor sign his or her own name to an opinion; for a professional
service corporation or partnership, an auditor signs the firm's name, thereby
extending responsibility for the report to the firm as a whole.

EXPLANATORY PARAGRAPHS AND MODIFICATIONS TO STANDARD REPORTS

An independent auditor adds an explanatory paragraph or otherwise modifies the wording of a standard report when:

▲ The auditor's opinion is based in part on the *report of another auditor*.
▲ The auditor wishes to *emphasize a matter* regarding the financial statements.
▲ The financial statements are affected by a *departure from generally accepted accounting principles*.
▲ Accounting principles have *not been applied consistently*.
▲ The financial statements are affected by an *uncertainty* concerning future events, the outcome of which is not susceptible to reasonable estimation at the date of the auditor's report.
▲ The *scope* of the auditor's examination is affected by conditions that preclude applying one or more auditing procedures considered necessary in the circumstances.
▲ Substantial doubt exists about an entity's ability to continue as a *going concern*.

For many of these circumstances, the type of opinion required depends on whether the effect of the circumstance is moderately material or highly material. The appropriate wording of audit reports for each circumstance is discussed and illustrated in the following sections.

Opinion Based in Part on Report of Another Auditor

An auditor may rely on the report of another auditor who examined the financial statements of an entity's subsidiary or other component. Reliance on another auditor's report does not preclude the issuance of an unqualified opinion, although it could if the opinion of the other auditor were qualified, adverse, or a disclaimer.

When an opinion is based partly on the report of another auditor, the auditors must decide who is the *principal auditor*, taking into consideration all relevant factors, such as (AU Sec 543):

▲ The materiality of financial statements examined by each auditor.
▲ The extent of each auditor's knowledge of the overall financial statements.
▲ The significance of financial statements examined in relation to the entity's activities taken as a whole.

The auditor who serves as the principal auditor must decide whether to refer in his or her report to the audit work of the other auditor. When no reference is made to another auditor's work, the principal auditor takes full responsibility for the work of the other auditor. However, if the principal auditor decides not to assume that degree of responsibility, his or her audit report should refer to the other auditor's work and clearly indicate the division of responsibility between the auditors.

To illustrate, assume that a principal auditor shares responsibility with another auditor who examined the financial statements of a consolidated subsidiary. Assuming an unqualified opinion is warranted, the principal auditor should disclose the division of responsibility in the introductory paragraph and refer to the report of the other auditor in the opinion paragraph; the scope paragraph is unchanged. An illustrative introductory paragraph and a partial opinion paragraph follow:

(Introductory Paragraph)

We have audited the consolidated balance sheets of ABC Company as of December 31, 19X2 and 19X1, and the related consolidated statements of income, retained earnings, and cash flows for the years then ended. These financial statements are the responsibility of the Company's management. Our responsibility is to express an opinion on these financial statements based on our audits. We did not audit the financial statements of B Company, a wholly-owned subsidiary, which statements reflect total assets of $_____ and $_____ as of December 31, 19X2 and 19X1, respectively, and total revenues of $_____ and $_____ for the years then ended. These statements were audited by other auditors whose report has been furnished to us and our opinion, insofar as it relates to the amounts included for B Company, is based solely on the report of the other auditors.

(Opinion Paragraph)

In our opinion, based on our audits and the report of other auditors, the consolidated financial statements referred to above present fairly . . .

Emphasis on a Matter

An independent auditor may wish to emphasize a matter and still issue an unqualified opinion. For example, an auditor may wish to point out that certain adjustments are reflected in the financial statements but not recorded in the books, as is customary for utility companies and other entities subject to federal and state regulatory acts. When emphasizing a matter in an audit report, the auditor makes no modification to the standard introductory, scope, or opinion paragraphs and describes the matter in an explanatory paragraph. Phrases such as "with the foregoing explanations" or the like should not be used in the opinion paragraph, since they tend to temper the meaning of the opinion expressed.

To illustrate, assume that an entity subject to the Interstate Commerce Act does not record in its books adjustments proposed by the auditor solely to conform the financial statements to generally accepted accounting principles. The resulting explanatory paragraph follows:

(Explanatory Paragraph)

As explained in Note X to the financial statements, certain adjustments have been made to the financial statements to conform to generally accepted accounting principles. These adjustments have not been recorded in the books.

Departure from GAAP

Generally accepted accounting principles include all the conventions, rules, and procedures which define accepted accounting practice at a particular point in time. In some cases an auditor must exercise professional judgment as to whether the accounting principles applied have general acceptance and are appropriate in the circumstances.

However, in the case of a departure from an accounting principle set forth in an official pronouncement (including extant Accounting Research Bulletins, Accounting Principles Board Opinions, and Statements of Financial Accounting Standards), professional ethics specifically prohibit expression of an unqualified opinion unless the auditor can demonstrate that due to unusual circumstances, adherence to the pronouncement would have rendered the financial statements misleading. In such cases, the auditor must describe the departure, and if practicable the approximate effects of the departure, and the reasons why compliance with the accounting principle would result in misleading financial statements. In practice, circumstances justifying such departures are rarely encountered. But, if the departure is justified, then it is appropriate for the auditor to issue an unqualified opinion with respect to conformity of the financial statements with generally accepted accounting principles.

In general, departures from generally accepted accounting principles arise from inadequate disclosure or inappropriate accounting principles. A qualified or adverse opinion should be issued when an audit conducted in accordance with generally accepted auditing standards reveals a material departure from generally accepted accounting principles. The degree of materiality of the misstatement resulting from the departure determines the type of opinion to be issued. These materiality judgments are based on such considerations as:

▲ The dollar magnitude of the resulting misstatement.
▲ The effect of the misstatement upon the amounts and presentation of other financial statement items.
▲ The impact of the misstatement on the financial statements taken as a whole.

Qualified Opinion. A qualified opinion resulting from a departure from generally accepted accounting principles requires an explanatory paragraph that discloses the principal effects of the misstatement and a qualification in the opinion paragraph. No changes are required in the introductory or scope paragraphs.

To illustrate, assume an entity omits overhead from the determination of inventory costs. The resulting explanatory paragraph and modified opinion paragraph follow:

(Explanatory Paragraph)

In valuing inventories, the company omits factory overhead from its cost. In our opinion, generally accepted accounting principles require inclusion of factory overhead in inventory. Had overhead been included, inventories at December 31, 19X2 and 19X1 would have been greater than the amounts shown on the balance sheet by $_____ and $_____, respectively, and net income, after giving effect to additional taxes that would have been payable for 19X2 and 19X1 would have been increased by $_____ and $_____, respectively.

(Opinion Paragraph)

In our opinion, except for the effect of omitting factory overhead from inventories, as discussed in the preceding paragraph, the financial statements referred to above present fairly . . .

Adverse Opinion. The effects of a departure from generally accepted accounting principles may be so material as to require an adverse opinion. In these circumstances the adverse opinion requires no changes to either the introductory or scope paragraphs. The report should include one or more explanatory paragraphs disclosing all the substantive reasons for the adverse opinion and the principal effects of the departure on financial position, results of operations, and cash flows. An adverse opinion paragraph follows the explanatory paragraph(s).

To illustrate, assume that a company carries property, plant, and equipment at appraisal values and that the effect of this departure from generally accepted accounting principles is so material as to preclude the auditor from issuing a qualified opinion. Illustrative explanatory and opinion paragraphs follow:

(Explanatory Paragraphs)

As discussed in Note C to the financial statements, the Company carries its property, plant, and equipment accounts at appraisal values, and provides depreciation on the basis of such values. Generally accepted accounting principles require that property, plant, and equipment be stated at an amount not in excess of cost, reduced by depreciation based on such amount, and that deferred income taxes be provided.

Because of the departure from generally accepted accounting principles identified above, as of December 31, 19X2 and 19X1, inventories have been increased $_____ and $_____ by inclusion in manufacturing overhead of depreciation in excess of that based on cost; property, plant, and equipment, less accumulated depreciation, is carried at $_____ and $_____ in excess of an amount based on the cost to the Company; and deferred income taxes of $_____ and $_____ have not been recorded; resulting in an increase of $_____ and $_____ in retained earnings and in appraisal surplus of $_____ and $_____, respectively. For the years ended December 31, 19X2 and 19X1, cost of goods sold has been increased $_____ and $_____, respectively, because of the effects of depreciation accounting and deferred income taxes of $_____ and $_____ have not been provided, resulting in an increase in net income of $_____ and $_____, respectively.

(Opinion Paragraph)

In our opinion, because of the effects of the matter discussed in the preceding paragraphs, the financial statements referred to above do not present fairly, in conformity with generally accepted accounting principles, the financial position of X Company as of December 31, 19X2 and 19X1, or the results of its operations or its cash flows for the years then ended.

Lack of Consistency

An explanatory paragraph is required when there has been an accounting change that materially affects an entity's financial statements. A qualified opinion is not required, though, unless management has not provided reasonable justification for the change, as required by Accounting Principles Board *Opinion No. 20,* "Accounting Changes." An illustration of an appropriately worded explanatory paragraph follows, and would appear in the audit report after the opinion paragraph.

(Explanatory Paragraph)

As discussed in Note X to the financial statements, the Company changed its method of computing depreciation in 19X2.

However, a qualified or adverse opinion is required if a newly adopted accounting principle is not generally accepted, the method of accounting for the effect of the change is not in conformity with generally accepted accounting principles, or management has not sufficiently justified the reason for the change. The materiality of the effect of the change determines the type of opinion to be issued.

Qualified Opinion. A qualification for lack of consistency requires no reference in the introductory or scope paragraph, a paragraph explaining the change, and a qualified opinion paragraph.

To illustrate, assume a client has not sufficiently justified a change from the last-in, first-out to the first-in, first-out method of determining inventory costs. The explanatory paragraph and modified opinion paragraph follow:

(Explanatory Paragraph)

As disclosed in Note X to the financial statements, the company has adopted the first-in, first-out method of determining inventory costs, whereas it previously used the last-in, first-out method. Although use of the first-in, first-out method is in conformity with generally accepted accounting principles, in our opinion, the company has not provided reasonable justification for seeking a change as required by Opinion No. 20 of the Accounting Principles Board.

(Opinion Paragraph)

In our opinion, except for the effects of the change in accounting principles discussed in the preceding paragraph, the financial statements referred to above present fairly . . .

Adverse Opinion. Lack of consistency may have such a material effect upon financial statements as to require an adverse opinion. In these circumstances, the adverse opinion requires no reference in the introductory or scope paragraphs, an explanatory paragraph that discloses all substantive reasons for the opinion and the principal effects of the change, and an adverse opinion paragraph.

To illustrate, assume the effect on financial statements of the above change in inventory cost flow method is so material as to preclude the auditor from issuing a qualified opinion. The wording of the above explanatory paragraph would not be changed. Rather, a second explanatory paragraph would be added that disclosed the effects of the change on the financial statements, and an adverse opinion paragraph would be presented, as illustrated earlier for departures from generally accepted accounting principles.

Uncertainty

Management commonly incorporates estimates of future transactions and events into the determination of some financial statement amounts or disclosures. Among these estimates are the useful lives of depreciable assets, the collectibility of accounts receivable, and the liability for product warranties. Although independent auditors are frequently able to substantiate the reasonableness of management estimates, the potential outcome of some transactions and events is not susceptible to reasonable estimation, thereby raising uncertainties about their ultimate resolution.

When uncertainties exist, the auditor must consider whether the situation requires an explanatory paragraph (with no mention in the opinion paragraph), or whether a qualified opinion or disclaimer of opinion is required. Generally, an explanatory paragraph, only, may be required when the matter is expected to be resolved at a future date, at which time sufficient evidence concerning the outcome of the matter is expected to become available. In contrast, a qualified opinion or disclaimer of opinion is required when the uncertainty arises from a scope limitation — i.e., evidence does (or did) exist but was not made available to the auditor because of management's record retention policies or a restriction imposed by management. Explanatory paragraphs resulting from uncertainties are discussed and illustrated next.

In deciding whether to add an explanatory paragraph for matters involving uncertainties unrelated to a scope limitation, the auditor must decide whether there is a remote likelihood, reasonable possibility, or probable chance of material loss resulting from the uncertainty. If management believes and the auditor is satisfied that there is only a *remote likelihood* of a material loss, the auditor would *not* add an explanatory paragraph. However, if management believes and the auditor is satisified that there is a *probable chance* of material loss, but management is unable to make a reasonable estimate of the loss, the auditor should add an explanatory paragraph.

If there is a *reasonable possibility* of material loss — that is, more than remote, but less than probable — the auditor should consider two additional matters in deciding whether to add an explanatory paragraph: the magnitude by which the reasonably possible loss exceeds the auditor's judgment of materiality, and whether the likelihood of material loss is closer to remote or to probable. For example, an auditor is more likely to add an explanatory paragraph as the amount of the reasonably possible loss becomes larger or the likelihood of occurrence increases.

When an auditor decides an explanatory paragraph is necessary, the paragraph should describe the matter giving rise to the uncertainty and indicate that its outcome cannot presently be determined, since the outcome depends on future events. No reference should be made in the introductory, scope, or opinion paragraphs, and the explanatory paragraph should follow the opinion paragraph. An example follows:

(Explanatory Paragraph)

As discussed in Note X to the financial statements, the Company is a defendant in a lawsuit alleging infringement of certain patent rights and claiming royalties and punitive damages. The Company has filed a counteraction, and preliminary hearings and discovery proceedings on both actions are in progress. The ultimate outcome of the litigation cannot presently be determined. Accordingly, no provision for any liability that may result upon adjudication has been made in the accompanying financial statements.

Qualified opinions and disclaimers of opinion resulting from scope limitations and their attendant uncertainties are discussed and illustrated next.

Scope Limitation

The scope of a financial statement audit is limited when conditions preclude applying necessary audit procedures. Limitations may result from client-imposed restrictions or from circumstances such as insufficient evidential matter, inadequate accounting records, or the timing of an auditor's work (e.g., when an engagement is accepted after year-end). Significant scope limitations ordinarily result in a qualified opinion or a disclaimer of opinion.

Qualified Opinion. A qualified opinion resulting from limitations on scope requires no change to the introductory paragraph, a modified scope paragraph, an explanatory paragraph preceding the opinion paragraph that explains the nature of the scope limitation, and a qualified opinion paragraph.

To illustrate, assume an auditor was unable to obtain audited financial statements supporting a client's investment in a foreign affiliate. Modifications to the scope paragraph and the resulting explanatory and opinion paragraphs follow:

(Scope Paragraph)

Except as discussed in the following paragraph . . .

(Explanatory Paragraph)

We were unable to obtain audited financial statements supporting the Company's investment in a foreign affiliate stated at $_____$ and $_____$ at December 31, 19X2 and 19X1, respectively, or its equity in earnings of that affiliate of $_____$ and $_____$, which is included in net income for the years then ended as described in Note X to the financial statements; nor were we able to satisfy ourselves as to the carrying value of the investment in the foreign affiliate or the equity in its earnings by other auditing procedures.

(Opinion Paragraph)

In our opinion, except for the effects of such adjustments, if any, as might have been determined to be necessary had we been able to examine evidence regarding the foreign affiliate investment and earnings, the financial statements referred to above present fairly . . .

Disclaimer of Opinion. Often, a limitation on the scope of an audit will be so significant as to require a disclaimer of opinion. Disclaimers for scope limitations require a modified introductory paragraph, omission of the standard scope paragraph, an explanatory paragraph explaining why the audit did not comply with generally accepted auditing standards, and an ''opinion'' paragraph explaining that the scope of the audit was not sufficient to warrant expressing an opinion.

To illustrate, assume that an opinion is disclaimed because a client did not take a physical inventory and evidence supporting the cost of property and equipment is no longer available. Appropriate modifications to the introductory paragraph and the resulting explanatory and opinion paragraphs follow:

(Introductory Paragraph)

We were engaged to audit the accompanying balance sheets of X Company as of December 31, 19X2 and 19X1, and the related statements of income, retained earnings, and cash flows for the years then ended. These financial statements are the responsibility of the Company's management.

(Explanatory Paragraph)

The Company did not take a physical inventory in 19X2 or 19X1, stated in the accompanying financial statements at $_____ as of December 31, 19X2, and at $_____ as of December 31, 19X1. Further, evidence supporting the cost of property and equipment acquired prior to December 31, 19X1, is no longer available. The Company's records do not permit the application of other auditing procedures to inventories or to property and equipment.

(Opinion Paragraph)

Since the Company did not take physical inventories and we were not able to apply other auditing procedures to satisfy ourselves as to inventory quantities and the cost of property and equipment, the scope of our work was not sufficient to enable us to express, and we do not express, an opinion on these financial statements.

Considering an Entity's Ability to Continue as a Going Concern

An entity is considered to be a going concern when it has the ability to continue in operation and meet its obligations. In the absence of evidence to the contrary, the ability of an entity to continue as a going concern is usually assumed in financial reporting.

Economic conditions within both the U.S. in general and some industries in particular, however, raise questions about the ability of some entities to continue meeting obligations without a substantial disposal of assets, restructuring of debt, externally forced revision of operations, or similar actions. As a result, auditors have questioned the going-concern assumption in some engagements, prompting the Auditing Standards Board to issue *Statement on Auditing Standards No. 59,* "The Auditor's Consideration of an Entity's Ability to Continue as a Going Concern," which requires that an auditor evaluate whether there is substantial doubt about a client's ability to continue as a going concern. The evaluation is based on evidence obtained through the completion of field work, and relates to a reasonable period of time in the future, not to exceed one year beyond the date of the financial statements audited.

Because of the going-concern assumption, an auditor does not ordinarily design audit procedures intended exclusively to search for evidence regarding an entity's continued existence. Nevertheless, under SAS No. 59, an auditor should evaluate whether there is substantial doubt about the going-concern assumption by considering the results of audit procedures designed and performed to achieve other audit objectives. For example, inquiry of an entity's legal counsel about litigation, claims, and assessments, discussed in Chapter 18, may reveal that a client has lost a judgment in litigation for uninsured claims that, in the aggregate, raise serious questions about the going-concern assumption. In addition, other evidence obtained in an audit may raise doubts, such as negative trends (e.g., recurring operating losses and working capital deficiencies), other indications of possible financial difficulties (e.g., loan defaults and denial of credit from suppliers), internal matters (e.g., work stoppages and loss of key management), and external matters (e.g., loss of principal customers or suppliers).

When audit evidence and inquiries indicate there is substantial doubt about continued existence, the auditor should consider management's plans for alleviating the problem and whether those plans can be implemented effectively. For example, if management plans to raise resources by disposing of selected assets, the auditor should consider the apparent marketability of the assets, possible effects on the entity's operations, and whether there are restrictions on disposing of the assets, such as loan covenants or encumbrances. After considering management's plans, and other evidence, an auditor may conclude that substantial doubt about the entity's ability to continue as a going concern is alleviated. In that case, the auditor should consider the need for disclosing in the financial statements the principal conditions that gave rise to doubt, but would not modify the standard audit report. However, if substantial doubt remains, an auditor should consider the recoverability and classification of recorded assets, and the amounts and classification of liabilities, and should modify the audit report. The following illustrates a modified report; the introductory, scope, and opinion paragraphs are unchanged. The paragraph would follow the opinion paragraph in the audit report.

(Explanatory Paragraph)

The accompanying financial statements have been prepared assuming that ABC Company will continue in existence as a going concern. As discussed in Note X to the financial statements, under existing circumstances there is substantial doubt as to the ability of ABC Company to continue as a going concern.

REPORTING ON COMPARATIVE FINANCIAL STATEMENTS

As illustrated in the report for Randolph International Corporation on page 764 and implied throughout this chapter, audit reports normally cover two or more fiscal years. In fact, the fourth standard of reporting requires no less, since the language of the standard — ". . . expression of opinion regarding the financial statements, *taken as a whole"* — should be considered to apply not only to the financial statements of the current period, but also to those of the one or more prior periods presented. However, reporting on comparative periods raises the problem of having different opinions in comparative years and the corresponding problem of updating a previously issued opinion. Each is discussed below.

Report with Differing Opinions

Because circumstances may change from period to period, an auditor could, for example, issue a qualified opinion for one year and express an unqualified opinion for the other. When this occurs, the auditor should disclose all substantive reasons for qualifying in an explanatory paragraph and alter the opinion paragraph accordingly. For example, the following illustrates a qualified opinion on the current year's financial statements and an unqualified opinion for the prior year; the unchanged introductory and scope paragraphs are not presented.

(Explanatory Paragraph)

The company has excluded, from property and debt in the accompanying 19X2 balance sheet, certain lease obligations that were entered into in 19X2 which, in our opinion, should be capitalized in order to conform with generally accepted accounting principles. If these lease obligations were capitalized, property would be increased by $_____, long-term debt by $_____, and retained earnings by $_____ as of December 31, 19X2, and net income and earnings per share would be increased (decreased) by $_____ and $_____, respectively, for the year then ended.

(Opinion Paragraph)

In our opinion, except for the effects on the 19X2 financial statements of not capitalizing certain lease obligations as described in the preceding paragraph, the financial statements referred to above present 'fairly, in all material respects, the financial position of X Company as of December 31, 19X2 and 19X1 . . .

Report with an Updated Opinion Different from a Previous Opinion

Auditors sometimes become aware during the current year's engagement of circumstances or events that affect the financial statements reported on in a prior year. For example, resolution in the current year of a matter that caused a qualified opinion, adverse opinion, or disclaimer of opinion in a prior year should result in an updated opinion for the prior year within the current report. In addition to an updated opinion paragraph, the report should also include an explanatory paragraph that discloses the date of the previous report, the type of opinion previously expressed, the circumstances or events that caused the auditor to express a different opinion in the prior year, and the fact that the auditor's updated opinion on the financial statements of the prior year is different from the previous opinion. The following illustrates an explanatory paragraph for a prior-year departure from generally accepted accounting principles, corrected in the current year; the introductory and scope paragraphs would not be changed, and neither would the opinion paragraph since an unqualified opinion is issued for both years in this example.

> (Explanatory Paragraph)
>
> In our report dated March 1, 19X2, we expressed an opinion that the 19X1 financial statements did not fairly present financial position, results of operations, and cash flows in conformity with generally accepted accounting principles because the Company did not provide for deferred income taxes with respect to differences between income for financial reporting purposes and taxable income. As described in Note X, the Company has restated its 19X1 financial statements to conform with generally accepted accounting principles. Accordingly, our present opinion on the 19X1 financial statements, as presented herein, is different from that expressed in our previous report.

REPORTING ON INFORMATION ACCOMPANYING OR DERIVED FROM AUDITED FINANCIAL STATEMENTS

Information included in basic financial statements is the primary concern in a financial statement audit and, therefore, the major focus of auditing standards. However, audit reports and the related financial statements are often published in annual reports which include a variety of additional information. In addition, audited financial statements are sometimes used to derive condensed or selected financial information. An auditor's responsibility for information accompanying or derived from his or her report and the basic financial statements depends on the nature of the information. In general, this information can be classified as:

▲ Supplementary information required by the Financial Accounting Standards Board (FASB) or the Governmental Accounting Standards Board (GASB).
▲ Segment information.
▲ Information in auditor-submitted documents.
▲ Condensed financial statements and selected financial data.
▲ Other information.

Supplementary Information Required by the FASB and GASB

In the late 1970s the Financial Accounting Standards Board (FASB) issued *Statement of Financial Standards No. 25,* "Suspension of Certain Accounting Requirements for Oil and Gas Producing Companies" (superseded by FASB Statement No. 69), and *No. 33,* "Financial Reporting and Changing Prices" (superseded by Statement No. 89), each of which permitted or required that additional information be disclosed to supplement an entity's basic financial statements. Since supplementary information required by the FASB or GASB for certain entities is an essential element of financial reporting, an auditor should apply certain limited procedures in accordance with SAS No. 52, "Omnibus Statement on Auditing Standards—1987." If the auditor determines that either an FASB or GASB pronouncement requires that an entity report supplementary information, then the following limited procedures should be performed:

▲ Inquire of management regarding the methods used to prepare the information, including (a) whether it is measured and presented within prescribed guidelines, (b) whether measurement or presentation methods have been changed from those used in the prior period and the reasons for any such changes, and (c) any significant assumptions or interpretations underlying the measurement or presentation.
▲ Compare the information for consistency with (a) management's responses to the preceding inquiries, (b) audited financial statements, or (c) other knowledge obtained during the audit.
▲ Consider whether representations on supplementary information should be included in the management representation letter (Chapter 18).
▲ Apply additional procedures, if any, that are prescribed in other SAS's for specific types of supplementary information.
▲ Make additional inquiries if applying the preceding procedures causes the auditor to believe that the information may not be measured or presented within applicable guidelines.

These procedures should be applied to any supplementary information that is currently required or may be required in the future by the FASB or GASB.

Because such required supplementary information is not part of the basic financial statements and is not audited (only limited procedures are applied), an independent auditor need not refer to the information in the audit report unless: the information is omitted, the auditor concludes that the measurement or presentation of the information departs materially from FASB or GASB guidelines, or the auditor is unable to complete the necessary procedures.

These three circumstances do not affect the opinion expressed on the financial statements. Thus, an auditor could still express an unqualified opinion, though an explanatory paragraph would be added to the standard report. This type of reporting is referred to as *exception reporting*. An auditor's standard report could note the omission of FASB- or GASB-required supplementary information as follows; the introductory, scope, and opinion paragraphs would not be changed:

(Explanatory Paragraph)

The Company has not presented (describe the supplementary information omitted) that the (Financial or Governmental) Accounting Standards Board has determined is necessary to supplement, although not required to be part of, the basic financial statements.

One specific example of FASB-required supplementary information is addressed in an auditing interpretation, which provides guidance relating to FASB Statement No. 69, "Disclosures about Oil and Gas Producing Activities." FASB Statement No. 69 requires that oil and gas producing entities disclose oil and gas reserve quantities (and changes in quantities) in annual financial statements. The limited procedures required in SAS No. 52 for FASB-required supplementary information should be applied to oil and gas information. The auditing interpretation requires additional procedures which specifically address estimates, among other things, used by management to compile supplementary oil and gas information.

Segment Information

Many large publicly traded corporations function within several different industries or industry segments, potentially making aggregated financial statements less meaningful than separate statements for each segment. For this reason, the FASB issued *Statement of Financial Accounting Standards No. 14,* "Financial Reporting for Segments of a Business Enterprise," requiring information about a public company's operations in different industries, foreign operations and export sales, and major customers as part of basic financial statements. In response, the Auditing Standards Executive Committee issued *Statement on Auditing Standards No. 21,* "Segment Information" (AU Sec. 435), providing guidance to independent auditors about audit procedures and reporting requirements for entities that disclose segment information in conformity with FASB Statement No. 14.

Procedures. Because segment information is reported as part of an entity's basic financial statements, SAS No. 21 requires the application of audit procedures, not limited procedures, as is the case with supplementary FASB- and GASB-required information. The audit procedures are neither sufficient nor intended to provide a basis for expressing an opinion on the segment information. Rather, the audit procedures required by SAS No. 21 are intended to provide a basis for concluding whether segment information is presented in conformity with FASB Statement No. 14 in relation to the financial statements taken as a whole. When an entity reports segment information in accordance with FASB requirements, the following audit procedures should be applied:

▲ Inquire of management concerning its methods of determining segment information, and evaluate the reasonableness of those methods in relation to the factors identified in FASB Statement No. 14.

▲ Inquire as to the bases of accounting for sales or transfers between industry segments and between geographic areas, testing for conformity with the bases of accounting disclosed.

▲ Test the disaggregation of financial statements into segment information. The tests should include (a) an evaluation of the entity's applications of the various percentage tests specified in FASB Statement No. 14 and (b) an analytical review of the segment information, including inquiries concerning relationships and items that appear unusual.

▲ Inquire as to the methods of allocating operating expenses incurred and identifiable assets used jointly by two or more segments, evaluate whether those methods are reasonable, and test the allocations to the extent considered necessary.

▲ Determine whether the segment information has been presented consistently from period to period and, if not, whether the nature and effect of the inconsistency are disclosed.

Reporting. Ordinarily, a standard audit report would not refer to segment information included in basic financial statements unless an auditor detects a material misstatement or omission or a change in accounting principle, or was unable to apply necessary audit procedures. The first situation represents a departure from GAAP and therefore requires either a qualified opinion or an adverse opinion, as illustrated earlier. In contrast, the second situation represents a scope limitation and therefore requires either a qualified opinion or a disclaimer, as illustrated earlier.

An auditor may also be requested to report separately on individual industry segments, in which case the procedures identified in SAS No. 21 would not be sufficient. A separate opinion on an individual industry segment would require a separate audit, encompassing all of the generally accepted auditing standards.

Information in Auditor-Submitted Documents

Independent auditors may submit to a client or others a document containing information in addition to basic financial statements and standard audit reports. For example, the additional information in *auditor-submitted documents* may relate to consolidating information, historical summaries extracted from basic financial statements, statistical data, or additional details about the basic financial statements. In 1980, the Auditing Standards Board issued *Statement on Auditing Standards No. 29,* "Reporting on Information Accompanying the Basic Financial Statements in Auditor-Submitted Documents" (AU Sec. 551), describing an auditor's responsibilities for reporting on auditor-submitted documents. When such information accompanies the basic financial statements, the auditor's report should:

▲ State that the examination has been made for the purpose of forming an opinion on the basic financial statements taken as a whole.

▲ Identify the accompanying information, either by descriptive title or by document page number.

▲ State that the accompanying information is presented for purposes of additional analysis and is not a required part of the basic financial statements.

▲ Include either an opinion on whether the accompanying information is fairly stated in all material respects in relation to the basic financial statements taken as a whole or a disclaimer of opinion, depending on whether the information has been subjected to auditing procedures applied in the audit of the basic financial statements.

The report may be added to a standard audit report or appear separately with the auditor-submitted documents. An example follows:

Our audit was made for the purpose of forming an opinion on the basic financial statements taken as a whole. The (identify accompanying information) is presented for purposes of additional analysis and is not a required part of the basic financial statements. Such information has been subjected to the auditing procedures applied in the examination of the basic financial statements taken as a whole.

Condensed Financial Statements and Selected Financial Data

Auditors are sometimes engaged to report on condensed financial statements or selected financial data that are derived from the audited financial statements of publicly traded companies. To guide auditors in these engagements, the Auditing Standards Board issued *Statement on Auditing Standards No. 42,* "Reporting on Condensed Financial Statements and Selected Financial Data" (AU Sec. 552), which provides separate guidelines for each type of engagement. The distinction between SAS No. 29, "Reporting on Information . . . in Auditor-Submitted Documents," and SAS No. 42 is that the former relates to situations where the auditor submits additional information concurrently with the audit report, whereas the latter relates to situations where the audit report may have been issued previously, thereby requiring an additional report.

Condensed Financial Statements. Condensed financial statements are presented in considerably less detail than complete statements and, therefore, are not presented in conformity with generally accepted accounting principles. As a result, an auditor should not report on condensed statements in the same manner as complete statements; to do so might lead users to assume erroneously that the condensed statements include all the disclosures necessary to constitute complete statements. Rather, each page of the condensed statements should be marked "condensed financial statements," and the independent auditor's report should indicate that the auditor has examined and expressed an opinion on the complete financial statements, show the date of the auditor's report on the complete statements, state the type of opinion expressed, and note whether, in the auditor's opinion, the information set forth in the condensed financial statements is fairly stated in all material respects in relation to the complete financial statements. An illustration follows:

> We have audited, in accordance with generally accepted auditing standards, the consolidated balance sheet of X Company and subsidiaries as of December 31, 19X1, and the related consolidated statements of income, retained earnings, and cash flows for the year then ended (not presented herein); and in our report dated February 15, 19X1, we expressed an unqualified opinion on those consolidated financial statements. In our opinion, the information set forth in the accompanying condensed consolidated statements is fairly stated, in all material respects, in relation to the consolidated financial statements from which it has been derived.

Selected Financial Data. An auditor may also be engaged to report on selected financial data that are included in a client-prepared document that contains previously issued audited financial statements. For example, a publicly traded corporation may include net sales or operating revenues and income or loss from continuing operations among other things in a filing under SEC regulation S-K. In these situations, an auditor's report should state that the auditor has examined and expressed an opinion on the complete financial statements, specify the type of opinion expressed, and indicate whether, in the auditor's opinion, the information set forth in the selected financial data is fairly stated in all material respects in relation to the complete financial statements. The explanatory paragraph would be similar to the paragraph illustrated above, except "selected financial data" would replace "condensed financial statements."

Other Information in Annual Reports

Annual reports typically include a variety of "other" information which is not examined by independent auditors. For example, annual reports often include a letter to stockholders from the chief executive officer, nonfinancial information by product line, and summaries of significant financial results of a five or ten-year period, among other information.

According to *Statement on Auditing Standards No. 8,* "Other Information in Documents Containing Audited Financial Statements" (AU Sec. 550), an auditor is not obligated to corroborate the "other" information. However, an auditor should read the information to determine whether the information or its manner of presentation is inconsistent with the financial statements. For example, if the chief executive officer's letter cites earnings per share of $5.25, the income statement should disclose the same amount. Should the client refuse to revise an inconsistency, the auditor should consider revising the audit report, withholding the report, or withdrawing from the engagement.

REPORTING ON FINANCIAL STATEMENTS PREPARED FOR USE IN FOREIGN COUNTRIES

U.S. corporations ordinarily prepare financial statements in conformity with accounting principles that are generally accepted in the United States, and auditors therefore examine these statements in accordance with the AICPA's generally accepted standards of auditing. However, as a result of a considerable influx of foreign capital into U.S. multinational and domestic corporations, it has become increasingly common for auditors to examine financial statements that are both prepared in conformity with accounting principles generally accepted in another country and intended for use outside the United States. For example, the financial statements of a U.S. domestic corporation may be prepared for inclusion in the consolidated statements of a non-U.S. parent, or, in contrast, they may be used to raise capital in another country. To guide auditors in these situations, the Auditing Standards Board issued *Statement on Auditing Standards No. 51*, "Reporting on Financial Statements Prepared for Use in Other Countries," which describes an auditor's obligation under U.S. and foreign auditing standards, and prescribes audit reports for use outside and within the United States.

General and Field Work Standards

Even when examining the financial statements of a U.S. corporation that are prepared in conformity with the accounting principles of another country, an auditor should comply with the U.S. general and field work standards. However, audit procedures may need to be modified, since the assertions embodied in financial statements prepared in conformity with foreign accounting principles may differ significantly from those embodied in statements prepared in conformity with U.S. accounting principles. For example, some foreign countries require that certain assets be revalued to adjust for the effects of inflation, and other countries neither require nor permit the recognition of deferred taxes and related party transactions. As a result, when reporting on financial statements prepared for use in other countries, an auditor should be familiar with the accounting principles accepted in the other country, and if necessary, he or she should consider consulting with foreign accountants.

Statements Used Outside the U.S. Only

When reporting on financial statements intended for use outside the U.S. *only,* the auditor should identify the statements examined, refer to a note that describes the basis of financial statement presentation, state that the audit was made in accordance with U.S. auditing standards, and include a paragraph that expresses an opinion on whether the statements are presented fairly in conformity with the basis described. The following illustrates:

(Introductory Paragraph)

We have audited the balance sheet of the International Company as of December 31, 19X2 and 19X1, and the related statements of income, retained earnings, and cash flows for the years then ended, which, as described in Note X, have been prepared on the basis of accounting principles generally accepted in (name of country). These financial statements are the responsibility of the Company's management. Our responsibility is to express an opinion on these financial statements based on our audits.

(Scope Paragraph)

We conducted our audits in accordance with auditing standards generally accepted in the United States (and in [name of country]). Those standards require that we plan and perform the audit to obtain reasonable assurance about whether the financial statements are free of material misstatement. An audit includes examining, on a test basis, evidence supporting the amounts and disclosures in the financial statements. An audit also includes assessing the accounting principles used and significant estimates made by management, as well as evaluating the overall financial statement presentation. We believe that our audits provide a reasonable basis for our opinion.

(Opinion Paragraph)

In our opinion, the financial statements referred to above present fairly, in all material respects, the financial position of the International Company at December 31, 19X2 and 19X1, and the results of its operations and its cash flow for the years then ended in conformity with accounting principles generally accepted in (name of country).

An auditor may also use the standard report of another country, but only if the report would be used by auditors in the other country in similar circumstances, and the auditor understands — and is in a position to make — the attestations contained in such a report.

Statements Used in the U.S.

If an auditor reports on financial statements prepared in accordance with accounting principles accepted in another country and those statements will have more than limited distribution in the United States, he or she should use the standard audit report illustrated earlier in this chapter, modified for departures from U.S. accounting principles. In addition, the auditor may include a separate paragraph in the report to express an opinion on whether the financial statements are presented in conformity with accounting principles generally accepted in the other country.

SUMMARY

The auditor's standard report, the product of an independent auditor's attest function, evolved from the American Institute of Accountants Committee on Cooperation with Stock Exchanges in the 1930s and includes several critical components. An audit report may express any one of four opinions: unqualified, qualified, adverse, or disclaimer. The type of opinion expressed depends on the specific circumstances and the level of materiality involved.

In general, an auditor's opinion relates only to the financial statements named in the audit report. An auditor is responsible, however, for certain types of information accompanying the financial statements. In some cases, the auditor's standard report should be modified to identify the accompanying information or to note exceptions. Exception reporting does not require that the auditor revise his or her opinion on the financial statements.

REFERENCES

Beresford, D. R., J. J. Doyle, and G. A. Kell, "On Trial — Voluntary Internal Control Reports." *Financial Executive* (September, 1980), pp. 14–19.

Carmichael, D. R. "The Auditor's Reporting Obligation: The Meaning and Implementation of the Fourth Standard of Reporting." *Auditing Research Monograph No. 1.* New York: AICPA, 1972.

Carmichael, D. R. "Client Imposed Restrictions on Scope." *Journal of Accountancy* (August, 1971), pp. 70–71.

Carmichael, D. R. "What Does the Independent Auditor's Report Really Mean?" *Journal of Accountancy* (November, 1974), pp. 83–87.

Causey, D. Y., Jr. *Duties and Liabilities of Public Accountants.* Homewood, Illinois: Dow Jones-Irwin, 1979.

Commission on Auditors' Responsibilities. *Report, Conclusions, and Recommendations.* New York: Commission on Auditors' Responsibilities, 1978, pp. 71–84.

Epavos, R. A., L. R. Paquette, and M. A. Pearson. "A Flow Chart Conceptualiza-

tion of Auditors' Reports on Financial Statements." *The Accounting Review*
(October, 1976), pp. 913–916.

Holsen, R. C. "Case History in Development of 'Subsequent Events' Statement."
Journal of Accountancy (February, 1970), pp. 70–71.

Nest, R. A. "Compliance with the Fourth Reporting Standard." *Journal of Accountancy* (July, 1965), pp. 63–64.

Pomeranz, F. "The Attest Function Trends and Prospects." *The CPA Journal* (April, 1979), pp. 41–47.

Rosenfeld, P. and L. Lorensen, "Auditors' Responsibilities and the Audit Report."
Journal of Accountancy (September, 1974), pp. 73–83.

Roth, J. L. "Breaking the Tablets: A New Look at the Old Opinion. *Journal of
Accountancy* (July, 1968), pp. 63–67.

QUESTIONS

1. From what origins did the independent auditor's attest function derive?
2. Trace the historical development of the content of audit reports in the U.S. from the 1930s to today.
3. Explain the significance of an audit report's date.
4. What is meant by dual dating an audit report?
5. To whom should an audit report be addressed?
6. Describe the purpose and major implications of a standard scope paragraph.
7. Describe the purpose and major implications of a standard opinion paragraph.
8. What should an auditor's opinion regarding generally accepted accounting principles be based on?
9. What is the meaning of an unqualified opinion?
10. Under what conditions is a qualified opinion ordinarily issued?
11. Under what conditions is an adverse opinion ordinarily issued?
12. How does a report disclaiming an opinion as a result of a scope limitation differ from a standard report?
13. Departures from generally accepted accounting principles may result in either a qualified or an adverse opinion, depending upon materiality. How are judgments about materiality made in these circumstances?
14. What type of opinions might an auditor issue if a newly adopted accounting principle is not generally accepted? Why?
15. Other than basic financial statements, what types of information could be included in financial reports?
16. Ordinarily, an audit report is not expanded to address supplementary FASB- or GASB-required information. However, in what circumstances might an auditor expand the report?
17. Why are limited — rather than audit — procedures required for supplementary FASB- or GASB-required information?
18. What is the purpose of reporting segment information in financial statements?
19. Under what conditions would a standard audit report refer to segment information?
20. What is an auditor's responsibility for reporting on auditor-submitted documents that accompany the basic financial statements?

MULTIPLE CHOICE QUESTIONS

1. An auditor is unable to determine the amounts associated with certain illegal acts committed by a client. In these circumstances the auditor would most likely

   a. Issue either a qualified opinion or a disclaimer of opinion.
   b. Issue an adverse opinion.
   c. Issue either a qualified opinion or an adverse opinion.
   d. Issue a disclaimer of opinion.   (AICPA Adapted)

2. Limitation on the scope of the auditor's examination may require the auditor to issue a qualified opinion or to disclaim an opinion. Which of the following would generally be a limitation on the scope of the auditor's examination?

   a. The unavailability of sufficient competent evidential matter.
   b. The engagement of the auditor to report on only one basic financial statement.
   c. The examination of a subsidiary's financial statements by an auditor other than the one who examines and reports on the consolidated financial statements.
   d. The engagement of the auditor after year-end.   (AICPA Adapted)

3. A CPA engaged to audit financial statements observes that the accounting for a certain material item is not in conformity with generally accepted accounting principles, and that this fact is prominently disclosed in a note to the financial statements. The CPA should

   a. Express an unqualified opinion and insert an explanatory paragraph emphasizing the matter by reference to the note.
   b. Disclaim an opinion.
   c. Not allow the accounting treatment for this item to affect the type of opinion because the deviation from generally accepted accounting principles was disclosed.
   d. Qualify the opinion because of the deviation from generally accepted accounting principles.   (AICPA Adapted)

4. An auditor includes an explanatory paragraph in an otherwise unqualified report in order to emphasize that the entity being reported upon is a subsidiary of another business enterprise. The inclusion of this middle paragraph

   a. Is appropriate and would *not* negate the unqualified opinion.
   b. Is considered a qualification of the report.
   c. Is a violation of generally accepted reporting standards if this information is disclosed in notes to the financial statements.
   d. Necessitates a revision of the opinion paragraph to include the phrase "with the foregoing explanation."   (AICPA Adapted)

5. The principal auditor is satisfied with the independence and professional reputation of the other auditor who has audited a subsidiary but wants to indicate the division of responsibility. The principal auditor should

   a. Modify the scope and opinion paragraphs of the report.
   b. Modify the explanatory and opinion paragraphs of the report.

c. *Not* modify the report except for inclusion of an explanatory middle paragraph.

d. Modify the opinion paragraph of the report.   (AICPA Adapted)

6. Addison Corporation is required to but does not wish to prepare and issue a statement of cash flows along with its other basic financial statements. In these circumstances the independent auditor's report on the Addison financial statements should include

a. A qualified opinion with an explanatory paragraph explaining that the company declined to present the required statement.

b. An unqualified opinion with an accurate and complete statement of cash flows prepared by the auditor and included in the auditor's report.

c. An adverse opinion stating that the financial statements, taken as a whole, are not fairly presented because of the omission of the required statement.

d. A disclaimer of opinion with a separate explanatory paragraph stating why the company declined to present the required statement.   (AICPA Adapted)

7. If an auditor wishes to issue a qualified opinion because the financial statements include a departure from generally accepted accounting principles, the auditor's report should have an explanatory paragraph referring to a note that discloses the principal effects of the subject matter of the qualification. The qualification should be referred to in the opinion paragraph by using language such as

a. "With the exception."
b. "When read in conjunction with the notes."
c. "With the foregoing explanation."
d. "Subject to the departure explained in the notes."   (AICPA Adapted)

8. When financial statements are prepared on the basis of a going concern and the auditor believes that the client may not continue as a going concern, the auditor should issue

a. A qualified opinion.
b. An unqualified opinion with an explanatory paragraph.
c. A disclaimer of opinion.
d. An adverse opinion.   (AICPA Adapted)

9. Keller, CPA, was about to issue an unqualified opinion on the financial statements of Lupton Television Broadcasting Company when a letter was received from Lupton's independent counsel. The letter stated that the Federal Communications Commission has notified Lupton that its broadcasting license will not be renewed because of some alleged irregularities in its broadcasting practices. Lupton cannot continue to operate without its license. Keller has also learned that Lupton and its independent counsel plan to take all necessary legal action to retain the license. The letter from independent counsel, however, states that a favorable outcome of any legal action is highly uncertain. On the basis of this information what action should Keller take?

a. Issue an unqualified opinion, with an explanatory paragraph that describes the matter giving rise to the uncertainty.

b. Issue an unqualified opinion if full disclosure is made of the dispute in a note to the financial statements.

   c. Issue an adverse opinion on the financial statements and disclose all reasons therefore.

   d. Issue a piecemeal opinion with full disclosure made of the license dispute in a note to the financial statements.   (AICPA Adapted)

10. If the auditor believes that required disclosures of a significant nature are omitted from the financial statements under examination, the auditor should decide between issuing.

   (a) A qualified opinion or an adverse opinion.
   b. A disclaimer of opinion or a qualified opinion.
   c. An adverse opinion or a disclaimer of opinion.
   d. An unqualified opinion or a qualified opinion.   (AICPA Adapted)

11. When an adverse opinion is expressed, the opinion paragraph should include a direct reference to

   a. A note to the financial statements which discusses the basis for the opinion.
   b. The scope paragraph which discusses the basis for the opinion rendered.
   (c) A separate paragraph which discusses the basis for the opinion rendered.
   d. The consistency or lack of consistency in the application of generally accepted accounting principles.   (AICPA Adapted)

12. An auditor's report on comparative financial statements should be dated as of the date of the

   a. Issuance of the report.
   (b) Completion of the auditor's field work.
   c. Latest financial statements being reported on.
   d. Last subsequent event disclosed in the statements.   (AICPA Adapted)

13. An auditor is confronted with an exception considered sufficiently material to warrant some deviation from the standard auditor's report. If the exception relates to a departure from generally accepted accounting principles, the auditor must decide between expressing a(an)

   a. Adverse opinion and an unqualified opinion.
   (b) Adverse opinion and a qualified opinion.
   c. Adverse opinion and a disclaimer of opinion.
   d. Disclaimer of opinion and a qualified opinion.   (AICPA Adapted)

14. The auditor's best course of action with respect to "other financial information" included in an annual report containing the auditor's report is to

   a. Indicate in the auditor's report that the "other financial information" is unaudited.
   b. Consider whether the "other financial information" is accurate by performing a limited review.
   c. Obtain written representations from management as to the material accuracy of the "other financial information."
   (d) Read and consider the manner of presentation of the "other financial information."   (AICPA Adapted)

PROBLEMS

19-1   Christine Burke, CPA, has completed field work for her examination of the Willingham Corporation for the year ended December 31, 1990, and now is in the process of determining whether to modify her report. Presented below are two independent, unrelated situations which have arisen.

Situation 1

In September 1990, a lawsuit was filed against Willingham to have the court order it to install pollution-control equipment in one of its older plants. Willingham's legal counsel has informed Burke that it is not possible to forecast the outcome of this litigation; however, Willingham's management has informed Burke that the cost of the pollution-control equipment is not economically feasible and that the plant will be closed if the case is lost. In addition, Burke has been told by management that the plant and its production equipment would have only minimal resale values and that the production that would be lost could not be recovered at other plants.

Situation 2

During 1990, Willingham purchased a franchise amounting to 20% of its assets for the exclusive right to produce and sell a newly patented product in the northeastern United States. There has been no production in marketable quantities of the product anywhere to date. Neither the franchiser nor any franchisee has conducted any market research with respect to the product.

Required:

In deciding the type of report modification, if any, Burke should take into account considerations such as:

  Relative magnitude
  Uncertainty of outcome
  Likelihood of error
  Expertise of the auditor
  Pervasive impact on the financial statements
  Inherent importance of the item

Discuss Burke's type of report decision for each situation in terms of the above and other appropriate considerations. Assume each situation is adequately disclosed in the notes to the financial statements. Each situation should be considered independently. In discussing each situation, ignore the other. It is not necessary for you to decide the type of report which should be issued.   (AICPA Adapted)

19-2   Upon completion of all field work on September 23, 1990, the following report was issued by Timothy Ross to the directors of The Rancho Corporation.

To the Directors of The Rancho Corporation:

   We have audited the balance sheet of The Rancho Corporation as of July 31, 1990 and the related statements of income and retained earnings. In accordance with your instructions, a complete audit was conducted.

   We conducted our audit in accordance with generally accepted auditing standards. An audit includes examining, on a test basis, evidence supporting the amounts and disclosures in the financial statements. We believe that our audit was appropriate in the circumstances.

In many respects, this was an unusual year for The Rancho Corporation. The weakening of the economy in the early part of the year and the strike of plant employees in the summer of 1990 led to a decline in sales and net income. After making several tests of sales records, nothing came to our attention that would indicate that sales have not been properly recorded.

In our opinion, with the explanation given above, and with the exception of some minor errors that are considered immaterial, the aforementioned financial statements present fairly, in all material respects, the financial position of the Rancho Corporation at July 31, 1990, and the results of its operations for the year then ended, in conformity with pronouncements of the Accounting Principles Board and the Financial Accounting Standards Board.

Timothy Ross, CPA
September 23, 1990

Required:

List and explain deficiencies and omissions in the auditor's report. The type of opinion (unqualified, qualified, adverse, or disclaimer) is of no consequence and need not be discussed.

Organize your answer by paragraph (introductory, scope, explanatory, and opinion) of the auditor's report.   (AICPA Adapted)

19-3   On January 15, 1991 Marc David, CPA, was engaged to audit the Kristin Manufacturing Company's December 31, 1990 financial statements. Kristin had taken a physical inventory on December 31, 1990; the resulting final priced inventory carrying value was $275,400 ($263,000 in 1989), which represented approximately 10% of total assets. David was unable to satisfy himself as to inventory quantities through other auditing procedures because of the nature of Kristin's inventory records.

Required:

Draft an appropriate audit report assuming no other circumstances require departure from a standard audit report.

19-4   Sturdy owns and operates a large office building in a desirable section of New York City's financial center. For many years the management of Sturdy Corporation has modified the presentation of their financial statements by:

1. Reflecting a write-up to appraisal values in the building accounts.
2. Accounting for depreciation expense on the basis of such valuations.

Wyley, a successor CPA, was asked to examine the financial statements of Sturdy Corporation for the year ended December 31, 1990. After completing the examination Wyley concluded that, consistent with prior years, an adverse opinion would have to be expressed because of the materiality of the apparent deviation from the historical-cost principle.

Required:

(1) Describe in detail the form of presentation of the explanatory paragraph of the auditor's report on the financial statements of Sturdy Corporation for the year ended December 31, 1990, clearly identifying the information contained in the paragraph. Do not discuss deferred taxes.

(2) Write a draft of the opinion paragraph of the auditor's report on the financial statements of Sturdy Corporation for the year ended December 31, 1990.

(AICPA Adapted)

19-5   Ross, Sandler & Co., CPAs, completed an audit of the 1990 financial statements of Fairfax Corporation on March 17, 1991, and concluded that an unqualified opinion was warranted. Because of a scope limitation arising from the inability to observe the January 1, 1989 inventory, the predecessor auditors, Smith, Ellis & Co. issued a report which contained an unqualified opinion on the December 31, 1989 balance sheet and a qualified opinion with respect to the statements of income, retained earnings, and cash flows for the year then ended.

The management of Fairfax Corporation has decided to present a complete set of comparative (1990 and 1989) financial statements in their annual report.

Required:

Prepare an auditor's report assuming the March 1, 1990 auditor's report of Smith, Ellis & Co. is not presented.   (AICPA Adapted)

19-6   Roscoe, CPA, has completed the audit of the financial statements of Excelsior Corporation as of and for the year ended December 31, 1990. Roscoe also audited and reported on the Excelsior financial statements of the prior year. Roscoe drafted the following report for 1990.

March 15, 1991

We have examined the balance sheet and statements of income and retained earnings of Excelsior Corporation as of December 31, 1990. Our examination was made in accordance with generally accepted auditing standards and accordingly included such tests of the accounting records as we considered necessary in the circumstances.

In our opinion, the above-mentioned financial statements are accurately prepared and fairly presented in accordance with generally accepted accounting principles in effect at December 31, 1990.

Roscoe, CPA
(Signed)

Other information:

(a) Excelsior is presenting comparative financial statements.
(b) Excelsior does not wish to present a statement of cash flows for either year.
(c) During 1990 Excelsior changed its method of accounting for long-term construction contracts and properly reflected the effect of the change in the current year's financial statements and restated the prior year's statements. Roscoe is satisfied with Excelsior's justification for making the change. The change is discussed in Note 12.
(d) Roscoe was unable to perform normal accounts receivable confirmation procedures, but alternate procedures were used to satisfy Roscoe as to the validity of the receivables.
(e) Excelsior Corporation is the defendant in a litigation, the outcome of which is highly uncertain. If the case is settled in favor of the plaintiff, Excelsior will be required to pay a substantial amount of cash which might require the sale of certain plant assets. The litigation and the possible effects have been properly disclosed in Note 11.
(f) Excelsior issued debentures on January 31, 1990, in the amount of $10,000,000. The funds obtained from the issuance were used to finance the expansion of plant facilities. The debenture agreement restricts the payment of future cash dividends

to earnings after December 31, 1993. Excelsior declined to disclose these essential data in the notes to the financial statements.

Required:

Consider all facts given and rewrite the auditor's report in acceptable and complete format incorporating any necessary departures from the standard report, assuming moderate materiality.

Do not discuss the draft of Roscoe's report, but identify and explain any items included in "Other information" that need not be part of the auditor's report.

(AICPA Adapted)

19-7   The following report was drafted by an audit assistant at the completion of an audit engagement and was submitted to the auditor with client responsibility for review. The auditor has reviewed matters thoroughly and has properly concluded that the scope limitation was not client-imposed and was not sufficiently material to warrant a disclaimer of opinion although a qualified opinion was appropriate.

To Carl Corporation Controller:

We have audited the accompanying financial statements of Carl Corporation as of December 31, 1990. These financial statements are the responsibility of the Company's management. Our responsibility is to express an opinion on these financial statements based on our audit.

We conducted our audit in accordance with generally accepted auditing standards. Those standards require that we plan and perform the audit to obtain reasonable assurance about whether the financial statements are free of material misstatement. An audit includes examining, on a test basis, evidence supporting the amounts and disclosures in the financial statements. An audit also includes assessing the accounting principles used and significant estimates made by management, as well as evaluating the overall financial statement presentation. We believe that our audit provides a reasonable basis for our opinion.

On January 15, 1990, the company issued debentures in the amount of $1,000,000 for the purpose of financing plant expansion. As indicated in Note 6 to the financial statements, the debenture agreement restricts the payment of future cash dividends to earnings after December 31, 1992.

The company's unconsolidated foreign subsidiary did not close down production during the year under examination for physical inventory purposes and took no physical inventory during the year. We made extensive tests of book inventory figures for accuracy of calculation and reasonableness of pricing. We did not make physical tests of inventory quantities. Because of this, we are unable to express an unqualified opinion on the financial statements taken as a whole. However:

Except for the scope limitation regarding inventory, in our opinion the accompanying balance sheet presents the financial position of Carl Corporation at December 31, 1990, subject to the effect of the inventory on the carrying value of the investment. The accompanying statements of income and of retained earnings present the incomes and expenses and the results of transactions affecting retained earnings in accordance with generally accepted accounting principles.

December 31, 1990

Pate & Co., CPAs

Required:

Identify all of the deficiencies in the above draft of the proposed report.

(AICPA Adapted)

19-8   The following tentative auditor's report was drafted by a staff accountant and submitted to a partner in the accounting firm of Better & Best, CPAs:

To the Audit Committee of
American Widgets, Inc.

We have audited the consolidated balance sheets of American Widgets, Inc., and subsidiaries as of December 31, 1990 and 1989, and the related consolidated statements of income, retained earnings, and cash flows, for the years then ended. These financial statements are the responsibility of the Company's management. Our responsibility is to express an opinion on these financial statements based on our audit. Other auditors examined the financial statements of certain subsidiaries and have furnished us with reports thereon containing no exceptions. Our opinion expressed herein, insofar as it relates to the amounts included for those subsidiaries, is based solely upon the reports of the other auditors.

As discussed in Note 4 to the financial statements, on January 8, 1991, the company halted the production of certain medical equipment as a result of inquiries by the Food and Drug Administration, which raised questions as to the adequacy of some of the company's sterilization equipment and related procedures. Management is not in a position to evaluate the effect of this production halt and the ensuing litigation, which may have an adverse effect on the financial position of American Widgets, Inc.

As fully discussed in Note 7 to the financial statements, in 1990 the company extended the use of the last-in, first-out (LIFO) method of accounting to include all inventories. In examining inventories, we engaged Dr. Irwin Same (Nobel Prize winner 1986) to test check the technical requirements and specifications of certain items of equipment manufactured by the company.

In our opinion, except for the effects, if any, on the financial statements of the ultimate resolution of the matter discussed in the second preceding paragraph, the financial statements referred to above present fairly, in all material respects, the financial position of American Widgets, Inc., as of December 31, 1990, and the results of operations, and its cash flows for the year then ended in conformity with generally accepted accounting principles.

To be signed by
Better & Best, CPAs

March 1, 1991, except
for Note 4 as to which
the date is January 8, 1991

Required:

Identify the deficiencies in the staff accountant's tentative report which constitute departures from the generally accepted standards of reporting.   (AICPA Adapted)

19-9   Lando Corporation is a domestic company with two wholly owned domestic subsidiaries. Michaels, CPA, has been engaged to audit the financial statements of the parent company and one of the subsidiaries and to act as the principal auditor. Thomas, CPA, has examined the financial statements of the other subsidiary whose operations are material in relation to the consolidated financial statements.

The work performed by Michaels is sufficient for Michaels to serve as the principal auditor and to report as such on the financial statements. Michaels has not yet decided whether to make reference to the audit made by Thomas.

Required:
What are the reporting requirements with which Michaels must comply if Michaels decides to name Thomas and make reference to the audit of Thomas?

(AICPA Adapted)

19-10   Most Statements on Auditing Standards interpret generally accepted auditing standards by providing independent auditors with guidance about procedures or reporting requirements related to the audit of basic financial statements. In contrast, SAS No. 8, "Other Information in Documents Containing Audited Financial Statements," and SAS No. 52, specifically the sections relating to supplementary information required by the FASB or GASB, do not directly relate to basic financial statements.

Required:
Explain the role of SAS No. 8 and SAS No. 52, given that a standard audit report relates to basic financial statements and SAS Nos. 8 and 52 to information outside the basic financial statements.

19-11   The complete set of financial statements for the Maumee Corporation for the year ended August 31, 1990, is presented on the following page.

Required:
List deficiencies and omissions in The Maumee Corporation's financial statements and discuss the probable effect of the deficiency or omission on the auditor's report. Assume that The Maumee Corporation is unwilling to change the financial statements or make additional disclosures therein.

Consider each deficiency or omission separately, and do not consider the cumulative effect of the deficiencies and omissions on the auditor's report. There are no arithmetical errors in the statements.

Organize your answer sheet in two columns as indicated below, and write your answer in the order of appearance within the general headings of Balance Sheet, Statement of Income and Retained Earnings, and Other.

Financial Statement Deficiency or Omission	Discussion of Effect on Auditor's Report

(AICPA Adapted)

The Maumee Corporation
Balance Sheet
August 31, 1990
(in Thousands of Dollars)

Assets

Cash		$ 103
Marketable securities, at cost which approximates market value		54
Trade accounts receivable (net of $65,000 allowance for doubtful accounts)		917
Inventories, at cost		775
Property, plant, and equipment	$3,200	
Less accumulated depreciation	1,475	1,725
Prepayments and other assets		125
Total assets		$3,699

Liabilities and Stockholders' Equity

Accounts payable	$ 221	
Accrued taxes	62	
Bank loans and long-term debt	1,580	
Total liabilities		$1,863
Capital stock, $10 par value (authorized 50,000 shares, issued and outstanding 42,400 shares)	$ 424	
Paid-in capital in excess of par value	366	
Retained earnings	1,046	
Total stockholders' equity		1,836
Total liabilities and stockholders' equity		$3,699

The Maumee Corporation
Statement of Income and Retained Earnings
For the Year Ended August 31, 1990
(in Thousands of Dollars)

Product sales (net of $850,000 sales returns and allowances)		$10,700
Cost of goods sold		8,700
Gross profit on sales		$2,000
Operating expenses:		
Selling expenses	$1,500	
General and administrative expense	940	2,440
Operating loss		$ (400)
Interest expense		150
Net loss		$ (590)
Retained earnings, September 1, 1989		1,700
		$1,110
Dividends:		
Cash — $1 per share	$ 40	
Stock — 6% of shares outstanding	24	64
Retained earnings, August 31, 1990		$1,046

OTHER REPORTS

20

Major topics discussed in this chapter are the following types of reports issued by independent accountants:

▲ *Reports on compilations and reviews of financial statements.*

▲ *Reports on interim financial information.*

▲ *Reports on internal control structure related matters noted in an audit.*

▲ *Reports prepared on a comprehensive basis of accounting other than GAAP.*

▲ *Reports on specified elements, accounts, or items of a financial statement, including special reports on agreed-upon procedures.*

▲ *Reports on compliance with contractual requirements.*

▲ *Letters for underwriters.*

▲ *Reports on financial forecasts and projections.*

▲ *Reports on personal financial statements.*

▲ *Reports on the application of accounting principles.*

The attest function is the predominant professional activity — and a standard audit report the predominant report — typically associated with independent public accountants. However, other professional activities and reports are also common in public accounting, though they usually represent a much smaller proportion of total billable hours for larger firms.

This chapter presents an introduction to a variety of nonaudit reports including those that express an opinion. In contrast with audit reports, discussed in Chapter 19, the reports issued for nonaudit services do not always express an opinion. Rather, they may express either *limited assurance* (sometimes called *negative assurance*) or no assurance at all. For nonaudit engagements, the term ''independent accountant'' is used rather than ''independent auditor.''

COMPILATIONS AND REVIEWS

Public accounting firms, particularly smaller firms, frequently prepare unaudited financial statements for nonpublicly traded clients. In general, prior to 1978 financial statements were deemed unaudited, as opposed to audited, if no audit procedures were applied or if the procedures applied were insufficient to warrant an opinion. Because an opinion was not warranted, independent accountants always issued a disclaimer of opinion to accompany unaudited statements.

Despite the guidance provided in the now superseded *Statement on Auditing Procedure No. 38,* "Unaudited Financial Statements" (1967) and an AICPA *Guide for Engagements to Prepare Unaudited Financial Statements* (1975), unaudited statements created considerable confusion over the years both for financial statement users and for independent accountants. Some users believed that accountants must have applied "some" procedures to prepare unaudited statements: not enough to issue an opinion, but certainly enough to develop minimum "assurances" about accounting data underlying the statements. As a result, these users occasionally placed more reliance on unaudited statements than was warranted. In contrast, independent accountants were uncertain about the extent of procedures to apply; indeed, should they apply any at all? As a result, the procedures applied in engagements to prepare unaudited statements varied among firms. The most noticeable effect of the confusion surrounding unaudited statements was a considerable number of legal actions against independent accountants, including *1136 Tenants' Corp. v. Max Rothenberg & Co.,* discussed in Chapter 4 in the context of engagement letters.

In 1978 the AICPA appointed a fifteen-member Accounting and Review Services Committee, a senior technical committee designated to issue pronouncements — *Statements on Standards for Accounting and Review Services (SSARS)* — about nonaudit services for nonpublic companies. The Committee issued SSARS No. 1, "Compilation and Review of Financial Statements," in 1978 and SSARS No. 2, "Reporting on Comparative Financial Statements," the following year. To date, six SSARS have been issued. The Statements replace the term "unaudited" financial statements with "compilations" and "reviews" of financial statements. An independent account is required to issue a report upon completion of a compilation or a review engagement. In general, compilation reports express no assurance about financial statements, and review reports express limited assurance.

Compilation of Financial Statements

A compilation of financial statements consists of "Presenting in the form of financial statements information that is the representation of management (owners) without undertaking to express any assurance on the statements."[1]

---

[1] Accounting and Review Services Committee, *Statement on Standards for Accounting and Review Services No. 1,* "Compilation and Review of Financial Statements" (New York: AICPA, 1978), par. 4.

In a compilation engagement an accountant merely compiles financial statements and no assurances are communicated to users about the integrity of financial data. Even though compilations require no audit procedures and no expression of assurance, SSARS No. 1 recognizes that because of potential liability, an accountant might feel uncomfortable compiling financial statements unless he or she also performs other accounting services for a client, such as adjusting the client's books.

When engaged to compile financial statements, an independent accountant should develop:

▲ A level of knowledge about the accounting principles and practices of the entity's industry, enabling the compilation of financial statements that are consistent with industry practice.

▲ A general understanding of the nature of an entity's business transactions, form of accounting records, stated qualifications of accounting personnel, and accounting basis for and form and content of financial statements.[2]

Although not required to perform any audit procedures, an accountant may become aware of errors, omissions, or other deficiencies in information supplied by a client. In such cases, the accountant should obtain additional or revised information. If the client refuses to provide the necessary information, the accountant should withdraw from the engagement.

Compiled financial statements should be accompanied by an accountant's report dated as of the date of completing the compilation. The report should describe the scope of the accountant's work, i.e., a compilation, and include a statement as to the nature and limitations of a compilation. The report should state explicitly that an audit was not performed and no opinion is expressed. A standard compilation report may be worded as follows:

Accountant's Compilation Report

The accompanying balance sheet of XYZ Company as of December 31, 19XX, and the related statements of income, retained earnings, and cash flows for the year then ended have been compiled by us.

A compilation is limited to presenting in the form of financial statements information that is the representation of management (owners). We have not audited

---

[2]*Ibid.*, par. 10–11.

or reviewed the accompanying financial statements and, accordingly, do not express an opinion or any other form of assurance on them.

Source: SSARS No. 1, par. 17.

Each page of the compiled financial statements should include a reference such as "See Accountant's Compilation Report." If not independent, an accountant may still perform compilation services, although he or she should add the following to the last paragraph of the compilation report: "We are not independent with respect to X Company."

Even though a compilation does not require determining whether financial statements conform with generally accepted accounting principles (GAAP), an accountant may become aware of material departures nevertheless. If a client does not revise the statements to conform with GAAP, an accountant should consider revising the standard compilation report. For example, assume an entity's financial statements report land at appraised value rather than cost. The second paragraph should be expanded and a new paragraph added to the standard compilation report as follows:

Accountant's Compilation Report:
Departure from GAAP

. . . However, we did become aware of a departure from generally accepted accounting principles that is described in the following paragraph.

As disclosed in note X to the financial statements, generally accepted accounting principles require that land be stated at cost. Management has informed us that the company has stated its land at appraised value and that, if GAAP had been followed, the land account and stockholders' equity would have been decreased by $_____.

Source: SSARS No. 1, par. 40.

Review of Financial Statements

A review of financial statements consists of "Performing inquiry and analytical procedures that provide the accountant with a reasonable basis for expressing limited assurance that there are no material modifications that should be made to the statements in order for them to be in conformity with generally accepted accounting principles or, if applicable, with another comprehensive basis of accounting."[3] Thus, on the basis of inquiry and analytical procedures, an accountant expresses *limited assurance,* thereby providing more assurance than a compilation, though less than an audit. Again because of potential litigation, an accountant might feel uncomfortable reviewing financial statements unless he or she also performs compilation or other accounting services for a client.

Ordinarily, an accountant's inquiry and analytical procedures should consist of the following:

▲ Inquiries concerning the entity's accounting principles and practices and the methods followed in applying them.

▲ Inquiries concerning the entity's procedures for recording, classifying, and summarizing transactions, and accumulating information for disclosure in the financial statements.

▲ Analytical procedures designed to identify relationships and individual items appearing unusual:
— Comparing financial statements with statements for comparable prior periods.
— Comparing financial statements with anticipated results, if available (e.g., budgets and forecasts).
— Studying relationships between financial statement elements expected to conform with predictable patterns.

▲ Inquiries concerning actions taken at meetings of stockholders, the board of directors, or committees of the board.

▲ Reading the financial statements to consider, on the basis of information coming to the accountant's attention, whether the statements appear to conform with GAAP.

▲ Obtaining reports from other accountants, if any, engaged to audit or review the financial statements of an entity's significant components, subsidiaries, and other investees.

▲ Inquiries of persons responsible for financial and accounting matters concerning:
— Whether the financial statements have been prepared in accordance with GAAP.
— Changes in the entity's business activities, or accounting principles and practices.
— Questions arising when performing inquiry and analytical procedures.
— Subsequent events that would have a material effect on the financial statements.[4]

_____

[3] *Ibid.,* par. 4.
[4] *Ibid.,* par. 27.

As with compilations, reviewed financial statements should be accompanied by an accountant's report dated as of the date of completing the review. The report should state that a review was performed in accordance with AICPA standards and that the financial statements are the representations of management (owners). The nature of a review should be described, and the report should expressly state that the scope of a review is substantially less than that of an audit. The assurance expressed in a review report is stated in a negative manner, i.e., the accountant is not aware of any material departures from GAAP. A standard review report encompassing these requirements follows:

Accountant's Review Report

We have reviewed the accompanying balance sheet of XYZ Company as of December 31, 19XX, and the related statements of income, retained earnings, and cash flows for the year then ended, in accordance with standards established by the American Institute of Certified Public Accountants. All information included in these financial statements is the representation of management (owners) of the XYZ Company.

A review consists principally of inquiries of company personnel and analytical procedures applied to financial data. It is substantially less in scope than an examination in accordance with generally accepted auditing standards, the objective of which is the expression of an opinion regarding the financial statements taken as a whole. Accordingly, we do not express such an opinion.

Based on our review, we are not aware of any material modifications that should be made to the accompanying financial statements in order for them to be in conformity with generally accepted accounting principles.

Source: SSARS No, 1, par. 35.

Negative Assurance

Each page of the reviewed financial statements should include a reference such as "See Accountant's Review Report."

A review does not provide a basis for determining whether financial statements conform with GAAP. However, when an accountant becomes aware of material departures from GAAP, the financial statements should be revised or the report modified. The following illustrates a modified review report assuming a departure from GAAP.

Accountant's Review Report:
Departure from GAAP

(First two paragraphs unchanged)

Based on our review, with the exception of the matter described in the following paragraph, we are not aware of any material modifications. . . .

As disclosed in note X to the financial statements, generally accepted accounting principles require that inventory cost consist of material, labor, and overhead. Management has informed us that the inventory of finished goods and work in process is stated in the accompanying financial statements at material and labor cost only, and that the effects of this departure from generally accepted accounting principles on financial position, results of operations, and changes in financial position have not been determined.

Source: SSARS No. 1, par. 40

INTERIM FINANCIAL INFORMATION

Independent accountants often review interim financial information, including interim information that (1) is presented alone and reported on or (2) accompanies annual audited statements. Prior to 1979, professional auditing standards precluded independent accountants from expressing any assurance in reports about interim financial statements; no more than a disclaimer of opinion could be issued. However, in 1979, the Auditing Standards Board issued *Statement on Auditing Standards No. 24,* "Review of Interim Financial Information," which allowed an independent accountant to express limited assurance by stating whether he or she was aware of any material modifications necessary to conform the information with generally accepted accounting principles. In 1981, the Board superseded SAS No. 24 with *Statement on Auditing Standards No. 36,* also entitled "Review of Interim Financial Information," which changed SAS No. 24 provisions relating to SEC-required information accompanying annual audited financial statements. SAS No. 36 (AU Sec. 722) provides guidance for conducting a review of interim information and the reporting applicable to such reviews.

Interim Review Procedures

Interim financial statements or summaries of selected interim data may be prepared monthly, quarterly, or at some other interval. Thus, in comparison with annual audits, independent accountants typically have less time available to develop information and documentation underlying interim financial information. As a result, costs, expenses, deferrals, and accruals are often estimated to a greater extent in interim than in annual financial statements.

A review of interim financial information under SAS No. 36 consists primarily of inquiries and analytical review procedures, which ordinarily should include (AU Sec. 722.06):

▲ Making inquiries concerning the accounting system and any significant changes in internal control structure.
▲ Performing analytical procedures to identify and provide a basis for inquiry about relationships and individual items that appear unusual. Analytical procedures include:
— Comparison of the financial information with comparable information for the immediately preceding interim period and for corresponding previous periods.
— Comparison of the financial information with anticipated results.
— Study of the relationships of elements of financial information that would be expected to conform with predictable patterns.
▲ Reading the minutes of meetings of stockholders, boards of directors, and committees of the board to identify actions that may affect the interim financial information.
▲ Reading the interim financial information to consider whether it conforms with GAAP.
▲ Questioning officers and other executives concerning:
— Whether the interim financial information has been prepared in accordance with GAAP.
— Changes in the entity's business activities or accounting principles.
— Matters about which questions have arisen.
— Events subsequent to the date of interim financial information that would have a material effect on the information.
— Obtaining written representations from management.

Reporting on Separate Interim Period Information

An accountant's report should accompany reviewed interim financial information and include a statement that the review was made in accordance with applicable AICPA standards. The report should identify the interim financial information reviewed, describe the nature of procedures performed, and state that the scope of a review of interim information is substantially less than that of an audit. The accountant's limited assurance is expressed in language identical to that of a review report under SSARS No. 1. A standard review report for interim period information may be worded as follows (AU Sec. 722.18):

> ### Accountant's Report on
> ### Interim Financial Information
>
> We have made a review of (describe information reviewed) XYZ Company as of September 30, 19XX and for the three-month and nine-month periods then ended, in accordance with standards established by the American Institute of Certified Public Accountants.
>
> A review of interim financial information consists principally of obtaining an understanding of the system for the preparation of interim financial information, applying analytical procedures to financial data and making inquiries of persons responsible for financial and accounting matters. It is substantially less in scope than an examination in accordance with generally accepted auditing standards, the objective of which is the expression of an opinion regarding the financial statements taken as a whole. Accordingly, we do not express such an opinion.
>
> Based on our review, we are not aware of any material modifications that should be made to the accompanying financial information (or statements) for them to be in conformity with generally accepted accounting principles.

Each page of the interim financial information should be clearly marked "unaudited."

As in compilations and reviews under SSARS No. 1, a review of interim financial information may reveal a material departure from GAAP, even though no audit procedures are performed. If a client does not revise the interim financial information, an accountant should consider revising the standard review report, describing the nature of the departure and effects on interim information. For example, assume a client excludes certain lease obligations from assets and liabilities that should be capitalized in accordance with *Statement of Financial Accounting Standards No. 13*, "Accounting for Leases." Modifications to the standard review report follow (AU Sec. 722.21):

> ### Accountant's Report on
> ### Interim Financial Information:
> ### Departure from GAAP
>
> (First two paragraphs unchanged)
>
> Based on information furnished us by management, we believe that the Company has excluded from property and debt in the accompanying balance sheet certain lease obligations that should be capitalized in order to conform with

generally accepted accounting principles. This information indicates that if lease obligations were capitalized at September 30, 19XX, property would be increased by $_____, and long-term debt by $_____, and net income and earnings per share would be increased (decreased) by $_____, $_____, $_____, and $_____, respectively, for the three-month and nine-month periods then ended.

Based on our review, with the exception of the matter described in the preceding paragraph, we are not aware of any material modifications. . . .

Interim Information Accompanying Audited Statements

SAS No. 36 also addresses the effect on a standard audit report when interim financial information accompanies audited financial statements. Securities and Exchange Commission Regulation S-K requires that certain quarterly data be presented as supplementary information "outside" the audited financial statements or in an unaudited note to the statements. An independent auditor should review the interim information in accordance with the procedures outlined earlier. However, a separate report is not issued, and a standard audit report need not refer to the quarterly information unless the information is either omitted or not reviewed, in which case the audit report should be modified (exception reporting).

REPORTING ON INTERNAL CONTROL STRUCTURE

As discussed in Chapter 7, in conjunction with a financial statement audit, an independent auditor is required to communicate to an entity's audit committee, or to individuals with a level of authority and responsibility equivalent to an audit committee, any significant deficiencies in the design or operation of internal control structure — i.e., reportable conditions — that could adversely affect the entity's ability to record, process, summarize, and report financial data. The auditor may also communicate material weaknesses in internal control under SAS No. 60, "Communication of Internal Control Structure Related Matters Noted in an Audit."

Independent accountants may also address an entity's internal control structure in three other types of reports:

▲ Reports expressing an opinion on an entity's internal control structure.
▲ Reports on internal control structure based on criteria established by regulatory agencies.
▲ Other special-purpose internal control reports.

The procedures to be applied and reports to be issued for engagements to report on internal control structure are described in SAS No. 30, "Reporting on Internal Control" (AU SEC. 642).

Reports Expressing an Opinion

An independent accountant may be engaged either by audit clients or by other entities to express an opinion on internal control structure. In either case, the objective of an independent accountant's review is to express an opinion on whether internal control structure provides management with reasonable, though not absolute, assurance that assets are safeguarded and that transactions are executed in accordance with management's authorization.

In order to express an opinion on an entity's internal control structure, an independent accountant examines all control procedures comprising the internal control structure by (1) planning the scope of the engagement, (2) reviewing the design of the structure, (3) testing prescribed control procedures, and (4) evaluating the results of the review of the design of the system and tests of controls. The auditor's consideration of internal control structure in conjunction with a financial statement audit is insufficient because the second standard of field work (the basis for considering internal control in an opinion audit) requires reviewing, testing, and evaluating only those controls an auditor intends to rely upon. The breadth and scope of an engagement to express an opinion on internal control structure are considerably greater than for a consideration of internal control structure under the second field work standard; the objective of a financial statement audit is to issue an opinion on financial statements, not on internal control structure.

An independent accountant's report expressing an opinion on internal control structure should include:

▲ A description of the scope of the engagement.
▲ The date to which the opinion relates.
▲ A statement that the establishment and maintenance of the structure is management's responsibility.
▲ A brief explanation of the broad objectives and inherent limitations of internal control structure.
▲ The accountant's opinion on whether the internal control structure taken as a whole was sufficient to meet the broad objectives of internal control insofar as those objectives pertain to the prevention or detection of errors or irregularities in amounts that would be material in relation to financial statements.

A standard report expressing an opinion on internal control structure may be worded as follows:

Accountant's Report Expressing an Opinion on
an Entity's Internal Control Structure

We have made a study and evaluation of the internal control structure of XYZ Company in effect at June 30, 19XX. Our study and evaluation was conducted in accordance with standards established by the American Institute of Certified Public Accountants.

The management of XYZ Company is responsible for establishing and maintaining the internal control structure. In fulfilling the responsibility, estimates and judgments by management are required to assess the expected benefits and related costs of control procedures. The objectives of an internal control structure are to provide management with reasonable, but not absolute, assurance that assets are safeguarded against loss from unauthorized use or disposition, and that transactions are executed in accordance with management's authorization and recorded properly to permit the preparation of financial statements in accordance with generally accepted accounting principles.

Because of inherent limitations in any internal control structure, errors or irregularities may occur and not be detected. Also projection of any evaluation of the internal control structure to future periods is subject to the risk that procedures may become inadequate because of changes in conditions, or that the degree of compliance with the procedures may deteriorate.

In our opinion, the internal control structure of XYZ Company in effect at June 30, 19XX, taken as a whole, was sufficient to meet the objectives stated above insofar as those objectives pertain to the prevention or detection of errors or irregularities in amounts that would be material in relation to the financial statements.

If one or more material weaknesses in internal control are detected, the opinion paragraph of the accountant's report could be modified as follows:

Accountant's Report Expressing an Opinion on
an Entity's Internal Control Structure:
Material Weaknesses

(First three paragraphs unchanged)

Our study and evaluation disclosed the following conditions in the internal control structure of XYZ Company in effect at June 30, 19XX, which, in our opinion, result in more than a relatively low risk that errors or irregularities in amounts that would be material in relation to the financial statements may occur and not be detected within a timely period.

(A description of the material weaknesses would follow.)

Reports Based on a Regulatory Agency's Criteria

Regulatory agencies sometimes require that regulated entities report on internal control structure. Some agencies accept reports similar to the preceding opinion report on internal control, while others require that the reports comply with specific evaluation and reporting criteria prescribed in agency-prepared guides, questionnaires, or other publications. Agency-prescribed criteria typically relate to specific aspects of internal control and sometimes to compliance with grant programs, regulations, or statutes.

An accountant's report based upon agency criteria should (AU Sec. 642.56):

▲ Clearly indicate the matters covered by the study.
▲ Indicate whether the study included tests of controls.
▲ Describe the objectives and limitations of internal control and of the accountant's evaluations.
▲ State the accountant's conclusions based upon the agency's criteria.
▲ State that the report is intended for use in connection with the purpose to which the report refers.

An illustrative report on a regulatory agency's criteria follows:

Accountant's Report on Internal Control Structure Based upon a Regulatory Agency's Criteria

We understand the XYZ Company has been awarded a grant of $_____ from (agency) for the period from (date) through (date) for use in accordance with the (title or description of program). We have made a study of those internal control procedures of XYZ Company that we considered relevant to the criteria established by (agency), as set forth in (section) of its audit guide, issued (date). Our study included tests of controls during the period from (date) through (date). Our study did not constitute an audit of any financial statements prepared by XYZ Company.

The management of XYZ Company is responsible for establishing and maintaining the internal control structure. In fulfilling their responsibility, estimates and judgments by management are required to assess the expected benefits and related costs of control procedures. The objectives of an internal control structure are to provide management with reasonable, but not absolute, assurance that assets are safeguarded against loss from unauthorized use or disposition, and that transactions are executed in accordance with management's authorization and recorded properly to permit the preparation of financial statements in accordance with generally accepted accounting principles.

Because of inherent limitations in any internal control structure, errors or irregularities may occur and not be detected. Also, projection of any evaluation of the structure to future periods is subject to the risk that procedures may become inadequate because of changes in conditions, or that the degree of compliance with the procedures may deteriorate.

We understand that procedures in conformity with the criteria referred to in the first paragraph of this report are considered by the (agency) to be adequate for its purpose in accordance with (name of act) and related regulations, and that procedures not in conformity with those criteria indicate some inadequacy for such purposes. Based on this understanding and on our study, we believe XYZ Company's procedures were adequate for the agency's purposes, except for the conditions described (reference to appropriate section of report), which we believe are material weaknesses in relation to the grant to which this report refers. In addition to these weaknesses, other conditions that we believe are not in conformity with the criteria referred to above are described (reference to appropriate section of report).

This report is intended for the information of XYZ Company and (agency) and should not be used for any other purpose.

Other Special-Purpose Reports

An accountant may also be engaged to issue other special-purpose reports on all or parts of internal control structure. Generally, special-purpose reports are designed for the restricted use of management, another independent accountant, or other specified third parties. Special-purpose reports will vary depending upon the circumstances, but ordinarily should (1) describe the scope and nature of the accountant's procedures, (2) disclaim an opinion on whether the internal control structure, taken as a whole, meets the control objectives of management, (3) state the accountant's findings, and (4) indicate the report is intended solely for management or specified third parties.

COMPREHENSIVE BASES OF ACCOUNTING OTHER THAN GAAP

In some circumstances, entities present financial statements prepared on a comprehensive basis of accounting other than GAAP. *Statement on Auditing Standards No. 14*, ''Special Reports'' (AU Sec. 621), addresses reporting standards for the following bases of accounting:

▲ The cash receipts and disbursements basis of accounting.

▲ A basis of accounting used to comply with a regulatory agency's requirements.

▲ A basis of accounting used to file income tax returns.

If financial statements are presented on a comprehensive basis other than GAAP, an accountant's report should include the following:

▲ A paragraph identifying the financial statements examined.

▲ A paragraph that:

— States, or preferably refers to a note that states, the basis of presentation used.

— Refers to a note describing how the basis of presentation differs from GAAP.

— States the financial statements are not intended to be presented in conformity with GAAP.

▲ A paragraph expressing the auditor's opinion on whether the financial statements are presented in conformity with the basis described.

An illustrative accountant's report for cash basis financial statements follows:

Accountant's Report on Cash Basis Financial Statements

We have audited the statements of assets and liabilities arising from cash transactions of XYZ Company as of December 31, 19XX, and the related statement of revenue collected and expenses paid for the year then ended. These financial statements are the responsibility of the company's management. Our responsibility is to express an opinion on these statements based on our audit.

As described in note X, the Company's policy is to prepare financial statements on the basis of cash receipts and disbursements; consequently, certain revenue and the related assets are recognized when received rather than when earned, and certain expenses are recognized when paid rather than when the obligation is incurred. Accordingly, the accompanying financial statements are not intended to present financial position and results of operations in conformity with generally accepted accounting principles.

In our opinion, the financial statements referred to above present fairly, in all material respects, the assets and liabilities arising from cash transactions of XYZ Company as of December 31, 19XX, and the revenue collected and expenses paid during the year then ended, in conformity with the basis of accounting described in note X.

REPORTS ON SPECIFIED ELEMENTS, ACCOUNTS, OR ITEMS OF A FINANCIAL STATEMENT

An independent accountant may be engaged by audit clients or other entities to report on specified financial statement elements, accounts, or items, as opposed to an entire set of financial statements taken as a whole. Reports for these engagements generally fall into one of two categories (AU Sec. 621.09): (1) a report expressing an opinion on the specified items or (2) a report relating to the results of applying agreed-upon procedures.

Reports Expressing an Opinion

When an independent accountant is engaged to express an opinion on specified financial statements items, an audit should be performed in accordance with applicable generally accepted auditing standards. The first standard of reporting does not apply, since the examination does not relate to financial statements, but only to specified elements. The accountant's report should describe the scope of the examination, specifying the elements, accounts, or items examined, and state whether the examination was made in accordance with generally accepted auditing standards. An illustrative report expressing an unqualified opinion on gross sales as a basis for determining rental payments follows:

> **Accountant's Report on Gross Sales for the Purpose of Computing Rental**
>
> We have audited the schedule of gross sales (as defined in the lease agreement dated March 4, 19XX, between ABC Company, as lessor, and XYZ Stores Corporation, as lessee) of XYZ Stores Corporation at its Main Street store, [City], [State], for the year ended December 31, 19XX. This schedule is the responsibility of the company's management. Our responsibility is to express an opinion on the schedule based on our audit.
>
> In our opinion, the schedule of gross sales referred to above presents fairly, in all material respects, the gross sales of XYZ Stores Corporation at its Main Street store, [City], [State], for the year ended December 31, 19XX, in conformity with the basis specified in the lease agreement referred to above.

Reports Relating to Agreed-Upon Procedures

An independent accountant may be engaged to apply agreed-upon procedures to specified financial statement items — procedures that are insufficient for expressing an opinion. For example, an entity might require a special report to help management evaluate selected creditor claims or the proposed acquisition of another entity.

According to *Statement on Auditing Standards No. 35,* "Special Reports — Applying Agreed-Upon Procedures to Specified Elements, Accounts, or Items of a Financial Statement," an accountant may accept these engagements provided the parties involved have a clear understanding of the procedures to be performed, and distribution of the report is restricted to named parties involved. Although the second and third standards of field work and the standards of reporting do not apply in engagements limited to agreed-upon procedures, the general standards and the first field work standard do apply.

SAS No. 35 requires that reports on specified financial statement elements, accounts, or other items should (AU Sec. 622.04):

▲ Indicate the specified elements, accounts, or items to which the agreed-upon procedures were applied.
▲ Indicate the intended distribution of the report.
▲ Enumerate the procedures performed.
▲ State the accountant's findings.
▲ Disclaim an opinion on the specified elements, accounts, or items.
▲ State that the report relates only to the elements, accounts or items specified, and not to the financial statements taken as a whole.

An illustrative accountant's report related to creditor claims follows:

Accountant's Report in Connection with Claims of Creditors

At your request, we have performed the procedures enumerated below with respect to the claims of creditors of XYZ Company as of May 31, 19XX, set forth in the accompanying schedules. Our review was made solely to assist you in evaluating the reasonableness of those claims, and our report is not to be used for any other purpose. The procedures we performed are summarized as follows:

1. We compared the total of the trial balance of accounts payable at May 31, 19XX, prepared by the company, to the balance in the company's related general ledger account.
2. We compared the claims received from creditors to the trial balance of accounts payable.
3. We examined documentation submitted by the creditors in support of their claims and compared it to documentation in the company's files, including invoices, receiving records, and other evidence of receipt of goods or services.

Our findings are presented in the accompanying schedules. Schedule A lists claims that are in agreement with the company's records. Schedule B lists claims that are not in agreement with the company's records and sets forth the differences in amounts.

Because the above procedures do not constitute an audit conducted in accordance with generally accepted auditing standards, we do not express an opinion on the accounts payable balance as of May 31, 19XX. In connection with the procedures referred to above, except as set forth in Schedule B, no matters came to our attention that caused us to believe that the accounts payable balance might require adjustment. Had we performed additional procedures or had we audited the financial statements in accordance with generally accepted auditing standards, other matters might have come to our attention that would have been reported to you. This report relates only to the accounts and items specified above and does not extend to any financial statements of XYZ Company, taken as a whole.

REPORTS ON COMPLIANCE WITH CONTRACTUAL AGREEMENTS OR REGULATORY REQUIREMENTS

In conjunction with an opinion audit, an independent auditor may be requested to report on an entity's compliance with contractual agreements, such as bond indentures or other debt covenants, or government regulatory requirements. An auditor's reporting obligation under SAS No. 14, "Special Reports" (AU Sec. 621), is to provide negative assurance either in a separate report or in a paragraph in the standard audit report. No assurance should be expressed unless the related financial statements have been audited. An illustrative separate report on compliance with a contractual agreement follows:

Auditor's Report on
Compliance with a Contractual Agreement

We have audited the balance sheet of XYZ Company as of December 31, 19X1, and the related statements of income, retained earnings, and cash flows for the year then ended, and have issued our report thereon dated February 16, 19X2. These financial statements are the responsibility of the company's management. Our responsibility is to express an opinion on these financial statements based on our audit.

> In connection with our audit, nothing came to our attention that caused us to believe that the Company was not in compliance with any of the terms, covenants, provisions, or conditions of sections XX to XX, inclusive, of the Indenture dated July 21, 19X0, with ABC Bank. However, it should be noted that our audit was not directed primarily toward obtaining knowledge of such noncompliance.

LETTERS FOR UNDERWRITERS

As discussed in Chapter 4, a registration statement must be filed with the Securities and Exchange Commission before an entity may publicly offer securities for sale. In most cases, an investment bank or other financial institution serves as an offering entity's *underwriter* by either purchasing the securities for resale or selling the securities in the entity's behalf. Thus, an underwriter is an intermediary between an offering entity and the investing public and, as a result, is a primary party to the registration process.

In accordance with the Securities Act of 1933, an underwriter is responsible to perform a "reasonable investigation" of financial and accounting data accompanying the registration statement. Because financial and accounting data are more within the realm of an accountant's, rather than underwriter's, area of expertise, underwriters engage independent accountants to perform professional services sufficient to issue a *letter for underwriters* (often called a "comfort letter") about the unaudited financial statements and schedules accompanying the registration statement. The comfort letter provides negative assurance and varies in content depending upon an underwriter's specific needs. Importantly, the purpose of a comfort letter is to provide assurance to an underwriter, not to the SEC. As a result, the letter is not filed with the SEC as part of the registration statement; rather, it is held by the underwriter and produced only as a defense against potential claims by securities purchasers.

SAS No. 49, "Letters for Underwriters" (AU Sec. 634), identifies the following items that an independent accountant would ordinarily refer to in a comfort letter (AU Sec. 634.06):

▲ The accountant's independence.
▲ Compliance as to form in all material respects of the audited financial statements and schedules included in the registration statement with the applicable accounting requirements of the Securities Act of 1933 and the related rules and regulations.
▲ Unaudited financial statements, condensed interim financial state-

ments, capsule information, or pro forma financial information included in the registration statement.

▲ Changes in selected financial statement items during a period subsequent to the date and period of the latest financial statements included in the registration statement.

▲ Tables, statistics, and other financial information included in the registration statement.

Because of the length and variety of comfort letters, a sample comfort letter is not illustrated. However, SAS No. 49, AU Sec. 634.48, includes twelve sample letters covering a wide range of circumstances confronted in practice.

FINANCIAL FORECASTS AND PROJECTIONS

An independent public accountant should not allow an entity to use his or her name in a manner that may lead users to believe the accountant vouches for the achievability of a financial forecast. However, as noted in Chapter 2, an accountant is not precluded from assisting an entity in preparing published forecasts and projections of financial position and results of operations.

As a result of considerable confusion about an independent accountant's responsibility in forecasts and the SEC's action in 1973 to lift a prohibition against financial forecasts, the AICPA's executive committees on accounting standards and on management advisory services each issued guidelines on accountants' involvement with forecasts. More recently, the Auditing Standards Board issued a *Statement on Standards for Accountants' Services on Prospective Financial Information* (1985), entitled "Financial Forecasts and Projections," which defines a "financial forecast" and a "financial projection," and sets forth standards and guidance for accountants concerning engagements to compile, examine, or apply agreed-upon procedures to prospective financial statements.

Forecasts and Projections

A *financial forecast* is a prospective financial statement that presents an entity's expected financial position, results of operations, and cash flows. Unlike audited, compiled, or reviewed financial statements, all of which are based on past transactions and events, forecasts are based on expected transactions and events and, as such, reflect the reporting entity's assumptions about conditions it expects to exist and the course of action it expects to take. A financial forecast may be expressed in specific monetary amounts as a single point estimate of forecasted results or as a range of monetary amounts.

In contrast, a *financial projection* is also a prospective financial state-

ment that presents an entity's expected financial position, results of operations, and cash flows, but is based on one or more hypothetical assumptions.
For example, a financial projection may be prepared to evaluate one or more
hypothetical courses of action — that is, in response to the question "What
would happen if . . . ?" Like a forecast, a financial projection may contain
a range of monetary amounts. Financial forecasts and projections are referred
to as *prospective financial statements*.

Compilation of Prospective Financial Statements

A compilation of prospective financial statements involves:

▲ Assembling the prospective financial statements based on the reporting
  entity's assumptions.
▲ Performing the required compilation procedures, including reading the
  prospective financial statements with their summaries of significant assumptions and accounting policies.
▲ Issuing a compilation report.

The summary of significant assumptions referred to above is essential to a
reader's understanding of the prospective financial statements. As a result, an
accountant should not compile prospective financial statements that omit a
summary of the significant assumptions or, in the case of a financial projection, that fail to disclose the hypothetical assumptions.

To illustrate a compilation report on prospective financial statements,
assume the Health Services Corporation engages an independent accountant
to prepare projected financial statements that will be used in negotiating a
plant expansion loan from the Boise Bank & Trust. A compilation report
follows:

Accountant's Compilation Report on a Financial Projection

We have compiled the accompanying projected balance sheet, statements of
income, retained earnings, and cash flows of the Health Services Corporation
as of December 31, 19XX, and for the year then ending, in accordance with
standards established by the American Institute of Certified Public Accountants.

The accompanying projection and this report were prepared for the Boise Bank
& Trust for the purpose of negotiating a plant expansion loan and should not
be used for any other purpose.

A compilation is limited to presenting in the form of a projection information
that is the representation of management and does not include evaluation of the

support for the assumptions underlying the projection. We have not audited the projection, and, accordingly, do not express an opinion or any other form of assurance on the accompanying statements or assumptions. Furthermore, even if the loan is granted and the physical plant is expanded, there will usually be differences between the projected and actual results, because events and circumstances frequently do not occur as expected, and those differences may be material. We have no responsibility to update this report for events and circumstances occurring after the date of this report.

Source: Financial Forecasts and Projections, par. 18.

Note in this case that there was only one hypothetical assumption: that the loan was granted.

Examination of Prospective Financial Statements

In an examination of prospective financial statements, an independent accountant renders an opinion. But unlike an opinion on audited financial statements, which provides assurance about whether the statements conform with GAAP, an opinion on prospective financial statements provides assurance on whether (1) the prospective financial statements conform with AICPA guidelines — i.e., the AICPA's "Financial Forecasts and Projections," and (2) the assumptions provide a reasonable basis for a forecast or projection. The following illustrates a standard report on the examination of a financial forecast:

Accountant's Report on an Examination of a Financial Forecast

We have examined the accompanying forecasted balance sheet, statements of income, retained earnings, and cash flows of XYZ Company as of December 31, 19XX, and for the year then ending. These forecasted financial statements are the responsibility of the company's management. Our responsibility is to express an opinion on these forecasted financial statements based on our examination made in accordance with standards for an examination of a forecast established by the American Institute of Certified Pubic Accountants.

In our opinion, the accompanying forecast is presented in conformity with guidelines for presentation of a forecast established by the American Institute of Certified Public Accountants, and the underlying assumptions provide a reasonable basis for management's forecast. However, there will usually be dif-

> ferences between the forecasted and actual results, because events and circumstances frequently do not occur as expected, and those differences may be material. We have no responsibility to update this report for events and circumstances occurring after the date of this report.

Note that, like the compilation report on financial projection illustrated earlier, the above report alerts readers that assumptions may not mirror future events and circumstances and that the accountant is under no obligation to update the report if future information casts doubt on earlier assumptions.

Applying Agreed-Upon Procedures to Prospective Financial Statements

Accountants are sometimes engaged to apply agreed-upon procedures to prospective financial statements for the express benefit of a specific third party, such as a commercial bank. However, these engagements may be accepted only if (1) the specified users have participated in establishing the nature and scope of the engagement and take responsibility for the adequacy of the procedures performed, (2) the report is distributed only to the specified user, and (3) the statements include a summary of significant assumptions. The agreed-upon procedures may be limited or extensive, but responsibility for their adequacy rests with the specified user.

In general, an accountant's report on the results of applying agreed-upon procedures should:

- ▲ Indicate the prospective financial statements covered.
- ▲ Indicate that use of the report is limited to the specified user.
- ▲ Enumerate procedures performed.
- ▲ If the procedures are less than those usually performed in an audit, disclaim an opinion on the statements and assumptions.
- ▲ State the accountant's findings.
- ▲ Indicate that the prospective results may not be achieved.
- ▲ State that the accountant assumes no responsibility to update the report.

PERSONAL FINANCIAL STATEMENTS

Much like businesses, individuals or families may also require audited financial statements, though for different reasons. For example, a political candidate may elect to disclose publicly his or her personal financial position or an individual may need personal statements to acquire bank credit when purchasing a business. Interestingly, personal financial statements differ markedly from financial statements prepared in accordance with GAAP. For example, assets are reported at estimated current values in personal financial statements, thereby requiring that the accountant attest to current value, a more difficult task than attesting to historical cost.

In 1982, the AICPA issued *Statement of Position 82-1*, "Accounting and Financial Reporting for Personal Financial Statements," followed the year after by *Personal Financial Statements Guide*, a guide to audit and non-audit engagements on personal financial statements. The *Guide* illustrates an unqualified report on the personal financial statements of a married couple.

Accountant's Report on Personal Financial Statements

We have audited the statement of financial condition of Mr. and Mrs. Robert V. Bracken as of December 31, 19XX, and the related statement of changes in net worth for the year then ended. These statements are the responsibility of Mr. and Mrs. Bracken. Our responsibility is to express an opinion on these statements based on our audit.

In our opinion, the financial statements referred to above present fairly, in all material respects, the financial position of Mr. and Mrs. Robert V. Bracken as of December 31, 19XX, and the changes in their net worth for the year then ended, in conformity with generally accepted accounting principles.

REPORTS ON THE APPLICATION OF ACCOUNTING PRINCIPLES

Occasionally, an accountant will report to a nonclient about the application of accounting principles. For example, the report might represent a "second opinion" or, in some cases, a proposal intended to obtain a new client. In 1986, the Auditing Standards Board issued *Statement on Auditing Standards No. 50*, "Reports on the Application of Accounting Principles," which provides guidance when an auditor reports in writing or orally on (1) the application of accounting principles or (2) a nonclient's audit opinion. A sample report follows:

Accountants' Report on the Application of Accounting Principles

We have been engaged to report on the appropriate application of generally accepted accounting principles to the specific transaction described below. This report is being issued to the XYZ Company for assistance in evaluating accounting principles for the described specific transaction. Our engagement has been conducted in accordance with standards established by the American Institute of Certified Public Accountants.

The facts, circumstances, and assumptions relevant to the specific transaction as provided to us by management of the XYZ Company are as follows:

(Text describing facts, circumstances, and assumptions.)

(Text discussing accounting principles.)

The ultimate responsibility for the decision on the appropriate application of generally accepted accounting principles for an actual transaction rests with the preparers of financial statements, who should consult with their continuing accountants. Our judgment on the appropriate application of generally accepted accounting principles for the described transaction is based solely on the facts provided to us as described above; should these facts and circumstances differ, our conclusion may change.

Source: SAS No. 50, par. 8.

SUMMARY

In addition to standard audit reports, accountants also issue other types of reports. Reports may be required for a variety of professional services including compilations and reviews of financial statements, reviews of interim financial information, reviews of internal control structure, and letters for underwriters, among others. Nonaudit reports typically express limited (negative) assurance or no assurance at all.

REFERENCES

American Institute of Certified Public Accountants. *Codification of Statements on Auditing Standards.* New York: American Institute of Certified Public Accountants.

American Institute of Certified Public Accountants. *Codification of Statements on Standards for Accounting and Review Services.* New York: American Institute of Certified Public Accountants.

American Institute of Certified Public Accountants. *Statement of Position 82-1.* New York: American Institute of Certified Public Accountants, 1982.

American Institute of Certified Public Accountants. *Statement on Standards for Accountants' Services on Prospective Financial Information,* "Financial Forecasts and Projections." New York: American Institute of Certified Public Accountants, 1985.

Brown, H. "Compilation and Review — A Step Forward." *The CPA Journal* (May, 1979), pp. 18–23.

Carmichael, D. R. "The Assurance Function — Auditing at the Crossroads." *Journal of Accountancy* (September, 1974), pp. 64–72.

Jones, W. J. and C. R. Ward. "Forecasts and Projections for Third-Party Use." *Journal of Accountancy* (April, 1986), pp. 100–102.

Kelley, T. P. "Compilation and Review — A Revolution in Practice." *The CPA Journal* (April, 1974), pp. 19–27.

Lambert, J. C. and S. J. Lambert III. "Review of Interim Financial Information." *The CPA Journal* (September, 1979), pp. 25–31.

Pallais, D. and G. M. Guy. "Prospective Financial Statements." *Journal of Accountancy* (April, 1986), pp. 90–99.

Weirich, T. R. and G. M. Pintar. "Interpretation and Flowchart of SSARS No. 1." *Journal of Accountancy* (November, 1979), pp. 60–65.

QUESTIONS

1. How does a standard audit report differ from nonaudit reports?
2. What created the confusion surrounding "unaudited" financial statements prior to SSARS No. 1?
3. Identify the case most responsible for the profession's response to the confusion about "unaudited" financial statements.
4. What senior technical committee of the AICPA is responsible for issuing pronouncements about nonaudit services for nonpublic entities?
5. What terminology is now used in place of "unaudited" statements for nonpublic entities?
6. What is a compilation of financial statements?
7. Identify the reporting requirements for financial statements compiled in accordance with SSARS No. 1.
8. What is a review of financial statements?
9. Describe the purpose and give examples of analytical procedures performed in conjunction with a review of financial statements.
10. Identify the reporting requirements for financial statements reviewed in accordance with SSARS No. 1.
11. In what situations might an independent accountant review interim financial information?
12. Why are costs, expenses, deferrals, and accruals often estimated to a greater extent in interim than annual financial statements?
13. In conjunction with an interim review, what inquiries are made of officers and other executives?
14. Identify the types of reports an independent auditor or accountant might issue on an entity's internal control structure.

15. What are the phases of an engagement designed to reach an opinion on an entity's internal control structure?
16. What is a "comprehensive basis of accounting other than GAAP"?
17. To what does an auditor's opinion relate when an entity's financial statements are prepared on a comprehensive basis of accounting other than GAAP?
18. What is the purpose of letters for underwriters?
19. What is the difference between a financial forecast and a financial projection?
20. What does a report on personal financial statements typically address?
21. Under what conditions might an independent accountant report on the application of accounting principles?

MULTIPLE CHOICE QUESTIONS

1. Which of the following would **not** be included in a CPA's report based upon a review of the financial statements of a nonpublic entity?

   a. A statement that the review was in accordance with generally accepted auditing standards.
   b. A statement that all information included in the financial statements is the representation of management.
   c. A statement describing the principal procedures performed.
   d. A statement describing the auditor's conclusions based upon the results of the review.   (AICPA Adapted)

2. A CPA who is **not** independent may issue a

   a. Compilation report.
   b. Review report.
   c. Comfort letter.
   d. Qualified opinion.   (AICPA Adapted)

3. The objective of a review of the interim financial information of a publicly held company is to

   a. Provide the accountant with a basis for the expression of an opinion.
   b. Estimate the accuracy of financial statements based upon limited tests of accounting records.
   c. Provide the accountant with a basis for reporting to the board of directors or stockholders.
   d. Obtain corroborating evidential matter through inspection, observation, and confirmation.   (AICPA Adapted)

4. A CPA's consideration of an entity's internal control structure in an audit

   a. Is generally more limited than that made in connection with an engagement to express an opinion on the internal control structure.
   b. Is generally more extensive than that made in connection with an engagement to express an opinion on the internal control structure.
   c. Is generally identical to that made in connection with an engagement to express an opinion on the internal control structure.

   d. Will generally result in the CPA expressing an opinion on the internal control structure.   (AICPA Adapted)

5. An auditor's report would be designated as a special report when it is issued in connection with which of the following?

   a. Financial statements for an interim period which are subjected to a limited review.

   (b) Financial statements which are prepared in accordance with a comprehensive basis of accounting other than generally accepted accounting principles.

   c. Financial statements which purport to be in accordance with generally accepted accounting principles but do not include a presentation of the statement of cash flows.

   d. Financial statements which are unaudited and are prepared from a client's accounting records.   (AICPA Adapted)

6. When asked to perform an examination in order to express an opinion on one or more specified elements, accounts, or items of a financial statement, the auditor

   a. May **not** describe auditing procedures applied.

   (b) Should advise the client that the opinion will result in a piecemeal opinion.

   c. May assume that the first standard of reporting with respect to generally accepted accounting principles does **not** apply.

   d. Should comply with the request only if they constitute a major portion of the financial statements on which an auditor has disclaimed an opinion based on an audit.   (AICPA Adapted)

7. A CPA has been engaged to audit financial statements that were prepared on a cash basis. The CPA

   (a.) Must ascertain that there is proper disclosure of the fact that the cash basis has been used, the general nature of material items omitted, and the net effect of such omissions.

   b. May not be associated with such statements which are not in accordance with generally accepted accounting principles.

   c. Must render a qualified report explaining the departure from generally accepted accounting principles in the opinion paragraph.

   d. Must restate the financial statements on an accrual basis and then render the standard report.   (AICPA Adapted)

8. When issuing a "comfort letter" to underwriters, the CPA should

   a. File a copy with the SEC.

   b. Disclaim an opinion.

   c. Avoid any reference to the CPA's independence.

   (d.) Express negative assurance.   (AICPA Adapted)

9. An auditor should not render a report on

   (a) The achievability of forecasts.

   b. Client internal control.

   c. Management performance.

   d. Quarterly financial information.   (AICPA Adapted)

PROBLEMS

20-1   A compilation of financial statements involves presenting management representations in the form of financial statements without expressing any degree of assurance. Nevertheless, even though no assurance is expressed, an independent accountant must comply with the provisions of SSARS No. 1, "Compilation and Review of Financial Statements."

Required:
(1) Identify the type of knowledge and understanding that an independent accountant should obtain in conjunction with a compilation engagement.
(2) How does an accountant inform users of the nature and limitations of a compilation?
(3) What actions should an independent accountant take when he or she becomes aware of a material departure from GAAP in financial statements compiled?

20-2   Kimberly Rossi, CPA, has been engaged by the Barrington Company, a nonpublicly held manufacturer of children's toys, to review Barrington's December 31, 1990 financial statements. Rossi accepts the engagement, performing inquiry and analytical procedures sufficient to provide a reasonable basis for expressing limited assurance that no material modifications are necessary to conform the statements with generally accepted accounting principles. While making inquiries of Barrington's chief financial officer, Rossi discovers that land is carried at appraised value rather than historical cost, and the company refuses to adjust the December 31, 1990 statements. All inquiries and analytical procedures are completed on January 28, 1991.

Required:
Prepare the review report Rossi would present to Barrington's board of directors, assuming the effect on financial statements of carrying land at appraised value has not been determined by management.

20-3   Loman, CPA, who has examined the financial statements of the Broadwall Corporation, a publicly held company, for the year ended December 31, 1990, was asked to perform a limited review of the financial statements of Broadwall Corporation for the period ending March 31, 1991. The engagement letter stated that a limited review does not provide a basis for the expression of an opinion.

Required:
(1) Explain why Loman's limited review will *not* provide a basis for the expression of an opinion.
(2) What are the review procedures which Loman should perform, and what is the purpose of each procedure? Structure your response as follows:

> *Procedure*   *Purpose of Procedure*

(AICPA Adapted)

20-4   The limitations on the CPA's professional responsibilities when associated with unaudited financial statements are often misunderstood. These misunderstandings can be substantially reduced by carefully following professional pronouncements and taking other appropriate measures.

Required:
The following list describes situations the CPA may encounter in his or her association with unaudited financial statements. Briefly discuss the extent of the CPA's
responsibilities and, if appropriate, the actions he or she should take to minimize any
misunderstandings. Number your answers to correspond with the numbering in the
following list.
1. A group of investors who own a farm which is managed by an independent agent
   engage a CPA to prepare quarterly unaudited financial statements for them. The
   CPA prepared the financial statements from information supplied by the independent agent. Subsequently, the investors find the statements were inaccurate because their independent agent was embezzling funds. The investors refuse to pay
   the CPA's fee and blame the CPA for allowing the situation to go undetected,
   contending that representations from the independent agent should not have been
   relied upon.
2. In comparing the trial balance with the general ledger, a CPA finds an account
   labeled "audit fees" in which the client has accumulated the CPA's quarterly
   billings for accounting services including the preparation of quarterly unaudited
   financial statements.
3. To determine appropriate account classification, a CPA reviewed a number of the
   client's invoices. The CPA noted in the working papers that some invoices were
   missing, but felt that they did not affect the unaudited financial statements and
   thus did nothing further. The client subsequently discovered that invoices were
   missing and contended that the CPA should not have ignored the missing invoices
   when preparing the financial statements and had a responsibility to at least inform
   the client that they were missing.
4. A CPA is engaged to review without audit the financial statements prepared by
   the client's controller. During the review, the CPA learns of several items which
   by generally accepted accounting principles would require adjustment of the statements and note disclosure. The controller agrees to make the recommended adjustments to the statements but refuses to add the notes because the statements
   are unaudited.   (AICPA Adapted)   ·

20-5   Assume you have been requested by the Upton Corporation to prepare a
report expressing an opinion on the entity's internal control structure. In each of the
five years Upton has been a client, you have issued an unqualified opinion on financial statements, and in each year your consideration of internal control structure in
accordance with the second field work standard has not revealed any reportable conditions. Because no reportable conditions have been detected, Ken Pontarelli, Upton's corporate controller, asks that you issue a report on internal control structure
without performing any additional procedures. Pontarelli says: "Simply issue the
opinion, stating it is based upon procedures performed during the audit. You know
as well as I do that additional procedures won't disclose anything significant. So why
make us pay for work that is a waste of time?"

Required
(1) Respond to Pontarelli's request, indicating why you could or could not issue an
    opinion on Upton Corporation's internal control structure.
(2) What are the similarities and differences between an accountant's report on in-
    ternal control in conjunction with an opinion audit and a report expressing an
    opinion on Upton Corporation's internal control structure.

20-6   Rose & Co., CPAs, has satisfactorily completed the audit of the financial statements of Bale & Booster, a partnership, for the year ended December 31, 1990. The financial statements which were prepared on the entity's income tax (cash) basis include footnotes which indicate that the partnership was involved in continuing litigation of material amounts relating to alleged infringement of a competitor's patent. The amount of damages, if any, resulting from this litigation could not be determined at the time of completion of the engagement. The prior years' financial statements were not presented.

Required:
Based upon the information presented, prepare an auditor's report which includes appropriate explanatory disclosure of significant facts.   (AICPA Adapted)

20-7   In order to obtain information that is necessary to make informed decisions, management often calls upon the independent auditor for assistance. This may involve a request that the independent auditor apply certain audit procedures to specific accounts of a company which is a candidate for acquisition and report upon the results. In such an engagement, the agreed-upon procedures may constitute a scope limitation.

At the completion of an engagement performed at the request of Uclean Corporation which was limited in scope as explained above, the following report was prepared by an audit assistant and was submitted to the auditor for review:

To: Board of Directors of Ajax Corporation

We have applied certain agreed-upon procedures, as discussed below, to accounting records of Ajax Corporation, as of December 31, 1990, solely to assist Uclean Corporation in connection with the proposed acquisition of Ajax Corporation.

We have examined the cash in banks and accounts receivable of Ajax Corporation as of December 31, 1990, in accordance with generally accepted auditing standards and, accordingly, included such tests of the accounting records and such other auditing procedures as we considered necessary in the circumstances.

In our opinion, the cash and receivables referred to above are presented fairly, in all material respects, as of December 31, 1990, in conformity with generally accepted accounting principles. We therefore recommend that Uclean Corporation acquire Ajax Corporation pursuant to the proposed agreement.

Required:
Comment on the proposed report describing those assertions that are:
a. Incorrect or should otherwise be deleted.
b. Missing and should be inserted.   (AICPA Adapted)

20-8   Roger Francoeur, a candidate for town council, is campaigning on a platform of open government and fiscal responsibility. During his campaign, Francoeur requests that you prepare personal financial statements, fully disclosing his financial position for the twelve month period ended June 30, 1990. Unfamiliar with the nature of personal financial statements, Francoeur asks that you explain the major similarities and differences between the financial statements and audit reports that are issued for personal and "corporate" financial statements.

Required:

Describe the major similarities and differences alluded to by Francoeur, indicating the rationale underlying each difference. Ignore differences related to the titles of financial statements.

20-9   Brown, CPA received a telephone call from Calhoun, the sole owner and manager of a small corporation. Calhoun asked Brown to prepare the financial statements for the corporation and told Brown that the statements were needed in two weeks for external financial purposes. Calhoun was vague when Brown inquired about the intended use of the statements. Brown was convinced that Calhoun thought Brown's work would constitute an audit. To avoid confusion Brown decided not to explain to Calhoun that the engagement would only be to prepare the financial statements. Brown, with the understanding that a substantial fee would be paid if the work were completed in two weeks, accepted the engagement and started the work at once.

During the course of the work, Brown discovered an accrued expense account labeled "professional fees" and learned that the balance in the account represented an accrual for the cost of Brown's services. Brown suggested to Calhoun's bookkeeper that the account name be changed to "fees for limited audit engagement." Brown also reviewed several invoices to determine whether accounts were being properly classified. Some of the invoices were missing. Brown listed the missing invoice numbers in the working papers with a note indicating that there should be a follow-up on the next engagement. Brown also discovered that the available records included the fixed asset values at estimated current replacement costs. On the basis of the records available, Brown prepared a balance sheet, income statement and statement of stockholder's equity. In addition, Brown drafted the notes but decided that any mention of the replacement costs would only mislead the readers. Brown suggested to Calhoun that readers of the financial statements would be better informed if they received a separate letter from Calhoun explaining the meaning and effect of the estimated replacement costs of the fixed assets. Brown mailed the financial statements and notes to Calhoun with the following note included on each page:

> The accompanying financial statements are submitted to you without complete audit verification.

Required:

Identify the inappropriate actions of Brown and indicate what Brown should have done to avoid each inappropriate action. Organize your answer sheet as follows:

Inappropriate Action	What Brown Should Have Done to Avoid Inappropriate Action

(AICPA Adapted)

PART V RESEARCH AND INTERNAL AND GOVERNMENTAL AUDITING

INTERNAL AND GOVERNMENTAL AUDITING

21

Major topics discussed in this chapter are the:

▲   *Distinctions among independent, internal, and governmental auditing.*

▲   *Scope of and need for internal and governmental auditing.*

▲   *Significance of independence to the internal audit function.*

▲   *Nature and types of internal operational audits.*

▲   *Relationship between internal and independent auditors.*

▲   *Nature and types of governmental audits.*

▲   *Single Audit Act of 1984.*

Independent, internal, and governmental auditing are distinctly different types of audit activities, and each provides unique professional responsibilities, opportunities, and challenges to its practitioners. This chapter, devoted exclusively to internal and governmental auditing, serves as a basis for comparing independent auditing — the focus of this book — with other audit activities practiced in the U.S. Figure 21-1 distinguishes independent, internal, and governmental auditing.

Independent auditing performed by CPA firms is a *societal control* which serves the needs of internal and, more importantly, external financial information users. *Independent* auditors conduct *financial statement opinion audits* and audit fees are paid directly by the organizations audited.

Internal auditing, in contrast, serves the organization and, as such, is an *organizational control* which measures and evaluates the effectiveness of other organized controls. Internal auditors conduct *operational audits* and are compensated by their employer organizations.

Governmental auditing is a *governmental control* which serves individual governmental entities at the federal, state, and local levels. Governmental audits are classified as *financial and compliance, economy and efficiency,* or *program results* audits and are usually conducted by government auditors, but in some cases by independent auditors. Governmental auditors are compensated by their employer organizations.

FIGURE 21-1

Distinguishing External, Internal, and Governmental Auditing

Activity	Type of Control	Type of Audit	Predominant Users
Independent auditing	Societal	Financial statement opinion audit	External financial information users
Internal auditing	Organizational	Operational audit	Internal organization members
Governmental auditing	Governmental	Financial and compliance audit Economy and efficiency audit Program results audit	Governmental entities

INTERNAL AUDITING

Like independent auditing, internal auditing had its roots in ancient times. In fact, independent and internal auditing had essentially the same beginnings; there was no distinction between the two prior to the nineteenth century.

Contemporary professional practice of internal auditing was born in 1941, when the first major internal auditing book, Victor Z. Brink's *Modern Internal Auditing,* was published, and the Institute of Internal Auditors was founded. *Modern Internal Auditing* is now in its third edition and still recognized as a major contribution to internal auditing thought. The Institute of Internal Auditors has grown from 24 charter members in 1941 to over 20,000 members and 130 chapters worldwide today. In four decades the Institute has done much to enhance the professional stature of internal auditors, including: approving a statement of responsibilities, developing a common body of knowledge, establishing continuing education and professional certification (Certified Internal Auditor) programs, and adopting standards for the professional practice of internal auditing along with a code of ethics. A summary of the general and specific standards of internal auditing is reproduced in Appendix A of this chapter, and the Institute of Internal Auditors Code of Ethics is in Appendix B.

Throughout the 1940s and '50s, internal audit activities in many organizations focused upon financial auditing, and internal audit departments were heavily involved in the review of financial statements. Today, however, internal auditing takes on a much broader perspective, as suggested in the Institute of Internal Auditor's *Statement of Responsibilities of Internal Auditors:*

> The objective of internal auditing is to assist all members of management in the effective discharge of their responsibilities by furnishing them with analyses, appraisals, recommendations and pertinent comments concerning activities reviewed. Internal auditors are concerned with any phase of business activity in which they may be of service to management. This involves going beyond the accounting and financial records to obtain a full understanding of the operations under review.

Given this objective, the Statement identifies several major internal audit activities:

▲ Reviewing and appraising the soundness, adequacy, and application of accounting, financial, and other operating controls, and promoting effective control at reasonable cost.

▲ Ascertaining the extent of compliance with established policies, plans, and procedures.

▲ Ascertaining the extent to which company assets are accounted for and safeguarded from losses of all kinds.

▲ Ascertaining the reliability of management data developed within the organization.

▲ Appraising the quality of performance in carrying out assigned responsibilities.

▲ Recommending operating improvements.

The objective and the six related activities describe the scope of *operational auditing,* the predominant activity of contemporary internal audit practice. Internal auditing is no longer confined to financial matters; it is much broader and much more pervasive.

Independence

An internal auditor must be independent of both the *personnel* and operational *activities* of an organization. Otherwise, the integrity of an internal auditor's conclusions and recommendations would be suspect. Note, however, that the term "independent auditor" normally refers to auditors in CPA firms, although internal auditors must still be independent to be effective. The Institute of Internal Auditors' *Statement of Responsibilities* underscores the significance of independence: "Independence is essential to the effectiveness of internal auditing. This independence is obtained primarily through organizational status and objectivity." Thus, the Institute identifies organizational status and *objectivity* as the primary means for achieving independence from personnel and activities, respectively.

Organizational Status. The *Statement of Responsibilities* discusses organizational status as follows:

> The organizational status of the internal auditing function and the support accorded to it by management are major determinants of its range and value. The head of the internal auditing function, therefore, should be responsible to an officer whose authority is sufficient to assure both a broad range of audit coverage and the adequate consideration of and effective action on the audit findings and recommendations.

Thus internal auditors should report to an organizational level above the levels audited; otherwise, an internal auditor may be inclined not to criticize peers or superiors. For example, an internal auditor who reports to the corporate controller may be reluctant to report weaknesses in the controller's activities and support staff — weaknesses that may be counterproductive to the organization's goals. On the other hand, an internal auditor who reports to the board of directors should not be reluctant to report weaknesses in staff levels below the board of directors, such as the corporate controller. The higher the organizational level reported to, the greater the range of an internal auditor's potential effectiveness.

In practice, internal auditors in most organizations have traditionally reported to the controller or another financial executive, such as the vice-president of finance. In recent years, however, internal auditing has become increasingly oriented toward operational control, oversight, and protection — all of which are major responsibilities of the board of directors. As a result of the increased emphasis on serving the needs of the board of directors, rather than management, internal auditing is moving further away from financial auditing, its traditional role, and closer toward operational auditing, its emerging role. This trend, and the resulting effect on the internal auditor's organizational status, is illustrated in the following excerpt from an article in the January 6, 1981 *Wall Street Journal:*

> Worries about foreign payoffs and corporate accountability prompt more firms to expand the clout of internal audit staffs. About a third of internal audit managers now report to boards of directors, instead of to controllers, says a poll by John Stork & Partners, a search firm.

Objectivity. The *Statement of Responsibilities* discusses objectivity as follows:

> Objectivity is essential to the audit function. Therefore, internal auditors should not develop and install procedures, prepare records, or engage in

any other activity which they would normally review and appraise and which could reasonably be construed to compromise the independence of the internal auditor. The internal auditor's objectivity need not be adversely affected, however, by determining and recommending standards of control to be applied in the development of the systems and procedures being reviewed.

Thus, internal auditors are not simply one of the organization's controls; they are a control over all other organizational controls. For this reason, internal auditors should not design and implement organizational controls. Rather, to maximize their objectivity, internal auditors should serve the organization as independent appraisers of existing controls. To design, implement, *and* audit controls could result in a conflict of interests; i.e., could an internal auditor objectively audit controls that he or she designed and implemented?

The Nature of Operational Auditing

Just as an independent financial statement opinion audit was described in Chapter 1 as a special application of the scientific method of inquiry, so too is an internal operational audit a special application of the scientific method. The objectives of internal and independent auditors differ, however, the logic underlying their audit activities is identical.

In general, internal operational audits are conducted for any one or more of six different purposes, all of which derive from the major internal audit activities listed earlier from the Institute of Internal Auditors' *Statement of Responsibilities*. These purposes are:

▲ Appraisal of controls
▲ Compliance
▲ Protection of assets
▲ Verification
▲ Appraisal of performance
▲ Recommendations for operating improvements

A discussion of the nature of each activity/purpose follows.

Appraisal of Controls. Organizations institute accounting, financial, and operating controls to assure compliance with organizational goals and objectives. The controls may take the form of policies, programs, and/or procedures. For example, a company may institute a *program* of recording and monitoring inventory spoilage in manufacturing plants as an *operating control* to achieve the *organizational objective* of reducing costs companywide. Although specific individual controls will vary, they all maintain a common framework:

Framework	Example
1. An objective	Reduce inventory spoilage costs.
2. Techniques for determining compliance with objective	Order raw materials in economic quantities to optimize inventory levels and, therefore, control spoilage costs.
3. Action regarding noncompliance	If spoilage costs increase, consider: a. Reassessing the variables in the economic order quantity model. b. Alternative methods of inventory storage.

When appraising controls, the internal auditor's purpose is to determine whether controls are sound and adequate. That is, are controls satisfactory in light of the organizational objectives for which they were designed? Appraisal of controls is a particularly significant operational audit activity since, as discussed earlier, internal auditing itself is an organizational control designed to measure and evaluate the effectiveness of other organizational controls.

Compliance. Instituting controls is absolutely meaningless unless the controls are complied with. Thus, the purpose of an operational audit for compliance is to determine whether specific control policies, programs, or procedures are operating satisfactorily. The focus of compliance reviews, however, is not necessarily upon dealing with the potential results of noncompliance (e.g., excess inventory spoilage), but upon preventing further noncompliance.

Protection of Assets. Closely related to compliance reviews are organizational audits designed to determine whether assets are properly accounted for and safeguarded from losses. Asset-protection reviews may be conducted both for liquid assets (e.g., cash and marketable securities) and for nonliquid assets (e.g., inventory and property, plant, and equipment), although the focus of each may differ since liquid assets are much more susceptible to irregularities and illegal acts. In either case, however, the internal auditor is concerned primarily with testing the effectiveness of those accounting, financial, and operating controls that were designed to account for and safeguard assets.

Verification. Unless accurate and reliable, management data are entirely useless. Thus, operational audits can be designed to verify the accuracy and reliability of internal management reports. As was the case with compliance reviews, the focus of verification reviews is not necessarily responding to the results of inaccurate or unreliable data; rather, the critical issue is promoting accuracy and reliability.

Management information systems are intended to provide input for management decisions. Thus, the information system should generate the most relevant, or useful, data for a particular type of decision. As a result, verification reviews are often designed to evaluate the relevance and usefulness of data as well as accuracy and reliability.

Appraisal of Performance. Employee performance is much more difficult to quantify than accounting or financial control compliance. As a result, interpretations and appraisals of employee performance can be tenuous at best. For example, employee performance is often influenced by variables other than extrinsic economic rewards, such as an employee's job satisfaction and acceptance among peers. Interpreting the effect of these and other variables on an employee's motivation to discharge his or her responsibilities adequately can be difficult, thereby suggesting that appraising employee performance can also be particularly difficult. Nevertheless, as a major organizational control over operational effectiveness, internal auditors are frequently called upon to appraise employee performance. Employee-performance reviews, however, can represent the one operational audit activity least consistent with the boundaries of an internal auditor's professional expertise.

Recommendations for Operating Improvements. Each of an internal auditor's operational audit activities should be designed to generate recommendations for improvements. When a reportable condition, error, irregularity, or illegal act is discovered, its results should be corrected and recommendations made to improve accountability. Although not itself an audit activity, recommending operating improvements as a result of any of the operational audit activities is a most significant by-product of the internal auditor's professional role. It is not enough for internal auditors to criticize; they must also be creative in developing recommendations for improvements.

The Operational Audit Approach

Although specific operational audit applications may differ depending upon the circumstances, most include several basic functions, each of which is related to the scientific method of inquiry. This is shown in Figure 21-2 and discussed in the following sections.

Management Requests. Management may request operational audits for any one or more of the six purposes discussed in the previous section. More

FIGURE 21-2

Relating the Scientific Method of Inquiry and Internal Operational
Audits

Scientific Method	Operational Audit Function
1. Observe and recognize a problem	*Management requests* an operational audit. *Familiarization* with the operational activity to be reviewed.
2. Formulate hypothesis	Overall *hypothesis:* The accounting, financial, or operating control is operating properly and relevant to the control's objective.
3. Gather relevant, verifiable evidence to test hypothesis	*Select* appropriate operational audit *procedures* and *gather* sufficient competent *evidential matter.*
4. Evaluate evidence	*Evaluate evidential matter* to determine if hypothesis is supported, refuted, or inconclusive. *Report* to appropriate organizational level.
5. Develop conclusions	

specifically, however, management may request that these reviews be applied
to the organization's:

▲ Electronic data processing facilities
▲ Financial management practices
▲ Quality control activities
▲ Research and development efforts
▲ Social responsibility
▲ Financial statement accounts

This list is by no means exhaustive. In fact, potential applications of
internal audit activities are almost limitless.

Familiarization. Soon after an operational audit is assigned, an internal auditor and his or her staff should attempt to familiarize themselves with the
specific operational activity to be reviewed. An operational audit should not
be conducted in a vacuum; rather, to maximize efficiency, preliminary information should be gathered and the audit planned in advance. Several preliminary considerations for familiarization are:

▲ Review internal audit workpaper files and reports generated in prior reviews of the operational activity.

▲ Discuss and coordinate the timing and scope of the review with the manager of the operational activity.

▲ Coordinate staff requirements with the director/manager of internal auditing to assure that the operational audit can be completed on time.

Hypothesis. Developing an overall hypothesis requires careful consideration of the objectives of the operational audit. For example, if the purpose of the review is to appraise controls, the internal auditor should determine the type of control policies, programs, and/or procedures to be reviewed and the purpose for which the control was designed. The operational audit hypothesis is then stated in terms of whether the control is desirable and potentially effective under the circumstances.

Selecting Procedures and Gathering Evidence. Operational audit procedures are selected in light of the overall hypothesis of the audit. Specific considerations in selecting procedures may include:

▲ The formality of the reviewed activity's information system; an informal system may preclude the internal auditor from reviewing all relevant information.

▲ Consideration of whether the control is designed to provide overall reasonableness or detailed compliance; more detailed compliance usually requires more detailed audit work.

▲ Overt evidence of problems, such as verbal admittance by employees of noncompliance with a prescribed control.

Selecting and gathering evidence is often an art, rather than a science. The internal auditor should attempt to gather the most appropriate evidence for the audit procedures selected. Evidence should be gathered in sufficient quantities to promote logical conclusions and should be of the highest quality available — written documents are generally of higher quality, though sometimes less informative, than informal verbal suppositions.

Evaluating Evidence and Reporting Results. In the context of auditing, evidence is the only basis for drawing conclusions. Thus, the evidence gathered should be evaluated objectively and in light of the overall operational audit hypothesis. In turn, audit conclusions should be communicated to appropriate organizational levels and within a reasonable time period. Unlike external audit reports, standardized internal audit reports are not common. Thus, the form and content of an internal audit report is usually left to the discretion of the internal auditor.

FIGURE 21-3
The Relationships Among Auditors and Users

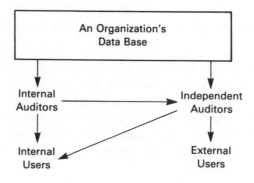

Relating Internal and Independent Auditing

Although internal and independent auditors use roughly the same audit methodology, they have *different objectives* when conducting audit activities. The objective of internal auditing is to assist management concerning activities reviewed, and the objective of independent auditing is to express an opinion on financial statements audited. In addition, internal and independent auditors serve the needs of *different user groups*. The needs of external users are not served by internal operational audits, and the needs of internal users are not served wholly by opinion audits. Thus, internal and independent auditing are separate and distinct independent appraisal activities.

Despite these differences, however, there is a relationship between internal and independent auditing, as illustrated in Figure 21-3. Both groups of auditors rely on the same data base. Also, internal users rely on both internal and independent auditors, and external users rely on independent auditors. Importantly, independent auditors can and often do rely upon an internal auditor's work when the internal audit function is strong. As a result, an organization's internal audit function can have an effect upon the scope of an independent auditor's examination.

Reliance on Internal Auditors. Statement on Auditing Standards No. 9 (AU Sec. 322), "The Effect of an Internal Audit Function on the Scope of the Independent Auditor's Examination," discusses an independent auditor's reliance on an internal auditor's work. The statement applies to reliance on both work performed by internal auditors as part of their normal duties and work completed by an internal auditor at an independent auditor's request (AU Sec. 322.02).

The strength of an organization's internal audit function is one among a series of variables considered by an independent auditor when planning and conducting an audit. Other variables, discussed more fully in earlier chapters, include materiality and potential audit risk. Independent auditors consider these other variables to determine their effect on the scope of a financial statement opinion audit. Importantly, the scope of an independent audit can be reduced if an organization's internal audit function is strong. Thus, the strength of an internal audit function and the scope of an independent audit are inversely related; as the strength of an internal audit function increases, the scope of an independent audit can decrease.

Competence and Objectivity. The *Codification of Statements on Auditing Standards* states that achieving an organization's control objectives ". . . depends on the competence and integrity of personnel, the independence of their assigned functions, and their understanding of the prescribed procedures." As a result of this language, SAS No. 9 requires that independent auditors review the competence and objectivity of internal auditors before their work is relied upon (AU Sec. 322.04). Competence can be reviewed by considering, for example, the organization's practices when hiring, training, promoting, and supervising internal auditors. Objectivity, in turn, can be reviewed by considering the organizational level to which internal auditors report. As discussed earlier in this chapter, objectivity and organizational status are closely related to an internal auditor's independence. Internal auditors cannot be considered independent from organizational levels at or above those to which they report. Thus, independent auditors cannot rely on internal audit work conducted for organizational levels at or above those to which an internal auditor reports; the internal auditor's objectivity and independence would be suspect.

Once deemed competent and objective, an internal auditor's work can be relied on, thereby reducing the scope of an independent audit. For example, assuming competence and objectivity, an internal auditor's flowcharts of an organization's accounting system could be relied on, thereby reducing the time required by an independent auditor to assess control risk. As another example, assuming competence and objectivity, an independent auditor may request that an internal auditor examine additions to property, plant, and equipment, thereby reducing the time required by an independent auditor to examine balances in the property, plant, and equipment account. As can be seen in these examples, an internal auditor's work can reduce the scope of an independent audit; the potential for using an internal auditor's work is almost limitless.

Evaluating an Internal Auditor's Work. Despite reviews of an internal auditor's competence and objectivity, an independent auditor should not accept an internal auditor's work "on blind faith"; the work should be evaluated before it is fully relied upon (AU Sec 322.08). An internal auditor's documentary evidence should be examined on a test basis to provide an independent auditor with a basis for judging the adequacy and appropriateness of:

▲ The scope of internal audit work.
▲ Audit programs.
▲ Working paper documentation.
▲ Conclusions reached.
▲ Any reports prepared.

In addition, the independent auditor should perform tests of some of the internal auditor's work. For example, if an internal auditor examined evidence in support of twenty-five additions to property, plant, and equipment, an independent auditor may examine evidence in support of a small number of the same additions. Of course, the independent auditor would then compare the results with those reached by the internal auditor.

Regardless of the quality of an internal auditor's work, all judgments on audit matters must be made by the independent auditor (AU Sec 322.11). The attest function is performed, not by the internal auditor, but by the independent auditor, who is responsible for the judgments leading to an attestation about financial statements.

GOVERNMENTAL AUDITING

As government has grown in scope, size, and complexity, so too has the need for governmental auditing. Accounting for and controlling U.S. governmental receipts and expenditures has resulted in the need for a staggering number of government clerks, accountants, and auditors.

The need for control over governmental revenues, appropriations, and expenditures should not be surprising. Federal, state, and local government is, actually, the largest "industry" in the U.S. Governmental spending at the federal, state, and local levels exceeds one third of the gross national product; further, employment at all three levels of government exceeds one sixth of the civilian nonfarm work force, and this figure excludes the military! No other "industry" similarly affects day-to-day commercial and personal life. In short, control through governmental auditing is essential, and the need continues to grow.

Annual budgets by federal, state, and local governments are generally incorporated into governmental accounting systems and financial reports; this is not the case in private-sector business organizations. Thus, annual budgets in conjunction with governmental financial reports are the primary focus of governmental audits.

Historical Development of Governmental Auditing

The dates of the earliest formal governmental budgets and financial reports are not known. However, it is known that Great Britain's Parliament instituted budgetary controls in the Magna Carta of 1215, although it was not until the end of the seventeenth century that Parliament assumed control of British crown expenditures in the form of annual appropriations. Since the origin of formal governmental budgets and reports is sketchy, so too is the origin of governmental auditing. However, the origin of governmental auditing in U.S. federal, state, and local governments is less uncertain.

The U.S. Budget and Accounting Act of 1921 created, among other things, the Bureau of the Budget, now the Office of Management and Budget. The Office of Management and Budget, in cooperation with the President, is responsible for preparing the annual federal budget. As a result of the overwhelming number of dollars and programs involved, the federal budget has created the need for accountability and control, both primary functions of governmental audits.

In contrast, no single event has affected state and local auditing quite so significantly. However, in the years since World War II, the growth in state and local governmental expenditures, employment, and public-service programs has actually exceeded that of the federal government. Such rapid growth and the resultant need for accountability and control have greatly expanded the need for state and local audits.

Events throughout and beyond the 1920s and the war years, then, created a distinct need for governmental auditing at the federal, state, and local levels. However, as discussed later in this chapter, the complexion of governmental auditing has changed markedly within the past two decades as critics cited the need for audits more closely aligned with the nature of governmental activities. Today, governmental audits can relate not only to a governmental entity's financial activities, but also to an entity's organizational structure and operations, much like internal auditing.

The Nature of Governmental Auditing

Governmental audits, like independent financial statement opinion audits and internal operational audits, are special applications of the scientific method of inquiry. Again, the logic underlying all three audit activities is identical, even though the objectives of independent, internal, and governmental auditors differ. Like independent and internal auditors, governmental auditors ascribe to professional standards and a code of ethics. The audit standards of the U.S. General Accounting Office (GAO) and the code of ethics of the Association of Government Accountants appear, respectively, in Appendices C and D of this chapter.

Prior to the 1960s, a governmental entity's performance was often monitored by financial and compliance audits, operational reviews, and special reviews and investigations of specific governmental activities. These audits, reviews, and investigations, however, focused primarily on financial accountability and therefore provided little information about whether a governmental entity:

▲ Managed or utilized financial resources economically and efficiently.

▲ Monitored inadequacies in information systems, administrative procedures, or organizational structure.

▲ Achieved the desired results and benefits and the objectives established by the legislature.

▲ Considered alternative actions which might reduce costs.

From the first two criticisms were born *economy and efficiency* governmental audits and from the final two, *program results* audits. These, in conjunction with *financial and compliance* audits, define the scope of governmental auditing.

An ideal audit of a governmental entity would include all three types of governmental audit activities. However, in practice, no more than one is usually performed, and financial and compliance audits predominate.

Financial and Compliance Audits

Headed by the Comptroller General of the United States, the U.S. General Accounting Office (GAO) is a nonpolitical federal agency responsible for conducting audits in behalf of Congress. In 1981, the GAO published revised *Standards for Audit of Governmental Organizations, Programs, Activities and Functions*,[1] an authoritative document which defines financial and compliance as follows:

> *Financial and compliance* — determines (a) whether the financial statements of an audited entity present fairly the financial position and the results of financial operations in accordance with generally accepted ac-

---

[1] U.S. General Accounting Office, *Standards for Audit of Governmental Organizations, Programs, Activities and Functions* (Washington: U.S. Government Printing Office, 1981). Pages 6–11 of this document, a summary of the standards, are reproduced in Appendix C of this chapter.

counting principles and (b) whether the entity has complied with laws and regulations that may have a material effect upon the financial statements.[2]

Financial and compliance audits are quite similar to independent financial statement opinion audits. The relationship between the scientific method of inquiry and independent auditing illustrated in Chapter 1 also applies to governmental financial and compliance audits. Both types of audits are conducted to determine whether financial statements are *presented fairly in accordance with generally accepted accounting principles* (GAAP). However, governmental financial and compliance audits also determine whether financial statements are presented in accordance with applicable *laws and regulations*.

Generally, financial statements of governmental entities are similar to those of private-sector business organizations and include results of operations, financial position, and changes in financial position. However, because governmental accounting is based on *budgets* and *funds* (sets of accounts segregated for a specific source of revenue, activity, or objective), the content and terminology of governmental financial reports differ somewhat from financial statements of a business enterprise. Further discussion of budgets and fund accounting is beyond the scope of this text. These topics are covered in governmental accounting texts.

Economy and Efficiency Audits

The GAO defines economy and efficiency as follows:

Economy and efficiency — determines (a) whether the entity is managing and utilizing its resources (such as personnel, property, space) economically and efficiently, (b) the causes of inefficiencies or uneconomical practices, and (c) whether the entity has complied with laws and regulations concerning matters of economy and efficiency.[3]

The purpose of governmental economy and efficiency audits is to determine whether operations are conducted economically and efficiently and, if not, to recommend cost-effective improvements. This, too, is the general purpose of internal operational audits. However, economy and efficiency audits are also concerned with whether an entity has complied with applicable laws and regulations.

The terms "economy" and "efficiency" are not synonymous. Economy

---

[2]*Ibid.*, p. 3.
[3]*Ibid.*

FIGURE 21-4

Relating the Scientific Method of Inquiry and Governmental Economy and Efficiency Audits

Scientific Method	Economy and Efficiency Audit Functions*
1. Observe and recognize a problem	*Management requires* an economy and efficiency audit. Obtain a *working knowledge* of the entity's purpose, systems, and operations.
2. Formulate hypothesis	Overall *hypothesis:* The governmental entity operates economically and efficiently in light of preferred practices.
3. Gather relevant, verifiable evidence to test hypothesis	*Select* appropriate economy and efficiency audit *procedures* and *gather* sufficient competent *evidential matter* about the entity's economy and efficiency.
4. Evaluate evidence 5. Develop conclusions.	*Evaluate evidential matter* to determine if hypothesis is supported, refuted, or inconclusive. *Report* to appropriate organizational level.

*Adapted in part from: F. Pomeranz, A. J. Cancellieri, J. B. Stevens, and J. L. Savage, *Auditing in the Public Sector* (Boston: Warren, Gorham & Lamont, 1976), p. 18.

implies appraising a governmental entity's performance in light of potential cost savings; i.e., could the entity have achieved the same or a higher level of performance at a lower cost? In contrast, efficiency implies appraising an entity's performance in light of the relationship between benefits and costs; i.e., were the benefits attained by the entity worth the cost incurred? For example, an entity could be economical by restricting costs but inefficient, in that additional costs may have resulted in worthwhile benefits. An effective entity should strive to optimize the relationship between economy and efficiency.

Actual economy and efficiency audits may differ depending upon the circumstances. However, most include some variation of the functions discussed in the following sections. The relationship of these functions to the scientific method of inquiry is illustrated in Figure 21-4. Note the similarity between the economy and efficiency audit functions in Figure 21-4 and the operational audit functions in Figure 21-2.

Management Requests and Working Knowledge. Once an economy and efficiency audit is requested by management, the auditing staff should obtain a working knowledge of the governmental entity's purpose, systems, and operations. This working knowledge or familiarity is particularly critical since in an economy and efficiency audit, the auditor is concerned primarily with potential cost reductions (economy) and potential improvements in the cost-benefit relationship (efficiency). Thus, the auditor should be familiar with those activities within an entity which are most susceptible to diseconomies and/or inefficiency.

Hypothesis. The overall hypothesis of an economy and efficiency audit is related to a governmental entity's performance in light of *preferred operating practices.* Preferred practices are those which have been economical and effective in the past for similar governmental entities. For example, if the transportation method of distributing material — a minimum cost quantitative technique for distributing materials from a series of supply warehouses to a series of demand points — is used successfully by a governmental supply depot in California, the transportation method may also be successful for a similar supply depot in New York. Thus, the critical issue is comparing current practices within the entity with preferred practices in other entities with an eye toward potential cost savings or potential improvements in the cost-benefit relationship.

Selecting Procedures and Gathering Evidence. Much like operational audit procedures, economy and efficiency audit procedures are selected in light of the overall audit hypothesis. Some of the considerations in selecting audit procedures may include:

▲ Existence of formal supervisory controls — lack of supervisory controls may result in uneconomical or inefficient employee performance, thereby requiring much greater audit scope.
▲ Entity's awareness of practices in similar governmental entities — lack of awareness may suggest the entity has some uneconomical or inefficient operations.

Selecting and gathering evidence for an economy and efficiency audit is related directly to the scope and importance of the activity or activities audited. More time and effort should be directed to more important activities. The quality and quantity of evidence gathered should be considered in light of the scope and importance of activities reviewed.

Evaluating Evidence and Reporting Results. The most significant consideration in evaluating evidence relates to the potential for improving economies and efficiencies. That is, does the evidence suggest the potential for either gaining cost savings or improving the cost-benefit relationship? Conclusions and recommendations should be communicated in writing to appropriate organizational levels within a reasonable time period.

Program Results Audits

In comparison with financial and compliance and economy and efficiency audits, program results audits are much more open-ended and subjective. The GAO defines program results as follows:

> *Program results* — determines (a) whether the desired results or benefits established by the legislature or other authorizing body are being achieved and (b) whether the agency has considered alternatives that might yield desired results at a lower cost.[4]

Unlike economy and efficiency audits, which focus on potential cost savings and improvements in the cost-benefit relationship, program results audits focus on whether the objectives of a program or activity are being met. In fact, no other type of audit conducted within the private or public sector is concerned so extensively with whether an entity has met its predetermined objectives. Program results audits are unique.

Pomeranz et al. cite several obstacles to performing a program results audit:

▲ Clearly defined goals and objectives are not always present in a given situation.
▲ Even where goals are adequately described, they may not be formally promulgated by the implementing agency as goals intended to be fulfilled.
▲ Goals may be misinterpreted at subordinate levels.
▲ Even where goals are explicit at each level, acceptable measurement criteria may not exist or may not be regularly and systematically applied and evaluated.[5]

Thus, program results audits are not as objective as other private and governmental audits and require a greater degree of imagination and creativity.

Given that objectives will differ markedly from program to program, no two program results audits are apt to be identical. Nevertheless, most should be somewhat consistent with the framework as discussed in the following

---

[4]*Ibid.*

[5]F. Pomeranz *et al., Auditing in the Public Sector* (Boston: Warren, Gorham & Lamont, 1976), p. 34.

FIGURE 21-5
Relating the Scientific Method of Inquiry and Governmental Program
Results Audits

Scientific Method	Program Results Audit Functions
1. Observe and recognize a problem	*Management requests* a program results audit. Determine which *objectives* are to be *reviewed*, and whether those objectives are formally promulgated.
2. Formulate hypothesis	Overall *hypothesis:* The governmental entity's activities are consistent with the objectives of the program reviewed.
3. Gather relevant, verifiable evidence to test hypothesis	*Select* appropriate program results audit *procedures* and *gather* sufficient competent *evidential matter* about whether (a) program objectives are interpreted properly at subordinate levels, and (b) the entity's activities are consistent with the objectives of the program reviewed.
4. Evaluate evidence 5. Develop conclusions	*Evaluate evidential matter* to determine if hypothesis is supported, refuted, or inconclusive. *Report* to appropriate organizational level.

sections. The relationship of program results audits to the scientific method of inquiry is illustrated in Figure 21-5.

Management Requests and Review of Objectives. Following assignment to a program results audit, an auditing staff should determine which of the governmental entity's objectives are to be reviewed and whether those objectives have been communicated throughout the entity. If not communicated, it is doubtful that the objectives are being met, thereby suggesting that the scope of the audit is apt to be rather expansive.

Hypothesis. In general, the overall hypothesis of a program results audit is related to a governmental entity's achieved results in light of preestablished program objectives. Note that the hypothesis is in no way concerned with financial operations, financial reports, or resource utilization. A program results audit focuses only upon established program objectives.

Selecting Procedures and Gathering and Evaluating Evidence. The methodology for measuring attainment of a program objective is tenuous, at best. For example, it would be difficult to measure whether a local municipality's Parks and Recreation Department achieved the objective of: "Improving the quality and availability of recreation sites throughout District A of the city." How should "quality" and "availability" be measured? As a result, selecting audit procedures and gathering and evaluating evidence will, as suggested earlier, require imagination and creativity. Figure 21-6, however, illustrates in some detail an auditor's decision process when selecting procedures and gathering and evaluating evidence for a program results audit. Note particularly that, since the entity audited is responsible for achieving its preestablished objectives, the decision process in Figure 21-6 requires that the entity attempt to generate both measurement criteria (step 3) and audit data (step 6). Some of the burden, therefore, is placed on the entity.

Reporting Results. Merely identifying failures to achieve desired program objectives in a program results audit is insufficient. An auditor should report in writing to appropriate organizational levels about (1) whether objectives are communicated throughout the entity, (2) whether objectives can be interpreted clearly, (3) achievement of program objectives, and (4) recommendations for planning future organizational activities in coordination with established objectives. Of course, the report should be communicated within a reasonable time period.

THE SINGLE AUDIT ACT OF 1984

Financial and compliance, economy and efficiency, and program results audits are performed by governmental or independent auditors for individual state governments, state agencies, and local governmental units such as cities, towns, counties, school and fire districts, and housing and airport authorities. Annually, the U.S. government grants over $100 billion to the states and to over 80,000 local governmental units for transportation, welfare, education, health services, and job training programs, among other things. To assure accountability for grant funds received, the federal government required periodic audits of each grant — that is, if a governmental unit participated in ten grant programs, then ten individual grant audits were required.

Because there was little coordination among federal, state, and local auditors, and because the requirements of each grant audit varied widely, the

GAO and the Joint Management Improvement Program (JMIP) reported in 1979 that grant-by-grant audits often resulted in considerable duplication of effort: the same internal controls were studied and evaluated, and the same accounting records were audited. In short, grant-by-grant audits were not cost effective. As a result, both the GAO and the JMIP recommended that grant-by-grant audits be abandoned and be replaced by a single audit of each governmental unit receiving federal assistance — that is, a single audit of the recipient entity rather than a separate audit of each grant received by the entity. In response, Congress enacted the Single Audit Act of 1984, which was intended to improve the financial management of state and local governments receiving federal funds, establish uniform audit requirements for federal grant recipients, promote efficient and effective use of audit resources, and ensure that federal departments and agencies rely on one audit only: the single audit.

Audit Coverage

The Single Audit Act applies to all governmental units which receive *any* federal assistance, although the requirements of the Act vary depending on the dollar amount of grant funds received:

▲ Governments receiving over $100,000 in grant funds per year, must perform the single audit annually.
▲ Governments receiving between $25,000 and $100,000 per year may *elect* a single audit or may comply with the audit requirements of the federal programs granting the funds.
▲ Governments receiving less than $25,000 per year are exempt from audit requirements, although adequate records and documents must be maintained.

Importantly, a single audit goes beyond generally accepted auditing standards in that the auditor *must* evaluate internal control structure and identify reportable conditions, even if the auditor does not rely upon the system to reduce the extent of substantive testing. In fact, the Single Audit Act strongly emphasizes, and thereby stresses, internal control and requires that tests of controls address five key areas:

▲ Allowable costs.
▲ Eligibility of grant recipients.
▲ Matching of costs with proper accounting periods.
▲ Proper allocation of indirect costs.
▲ Special grant requirements and periodic reports.

In general, costs charged to the grant programs selected for testing are tested by the following criteria.

FIGURE 21-6
A Program Results Audit: An Auditor's Decision Process

Description	Step
Does the entity have clearly defined objectives?	1
Clearly defined objectives must be developed by the entity (or appropriate body-Congress, State, etc.).	2
Have quantified and measurable criteria been identified?	3
The entity must identify measurement criteria for use in judging effectiveness.	4
Are the measurement criteria relevant and valid?	5
Have data been accumulated for measurement against identified criteria?	6

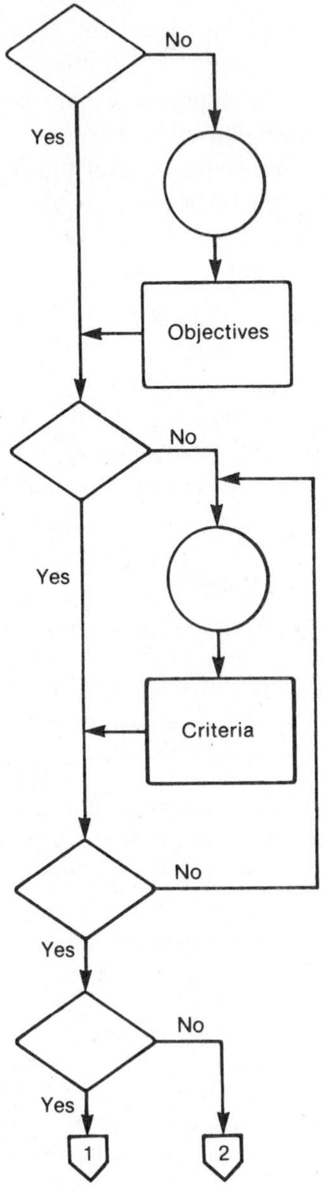

The entity should accumulate
data on:
    (1) Resources used
    (2) Results achieved.   7

Have accurate data been appropriately accumulated?   8

Analyze and evaluate data in
relation to objectives and
document findings.   9

Discuss findings with appropriate entity employees to:
    (1) Identify any additional
        factors that should be
        considered to place the
        finding in proper
        perspective.
    (2) Enable the entity to
        take immediate correc-
        tive action if deemed necessary.   10

No

Yes

Finding

LEGEND: Decision/Branching: · · · · · · · · · ·

                Process: · · · · · · · · · · · ·

     Report or Document: · · · · · · · · · · · ·

▲ Are the costs reasonable and necessary?

▲ Do the costs conform to applicable grant requirements?

▲ Are the costs net of applicable credits such as purchase discounts?

▲ Do the costs exclude those properly chargeable to other federal financial assistance programs?

▲ Did costs receive advance approval and, where necessary, were they procured competitively?

Audit Report

To comply both with the Single Audit Act and the GAO's *Standards for Audit of Governmental Organizations, Programs, Activities, and Functions,* an auditor should issue a report covering the following separate but interrelated reports:

▲ The standard auditor's report on the financial statements.

▲ A report on the study and evaluation of internal control structure for (a) those controls studied and evaluated as part of the examination of the financial statements, and (b) those controls studied and evaluated as required by the Single Audit Act.

▲ A report on the results of the testing of compliance with the laws and regulations pertaining to each major federal assistance program.

Although sweeping and far-reaching, the Single Audit Act does not limit the authority of federal agencies to conduct additional audits as deemed necessary. However, the single audit is *the* definitive audit of federal assistance programs, and as a result, additional audits must be done at the cost of the federal agency, not at the cost of the grant recipient.

SUMMARY

Independent, internal, and governmental auditing are separate and distinct appraisal activities. Independent auditing is a societal control; internal auditing, an organizational control; and governmental auditing, a governmental control.

To be effective, internal auditors should be independent of both the personnel and activities audited. Lacking independence, an internal auditor's conclusions and recommendations are apt to be biased.

Internal operational audits are conducted for purposes of appraising controls, compliance, asset protection, verification, appraising performance, and recommending operating improvements. The approach to operational audits is consistent with the scientific method of inquiry and is intended to determine whether relevant accounting, financial, or operating controls are functioning properly.

Independent auditors often rely on the work of internal auditors, assuming the internal audit function is strong. However, before relying on their work, independent auditors should determine whether the internal auditors are competent and objective and should evaluate the adequacy and appropriateness of the internal auditor's work.

Governmental audits, too, are consistent with the scientific method and classified as financial and compliance, economy and efficiency, or program results. Financial and compliance audits are similar to financial statement opinion audits, and economy and efficiency audits are similar to internal operational audits. Program results audits, however, are unique and are designed to determine whether a governmental entity's activities are consistent with the objectives of the program reviewed.

APPENDIX A
SUMMARY OF GENERAL AND SPECIFIC STANDARDS FOR THE PROFESSIONAL PRACTICE OF INTERNAL AUDITING

100 *Independence* — Internal auditors should be independent of the activities they audit.

110 *Organizational Status* — The organizational status of the internal auditing department should be sufficient to permit the accomplishment of its audit responsibilities.

120 *Objectivity* — Internal auditors should be objective in performing audits.

200 *Professional Proficiency* — Internal audits should be performed with proficiency and due professional care.

The Internal Auditing Department

210 *Staffing* — The internal auditing department should provide assurance that the technical proficiency and educational background of internal auditors are appropriate for the audits to be performed.

220 *Knowledge, Skills, and Disciplines* — The internal auditing department should possess the knowledge, skills, and discipline needed to carry out its audit responsibilities.

230 *Supervision* — The internal auditing department should provide assurance that internal audits are properly supervised.

The Internal Auditor

240 *Compliance with Standards of Conduct* — Internal auditors should comply with professional standards of conduct.

250 *Knowledge, Skills, and Disciplines* — Internal auditors should possess the knowledge, skills, and disciplines essential to the performance of internal audits.

260 *Human Relations and Communications* — Internal auditors should be skilled in dealing with people and in communicating effectively.

270 *Continuing Education* — Internal auditors should maintain their technical competence through continuing education.

280 *Due Professional Care* — Internal auditors should exercise due professional care in performing internal audits.

300 *Scope of Work* — The scope of the internal audit should encompass the examination and evaluation of the adequacy and effectiveness of the organization's system of internal control and the quality of performance in carrying out assigned responsibilities.

310 *Reliability and Integrity of Information* — Internal auditors should review the reliability and integrity of financial and operating information and the means used to identify, measure, classify, and report such information.

320 *Compliance with Policies, Plans, Procedures, Laws, and Regulations* — Internal auditors should review the systems established to ensure compliance with those policies, plans, procedures, laws, and regulations which could have a significant impact on operations and reports and should determine whether the organization is in compliance.

330 *Safeguarding of Assets* — Internal auditors should review the means of safeguarding assets and, as appropriate, verify the existence of such assets.

340 *Economical and Efficient Use of Resources* — Internal auditors should appraise the economy and efficiency with which resources are employed.

350 *Accomplishment of Established Objectives and Goals for Operations or Programs* — Internal auditors should review operations or programs to ascertain whether results are consistent with established objectives and goals and whether the operations or programs are being carried out as planned.

400 *Performance of Audit Work* — Audit work should include planning the audit, examining and evaluating information, communicating results, and following up.

410 *Planning the Audit* — Internal auditors should plan each audit.

420 *Examining and Evaluating Information* — Internal auditors should collect, analyze, interpret, and document information to support audit results.

430 *Communicating Results* — Internal auditors should report the results of their audit work.

440 *Following Up* — Internal auditors should follow up to ascertain that appropriate action is taken on reported audit findings.

500 *Management of the Internal Auditing Department* — The director of internal auditing should properly manage the internal auditing department.

    510 *Purpose, Authority, and Responsibility* — The director of internal auditing should have a statement of purpose, authority, and responsibility for the internal auditing department.

    520 *Planning* — The director of internal auditing should establish plans to carry out the responsibilities of the internal auditing department.

    530 *Policies and Procedures* — The director of internal auditing should provide written policies and procedures to guide the audit staff.

    540 *Personnel Management and Development* — The director of internal auditing should establish a program for selecting and developing the human resources of the internal auditing department.

    550 *External Auditors* — The director of internal auditing should coordinate internal and external audit efforts.

    560 *Quality Assurance* — The director of internal auditing should establish and maintain a quality assurance program to evaluate the operations of the internal auditing department.

APPENDIX B
THE INSTITUTE OF INTERNAL AUDITORS' CODE OF ETHICS

INTRODUCTION:

Recognizing that ethics are an important consideration in the practice of internal auditing and that the moral principles followed by members of *The Institute of Internal Auditors, Inc.*, should be formalized, the Board of Directors at its regular meeting in New Orleans on December 13, 1968, received and adopted the following resolution:

WHEREAS the members of *The Institute of Internal Auditors, Inc.*, represent the profession of internal auditing; and

WHEREAS managements rely on the profession of internal auditing to assist in the fulfillment of their management stewardship; and

WHEREAS said members must maintain high standards of conduct, honor and character in order to carry on proper and meaningful internal auditing practice;

THEREFORE BE IT RESOLVED that a Code of Ethics be now set forth, outlining the standards of professional behavior for the guidance of each member of *The Institute of Internal Auditors, Inc.*

In accordance with this resolution, the Board of Directors further approved of the principles set forth.

INTERPRETATION OF PRINCIPLES:

The provisions of this Code of Ethics cover basic principles in the various disciplines of internal auditing practice. Members shall realize that individual judgment is required in the application of these principles. They have a responsibility to conduct themselves so that their good faith and integrity should not be open to question. While having due regard for the limit of their technical skills, they will promote the highest possible internal auditing standards to the end of advancing the interest of their company or organization.

ARTICLES:

   I. Members shall have an obligation to exercise honesty, objectivity, and diligence in the performance of their duties and responsibilities.

  II. Members, in holding the trust of their employers, shall exhibit loyalty in all matters pertaining to the affairs of the employer or to whomever they may be rendering a service. However, members shall not knowingly be a part to any illegal or improper activity.

 III. Members shall refrain from entering into any activity which may be in conflict with the interest of their employers or which would prejudice their ability to carry out objectively their duties and responsibilities.

 IV. Members shall not accept a fee or a gift from an employee, a client, a customer, or a business associate of their employer without the knowledge and consent of their senior management.

  V. Members shall be prudent in the use of information acquired in the course of their duties. They shall not use confidential information for any personal gain nor in a manner which would be detrimental to the welfare of their employer.

 VI. Members, in expressing an opinion, shall use all reasonable care to obtain sufficient factual evidence to warrant such expression. In their reporting, members shall reveal such material facts known to them, which, if not revealed, could either distort the report of the results of operations under review or conceal unlawful practice.

VII. Members shall continually strive for improvement in the proficiency and effectiveness of their service.

VIII. Members shall abide by the bylaws and uphold the objectives of *The Institute of Internal Auditors, Inc.* In the practice of their profession, they shall be ever mindful of their obligation to maintain the high standard of competence, morality, and dignity which *The Institute of Internal Auditors, Inc.*, and its members have established.

APPENDIX C
SUMMARY OF STANDARDS FOR AUDIT OF
GOVERNMENTAL ORGANIZATIONS, PROGRAMS,
ACTIVITIES AND FUNCTIONS

GENERAL STANDARDS

1. Qualifications: The auditors assigned to perform the audit must collectively possess adequate professional proficiency for the tasks required.
2. Independence: In all matters relating to the audit work, the audit organization and the individual auditors, whether government or public, must be free from personal or external impairments to independence, must be organizationally independent, and shall maintain an independent attitude and appearance.
3. Due professional care: Due professional care is to be used in conducting the audit and in preparing related reports.
4. Scope impairments: When factors external to the audit organization and the auditor restrict the audit or interfere with the auditor's ability to form objective opinions and conclusions, the auditor should attempt to remove the limitation or, failing that, report the limitation.

EXAMINATION AND EVALUATION (FIELD WORK) AND
REPORTING STANDARDS FOR FINANCIAL AND
COMPLIANCE AUDITS

1. AICPA Statements on Auditing Standards for field work and reporting are adopted and incorporated in this statement for government financial and compliance audits. Future statements should be adopted and incorporated, unless GAO excludes them by formal announcement.
2. Additional standards and requirements for government financial and compliance audits.
   a. Standards on examination and evaluation:
      (1) Planning shall include consideration of the requirements of all levels of government.
      (2) A review is to be made of compliance with applicable laws and regulations.
      (3) A written record of the auditors' work shall be retained in the form of working papers.
      (4) Auditors shall be alert to situations or transactions that could be indicative of fraud, abuse, and illegal expenditures and acts and if such evidence

exists, extend audit steps and procedures to identify the effect on the entity's financial statements.

b. Standards on reporting:

(1) Written audit reports are to be submitted to the appropriate officials of the organization audited and to the appropriate officials of the organizations requiring or arranging for the audits unless legal restrictions or ethical considerations prevent it. Copies of the reports should also be sent to other officials who may be responsible for taking action and to others authorized to receive such reports. Unless restricted by law or regulation, copies should be made available for public inspection.

(2) A statement in the auditors' report that the examination was made in accordance with generally accepted government auditing standards for financial and compliance audits will be acceptable language to indicate that the audit was made in accordance with these standards.

(3) Either the auditors' report on the entity's financial statements or a separate report shall contain a statement of positive assurance on those items of compliance tested and negative assurance on those items not tested. It shall also include material instances of noncompliance and instances or indications of fraud, abuse, or illegal acts found during or in connection with the audit.

(4) The auditors shall report on their study and evaluation of internal accounting controls made as part of the financial and compliance audit. They shall identify as a minimum: (a) the entity's significant internal accounting controls, (b) the controls identified that were evaluated, (c) the controls identified that were not evaluated (the auditor may satisfy this requirement by identifying any significant classes of transactions and related assets not included in the study and evaluation), and (d) the material weaknesses identified as a result of the evaluation.

(5) Either the auditors' report on the entity's financial statements or a separate report shall contain any other material deficiency findings identified during the audit not covered in (3) above.

(6) If certain information is prohibited from general disclosure, the report shall state the nature of the information omitted and the requirement that makes the omission necessary.

EXAMINATION AND EVALUATION STANDARDS FOR ECONOMY AND EFFICIENCY AUDITS AND PROGRAM RESULTS AUDITS

1. Work is to be adequately planned.
2. Assistants are to be properly supervised.
3. A review is to be made of compliance with applicable laws and regulations.
4. During the audit a study and evaluation shall be made of the internal control system (administrative controls) applicable to the organization, program, activity, or function under audit.

5. When audits involve computer-based systems, the auditors shall:
   a. Review general controls in data processing systems to determine whether (1) the controls have been designed according to management direction and known legal requirements and (2) the controls are operating effectively to provide reliability of, and security over, the data being processed.
   b. Review application controls of installed data processing applications upon which the auditor is relying to assess their reliability in processing data in a timely, accurate, and complete manner.
6. Sufficient, competent, and relevant evidence is to be obtained to afford a reasonable basis for the auditors' judgments and conclusions regarding the organization, program, activity, or function under audit. A written record of the auditors' work shall be retained in the form of working papers.
7. The auditors shall:
   a. Be alert to situations or transactions that could be indicative of fraud, abuse, and illegal acts.
   b. If such evidence exists, extend audit steps and procedures to identify the effect on the entity's operations and programs.

REPORTING STANDARDS FOR ECONOMY AND EFFICIENCY AUDITS AND PROGRAM RESULTS AUDITS

1. Written audit reports are to be prepared giving the results of each government audit.
2. Written audit reports are to be submitted to the appropriate officials of the organization audited and to the appropriate officials of the organizations requiring or arranging for the audits unless legal restrictions or ethical considerations prevent it. Copies of the reports should also be sent to other officials who may be responsible for taking action on audit findings and recommendations and to others authorized to receive such reports. Unless restricted by law or regulation, copies should be made available for public inspection.
3. Reports are to be issued on or before the dates specified by law, regulation, or other special arrangement. Reports are to be issued promptly so as to make the information available for timely use by management and by legislative officials.
4. The report shall include:
   a. A description of the scope and objectives of the audit.
   b. A statement that the audit (economy and efficiency or program results) was made in accordance with generally accepted government auditing standards.
   c. A description of material weaknesses found in the internal control system (administrative controls).
   d. A statement of positive assurance on those items of compliance tested and negative assurance on those items not tested. This should include significant instances of noncompliance and instances of or indications of fraud, abuse, or illegal acts found during or in connection with the audit. However, fraud, abuse, or illegal acts normally should be covered in a separate report, thus permitting the overall report to be released to the public.

e. Recommendations for actions to improve problem areas noted in the audit and to improve operations. The underlying causes of problems reported should be included to assist in implementing corrective actions.

f. Pertinent views of responsible officials of the organization, program, activity, or function audited concerning the auditors' findings, conclusions, and recommendations. When possible their views should be obtained in writing.

g. A description of noteworthy accomplishments, particularly when management improvements in one area may be applicable elsewhere.

h. A listing of any issues and questions needing further study and consideration.

i. A statement as to whether any pertinent information has been omitted because it is deemed privileged or confidential. The nature of such information should be described, and the law or other basis under which it is withheld should be stated. If a separate report was issued containing this information it should be indicated in the report.

5. The report shall:

a. Present factual data accurately and fairly. Include only information, findings, and conclusions that are adequately supported by sufficient evidence in the auditors' working papers to demonstrate or prove the bases for the matters reported and their correctness and reasonableness.

b. Present findings and conclusions in a convincing manner.

c. Be objective.

d. Be written in language as clear and simple as the subject matter permits.

e. Be concise but, at the same time, clear enough to be understood by users.

f. Present factual data completely to fully inform the users.

g. Place primary emphasis on improvement rather than on criticism of the past; critical comments should be presented in a balanced perspective considering any unusual difficulties or circumstances faced by the operating officials concerned.

APPENDIX D
THE ASSOCIATION OF GOVERNMENT ACCOUNTANTS' CODE OF ETHICS

A. *Introduction.* The Association of Government Accountants is a national professional organization most of whose members are primarily engaged in government accounting, auditing, budgeting, and related financial management activities.

The membership represents most government agencies as well as industrial, educational, and private personal service organizations having an interest in government programs.

The Association of Government Accountants' major program objectives are to:

Unite professional financial managers in government service to perform more efficiently for their own development and thereby for the benefit of the government and
society.

Encourage and provide an effective means for interchange of work-related and
professional ideas.

Aid in improving general financial management and accounting and auditing techniques and concepts.

Improve financial management education in all levels of government and universities.

B. *Purpose of the Code.* In order to foster the highest professional standards and
   behavior, and exemplary service to the government, this Code of Ethics has been
   developed as guidance for the members of the Association of Government Accountants, and for the information of their employers.
C. *Definitions.* In instances where reference is made to a member, it is intended to
   include all classes of membership. Where reference is made to employer, it is
   intended to apply to a government agency as an entity, and to a non-government
   organization to the extent the principle is considered applicable.
D. *Explanations.* To better understand each ethical principle, a justification or explanation is provided to indicate where and how motivation or proscription of action
   is intended.
E. *Ethical Principles.*

Personal Behavior

1. A member shall not engage in acts or be associated with activities which are
   contrary to the public interest or discreditable to the Association of Government Accountants.
   (This principle cautions members to avoid actions which adversely affect the
   public interest and the professional image of the Association.)
2. A member shall not engage in private employment or hold himself out as an
   independent practitioner for remuneration except with the consent of his employer, if required.
   (This principle identifies a restriction against earnings which result from the
   use of a member's professional qualifications, without the express approval
   of his employer, if required.)
3. A member shall not purposefully transmit or use confidential information
   obtained in his professional work, for personal gain or other advantage.
   (This principle prohibits the improper use of official position or office for
   strictly personal purpose, monetary, or otherwise.)
4. A member shall adhere to the Standards of Conduct promulgated by his
   employer.
   (This principle, for example, endorses the commitment of Federal employees
   to recognize the Standards of Conduct prescribed by their government agencies pursuant to Executive Order 11222 of May 8, 1965, (30 F. R. 6469),
   and the Code of Ethics for government services adopted by the Congress on
   July 11, 1958.)

Professional Competence and Performance

5. A member shall strive to perform the duties of his position and supervise the work of his subordinates, with the highest degree of professional care.
(This principle emphasizes the requirement for a member to give special attention to the professional aspects of his work, and not to condone substandard performance at any level within his responsibility.)

6. A member shall continually seek to increase his professional knowledge and skills, and thus to improve his service to employers, associates and fellow members.
(This principle stresses the importance of professional development and the use of professional skills in helping his colleagues and employers.)

7. A member shall render opinions, observations or conclusions for official purposes only after appropriate professional consideration of the pertinent facts.
(This principle stresses the importance of avoiding unsupported opinions involving professional judgments which could cause inappropriate official actions.)

8. A member shall exercise diligence, objectivity and honesty in his professional activities and be aware of his responsibility to disclose improprieties that come to his attention.
(This principle places the responsibility upon a member to exercise moral and independent judgment and to disclose to appropriate authorities illegal, improper or unethical practices noted in the course of his work.)

9. A member shall be aware of and strive to apply requirements and standards prescribed by authorized government agencies, which may be applicable to his work.
(This principle recognizes that special professional criteria are promulgated by authorized government agencies at the Federal, State and Local levels which require attention in certain assignments.)

Responsibility to Others

10. In the performances of any assignment, a member shall consider the public interest to be paramount.
(This principle stresses a member's foremost concern for the public interest in any specific work situation involving competing interests.)

11. A member shall not engage in any activity or relationship which creates or gives the appearance of a conflict with his responsibilities to his employer.
(This principle cautions against becoming involved in situations where a member's official or personal activities are inconsistent with his responsibilities to his employer.)

12. In speaking engagements or writings for publication, a member shall identify personal opinions which may differ from official positions of his employer.
(This principle stresses the need to avoid inappropriate interpretations by the public from speeches or articles by members which reflect personal rather than official viewpoints of their employers.)

REFERENCES

American Institute of Certified Public Accountants. *Auditing Standards Established by the GAO: Their Meaning and Significance for CPAs.* New York: American Institute of Certified Public Accountants, 1973.

Arthur Andersen & Co. *Single Audit.* Chicago: Arthur Andersen, 1984.

Brink, V. Z., J. A. Cashin, and H. Witt. *Modern Internal Auditing: An Operational Approach,* 3d ed. New York: The Ronald Press Company, 1973.

Broadus, W. A., Jr., and J. D. Comtois. "The Single Audit Act: A Needed Reform." *Journal of Accountancy* (April, 1985), pp. 62–70.

Henderson, G. V., Jr., and M. Hernandez. "A Generalized Approach to the Operational Audit of Management Information." *The Internal Auditor* (June, 1979), pp. 70–76.

The Institute of Internal Auditors, Inc. *Standards for the Professional Practice of Internal Auditing.* Altamonte Springs, Fla.: The Institute of Internal Auditors, Inc., 1978.

Municipal Finance Officers Association of the United States and Canada. *Governmental Accounting, Auditing, and Financial Reporting.* Chicago: Municipal Finance Officers Association of the United States and Canada, 1980.

Office of Management and Budget Circular A-102 (and Attachments A through P thereto). *Uniform Requirements for Assistance to State and Local Governments.* Washington, D.C., January, 1981.

Office of Management and Budget Circular A-128. *Audits of State and Local Governments.* Washington, D.C., April 12, 1985.

Pomeranz, F., *et al. Auditing in the Public Sector.* Boston: Warren, Gorham & Lamont, 1976.

Sawyer, L. B. *The Practice of Modern Internal Auditing.* Altamonte Springs, Fla.: The Institute of Internal Auditors, Inc., 1973.

Sawyer, L. B. "Internal Auditing: Yesterday, Today, and Tomorrow." *The Internal Auditor* (December, 1979), pp. 23–32.

Scott, G. A., "How to Obtain — and Handle — Engagements to Audit Government Entities." *The Practical Accountant* (September 1987), pp. 79–96.

State and Local Government Committee. *Audits of State and Local Governmental Units,* rev. ed. New York: American Institute of Certified Public Accountants, 1986.

Statts, E. B. "Governmental Auditing — Yesterday, Today, and Tomorrow." *The GAO Review* (Spring, 1976), pp. 1–9.

U.S. General Accounting Office. *Standards for Audit of Governmental Organizations, Programs, Activities and Functions.* Washington: U.S. Government Printing Office, 1981.

QUESTIONS

1. Distinguish independent, internal, and governmental auditing.
2. Cite several significant events in the development of contemporary internal auditing in the U.S.
3. What are the major internal audit activities identified in the Institute of Internal Auditor's *Statement of Responsibilities of Internal Auditors*?
4. What are the primary sources of an internal auditor's independence as identified

in the Institute of Internal Auditor's *Statement of Responsibilities of Internal Auditors*?

5. Outline the overall approach to an internal operational audit. How is this approach similar to other types of audit activities?

6. How are internal and independent auditing related?

7. What requirements does SAS No. 9, "The Effect of an Internal Audit Function on the Scope of the Independent Auditor's Examination," impose upon independent auditors regarding internal auditors?

8. Even though internal and governmental auditors serve different user groups, their audit activities are sometimes similar. How are they similar?

9. What creates the demand for federal, state, and local governmental audits?

10. What is the purpose of financial and compliance audits, and how are they similar to financial statement opinion audits?

11. The purpose of governmental economy and efficiency audits is to determine whether operations are conducted economically and efficiently. Distinguish the terms "economy" and "efficiency."

12. What are program results audits? What special problems do they present to auditors?

MULTIPLE CHOICE QUESTIONS

1. The independence of the Internal Auditing Department will most likely be assured if it reports to the

   a. President.
   b. Controller.
   c. Treasurer.
   d. Board of Directors.
   e. Vice-President of Finance.

2. A major responsibility of internal auditing is to

   a. Install sound accounting, financial, and operating controls at reasonable cost.
   b. Ascertain the extent of compliance with established policies, plans, and procedures.
   c. Account for the company's assets and safeguard them from losses.
   d. Develop reliable management data.
   e. All of the above.

3. In comparison to the independent auditor, an internal auditor is more likely to be concerned with

   a. Legal and regulatory compliance.
   b. Cost accounting procedures.
   c. Operational auditing.
   d. Internal control structure.

4. Taylor Sales Corp. maintains a large full-time internal audit staff which reports directly to the chief accountant. Audit reports prepared by the internal auditors indicate that the system is functioning as it should and that the accounting records are reliable. The independent auditor will probably

a. Eliminate test of controls.
b. Increase the depth of the assessment of control risk.
c. Avoid duplicating the work performed by the internal audit staff.
d. Place limited reliance on the work performed by the internal audit staff.

5. When an independent auditor decides that the work performed by internal auditors may have a bearing on the nature, timing, and extent of contemplated audit procedures, the independent auditor should plan to evaluate the objectivity of the internal auditors. Relative to objectivity, the independent auditor should

a. Consider the organizational level to which internal auditors report the results of their work.
b. Review the quality control program in effect for the internal audit staff.
c. Examine the quality of the internal audit reports.
d. Consider the qualifications of the internal audit staff.

6. Governmental auditing often extends beyond examinations leading to the expression of opinion on the fairness of financial presentation and includes audits of efficiency, economy, effectiveness, and also

a. Accuracy.
b. Evaluation.
c. Compliance.
d. Internal control structure.

7. Operational audits generally have been conducted by internal auditors and governmental audit agencies but may be performed by certified public accountants. A primary purpose of an operational audit is to provide

a. A means of assurance that internal controls are functioning as planned.
b. Aid to the independent auditor, who is conducting the examination of the financial statements.
c. The results of internal examinations of financial and accounting matters to a company's top-level management.
d. A measure of management performance in meeting organizational goals.

8. A governmental auditor is performing an audit of the city of Pawtucket, Rhode Island. The auditor's objective is to determine whether the city's financial statements are fairly stated and whether the city has complied with laws and regulations that may have a bearing on the financial statements. This is an example of which of the following types of audits

a. Financial statement opinion audit.
b. Operational audit.
c. Financial and compliance audit.
d. Economy and efficiency audit

9. Program results audits differ from other types of audits because

a. Materiality is ignored.
b. The efficiency of a governmental unit's operations is emphasized.

   c. The auditor must first establish objective measures of the program's objectives.

   d. Program results audits can be performed by governmental auditors only.

10. The Single Audit Act evolved because

   a. Grant-by-grant audits were not cost effective.

   b. Congress preferred that governmental auditors emphasize grant contracts rather than financial statements.

   c. There was a need for audits that deemphasized grants that were immaterial to the financial statements.

   d. The General Accounting Office was overburdened with grant audits.

PROBLEMS

21-1   B. J. Machine Company is considering developing an internal audit department. A few years ago, the company began an expansion program which included the acquisition of new businesses, some of which are located quite far from the home office. B. J. Machine has retained the existing managements in most past acquisitions and expects to continue to do so. The corporate organization is decentralized, with the parent company (B. J. Machine) setting the general policies. Division and subsidiary managements are quite autonomous; their performance is measured against budgets and return-on-investment targets established at the beginning of each year. The separate units of B. J. Machine manufacture and market their own products. The present companywide sales volume is $150,000,000.

   B. J. Machine has been audited by the CPA firm in which you are a manager. You have supervised the audit of B. J. Machine for the past three years. You have been asked by B. J. Machine Company to prepare a report on the activities that could be undertaken by an internal audit department.

Required:
(1) Prepare a report which describes:
   (a) The different objectives of the independent and internal auditor.
   (b) The types of audits that an internal audit department might be expected to perform.
   (c) The relationship of the internal auditor to the independent auditor.
(2) The company has indicated that you will be asked to head the internal audit department if it is established. Describe the changes in your audit philosophy and in your relationship to the firm management that you believe should occur if you were to take this job.   (CMA Adapted)

21-2   Amelia Barba, a local real estate broker, is a newly appointed member of the Board of Directors of Pennset Corporation. At a recent Board meeting, called to discuss the financial plan for 1990, Barba discovered two planned expenditures for auditing. In the Controller's Department budget she found an amount designated for internal audit activity, and in the treasurer's budget she found an estimate for the 1990 annual audit by a CPA firm.

   Barba couldn't understand the need for two different expenditures for auditing.

Since the CPA fee for the annual audit was less than the cost of the internal audit activity, she proposed eliminating the internal audit function.

Required:
(1) Explain to Barba the different purposes served by the two audit activities.
(2) What benefits does the CPA firm performing an audit derive from the existence of an internal audit function?   (CMA Adapted)

21-3   Many internal audit organizations report to a level of authority below either the Board of Directors or the chief executive officer. In these cases, there could be some doubt as to the objectivity and independence of the internal audit coverage and reporting.

   The organization chart given below is an example of such a situation.

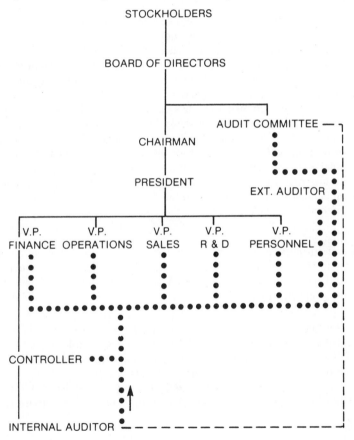

LEGEND

—— Administrative responsibility

––– Functional responsibility

●●●● Report of internal audit findings as appropriate

Required:
Cite three advantages and three disadvantages to the internal audit operation of the organization form and the responsibilities depicted by the chart.　　　(IIA Adapted)

21-4　　You have just been appointed to establish an internal audit function in a large national organization with 15,000 employees in various locations. The company is engaged in manufacturing and marketing commercial products. Its customers are mainly in the wholesale, manufacturing, and warehousing businesses.

Required:
Describe at least four important initial steps you would take preparatory to setting up an overall audit plan.　　　(IIA Adapted)

21-5　　Over the last several years Hobbie, Inc., has expanded and diversified its operations, resulting in growth of sales and profit. Two years ago the Hobbie management established an internal audit function. The Internal Audit Department is responsible for evaluating and recommending modifications in control procedures, reviewing operating practices to promote efficiency and economy, and conducting special inquiries at management's direction.

　　As in prior years, Hobbie, Inc., has engaged Plautz & Associates as its independent auditor. The partner from Plautz & Associates who is in charge of the Hobbie audit has made an appointment with the manager of Hobbie's Internal Audit Department to discuss the development of the Internal Audit Department, including new personnel and new activities, during its second year of operation.

　　The partner needs this information to plan the scope of the audit and to determine the amount of direct assistance, in the form of audit tests, that will be needed from the Internal Audit Department.

Required:
The scope of an independent audit can be modified if a good Internal Audit Department exists in the client firm. What characteristics of Hobbie's Internal Audit Department and its work should Plautz & Associates evaluate when establishing the scope of its independent audit?　　　(CMA Adapted)

21-6　　The Internal Auditing Department of a large service entity is organizationally responsible to the controller, who, in turn, is responsible to the president. As part of the internal audit responsibility, regular audits are performed of payroll, general accounting, accounts receivable, and accounts payable.

　　Because these activities also report to the controller, criticism is frequently made that the internal auditor cannot be objective when auditing such activities.

Required:
Following are two solutions that might eliminate the criticism. Describe briefly two advantages and two disadvantages of each of these solutions.
(a) The Internal Auditing Department could send directly to the president audit reports concerning activities under the supervision of the controller.
(b) The Director of Internal Auditing could discuss the organizational problem with the independent auditors and ask them to make a recommendation which would eliminate the criticism.　　　(IIA Adapted)

21-7   Supervision of internal auditors is necessary to provide guidance and direction.

Required:
Discuss three factors that internal auditing supervisors should consider when overseeing staff auditors on internal audit assignments.   (IIA Adapted)

21-8   MoCom, Inc., is a diversified company composed of several wholly owned subsidiaries. Dason Company, one of the subsidiaries, was acquired in 1980. MoCom, Inc., retained the Dasom management and gave it substantial autonomy, allowing the company to operate as it had before the acquisition took place.

Dasom Company manufactures window fans and sells them directly to retailers throughout the Midwest. Dasom's obligation to retailers and the final consumer on new fans ends after a 12-month warranty period. A significant portion of company revenue comes from the sale of fan replacement parts to retailers and appliance service centers.

Fans and replacement parts are sold on a 30-day open account basis to all customers whose credit has been approved by the Credit Department. The Credit Department has a set of formalized standards which are used to evaluate a customer's credit standing. In addition, a performance file is maintained for all approved customers in order to keep a current record of customers' activities (sales, returns, payments) with the company; this file is reviewed periodically to identify any customers whose credit standing should be modified.

During the spring of 1990, several changes were made in key positions in the Sales Department due to retirements, promotions, and normal attrition. The credit manager and sales manager were two of the key personnel changes.

The new sales manager revised the sales program to increase sales volume. The program has been successful, and the salespeople have submitted a large number of orders from new customers all of which require credit approval.

The new credit manager was not completely content with the present credit standards, feeling they were too strict and would limit the success of the new sales programs. Consequently, the new credit manager did not apply the standards as stringently as the former manager. In addition, sales were made to some customers on the basis of a cursory credit evaluation due to the backlog of credit approvals which had resulted from the increased sales effort.

The increased activity in the Credit Department has had two other consequences: the performance file has not been kept up to date; some new customer records have not been added to the file on a timely basis; and the customers' records have not been kept current. In addition, there has not been the usual follow-up on past-due accounts. Normally, the salespeople are expected to get approval before attempting to make sales to customers with past-due accounts. Further, they are required to make personal visits to the customers who are unusually slow in making payments. However, the Credit Department has not been providing the salespeople with the information needed to carry out these responsibilities.

MoCom management seldom interferes with the management of subsidiary operations. Only when analysis of the financial reports or other information indicates a problem may exist does it become involved with the activities of the subsidiary. Recent analyses have shown that Dasom's accounts receivable balance is growing too rapidly. In the past 12 months the average collection period has more than doubled from 35 days to 80 days. This would seem to indicate that Dasom is experiencing an increase in overdue accounts. MoCom has directed its Internal Audit Department to review Dasom's accounts receivable procedures to determine the problem, if any, and recommend corrective measures.

MoCom's internal auditors applied the following procedures in their examination of Dasom Company:

1. Reviewed a flowchart of the entire sales, accounts receivable, and cash receipts system.
2. Prepared an aged trial balance of the outstanding accounts receivable.
3. Reviewed the procedures employed to follow up on overdue accounts.
4. Reviewed the formal credit standards that are to be employed in evaluating and approving new customers and reevaluating old accounts.

The information obtained by the internal auditors can be summarized as follows:

1. All sales and collections on account are recorded promptly and properly in the company records.
2. Invoices and monthly statements are mailed to customers on a regular and timely basis.
3. Dasom has approximately 1,500 customers and the average invoice is for $2,000.
4. The age of the accounts receivable has increased significantly, and the accounts over six months old have tripled while sales have doubled.
5. Credit has been extended to some customers whose accounts are over six months old, and a few accounts have unusually high balances which built up over the last six to nine months.
6. The formal credit standards are judged to be adequate in evaluating and approving new customers and are similar to standards used by other firms in the industry.
7. The follow-up procedures to be conducted by the sales personnel were not being carried out.

The audit report filed by the evaluation team made the following recommendation:

"In light of the fact that the overdue accounts are growing at a rapid rate and the follow-up collection procedures cannot be carried out because of the high sales volume, we recommend that the services of a reputable collection agency be engaged to collect all accounts over 60 days old. The collection industry averages 75% effectiveness and generally charges a fee of 30% of the amounts collected. While this fee is high, Dasom Company and MoCom, Inc., cannot afford to allow these overdue accounts to remain outstanding."

Required:
(1) Evaluate the procedures employed by the internal auditors of MoCom, Inc., in their examination of Dasom Company's accounts receivable, and identify areas, if any, for which additional procedures should have been considered by the internal auditors during their examination.
(2) Assuming the audit procedures you believe necessary were carried out and revealed the facts presented regarding Dasom's accounts receivable procedures, would you agree with the internal auditors' recommendation? If you would not agree with their recommendation, present an alternative recommendation. Support your answer in either case.   (CMA Adapted)

21-9   Heretofore, senior executives have not read your internal audit reports. You believe that these executives should be interested in receiving copies of your reports, particularly because you have expanded your audit program to cover operations throughout the entire organization.

Required:
Identify three qualities — in terms of form and/or content — of internal audit reports which you believe will help capture and hold the interest of senior executives.

(IIA Adapted)

21-10   During the audit of purchasing and inventory operations, the internal auditor discovers that significant quantities of purchased materials are not actually in stock nor accounted for. Stock records, controlled by the warehouse supervisor, do not reflect shortages; and the inventory reports appear to have been altered. The internal auditor suspects that the warehouse supervisor, who has the greatest opportunity to remove materials for personal gain, altered the reports.

The auditor immediately notifies the department manager; and, together, they confront the suspected supervisor. The supervisor offers no explanation for the shortages and denies any wrongdoing. The department manager immediately suspends the supervisor, pending further investigation, and informs the warehouse employees of the situation. Since no adequate explanation for the shortages was obtained, the auditor contacts the security unit for assistance.

Required:
The actions of the auditor and the department manager could hinder the conduct of a successful investigation and could subject the company to legal proceedings. List four such actions and briefly discuss the possible adverse effect of each.

(IIA Adapted)

21-11   The agenda of a forthcoming meeting of the Audit Committee of the Board of Directors indicates that you are to discuss coordination between independent and internal auditors.

Required:
(1) List five advantages of a program of coordination between independent and internal auditors.
(2) List five essential ingredients in establishing effective coordination between independent and internal auditors.   (IIA Adapted)

21-12   One early definition and discussion of internal control structure states: "Internal control comprises the plan of organization and all of the coordinate methods and measures adopted within a business to safeguard its assets, check the accuracy and reliability of its accounting data, promote operational efficiency, and encourage adherence to prescribed managerial policies. This definition possibly is broader than the meaning sometimes attributed to the term. It recognizes that a 'system' of internal control extends beyond those matters which relate directly to the function of the accounting and financial departments."

Required:
(1) Identify the elements of this definition which are particularly applicable to operational audits performed by internal auditors and relate them to the objectives of operational auditing.

(2) An operational audit of any particular functional segment of a business may entail three distinct yet related areas of investigation: policy, control, and evaluation of performance. Discuss in general terms the audit methodology which might be applicable to each phase.   (IIA Adapted)

21-13   Your company's management is considering a proposal which would require the internal auditors to participate in collecting the bids and controlling the competitive bidding practices in the Purchasing Department.

Required:
Discuss your response to the above proposal to involve the internal auditors in a line function in relation to (a) a short-term or long-term assignment and (b) its possible impact on the effectiveness of your normal audit program in the purchasing area.
                                                                    (IIA Adapted)

21-14   Jones and Todd, a local CPA firm, received an invitation to bid for the audit of a local, federally assisted program. The audit is to be conducted in accordance with the audit standards published by the General Accounting Office (GAO), a federal auditing agency. Jones and Todd has become familiar with the GAO standards and recognizes that the GAO standards are concerned with more than the financial aspects of an entity's operations. The GAO standards broaden the definition of auditing by establishing that the full scope of an audit should encompass the following elements:
1. An examination of financial transactions, accounts, and reports, including an evaluation of compliance with applicable laws and regulations.
2. A review of efficiency and economy in the use of resources, such as personnel and equipment.
3. A review to determine whether desired program results are effectively achieved.
    Jones and Todd has been engaged to perform the audit of the program, and the audit is to encompass all three elements.

Required:
(1) Jones and Todd should perform sufficient audit work to satisfy the financial and compliance element of the GAO standards. What should such audit work determine?
(2) After making appropriate review and inquiries, what uneconomical practices or inefficiencies should Jones and Todd be alert to, in satisfying the efficiency and economy element encompassed by the GAO standards?
(3) After making appropriate review and inquiries, what should Jones and Todd consider to satisfy the program results element encompassed by the GAO standards?
                                                                    (AICPA Adapted)

21-15   Monte Carlo is executive vice-president of a major automobile manufacturing company. Carlo was recently elected mayor of Detroit. Prior to assuming office, he calls on you, his CPA, for advice. He asks you to explain the major similarities and differences between a financial and compliance audit for a large city and a financial statement opinion audit for an industrial corporation.

Required:
Describe the major similarities and differences between a governmental financial and compliance audit and an independent financial statement opinion audit of a business enterprise.

21-16   Devlin & Bruce, CPAs, has been engaged to perform the audit of a local, federally funded Housing Allowance Program. The objective of the program is to increase the housing standards of Agana County through subsidized rent payments. The program, however, has been criticized by local authorities for failing to achieve "significant results" during its two years of existence. You have been assigned to plan an audit examination.

Required:
(1) What matters would you take into consideration when planning the Housing Allowance engagement?
(2) Apply the scientific method of inquiry to the engagement, giving examples of procedures and measurement criteria you deem appropriate.

21-17   As a GAO auditor, you have been assigned to perform an audit of a Department of Education Hot Lunch Program. The Department had instructed all schools to order commodities in economical institutional-size packages to the extent possible.

In eight of the twenty-two schools covered by the review, you have found purchases in smaller-size packages. You estimate resulting additional costs to total $10,000 per month, per school. Considering the escalation in food prices, it was evident that bulk purchasing was essential due to favorable quantity discounts. Department of Education officials stated that although bulk purchases were encouraged, they were not mandated.

Required:
(1) Refer to the GAO general standards in Appendix C. What is the scope of the above audit? Explain.
(2) Draft a paragraph summarizing the recommendations you would include in a report to the Department of Education.

RESEARCHING AUDIT PRACTICE PROBLEMS

22

Major topics discussed in this chapter are the:

▲ *Importance of and need for research in audit practice.*

▲ *Auditor's approach to researching nonroutine accounting and auditing problems.*

▲ *Manual and computer-assisted research sources available for accounting and auditing research.*

L ike other professional decision makers, auditors are bounded by their own experience, expertise, and rationality. No one auditor has all the "answers"; experience and expertise yield some answers in some cases, but rationality should suggest that additional sources be consulted when experience and expertise are insufficient. The AICPA's third general standard — due professional care — requires no less.

This chapter is an introduction to an auditor's approach to researching nonroutine audit practice problems. The chapter begins with a discussion of the importance of, and need for, audit research. In turn, an auditor's research approach is outlined, and selected manual and computer-assisted research sources are discussed.

THE IMPORTANCE OF RESEARCH IN AUDIT PRACTICE

An auditor cannot function in a vacuum, relying solely upon prior experience to solve difficult or unfamiliar audit practice problems. Business transactions and authoritative pronouncements are becoming far too complex — and the potential consequences of legal liability far too severe — for an auditor to ignore the wealth of manual and computer-assisted research tools currently available. Indeed, accounting and auditing research are not limited to academics and the research departments of national public accounting firms. Rather, research is a normal recurring activity of all auditors and, equally important, is recognized either implicitly or explicitly in no less than three citations within the authoritative professional literature: the first and third general standards and Rule 201 of the AICPA Code of Professional Conduct.

In discussion related to the first general standard — adequate technical training and proficiency — the *Codification of Statements on Auditing Standards* implicitly recognizes the importance of research in referring to an auditor's obligation to be continually aware of developments within the profession, particularly technical pronouncements (AU Sec. 210.04):

> The independent auditor's formal education and professional experience complement one another; each auditor exercising authority upon an engagement should weigh these attributes in determining the extent of his supervision of subordinates and review of their work. It should be recognized that the training of a professional man includes a continual awareness of developments taking place in business and in his profession. He must study, understand, and apply new pronouncements on accounting principles and auditing procedures as they are developed by authoritative bodies within the accounting profession.

Thus, research is significant to an auditor's training from the viewpoint of providing an awareness of authoritative pronouncements that may impact a particular client's business transactions and reporting. Research is important not only when a significant question arises, but also in pointing to significant questions that should have arisen.

In a second, though again implicit, reference to the importance of research, the *Codification of Statements on Auditing Standards,* in discussing the third general standard — due professional care — cites *Cooley on Torts,* which notes that (AU Sec. 230.03): "Every man who offers his service to another . . is understood as holding himself out to the public as possessing the degree of skill commonly possessed by others in the same employment. . . ." Certainly, the ability to research nonroutine accounting and auditing issues is embraced within an auditor's special skills.

An explicit reference to research appears in Interpretation 201-1, "Competence," an interpretation of Rule 201 of the AICPA Code of Professional Conduct. The interpretation explicitly draws a relationship between audit research and professional conduct, stating in part that:

> The member may have the knowledge required to complete an engagement professionally before undertaking it. In many cases, however, additional research or consultation with others may be necessary during the course of the engagement. This does not ordinarily represent a lack of competence, but rather is a normal part of the professional conduct of an engagement.

Clearly, research is an integral part of an auditor's professional activity. Researching a problem does not suggest an auditor is incompetent; failing to research a problem completely and effectively, however, does.

THE NEED FOR RESEARCH

Generally, an auditor conducts research in response to either client requests for technical advice or nonroutine accounting or auditing problems arising for particular audit engagements. In either case, an auditor's research method is similar, although the potential impact upon an auditor's independence and the form for documenting solutions may differ.

Client Requests

Even when an auditor is not actively involved in the planning, interim, or year-end stages of a continuing engagement, a client may request technical advice about the accounting and reporting implications of a planned or completed transaction. For example, before entering into a business combination as investor, a client may request technical advice about whether the planned transaction is likely to be accounted for as a purchase or pooling of interests, and the likely effect on the client's reported postcombination financial position.

Clients should be encouraged to solicit an auditor's technical advice, particularly when internal accounting personnel are neither skilled nor experienced in conducting accounting and auditing research. In the interest of providing a client with the most useful information for decision making, clients should be encouraged to seek advice before, rather than after, a transaction is completed. Before a transaction is completed, an auditor can provide advice about alternative means for structuring a transaction. However, after a transaction is completed, opportunities for management to consider alternatives are lost.

After research is completed, an auditor should communicate the results to management in a formal memorandum that summarizes both the issues raised and conclusions reached. In order to remain independent, an auditor can provide a client with technical advice only, not with a decision. Financial statements are management's representations, not the auditor's.

Accounting or Auditing Problems

In addition to client requests for technical advice, auditors also conduct research for nonroutine accounting or auditing problems arising for particular engagements. To the extent possible, an auditor should attempt to isolate and resolve nonroutine accounting or auditing problems early in an engagement, preferably during the planning or interim stage. Ideally, all problems should be resolved before year-end, except those specifically arising from year-end substantive procedures or subsequent events. At year-end, an auditor's efforts

FIGURE 22-1
An Accounting and Auditing Research Approach

1. Observe and recognize a problem.
2. Summarize pertinent issues related to the problem and document a ''trail''
   from which to select appropriate research sources.
3. Select appropriate manual and/or computer-assisted research sources.
4. Evaluate research sources and develop and document conclusions.

are devoted predominantly toward obtaining sufficient competent evidential
matter, leaving little time for involved research.

As with client-requested advice, research related to accounting or auditing problems arising during an engagement should be documented, summarizing issues raised and conclusions reached. Aside from summarizing issues
and conclusions, research documentation can also be instrumental in demonstrating an auditor's partial compliance with the first and third general standards and with the AICPA Code of Professional Ethics' Rule 201.

A RESEARCH APPROACH

In order to reach reasoned, supportable conclusions to nonroutine accounting and auditing problems, an auditor needs a logical research approach,
not unlike the scientific method of inquiry introduced in Chapter 1. An appropriate accounting and auditing research approach appears in Figure 22-1
and is discussed in the following sections.

Observing and Recognizing Problems

Observing and recognizing a problem is obviously the first step in reaching a viable solution. However, unless a client specifically requests technical
advice, the identity of issues and problems requiring research is not always
obvious. An auditor's ability to recognize researchable problems is largely
dependent upon his or her (1) understanding of a client's business, industry,
and accounting policies and procedures, and (2) awareness of recent and relevant pronouncements.

Business, Industry, and Accounting. To be effective, an auditor should
have an adequate understanding of a client's industry or industries, since a

particular industry may present a unique set of accounting and auditing problems. On the other hand, no two clients are apt to be identical, suggesting that individual clients — even those operating within the same industry — could, as a result of dissimilar business objectives and management philosophy, present unique accounting and auditing problems. In short, an auditor should be knowledgeable of accounting and reporting problems unique both to particular industries and to particular clients.

Recent and Relevant Pronouncements. Within the past two decades, and particularly the past few years, a seemingly overwhelming number of technical pronouncements have been issued by a variety of private-sector bodies, including the Financial Accounting Standards Board and the Securities and Exchange Commission. Certainly, no one practicing auditor could be expected to be completely familiar with all of the accounting, auditing, and reporting ramifications of each pronouncement. However, there is no excuse for a competent auditor to be unaware of pronouncements affecting current clients. As a result, an auditor should keep abreast of recent and proposed pronouncements and consider their applicability to each client.

Summarizing Pertinent Issues

A problem cannot be solved if not properly defined. Thus, before attempting to solve an accounting or auditing problem, an auditor should be thoroughly familiar with the research problem as well as all related and pertinent issues. Although the facts related to each individual research problem are apt to differ, an auditor should consider the following as a minimum:

▲ A clear, concise, and unambiguous statement of the problem.
▲ An indication of whether the problem involves:
  — accounting principles,
  — auditing standards or procedures,
  — reporting to regulatory bodies, and/or
  — specialized industries.
▲ An indication of whether the research solution will be used by:
  — the client in accounting for a planned or completed transaction or economic event,
  — the auditor in connection with a professional engagement, or
  — a client's attorney in connection with threatened or pending litigation.
▲ Materiality and risk.

Regardless of whether the research problem was initiated by a client or an auditor, each of the above considerations should be clearly documented, leaving a "trail" from which to select appropriate research sources and seek viable solutions.

Selecting Research Sources

Once a problem has been recognized and pertinent issues summarized, an auditor then selects manual and/or computer-assisted research sources appropriate in the circumstances. Although the major research sources contain key-word indexes and are relatively easy to use, the search for solutions is a creative process, in part because difficult issues are apt to require investigating several sources. For example, for publicly traded companies, an auditor must consider both private-sector pronouncements (e.g., Statements of the Financial Accounting Standards Board) and governmental regulations (e.g., Securities and Exchange Commission Regulation S-X). Some specific research sources are discussed later in this chapter.

Evaluating Research Sources and Developing Conclusions

The final phase of accounting and auditing research involves evaluating research sources and developing conclusions. The validity of conclusions reached depends upon (1) the auditor's ability to evaluate and interpret research findings and (2) the proficiency and care exercised in the earlier phases of the research. Unless the relevant issues are properly defined and appropriate research sources selected, the auditor cannot draw reasoned and informed conclusions.

According to AICPA Code of Conduct Rules 202 and 203, an auditor cannot permit his or her name to be associated with financial statements unless he or she has complied with generally accepted auditing standards (GAAS), and unless the statements are presented in accordance with generally accepted accounting principles (GAAP). As a result, when conducting research, an auditor's conclusions should be based upon the most current and authoritative interpretations of auditing and accounting standards.

Of course, conscientious interpretations of either generally accepted accounting principles or generally accepted auditing standards can result in alternative solutions. For instance, both straight-line and accelerated depreciation are generally accepted, and either may be appropriate in a particular situation. Thus, in evaluating accounting and auditing research sources, an auditor is apt to consider alternative conclusions — or indeed he or she may conclude any one of several alternatives is appropriate. As a result, the auditor should document the alternatives considered, the research sources consulted, and any additional implications resulting from the research process, thereby continuing the research "trail" begun when summarizing pertinent issues. If the research problem was initiated by a client's request for technical advice, the auditor should issue a memorandum to the client, clearly indicating the problem, research trail followed, and conclusions reached.

MANUAL RESEARCH SOURCES

Several authoritative research sources are available to an auditor, including those listed in Figure 22-2 and discussed briefly in the following sections.

Professional Standards

The AICPA's two professional standards volumes listed in Figure 22-2 include currently effective pronouncements related to auditing and public accounting practice. The volumes may be subscribed to in looseleaf form or purchased in bound form.

Volume I. As noted earlier in this book, *Statements on Auditing Standards* are interpretations of generally accepted auditing standards, and are issued by the Auditing Standards Board, the senior technical body of the AICPA designated to issue auditing pronouncements. Under Rule 202 of the AICPA Code of Professional Conduct, an Institute member must be prepared to justify departures from SASs. The Auditing Standards Division of the AICPA issues *Interpretations* of SASs in question and answer form that are designed to provide timely guidance on the application of the SASs interpreted. For example, SAS No. 39, "Audit Sampling," discussed in Chapters 10 and 11, states that there may be reasons other than sampling for an auditor to examine less than 100 percent of the items comprising an account balance or class of transactions. But, what might those other reasons be? An auditing interpretation (AU Sec. 9350) answers the question by stating that examining less than 100 percent of the items would not be sampling if (1) the auditor does not intend to extend an audit conclusion to the entire population, (2) the entire population is examined, (3) tests of controls are performed on a control procedure that does not produce documentation, or (4) the auditor is applying analytical procedures as a substantive test.

The AICPA's *Statement on Standards for Accountants' Services on Prospective Financial Information* and *Statements on Standards for Attestation Engagements,* issued jointly by the Auditing Standards Board and the Accounting and Review Services Committee, are codified within the AICPA's SASs, but are issued as separate pronouncements because they relate to issues beyond the scope of audit practice. For example, the statement on prospective

FIGURE 22-2
Manual Research Sources

Professional Standards:
  Volume I:
    Statements on Auditing Standards
    Auditing Interpretations
    Statement on Standards for Accountants' Services on Prospective Finan-
      cial Information
    Statements on Standards for Attestation Engagements
  Volume II:
    Statements on Standards for Accounting and Review Services
    Accounting and Review Services Interpretations
    Code of Professional Ethics
    Bylaws of the AICPA
    Statements on International Accounting Standards
    International Auditing Guidelines
    Statements on Standards for Management Advisory Services
    Statements on Quality Control Standards
    Statements on Responsibilities in Tax Practice
  FASB Accounting Standards: Current Text
Exposure Drafts
Discussion Memoranda
Statements of Financial Accounting Concepts
Accounting Trends and Techniques
Financial Report Surveys
Industry Audit Guides
Industry Accounting Guides
Statements of Position
Accounting Research Studies
Audit Research Monographs
Auditing Procedure Studies
Accountant's Index
Commerce Clearing House Accounting Articles
Index to Accounting and Auditing Technical Pronouncements
Issues Papers of the Accounting Standards Division
AICPA Technical Information Service
AICPA Audit and Accounting Manual
Securities and Exchange Commission
Journal Articles and Books

financial information relates to financial forecasts and projections, which are compiled and reviewed by the auditor but are not audited per se.

Volume II. Professional standards Volume II includes a variety of pronouncements, publications, and guidelines all related to professional accounting and auditing services. *Statements on Standards for Accounting and Review Services* are issued by the AICPA's Accounting and Review Services Committee, the senior technical committee designated to issue pronouncements about unaudited financial statements or other unaudited financial information of a nonpublic entity. Under Rule 204 of the AICPA Code of Professional Conduct, an Institute member must be prepared to justify departures from the committee's Statements. *Accounting and Review Services Interpretations* are issued periodically. Although an Interpretation is not as authoritative as a pronouncement of the Accounting and Review Services Committee, an Institute member could be requested to justify departures if his or her work were questioned.

The *Code of Professional Conduct*, including the Principles of Professional Conduct, the Rules of Conduct, Interpretations, and Ethics Rulings, all of which were introduced in Chapter 2, are included in Volume II. The volume also includes the *AICPA Bylaws*, which set forth standards for admission to membership in the Institute, election of the Institute's Council, board of directors, and officers, and membership termination and disciplinary sanctions.

Statements on International Accounting Standards, issued by the International Accounting Standards Committee, are designed to formulate uniform accounting standards for world-wide acceptance. The Committee has issued standards on a variety of issues including accounting for business combinations, capitalization of borrowing costs, and related party disclosures. *International Auditing Guidelines* are issued by the International Auditing Practices Committee of the International Federation of Accountants. The guidelines — and the international accounting standards — are not enforceable under the AICPA Code of Professional Conduct, and would have to be adopted specifically by the Auditing Standards Board in order to govern the audit of a U.S. based multinational corporation. Volume II includes each Guideline together with any significant differences from U.S. generally accepted auditing standards.

Statements on Management Advisory Services are issued by the AICPA's Management Advisory Services (MAS) Committee. The Statements relate to conducting an advisory services practice and three have been issued to date: definitions and standards for MAS, MAS engagements, and MAS consultants. An Institute member must justify departures from the committee's Statements.

Only one *Statement on Quality Control Standards,* entitled "System of Quality Control for a CPA Firm", was issued by the Quality Control Standards Committee, the now defunct senior technical committee of the Institute designated to issue pronouncements on quality control. The Statement gives authority to the elements of quality control for CPA firms introduced in Chapter 1.

The AICPA's Division of Federal Taxation issues *Statements on Responsibilities in Tax Practice* designed to identify tax practice standards and delineate the extent of a tax practitioner's responsibility to clients, the public, government, and the profession. Statements have been issued about a variety of topics including the use of estimates in tax returns, advice to clients, and positions contrary to Treasury Department or Internal Revenue Service interpretations.

FASB Accounting Standards. The FASB's Accounting Standards, current text, consists of two volumes, general standards and industry standards, and may be subscribed to in looseleaf form or purchased in bound form. The volumes codify all currently effective pronouncements related to generally accepted accounting principles, and therefore are a primary source for researching accounting problems. Thus, the volumes include all extant (1) *Accounting Research Bulletins* issued by the AICPA Committee on Auditing Procedure from 1938–1959, (2) *Opinions* and *Interpretations* issued by the AICPA Accounting Principles Board from 1959–1973, and (3) Statements, Interpretations, and Technical Bulletins issued by the Financial Accounting Standards Board since 1973.

Other Sources

In addition to the Professional Standards Volumes, other manual research sources exist and are listed in Figure 22-2. Several authoritative bodies issue *Exposure Drafts,* providing advance notice to the financial community of proposed technical pronouncements. Though not authoritative, Exposure Drafts can provide a valuable research source when no other authoritative pronouncements exist for a particular issue, or when an existing pronouncement is likely to be superseded. The Financial Accounting Standards Board sometimes precedes Exposure Drafts with *Discussion Memoranda,* documents that present issues — not the Board's position — for discussion within the financial community. Discussion memoranda can also provide research information, although they do not reveal the Board's likely position.

Statements of Financial Accounting Concepts are issued by the Financial Accounting Standards Board, and are intended to establish underlying objectives and concepts of accounting. In contrast with Statements of Financial Accounting Standards, the Statements of Financial Accounting Concepts do not constitute generally accepted accounting principles, and therefore need not be followed under Rule 203 of the AICPA Code of Professional Conduct.

Statements of Position are issued by the AICPA Accounting Standards Executive Committee, the senior technical body designated to promulgate the Institute's position on accounting matters. Statements of Position are not enforceable under the AICPA Code of Professional Conduct; rather, they are intended to influence the authoritative bodies that issue pronouncements which are enforceable.

The AICPA publishes a particularly useful guide to accounting disclosures, *Accounting Trends and Techniques,* an annual survey of over 600 annual reports. *Financial Report Surveys,* published by the AICPA, also illustrate accounting disclosures, though for only a single issue, such as an entity's disclosure of accounting policies.

Industry Audit Guides are issued by the AICPA, and intended as guidelines for auditors about individual industries, such as hospitals and state and local governments. In general, the guides describe auditing issues related to an industry's particular characteristics, problem areas, and other peculiarities. The AICPA also issues *Industry Accounting Guides,* intended to fulfill a role similar to audit guides, though related instead to accounting and reporting issues.

Accounting Research Studies and *Audit Research Monographs,* issued by the AICPA, are each intended to represent extensive studies about difficult or controversial issues. Research studies have been issued for topics such as business combinations and generally accepted accounting principles, and research monographs for topics such as internal control structure.

The *Accountant's Index,* published annually by the AICPA, lists titles by authors and subjects added to the Institute's New York library, and covers a wealth of accounting, auditing, tax, and management advisory services literature. Commerce Clearing House's *Accounting Articles,* updated monthly, is an index and synopsis of published accounting articles, though it covers less material than the Accountant's Index. Both the Accountant's Index and Accounting Articles are excellent sources for locating *periodicals* — and in the case of the Index, for locating books — relevant to a research issue.

Since 1977, the AICPA has published a key-word *Index to Accounting and Auditing Technical Practice,* compiled from information supplied by a national public accounting firm. The Index incorporates references from all relevant AICPA, FASB, Governmental Accounting Standards Board, and Securities and Exchange Commission pronouncements.

The AICPA's *Technical Information Service* (TIS) is available to answer

FIGURE 22-3
Computer-Assisted Research Sources

National Automated Accounting Research System (NAARS)
LEXIS
DISCLOSURE II
EXCHANGE
NEXIS
INFOBANK
ABI/INFORM

member questions about a variety of issues including accounting principles and auditing standards. Although member questions are researched by qualified CPAs, responses do not carry the full authority of the AICPA. Rather, they represent the personal opinion of the TIS researcher, since only a senior AICPA committee can promulgate official pronouncements. The TIS program also includes *Technical Practice Aids,* published questions and answers about technical and professional issues. Like other aspects of TIS, Technical Practice Aids do not carry the authority of Institute pronouncements.

The *Audit and Accounting Manual,* an AICPA technical practice aid, includes guidelines and sample programs, questionnaires, and work sheets for a variety of practice considerations, such as engagement planning and administration, audit approach (including internal control structure questionnaires, tests of controls, and audit programs), internal control structure, and financial statements. The manual is prepared by the Institute's Technical Information Division and is not authoritative.

The *Securities and Exchange Commission* (SEC) is an important source when researching problems of publicly traded entities. For example, an entity must comply with SEC Financial Reporting Releases in filings under the Securities Acts, thus illustrating the SEC's potential influence on generally accepted accounting principles and auditing standards.

COMPUTER-ASSISTED RESEARCH SOURCES

In conjunction with manual research sources, an auditor could use one or more computer-assisted sources, including those listed in Figure 22-3. Each source is discussed briefly below.

NAARS

The National Automated Accounting Research System (NAARS) is a full-text (i.e., includes every word of a selected research document) research data base developed jointly by the AICPA and Mead Data Central, Inc. NAARS is accessible by authorized subscribers through off-site computer terminals located, for example, in a CPA firm's office.

Research Files. NAARS maintains a periodically updated library, organized into files. Each file is separately researchable and consists of documents related by both origin and physical makeup. Five NAARS files are listed and briefly discussed below:

▲ Annual Report File
▲ Accounting Literature File
▲ Management Discussion and Analysis File
▲ Prospectus File
▲ Technical Practice Aids File

The *Annual Report File* includes several thousand annual reports for companies listed on the New York and American stock exchanges and for companies traded over the counter. Only the two most recent annual reports for each company are contained within the file, although prior reports are contained on archive tapes. Among other things, the *Accounting Literature File* includes many of the manual research sources discussed earlier. For example, the file includes Statements on Auditing Standards; Auditing Interpretations; Opinions and Statements of the Accounting Principles Board; and Statements, Interpretations, and Technical Bulletins of the Financial Accounting Standards Board. Although the Accounting Literature File contains many sources available manually, the file provides the added features of being (1) up-to-date, thereby eliminating the danger of overlooking the most current research sources available, and (2) easily accessible from one terminal site, thereby minimizing the time needed to accumulate research sources.

The *Management Discussion and Analysis File* includes the full text of reports by management and other analyses contained within hundreds of annual reports. Reports by management have gained increasing prominence in recent years, and particularly since the mid-to-late 1970s. Thus, the reports are relatively new, thereby underscoring the value of the Management Discussion and Analysis File when advising clients about proposed management reports.

The *Prospectus File* includes prospectuses filed by companies in conjunction with the initial offering and sale of securities under the Securities Act of 1933. Of course, the *Technical Practice Aids File* includes AICPA technical practice aids, published questions and answers about practical issues identified earlier.

Research Approach. NAARS research requires no particular computer programming capabilities. Rather, NAARS is in a conversational mode, allowing an auditor to communicate directly with the system through simple command statements typed on a terminal's keyboard.

The search process requires that an auditor enter unique key words or phrases most likely to be associated with a research problem. For example, if interested in a particular financial statement disclosure, an auditor would enter key words or phrases according to a specified search request format. On command, NAARS searches the Annual Report File and indicates the number of annual reports containing the key words or phrases. When requested, NAARS displays or prints any or all of the disclosures found. As with any search, whether manual or computer-assisted, an auditor's efficiency and effectiveness depends heavily upon the selection of key words or phrases. For example, when researching treasury stock disclosures, the key phrase "stockholders' equity" would be much too broad, since every annual report included in the Annual Report File is likely to contain a stockholders' equity section.

LEXIS

While NAARS is an accounting and auditing tool, LEXIS is a tax research tool, also developed jointly by the AICPA and Mead Data Central, Inc. Like NAARS, LEXIS includes researchable files, accessed by key words or phrases. For example, the LEXIS Federal Tax Library includes (1) the Internal Revenue Code, (2) Treasury Department Regulations, (3) decisions of courts hearing tax cases, and (4) Public Laws and related House, Senate, and Conference Committee Reports. LEXIS is a particularly valuable and efficient means for tax research, since, like NAARS' Accounting Literature File, the Federal Tax Library contains a wealth of ever-changing research information that is both up-to-date and easily accessible.

DISCLOSURE II

DISCLOSURE II, a service offered by Disclosure, Inc., provides statistical information from SEC filings of over 9,000 publicly traded companies. However, unlike NAARS, DISCLOSURE II provides abstracts of a company's public filings, not entire filings. For each company DISCLOSURE II maintains a profile which includes the state of incorporation, stock exchange (if any), ticker symbol, standard industrial classification (SIC) code, business description, auditor, type of audit report and filings for the previous eighteen months, and names of parent and subsidiary companies, among other things. Information in the DISCLOSURE II files, but not in NAARS, includes compilations of auditor changes; the names, titles, age, and remuneration of officers and directors; and the specific numbers of shareholders and employees.

EXCHANGE

Occasionally, auditors are interested in information related to a specific industry rather than a specific company. For these types of data searches, EXCHANGE, offered by Mead Data Central, Inc. (operators of the NAARS data files), maintains industry reports and analyses, such as industry trends and statistics. Information for the EXCHANGE library is supplied by brokerage houses and investment research firms. One of the EXCHANGE files, called INDEX 2, lists all covered industry categories alphabetically and abbreviations of the sources of information.

Background Information, Articles, and Wire Services

A variety of computer-assisted sources are available when an auditor wishes to research information not directly related to financial accounting and disclosure, such as published articles and news releases about stockholder meetings, bond rating changes, and key personalities in business and government. Among the currently available research sources are NEXIS, INFO-BANK, and ABI/INFORM, all of which can be used to gain familiarity with a present or potential client, or to prepare a speech or article.

The NEXIS library contains the full text of current articles from newspapers, magazines, and wire services. Among the sources included are *Newsweek, U.S. News & World Report, Business Week,* the *Congressional Quarterly Almanac, Dun's Review,* the *Washington Post,* and the Associated Press world, national, and business wires. INFOBANK, a part of the LEXIS library, contains the full text of the *New York Times* from June 1, 1980 to the present and abstracts of pieces from about 100 other periodicals such as *The New Yorker, The Chicago Tribune, The Wall Street Journal, Barron's, Fortune,* and the *Financial Times.* In turn, ABI/INFORM contains abstracts of articles from over 650 worldwide business and management journals. The abstracts are generally no more than 250 words in length, and are drawn from such areas as accounting, finance, management, retailing, and advertising.

Although all these sources — as well as NAARS, LEXIS, DISCLO-SURE II, and EXCHANGE — are invaluable research sources, they do present some disadvantages. For example, different terminals or personal computers may be necessary to access different systems. Thus, some research services may not be compatible with an auditor's computer facilities. In addition, some of the services duplicate files offered by other services, and all the services use different descriptor codes and search strategies, thereby requiring that an auditor become familiar with each service used. Although the services collectively suffer from disadvantages, they are extraordinary research tools individually and provide significant advantages over manual research sources. In short, there are deficiencies, but they are neither insurmountable nor sufficient reason to overlook computer-assisted research.

SUMMARY

In many instances an auditor is confronted with nonroutine audit practice problems, necessitating a research approach for reaching viable solutions. An appropriate approach would involve observing and recognizing researchable problems, summarizing pertinent issues related to the problem, selecting and evaluating appropriate research sources, and developing conclusions.

Both manual and computer-assisted research sources are available for an auditor's use in researching accounting and auditing problems. The manual sources include professional standards volumes and a number of other materials such as industry audit guides, the Accountant's Index, and the AICPA Audit and Accounting Manual. Computer-assisted sources include the National Automated Accounting Research Service, LEXIS, DISCLOSURE II, EXCHANGE, NEXIS, INFOBANK, and ABI/INFORM. The sources are central to solving nonroutine audit practice problems, and as a result are indispensable to audit practitioners.

REFERENCES

American Institute of Certified Public Accountants. "Accounting and Auditing Research," in *Professional Training Programs: Taking Charge of Small Engagements, Level II*. New York: AICPA, 1988.

Gale, A. "A Breakthrough in Disclosure Retrieval." *Journal of Accountancy* (September, 1978), pp. 86–90.

Gale, A. "Computerized Research: An Advanced Tool." *Journal of Accountancy* (January, 1982), pp. 73–84.

Gale, A. "Data Bases: An Accountant's Choice." *Journal of Accountancy* (December, 1985), pp. 111–122.

Goodman, H. "NAARS: The CPA's Electronic Shoebox." *Journal of Accountancy* (December, 1985), pp. 125–132.

Moe, P. "How to Research an Accounting or Auditing Problem." *The Practical Accountant* (June, 1979), pp. 60–67.

Weirich, Thomas R., and Alan Reinstein. *Accounting & Auditing Research: A Practical Guide.* 2d ed., Cincinnati: South-Western Publishing Co., 1988.

QUESTIONS

1. Does the professional literature require that an auditor be proficient in conducting accounting and auditing research?
2. Under what general circumstances does an auditor ordinarily conduct research?
3. Outline and describe a research approach appropriate for solving accounting and auditing problems.
4. Identify the pertinent issues an auditor should consider when defining an accounting or auditing research problem.
5. What impact do AICPA Code of Ethics Rule 202, "Auditing Standards," and Rule 203, "Accounting Principles," have upon researching accounting and auditing problems?
6. What is meant by a "research trail"?
7. In addition to the professional standards volumes, what manual research sources are available to an auditor?
8. Compare and contrast the National Automated Accounting Research System (NAARS) and LEXIS.
9. What advantage does the NAARS Accounting Literature File have over the AICPA's professional standards volumes?
10. Identify and briefly describe the computer-assisted research sources other than NAARS and LEXIS.

MULTIPLE CHOICE QUESTIONS

1. Researching nonroutine audit practice problems:

   a. Is not required when an auditor's practice has not previously confronted the problem.
   b. Suggests that the auditor is not competent with respect to the problem confronted and, therefore, should not have accepted the engagement.
   c. Is recommended under Ethics Rule 201, and does not necessarily represent a lack of competence.
   d. Is performed only by academics and the research departments of public accounting firms.

2. The proper sequence of accounting and audit research is to:

   a. Select research sources, recognize the problem, summarize pertinent issues, evaluate and document conclusions.
   b. Recognize the problem, summarize pertinent issues, select research sources, evaluate and document conclusions.
   c. Recognize the problem, select research sources, summarize pertinent issues, evaluate and document conclusions.
   d. Summarize pertinent issues, recognize the problem, select research sources, evaluate and document conclusions.

3. In reaching conclusions about nonroutine accounting and auditing problems, an auditor is *not* required to justify departures from:

    a. Statements on Auditing Standards.
    b. International Auditing Guidelines issued by the International Federation of Accountants.
    c. Statements of Financial Accounting Standards of the Financial Accounting Standards Board.
    d. Statements on Standards for Accounting and Review Services issued by the Accounting and Review Services Committee.

4. Which of the following computer-assisted research sources includes selected information from publicly traded companies' annual 10-K filings with the Securities and Exchange Commission?

    a. NAARS.
    b. INFOBANK.
    c. EXCHANGE.
    d. DISCLOSURE II.

PROBLEMS

22-1 The scientific method of inquiry is a logical, evaluative framework for reaching reasoned, supportable conclusions. As explained in Chapters 1 and 21, the scientific method is equally applicable to external, internal, and governmental auditing.

Required:
Explain the relationship between the scientific method of inquiry and an auditor's approach to solving accounting and auditing research problems.

22-2 The first and third general standards of the AICPA's generally accepted auditing standards require that an audit be performed by a person or persons having *adequate technical training and proficiency* and that *due professional care* be exercised in performing the audit and preparing a report. Although the relationship of these two standards to audit practice is stated explicitly in the AICPA's *Codification of Statements on Auditing Standards,* their relationship to accounting and auditing research is only implicit.

Required:
(1) Discuss the relationship between (a) accounting and auditing research and (b) the practice of external auditing.
(2) Defend the applicability of the first and third general standards to accounting and auditing research.

22-3 The AICPA's two professional standards volumes have long been an invaluable manual research source for practicing CPAs. Their value stems primarily from the fact that the full text of all of the extant pronouncements are codified for a variety of private-sector authoritative bodies, including the Auditing Standards Board and the Financial Accounting Standards Board.

Required:

(1) Contemporary auditing requires that currently effective (extant) pronouncements be applied in professional engagements. Of what value, if any, are superseded pronouncements to accounting and auditing research?
(2) List and indicate the scope of the research sources included within the AICPA's professional standards volumes.

22-4   The National Automated Accounting Research System (NAARS) is a computer-assisted accounting and audit research tool available to authorized subscribers. Not surprisingly, NAARS has revolutionized accounting and auditing research by creating full-text research files that contain a myriad of potentially useful data sources.

Required:

(1) Describe the NAARS research process.
(2) Identify and indicate the contents of the NAARS research files.

22-5   Jillian Bracken, CPA, was recently assigned as in-charge auditor for the Rumford Company, a manufacturer of corrugated cardboard and paper products. From a review of prior-year working papers, Bracken discovers that controls over receivables were not relied on during the 1989 audit. However, early in 1990 Rumford installed a new system which Christopher Rossi, Rumford's controller, called, "an enormous improvement." Rossi also states that the company's billings are always mailed as of the last business day of the month and that "the auditors should be able to rely on the system, and thereby reduce both the extent of substantive tests at year-end and our audit bill."

Required:

(1) What specific problem does Bracken face in planning the Rumford engagement?
(2) Which of the research sources discussed in the chapter could Bracken rely on to address the problem in (1) above?

INDEX